Encyclopedia of Feminist Literary Theory

Advisory Board

Encyclopedia of
Feminist Literary Theory

Editor
Elizabeth Kowaleski-Wallace

GARLAND PUBLISHING, INC.
New York & London
1997

Library of Congress Cataloging-in-Publication Data

Encyclopedia of feminist literary theory / edited by Elizabeth Kowaleski-Wallace.
        p.   cm. — (Garland reference library of the humanities ;
vol. 1582)
     Includes bibliographical references and index.
     ISBN 0-8153-0824-8 (alk. paper)
     1. Feminist literary criticism—Dictionaries.   I. Kowaleski-Wallace,
Elizabeth, 1954–   II. Series.
PN98.W64E53   1997
801'.95'082—dc20   96-34754
                                                     CIP

Cover design: Lawrence Wolfson Design, New York

Printed on acid-free, 250-year-life paper
Manufactured in the United States of America

Contents

Preface

The mission of this encyclopedia is to map out the vast intellectual territory that has arisen mostly since the 1970s, due to the efforts of feminist literary scholars and critics in the United States and Great Britain. While encyclopedias of literary theory are currently accessible, and while encyclopedias of feminism are also available, this encyclopedia concerns itself uniquely with the crossing of the social, political, and intellectual force that is feminism and the major literary and theoretical movements of our time. Within the covers of a single volume, students, scholars, and the general public will find key words, topics, names, and critical terminology pertinent to the field of feminist literary theory. The encyclopedia offers all readers the opportunity to find, in consolidated form, the precise significance of a given theoretical movement or idea within a feminist literary context, and it also suggests how feminist theory may have affected the development of emerging ideas or intellectual practices.

Undergraduates and general readers using the encyclopedia will find, in quick and convenient form, a precise definition of any number of important terms—such as "Essentialism," the "Gaze," "Homosociality," or "Sororophobia." They will also find short entries designed to summarize the salient ideas of critics working in the field. We have aimed to include as many feminist literary critics as possible, with the sole criterion that their work be generally recognized as having made a significant contribution to feminist literary theory. Longer overview entries, on topics ranging from "Pornography" to "Violence," from "Beauty" to "War," offer discussions of the major theoretical points relevant to a feminist literary discussion of the topic. In addition, entries organized around literary periods or fields, such as "Medieval Studies," "Shakespeare," or "Romanticism," survey the chief points of intersection between that field and feminist literary theory, suggesting along the way how feminist theory has altered our understanding. Where the period entries seem disproportionate—Victorian Studies yielding more cross-references than Medieval Studies, for example—this reflects the current status of the field; feminist literary theorists have historically gravitated more toward some fields than others, though the situation remains in flux.

Purposefully omitted from the entry list are two terms in particular: "feminism" and "feminist." Rather than define these terms, we have preferred to let the entries suggest a multiplicity of possibilities. As is often stated, feminism is an idea best spoken of in the plural, as feminisms, while the related term "feminist" is hotly contested even as I write. Nonetheless, feminism can be said to refer to a constellation of social and political ideas, chief among them the recognition that gender inequality continues to be a pressing concern in contemporary society, and that an activist agenda in response to the status quo is necessary. More recently, feminism has concerned itself with class and race oppression, often painfully interrogating its own relationship to both class and racial politics. "Feminist," as an adjective, functions in relation to "feminism." It implies an intellectual commitment to achieving gender, class, and racial equality, and it often sees all aspects of culture—especially literature—as contested sites. Feminist literary theory, then, engages with the political and social goals of feminism, and it concentrates on literary culture and theory as a possible site of struggle and as a means of eventual change.

Each entry in the encyclopedia is accompanied by a bibliography designed both to help in the definition of the term and to lead to further study. Graduate students in particular may find these bibliographies useful as a point of departure for further research. Certainly, however, a key virtue of this encyclopedia is that it accumulates bibliographical references for so many important and often-cited works within a single volume. In this way, instructors will find that it is also a useful tool in the preparation of course materials or syllabi. It is our hope that all readers using the encyclopedia will gain immediate access to the vast territory of feminist literary theory; that they will quickly accumulate useful information on a broad range of subjects; and that they will use the encyclopedia as a point of departure for future work, as the territory continues to expand and develop.

The scope of this encyclopedia is all aspects of feminist theory, with most emphasis on the terminology produced in the United States and Great Britain since the 1970s, though items significant to the history of feminist theory are also featured. The encyclopedia provides reference to some terms from French feminist theory, when such terms have influenced Anglo American theory. Because literary criticism draws heavily upon other disciplines, including sociology, psychology, philosophy, history, anthropology, and law, terms from such disciplines also occasionally appear in the encyclopedia. (See, for example, "Family Systems Theory," "Feminist Jurisprudence," "Separate Spheres," or "Traffic in Women.") Though the terminology of women's studies is often difficult to distinguish from that of feminist literary theory, we have included topics from women's studies when those subjects have also been discussed in a literary and theoretical context. In addition, special efforts have been made to locate salient terms relevant to the critical discourses of African American feminist studies, Chicana studies, other ethnic studies, lesbian and gay studies, and feminist film studies, whenever these discourses have intersected with feminist theory.

It could be said that three major movements in particular have had the greatest impact upon feminist literary theory: psychoanalysis, poststructuralism, and Marxism. By now, each of these movements has given rise to a large vocabulary of its own. Here those three movements are amply referred to, either through overview entries that discuss their connections to feminist literary theory (see "Marxism" or "Psychoanalysis"), or through biographical or topical entries that also make important linkages (see, for example, "Hysteria," "Lacan, Jacques," or "Materialist Feminism"). The entry list pays special attention to terminology within these movements—to terms such as "binary opposition," "différance," "other," "phallus"—in order to arrive at the fullest possible understanding.

The index is designed to facilitate reference between and among entries. A reader might move logically from an overview entry, to a shorter definition; or the consultation of a short definition might lead her to an overview description. In either case, use of the index will ensure maximum coverage of a topic. Needless to say, the index can also help locate terms, names, or topics not appearing in the entry list.

As this project comes to a close, it is clear that the business of collecting materials relevant to feminist literary theory could easily take us into the next century. Nonetheless, this encyclopedia has its "resting"—if not its "end" point—in work largely produced by 1994, and the bibliographies are inclusive through that moment. It is now almost impossible to think back to the time before feminist literary theory was an identifiable subject in the Modern Language Association bibliography, back to the day—a scant twenty-five years ago—when the very idea of a seminar in feminist literary theory would have been outrageous. To bring this project to closure is, then, to acknowledge with gratitude the struggle of all those who worked to establish legitimacy for the field. A work like this, however massive in its proportion, can never do full justice to their accomplishment.

On the day-to-day level, many individuals facilitated the completion of this encyclopedia. First, the contributors are to be commended for responding professionally and for attending so promptly to deadlines. Several research assistants participated in day-to-day operations: Dagmara Dobzrynski, Michael Enos, and Sandra Schneible. Boston College generously awarded several Research Expense Grants to help with the preparation of the manuscript. James D. Wallace provided invaluable technological assistance. In the early days of the project, Paula Ladenberg was a major source of guidance and support. The editorial board—Rosalind Ballaster, Lois Brown, Helena Michie, Frances Restuccia, Kristina Straub, and Robyn Warhol—supplied counsel and wisdom. Lastly, Sara Quay was much more than an assistant. Participating in this project since its very first moment, she performed feats both small and big, from the most mundane correspondence, to acting as an emissary for the encyclopedia, to writing entries, to speaking at MLA about our project. This encyclopedia is dedicated to her and to her future as a feminist literary critic of the first order.

Elizabeth Kowaleski-Wallace

Contributors

Afzal-Khan, Fawzia
Montclair State College

Agigian, Amy
Brandeis University

Anderson, Antje Schaum
Rice University

Astyk, Sharon
Brandeis University

Baker, Lori A.
Providence, Rhode Island

Ballaster, Ros
Oxford University

Balsamo, Anne
Georgia Institute of Technology

Barker, Joanne Marie
University of California, Santa Cruz

Bennett, Alexandra
Brandeis University

Bilger, Audrey
Claremont McKenna College

Blansett, Lisa
University of North Carolina, Chapel Hill

Boelcskevy, Mary Anne Stewart
Harvard University

Boufis, Christina
CUNY Graduate School

Bové, Carol Mastrangelo
Westminster College

Bowers, Terence
University of Chicago

Bowers, Toni
University of Pennsylvania

Bretzius, Stephen
Louisiana State University

Bromberg, Pamela Starr
Simmons College

Brown, Lois
Cornell University

Brown, Monica A.
Ohio State University

Brunk, Terence
Rutgers University

Brush, AnJanette
State University of New York, Buffalo

Burdan, Judith
James Madison University

Carpenter, Mary Wilson
Queen's University

Carson, James
Kenyon College

Carter, Mia E.
University of Texas, Austin

Chedgzoy, Kate
Liverpool University

Clarke, Jennifer
State University of New York, Stony Brook

Cody, Lisa
Stanford University

Conboy, Sheila
Stonehill College

Conry, Clare E.
Boston College

Cosentino, J. Nicole
Chapel Hill, North Carolina

Creadick, Anna
University of Massachusetts, Amherst

Creef, Elena
Wellesley College

Crosby, Janice
Baton Rouge, Louisiana

Cross, Ashley J.
Illinois Benedictine College

Cutter, Martha J.
University of Connecticut

da Silva, Stephen
Rice University

Dacey, Beth
Boston College

Daileader, Celia R.
University of Alabama

Dallas, Phyllis Surrency
Georgia Southern University

Danahey, Mary A.
Boston College

Deal, Michelle L.
University of Vermont

Disenhaus, Nancy
University of Vermont

Dougherty, Mary V.
Rutgers University

Draper, Ellen
Simmons College

Dropick, A.M.
Princeton University

Dulan, Jo
Wayne State University

Eby, Clare Virginia
University of Connecticut

Espinoza, Dionne
Cornell University

Fish, Cheryl
CUNY, Graduate Center

Folsom, Marcia McClintock
Wheelock College

Frankson, Susan M.
Minneapolis, Minnesota

Gamer, Michael Crews
University of Pennsylvania

Geronimo, Anna
State University of New York, Buffalo

Gillooly, Eileen
Columbia University

Golden, Catherine
Skidmore College

Goldstein, Nancy
Connecticut College

Gormly, Kathleen
University of Vermont

Goulding, Susan
New York University

Grathwol, Kathleen B.
Brandeis University

Gray, Janet
Princeton University

Greenberg, Judith Ann
Yale University

Greenberg, Nina Manasan
University of Central Florida

Gullette, Margaret Morganroth
Radcliffe Seminars

Hames, Gina
Carnegie Mellon University

Hanselman, Sarah Amyes
Tufts University

Harris, Marla
Brandeis University

Hawkins, Kay
Lakewood, Ohio

Herndl, Diane Price
New Mexico State, Las Cruces

Hicks, Kim
University of Massachusetts, Amherst

Hodge, Jon
Tufts University

Hohmann, Marti
Harvard University

Hollenberg, Donna Krolick
University of Connecticut

Hunter, Dianne
Trinity College

Inness, Sherrie A.
Miami University

Isikoff, Erin
Columbia University

Ivers, Jenna
Brandeis University

Jadwin, Lisa
St. John Fisher College

Jerinic, Maria
State University of New York, Stony Brook

Johnson, Ronna C.
Tufts University

Jones, Therese
University of Colorado, Boulder

Kader, Cheryl
Beloit College

Kahn, Robbie Pfeufer
University of Vermont

Kapila, Shuchi
Cornell University

Kaufman, Heidi N.
University of New Hampshire

Kennedy, Colleen
College of William and Mary

King, Sigrid
Francis Marion University

Koch, Emily
Brandeis University

Kowaleski-Wallace, Beth
Boston College

Kurian, Manju
University of Vermont

Lemire, Elise
Rutgers University

Lesnik-Oberstein, Karín
Oxford University

Lewes, Darby
Lycoming College

Lieske, Pam
University of Massachusetts, Amherst

Lobanov-Rostovsky, Sergei
Kenyon College

Looser, Devoney
Indiana State University

Lynch, Deidre
State University of New York, Buffalo

McGrath, Lynette
West Chester University

Mackie, Erin
Washington University

Mackin, Kathleen
State University of New York at Buffalo

Maier, Carol
Kent State University

Malina, Debra
Boston College

Mangum, Teresa
University of Iowa

Marcus, Lisa
Rutgers University

Margolis, Harriet E.
Victoria University

May, Ron
Baton Rouge, Louisiana

Mazella, David
University of Houston

Mazzio, Carla J.
Harvard University

Medoff, Jeslyn
Swampscott, Massachusetts

Mercier, Cathryn M.
Simmons College

Miller, Diane Helene
University of Georgia

Miller, Naomi J.
University of Arizona

Mizejewski, Michele
Boston College

Mooney, Susan M.
Stonehill College

Moss, Betty
University of South Florida

Moya, Paula
Cornell University

Mukherjee, Ankhi
Rutgers University

Nadeau, Carolyn A.
Pennsylvania State University

Nakamura, Lisa
CUNY Graduate Center

Paige, Linda Rohrer
Georgia Southern University

Pallis, Patricia LaRose
Tolland, Connecticut

Parsons, Clare Olivia
Harvard University

Pawlowski, Merry M.
California State University, Bakersfield

Pelzer, Linda C.
Wesley College

Perrakis, Phyllis Sternberg
University of Ottawa

Picklesimer, Claudette
Boston College

Pines, Davida
Brandeis University

Plimpton, Pamela
University of Oregon

Pollak, Ellen
Michigan State University

Postol, J.S.
Boston College

Quay, Sara E.
Brandeis University

Quinn, Laura
Allegheny College

Rado, Lisa
University of Michigan

Raimon, Eve Allegra
University of Southern Maine

Ray, Sangeeta
University of Maryland

Rees, Emma L.E.
University of East Anglia

Reilly, Susan P.
Boston College

Reitz, Caroline
Brown University

Reynolds, Bryan
Harvard University

Richardson, Alan
Boston College

Rigsby, Roberta K.
Indiana University of Pennsylvania

Roach, Susan
Louisiana Tech University

Roberts, Kimberley
University of Virginia

Rogers, Deborah D.
University of Maine at Orono

Rossman, Dara Tomlin
Brandeis University

Savelson, Kim
Brandeis University

Schneller, Beverly
Millersville University

Seamon, Hollis
College of Saint Rose

Seshadri-Crooks, Kalpana
Boston College

Sharon-Zisser, Shirley
Tel Aviv University

Sharp, Lynn L.
Costa Mesa, California

Sheffield, Elisabeth
University of Illinois

Sielke, Sabine
Freie Universität, Berlin

Sikorski, Grace
Pennsylvania State University

Slater, Tracy
Brandeis University

Singley, Carol J.
Rutgers University

Smedman, Lorna J.
CUNY Graduate Center

Smith, Patricia Juliana
University of Connecticut

Sosnoski, Karen
Brandeis University

Spahr, Juliana
State University of New York, Buffalo

Stanbury, Sarah
College of the Holy Cross

Stein, Karen F.
University of Rhode Island

Stenson, Linnea A.
Macalester College

Stern, Rebecca F.
Rice University

Sullivan, Megan
University of Rhode Island

Swanson, Diana L.
Northern Illinois University

Sweeney, Susan Elizabeth
College of the Holy Cross

Tabron, Judith
Brandeis University

Taylor, Susan B.
University of Colorado, Boulder

Tedrowe, Melissa
University of Illinois, Champaign-Urbana

Temple, Kathyrn
Georgetown University

Thompson, Deborah
University of Alberta

Thompson, James
University of North Carolina, Chapel Hill

Thompson, Mary
Bowling Green State University

Thomson, Rosemarie Garland
Howard University

Thorn, Jennifer
Duke University

Travis, Jennifer
Brandeis University

Ty, Eleanor
Wilfed Laurier University

Vallone, Lynne
Texas A&M University

Volz, Tracy M.
Rice University

Wahl, Wendy C.
University of Vermont

Ward, Jenifer K.
Rhodes College

Warhol, Robyn R.
University of Vermont

Waters, Sarah
London, England

Weiner, Deborah
University of Rochester

Wells, Christopher
Brandeis University

West, Kathryn
Bellarmine College

Willis, Julia
Rutgers University

Wilson, Anna
Bowdoin College

Winter, Kari J.
University of Vermont

Witt, Doris
University of Iowa

Yavneh, Naomi
University of South Florida

Zimnik, Nina
New York, New York

Encyclopedia of
Feminist Literary Theory

A

Abel, Elizabeth

Elizabeth Abel served as guest editor for a special issue of *Critical Inquiry* in 1981, "Writing and Sexual Difference," which appeared in book form in 1982. These essays mark a shift in the history of feminist literary theory from "recovering a lost tradition to discovering the terms of confrontation with the dominant tradition," from "unwieldy global questions about female writing" to "specific historical studies of the ways women revise prevailing themes and styles."

With Emily K. Abel, she edited *The Signs Reader: Women, Gender, and Scholarship*, which collects the most influential of the first thirty articles to appear in *Signs*. With Marianne Hirsch and Elizabeth Langland, Abel edited *The Voyage In: Fictions of Female Development*, drawing attention to the traditional lack of consideration of gender in studies of novels of development.

Abel's *Virginia Woolf and the Fictions of Psychoanalysis* demonstrates that Woolf engaged her novels in the same set of terms that dominated the discourse on gender development being shaped by psychoanalysts (Sigmund Freud and Melanie Klein) and social anthropologists in the 1920s. In chapters praised for their textual analysis and their contextualization, Abel reads Woolf's texts both against one another and against the psychoanalytic texts, providing new insights into Woolf's artistry and ideas and into the fictionality—the narrative structures and choices of—psychoanalysis. For example, Abel argues that *Mrs. Dalloway* (1925) anticipates a female developmental sequence similar to the one that Freud will describe in his essays on female sexuality (1925–1933), yet challenges Freud's ideas of the "normal." Notably, Abel describes a shift in Woolf's own position, a shift produced by fascism's appropriation of ideologies of motherhood that led her closer to Freud in expounding a patrocentric view. For instance, the woman writer thinking back through her literary foremothers in *A Room of One's Own* becomes the "daughter of an educated man" in *Three Guineas*. Finally, Abel examines the similar but inverse responses of Woolf and Freud to fascism in *Between the Acts* (1941) and *Moses and Monotheism* (1939), respectively; both envision fascism as a disastrous endpoint, but Freud sees it as the decline of patriarchy, while Woolf discerns a conclusive triumph of patriarchy.

In "Black Writing, White Reading: Race and the Politics of Feminist Interpretation," Abel explores the complexities of "crossing racial boundaries in reading." Here as in all her work, Abel demonstrates that, as she phrases it in the introduction to *Writing and Sexual Difference*, "textual politics are neither trivial nor obvious: they reflect larger political contexts."

Kathryn West

References

Abel, Elizabeth. "Black Writing, White Reading: Race and the Politics of Feminist Interpretation." *Critical Inquiry* 19 (1993): 470–498.

———. "(E)Merging Identities: The Dynamics of Female Friendship in Contemporary Fiction by Women." *Signs* 6 (1981): 413–435.

———. "The Golden Notebook: 'Female Writing' and 'The Great Tradition.'" In *Critical Essays on Doris Lessing*, edited by Claire Sprague and Virginia Tiger,

101–107. Boston: G.K. Hall, 1986.

———. "Resisting the Exchange: Brother-Sister Incest in Fiction by Doris Lessing." In *Doris Lessing: The Alchemy of Survival*, edited by Carey Kaplan and Ellen Cronan Rose, 115–126. Athens: Ohio University Press, 1988.

———. *Virginia Woolf and the Fictions of Psychoanalysis*. Chicago: University of Chicago Press, 1989.

———, ed. *Writing and Sexual Difference. Essays from a Special Issue of* Critical Inquiry. Chicago: University of Chicago Press, 1982.

———, and Emily K. Abel, eds. *The Signs Reader: Women, Gender, and Scholarship*. Chicago: University of Chicago Press, 1983.

———, Marianne Hirsch, and Elizabeth Langland, eds. *The Voyage In: Fictions of Female Development*. Hanover, N.H.: University Press of New England, 1983.

Abortion

If, ordinarily, the term "abortion" lends itself either to termination of the embryo or fetus in utero, either naturally or externally induced, feminist readings of the act have looked resolutely at situations involving the operation of will or choice. They concentrate on the multiplex, conflicted agency of the woman who must choose, and on human maternity, which lies beleaguered and misunderstood at the center of the question of abortion.

That action itself is what Judith Wilt called "the undoing of the not yet done," and it can appear to dislocate language, perpetrating violence on it, by dismantling the binaries of subject and object, agent and victim. In her essay, "Apostrophe, Animation, and Abortion," Barbara Johnson discusses abortion poems by women poets, using the rhetorical structure of the apostrophe schematically. Because language inevitably animates whatever it addresses, rhetoric can always have already answered "yes" to the question of whether a fetus is a live human, she says. The life-instilling energies of the address are, however, problematized when the lyric speaker is also the death-dealing agent, but one who is unsure of the precise degree of human animation that existed in that entity "killed"; the uncertainty of the fetus's status as an object brings about the speaker's concomitant instability as controlling subject. The clear-cut distinctions between subject and object assume Byzantine ambiguities when the "self" seems to be controlled by the "other" it has anthropomorphized through language, and the mother/speaker is seen to become the addressee. Language, by simultaneously granting women the right to choose, and the right to mourn, humanizes both mother and aborted child, and gives away its "inadequacy . . . to resolve the dilemma without violence."

Judith Wilt, in her *Abortion, Choice, and Contemporary Fiction: The Armageddon of the Maternal Instinct*, elaborates on this dilemma of making a choice in the shadow of other choices, none of which are good. In her preface, Wilt states, "A woman's freedom to abort a fetus is a monstrous, a tyrannous, but a *necessary* freedom in a fallen world." What is ironic is that, in an unfallen world, there would be no necessity, and therefore no freedom: freedom follows from dire necessity and is "coterminous with it." In the case of abortion, agency is not necessarily autonomous, and the subject is the object of violence at the same time, and the agent the victim. As Johnson says, she who wields choice has not necessarily chosen the conditions under which she must choose. If the issue in abortion is that of maternal choice, that choice is not simply between violence and nonviolence; it is negotiated between the registers of discernible violence to a fetus, and the complex, less perceptible violence to "an involuntary mother and/or an unwanted child."

Both Johnson and Wilt talk about the powerful taboo that is violated when a woman ceases to speak about the death of children in terms of loss, and both think that the taboo is not just patriarchal horror at woman's rebuttal of motherhood. Rather, the taboo relates more deeply to the archetypal reliance of all humans upon maternity as an instinct that swamps consciousness, unmindful of choice. Abortion signals "the Armageddon of the maternal instinct," writes Wilt: the last days, not of maternity, but of maternity as an instinct that precludes choice. In her study, Wilt poignantly evokes "the line we once crossed from the all-desiring imaginary to the rational symbolic," from the idyllic limitlessness of a world where choice is redundant because no alternative excludes another, to the world we mostly think we have to live in, the world of either/or. The prochoice worldview is thus entrenched in the Lacanian symbolic, "ready to speak, ready to plan, ready for the long, complex arc of reasoned thought toward best possible choice." It is a reaching after female selfhood, a will to augment the delivery of babies with the deliverance of mothers.

Ankhi Mukherjee

References

Johnson, Barbara. "Apostrophe, Animation, and Abortion." *Diacritics* 16 (1987): 29–39.

Wilt, Judith. *Abortion, Choice, and Contemporary Fiction: The Armageddon of the Maternal Instinct.* Chicago and London: University of Chicago Press, 1990.

Acquired Immune Deficiency Syndrome

AIDS was identified as a distinct disease entity in 1981, emerging at a particular historical moment that, as Jeffrey Weeks argues, constructed it as a cultural entity as much as a tragic individual and collective experience. A postmodern epidemic, HIV/AIDS engendered a crisis not only in the discovery and management of a new infectious agent, but also in the representations of the disease. Thus, feminists have had to identify, challenge, and subvert the meanings of HIV/AIDS produced by government agencies, the medical industry, and mass media.

One such example is Paula Treichler's 1987 essay on AIDS, gender, and biomedical discourse, in which she posed this question: how can we account for the striking silence on the topic of women in AIDS discourse when a relationship between women and AIDS has existed for the known lifespan of the disease? The linking of women and silence in some linguistic shape or other has become a common starting point for literary analyses, epidemiological overviews, and social histories concerned with American women and HIV/AIDS. Treichler, Jan Zita Grover, Gena Corea, and Cindy Patton among others have theorized women's silence and invisibility from two perspectives. The first is that the scientific construction of HIV/AIDS as a male disease that placed women under the literal rubric of "Other" in the pie-shaped charts of risk groups made them invisible, and as that construction was consistently reinscribed in biomedical, popular, and literary discourses, the monolithic identities of those at risk and not at risk were continually reinforced, making them virtually impossible to dislodge. The second is that the erasure and

marginalization of women as evidenced in silence and absence or by stereotypical and distorted roles such as ministering angel, innocent victim, maternal vessel, and demonized prostitute are another expression of the entrenched attitudes of sexism. These attitudes reduce women's access to information, resources, and political power, and they are a sign of the oppressive institution of patriarchy, which perpetuates male control over women's labor time, sexuality, and reproductive capabilities.

Consequently, feminist scholars and artists have had a simultaneous project: deconstructing HIV/AIDS as a male disease and reconstructing it as a women's issue to encourage resistant strategies, alternative representations, and what Katie Hogan describes as an oppositional sensibility, one that assumes an interlocking oppression of gender, sexuality, race, and class and finds expression in renderings that neither eschew politics nor sacrifice imagination. In equal measures of irony and optimism, feminists like Biddy Martin, and Sue O'Sullivan note that silence and invisibility are being transfigured as openings and spaces for the public discussion of ourselves and our sexualities, despite renewed repressions.

The ways in which women infected with and affected by HIV/AIDS are filling up the silence and making themselves visible are diverse and radical, exemplifying a resistant and visionary feminist consciousness that constructs a self in relation or opposition to the categories forced upon them and gives that self over for and to other women. For example, Tessa Boffin's glossed pictorial fantasy "Angelic Rebels" addresses safer sex practices for lesbians, women virtually ignored in educational campaigns; Andrea Rudd and Darien Taylor's international anthology, *Positive Women: Voices of Women Living with AIDS*, offers women the opportunity to proclaim their identity as HIV-infected individuals and connect with others through personal testimony, poetry, and art; the text of Karen Finley's performance piece "We Keep Our Victims Ready" reads as a powerful indictment of institutions and a terrorist attack on cultural attitudes; the captioned photographs of Ann Meredith in "Until that Last Breath: Women with AIDS" convey the corporeal presence of women who are living with the physical, emotional, and spiritual demands of chronic disease, as well as transgressing the imaginary boundaries that separate risk populations from "general populations" and collapse the medical hierarchy of exposure categories.

Judith Laurence Pastore writes that literary AIDS reinforces the contemporary conviction that just as there is no separation between private and public, there can be none between art and politics. Thus she foregrounds the challenge to feminist theorists and critics for describing and evaluating materials that might be personal or collective, confrontational or didactic, sentimental or ironic, traditional or experimental.

Therese Jones

References

Boffin, Tessa, and Sunil Gupta, eds. *Ecstatic Antibodies: Resisting the AIDS Mythology*. London: Rivers Oram, 1990.

Corea, Gena. *The Invisible Epidemic: The Story of Women and AIDS*. New York: HarperCollins, 1992.

Finley, Karen. *Shock Treatment*. San Francisco: City Lights, 1990.

Grover, Jan Zita. "AIDS, Keywords and Culture." In *Cultural Studies Now and in the Future*, edited by Cary Nelson, Lawrence Grossberg, and Paula A. Treichler, 227–240. New York: Routledge, 1992.

Hogan, Katie. "Speculations on Women and AIDS." *Minnesota Review* (Spring/ Summer 1993): 84–94.

Martin, Biddy. "Sexual Practice and Changing Lesbian Identities." In *Destabilizing Theory: Contemporary Feminist Debates*, edited by Michele Barrett and Ann Philips, 93–119. Stanford: Stanford University Press, 1992.

Meredith, Ann. "Until that Last Breath: Women with AIDS." In *AIDS: The Making of a Chronic Disease*, edited by Elizabeth Fee and Daniel Fox, 229–244. Berkeley: University of California Press, 1992.

O'Sullivan, Sue, and Kate Thomson, eds. *Positively Women: Living with AIDS*. London: Sheba Feminist Press, 1992.

Nelson, Emmanuel, ed. *AIDS: The Literary Response*. Boston: Twayne, 1992.

Pastore, Judith Laurence, ed. *Confronting AIDS through Literature: The Responsibilities of Representation*. Urbana: University of Illinois Press, 1993.

Patton, Cindy. *Inventing AIDS*. New York: Routledge, 1990.

Rudd, Andrea, and Darien Taylor, eds. *Positive Women: Voices of Women Living with AIDS*. Toronto: Second Story, 1992.

Treichler, Paula A. "AIDS, Gender, and Biomedical Discourse: Current Contests for Meaning." In *AIDS: The Burdens of History*, edited by Elizabeth Fee and Daniel Fox, 191–266. Berkeley: University of California Press, 1987.

Weeks, Jeffrey. *Sex, Politics, and Society: The Regulation of Sexuality since 1800*. New York: Longmans, 1981.

Adams, Parveen

Parveen Adams has been most influential as a co-founder and editor of, and contributor to, the British socialist-feminist journal *m/f* (1978–1986). Adams's approach is based partially on the discourse theory of the French theorist Michel Foucault, partially on critiques of traditional Marxist analyses, but most importantly on the psychoanalytic theories of Sigmund Freud and the French analyst Jacques Lacan. Adams offers an extensive critique of essentialist feminist views, which portray "woman" as a unitary category with trans-historical or transcultural traits. Instead, the category of "woman" is seen as being constructed in many ways in cultural and historical practices that produce sexual difference. Importantly, Adams therefore goes further than ideas of the social construction of gender: in her work the very subject itself is constructed too, and there is no essential woman or man who is genderless until acted upon by historical or social forces. Psychoanalysis is also used by Adams to argue that gender is a powerful psychic reality in the Freudian unconscious, and that this interacts in complex ways with constructions of "woman" on many levels. Adams argues that society constructs many "women" for its own practices, such as in law, medicine, and politics: these are not disciplines that act upon women merely, but that simultaneously create the women they act upon. Adams has written about many of these constructions of "women" in relation to politics, motherhood, the body, representation, sexuality, and the family.

Karín Lesnik-Oberstein

References

Adams, Parveen. "The Art of Analysis: Mary Kelly's Interim and the Discourse of the Analyst." *October* 58 (1991): 81–96.

———. "Of Female Bondage." In *Between Feminism and Psychoanalysis*, edited by Teresa Brennan, 247–265. London and New York: Routledge, 1989.

———, ed. *Language in Thinking: Selected Readings*. Harmondsworth: Penguin, 1972.

———, and Elizabeth Cowie, eds. *The Woman in Question*. London: Verso, 1990. Cambridge: MIT Press, 1990.

Adolescence

Although adolescence is defined biologically as the period of life beginning with puberty and ending at maturity, its social and psychological parameters are more difficult to determine. The *Oxford English Dictionary,* 2nd edition, defines adolescence as lasting from twelve to twenty-one in females and fourteen to twenty-five in males. Most social historians agree that adolescence is a relatively modern phenomenon, coming into linguistic currency only in the twentieth century and arising out of educational, demographic, and industrial changes in the nineteenth century. For feminist theorists, adolescence raises additional problems of definition: not only has the developmental stage been conceived in primarily male-biased ways, but these ideas may not hold true for women. The subject of adolescence is of interest to feminist literary critics not only because so many novels center around adolescent protagonists, but also because these heroines confront the social and psychological ramifications of being a woman in a patriarchal society.

While the study of adolescence is relatively recent, it is only in the last twenty years—and under the second wave of feminism—that feminist theorists have reexamined female adolescence, positing new developmental patterns that differ from male models. Following Freud, most psychoanalysts believe that biology alone determined the psychosexual processes of adolescence, which for girls was thought to seal their passive role in life. The main tasks of adolescence—separation and individuation—which involve relinquishing family ties in favor of new love objects, are often perceived to be more conflicted in girls' development.

Adolescence is thought to be successfully completed when sexual identity and personality is consolidated, and the individual becomes an autonomous adult integrated into society. But this same definition casts girls' coming of age as both more troubled and less successful than boys'. Though Margaret Mead in *Coming of Age in Somoa* asserts that cultural not biological factors account for any storm and stress during puberty, it was not until the 1970s and 1980s that feminist psychologists looked again at social influences to explain differences between the sexes during development.

In *The Reproduction of Mothering,* social psychologist Nancy Chodorow finds that women have more fluid ego boundaries than men, a result not of a failed ability to develop an autonomous self but of asymmetrical child-rearing, which fosters a girl's close identification with her mother. As a result, Chodorow claims that girls, unlike boys, come to define their personality in relation to others, and that during adolescence they do not completely relinquish their strong maternal bond.

This emphasis on the contextual nature of women's development is a point taken up by Carol Gilligan in *In a Different Voice.* Gilligan finds an "ethic of care" in young women's moral development that depends on a network of relationships rather than abstract notions of justice. Furthermore, Gilligan notes a self-silencing on the part of adolescent girls, a fear not only of hurting others but of not being heard, a topic she pursues in *Meeting at the Crossroads: Women's Psychology and Girls' Development.*

For feminist literary theorists, reexaminations of female development by social psychologists in the 1970s and 1980s have interesting correlations to literary form. Ideas about development are reflected in the *bildungsroman,* or novel of formation, which traditionally follows the growth of a protagonist from childhood to adulthood and has been seen mostly in terms of male experience. Similar to new psychoanalytic models that recast development in terms of gender, feminist critics have charted specifically female versions of the *bildungsroman.* The essays in *The Voyage In: Fictions of Female Development,* edited by Elizabeth Abel, Marianne Hirsch, and Elizabeth Langland, reinterpret traditional literary forms to find patterns of development that have been overlooked primarily because they do not fit male-defined plots. The conclusion to George Eliot's *The Mill on the Floss,* for example, in which the heroine, Maggie Tulliver, drowns in a flood with her brother, is read not as "artistic failure" but as paradigmatic of a young women's profoundly different developmental experience. As the editors of *The Voyage In* point out in their introduction, Eliot's heroine chooses not to surrender elemental family ties, thus demonstrating the embedded and relational nature of woman's identity.

Adolescence also has been seen as a time to choose a path in life, but it is undoubtedly true that society has offered fewer choices for women. Thus feminist critics such as Annis Pratt and Barbara White find that in many novels coming of age is marked by images of imprisonment, madness, dwarfing and maiming, a "growing down" rather than a "growing up." The awkward heroine of Carson McCullers's *The Member of the Wedding*, Frankie Addams—as White demonstrates in *Growing Up Female*—exemplifies the ambivalent nature of the female adolescent: coming of age often involves a loss of self. Moreover, as women have been marginalized by patriarchy, the female adolescent is even more of an outsider, a point made by Patricia Meyer Spacks in *The Adolescent Idea*.

Examining the subject of adolescence in literature invites comparison to social expectations of women in "real life." Not only is adolescence an actual period for gender-role formation, but a culture's ideas about development are reflected in literary form. As a relatively recent social construct, adolescence—and female adolescence in particular—is just now being rigorously questioned. We might continue to ask if there are additional developmental differences between women and men that also have been overlooked by critics. If so, how do we theorize these differences and how are they reflected in literature? Feminist theories of development, as Bonnie Zimmerman states in her article "Exiting from Patriarchy: The Lesbian Novel of Development," must also include homosexual identity formation, as the coming out process is a significant theme in lesbian novels of development. Future explorations of adolescence might focus on different class and multicultural accounts of this transitional period, for adolescence is still formulated mainly in white, middle-class, and heterosexual terms. Feminist theory continues to yield a wealth of insight into these differences, and, together with feminist praxis, which advances the position of women in society, the opportunities for young women coming of age will undoubtedly expand.

Christina Boufis

References

Abel, Elizabeth, Marianne Hirsch, and Elizabeth Langland, eds. *The Voyage In: Fictions of Female Development*. Hanover, N.H.: University Press of New England, 1983.

Bakerman, Jane S., and Mary Jean DeMarr. *Adolescent Female Portraits in the American Novel, 1961–1981: An Annotated Bibliography*. New York: Garland, 1983.

Brown, Lyn Mikel and Carol Gilligan. *Meeting at the Crossroads: Women's Psychology and Girls' Development*. Cambridge, Mass.: Harvard University Press, 1992.

Chodorow, Nancy. *The Reproduction of Mothering: Psychoanalysis and the Sociology of Gender*. Berkeley: University of California Press, 1978.

Dalsimer, Katherine. *Female Adolescence: Psychoanalytic Reflections on Works of Literature*. New Haven: Yale University Press, 1986.

Gilligan, Carol. *In a Different Voice: Psychological Theory and Women's Development*. Cambridge: Harvard University Press, 1982.

Pratt, Annis. *Archetypal Patterns in Women's Fiction*. Bloomington: Indiana University Press, 1981.

Rosowski, Susan J. "Writing against Silences: Female Adolescent Development in the Novels of Willa Cather." *Studies in the Novel* 21 (1989): 60–77.

Spacks, Patricia Meyer. *The Adolescent Idea: Myths of Youth and the Adult Imagination*. New York: Basic, 1981.

Troester, Rosalie R. "Turbulence and Tenderness: Mothers, Daughters, and Othermothers in Paule Marshall's *Brown Girl, Brownstones*." *Sage: A Scholarly Journal on Black Women* 1 (1984): 13–16.

White, Barbara A. *Growing Up Female: Adolescent Girlhood in American Fiction*. Westport, Conn.: Greenwood, 1985.

Yalom, Marilyn. "Towards a History of Female Adolescence: The Contribution of George Sand." In *George Sand: Collected Essays*, edited by Janis Glasgow, 204–215. Troy, N.Y.: Whitson, 1985.

Zimmerman, Bonnie. "Exiting from Patriarchy: The Lesbian Novel of Development." In *The Voyage In: Fictions of Female Development*, edited by Elizabeth Abel et al., 244–257. Hanover, N.H.: University Press of New England, 1983.

Aesthetics
See FEMINIST AESTHETICS

Aesthetics of Response
See READER RESPONSE CRITICISM

Age (Aging)

Now almost required in feminist theory lists (along with gender, class, race and ethnicity, and sexual orientation), age has nevertheless been underutilized by literary critics, theorists, reviewers, and dictionary editors. Feminist literary theory, like other theoretical approaches, still often posits a subject without age; some critics use the age categories as if they were natural or essential. In the 1990s however, feminist age theory is developing, in a shift marked by nomenclature, from "literary gerontology" toward "age studies."

Literary gerontology studies primarily the elderly, through literature, film, and so on, and initially aimed to expand the field of gerontology by insisting on humanistic approaches. Age studies, named by Margaret Morganroth Gullette in a 1993 essay entitled "Creativity, Gender, Aging," is also an interdisciplinary study of culture. It understands age more explicitly as a set of historical and cultural concepts (like gender or race) useful for investigating how a culture builds age constructions and reproduces them in "all formulations of life events," as Kathleen Woodward explains. A social-constructionist approach to age allows us to understand discourses, institutions, and material conditions as producers of age categories and attributes, power differentials, emotions like dread of aging, and systems that interlock age and gender. The age-connected categories of American culture, which include "adolescence" and "Generation X," the "Baby Boomers" and the "midlife crisis," "old age," "stages," "transitions," "the life course," and the processes known as "life-course development" and "aging," although popularly accepted as empirical, must all be thought of as discursive or ideological constructs open to theorization. Gullette has argued that the dominant culture provides a "master (life-course) narrative" of peak and decline for both men and women, and she has termed the decline story the dominant "age ideology" of our culture.

Beginning in the nineteenth century, feminism issued a call for women to speak for themselves, and, particularly in the current wave, women of all ages have responded through oral histories, autobiography, fiction, and poetry. Some have reconfigured the ages of life, the life course, and women's development in untraditional and liberating ways. Since the eighties, bibliographies and anthologies have appeared, focused on primary protagonists identified as "old" (as in collections edited by Sandra Martz, *When I Am an Old Woman I Shall Wear Purple* and Jo Alexander, *Women and Aging*). Criticism, too, concerned "images" of old women in individual works. Finally, work on representations of the middle years of life (some of it influenced by midlife research in psychology, anthropology, history, and sociology) opened up two possibilities: theorizing the entire life course as socially constructed and considering the limits of social construction.

In age studies in literature the most promising avenue of analysis deals with narrative or groups of novels. In general, narrative produces age effects in characters and represents temporality, by means of standard devices: plots of progress or decline that are linked to chronological ages, characterization through age—"appropriate" attributes, flashbacks, tropes for elapsed time, realistic dialogue about what it feels like to be "aging." A series of novels written over a writer's life course may also represent temporality implicitly, argues Margaret Gullette. Any text—popular or "scientific"—may keep in circulation fragments of the master narrative of decline, along with the idea of the ages and the "entrance" into aging. At ages called young, subjects are socialized into learning the age stages and how to apply the categories to themselves.

Studies of the fictions of female temporality have appeared, inevitably looking past the romance ending of what we can now label as the narrative of youth. These studies, contest rather than support the master narrative by utilizing countercultural terms such as "midlife progress narrative" (in the words of Margaret Gullette, who also looks at men's midlife fiction), *Vollendungsroman*, or "novel of completion" (Constance Rooke's terms), and *Reifungsroman*, or "novel of ripening" (Barbara Frey Waxman's term). Waxman finds feminist writers "turning a bipolar concept of youth and age into that of an age continuum." A few critics, such as Kathleen Woodward and Anne Wyatt-Brown, are studying "late-life creativity," not necessarily to reify a "style" distinctive to "later" life but to extend creativity across the life course.

Age studies in the humanities are also enriching the interactions between literary theory and theory in other disciplines. In *Aging and Its Discontents* and other essays, Kathleen Woodward has produced subtle work bridging literary texts, psychoanalysis, and humanistic gerontology. *Aging and Gender*, edited by Wyatt-Brown and Rossen, models various approaches to writers' creative lives from literary criticism and the social sciences.

If many feminists have in fact been writing about young women when purporting to treat "women," writing from the point of view of daughters when purporting to treat "mothers and daughters," writing about the elderly when purporting to treat "aging," future work must resolve to take age issues into account in a much more self-conscious way. If aging in a particular culture changes relations between men and women (by, say, increasing or lessening acculturated differences), and if men's stages are constructed in relationship to women's, and vice versa, age studies will require rethinking feminism's relationship to the study of men. If being aged by culture changes identity across the life course, how does this affect essentialism and the category "woman"? As (some) older women achieve greater economic power and status than any have in the past, how will that affect the cultural imagination and subjectivity of young women, retired women, midlife women, and men?

Feminist literary and cultural theory has much to incorporate and offer, particularly those branches already allied with the construction of subjectivity, cultural studies, and a historicized psychodynamics. Age studies, bound to be cross-disciplinary and multicultural, might utilize age-oriented work on such issues as "age hierarchies," the effects of the historical cohort, the construction of new "characters" in the social text (as Margaret Gullette suggests in "Inventing the 'Postmaternal' Woman"), the invention of the "life course" as a standardized set of stages and goals, the economics of the life course, and emotionology (the construction of the feelings, including, conceivably, fear of death). Much work remains to be done in extending the idea that discourses are liable to be age-graded as well as gendered or racialized.

The term "aging" in particular needs to be theorized. It is often used as synonymous with "old age." This may continue because of unconscious ageism that wishes to attach everything emotionally connected with aging to "the old"; because of disciplinary practices (for example, anthropology uses "elders" as informants, and historical research often deals with eras when "old" and "young" were the major life-course binary); and because literary gerontology accepted the assumption of gerontology that the elderly were separate and alone subject to "aging" discourses and practices. Feminist activism from the beginning has intervened to improve socioeconomic and discursive conditions for "older" women (who are disproportionately poor). One of the most powerful voices for activism was Simone de Beauvoir's in the first half of *La Vieillesse* (translated as *Old Age* in England, and in the United States as *The Coming of Age)*. Some work on age still reifies aging based on the medical model, a kind of biological essentialism that constructs markers—major events—(notably "the Change") in women's lives. Feminist work in fields such as epidemiology, endocrinology, and sociology is weakening the medical model. Age theory needs to argue that the single concept "aging" now covers and confuses socially produced diseases (caused by pollution, poverty, and hazardous work) that take years to show themselves, cultural forms that produce social aging, and bodily and mental age processes; it may be that when all the external forces are accounted for, little may remain to constitute biological age processes.

Theorists will eventually want to consider what elements (including biases toward youth and the youth genres in canonical literature, in contemporary culture, university culture, and the feminist movement itself) delayed their consideration of age so long after it had proved itself compelling in social and medical research and yet remained in need of the intensity created by sensitive analysis of texts, and the clarifications and urgency of debate that theory can provide.

Margaret Morganroth Gullette

References

Alexander, Jo, ed. *Women and Aging: An Anthology by Women.* Corvallis: Calyx, 1986.

Gullette, Margaret Morganroth. "Creativity, Gender, Aging." In *Aging and Gender in Literature: Studies in Creativity*, edited by Anne M. Wyatt-Brown and Janice Rossen, 19–48. Charlottesville: University Press of Virginia, 1993.

———. *Cultural Combat. The Politics of the Midlife.* Charlottesville: University Press of Virginia, 1997.

———. "Inventing the 'Postmaternal' Woman: Idle, Unwanted, and Out of a Job." *Feminist Studies* 21 (1995): 221–253.

———. *Safe at Last in the Middle Years.* Berkeley: University of California Press, 1988.

Martz Sandra, ed. *When I Am an Old Woman, I Shall Wear Purple.* Manhattan Beach, Calif.: Papier Maché Press, 1987.

Rooke, Constance. "Old Age in Contemporary Fiction." In *Handbook of the Humanities and Aging*, edited by Thomas Cole, David Van Tassell, and Robert Kastenbaum, 241–257. New York: Springer, 1992.

Waxman, Barbara Frey. *From the Hearth to the Open Road. A Feminist Study of Aging in Contemporary Literature.* Westport, Conn.: Greenwood, 1990.

Woodward, Kathleen. *Aging and Its Discontents: Freud and Other Fictions.* Bloomington: Indiana University Press, 1991.

———. "Late Theory, Late Style." In *Aging and Gender in Literature: Studies in Creativity,* edited by Anne M. Wyatt-Brown and Janice Rossen, 82–101. Charlottesville: University Press of Virginia, 1993.

———. "Tribute to the Older Woman: Psychoanalytic Geometry, Gender, and the Emotions." In *Psychoanalysis, Feminism, and the Future of Gender*, edited by Joseph H. Smith and Afaf M. Mahfouz, 91–108. Baltimore: Johns Hopkins University Press, 1993.

Wyatt-Brown, Anne M. "The Coming of Age of Literary Gerontology." *Journal of Aging Studies* 4 (1990): 299–315.

———, and Janice Rossen, eds. *Aging and Gender in Literature: Studies in Creativity.* Charlottesville: University Press of Virginia, 1993.

AIDS

See ACQUIRED IMMUNE DEFICIENCY SYNDROME

Alarcón, Norma

Both as general editor of *Third Woman*, an independent press dedicated to the publication of new writing and criticism by women of color, and as a literary critic, Alarcón has been a key figure in the fields of Chicana literary criticism and theory in particular and in the area of writing by women of color more generally. Alarcón seeks to examine the usefulness of Anglo and French feminist literary theories for understanding and explaining Chicana literature, while at the same time forging a specifically Chicana feminist theoretical viewpoint. More recently, she has moved beyond a merely literary understanding of Chicana feminist theories to assert the importance of situating Chicanas both within the political-economic context of the United States and within the new international division of labor (1990). Furthermore, she argues that the Chicana critic's and intellectual's positioning in relation to the fields of women's studies and Chicano studies necessitates that Chicanas in the academy create another disciplinary space from which to speak.

Her criticism is notable for showing how French feminist theory, specifically the work of Julia Kristeva and Luce Irigaray, can be useful in analyzing Chicana literature. In doing this, she does not merely provide a critical and useful application of the theory to the text; rather, she explores the limits of French feminist theory with respect to Chicana literature, history, and culture (1987). She has also demonstrated how some Anglo feminist theories, such as the feminist standpoint theory proposed by Allison Jaggar, participate in the silencing of the voices of women of color because in privileging the heterosexual relation within an assumed homogeneous social space, they prioritize gender oppression over oppression on the basis of race, class, and sexuality (1990). Furthermore, in comparing theories generated by Mexican writers such as Rosario Castellanos and Chicana writers such as Gloria Anzaldúa to those of French feminists like Julia Kristeva (1992), she reveals their affinities, while also drawing attention to the various geographical locations in which theory is produced and the inequities involved in the way these locations influence their reception. Finally, and perhaps more important, she asserts the specificity of Chicana cultural identity while also underscoring the need for building coalitions with other Third World women both within and without the United States.

Both Alarcón's work as publisher of Third Woman press and her literary theory and criticism have played a critical role not only in making available salient literature by women of color, but also in enabling a sophisticated understanding of the intersection of race, class, gender, and sexuality as it is expressed by the multiply positioned woman of color.

Dionne Espinoza

References

Alarcón, Norma. "Chicana Feminism: In the Tracks of 'the' Native Woman." *Cultural Studies* 4 (1990): 248–256.

———. "Chicana's Feminist Literature: A Revision through Malinztin/ or Malintzin: Putting Flesh Back on the Object." In *This Bridge Called My Back: Writings by Radical Women of Color*, edited by Gloria Anzaldúa and Cherríe Moraga, 182–190. New York: Kitchen Table: Women of Color Press, 1981.

———. "Making 'Familia' from Scratch: Split Subjectivities in the Work of Helena María Viramontes and Cherríe Moraga." In *Chicana Creativity and Criticism: Charting New Frontiers in American Literature*, edited by María Herrera-Sobek and Helena María Viramontes, 147–159. Houston, Tex.: Arte Publico, 1987.

———. *Ninfomanía: El discurso feminista en la obra poética de Rosario Castellanos*. Madrid, Spain: editorial pliegos, 1992.

———. "The Theoretical Subject(s) in *This Bridge Called My Back* and Anglo-American Feminism." In *Making Face, Making Soul: Haciendo Caras*, edited by Gloria Anzaldúa, 356–369. San Francisco: Spinsters/Aunt Lute, 1990.

Amazon

This term has Latin and Greek roots and goes back to literature of the Classical period. The *Oxford English Dictionary* cites the origin of the word as a description of "a race of female warriors alleged by Herodotus, etc. to exist in Scythia," but traces it further to include a "female warrior," a "very strong, tall, or masculine woman," or, more generally, as a reference to the "sexual habits" of those women. The *OED* definition reflects the controversial nature of the Amazonian ideal that has caused division among feminists over whether to adopt the Amazon as a role model.

The origin of the Amazon's story is a source of debate. Some critics believe that the Amazon began as a male-created myth in Greek legends, while others believe that the amazons could have been based on actual societies of goddess-worshiping women living around the Black Sea or in North Africa. The word *Amazon* can be traced back to the word *a mazos*, for "breastless," because of the story that these warrior women would remove one breast in order to more easily use their weapons. While the Amazons were fierce fighters, usually opponents of Heracles or Theseus in myth, they eventually succumbed to their male opponents either through death or matrimony, as in the story of Heracles's removal of the girdle from Hippolyte. Recent analyses of the Amazon myth by Paige duBois and William Blake Tyrrell demonstrate how the Amazons' role in Antiquity was marginal until they could be conquered. Abby Wettan Kleinbaum's *The War against the Amazons* asserts that defeat of an Amazon helped demonstrate the heroic nature of a male figure and enhanced his sense of "worth and historical significance."

After the Classical period, Amazons continued to appear in literature but began to be appropriated by women to dramatize possibilities for female strength and independence. In medieval France, Christine de Pizan used the Amazons as a positive image for women in her *Livre de la cité des dames*. In Renaissance English literature, Amazons frequently appear as the "other" in travel narratives of colonial exploration in the New World. The Amazon was frequently figured diametrically as either a virgin (as Radigund in *The Faerie Queene*) or a "woman who uses her strength for non-virtuous, specifically lustful ends." Several essays in *Playing with Gender: A Renaissance Pursuit* demonstrate that Amazons also appeared in Renaissance works that questioned gender categories, with men disguised as Amazons (as in Philip Sidney's *New Arcadia*). During the eighteenth century, writers used the Amazonian myth to construct "political and social theories and to signify "the representation of difference." In the nineteenth century, J.J. Bachofen described an Amazonian stage of cultural development common "to all humanity," which was "only slightly higher or more advanced than pure animal existence." This juxtaposition of the Amazon with the "animal" has caused some twentieth-century feminists, like bell hooks, to problematize the Amazonian model.

Contemporary Amazons appear in the "Wonder Woman" comic strip of the 1940s, science fiction, Maxine Hong Kingston's *Woman Warrior*, and Monique Wittig's *Les Guérillères*. The contemporary figure of the Amazon is not for Wittig "a romantic figure evoked in nostalgia for a prepatriarchal past"; instead, she "is the activist lesbian feminist of the present fighting to transform the future." Jessica Salmonson's recent *Encyclopedia of Amazons* chronicles the amazing variety of forms in which the Amazon myth has manifested itself in different cultures. The Amazon provides contemporary feminists with a model of "political power, of military prowess, and a role model of autonomy and hence dignity." Many twentieth-century lesbians follow the example of Natalie Clifford Barney, who "embraced the title" of Amazon as a clear reflection of her sexual preference, as well as her masculine habits. Although in its earliest stages the image of the Amazon may have been used by men to reinforce their own heroic myth, it has since been appropriated by feminists to express women's "independence and power."

Sigrid King

References

Brink, Jean R., Maryanne C. Horowitz, and Allison P. Coudert, eds. *Playing with Gender: A Renaissance Pursuit*. Urbana: University of Illinois Press, 1991.

Brown, Laura. *Ends of Empire: Women and Ideology in Early Eighteenth-Century English Literature*. Ithaca, N.Y.: Cornell University Press, 1993.

Crowder, Griffin Diane. "Amazons and Mothers? Monique Wittig, Hélène Cixous and Theories of Women's Writing." *Contemporary Literature* 24 (1983): 117–144.

DuBois, Paige. *Centaurs and Amazons: Women and the Pre-History of the Great Chain of Being*. Ann Arbor: University of Michigan Press, 1982.

hooks, bell. *Ain't I a Woman: Black Women and Feminism*. Boston: South End, 1981.

Kingston, Maxine Hong. *The Woman Warrior*. New York: Knopf, 1976.

Kirk, Ilse. "Images of Amazons: Marriage and Matriarchy." In *Images of Women in Peace and War*, edited by Sharon Macdonald, Pat Holden, and Shirley Ardener, 27–39. Madison: University of Wisconsin Press, 1989.

Kleinbaum, Abby Wettan. *The War against the Amazons*. New York: McGraw-Hill, 1983.

Salmonson, Jessica Amanda. *The Encyclopedia of Amazons: Women Warriors from Antiquity to the Modern Era*. New York: Paragon House, 1991.

Shepherd, Simon. *Amazons and Warrior Women: Varieties of Feminism in Seventeenth-Century Drama*. Sussex: Harvester, 1981.

Tyrrell, William Blake. *Amazons: A Study in Athenian Mythmaking*. Baltimore: Johns Hopkins University Press, 1984.

Wittig, Monique. *Les Guérillères*. Translated by David Le Vay. New York: Avon, 1969.

American Studies

American Studies combines traditional historiography, which focuses on political figures and great events, with a cultural approach, which borrows the conceptual and methodological tools of such fields as literary studies, anthropology, sociology, and psychology in order to study society in its entirety.

In its first few decades of existence after the Second World War, American Studies limited its focus to "high" culture, and thus to texts written predominantly by middle-class, white men. Ralph Waldo Emerson was thus thought to reveal more about "the American mind" than, say, Davy Crockett or Sojourner Truth. Scholars believed all of American culture was the product of this dominant group. Later, following developments in the 1950s and '60s, American Studies expanded its focus, employing a much more pluralistic sense of America as constitutive of many cultures. The cultural productions of the working class, African Americans, and women were studied. In terms of its impact on feminist scholarship, this expansion of the American Studies focus occasioned an explosion of interest in women's cultural productions throughout American history.

After its birth in the years surrounding the Second World War, American Studies was institutionalized with the development of degree programs at American universities in the 1930s, 1940s, and 1950s. By often calling themselves American Civilization departments, such departments signaled their defensiveness against older European cultures. They wanted to stress American exceptionalism. Inaugurated by Henry Nash Smith in 1950 and followed by R.W.B. Lewis, Leo Marx, and others, the so-called Myth and Symbol school within American Studies argued for other myths as well: the myth of the American mission in the "New World" as one which in many ways continued to define American culture over the centuries; the myth of the American as Adam in the new Eden; the myth of the American as the democratic and self-reliant man. These and other scholars of the period looked no further than "high brow" literature for their so-called defining myths. This tendency is perhaps best exemplified by another first generation study of America, F.O. Matthiessen's *American Renaissance: Art and Expression in the Age of Emerson and Whitman*. Matthiessen held that Whitman, Thoreau, Melville, Emerson, and Hawthorne were all engaged in elaborating the myth of the democratic man.

As Matthiessen's study makes clear, in answer to Crevecoeur scholars had argued implicitly that to be an American meant to be male, white, Protestant, middle class, and usually from the Northeast, at least insofar as all of the supposedly defining myths were propagated by such men. This assumption was first challenged in the 1950s with the development of the New Social History led by Raymond Williams in Britain. Williams argued that the working classes produce their own cultures and, therefore that scholars need to attend to their texts. In doing so, he both expanded the definition of a text from the previously narrow focus on "high brow" culture and successfully challenged the idea of a unified American culture.

Because of the civil rights and women's movements of the 1960s, American Studies further expanded its focus to include African Americans and women. The first great debate about women's culture in America was the feminization debate. In the 1960s, Barbara Welter detailed the "Cult of True Womanhood" as the nineteenth-century view that women must be pious, pure, domestic, and submissive. Then, in *The Feminization of American Culture*, Ann Douglas argued that the devotion to this ideal, and the creation of sentimental novels that espoused it, impoverished all of nineteenth-century American culture, leaving the early twentieth-century without either the intellectual rigor of the older Calvinist tradition or a comprehensive feminism with which to replace it. In *Sensational Designs: The Cultural Work of American Fiction, 1790–1865*, Jane Tompkins countered that "the popular domestic novel of the nineteenth century represents a monumental effort to reorganize culture from woman's

point of view." Other scholars such as Mary Kelley and Janice Radway joined Tompkins in her reassessment of women writers. In *Reading the Romance: Women, Patriarchy, and Popular Literature*, Radway presents a study of Harlequin romance readers which, in the true interdisciplinary spirit of American Studies, includes detailed economic analyses of the publishing industry, literary analyses of the texts themselves, interviews with the women readers, and the use of feminist psychology. She argues that, contrary to popular belief, romances provide women with important means of attaining self-worth and that the act of reading them can be used as a means of intervention in a world otherwise hostile to the desires of wives and mothers.

Still others have recast specific American Studies theses. Annette Kolodny, in *The Land before Her: Fantasy and Experience of the American Frontiers, 1630–1860*, found that women did not share the fantasy delineated in Henry Nash Smith's *Virgin Land: The American West as Symbol and Myth*, a fantasy that she showed to be based on a decidedly male psychosexual fantasy of possessing sexualized landscape. Jane Tompkins explored the way in which the American canon, exemplified by Matthiessen's focus, was constructed. It is not, she claims, that Nathaniel Hawthorne's work has intrinsic and thus ahistorical merit. Rather, twentieth-century academic culture began to privilege the themes Hawthorne explored and thus has revered his work over that of the widely popular white women novelists of the nineteenth century, work that also shaped American culture.

All of these studies, except for Welter's, were influenced by poststructuralism, most notably by the work of Michel Foucault and Jacques Derrida, and thus are built on the theoretical assumption that there is a fundamental relationship between power and knowledge. In other words, language, not merely politics and economics, is now thought to be capable of transforming material social practice. When texts by white males are celebrated to the detriment of texts by others, this has a profound impact on social life; only one version of culture is thought to be "authentic" and thus worthwhile.

In looking forward, feminist scholars of American Studies such as Alice Kessler-Harris, Linda Kerber, and Elizabeth Fox-Genovese argue that feminist scholarship within American

Studies must now turn its focus from women's culture in its particularity, if indeed there can even be said to be one women's culture given the diversity of women's experiences in America, to the relationship between cultures and between cultural myths, most notably between those that are canonical and those that are marginalized. How, for example, have the culturally privileged myths shaped women's subcultures and vice versa, especially given that this is a relationship infused with power?

Since expanding its definition of a text to include texts other than those considered canonical, and since concomitantly developing a multicultural perspective, American Studies has seen and contributed to an explosion of scholarly inquiry into the lives and cultural productions of American women.

Elise Lemire

References

Douglas, Ann. *The Feminization of American Culture.* New York: Knopf, 1977. New York: Doubleday, 1988.

Fox-Genovese, Elizabeth. "Between Individualism and Fragmentation: American Culture and the New Literary Studies of Race and Gender." *American Quarterly* 42 (1990): 7–34.

Gleason, Philip. "World War II and the Development of American Studies." *American Quarterly* 36 (1984): 343–358.

Kelley, Mary. *Private Woman, Public Stage: Literary Domesticity in Nineteenth-Century America.* New York and Oxford: Oxford University Press, 1984.

Kerber, Linda K. "Diversity and the Transformation of American Studies." *American Quarterly* 41 (1989): 415–431.

Kessler-Harris, Alice. "Cultural Locations: Positioning American Studies in the Great Debate." *American Quarterly* 44 (1992): 299–312.

Kolodny, Annette. *The Land before Her: Fantasy and Experience of the American Frontiers, 1630–1860.* Chapel Hill: University of North Carolina Press, 1984.

Kuklick, Bruce. "Myth and Symbol in American Studies." *American Quarterly* 24 (1972): 435–450.

Lewis, R.W.B. *The American Adam: Innocence, Tragedy, and Tradition in the Nineteenth Century.* Chicago: University of Chicago Press, 1955.

Marx, Leo. *The Machine in the Garden: Technology and the Pastoral Ideal in America.* London: Oxford University Press, 1964.

Matthiessen, F.O. *American Renaissance: Art and Expression in the Age of Emerson and Whitman.* London: Oxford University Press, 1941.

Radway, Janice A. *Reading the Romance: Women, Patriarchy, and Popular Literature.* Chapel Hill and London: University of North Carolina Press, 1984.

Shank, Barry. "A Reply to Steven Watts's 'Idiocy.'" *American Quarterly* 44 (1992): 439–449.

Smith, Henry Nash. *Virgin Land: The American West as Symbol and Myth.* Cambridge: Harvard University Press, 1950.

Tompkins, Jane. *Sensational Designs: The Cultural Work of American Fiction, 1790–1865.* New York and Oxford: Oxford University Press, 1985.

Watts, Steven. "The Idiocy of American Studies: Poststructuralism, Language, and Politics in the Age of Self-Fulfillment." *American Quarterly* 43 (1991): 625–660.

Welter, Barbara. "The Cult of True Womanhood." In *Dimity Convictions: The American Woman in the Nineteenth Century,* 21–41. Athens: Ohio University Press, 1976.

Williams, Raymond. *Culture and Society, 1780–1950.* [1958]. London: Penguin, 1961.

Androgyny

The term "androgyne," combining the Greek words for man and woman, describes a human who possesses the characteristics of both sexes, a figure that appears widely in ancient mythology and religion. Virginia Woolf introduced the concept of androgyny into feminist discourse in the last chapter of *A Room of One's Own.* There she seeks to counter the binary division of gender by suggesting that while bodies are divided into two sexes, minds contain both, although: "in the man's brain, the man predominates over the woman, and in the woman's brain, the woman predominates over the man." Woolf develops Samuel Taylor Coleridge's idea that a great mind is androgynous, explaining that the two sexes within each mind must fuse and cooperate to foster wholeness and creativity. Significantly, Woolf's examples of androgynous writers are all male: Shakespeare, Keats, Sterne, Cowper, Lamb, Coleridge himself, and Proust. The lack of any women writers on this list reveals the depth of male dominance even in the work of Woolf, one of the pioneers of feminist literary theory, and also points to the tendency of androgyny to be employed in conservative or male-centered analysis that stresses the gains available to men who do not suppress their "feminine" traits. Woolf further develops the androgynous ideal in her novel *Orlando*, whose protagonist moves through the centuries, first as a man, then as a woman.

Androgyny was embraced as a utopian goal by a number of feminists in the late 1960s. In *Toward a Recognition of Androgyny* Carolyn Heilbrun advocates "movement away from sexual polarization and the prison of gender" toward the ideal of androgyny, which would liberate individuals from the "confines of the appropriate." Heilbrun grounds her argument in evidence of androgyny in classical Greek and English canonical literature, and then engages in an extended discussion of the "female hero" in the English novel. Finally, she presents the Bloomsbury group as exponents of androgyny, both in their lives and writing, with particular focus on Lytton Strachey and Virginia Woolf. Arguing for equality, Heilbrun's analysis belongs to the tradition of liberal feminism. She warns against confusing androgyny with feminism, explaining that although these approaches appear identical in an age of great sexual polarization and great patriarchal power, the reader identifies equally with male and female characters in an androgynous novel, but only with the female hero in a feminist work.

The concept of androgyny may also be seen as a precursor to the postmodern analysis of gender as socially constructed and to the contemporary interest in cross dressing and transsexualism as a means of investigating the performative nature of gender. However, the utopian ideal of androgyny tends to deny the real historical differences and conflicts created by the gender system and to ignore the importance of political struggle, as well as other categories of social and cultural inequality. While androgyny no longer occupies a central position in current feminist literary theory, it does continue to be employed by critics in significant numbers, often to discuss writers whose texts or characters in some way challenge prevailing gender norms. The most recent comprehensive and theoretically sophisticated study of an-

drogyny is Kari Weil's *Androgyny and the Denial of Difference*. After a theoretical investigation of the distinction between androgyny and hermaphroditism and a discussion of fictional representations of the androgyne in nineteenth-century France, Weil presents a historical analysis of feminist critical responses to the concept of androgyny.

Pamela Starr Bromberg

References

Fox-Genovese, Elizabeth. *Feminism without Illusions*. Chapel Hill: University of North Carolina Press, 1991.

Heilbrun, Carolyn G. *Toward a Recognition of Androgyny*. New York: W.W. Norton, 1973.

Jaggar, Alison M. *Feminist Politics and Human Nature*. Totowa, N.J.: Rowman and Allanheld, 1983.

Weil, Kari. *Androgyny and the Denial of Difference*. Charlottesville: University Press of Virginia, 1992.

Woolf, Virginia. *Orlando*. New York: Harcourt Brace Jovanovich, 1928.

Woolf, Virginia. *A Room of One's Own*. New York: Harcourt Brace Jovanovich, 1929.

Anglo American Feminist Criticism

Anglo American feminist criticism is an approach to literature that analyzes literary texts, the conditions of their production, reception, circulation, and their cultural effects from the perspective of gender difference. Though fully developing in the 1960s under the influence of the third wave of the American feminist movement and in reaction against New Critical modes of interpretation, Anglo American feminist criticism has had a long tradition that has advanced its major concerns for more than two hundred years. The major steps that Anglo American feminist criticism has taken since the late 1960s were already anticipated by Mary Wollstonecraft's critique of Milton's and Rousseau's images of women, Margaret Fuller's exploration of strong female figures in mythology and literature, Virginia Woolf's analysis of women's disadvantaged position in cultural production, and Simone de Beauvoir's claim that women are not born, but made women.

So far, Anglo American feminist criticism has gone through four phases, moving from the early images-of-women criticism through a preoccupation with women's writing and its tradition to a phase of theoretization induced by Continental poststructuralist and psychoanalytic thought and fundamental to the presently dominant gender critique. The major changes that characterize this development are conceptual and concern the notion of the literary text itself, of self and subjectivity, of the relation between cultural representation and historical reality, and consequently of our understanding of culture as such. In the course of these conceptual modifications the object of feminist literary analyses has shifted from the portrayal of women in men's writing to the construction of gender in both male and female authors' literary texts.

Images-of-women criticism as represented by Susan Koppelman Cornillon's *Images of Women in Fiction*, for instance, focused on stereotypical and thus supposedly "unreal" characterizations of women in texts by male as well as female authors. Instead of these "false" images of women, critics called for faithful reproductions of "real life" female figures. Kate Millett's critique of Lawrence, Miller, and Mailer, in contrast, underscored the correlation between the sexual politics of the literary text and its cultural realities. In this way, Millett anticipated central issues of gender analysis. At the same time, she shared with other feminist critics of the time a problematic and oftentimes prescriptive notion of the literary text as mimetic reflection of real experience that ignored the literariness of literature and simplified the relation between author and text as well as between text and reality.

In search for different, that is more self-reliant female characters, feminist criticism turned to literature by women that was still considered a marginal and minor phenomenon within literary history. What followed was a phase of intense search and research: feminist critics such as Mary Helen Washington, Elaine Showalter, Ellen Moers, Sandra M. Gilbert, and Susan Gubar discovered and rediscovered, collected and edited, read and reinterpreted women's literature, in this way claiming and constructing a female literary tradition. This documentation was an immensely eye-opening and productive, yet nonetheless contradictory enterprise that bred its own hierarchies and principles of exclusions. Focused on texts that thematize "female experience" and identity explicitly, feminist literary criticism tended to dismiss modernist texts that problematize gen-

der in more mediated ways. At the same time, however, the preoccupation with a countertradition of women's writing raised the question of a specific female aesthetic and discourse that required more careful textual analyses and provoked a turn toward Continental theory.

The confrontation between Anglo American feminist criticism and French "feminist" theory began in the late 1970s as an initially quite polemical exchange between two distinct approaches and sets of concerns: between a primarily sociologically and historically oriented literary criticism focused on questions of female identity, authorship, and authority and a system of thought based on European philosophy, linguistics, Lacanian psychoanalysis, and Derridean deconstruction. This critique privileged writing, considered subjectivity a position in discourse, and was concerned not with the literary construction of a strong female self, but with the crisis of the male philosophical subject.

The work of Julia Kristeva, Luce Irigaray, and Hélène Cixous, among others, was met with much resistance against its supposed ahistoricism, antiempiricism and essentialism and was only rarely adapted for literary analysis. Still, the impact of its discussion, mediated by critics such as Alice Jardine and Jane Gallop, was manifold and deeply affected both practice and theory of Anglo American feminist literary criticism. The encounter with continental subject theories altered feminist conceptions of self and language, which in turn provoked a revaluation of modernist literature and of disruptive elements in literary texts by women. The emphasis that revisionary psychoanalysis placed on the return of the pre-Oedipal in writing refocused feminist attention on the female body and desire in language. The poststructuralist privileging of *différance* (versus identity) finds an analogy in the differentiation of Anglo American feminist criticism into multiple, heterogeneous positions such as lesbian, black, and Marxist feminism. Most important, however, is that the reconceptualization of subjectivity and language has displaced the term "sexual difference" and its primarily biological reference by the concept of gender, which acknowledges that differences between the sexes are not naturally given but always already culturally constructed.

The contemporary notion that both gender and sex are constructed in discourse indicates that identity itself has ceased to center around the sexual binarism of male and female. It has instead turned into "the concept of a multiple, shifting, and often self-contradictory identity . . . made up of heterogeneous and heteronomous representations of gender, race, and class, and often indeed across languages and cultures" (Teresa de Lauretis). Accordingly, Anglo American feminist criticism is no longer concerned with the literary productions of a supposedly separate and "other" female culture. As gender critique it focuses on a culture that not only constructs male and female subjects differently at different times but that is being constructed by means of a literary practice that collaborates, interferes with, and possibly subverts, but in any case produces the cultural fictions that make up our sense of the real.

Sabine Sielke

References

Abel, Elizabeth, ed. *Writing and Sexual Difference*. Chicago: University of Chicago Press, 1982.

Cornillon, Susan Koppelman, ed. *Images of Women in Fiction: Feminist Perspectives*. Bowling Green, Ohio: Bowling Green University Press, 1972.

de Lauretis, Teresa, ed. *Feminist Studies/ Critical Studies*. Bloomington: Indiana University Press, 1986.

Eisenstein, Hester, and Alice Jardine, eds. *The Future of Difference*. Boston: G.K. Hall, 1980.

Gates, Henry Louis, Jr., ed. *Reading Black, Reading Feminist. A Critical Anthology*. New York: Meridian, 1989.

Gilbert, Sandra M., and Susan Gubar. *The Madwoman in the Attic. The Woman Writer and the Nineteenth-Century Literary Imagination*. Bloomington: Indiana University Press, 1979.

Greene, Gayle, and Cora Caplan. *Making a Difference: Feminist Literary Theory*. London: Methuen, 1985.

Miller, Nancy, ed. *The Poetics of Gender*. New York: Columbia University Press, 1986.

Millett, Kate. *Sexual Politics*. New York: Doubleday, 1969.

Moi, Toril. *Sexual/Textual Politics: Feminist Literary Theory*. London: Methuen, 1985.

Showalter, Elaine. *A Literature of Their Own. British Women Novelists from Brontë to Lessing*. Princeton: Princeton University Press, 1977.

———, ed. *New Feminist Criticism*. New York: Pantheon, 1985.

———, ed. *Speaking of Gender*. New York: Routledge, 1989.

Todd, Janet. *Feminist Literary History*. New York: Routledge, 1988.

Warhol, Robyn, and Diane Price Herndl, eds. *Feminisms. An Anthology of Literary Theory and Criticism*. New Brunswick, N.J.: Rutgers University Press, 1991.

Anorexia

Anorexia nervosa, bulimia nervosa, and other compulsive eating disorders have come to be understood as sociologically informed physical illnesses that can be characterized as both products and critiques of patriarchy, while the sufferers are seen as both the victims and heroines of capitalism. Because anorexia can be interpreted as an extreme result of sexual objectification as it problematizes the struggle of "reading the female body," feminist literary theorists have adopted the project of studying this disease and theorizing about its origins and manifestations—replacing psychologists and other social scientists as its major critics.

In the nineteenth century, physicians described two versions of the disease—anorexia mirabilis, or prolonged religious fasting, and anorexia nervosa, a gastrointestinal symptom related to female hysteria. William Gull in Great Britain and Charles Lasegue in France named the disease almost simultaneously in the late 1870s, and little was known about the disease outside the medical community until almost a century later. Sufferers were isolated, force fed, and counseled by clergy. One of the earliest-known and most famous anorexics is Samuel Richardson's eighteenth-century Clarissa Harlowe, whose suffering synthesizes internal and external forces of desire and control in what she calls an "effectual remorse," which is the eventual instrument of her death.

In 1981, Kim Chernin revolutionized the study of anorexia in her book *The Obsession: Reflections on the Tyranny of Slenderness*, by arguing that the disease is an internalized "alienation from the body" and a relinquishing of the potential for female power. Interpretations of anorexia then began to examine how severe the division between body and mind can be, arguing that the misogynist fear of the "unruly" female body was characterized in women as a refusal to leave a preadolescent bodily state.

Later, in *The Hungry Self: Women, Eating & Identity*, Chernin expanded her hypothesis to include a theory stating that anorexics are invested in an act of separating from and "surpassing" their mothers.

Currently, the disease is often interpreted as a more literal manifestation of a modern cultural ideal (a simple desire to be permanently thin) or as a neurotic desire for control in women who feel powerless regarding other aspects of their lives. *Fasting Girls: The Emergence of Anorexia Nervosa as a Modern Disease* by Joan Jacobs Brumberg examines how anorexia has evolved from the Victorian era (before thinness was equated with female desirability) into the twentieth century, where issues of perfection and individual achievement have complicated the realms of female sexuality and family life. The female body, along with the changing sociopolitical roles of women, has become a convenient text in which to find physical manifestations of misogynist ideologies (internalized) that are no longer acceptable as overt social dogma. In other words, the apparent rise in anorectic behavior and sicknesses is arguably a direct inverse correlative of the social strides made in the public sphere since the women's movement. Thus, the public sphere has literally begun to devour the private sphere in the most extreme form of body policing. The disease, therefore, may be read as a somewhat logical response to a set of unreasonable social requests directed most forcefully at adolescent girls and young women.

In 1989, Roberta Pollack Seid published *Never Too Thin: Why Women Are at War with Their Bodies*, adding to the definition of anorexia by revealing that the emergence of the health and fitness craze is little more than a disguise for the same sickness. In addition, Susan Bordo in *Unbearable Weight: Feminism, Western Culture, and the Body* offers an explanation of the switch from mere "thinness" to rockhard "fitness," that highlights both the need for "self-management in consumer culture" and the subsequent acceptability of desire allowed a more "traditionally male body."

Feminists also provide more candid critiques of the hypercapitalistic fashion industry and other medias' involvements in the maintenance of body-image and eating disorders, and they have begun to illustrate the correlation between wealth and the thinness obsession. Maud Ellmann argues that middle-class dieters experience a "nostalgia for the lost experience of need." Until recently, anorexia was a predominantly white, middle-class disease, but the growing inclusion of black, Asian, and Latin American models in high fashion has resulted in a demographic expansion of the disease. Anorectic behavior in the lower classes are complicated by financial anxiety—nutritious foods and exercise options are inaccessible, while there is an overabundance of inexpensive, high-fat, low-nutrition foods.

Feminism's interest in the subject of eating disorders is relatively young. A parallel increase can be found feminist analyses of subsistence needs and issues of starvation in developing countries. The majority of people starving from poverty and drought in the world are women and, by extension, their children, so this epidemic occurrence of anorexia and bulimia (with approximately 150,000 current sufferers in the United States alone) seems all the more significant and ironic. Feminist theorists in the future would do well to ask what the relationship between these two issues is and what a potential strategy for diffusing both voluntary and involuntary hunger would incorporate.

Jenna Ivers

References

Bordo, Susan. *Unbearable Weight: Feminism, Western Culture, and the Body.* Berkeley: University of California Press, 1993.

Bruch, Hilde. *The Golden Cage: The Enigma of Anorexia Nervosa.* New York: Vintage Books, 1979.

Brumberg, Joan Jacobs. *Fasting Girls: The Emergence of Anorexia Nervosa as a Modern Disease.* Cambridge: Harvard University Press, 1988.

Chernin, Kim. *The Hungry Self: Women, Eating & Identity.* New York: Times, 1985.

———. *The Obsession: Reflections on the Tyranny of Slenderness.* New York: Harper and Row, 1981.

Ellmann, Maud. *The Hunger Artists: Starving, Writing, and Imprisonment.* Cambridge: Harvard University Press, 1993.

Fraad, Harriet. "Anorexia Nervosa: The Female Body as a Site of Gender and Class Transition." *Rethinking Marxism* 3 (1990): 79–99.

Liu, Aimee. *Solitaire.* New York: Harper and Row, 1979.

Michie, Helena. *Flesh Made Word: Female Figures and Women's Bodies.* New York: Oxford University Press, 1987.

Richardson, Samuel. *Clarissa or the History of a Young Lady*. New York: Modern Library, 1950.

Seid, Roberta Pollack. *Never Too Thin: Why Women Are at War with Their Bodies*. New York: Prentice Hall, 1989.

Shute, Jenefer. *Life-Size*. Boston: Houghton Mifflin, 1992.

Wolf, Naomi. *The Beauty Myth: How Images of Women Are Used against Women*. New York: William Morrow, 1991.

Antifeminism

Antifeminism may be simply defined as the opposition to feminism. Like feminism, antifeminism focuses on the role of woman at work, at home, in society, and in the culture. And, like feminism, antifeminism promotes a complex political, social, and cultural agenda. Antifeminists often take their cues from feminists, speaking out against current feminist platforms and against feminists themselves. Although antifeminism may involve misogyny, it is important to distinguish between these attitudes toward women: whereas misogynists distrust and hate all women, antifeminists promote subordinate models of womanhood and abhor any women who reject such models.

Shifts in antifeminist thinking over history reflect actual feminist gains, as antifeminism changes its tactics in an attempt to stay one step ahead of feminism. For example, antifeminists in early twentieth-century England and the United States opposed female suffrage, but by the end of the century women's right to vote was securely established, and antifeminists moved on to other targets, such as abortion and childcare issues.

Three studies in particular provide a good overview of American antifeminism. Cynthia Kinnard's annotated bibliography *Antifeminism in American Thought* traces nineteenth- and early-twentieth-century antifeminist themes, correlating heightened periods of antifeminism with each new suffrage campaign. Susan Marshall's essay "Who Speaks for American Women?: The Future of Antifeminism" examines American antifeminist movements of the last third of the twentieth century. The most influential survey of late-twentieth-century antifeminism is journalist Susan Faludi's *Backlash: The Undeclared War against American Women*. Faludi argues that antifeminist backlashes occur when small feminist advances have been made and that antifeminists exaggerate the successes of the women's movement in order to sensationalize and stigmatize feminist issues.

Antifeminism is by no means the sole province of men. Kinnard points out that almost half of the antifeminist books and pamphlets and nearly one-third of the articles in her bibliography were written by women. Phyllis Schlafly's Eagle Forum and Beverly LaHaye's Concerned Women for America spearheaded the antifeminist campaign to defeat the Equal Rights Amendment. Both Marshall and Faludi highlight the paradox inherent in the female antifeminist activist's position: such women often make a public career of campaigning against women's right to a public life. *Amazons, Bluestockings, and Crones: A Feminist Dictionary* nails down this paradox by defining an antifeminist as a "woman who claims the only place for woman is in the home and who has come out of the home to prove it."

To discredit feminist advocates, antifeminists frequently invoke myths about women's innate inferiority to men. Like other antifeminist arguments, these vary over time. Ancient views about "wandering wombs" and nineteenth-century beliefs about women's underdeveloped brains are no longer widely held; however, arguments based upon the fragility of the female reproductive system and women's intrinsically domestic nature are still advanced to discourage women from seeking equality with men.

In the 1980s and 1990s, debates over curriculum- and canon-formation within the academy led to an outpouring of antifeminist sentiments both on and off campus. Opponents of feminist criticism and women's studies, such as Dinesh D'Souza and Camille Paglia, filled lecture halls, made the news, and appeared in a variety of publications. They accused feminists of holding the university system hostage, of lowering the standards of intellectual debate by introducing political biases into hitherto nonpartisan classrooms, and of wearying students and colleagues with their incessant "whining."

Antifeminists do not always content themselves with throwing insults at the opposition. In its most extreme form, antifeminism can lead to violence against women: around the globe, women have been imprisoned, tortured, and killed for violating patriarchal codes. A brutal instance of antifeminist violence occurred at the University of Montreal in December 1989. "You're all fucking feminists," shouted Marc Lepine as he opened fire on an engineering class, after first separating the women from the men. He killed fourteen women and wounded nine more because he felt that feminists had invaded traditional male territory.

Audrey Bilger

References

"Anti-feminism" and "Anti-feminist." In *Amazons, Bluestockings, and Crones: A Feminist Dictionary* [1985], edited by Cheris Kramarae and Paula A. Treichler. London: Pandora, 1992.

Faludi, Susan. *Backlash: The Undeclared War against American Women.* New York: Crown, 1991.

Kinnard, Cynthia D. *Antifeminism in American Thought: An Annotated Bibliography.* Boston: G.K. Hall, 1986.

Marshall, Susan. "Who Speaks for American Women?: The Future of Antifeminism." *Annals of the American Academy of Political and Social Science* (1991): 50–62.

Spender, Dale. *Women of Ideas and What Men Have Done to Them.* London: Routledge and Kegan Paul, 1982.

Anxious Power

This term describes women's ambivalence toward language, and the representation of that ambivalence in literature by women. It is grounded in both Anglo American and French feminist theory—especially Sandra M. Gilbert's and Susan Gubar's "anxiety of authorship" and Julia Kristeva's notion of *écriture féminine.* Anxious power thus bridges the gap between the social construction of women's reading and writing, and a female poetics.

The adjective "anxious" links this term with Harold Bloom's "anxiety of influence" and Gilbert's and Gubar's "anxiety of authorship." Bloom is concerned with Oedipal configurations in male literary history, and Gilbert and Gubar with nineteenth-century women's identities as writers. Anxious power, on the other hand, refers both to women's perceptions of themselves in relation to male authorship, and to the various formal strategies with which women express their anxiety about the power conferred by reading and writing. In an overwhelmingly masculine literary tradition, the female reader often must read against herself or adopt a male point of view, while the female writer worries about her authorial legitimacy. But if discourse is the site of a woman's powerlessness, it also enables her to articulate and even transcend her plight. Inevitably, then, the acts of reading and writing—and even language itself—can evoke in women conflicting feelings of anxiety and empowerment.

This ambivalence affects the form of women's literature, which often incorporates a range of choices rather than deciding among them. Kristeva describes *écriture féminine* in similar terms to these; however, anxious power traces the distinguishing characteristics of women's writing to social constructions of femininity, rather than to the body. In narrative, for example, female writers often express their ambivalence toward language with such formal strategies as dialogic narration, mixed genres, *mises en abyme,* and open endings. The recurrence of these and other manifestations of anxious power constitutes a distinctly female literary tradition.

Carol J. Singley and Susan Elizabeth Sweeney first coined this term in an essay on forbidden reading and ghostly writing in a story by Edith Wharton. Their co-edited book develops the implications of anxious power more fully: how has woman's historical exclusion from literature shaped the form of her writing? How can we identify a woman's language? How have women reproduced, revised, or transformed masculine literary genres? How have women turned their anxiety into a source of power? Anxious power is a valuable concept that allows critics to combine feminist study of women's experiences with formalist analysis of how those experiences are expressed in literature.

Carol J. Singley
Susan Elizabeth Sweeney

References

Bloom, Harold. *The Anxiety of Influence: A Theory of Poetry.* New York: Oxford University Press, 1973.

Gilbert, Sandra M., and Susan Gubar. *The Madwoman in the Attic: The Women Writer and the Nineteenth-Century Literary Imagination.* New Haven: Yale University Press, 1979.

Kristeva, Julia. "La femme, ce n'est jamais ca." Translated by Marilyn A. August. In *New French Feminism,* edited by Elaine Marks and Isabel de Courtivron, 137–141. Amherst: University of Massachusetts Press, 1980.

Singley, Carol J., and Susan Elizabeth

Sweeney, eds. *Anxious Power: Reading, Writing, and Ambivalence in Narrative by Women*. Albany: State University of New York Press (Series in Feminist Criticism and Theory), 1993.

———, and Susan Elizabeth Sweeney. "Forbidden Reading and Ghostly Writing: Anxious Power in Wharton's 'Pomegranate Seed.'" *Women's Studies* 20 (1991): 177–203.

Anzaldúa, Gloria

With the publication of *This Bridge Called My Back: Writings by Radical Women of Color*, Gloria Anzaldúa, together with co-editor Cherríe Moraga, helped institute a movement toward a specifically U.S. Third-World feminism. The book, which was subsequently adopted as a text by women's studies programs across the country, was the first of its kind to bring together writings by radical U.S. women of color. Conceived as a response to the exclusionary theories and practices arising from the racism and classism of Anglo American feminism, the book represents an early effort to theorize a feminist politics that takes into account the multiple oppressions of race, class, and sexuality. Anzaldúa's essay in that collection, "La Prieta," analyzes the contradictory complicity of the Chicana mother in the perpetration of the racist, sexist, classist, and heterosexist ideologies that place herself and her daughters at the margins of U.S. society. By exposing the shame resulting from the internalized racism she learned from her mother, even as she affirms the pride she feels in her mother, Anzaldúa undermines the dialectic of duality (good/evil, light/dark, male/female, and so on) that inevitably places the woman of color on the wrong side of the slash. This, together with her refusal to choose only one from among an array of possible identities assigned to her (such as Chicana, feminist, or lesbian), anticipates the "mestiza consciousness" Anzaldúa articulates as a strategy of survival in *Borderlands*.

In *Borderlands/La Frontera: The New Mestiza* Anzaldúa introduces her image of the U.S.-Mexican border as a "1,950-mile-long open wound" where "the Third World grates against the first and bleeds." In Anzaldúa's depiction of it, the border, in addition to being a real geographic space, is the metaphorical site of the collision between her unconscious and conscious selves. As such, it is the psychic location within which Chicanas—as Third-World women growing up in the First World, as educated daughters of illiterate parents, and as feminists or lesbians growing up in a patriarchal heterosexist society—must struggle to reconcile their cultural contradictions. Anzaldúa's image of the borderlands has been taken up by Chicano/a theorists, as well as by some postmodern literary theorists who have found it useful as a metaphor for the postmodern condition.

As a Chicana *tejana* lesbian-feminist poet and fiction writer who has worked to create a space from which, and within which, Chicanas and other women of color can be heard, Gloria Anzaldúa has been instrumental in the development of a U.S. Third World feminist consciousness, as well as in the dissemination and understanding of literature written by women of color in the United States.

Paula Moya

References

Anzaldúa, Gloria. *Borderlands/La Frontera: The New Mestiza*. San Francisco: Spinsters/Aunt Lute, 1987.

———, ed. *Making Face, Making Soul: Haciendo Caras: Creative and Critical Perspectives by Women of Color*. San Francisco: Spinsters/Aunt Lute, 1990.

———, and Cherríe Moraga, eds. *This Bridge Called My Back: Writings by Radical Women of Color*. Watertown, Mass.: Persephone, 1981.

Archetypal Criticism

Archetypal criticism is an interdisciplinary activity using ideas drawn or developed from the psychology of C.G. Jung to illuminate literary works. Jos van Meurs's bibliography covers most of this work in English published between 1920 and 1980, the quality of which varies widely.

Feminist archetypal criticism views Jung's ideas and those of associated thinkers with more skepticism, while recognizing aspects of those ideas as useful in furthering the feminist project of reappraising both women writers' work and male authors' representations of women and "the feminine." In particular, feminist archetypal critics contest the conventional Jungian view of anima and animus, see archetypes as changeable cultural constructs rather than genetically programmed absolutes, and view women writers as reflecting and contributing to the development of new archetypes. In conventional Jungian thought, the anima is the intrapsychic feminine aspect of a man; and the animus, correspondingly, is the masculine element in a woman's psyche. Feminists have opposed this model's unproven symmetry and its collusion with gender stereotypes (see Christ; Goldenberg). Feminist archetypal critics have found male figures in women's works to occupy lesser or different positions than Jungian theory would predict; have found some female figures in women's works to function as animas; and have found many adherents to anima theory to attend too little to the projective aspects of male writers' female characters. Feminist archetypal critics also have taken a larger view of "archetype" and "myth" than that encompassed in a conventional Jungian perspective. Looking back past the patriarchal level of myth (see Spretnak) and looking around at a variety of women writers and artists (see Lauter), feminist archetypal critics have opposed the essentialism that can overtake Jungian discussions of "the feminine," and they have seen women's mythmaking as an actively revisionist process (see Ostriker).

Feminist archetypal criticism represents a daring appropriation, rather than a rote application, of Jung's ideas, yet feminist archetypal critics in general have not belabored this point. To accurately comprehend feminist archetypal criticism, the student of this subject therefore must be wary of false definitions offered by those outside the field. In particular, critics uninformed about but inimical to feminist archetypal criticism often fail to distinguish between women Jungians and feminist archetypal critics. Also, in objecting to feminist archetypal work as neglecting the social dimension of the feminist struggle, critics betray a dualistic habit of thought that opposes intrapsychic to social processes.

The small body of published feminist archetypal criticism deals primarily with women writers and often with their women characters, who resist the identities socially imposed on them. In looking for women's reality beneath concealing patriarchal versions, feminist archetypal criticism often refers to mythic patterns. Feminist archetypal criticism reflects tendencies evident in feminist criticism generally—moving from a concern with women writers (in the 1970s and early 1980s) to a more self-conscious stance (beginning in the mid 1980s) in which theory is explicitly discussed rather than being shown only in practice. Annis Pratt's *Archetypal Patterns in Women's Fiction* described patterns of psychological development, markedly different from those found in male writers' work, discovered as a result of an extensive survey of novels in English written by women. Pratt found that the female hero's development is disrupted at each stage "by social norms dictating powerlessness for women," so that she can find fulfillment only in a green world apart from men or as an outcast from society. Estella Lauter's *Women as Mythmakers* underlined the interdisciplinary nature of feminist archetypal criticism in discussing both poetry by Canadian and U.S. writers and visual art by European, South-American, and U.S. women. Lauter's work made a case for women as changers, rather than simply transmitters, of archetypes. *Feminist Archetypal Theory*, edited by Lauter and Carol S. Rupprecht, also defined feminist archetypal criticism as a thoroughly interdisciplinary enterprise by considering archetypal theory in relation to literature, art, religion, psychotherapy, and dreams. This collection includes a very useful essay by Pratt describing the theoretical underpinnings of feminist archetypal work. The collection in general, though, is best read together with two careful reviews of it by Douglas and Wagner that discuss problems as well as advantages associated with the book's scope. Most recently, an essay by Roberta Rigsby provides a metaview of concerns related to feminist archetypal criticism. Her essay discusses prohibitions against the use of feminist archetypal criticism; the relation of such criticism to archetypal psychology; the values shared by this criticism and psychology; and the benefits of incorporating feminist archetypal criticism into the feminist repertoire.

Feminist archetypal criticism has shown itself a lively, self-reflective branch of feminist literary scholarship. However, it would be enhanced by more explicit attention to the connection of political action with personal change; more analyses of works by male authors; attention to non-Western writers; and more conscious consideration of women's realities and experiences as plural. Consideration of affinities with the Jungian Developmental (London) School also might prove fruitful. Though often resisted because misunderstood, feminist archetypal criticism already has proven its value and bids fair to flourish.

Roberta K. Rigsby

A

References

Christ, Carol P. "Some Comments on Jung, Jungians, and the Study of Women." *Anima* 3 (1977): 66–69.

Davis, Cynthia A. "Archetype and Structure: On Feminist Myth Criticism." In *Courage and Tools: The Florence Howe Award for Feminist Scholarship 1974–1989,* edited by Joanna Glasgow and Angela Ingram, 109–118. New York: Modern Language Association, 1990.

Douglas, Claire. "The Animus: Old Women, Menopause and Feminist Theory." Review of *Feminist Archetypal Theory*, edited by Estella Lauter and Carol S. Rupprecht, and two other books. San Francisco: *Jung Institute Library Journal* 6 (1986): 1–20.

Goldenberg, Naomi. "A Feminist Critique of Jung." *Signs* 2 (1976): 443–449.

Lauter, Estella. *Women as Mythmakers: Poetry and Visual Art by Twentieth-Century Women.* Bloomington: Indiana University Press, 1984.

———, and Carol S. Rupprecht, eds. *Feminist Archetypal Theory: Interdisciplinary Re-Visions of Jungian Thought.* Knoxville: University of Tennessee Press, 1985.

Ostriker, Alicia. "The Thieves of Language: Women Poets and Revisionist Mythmaking." *Signs* 8 (1982): 68–90.

Pratt, Annis, with Barbara White, Andrea Loewenstein, and Mary Wyer. *Archetypal Patterns in Women's Fiction.* Bloomington: Indiana University Press, 1981.

Rigsby, Roberta K. "Feminist Critics and Archetypal Psychology: What's in It for Us?" *LIT: Literature, Interpretation, Theory* 2 (1991): 179–200.

Spretnak, Charlene. "Problems with Jungian Uses of Greek Goddess Mythology." *Anima* 6 (1979): 23–33.

van Meurs, Jos, with John Kidd. *Jungian Literary Criticism, 1920–1980: An Annotated Critical Bibliography of Works in English (with a Selection of Titles after 1980).* Metuchen, N.J.: Scarecrow, 1988.

Wagner, Ursula. "Feminism and Archetypal Theory." Review of *Feminist Archetypal Theory*, edited by Estella Lauter and Carol S. Rupprecht. San Francisco: *Jung Institute Library Journal* 6 (1986): 21–32.

Armstrong, Nancy

In her book *Desire and Domestic Fiction*, Nancy Armstrong links the history of gender and sexuality to the history of the novel and explores the feminizing effects of domestic fiction. She articulates an important connection between the formation of bourgeois subjectivity and the rise of the novel. Arguing from a Foucauldian position, Armstrong describes how authors such as Samuel Richardson, Jane Austen, and the Brontë sisters psychologize political information and gender it as female. This displacement of political identity in domestic fiction forged an alternative form of political power that was contained within the private domestic sphere and brought under a woman's supervision. This evolving domestic economy served as the basis for revising traditional economic practices and ultimately led to the formation of a powerful, unified middle class.

In "Occidental Alice," Armstrong studies nineteenth-century photographs of diseased prostitutes, colonized women, and illustrations of monstrous women in children's literature in order to explore the "double-bodied woman's" role in redefining Victorian culture's sense of self and other. She reads Lewis Carroll's *Alice's Adventures in Wonderland* as the prototype of mad female consumerism. Armstrong's interest in colonialism and the construction of political identity also informs *The Imaginary Puritan*, a book in which she and co-author Leonard Tennenhouse argue that previous historical accounts of modernity are insufficient because they fail to consider the significance of "discursive practices." Despite its sometimes controversial reception, Armstrong's scholarship provides valuable insights into the relationship between gender, politics, and poetics.

Tracy M. Volz

References

Armstrong, Nancy. *Desire and Domestic Fiction: A Political History of the Novel.* New York: Oxford University Press, 1987.

———. "Occidental Alice." *differences: A Journal of Feminist Cultural Studies* 2 (1990): 3–38.

———, and Leonard Tennenhouse. *The*

Imaginary Puritan. Berkeley: University of California Press, 1992.

———, Leonard Tennenhouse, et al., eds. *The Violence of Representation: Literature and the History of Violence.* London: Routledge, 1989.

Asian American Feminist Literary Theory

Anyone surveying the U.S. Third World literary scene the past two decades cannot help but notice the dramatic increase in the production and publication of new works by both Asian American creative writers and feminist scholars that engage in the critical interrogation of the interstices of race, class, gender, sexuality, culture, and cultural nationalism. However, just as one hundred years of Asian American literary history have long been marginalized within the canonical blindspot of traditional American literary studies, so too has the growing body of recent Asian American feminist work been largely overlooked by mainstream Anglo American feminist criticism. To date, there has not yet been the same attention and focus on Asian American feminist criticism that African American, Chicana/Latina, and Native American feminist writings have received; nonetheless, the diverse field that can be named Asian American feminist cultural criticism—particularly the work by literary scholars—has not only gained enormous ground but must now be reckoned with as a legitimate new critical terrain in the continuum of what has been called U.S. Third World feminism.

Elaine Kim's groundbreaking work *Asian American Literature: An Introduction to the Writings and Their Social Context* offers a strategic point of departure for anyone wishing to begin both a study of Asian American literature and feminist criticism. As the first book-length examination of its kind, Kim produces both an outstanding literary history as well as a bibliography of Asian American writings since the late nineteenth century. This study is noteworthy for its foregrounding of the literature within a distinctly sociohistorical and cultural framework. Kim's discussion of how both Asian American male and female writers have constructed racialized and gendered representations of "Asian American consciousness" is particularly valuable, as is her book's final chapter, which includes a discussion of the distinct genre of Asian American feminist writings that emerged in the late 1970s and early 1980s.

Amy Ling's *Between Worlds: Women Writers of Chinese Ancestry* may also be considered as part of this first wave of Asian American feminist literary criticism. Like Kim, Ling writes out of a similar desire to unearth previously unknown writings by Asian Americans—particularly the work of women of Chinese ancestry. She is also one of the first Asian American literary critics to borrow from W.E.B. DuBois's powerful concept of "divided consciousness" as she theorizes the historical predicament of Asian Americans who are constructed as forever foreign and alien within dominant American culture. *Between Worlds* specifically examines the problematic of Asian American women of color who both write and speak out of their doubly displaced racial and gendered positioning to produce what feminist critic Elaine Showalter has elsewhere named the "double-voiced discourse" of women.

Such a "double-voiced" discourse has also been the subject of U.S. Third World feminist criticism that further argues that conditions of linguistic and cultural displacement, political and economic marginalization, and historical invisibility and silence produce an even more complexly positioned and "multiply voiced" female subject. Indeed, it may be useful here to consider some of the Asian American feminist writings of the late 1970s and 1980s as part of the early genealogy of both contemporary Asian American and U.S. Third World feminist criticism. In particular, the creative and critical writings of Nellie Wong, Mitsuye Yamada, and Merle Woo—as featured in the 1981 landmark feminist publication *This Bridge Called My Back*—are among the first to articulate specifically Asian American or "Yellow feminist" positions. Their work also raises such provocative contemporary questions as what counts as legitimate theoretical discourse within academic institutions? Yamada's essays in *Bridge*, "Invisibility is an Unnatural Disaster: Reflections of an Asian American Woman" and "Asian Pacific American Women and Feminism" still stand as two of the most powerful articulations of Asian American women's multiple marginalization within both dominant American culture and what has been retrospectively called the "white women's movement" of the 1970s and 1980s.

Literary critic Lisa Lowe has been one of the first to chart how the multiplicitous nature of Asian American difference also offers a powerful deconstructive tool for cultural politics. By utilizing numerous examples from Asian American women's texts, she demonstrates how Asian American discussions of ethnicity and identity have been highly contested, unfixed, and heterogeneous, thus challenging the perspective from which the majority culture has historically grouped Asian Americans into a singular and homogeneous category. Ironically, Lowe also notes how essentialist notions of Asian American identity, culture, and politics have resulted in internal debates where Asian American feminists who dare to challenge Asian American sexism have been cast as "assimilationists" by male critics who accuse them of betraying Asian American "nationalism." Such debates as recorded by Elaine Kim, King-Kok Cheung, and Shirley Geok-lin Lim, reveal not only a masculinist desire for a fixed, culturally pure, and "authentic" Asian American discourse, but also an underlying unease with the hybridizing of Asian American culture—denounced as "fake"—and the growing presence of Asian American feminism. Indeed, Lim's discussion of these debates also maps out the current complex intersections of both Asian American feminism and ethnic literary theory.

If the making of Asian American culture can be described as "nomadic," "unsettled," and taking place in the "travel between cultural sites" (as Lisa Lowe writes), then the same may also be said of the current production of Asian American feminist literary criticism, which continues to grow, in unprecedented manner, not only from multiple locations but multivocal critical positions as well. Several book-length studies and critical anthologies have emerged in the past few years that have already shifted the direction of Asian American literary studies. Sauling Wong's *Reading Asian American Literature* and King-Kok Cheung's *Articulate Silences* both mark a departure from earlier Asian American critical studies in terms of examining the formal, thematic, and "intertextual" elements of the literature in addition to insisting upon the importance of placing them in their social and historical contexts. Of these two studies, Cheung's work is situated more specifically within a feminist framework. She herself states that her book is "in dialogue with recent feminist theories about women's poetics" as she examines the different modalities of "Asian American silence" in the work of women writers Maxine Hong Kingston, Hisaye Yamamoto, and Joy Kogawa. Shirley Lim and Amy Ling's *Reading the Literatures of Asian America* also

breaks new ground as the first published collection of critical essays by a variety of scholars addressing issues of identity politics, race and gender, borders and boundaries, and the politics of representation and self-representation. Lim has also recently edited a collection of essays on approaches to teaching Maxine Hong Kingston's *The Woman Warrrior*. Given *The Woman Warrior's* unique double status as the only Asian American text to be included in the American literary canon as well as its distinction as the "most taught" work of American literature (by a living author) in college classrooms across the country, these essays combine—in both provocative and practical manner—feminist and multicultural pedagogies and criticism. Elaine Kim and Norma Alarcón have also co-edited a collection of critical essays on Korean American writer Theresa Hak Kyung Cha's postmodern feminist text *Dictee*. Born out of a similar sense of pedagogical "urgency," *Writing Self/Writing Nation* not only represents five different Asian American feminist approaches (including one visual essay by artist Yong Soon Min) to the relations between nation, narratives, "home," and feminist identities, but also intervenes in the contemporary criticism of *Dictee*, which has either overlooked or marginalized Korea and Korean America in its discussions.

One final area of new scholarship that has just begun to reshape current directions in Asian American literary and gender studies has emerged out of the site known as Queer Asian American cultural criticism and theory. It is significant that while queer Asian American scholars and writers have had a presence for decades, it is only recently that Asian American "Queer Theory" has had visibility in Asian American studies. Indeed, the primary academic journal in the field, *Amerasia Journal*, has only just addressed the topic of "other Asian and Pacific American sexualities" in a special 1994 double issue volume, "Dimensions of Desire," devoted to the critical and creative work of lesbian, gay, and bisexual scholars and writers. While a book-length collection of critical essays in Queer Asian American literary studies is currently in the planning stages (from Temple University Press), one can find a general introduction to the range of writings and critical stakes in Alice Hom's and Ming-Yuen S. Ma's excellent joint dialogue on "Asian Pacific Islanders Lesbian and Gay Writing," which carefully identifies, examines, and locates various individual and collective projects that have emerged in the last two decades.

Elena Tajima Creef

References

Alarcón, Norma. "The Theoretical Subject(s) of *This Bridge Called My Back* and Anglo-American Feminism." In *Making Face, Making Soul: Haciendo Caras*, edited by Gloria Anzaldúa, 356–369. San Francisco: Spinsters/Aunt Lute, 1990.

Anzaldúa, Gloria, and Cherríe Moraga, eds. *This Bridge Called My Back: Writings by Radical Women of Color*. New York: Kitchen Table: Women of Color Press, 1981.

Cheung, King-Kok. *Articulate Silences: Hisaye Yamamoto, Maxine Hong Kingston, Joy Kogawa*. Ithaca, N.Y., and London: Cornell University Press, 1993.

———. "The Woman Warrior Versus the Chinaman Pacific: Must a Chinese American Critic Choose between Feminism and Heroism?" In *Conflicts in Feminism,* edited by Marianne Hirsch and Evelyn Fox Keller, 234–251. New York: Routledge, 1990.

———, and Stan Yogi, eds. *Asian American Literature: An Annotated Bibliography*. New York: Modern Language Association, 1988.

Hom, Alice Y., and Ming-Yuen S. Ma. "Premature Gestures: A Speculative Dialogue on Asian Pacific Islander Lesbian and Gay Writing." In *Critical Essays: Gay and Lesbian Writers of Color*, edited by Emmanuel S. Nelson, 21–51. New York and London: Haworth, 1993.

Kim, Elaine. *Asian American Literature: An Introduction to the Writings and Their Social Context*. Philadelphia: Temple University Press, 1982.

———. "Such Opposite Creatures." *Michigan Quarterly Review* Winter (1990): 68–93.

———, and Norma Alarcón, eds. Writing *Self/Writing Nation: A Collection of Essays on* Dictee *by Theresa Hak Kyung Cha*. Berkeley: Third Woman, 1994.

Lim, Shirley Geok-lin. "Feminism and Ethnic Literary Theories in Asian American Literature." *Feminist Studies* 19 (1993): 571–595.

———, ed. *Approaches to Teaching Kingston's* The Woman Warrior. New York: Modern Language Association, 1991.

———, and Amy Ling, eds. *Reading the Literatures of Asian America*. Philadelphia: Temple University Press, 1992.

Ling, Amy. *Between Worlds: Women Writers of Chinese Ancestry*. New York and Oxford: Pergamon, 1990.

Lowe, Lisa. "Heterogeneity, Hybridity, Multiplicity: Marking Asian American Differences." *Diaspora* 1 (1991): 24–44.

Wong, Nellie, Merle Woo, and Mitsuye Yamada. *3 Asian American Writers Speak out on Feminism*. San Francisco: San Francisco Radical Women, 1979.

Wong, Sauling. *Reading Asian American Literature: From Necessity to Extravagance*. Princeton: Princeton University Press, 1993.

Astell, Mary

Mary Astell (1666–1731), the author of two anonymous pamphlets, *A Serious Proposal to the Ladies* (1694) and *Some Reflections upon Marriage* (1700), is often cited today as "the first English feminist." In her own time, this unmarried daughter of a Newcastle coal merchant was probably best known as an Anglican/Tory polemicist. She was also a fine poet, letter writer and philosopher. The first part of Astell's *Serious Proposal* considered the structure and viability of a Protestant educational community for unmarried women funded by their dowries. Residents would be steered toward the study of philosophy (especially Descartes) and religious orthodoxy in place of reading "idle *Novels* and *Romances*." The second part (1697) went on to apply the Cartesian system to the lives of middle-class women. *Reflections upon Marriage* expanded Astell's feminist debate with philosophy into the realm of politics, this time through a challenge to the ascendancy of contract theories of government in England; Astell noted that critics of absolutist monarchy (John Locke's *Second Treatise on Government* of 1689 is a primary target) continued to endorse patriarchal rule by husbands in marriage. Paradoxically, Astell's conservative High Church politics led her to an acerbic and witty early feminist critique of the exclusion of women from the doctrines of Enlightenment theory and the development of less arbitrary forms of political government in Europe.

Ros Ballaster

References

Gallagher, Catherine, "Embracing the Absolute: The Politics of the Female Subject in Seventeenth-Century England." *Genders* 1 (1988): 24–39.

Hill, Bridget, ed. *The First English Feminist: Reflections on Marriage and Other Writings by Mary Astell*. New York: St. Martin's, 1986.

Perry, Ruth. *The Celebrated Mary Astell: An Early English Feminist*. Chicago: University of Chicago Press, 1986.

Atwood, Margaret

Poet, fiction writer, literary critic, and essayist. A passionately political writer, Atwood has in interviews resisted narrow labeling as a feminist, primarily because of her deep distrust of categorization and her concern about the limitations of language as well as her insistence on the variety of women and feminisms. But she believes absolutely in the rights of women and in her central project of telling women's stories and uncovering the ways in which culture and discourse construct social identity and gender.

Atwood's early poetry and novels, including *The Edible Woman* and *Lady Oracle*, explore the construction of femininity as the insidious division of the female subject self into object and image. Employing characteristic satire and verbal irony Atwood creates "everywomen," ordinary protagonists whose entrapment in the ideology of their commercial, patriarchal societies is representative. Atwood writes prose with a poet's sensitivity to linguistic meaning, and carefully recorded experience often takes on symbolic weight in her fiction. In the brief essay "What Is a Woman's Novel" she calls herself one of the "literalists of the imagination" and writes that "metaphor leads me by the nose." Her brilliant exploration of the ways in which culture and ideology operate through language has anticipated many of the central tenets of later feminist theorists.

Atwood's identity as a Canadian writer has been instrumental in providing her with a critical vantage point on North American culture. Her publication in 1972 of *Survival: A Thematic Guide to Canadian Literature* proved a catalyst in the recognition and recovery of the Canadian literary tradition and its prominent women writers. The Canadian perspective is central in many of her works, including *The Journals of Susanna Moodie* (1970) and the novel *Surfacing* (1972), and contributes to her insight into the experiences of colonization at the level of history and metaphor, a subject she explores in *Bodily Harm*.

Atwood's fiction has developed toward a more comprehensive understanding of women's oppression as part of a greater nexus of political, social, and economic domination, the urge to control, possess, and use rather than imaginatively perceive and love the other—whether it be nature, woman, people of color, or colonized territories. *The Handmaid's Tale* presents a dystopic vision of late twentieth-century North American society. Atwood, working in the literary tradition of prophetic satire, extrapolates from the Puritan past and contemporary political scene to create the totalitarian regime of Gilead.

Atwood's recent novel *Cat's Eye* is an intricately structured story of recovering the past, particularly the intense and painful world of young girls' friendships and socialization into femininity. Atwood continues the process of recovering the past through a feminist consciousness in *The Robber Bride*.

Pamela Starr Bromberg

See also FAIRY TALES

References

Atwood, Margaret. *Bodily Harm*. 1982. New York: Bantam, 1983.

———. *Cat's Eye*. New York: Doubleday, 1988.

———. *The Edible Woman* [1969]. New York: Bantam, 1991.

———. *Good Bones and Simple Murders*. New York: Doubleday, 1994.

———. *The Handmaid's Tale* [1985]. New York: Fawcett, 1986.

———. *Lady Oracle* [1976]. New York: Fawcett, 1986.

———. *The Robber Bride*. New York: Doubleday, 1993.

Bouson, J. Brooks. *Brutal Choreographies: Oppositional Strategies and Narrative Design in the Novels of Margaret Atwood*. Amherst: University of Massachusetts Press, 1993.

Davidson, Arnold E., and Cathy N. Davidson, eds. *The Art of Margaret Atwood: Essays in Criticism*. Toronto: Anansi, 1981.

Greene, Gayle. *Changing the Story: Feminist Fiction and the Tradition*. Bloomington: Indiana University Press, 1991.

Hite, Molly. *The Other Side of the Story: Structures and Strategies of Contemporary Feminist Narratives*. Ithaca, N.Y.: Cornell University Press, 1989.

Ingersoll, Earl G., ed. *Margaret Atwood Conversations*. Princeton, N.J.: Ontario Review, 1990.

McCombs, Judith, and Carole L. Palmer. *Margaret Atwood: A Reference Guide*. Boston: G.K. Hall, 1991.

————, ed. *Critical Essays on Margaret Atwood*. Boston: G.K. Hall, 1988.

Rao, Eleonora. *Strategies for Identity: The Fiction of Margaret Atwood*. New York: Peter Lang, 1993.

Van Spanckeren, Kathryn, and Jan Garden Castro, eds. *Margaret Atwood: Vision and Forms*. Carbondale: Southern Illinois University Press, 1988.

Wilson, Sharon Rose. *Margaret Atwood's Fairy-Tale Sexual Politics*. Jackson: University Press of Mississippi, 1993.

Auerbach, Nina

With the publication of *Woman and the Demon: The Life of a Victorian Myth*, scholar Nina Auerbach imbues the "Angel in the House," the model of selflessness and passivity, with a demonic, subversive energy, a verve that defies Virginia Woolf's popular, but repressive, interpretation of Victorian womanhood. Beyond the translucent disguise of "angel," Auerbach reconstructs woman as dangerous, creative, transcendent, and dominant. Enthralled with female energy and with woman's ability to transform her role in history, Auerbach illumines myth as a powerful and important vehicle for feminist criticism.

Auerbach's penetration of familiar Victorian masks is nowhere more pronounced than in her reimagining of familiar myths: of fallen women, of old maids and whores, of mermaids and serpent women. Implicit in this myth-making is the reinvestment of power—the angel disguises the militant, the old maid masks the whore. In *Romantic Imprisonment*, Auerbach even recasts the orphan and the outcast: the "alien and excluded snatch from the wield over citizens who think they are safe."

Proving herself a premiere critic of Victorian culture, Auerbach rereads major literary figures, such as Jane Austen, Lewis Carroll, George Eliot, and Christina Rossetti, and exposes her readers as well to the writings of lesser known female authors, such as Ellen Wood and Frances Power Cobbe. As she reconstructs Victorian culture (fiction, theater, art, and myth), Auerbach invites us to partake in the remolding of our own culture, our own myths. Implicit in this transfiguration looms the possibility of reimagining ourselves as we reimagine others. Investigating the figure's historical antecedents and acknowledging the British and American "thirst" for the vampire, Auerbach's latest book, *Our Vampires, Ourselves*, examines the role of the horrifying, yet titillating undead. In its extreme adaptability and mutability, Auerbach argues, the vampire changes with the body politic, infusing itself into our literature and film, from Stoker's early *Dracula* to Jewelle Gomez's *The Gilda Stories*.

Linda Rohrer Paige

References

Auerbach, Nina. "Alice and Wonderland: A Curious Child." In *Lewis Carroll: Modern Critical Views*, edited by Harold Bloom, 31–44. New York: Chelsea House, 1987.

————. *Communities of Women: An Idea in Fiction*. Cambridge: Harvard University Press, 1978.

————. "Dickens and Acting Women." In *Dramatic Dickens*, edited by Carol Hanbery MacKay, 81–86. New York: St Martin's, 1989.

————. *Ellen Terry: Player in Her Time*. New York: Norton, 1987.

————. "Engorging the Patriarchy." In *Historical Studies and Literary Criticism*, edited by Jerome J. McGann, 229–239. Madison: University of Wisconsin Press, 1985.

————. "Jane Austen and Romantic Imprisonment." In *Jane Austen in a Social Context*, 9–27. Totowa, N.J.: Barnes and Noble, 1981.

————. Foreword to *Old Maids to Radical Spinsters: Unmarried Women in the Twentieth-Century Novel*, edited by Laura L. Doan, ix-xv. Urbana: University of Illinois Press, 1991.

————. *Our Vampires, Ourselves*. Chicago: University of Chicago Press, 1995.

————. *Private Theatricals: The Lives of the Victorians*. Cambridge: Harvard University Press, 1990.

————. *Romantic Imprisonment: Women and Other Glorified Outcasts*. New

York: Columbia University Press, 1986.

———. "Victorian Players and Sages." In *The Performance of Power: Theatrical Discourse and Politics*, edited by Sue-Ellen Case and Janelle Reinelt, 183–198. Iowa City: University of Iowa Press, 1991.

———. "Why Communities of Women Aren't Enough." *Tulsa Studies in Women's Literature* 3, nos. 1–2 (1984): 153–157.

———. *Woman and the Demon: The Life of a Victorian Myth*. Cambridge: Harvard University Press, 1982.

———, and U.C. Knoepflmacher, eds. *Forbidden Journeys: Fairy Tales and Fantasies by Victorian Women Writers*. Chicago: University of Chicago Press, 1992.

Authority

The basis of the theory of poetic and literary influence described by Harold Bloom (and reconsidered in terms of feminist literary theory by Sandra Gilbert and Susan Gubar, and Jane Spencer). For Bloom, poetry is "the anxiety of influence" experienced by each "Strong Poet" through the paradigm of the "Family Romance." Gilbert and Gubar argue that women writers do not have a place in Bloom's model of poetic theory because his theory is an "analysis of the patriarchal poetics" of our culture. The authority of the patriarchy "has imprisoned" women. Jane Spencer posits that there is a female literary authority in addition to the male, one that began to be realized in the eighteenth century and whose foundation was "the authority of the mother."

Although six of the eight *Oxford English Dictionary*'s definitions of authority include the word "power," authority is clearly more than the power—the "ability" or "control"—that is a part of its definition. In fact, for Hannah Arendt, authority that uses power is not authority at all; "authority demands obedience," but does not coerce it. For Bloom, a "Strong Poet" cannot elude the influence generated by the poet who serves as authority; each poem that poet writes is an attempt to prevail over and to become the authority. Here, Gilbert and Gubar are able to illustrate most effectively the dilemma of the woman writer confronting authority: for her, the authority is more than the "forefather," but is moreover the patriarchal tradition that literature has absorbed. Using Bloom's terms, Gilbert and Gubar describe Milton as "the great Inhibitor" because his work is at the heart of Western literature, and in that work Milton identifies "woman's secondness, her otherness," and her banishment from the poetic tradition.

Spencer's designation of a separate female literary authority begins to illustrate the ways in which women's writing "contained the potential for radically subverting" the patriarchal authority Gilbert and Gubar describe. What Spencer describes rests less upon the power that the patriarchal tradition utilizes, and more upon the image of a mother who ensures the correct moral foundation. This description is allied to the ideas of "credit" and "credibility" that Samuel Johnson uses as part of his definition of authority (1755), and it indicates that, even in situations where women are excluded from positions of power, they still may be able to exercise authority.

Susan Goulding

References

Arendt, Hannah. What Is Authority?" In *Between Past and Future: Eight Exercises in Political Thought* [1954], 91–141. New York: Viking, 1961.

Bloom, Harold. *The Anxiety of Influence: A Theory of Poetry*. New York: Oxford University Press, 1973.

Gilbert, Sandra M., and Susan Gubar. *The Madwoman in the Attic: The Woman Writer and the Nineteenth-Century Literary Imagination*. New Haven: Yale University Press, 1979.

Johnson, Samuel. *A Dictionary of the English Language* [1755]. Vol. 1. New York: AMS, 1967.

Oxford English Dictionary. 2nd ed., Vol. 1. Oxford: Clarendon, 1989.

Spencer, Jane. "'Of Use to Her Daughter': Maternal Authority and Early Women Novelists." In *Living By the Pen: Early British Women Writers*, edited by Dale Spender, 201–211. New York: Teachers College, 1992.

Autobiography

Many feminists studying autobiography from varied theoretical perspectives agree on the importance of making visible women's interpretations of their own historically grounded lives; to do so is to expand and to change a male privileged understanding of history, even a male privileged understanding of women's lived experiences. Similarly, to study women's personal narratives, including diaries, journals, and letters that previously have not been valued as "literature" is to question and to take feminist responsibility for the standards by which we make literary evaluations.

More problematically, autobiography plunges feminist critics into complex issues of identity and difference. In arguing for the importance of women's autobiographies, feminists must assert that the gender of the author matters and by implication that the author her "self" matters to our understanding of her text. Feminists are challenged to claim the political power that may be enacted by a woman writing about herself without falling back on romantic, totalizing notions of womanhood or authorship. Recent feminist theorizing about autobiography grapples with, rather than obscures, the numerous and sometimes extreme differences within women's autobiography and within particular women's autobiographies.

In the late 1970s and early 1980s, feminist critics of autobiographies began to speculate about the possible instructive differences between women's life writings and men's. For example, in *Imagining a Self: Autobiography and Novel in Eighteenth-Century England*, Patricia Spacks suggests that eighteenth-century women's lived circumstances and written self-presentations show signs of being more severely restricted by society than those of their male counterparts; thus, she argues, women's life writings from this period give us a particularly clear example of how cultural forces help to shape an individual's identity. Mary Mason compares the autobiographies of Julian of Norwich, Margery Kempe, Margaret Cavendish, and Anne Bradstreet to argue that they are thematically linked by a preoccupation with the definition of self in relation to other. She sees this elemental preoccupation "as more or less constant in women's life writing—this is not the case in men's life writing." Estelle C. Jelink argues in a much more broadly transhistorical fashion that women's quite different cultural experience from men's "as far back as Augustine" accounts for a very different female autobiographical style: more fragmented, less publicly oriented, more experimental, more creative. Jelink suggests that male autobiographies have informed our standards for "good" autobiographies, and this is why women's "different" autobiographies have been largely ignored.

Feminist critics of the late 1980s to the present seek to discover new feminist understandings not so much in the differences between women's and men's autobiographical writings, but in the connections and disconnections between autobiographies of women of different racial, sexual, class, ethnic, and geographical backgrounds. Feminists approach the study of women's autobiographical differences from their own differing theoretical and political perspectives. In *The Female Autograph*, for example, Domna Stanton excises the "bio" from her study in order to demonstrate her postmodernist feminist belief that, while the assertion of the female subject in writing is an act of power, the bio/self is not self-enclosed or self-referential, rather, "Its life-lines came from and extend[ed] to others." In *De/Colonization and the Politics of Discourse in Women's Autobiographical Practices*, Julia Watson and Sidonie Smith express dissatisfaction with postmodernist claims of this sort. They argue that to insist all subjects or even all women subjects have been "colonized" by multiple cultural forces is to trivialize the very specific "colonial relationships which exist today." Elizabeth Fox-Genovese, who studies women's life writings within the Afro-American tradition, identifies a feminist need to recognize both the "distinctiveness" of particular groups as well as the particularity of differently situated individuals within these groups. As Doris Sommer examines in relation to her own studies of Latin American women's testimonials, our abilities to "recognize" each other's distinctive, community based self-inscriptions (and to write about them) is often mediated by power imbalances, by problems with translations and editing, by contradictory cultural assumptions about self and community. Nancy Miller wonders in *Getting Personal* if "personal criticism," the interweaving of life story into critical text, may be one method feminists can use to help "undermine the unselfconscious, exclusionary speaking self."

If the study of women's autobiography influences how we write and teach it may also influence how we live. Carolyn Heilbrun in *Writing a Woman's Life* urges that as women's varied life "events, decisions, and relationships" become increasingly visible to us, so will our own varied choices, decisions, and political responsibilities.

Karen Sosnoski

References

Benstock, Shari, ed. *The Private Self: Women's Autobiographical Writings.* Chapel Hill: University of North Carolina Press, 1988.

Cline, Cheryl. *Women's Diaries, Journals and Letters. An Annotated Bibliography.* New York and London: Garland, 1989.

Fox-Genovese, Elizabeth. "TO WRITE MY SELF: The Autobiographies of Afro-American Women. " In *Feminist Issues in Literary Scholarship*, edited by Shari Benstock, 161–167. Bloomington and Indianapolis: Indiana University Press, 1987.

Heilbrun, Carolyn G. *Writing a Woman's Life.* New York and London: W.W. Norton, 1988.

Jelink, Estelle C. *The Tradition of Women's Autobiography from Antiquity to the Present.* Boston: Twayne, 1986.

Mason, Mary. "The Other Voice: Autobiographies of Women Writers." In *Autobiography: Essays Theoretical and Critical,* edited by James Olney, 207–235. Princeton: Princeton University Press, 1980.

Miller, Nancy K., ed. *Getting Personal: Feminist Occasions and Other Autobiographical Acts.* New York and London: Routledge, 1991.

Sommer, Doris. "'Not Just a Personal Story': Women's Testimonies and the Plural Self." In *Life/Lines: Theorizing Women's Autobiography,* edited by Bella Brodzki and Celeste Schenck, 117–130. Ithaca, N.Y., and London: Cornell University Press, 1988.

Spacks, Patricia. *Imagining a Self: Autobiography and Novel in Eighteenth-Century England.* Cambridge: Harvard University Press, 1976.

Stanton, Domna. "Autogynography: Is the Subject Different?" In *The Female Autograph: Theory and Practice of Autobiography from the Tenth to the Twentieth Century*, edited by Domna C. Stanton, 3–20. Chicago and London: University of Chicago Press, 1987.

Watson, Julia, and Sidonie Smith, eds. *De/colonizing the Subject: The Politics of Gender in Women's Autobiography.* Minneapolis, Minn.: Minneapolis University Press, 1992.

Auto-eroticism

See EROTICISM

Autonomy

A term used to signify both agency and authority. By definition, autonomous individuals possess a sense of self-determination that leads them to fashion their own lives and, in so doing, to attempt to influence the lives of others. Feminists have redefined the term to incorporate affiliation with and connection to others with whom they share identity or commonality. Thus, for feminists, autonomy is socially constituted; it derives from the position of strength created by sustained personal relationships with others.

Feminist theorists challenge a number of preexisting notions of the concept of autonomy. With its emphasis upon freedom and equality, Western humanism, for instance, has long made autonomy one of its basic tenets. Some feminists argue, however, that concepts of freedom and equality privilege the individual, who can assert a self only in competition with others who seek the same state of being and who exercise their own sense of power and authority to achieve it. The result is an oppressive hierarchical structure wherein those with power are accorded agency and authority; those without are relegated to a subordinate position and thus denied autonomy. In other words, for feminists, the most persistent notion of autonomy makes it a struggle concept.

As a struggle concept, autonomy has little meaning or value for some feminists. They recognize that the tradition's masculine bias, its privileging of subjectivity, denies women, who have been marginalized, objectified, and rendered powerless by patriarchal social structures, the freedom and equality to exercise their will and to act on their needs and desires. Their subordinate position denies them the power, and thus the potential, for agency and self-determination.

Other feminists have met with equal skepticism postmodern efforts to deconstruct the subject and render it meaningless. Those who have long assumed their subjectivity and who have accepted autonomy as their right, chiefly white, Western males, find little to fear in the notion that subjectivity is a fiction, a construct of language or an effect of discourse. However, those who have traditionally been denied subjectivity find the postmodernist project disheartening, for it undermines feminist efforts to assert agency and authority as just the point when they are beginning to articulate and to assert their subjectivity.

Feminist concepts of autonomy thus derive from an understanding of gender and power relations. Oppressed groups, feminists assert, can achieve self-determination, but only by reconceptualizing power. Autonomy is realized not through competition, but through affiliation with and connection to others. Commonality creates the position of strength from which agency and authority issue forth. Thus, autonomy shares one of its most important characteristics—its relational nature—with feminist concepts of self. Just as individuals develop a sense of self through a complex web of private, personal, and social relationships, so do they achieve autonomy.

Despite their insistence on the relational nature of autonomy and their skepticism of any position that discounts the social construction of difference, feminists have tended to take white Western women's experiences as the norm and generalize from them a shared and universal female oppression. Such a stance, however, fails to acknowledge the power differences between women, especially those distinguishing white women from women of color. Consequently, feminist theorists are now developing an autonomy of color that articulates the independent experiences of African American and other ethnic women and thereby recognizes their distinct feminisms.

Autonomous selfhood is not an outmoded fiction for feminists. Having internalized the cultural norm of inferiority that women's subordinate positions engender, they continue to make the conscious assertion of separate identity a pressing concern. Certainly the extent to which women writers articulate their ideas in autobiography and novels of self-discovery attests to the continued importance of autonomy, even in the face of postmodernism.

Linda C. Pelzer

References

Felski, Rita. *Beyond Feminist Aesthetics: Feminist Literature and Social Change.* London: Hutchinson Radius, 1989.

Flax, Jane. *Thinking Fragments. Psychoanalysis, Feminism, and Postmodernism in the Contemporary West.* Berkeley: University of California Press, 1990.

Gilligan, Carol. *In a Different Voice: Psychological Theory and Women's Development.* Cambridge: Harvard University Press, 1982.

McDowell, Deborah E. "New Directions for Black Feminist Criticism." *Black American Literature Forum* 14 (1980). Reprinted in *New Feminist Criticism: Essays on Women, Literature and Theory,* edited by Elaine Showalter, 186–199. New York: Pantheon, 1985.

McNay, Lois. *Foucault and Feminism: Power, Gender, and the Self.* Boston: Northeastern University Press, 1992.

Miller, Jean Baker, ed. *Psychoanalysis and Women.* Boston: Beacon, 1976.

Smith, Barbara. "Toward a Black Feminist Criticism." In *The New Feminist Criticism: Essays on Women, Literature and Theory,* edited by Elaine Showalter, 168–185. New York: Pantheon, 1985.

A

B

Bakhtin, Mikhail

Russian formalist critic (1895–1975). The foundation for all Bakhtin's analyses of literature, culture, psychology, and ethics is his theory of "dialogics." Bakhtin argues that each discursive action (both spoken and written, simple and complex) is not simply the immediate interaction between the speaker, listener, and context. Instead, it is a link in a complex chain of other utterances." Every discursive action, then, is always in the process of dynamic interaction and struggle with the "other's thoughts, and is filled with echoes and reverberations of previous utterances." This basic theory of dialogics informs Bakhtin's analysis and appreciation of what he calls the "polyphonic novel." Using Dostoevsky's work as a prime example, Bakhtin celebrates the novel as the literary genre with the greatest potential to preserve and renew cultural, social, and ideological "voices." By allowing various worldviews and ideologies to interact dialogically, the polyphonic novel affirms the plurality of independent and fully valid "voices" and consciousnesses in culture. However, Bakhtin's dissertation on Rabelais, which posits a theory of the "carnivalesque" in culture and literature, argues that harmony and affirmation are not the only outcomes of such dialogic interaction. According to this theory, carnival is the wedding of antithetical elements such as the sacred and the profane, and the ritualistic defiance of laws, prohibitions, and restrictions through the inversion of hierarchies. Nonetheless, carnival temporarily establishes new relationships between cultural elements by bringing otherwise marginalized elements to the center to call into question official social orders.

Although feminists might object to using Bakhtin's theories because they ignore specific questions of gender, some have found them to be useful in exploring several key feminist issues. For example, Bakhtin's theory of dialogics supports the feminist claim to a women's literary tradition that preserves and affirms feminine "voices" through an intertextual "chain." Bakhtin's theory of the carnivalesque in literature explains further how the "voice" of the marginalized feminine is engaged in a dynamic struggle against the dominant or official patriarchal "voice" in the polyphonic text. It also exposes how power dynamics might be challenged and subverted through inversion and parody, two common feminist strategies for critiquing the patriarchal elements in culture and literature. Moreover, Bakhtin's theories provide feminists with a useful methodology with which to read literature, analyze characters, identify dynamics among voices within texts, and even to gain a new perspective on feminist theory itself. For example, Susan Kehde argues that Bakhtin's theory of carnivalesque is a way to "empower the feminist critic at least to listen to marginalized voices" in the literary texts of canonical authors such as Henry James. Jaye Berman examines how Donald Barthelme's postmodern female characters are engaged in a carnivalesque critique of dominant patriarchal culture. Mary O'Connor uses Bakhtin's theory of the self to understand the multivocal potential in texts written by black women. Gail Schwab has utilized the Bakhtinian dialogic linguistic model to reinterpret Luce Irigaray's feminist theory. One will find that generally Bakhtin's theories agree with several feminist assumptions, methodologies, and objectives, most significantly in their attention to the "other."

Grace Sikorski

References

Bakhtin, Mikhail. *Art and Answerability: Early Philosophical Essays by M.M. Bakhtin.* Edited by Michael Holquist and Vadim Liapunov. Translated by Vadim Liapunov. Austin: University of Texas Press, 1990.

———. *The Dialogic Imagination: Four Essays by M.M. Bakhtin.* Edited by Michael Holquist. Translated by Caryl Emerson and Michael Holquist. Austin: University of Texas Press, 1981.

———. *Problems of Dostoevsky's Poetics.* Edited and translated by Caryl Emerson. Minneapolis: University of Minnesota Press, 1984.

———. *Rabelais and His World.* Translated by Helene Iswolsky. Cambridge: MIT Press, 1968.

———. *Speech Genres and Other Late Essays.* Edited by Caryl Emerson and Michael Holquist. Translated by Vern W. McGee. Austin: University of Texas Press, 1986.

Bauer, Dale. *Feminist Dialogics: A Theory of Failed Community.* Albany: State University of New York Press, 1988.

———, and S. Jaret McKinstry, eds. *Feminism, Bakhtin, and the Dialogic.* Albany: State University of New York Press, 1991.

Hohne, Karen, and Helen Wussow, eds. *A Dialogue of Voices: Feminist Literary Theory and Bakhtin.* Minneapolis: University of Minnesota Press, 1994

Bal, Mieke

Mieke Bal may be best known for her accessible summary of narratology, the theory of narrative structure. She has since developed key narratological concepts, relating to perspective and subjectivity, for application in a feminist criticism that draws as well on psychoanalytic, semiotic, and political approaches to literature. In her 1984 article "The Rhetoric of Subjectivity," Bal developed a theory of "narrative subjectivity" and its ideological effects. That theory and Bal's application of it to the story of Samson and Delilah set the stage for a series of feminist interpretations of Bible stories. More recently, she has broadened her scope to include the interpretation of visual art. In all her work, Bal uses a variety of relevant approaches to complement and interrogate one another in an evolving, interdisciplinary feminist criticism.

This criticism reveals the political implications not only of the objects of study, but also of the methodologies that are used to analyze them.

Bal examines the need on the part of readers of narrative to carve out a "subject position" for themselves—a perspective with which they can, in a sense, "identify"—in order to make sense of texts. By directing us toward the construction of male-oriented and often misogynist perspectives, argues Bal, narratives often force us to interpret them in misogynistic ways. They give us cues that force us to refer to, build upon, and thereby tacitly assent to many of the "myths" that justify patriarchy. This is especially true in the case of Bible stories, which have been told and retold from many perspectives and for many audiences, but almost invariably with unwritten sexist assumptions. Bal thus demonstrates narrative's subtle ideological manipulation of its reader.

In her book-length study of Biblical love stories (*Lethal Love*), Bal challenges the authority of traditional literary critical approaches to the Bible. She argues that there is a powerful partnership "between ideological dominance and specific forms of representation." In addition to dissecting the "dominant misogynist readings" of Biblical texts, *Lethal Love* exposes the unstated political assumptions behind the allegedly "scientific" analytic tools of narratology upon which Bal has drawn. It thus extends her critique of patriarchal discourses and their claims to "objectivity."

Debra Malina

References

Bal, Mieke. *Lethal Love: Feminist Literary Readings of Biblical Love Stories.* Bloomington: Indiana University Press, 1987.

———. *Narratology: Introduction to the Theory of Narrative.* Translated by Christine Van Boheemen. Toronto: University of Toronto Press, 1985.

———. "The Rhetoric of Subjectivity." *Poetics Today* 5 (1984): 337–376.

Bambara, Toni Cade

Bambara is an extraordinary example of a writer whose work integrates the personal and the political: a self-described "Pan-Africanist-socialist-feminist," her experiences as a social worker and activist provided motive and material for her essays and fiction, which resonate with themes of responsible selfhood within an organic black community and of the political and sexual tensions generated by the black woman's unique status (black and female). Accordingly, her writing is consistently informed by the dynamics of conflict, the problems that arise from violation of natural contracts with self, family, friends, ancestors, and God. In her prose essays and fiction she focuses not only on issues of gender roles and the damaging effects of sexism, but also on the importance of "wholeness" and balance in material and spiritual life. In her novel *The Salt Eaters*, as well as in her short stories, she offers an exploration of these conflicts through a feminine consciousness situated within the context of the political and personal imperatives of the black woman. The demythologizing and marginalization of the black male and the foregrounding of feminine desire and power are part of a strategy to neutralize gender distinctions: her goal is to promote selfhood and blackhood—not ideals of the "masculine" and the "feminine."

Grounded in the tradition of African American oral culture, her fiction provides insights into how knowledge and wisdom are shared, especially among women. Whether engaging in conversation or communicating with "spirit kin," her female characters participate in rites of initiation and healing through oral discourse. Her stories also offer superb examples of urban and Southern black vernacular, flavored by jazz, blues, and gospel modes and punctuated by call-and-response and "signifying" practices.

Claudette Picklesimer

References

Bambara, Toni Cade. *Gorilla, My Love*. New York: Random House, 1972.

———. *The Salt Eaters*. New York: Random House, 1980.

———. *The Sea Birds Are Still Alive: Collected Stories*. New York: Random House, 1977.

———, ed. *The Black Woman: An Anthology*. New York: American Library, 1970.

Barrett, Michèle

Primarily sociological in scope, Michèle Barrett's attempts to synthesize Marxist and feminist accounts of social relations have nevertheless inspired and influenced cultural and literary critics alike. Her 1980 *Women's Oppression Today*—though flawed, as she herself later acknowledged, by ethnocentrism—remains persuasive in its insistence that sexual oppression preexisted capitalism, and seems likely to outlast it. Her more recent work considers the further shifts and complications of that debate under the impact of poststructuralism.

Barrett's fascination with the processes and problems of ideology and cultural production has made her an occasional but insightful literary critic. In her pioneering edition of Virginia Woolf's essays on *Women and Writing* she elucidated the tension between the materialist and the apolitical in Woolf's critical vision. In "Feminism and the Definition of Cultural Politics" she challenged the "gynocritical" celebration of women's art, arguing that if meanings are socially constructed, there can be no inherently feminist text, and no natural aesthetic hierarchies.

Barrett understands literary texts to be important sites of ideological contest and negotiation, but cautions us against overprivileging literature in our analyses of social production and reproduction. Most usefully, perhaps, she encourages us to take a critical, historicizing stance on our own reading, writing, and theorizing habits.

Sarah Waters

References

Barrett, Michèle. "Feminism and the Definition of Cultural Politics." In *Feminism, Culture and Politics*, edited by Rosalind Brunt and Caroline Rowan, 37–58. London: Lawrence and Wishart, 1982.

———. *Women's Oppression Today: Problems in Marxist Feminist Analysis*. London: Verso, 1980. Rev. ed. London: Verso, 1988.

———. "Words and Things: Materialism and Method in Contemporary Feminist Analysis." In *Destabilizing Theory: Contemporary Feminist Debates*, edited by Michèle Barrett and Anne Philips, 201–219. Cambridge: Polity, 1992.

Baudrillard, Jean

In *Seduction*, Baudrillard equates seductive skill with femininity, arguing that "the feminine" is actually the most powerful force in society; although the feminine does not oppose the masculine, it exerts more power and control than does the masculine. Thus, for Baudrillard, the

B

real source of power lies not in controlling reality, but in learning how to manipulate the world of appearances, of surfaces and copies. Seduction, through its use of artifice, is the most powerful procedure within what Baudrillard terms this "world of appearances." Feminist literary critics have found Baudrillard's theory of seduction useful because it helps to describe how seduction works on a textual level. For example, this theory can illuminate seduction between narrators and readers. On the other hand, feminists have also questioned the accuracy of Baudrillard's claim: arguing for femininity's dominance suggests an inability to recognize the condition of women, as those who are usually seen as the agents of femininity. Furthermore, to be feminine is also to be the object of another's gaze; Baudrillard's theory of seduction does not acknowledge this, or the way in which objectification takes power away from women.

Wendy C. Wahl

References

Baudrillard, Jean. *Seduction*. Translated by Brian Singer. New York: St. Martin's, 1990.

———. *Selected Writings*. Edited by Mark Poster. Stanford: Stanford University Press, 1989.

———. *Simulations*. Translated by Paul Foss, Paul Patton, and Philip Beitchman. New York: Semiotexte, 1983.

Gallop, Jane. "French Theory and the Seduction of Feminism." In *Men in Feminism*, edited by Alice Jardine and Paul Smith, 111–115. New York: Methuen, 1987.

Ross, Andrew. "Baudrillard's Bad Attitude." In *Seduction and Theory: Readings of Gender, Representation, and Rhetoric*, edited by Dianne Hunter, 214–225. Urbana: University of Illinois Press, 1989.

Schor, Naomi. "Cartes Postales: Representing Paris 1900." *Critical Inquiry* 18 (1992): 188–244.

Baym, Nina

With her book *Woman's Fiction: A Guide to Novels by and about Women in America, 1820–1870*, literary critic Nina Baym led the way in recovering the work of antebellum American women writers. Half of the literature published by Americans between 1820 and 1870 was by white women and was, in its day, immensely popular. But until the work of Baym and others, it was ignored or denigrated by scholars.

In "Melodramas of Beset Manhood: How Theories of American Fiction Exclude Women Authors," anthologized with her other important articles in *Feminism and American Literary History*, Baym explained how literary theory has systematically excluded these women writers from the American canon. She examined the presumptions of those studies that created a canon of white, middle-class men such as Melville and Thoreau. Early American literary critics wanted a literature that was equal to the presumed greatness of the new nation. Literary greatness thus became synonymous with "Americanness." For these critics, the classic story of America was about that individual who left society behind so as to create a personally crafted destiny. Baym explained how this myth is necessarily predicated on "a certain believable mobility" available only to a man. Furthermore, his mobility was portrayed as hindered by a society imagined as primarily female. The wilderness he runs to is his fantasy of what women should provide, namely total gratification. Because women writers were unable realistically to portray mobile female protagonists and because they did not care to perpetuate a myth in which they were either the enemy or completely self-effacing, their fiction told different stories and was thus later ignored by literary critics. Much of Baym's work has been devoted to unearthing their many stories.

Most notably, in *Woman's Fiction*, Baym recovered one of the most often repeated stories of the antebellum period that had previously been ignored by literary critics. After an extensive review of the women authors of the period and the plots of their novels, Baym concluded that each novel tells the same story of a young girl deprived of all support who is thus obliged to make her own way in the world. Viewed this way, such literature does not seem to advocate women's conformity to patriarchal stipulations, as had often been argued, but rather offers a "pragmatic feminism." At the end of most of the novels, a happy marriage symbolizes not conformity, but rather the heroine's success in triumphing over adversity.

Baym's work has been instrumental in creating a more accurate history of nineteenth-century American literature, a history in which women were active participants.

Elise Lemire

References

Baym, Nina. *Feminism and American Literary History*. New Brunswick, N.J.: Rutgers University Press, 1992.

———. "Rewriting the Scribbling Women." *Legacy* 2 (1985): 3–12.

———. "The Rise of the Woman Author." In *Columbia Literary History of the United States*, edited by Emory Elliott, 289–305. New York: Columbia University Press, 1988.

———. "Thwarted Nature: Nathaniel Hawthorne as Feminist." In *American Novelists Revisited: Essays in Feminist Criticism*, edited by Fritz Fleischmann, 58–77. Boston: G.K. Hall, 1982.

———. *Woman's Fiction: A Guide to Novels by and about Women in America, 1820–1870*. Ithaca, N.Y.: Cornell University Press, 1978.

Beard, Mary

Mary Ritter Beard (1876–1958) made her greatest contribution as a pioneer in feminist cultural studies by arguing that women in the nineteenth and twentieth centuries were important historical actors, and by pointing out that nineteenth-century feminists must be viewed within the economic, political, and social currents within which they lived. These two assertions, which today seem commonplace among feminist scholars, were significant breakthroughs in feminist thought and research. She attempted to form a feminist theory of history. She argued that women have played a very active part in history, and that without a knowledge or written record of women's contributions, our knowledge of history would continue to be not only incomplete but inaccurate.

Mary Beard's most famous and powerful work, *Woman as Force in History*, argued that regaining the history of women, namely the history of arenas inhabited by women rather than those exclusively the purview of men, not only shows women as historical agents, but also serves to empower women now. Change the definition of what history is, she argued, rather than "adding" something about women to the existing history paradigm. Current contemporary feminist analyses have been influenced by the nascent ideas of Mary Beard and her constant struggle to show women as central to the construction of culture.

Gina Hames

References

Beard, Mary Ritter. *America through Women's Eyes*. New York: Greenwood, 1933. 2nd ed. New York: Greenwood, 1969.

———. *Woman as Force in History: A Study in Traditions and Realities*. New York: Macmillan, 1946. 2nd ed. New York: Persea, 1987.

Cott, Nancy F., ed. *A Woman Making History: Mary Ritter Beard through Her Letters*. New Haven: Yale University Press, 1991.

Lane, Ann J. *Mary Ritter Beard: A Source Book*. Boston: Northeastern University Press, 1977; 2nd ed. Boston: Northeastern University Press, 1988.

Beauty

The physical ideals of face and form have generated critical attention in the feminist community because women have traditionally been judged exclusively according to these criteria. Aesthetic evaluation objectifies; women seen as beautiful or as ugly by others cannot subjectify themselves as anything else, cannot define themselves in other terms, or by other categories, such as personal achievement. Theoretically, to be appraised purely according to one's physical nature subjects women to secondary status in culture. Practically, rituals of beauty enslave women so that they have neither the time nor the energy left over for success in other spheres. Historically, the beautiful woman, like any other aesthetic artifact, has been treated as a charming possession, as a valuable sort of chattel. In so many ways, the constant struggle for a pleasing appearance has contributed to the suppression of women's potential and to the politics of their marginalization.

Simone de Beauvoir, in *The Second Sex*, was among the first to point out that the female body does not have "transcendence" but rather "immanence": "it is not for such a body to have reference to the rest of the world, it must not be the promise of things other than itself." Instead of projecting the "personality" of its subject, beauty arouses a response—desire—in its observer. De Beauvoir argues that the beautiful body "must present the inert and passive qualities of an object," suppressing its own subjectivity in order to reflect that of a possessor.

With de Beauvoir, feminism began the

search for the sources of this objectification of the female body. Sherry B. Ortner's article, "Is Female to Male as Nature Is to Culture?" written in homage to de Beauvoir, examines how women have been associated with the physical (with their body and its functions) and hence the natural sphere, and thus devalued by the cultural (intellectual and technological) sphere associated with men. Beauty as an anatomical quality participates in constructing women as nature; Ortner's work suggests the irony that women become cultural objects through a persistent link between them and culture's opposite, nature.

The feminist study of beauty as a cultural object, as a cultural commodity, has gained steam only in the 1980s. And with this intensification of interest in beauty has come an increased resistance to it as an ideological construct. Robin Tolmach Lakoff and Raquel L. Scherr, in *Face Value: The Politics of Beauty*, discuss the connections between beauty and power. Through discussions of the history, psychology, and politics of personal appearance, Lakoff and Scherr attempt to define beauty as "power over other people" and to deny it the ability to separate "woman from woman, women from men, and race from race." Beauty achieves its power from its exchange value; like money it is "currency" that is "symbolic" of a value located elsewhere. When women can see beauty as a "deindividualized possession" subject to "standardization," they can begin to understand its politics and perhaps choose not to identify with it.

Similarly, Susan Brownmiller's *Femininity* dissects the different commodities or components of beauty, including body, hair, clothes, voice, skin, and movement, in order to demystify the aesthetics of "femininity" and engage women in some "hard reckoning" about themselves. Like Lakoff and Scherr, Brownmiller attempts to investigate a female construct "built upon a recognition of powerlessness" and bring women an "awareness . . . of a feminine ideal . . . used to perpetuate inequality between the sexes." Rita Freedman's *Beauty Bound* explores the "social myth" of beauty in all its twentieth-century manifestations in order to enable women to "loosen" the "bonds of beauty," which damage their mental health. Naomi Wolf's political manifesto, *The Beauty Myth*, hopes to free women to enjoy political and social liberation by flushing out and challenging the "last one remaining of the old femi-nine ideologies that still has the power to control" women.

Instead of allowing women to be identified by their outward appearance, to live as objects of society's gaze, feminists have begun to listen to women's versions of beauty and nonbeauty, lived from the inside. Wendy Chapkis's *Beauty Secrets* replaces "the still life of unchanging 'perfection'" with the voices of "creatures so lively and diverse as womankind." Chapkis collects memoirs in which women express their anger in confronting existing notions of beauty and their joy in learning to redefine them.

But the most recent addition to the bibliography on beauty reformulates it from the outside. Francette Pacteau, in *The Symptom of Beauty*, again addresses beauty "'in the eye of the beholder.'" Indeed Pacteau conceives of physical perfection as an ideology in which no ideal women are present, as a fantasy having only to do with the spectator. Pacteau's work concerns the "act of attribution," not the attribute. She uses psychoanalytic theory to examine the fantasy of beauty, which she reads as "symptoms" of a cultural disease of repression. Although Pacteau looks at men creating beauty, she writes a feminist critique of the male "fantasy which frames it."

Sustained readings of Freud (beauty as sexuality) also appear in Arthur Marwick's *Beauty in History*. And a discussion of Lacan (beauty and the mirror) appears in two studies of beauty within the academic disciplines of literature and film, Jenijoy La Belle's *Herself Beheld* and Laura Mulvey's *Visual and Other Pleasures,* respectively. The interpersonal politics of beauty often intertwine with the personal politics of the psyche.

Erin Isikoff

References

Brownmiller, Susan. *Femininity*. New York: Fawcett Columbine, 1984.

Chapkis, Wendy. *Beauty Secrets: Women and the Politics of Appearance*. Boston: South End, 1986.

de Beauvoir, Simone. *The Second Sex*. Translated by H.M. Parshley. New York: Knopf, 1952. New York: Vintage Books, 1974.

Freedman, Rita. *Beauty Bound*. Lexington, Mass.: Lexington, 1986.

La Belle, Jenijoy. *Herself Beheld: The Literature of the Looking Glass*. Ithaca, N.Y.: Cornell University Press, 1988.

Lakoff, Robin Tolmach, and Raquel L. Scherr. *Face Value: The Politics of Beauty*. Boston: Routledge and Kegan Paul, 1984.

Marwick, Arthur. *Beauty in History: Society, Politics, and Personal Appearance c. 1500 to the Present*. London: Thames and Hudson, 1988.

Mulvey, Laura. *Visual and Other Pleasures*. Bloomington: Indiana University Press, 1989.

Ortner, Sherry B. "Is Female to Male as Nature Is to Culture?" In *Women, Culture, and Society*, edited by Michelle Zimbalist Rosaldo and Louise Lamphere, 67–87. Stanford: Stanford University Press, 1974.

Pacteau, Francette. *The Symptom of Beauty*. Cambridge: Harvard University Press, 1994.

Wolf, Naomi. *The Beauty Myth: How Images of Beauty Are Used against Women*. New York: William Morrow, 1991. New York: Anchor, 1992.

Beauvoir, Simone de

Teacher, philosopher, political activist, existentialist, and feminist, Beauvoir was one of the best known French writers and thinkers of the twentieth century. A central figure in left-wing French intellectual circles, Beauvoir also wrote novels, a play, and nonfiction ranging from autobiography to travelogues to political commentary; however, she is best known for her analysis of the social construction of femininity in her seminal work, *The Second Sex*. Although she herself was unmarried, financially independent, professionally successful, and quite removed from the domestic sphere of most women, Beauvoir boldly wrote that women had not been given equality, and called into question existing laws, religions, customs, and traditions. In demanding that society and all of its structures be evaluated, Beauvoir inspired a generation of women to change the course of their lives to their own advantage. Initially creating a furor due to its frank discussion of female sexuality, as well as its glaring indictment of patriarchy, *The Second Sex* is today regarded as the bible of the women's liberation movement.

Originally published in two volumes, *The Second Sex* is a comprehensive, well-documented scholarly treatise on the historical and contemporary situation of women in Western culture examined from an existential position. Drawing extensively from biology, psychology, literature, history, and the autobiographies of contemporary Western women, Beauvoir details how, for centuries, women have been reduced to passive objects for men, and then offers two corollaries. First of all, that man conceiving of himself as the essential being, the subject, has constructed woman into the unessential being, the negative object, and the Other. Secondly, that there is no such thing as feminine nature and that all notions of femininity are artificial. "One is not born," writes Beauvoir "but rather becomes a woman. No biological, psychological, or economic fate determines the figure that the human female presents in society; it is civilization as a whole that produces this creature, intermediate between male and eunuch; which is described as feminine."

Women, Beauvoir argues, have been forced by social tradition into making their choices from a secondary or inferior position in relation to men, and have in many ways been treated as though they were members of a racial minority. Because dependence is the essence of "femininity," women are brought up without ever being impressed with the necessity of taking charge of their own existence. Men, instead, have taken it over and in the process have oppressed women.

Depriving women of the human dignity of both professional and intellectual equality with men, Beauvoir explains, has not only restricted women's cultural contributions, but has also created persuasive social injustices and has tended to violate sexual relations between man and woman. Men, as oppressors, cannot be expected to make a move of gratuitous generosity; it is instead up to the women of the world to fully emancipate themselves. The essential means by which women will eventually be freed from their dependence on men is through economic emancipation, which can usually be achieved only if birth control is practiced. Convinced that the rise of socialism would put an end to the tyranny of women, Beauvoir concludes *The Second Sex* by solemnly urging men and women to join hands as "comrades, friends, and partners" in a common struggle to "abolish the enslavement of half of humanity."

In 1974, Beauvoir published *All Said and Done*, the last of her four-volume autobiography. Returning to a notion that she had espoused twenty-one years earlier in *The Second Sex,* she wrote that "all male ideologies are di-

rected at justifying the oppression of women—
[and that] women are so conditioned by society that they consent to this oppression." But,
for Beauvoir, women's rights were inseparable
from human rights, and whenever the opportunity arose she took a stand against oppression,
be it of the individual or the group, lending her
name to journals, organizations, public meetings, and petitions. Simone de Beauvoir's feminism, in short, was based on her own doctrine
and philosophy: the need to take action.

J.S. Postol

References

Bair, Deirdre. *Simone de Beauvoir: A Biogra-
phy.* New York: Summit, 1990.
Beauvoir, Simone de. *All Said and Done.* New
York: Putnam, 1974.
———. *The Coming of Age.* New York:
Putnam, 197(?).
———. *Force of Circumstances.* New York:
Putnam, 1965.
———. *Memoirs of a Dutiful Daughter.*
Cleveland: World, 1959.
———. *The Second Sex.* New York: Knopf,
1953.
Francis, Claude, and Gontier. *Simone de
Beauvoir: A life. A love story.* New York:
St. Martin's, 1987.

Belsey, Catherine

For many students and critics in the 1980s, their
first memorable encounter with poststructuralism was via Catherine Belsey's *Critical Practice,* a persuasive and accessible introduction to
the theories of Saussure, Barthes, Lacan,
Derrida, and Macherey, that demonstrated their
revolutionary implications for literary studies.
Belsey challenged the alliance between traditional criticism and "classic realism," the dominant modern fictional mode. Both, she argued,
perform the work of liberal humanist ideology
and naturalize its version of class and gender
relations. She called for a radical new reading
practice that would address itself to textual pluralities and instabilities, rather than collude
with classic realism in smoothing over ideological tensions.

Belsey has continued her poststructuralist
interrogation of liberal humanism, seeking particularly to restore a history to its apparently
ahistorical gendered subjects. *The Subject of
Tragedy* examines Renaissance drama to consider the problematical relationship between the

liberal humanist "Man," and the women who
were denied a stable subject-position in early
modern society. While writing of the period
delineates a new male subjectivity that is interior, cohesive, and fixed, she argues, the female
subject remains fragmented, her speech discontinuous or inaudible.

Liberal humanism's patriarchal allegiances,
Belsey implies, continue to oppress its female
subjects. However, by exposing the history of
the discourses and categories that offer themselves as "common sense," she not only invites
us to speculate upon our own political practices,
but also alerts us to the possibility of cultural
change.

Sarah Waters

References

Belsey, Catherine. *Critical Practice.* London:
Methuen, 1980.
———. *John Milton: Language, Gender,
Power.* Oxford: Basil Blackwell, 1988.
———. *The Subject of Tragedy: Identity and
Difference in Renaissance Drama.* Lon-
don: Methuen, 1985.
———, and Jane Moore, eds. *The Feminist
Reader: Essays in Gender and the Poli-
tics of Literary Criticism.* Basingstoke:
Macmillan, 1989.

Benjamin, Jessica

In *The Bonds of Love* psychoanalyst Jessica
Benjamin overturns the cultural assumption
that identity arises through separation from the
mother, exposing misogynist logic underlying
this idea. To Benjamin, children need to "grow
sovereign within relationship" to the mother, a
creative tension she calls "mutual recognition."
All ensuing relationships are based on mutual
recognition, which protects against domination
of, or from, the other. For literary theory, Benjamin enables new readings of the mother/child
bond, family, child development, and relations
of domination in private and public life.

Benjamin contributes to psychoanalytic,
social, and feminist theory. In asserting the view
that domination is "natural," Freud and Hegel
fail to see that the need to control the other
occurs when mutual recognition breaks down.
Object-relations theory, seeing the mother as a
mirror for the child, overlooks that her separate
existence allows her to grant a child full recognition. Liberal theory's belief in individuation,
objectivity, and freedom slights social and pri-

mary emotional bonds. This lack of nurturance, not absence of paternal authority, causes cultural malaise. For feminist theory, Benjamin presents the mother as an agent of both connection and separation; drawing upon infant research, she affirms the interactive human infant, and she explains erotic domination (typically, the woman is submissive) as a distorted form of mutual recognition.

Benjamin rehabilitates maternal presence, brings infants as active agents to view, and reveals the psychological origins of the gendered, dominant values of the culture. Literary theory benefits from Benjamin's vision of "mutual recognition" by testing theories and relationships in the text.

Robbie Pfeufer Kahn

References

Benjamin, Jessica. "The Alienation of Desire: Women's Masochism and Ideal Love." In *Psychoanalysis and Women: Contemporary Reappraisals*, edited by Judith Alpert, 113–138. Hillsdale, N.J.: Analytic, 1986.
———. "Authority and the Family Revisited; or, A World without Fathers?" *New German Critique* 13 (1978): 35–58.
———. *The Bonds of Love: Psychoanalysis, Feminism, and the Problem of Domination.* New York: Pantheon, 1988.
———. "The End of Internalization: Adorno's Social Psychology." *Telos* 32 (1977): 42–64.

Benstock, Shari

Benstock has written on a broad array of subjects, ranging from James Joyce to women's autobiographical theory. In her book *Textualizing the Feminine: On the Limits of Genre*, Benstock combines Derrida's theories of epistolary form with Kristeva's influence of writing the feminine to understand the connection between women's bodies, or biological identities, and women's textuality. Benstock offers a useful analysis of French linguistic theory, while illustrating how rhetoric can be used to produce a distinctly feminine text.

In *Women of the Left Bank: Paris 1900–1940*, a biography of expatriate women artists, Benstock argues that these women were unified by their desire to flee patriarchal constraints and to construct limits for themselves in a new space. *Women of the Left Bank*, both a critical and biographical study, makes a significant

contribution to feminist scholarship by extending literary modernism to study this community of women writers. Benstock illustrates the differences that mark each woman's search for identity, artistic expression, and her place in a patriarchal world.

Benstock's work is important for her focus on women's writing that illustrates places where genre, specifically autobiography, and gender intersect. Her research includes various autobiographical texts and theories of autobiography. Both lend to her search to understand women's writing not only as different, outside or "other" from the tradition of male writing, but also as a discourse that is distinctly female. Benstock's work deconstructs the dichotomy of "public" male writing and "private" female writing by accounting for the way each one has been constructed by social patterns and power structures.

Heidi N. Kaufman

References

Benstock, Shari. *Textualizing the Feminine: On the Limits of Genre.* Norman: University of Oklahoma Press, 1991.
———. *Women of the Left Bank: Paris 1900–1940.* Austin: University of Texas Press, 1986.
———, ed. *Feminist Issues in Literary Scholarship.* Bloomington: Indiana University Press, 1987.
———, ed. *The Private Self: Theory and Practice of Women's Autobiographical Writings.* Chapel Hill: University of North Carolina Press, 1988.

Bilingualism

A writer's use of more than one language is a topic of increasing interest to feminist theorists. Not all of them would agree with Susanne de Lotbinière-Harwood's assertion that, because all languages are manmade, bilingualism is universal among women. But they would certainly accept her belief that "language is never neutral" and that it is intimately linked to gender. In their efforts to understand this linkage, and its implications for writers, texts, and readers, feminist theorists focus on the varied ways in which writers work deliberately with "different Englishes" (Amy Tan) or with a mix of English and another language or languages.

Because bilingual writers alter the very fabric of language, their work is experimental by definition. As Diane P. Freedman has observed, however, such experimentation arises "not so much from a postmodern plight or post-structuralist perspective" as from what poet Gloria Anzaldúa has referred to as life in the "borderlands" between languages and cultures. Like Maxine Hong Kingston, who explains that she will write English as she speaks it, "with Chinese accents" (Rabinowitz), Anzaldúa writes across the multiple borders she has experienced as a woman, a Chicana, and a lesbian. She describes her aesthetics as that of a new "mestiza consciousness" that both explores and seeks to counter in language the polarities and concomitant inequalities that she finds in Western thought and practices.

The extent to which bilingualism can be said to characterize the work of individual writers varies greatly. In her novel *Singing Softly/Cantando bajito*, for example, Carmen Monteflores interweaves Spanish and English continually, as if they were one language, although translations are provided in italics within the text. Other writers use a second language more sparingly, and without providing translations, as Tsitsi Dangarembga has done with Shona in *Nervous Conditions* (and Sandra Cisneros has done in *"Woman Hollering Creek" and Other Stories*. In each instance, however, the reader is placed in a position described by Debra Castillo as one of "subjunctivity"—that of "an unexpected space" in which it is necessary to participate in the "working" of a text. Such participation can also be identified as the activity (as opposed to the product) of translation; in the absence of "linguistic unity in English" (Castillo), it is up to the reader to construct "meaning."

Another aspect of bilingualism has been studied by Patricia Yaeger, who has discussed the creation of bilingual heroines as an "emancipatory strategy" in women's writing. Although men have also used bilingual characters to probe and challenge the constraints of language, Yaeger maintains that in their bi- and multilingual protagonists women have "surpassed their male contemporaries in ingenuity." Yeager's work focuses largely on nineteenth-century writers, and she draws heavily on the work of French feminist theorists. Nevertheless, there are numerous and provocative intersections between her affirmations and Anzaldúa's mestiza struggle or the "political agenda" and the re-imagining of America identified by Kingston. Future work in bilingualism will need to explore both those intersections and the characteristics that identify a specifically feminist bilingual writing practice.

Carol Maier

References

Anzaldúa, Gloria. *Borderlands/"La frontera": The New Mestiza*. San Francisco: Spinsters/Aunt Lute, 1988.

Castillo, Debra. "In a Subjunctive Mood: Denise Chávez, Maxine Hong Kingston, and the Bicultural Text." In *Talking Back: Toward a Latin American Feminist Literary Criticism*, edited by Debra A. Castillo, 260–292. Ithaca, N.Y.: Cornell University Press, 1992.

Cisneros, Sandra. *"Woman Hollering Creek" and Other Stories*. New York: Random House, 1991.

Dangarembga, Tsitsi. *Nervous Conditions*. Seattle: Sed Press, 1989.

de Lotbinière-Harwood, Susanne. *Re-belle et infidèle/The Body Bilingual*. Montreal: Les éditions du remue-ménage/Women's Press, 1991.

Freedman, Diane P. *An Alchemy of Genres: Cross-Genre Writing by American Feminist Poet-Critics*. Charlottesville: University Press of Virginia, 1992.

Humm, Maggie. "Translation as Survival: Zora Neale Hurston and La Malincha." *Fiction International* 17 (1987): 119–129.

Jouve, Nicole Ward. "Her Legs Bestrid the Channel": Writing in Two Languages." In *Women Writing: The Challenge to Theory*, edited by Moira Monteith, 34–53. Brighton: Harvester, and New York: St. Martin's, 1986.

Monteflores, Carmen. *Singing Softly/Contando bajito*. San Francisco: Spinster/Aunt Lute Press, 1989.

Rabinowitz, Paula. "Eccentric Memories: A Conversation with Maxine Hong Kingston." *Michigan Quarterly Review* 26 (1987): 177–187.

Tan, Amy. "Mother Tongue." *Three Penny Review* (Fall 1990): 7–8.

Yaeger, Patricia. *Honey-Mad Women: Emancipatory Strategies in Women's Writing*. New York: Columbia University Press, 1988.

Binary Opposition

A term that refers to the duality of thought and

language that informs Enlightenment, or Modern, epistemology, a duality that is insistently critiqued by Jacques Derrida and by certain feminist theorists, among them Hélène Cixous. Binary oppositions, or dualities, include male/female, active/passive, mind/body, subject/object, rational/irrational, presence/absence, self/other. This duality implies that each binary concept requires its opposite for the construction of its meaning. For instance, the concept of male requires the concept of female, its oppositional element, in order to construct its meaning; similarly, the concept of rationality depends upon the concept of the opposing irrationality for the construction of its meaning.

Feminists challenge binary oppositions precisely because they imply hierarchies, since hierarchies imply control or dominance. Further, feminists assert that dualisms are gendered, that they reflect the fundamental dichotomy of male/female, wherein the male is privileged over the female. This basic male/female dichotomy accounts, then, for the privileged status of such elements as the active (male) over the passive (female); the mind (male) over the body (female); and the rational (male) over the irrational (female), with the male element of the binary opposition being the dominant and the female element being the subordinate. In this way, the duality always asserts a superiority of the masculine over the feminine.

Different feminist approaches struggle with resisting and challenging this male/female dualism. One approach, based in the liberal humanist tradition, attempts to incorporate the female into the male realm, thereby removing the privileged status accorded to the masculine. For example, woman might claim status as an active being, denying her conventional association with the passive. Another approach, associated with radical feminists, attempts to reverse the privileging by valorizing the female element. Here woman might claim irrationality as a superior way of knowing. A third approach, linked to French feminism or poststructuralism, rejects the entire construct of dualistic thought and attempts to transform or displace the binary foundation of Western epistemology. For example, woman might challenge the mind/body dichotomy, transforming the implied hierarchy through deployment of alternative discursive formations of meaning that embrace plurality rather than linearity.

Betty Moss

References

Cixous, Hélène. *The Newly Born Woman.* Translated by Betsy Wing. Minneapolis: University of Minnesota Press, 1986.
———. "Sorties." Translated by Ann Liddle. In *New French Feminisms*, edited by Isabelle de Courtviron and Elaine Marks, 90–98. New York: Schocken Books, 1981.
Derrida, Jacques. *Of Grammatology.* Translated by Gayatri Spivak. Baltimore: Johns Hopkins University Press, 1976.
———. *Writing and Difference.* Translated by Alan Bass. Chicago: University of Chicago Press, 1978.
Moi, Toril. *Sexual/Textual Politics.* New York: Routledge, 1985.
Tong, Rosemarie. *Feminist Thought: A Comprehensive Introduction.* San Francisco: Westview, 1989.

B

Biological Determinism

Biological theories have justified social inequality in Western culture for over two thousand years, providing "explanations" for the physical, mental, and moral "inferiority" of women, people of color, ethnic minorities, the lower and working classes, and lesbians and gay men. Biological determinists assert that differences in character traits, behavior, social relationships, and social and economic status between women and men are based on biological differences, be those differences the result of evolution or God's creation. The implication of such theories is that change in gender roles and hierarchy is impossible or, if possible, dangerous, immoral, regressive, or antievolutionary.

In Western culture, theories proposing that gender differences and women's inferior status are biologically determined probably begin with the assertion of the Greek philosopher Aristotle (384–322 B.C.E.) that women perform only a passive function in reproduction, serving merely as the vessel for the sperm, which forms the entire fetus. Ideas about women's essentially flawed, inferior, carnal, and sinful nature, based on the story of the Creation and the Fall in the biblical book of Genesis, have also been prominent in many phases of Christian church history, including the Middle Ages, the Renaissance, and the Enlightenment, and in many different sects and denominations. While modern biology has proved Aristotle's idea false, assumptions about women's passivity, irrationality, emotionality, inherently nurturing nature, physical and mental weakness, and abnormality compared to a male norm still underlie much biological, sociological, and psychological theory, research, and practice.

In the nineteenth century, doctors in America and Britain conceptualized women's reproductive systems as inherently pathological, arguing that women were constitutionally incapable of laboring in the public world and that higher education would cause atrophy of the uterus and the breasts. Woman's "weaker frame" signaled a weaker mind; she needed all her vital energy for reproduction. (These arguments, of course, ignored all the work women, especially workingclass and slave women, were actually doing.) Some scientists used Charles Darwin's theory of evolution to argue that the demands of the women's suffrage movement were evolutionarily retrogressive. In the early twentieth century, Sigmund Freud's theories constituted a different version of biological determinism, which also entered into the ongoing debate over the "Woman Question." Freud's theories of female psychosexual development stress that a girl's achievement of "normal femininity" entails realizing her "original sexual inferiority" and passing "from her masculine [clitoral] phase to the feminine [vaginal] one to which she is biologically destined." Freud suggests that true femininity entails passive sexuality and subordinate wifehood and motherhood, and that these roles, though mediated by family and personal history, are essentially biologically based. For Freud, women's supposed failure to make substantial contributions to civilization rests on biological grounds. The eugenics movement of the late nineteenth and early twentieth centuries, based on social Darwinism, put biological determinism into practice, calling for fewer children from the "unfit," more from the "fit." Adolf Hitler's and the Third Reich's "Final Solution" for the problem of "genetic inferiors" was perhaps the most horrendous application of biologically determinist ideas since the witch burnings of the European Renaissance.

The 1970s, another time of ferment about the "Woman Question," saw the most recent development in biological determinist theories: sociobiology. Sociobiologists' theories have implications for race and class but they focus most persistently on gender roles, behavior, and traits. These theories assert that the differences between the sexes can be accounted for by their different strategies for, as Ruth Bleier writes, "maximizing their [genetic] fitness through the reproduction of the largest possible number of offspring." Other biologists and psychologists focus on hormones and brain structure as responsible for gender differences. These scientists claim to document gender differences in intelligence, aggression, spatial ability, math and verbal ability, emotional instability, and nurturing versus competitive behavior, and to explain these differences in terms of biology.

Over the past several decades, feminist scholars have investigated the history of biological theories and their impact on women as social beings and as artists, and have developed a critique of the assumptions and methods of the current medical, biological, and psychological studies that argue for biological determinism. Fausto-Sterling and Bleier, for example, critique these studies as methodologically flawed, androcentric, ethnocentric, and based on unsupported assumptions about gender that serve the status quo. They point out that current biological determinists justify women's oppression by explaining current social conditions as genetic in origin. For example, the high rate of rape, wife abuse, and other forms of violence against women are allegedly the combined result of men's genetically predetermined, uncontrollable mating urge and women's hysterical tantrums caused by the premenstrual syndrome.

Fausto-Sterling and Bleier also critique the nature versus nurture, biological versus social determinism argument underlying much of the debate on this topic, saying that it sets up a false dichotomy. (The feminist debate over essentialism versus social constructionism is in part another version of this controversy.) They argue instead that human personalities, behavior, capacities, social and cultural forms, and even physical capabilities develop through a complex, ongoing, two-way interaction between biology and social environment. They claim it is impossible to single out any behavior or ability as purely biological in origin.

The contemporary debates and prevailing attitudes about women's nature and capabilities affect the conditions for the production and reception of women's writing at any particular point in time. Such debates and attitudes influence how a woman writer thinks and feels about whether and how she can or should write and what she can or should write about. Assumptions about women's "natural" affinities and abilities have been and are used to trivialize the achievement of women writers and to misread their work. And finally, feminist literary critics since Virginia Woolf's *A Room of One's Own* have discussed the concept of a "woman's sentence" or a woman's style, and to what extent it is shaped by woman's body.

Diana L. Swanson

References

Arditti, Rita, Pat Brennan, and Steve Cavrak, eds. *Science and Liberation*. Boston: South End, 1980.

Barker-Benfield, G.J. *The Horrors of the Half-Known Life*. New York: Harper and Row, 1977.

Bleier, Ruth. *Science and Gender: A Critique of Biology and Its Theories on Women*. New York: Pergamon, 1984.

Ehrenreich, Barbara, and Deirdre English. *For Your Own Good: 150 Years of the Experts' Advice to Women*. Garden City, N.Y.: Doubleday, 1978.

Fausto-Sterling, Anne. *Myths of Gender: Biological Theories about Women and Men*. New York: Basic, 1985. Rev. ed., 1992.

Freud, Sigmund. "Femininity" [1933]. In *New Introductory Lectures on Psychoanalysis*, translated and edited by James Strachey, 99–119. New York: W.W. Norton, 1965.

Goldberg, Stephen. *The Inevitability of Patriarchy*. New York: William Morrow, 1974.

Harding, Sandra. *The Science Question in Feminism*. Ithaca, N.Y.: Cornell University Press, 1986.

———. *Whose Science, Whose Knowledge? Thinking from Women's Lives*. Ithaca, N.Y.: Cornell University Press, 1991.

Lowe, Marian, and Ruth Hubbard, eds. *Woman's Nature: Rationalizations of Inequality*. New York: Pergamon, 1983.

Wilson, E.O. *Sociobiology: The New Synthesis*. Cambridge: Harvard University Press, 1975.

Woolf, Virginia. *A Room of One's Own* [1929]. New York: Harcourt Brace Jovanovich, 1975.

Birth

The province of women, and generally supposed to be the most natural of events, giving birth may be defined as the bearing of offspring. It can be a natural, fulfilling process, or it can threaten the individual's creative urge, or even life itself, because of the dangers to which practitioners—midwives and doctors—can submit the woman. Despite the fact that birth is not a universal experience, in that it differs across, or even within, cultures, it has for centuries been used in literature to symbolize the growth of the text in the mind. This metaphorical relationship between creation and procreation has been analyzed by feminist literary theorists approaching the topic from a variety of standpoints.

Figurative use of birth has been largely appropriated by men to apply to industrial or technological processes from which women, by virtue of a lack of opportunity, are for the most part excluded. Further, the very community within which the birth occurs may place linguistic ideological restraints upon the new baby and those who have given birth, as Bob Hodge demonstrates in "Birth and the Community." Examining birth certificates, announcements of births in newspapers, and greeting cards designed for congratulation on the occasion of a birth, Hodge shows how, from the very moment of birth, human beings have ideological instruments operating upon their lives.

In 1979, Hélène Cixous wrote in "Sorties" of her anxieties that women, in positing maternity as a product of, or service for, capitalism, were actually repressing other women who wanted to have babies. The gestational drive, Cixous argued, like writing, is a vital experience for some women, an opportunity to discover myriad possibilities within the self, signifying women's vast reserves of energy.

Susan Stanford Friedman's 1987 article, "Creativity and the Childbirth Metaphor," is perhaps the best overview and analysis of the use of birth to signify creativity in literary works. Friedman demonstrates how an appreciation of the differences of use to which male and female writers put this metaphor can wrest it from accusations of biological determinism, and can lead one to postulate that it is the ultimate *écriture féminine*. Because of the biological impossibility of the situation, the metaphor is incongruous and can fail if the reader is aware that the writer is male. Of course the metaphor is still literally untrue when applied to women—books are not babies—but it can be enabling, a woman's ability to procreate arguably predisposing her to create literary works.

Friedman documents various interpretations of male use of the birth metaphor. Since men have a less involved role in gestation, they use art as a compensation. Further, control over creative art goes some way to dealing with their fear of most women's inherent capability to create in a biological sense. Male writers do not use the metaphor as a tribute to women's powers, the elevation of procreativity rather making it seem the most important thing women are capable of performing, and so ignoring their art.

Seven major uses to which women writers put the birth metaphor are identified by Friedman. First, writers like Elinor Wylie use it in a straightforward way, to illustrate the mutual exclusivity of creation and procreation. Second, in the early nineteenth-century, Mary Shelley elaborated upon this usage in describing her fears that creativity and procreativity were not compatible, despite any hopes she may have harbored to the contrary. Next, Friedman describes how Sylvia Plath's use of the birth metaphor told directly of the actual dangers of the attempt to combine motherhood and life as an artist. Erica Jong, a more contemporary writer, changed her attitude following her pregnancy—in her essay "Creativity vs. Generativity" she condemns the metaphor. Fifth, H.D. regarded the metaphor as a tool that could illuminate her own writing. Anais Nin, Friedman avers, saw the metaphor as delineating a specifically female discourse, but reminded the reader that men had an essential role in the procreative process—in this respect, it is not something women can do alone. Finally, Friedman identifies use of the metaphor as central to a specifically female discourse. Friedman illustrates all these uses comprehensively, concluding that since women are oppressed when patriarchal systems appropriate their bodies and means of reproduction, women can regain control "through the labor of the mind pregnant with the word."

Emma L.E. Rees

References

Castle, Terry J. "La'bring Bards: Birth *Topoi* and English Poetics." *Journal of English and Germanic Philosophy* 78 (1979): 193–208.

Cixous, Hélène. "Sorties." In *The Newly Born Woman*. Translated by Betsy Wing. Minneapolis: University of Minnesota Press, 1989.

Corea, Gena. *The Hidden Malpractice: How American Medicine Treats Women as Patients and Professionals*. New York: William Morrow, 1977.

Friedman, Susan Stanford. "Creativity and the Childbirth Metaphor: Gender Difference in Literary Discourse." *Feminist Studies* 13 (1987): 49–82.

Gubar, Susan. "'The Blank Page' and the Issues of Female Creativity." *Critical Inquiry* 8 (1981): 243–264.

Hodge, Bob. "Birth and the Community." In *Language and Control*, edited by Roger Fowler, 175–184. Boston: Routledge and Kegan Paul, 1979.

Ostriker, Alicia. "Body Language: Imagery of the Body in Women's Poetry." In *The State of Language*, edited by Leonard Michaels and Christopher Ricks, 247–263. Berkeley: University of California Press, 1980.

Rich, Adrienne. *Of Woman Born: Motherhood as Experience and Institution*. New York: W.W. Norton, 1976.

Black Feminist Criticism (African American)

Black feminist criticism is an approach to literature that is informed not only by issues of race and gender, but also by class, history, and culture. According to feminist critic Deborah McDowell, black feminist criticism is done by "black feminist critics who analyze the works of Black female writers from a feminist or political perspective." Critic Valerie Smith offers a more inclusive definition inspired by the idea that "reclaim[ing] the black feminist project from those who are not black women . . . would be to define the field too narrowly." According to Smith, the field should be understood as a practice, a "way of reading inscriptions of race (particularly but not exclusively blackness), gender (particularly but not exclusively womanhood), and class in modes of cultural expression." The identity politics of a black feminist critical project continues to be a highly charged issue within the field.

In her 1977 essay "Toward a Black Feminist Criticism," Barbara Smith outlined the desired black feminist critical project of the future. In this historic and frequently anthologized statement, Smith declared that black feminist criticism should be borne of a political consciousness and "embod[y] the realization that the politics of sex as well as the politics of race and class are crucially interlocking factors in the works of black women writers." Since the late 1970s, black feminist critics have been committed to "restoring a lost tradition" (Wall) of African American women's writing, renaming appropriate principles of Anglo American and European criticism, and creating new nonderivative theories of identity, race, sexuality, narrative, orality, and other concepts. Such work is characteristic of distinct phases in black feminist criticism. This theory does not develop in a strict linear fashion. Its stages of development are cyclical and thus respond to the ongoing recovery and republication of African American writings that are central to the work of scholars in African American studies.

According to Valerie Smith, "archaeological projects" constitute the first stage of black feminist criticism. In this first stage, a wide range of editorial projects make African American women's writing accessible. Some of the pioneering archaeological projects include Toni Cade Bambara's *The Black Woman: An Anthology*, Mary Helen Washington's *Black-eyed Susans: Classic Stories by and about Black Women*, Mari Evans's *Black Women Writers (1950–1980): A Critical Evaluation*, and Anne Allen Shockley's *Afro-American Women Writers, 1746–1933: An Anthology and Critical Guide*. Additional archaeological projects include the republication of invaluable primary texts including Henry Louis Gates's edition of Harriet Wilson's 1861 *Our Nig*, Jean Fagan Yellin's edition of Harriet Jacobs's 1859 *Incidents in the Life of a Slave Girl*, and first-time compilations such as Frances Smith Foster's edition of three newly discovered serialized novels by Frances Harper. Multivolume sets such as the Schomburg Library series of works by nineteenth-century black women writers and other anthologies of black women's writing illustrate the perpetual archaeological project of black feminist criticism. Publication efforts such as these lead to textual analysis, the second stage of black feminist criticism.

Archaeological projects, or to borrow from Ann duCille, "recovery and reconnaissance missions" and textual analysis have been increasingly empowered by sophisticated black feminist theoretical works. Like the primary works, these critical writings challenge a number of generic assumptions, anxieties about the canon, concepts of tradition, authenticity, intertextuality, narrative devices, and more. Black feminist scholars have been considering black women's texts in relation to a number of compelling issues such as marginalization, hegemony, self-discovery, alterity, and orality. Quite often, such projects are capable of, if not

intent on, destabilizing "narrative relations that enshrine configurations according to genre, gender, culture, or models of behavior and personality" (V. Smith). In such discourse, diverse theoretical models contribute to a host of black feminist theoretical enterprises. Hortense Spillers's application of Freudian and psychoanalytic theory to articulate the metaphysics of racial identity and dimensions of black women's sexuality and Deborah McDowell's applications of reader-response theory in her work on audience and African American authors are among the best examples of this dialogic quality of black feminist criticism.

In contemplating such charged topics as radical subjectivity, essentialism, and representations of the black body, both black feminist criticism and the primary texts it refers to are endowed with a sociocultural immediacy. The work of Claudia Tate, Ann duCille and Hazel Carby for example, simultaneously recuperates the historic nineteenth- and turn-of-the-century circumstances, duties, and visions of African American women writers even as it offers us new critical tools with which to assess the foundations of twentieth-century black literary traditions. Black feminist critics have documented crucial links between nineteenth- and twentieth-century writers who consistently explore the tensions in inter- and intraracial politics. The African American women's literary tradition is host to some of the most insightful portraits of African American communities, women's social and political solidarity, female liberation, and creativity.

Many black feminist critics are concerned that their work be directly connected to black women's experiences. Barbara Christian has urged scholars not to succumb to the "race for theory" but produce a black feminist criticism that is "rooted in practice." Such directives have resulted in a wide variety of critical projects, ranging from collected scholarly essays on the Hill/Thomas hearings to conferences on the conditions and future of black women in and associated with academia, and essays that discuss scholars' convergence on African American women's literature and hypothesize about the subtexts of this contemporary interest. Since its inception, black feminist critics have challenged the academy's theoretical and canonical oversights. Ann duCille, bell hooks, Audre Lorde, Barbara Smith, Hortense Spillers, and others have decried the misrepresentation of African American experiences, and the racial and sexual politics that contribute to the dismissal of highly respected and pioneering work by black feminist scholars.

Debates about privilege, appropriation, and critical license are important to black feminist critics as black feminist criticism and African American studies become increasingly popular, commodified, and theoretically attractive fields. A number of critics are concerned with the visible commodification of African American women's literature and the corresponding commodification of black feminist theory by critics who do not have sufficient training in the field or who proceed to relegate the primary and critical works of black women to a "posterior position" (duCille) even as they propose to privilege them. Black feminist critics have consistently protested the use of convenient and dangerous metaphors and analogies in which race, blackness, and black women are not reckoned with as complex entities or as having particular subject positions. As they respond to various critical faux pas and attempt to clarify the trajectories of black feminist criticism, black feminist critics have called for responsible scholarship, a "sane accountability" (B. Smith), or proposed "complementary theorizing" (duCille) as an antidote to cooptive criticism and means of further improving the field.

Since its formal beginnings in the 1970s, numerous pressures have come to bear on black feminist criticism. In 1977, Barbara Smith hoped that black feminist criticism would be "highly innovative, embodying the daring spirit of [African American women's] works themselves." To date, some of the most highly innovative theoretical work ever done has been produced by black feminist critics.

Lois Brown

References

Bambara, Toni Cade, ed. *The Black Woman: An Anthology.* New York: New American Library, 1970.

Carby, Hazel. *Reconstructing Womanhood.* New York: Oxford University Press, 1987.

Christian, Barbara. *Black Feminist Criticism.* New York: Pergamon, 1985.

———. "The Race for Theory." *Cultural Critique* (1987): 51–63.

duCille, Ann. "The Occult of True Black Womanhood: Critical Demeanor and Black Feminist Studies." *Signs* 19 (1994): 591–629.

Evans, Mari, ed. *Black Women Writers (1950–1980): A Critical Evaluation.* Garden City, N.Y.: Anchor/Doubleday, 1983.

Harper, Frances. *Iola Leroy, or Shadows Uplifted,* edited by Frances Smith Foster. New York: Oxford University Press, 1988.

Hull, Gloria, Patricia Bell Scott, and Barbara Smith, eds. *All the Women are White, All the Blacks Are Men, but Some of Us Are Brave.* Old Westbury, N.Y.: Feminist, 1982.

Jacobs, Harriet. *Incidents in the Life of a Slave Girl,* edited by Jean Fagan Yellin. Cambridge: Harvard University Press, 1987.

Joyce, Joyce. "The Black Canon: Reconstructing Black American Literary Criticism." *New Literary History* 18 (1987): 335–344.

McDowell, Deborah. "New Directions for Black Feminist Criticism." In *The New Feminist Criticism,* edited by Elaine Showalter, 186–199. New York: Pantheon, 1985.

Pryse, Marjorie, and Hortense Spillers, eds. *Conjuring: Black Women, Fiction, and Literary Tradition.* Bloomington: Indiana University Press, 1985.

Schockley, Ann Allen, ed. *Afro-American Women Writers, 1746–1933: An Anthology and Critical Guide.* Boston: G.K. Hall, 1988.

Smith, Barbara. "Toward a Black Feminist Criticism." In *All the Women are White, All the Blacks are Men, but Some of Us Are Brave: Black Women's Studies,* edited by Barbara Smith, 157–175. Old Westbury, N.Y.: Feminist, 1982.

Smith, Valerie. "Black Feminist Theory and the Representation of the "Other." In *Changing Our Own Words,* edited by Cheryl Wall, 38–57. New Brunswick, N.J.: Rutgers University Press, 1989.

Wall, Cheryl. *Changing Our Own Words: Essays on Criticism, Theory and Writing by Black Women.* New Brunswick, N.J.: Rutgers University Press, 1989.

Washington, Mary Helen, ed. *Black-eyed Susans: Classic Stories by and about Black Women.* Garden City, N.Y.: Anchor Books, 1975.

Wilson, Harriet E. *Our Nig,* edited by Henry

Louis Gates. New York: Random House, 1983.

Black Feminist Criticism (other than African American)

In Britain the term "black" is used to designate a broad spectrum of people including Asians, Africans, Caribbeans, Latin Americans, and Arabs. In America, on the other hand, the term black is used primarily to identify African Americans and to distinguish them from other nonwhite races that make up a significant proportion of the current population. Even as this distinction helps underline the specific history of African Americans in the United States, it also helps further the racist policy of the dominant group in control by producing a racial hierarchy within the various oppressed racial groups. In the United States, feminists from the various nonwhite races have tried to bridge differences by calling themselves women of color. This designation has the same unifying potential that the term "black," in its usage by British feminist groups, has achieved. In the United States then, "women of color" rather than "black" is the preferred characterization. "Women of color" identifies a political constituency, a sociopolitical designation for people of Asian, African, Arab, Caribbean, and Latin American descent as well as native peoples of the United States.

Even though coalitions across racial boundaries are hard to form and even more hard to maintain given the hegemonic policy of divide and conquer, feminists of color insistently try to come to terms with their internalized racism, cross racial hostility, and homophobia. The editors of the groundbreaking anthology *This Bridge Called My Back: Writing by Radical Women of Color*, Cherríe Moraga and Gloria Anzaldúa, outline the major areas of concern for the political mobilization of black women. They emphasize the acknowledgment of color as the first step toward radicalism, followed by the need to confront racism in the women's movement, the recognition of cultural, class, and sexual differences that divide women of color, and finally they stress the importance of writing as a tool for self-preservation and revolution. Almost a decade after the publication of *This Bridge*, Anzaldúa edited a second collection, *Making Face, Making Soul: Haciendo Caras*, in order to foreground more black women's voices. The anthology combines testimonials, poems, stories, and critical essays that focus on the corrosive legacy of racism, the empowering strategies of personal and cultural decolonization, the importance of speech and writing by and for women of color, the necessity for the formation of interethnic communities, and the significance of different and radical epistemologies in a homogenizing intellectual arena.

Gayatri Chakravorty Spivak, a foremost postcolonial critic, foregrounds the necessity for "First World" feminists to unlearn the privilege of their elite education and avoid turning the "Third World woman" into an authenticating signature for academic feminism in *In Other Worlds* and *The Postcolonial Critic*. In another of her contributions, "Three Women's Texts and a Critique of Imperialism," she examines the "worlding" of the "Third World" in Western feminist examinations of certain often-read texts such as *Jane Eyre* and *Frankenstein*.

Ngambika: Studies of Women in African Literature and *Women Writers in African Literature Today* go beyond a mere recording of African women's writing. These two volumes, as well as a special issue of *Research in African Literatures*, introduced by Rhonda Cobham, examine the importance of a black feminist consciousness and issues of gender and race in African critical and creative practices. *Out of the Kumbla: Caribbean Women and Literature* attempts to do the same for Caribbean women's writing.

Ketu Katrak's essay "Decolonizing Culture: Toward a Theory for Postcolonial Women's Texts" draws upon the work of a number of non-Western feminists and activists to produce an oppositional theoretical model for the study of postcolonial women's texts. Lata Mani in "Multiple Mediations: Feminist Scholarship in the Age of Multinational Reception" explores the issues of positionality and location in the production and circulation of global theories of feminism. *Third World Women and the Politics of Feminism* includes essays that address the production of knowledge by and about women in Asia, the Caribbean, the Middle East, South America, and the United States. Chandra Mohanty's essay "Under Western Eyes: Feminist Scholarship and Colonial Discourses," the first significant critical examination of the production of the "Third World woman" as a monolithic subject in some Western feminist texts, is reprinted in this collection. Trinh T. Minh-ha in *Woman, Native Other* illustrates the fundamentally gendered and racial nature of anthropological study by uncovering the continuity between definitions of the "native" (male) and the "Third World" woman. Rey Chow's book *Woman and Chinese Modernity: The Politics of Reading between West and East* uses psychoanalytic theories to read the obsession with the construction of the figure of woman in texts about modern China. And last but not the least, *Motherlands: Black Women's Writing from Africa, the Caribbean and South Asia* examines a number of representative texts by women writers using feminist theories to address issues of language, culture, and female consciousness.

Future critical work should continue to challenge and reexamine existing feminist praxis within a cross-cultural and international framework. Faced by constant effacement of the pluralities of their selves by white society, women of color have to pursue their search for a politics of unity based on an ongoing critical recognition of the politics of gender, race, and sexuality in the construction of their identities.

Sangeeta Ray

References

Anzaldúa, Gloria, ed. *Making Face, Making Soul: Haciendo Caras*. San Francisco: Spinsters/Aunt Lute, 1990.

Chow, Rey. *Woman and Chinese Modernity: The Politics of Reading between West and East*. Minneapolis: University of Minnesota Press, 1991.

Cobham, Rhoda, and Chikwenye Okonjo Ogunyemi, eds. *Research in African Literatures: Special Issue on Women's Writing* 19 (1988).

Davies, Carol Boyce, and Elaine Fido, eds. *Out of the Kumbla: Caribbean Women and Literature*. Trenton, N.J.: Africa World, 1990.

———, and Anne Adams Graves, eds. *Ngambika: Studies of Women in African Literature*. Trenton, N.J.: Africa World, 1986.

Jones, Eldred, Marjorie Eustace, and Palmer Eustace, eds. *Women Writers in African Literature Today*. London: Currey, 1987.

Katrak, Ketu. "Decolonizing Culture: Toward a Theory for Postcolonial Women's Texts." *Modern Fiction Studies* 35 (1989): 157–179.

Mani, Lata. "Multiple Mediations: Feminist Scholarship in the Age of Multinational Reception." *Feminist Review* 35 (1990): 24–41.

Minh-ha, Trinh T. *Woman, Native Other*. Bloomington: Indiana University Press, 1989.

Mohanty, Chandra Talpade, Ann Russo, and Lourdes Torres, eds. *Third World Women and the Politics of Feminism*. Bloomington: Indiana University Press, 1991.

Moraga, Cherríe, and Gloria Anzaldúa, eds. *This Bridge Called My Back: Writings by Radical Women of Color*. New York: Kitchen Table: Women of Color Press, 1983.

Nasta, Susheila. *Motherlands: Black Women's Writing from Africa, the Caribbean, and South Asia*. New Brunswick: Rutgers University Press, 1992.

Research in African Literatures 9 (1988).

Spivak, Gayatri Chakravorty. *In Other Worlds*. New York: Methuen, 1987.

———. *The Postcolonial Critic*. Edited by Sarah Harasym. New York: Routledge, 1990.

———. "Three Women's Texts and a Critique of Imperialism." In *"Race," Writing, and Difference*, 262–280. Chicago: University of Chicago Press, 1986.

Blues

African American cultural critics and theorists widely agree that the blues infuse the heart and soul of African American culture. To understand the significance of blues to feminist theory, one must understand the cultural significance of blues in general.

Houston Baker defines the blues as the matrix of African American discourse, "a web of intersecting, crisscrossing impulses always in productive transit . . . the multiplex, enabling *script* in which Afro-American cultural discourse is inscribed." Blues artists refuse "to be pinned down to any final, dualistic significance. Even as they speak of paralyzing absence and ineradicable desire, their instrumental rhythms suggest change, movement, action, continuance, unlimited and unending possibility." Resistance to unitary or binary ideological narratives is a primary goal of most contemporary feminist theory; thus, the blues offer fertile possibilities for feminist performers. When singing, writing, or otherwise playing (with) the blues, black women subvert patriarchal as well as white supremacist narratives. They assert multiple sexual identities, name their own transgressive desires, protest against violence, threaten revenge for wrongs, and celebrate freedom of movement.

The idea that blues are simply mournful songs about victimization is a common but uninformed misperception. Ralph Ellison, describing Richard Wright's literary achievement in writing *Black Boy*, argues that "the blues is an impulse to keep the painful details and episodes of a brutal experience alive in one's aching consciousness, to finger its jagged grain, and to transcend it, not by the consolation of philosophy but by squeezing from it a near-tragic, near-comic lyricism. As a form, the blues is an autobiographical chronicle of personal catastrophe expressed lyrically." The blues, then, is an impulse, a sensibility, an affirmation that can be expressed through multiple artistic mediums: music, writing, painting, sculpture, and so on.

James Baldwin gave the blues unsurpassed expression in his story "Sonny's Blues" when he described the socially transformative power of the blues. Baldwin suggests that the blues artist creates his or her art, risking "ruin, destruction, madness, and death, in order to find new ways to make us listen. For, while the tale of how we suffer, and how we are delighted, and how we triumph is never new, it always must be heard." Like feminist artists, the blues performer "fill[s] the air with life," with his or her own life, which contains the lives of many other people as well. Through the blues, the artist and the audience lament the tragedies of their lives, but also discover "how we could cease lamenting." Freedom is imagined and expressed in the blues: the audience finds freedom through listening and the artist finds freedom when the audience listens, in reciprocal empowerment.

Since the beginning of the twentieth century, African American women's blues have been a particularly radical site of feminist and African American resistance and self-affirmation. In performing the blues, African American women bring together the transformative powers of feminist politics and the African American blues matrix. Hazel Carby's path-breaking work on women's blues argues that because women blues singers existed from the outset outside the pale of respectability, they "frequently appear as liminal figures that play out and explore the various possibilities of a sexual existence; they are representations of women who attempt to manipulate and control their construction as sexual subjects." The revolutionary potentialities of women blues artists is a rich field of study that has only begun to be mined.

Kari J. Winter

References

Baker, Houston A. *Blues, Ideology, and Afro-American Literature: A Vernacular Theory*. Chicago: University of Chicago Press, 1984.

Baldwin, James. "Sonny's Blues." In *Going to Meet the Man*, 101–141. New York: Dial, 1965.

Carby, Hazel. "It Jus Be's Dat Way Sometime: The Sexual Politics of Women's Blues." *Radical America* 20 (1986): 9–22.

Ellison, Ralph. "Richard Wright's Blues." In *Shadow and Act*, 77–94. New York: Vintage, 1953.

Murray, Albert. *Stomping the Blues*. New York: Da Capo, 1976.

Body

Perhaps more than any other term, "body" defies the disciplinary boundaries of feminism, as attention to the gendered body is found not only in literary, but also in historical, psychoanalytic, philosophical, and sociological inquiry. Interdisciplinary fields such as gender studies and cultural studies are now exploring our understanding of how the body—particularly the female body—has been constructed through ideologies, discourses, and practices. Thus, work in a wide range of fields has profoundly influenced the study of literature.

As early as 1949, Simone de Beauvoir's *The Second Sex* articulated the difference between biological sex and social "gendering." Women, de Beauvoir argues, are not born but made. In addition, her critique of binary oppositions—in which women are linked to the body, men to the mind—creates the terms for later feminist theory on the body. De Beauvoir's work helped launch the contemporary women's liberation movement in France, and her social tract lay the groundwork for the later (1970s) feminist theories of Hélène Cixous, Luce Irigaray, and Julia Kristeva.

Important to literary studies is the attention that French feminists give to language, which they argue has been claimed by men and used to objectify and master the "other" (woman), hence stealing her voice and speaking for her. Certainly the most famous injunction for women to create a language of their own is Hélène Cixous's command: "Write yourself. Your body must be heard." Cixous is particularly concerned that Western oppositions such as mind/body (associated directly with man/woman) are explicitly binary, but implicitly hierarchical: man ~ woman, mind ~ body. For Cixous, a language—usually associated with the mind—which instead exults in its relationship to the body would break down the classic opposition and allow writing a new material dimension. Feminist theories that elaborate the possibilities for women's writing rely heavily on psychoanalytic models. They suggest, for example, that women may have more access to a pre-Oedipal mother-child fusion that manifests itself in repetitive, rhythmic, untraditional discourse (Kristeva); or that woman's "diversified" and complex sexual experience operates in an antilogical way, which can be reflected in a language that might seem "incoherent" by conventional standards (Irigaray).

French feminist claims for a language emerging from the body of "woman" initially offered European and American women a powerful political tool for social change, but such theories met with important critiques in the early 1980s. Many feminists questioned the inherent essentialism in such a construction of "woman" as an ahistorical and unchanging identity. Women of color and lesbians asked how white academic women could speak for the bodily experiences of all women (any more than men could speak for all human beings) and called attention to heterosexist presumptions (Smith). Thus, the very category "women" was called into question, severely hampering the potential for a feminist politics grounded in the body. Feminist theorists working at the intersection of feminism and postmodernism go so far as to argue that our experience of the body is mediated by discourse, "by a presentation of the body, the body image" (Adams). They suggest, in the words of Janet Wolff, "that there is no body outside discourse."

At the same time that feminist theorists debated the relationship of the female body to discursive practices, visual theorists explored the construction of the female body as object of the male gaze. John Berger's influential study *Ways of Seeing* argues that in the history of painting, the bodies of women are displayed for the proprietary claims of male viewers, and feminist studies of film confirm a similar representation of the female body for the male gaze. Laura Mulvey's now classic essay on gendered positioning in spectatorship initiated an enormous feminist debate that raised questions about whether women can ever "own the gaze, and about the possibilities for a female desire unfettered by the cultural construction of women as objects of desire (Kaplan, Benjamin).

These analyses, built once again from psychoanalytic models, carry over into examinations of mass culture, exposing the prevalent commodification, woman's "otherness." Judith Williamson, for instance, surveys contemporary advertising and explores how the representation of "natural" women and foreigners makes these groups "primitives" for capitalist society to appropriate. So material are women's bodies to the reproduction of capitalist culture that they can be sold—or used to sell other products. And women come to participate in their own commodification by adopting systems of self-scrutiny in which they constantly measure their individual attributes against valued cultural norms.

In fact, much feminist scholarship—beginning in the mid 1980s—employs the theories of Michel Foucault to examine women's ways of disciplining the body. Foucault argues that in modern society, human beings enact an elaborate regulation of their bodies; they "discipline and punish" in order to maximize bodily control and efficiency. Institutions often require this control, but the practice of restraint is ultimately internalized by the individual. Although Foucault makes no distinctions between men and women, feminist theorists have used his terms as a starting point to consider the production of femininity—the specific regulatory practices that shape female subjectivity. Sandra Lee Bartky explores "the disciplinary practices a woman must master in pursuit of a body of the right size and shape that also displays the proper styles of feminine motility," as well as the practice of ornamenting that body through specific regimes of skin care, hair care, and makeup. The kind of self-surveillance women enact in their "proper" concern about weight, clothing, and makeup constitutes "a form of obedience to patriarchy."

Other theorists, like Susan Bordo, examine such predominantly female maladies as anorexia nervosa in light of Foucault's concept of discipline. Indeed, the work of Bordo, Bartky, and Judith Butler combines to suggest that gender itself is a matter of "performance." Butler contends that such imitative acts as "drag," by apparently mimicking gender identity, reveal "the imitative structure of gender itself." This structure Butler characterizes as "a fantasy instituted and inscribed on the surface of bodies," which posits an illusion of unity in the service of reproductive heterosexuality.

The body has been at the center of contemporary feminist theory because it offers a material locus for the critique of Western culture. This general interest has affected the study of literature in a variety of ways—through studies of literary texts in specific historical periods, through explorations of particular genres, or through examinations of the representation of specific bodily experiences like childbirth, illness, or rape.

One important work that raises issues about the meanings of the body at a particular historical moment is Helena Michie's *The Flesh Made Word: Female Figures and Women's Bodies*. Michie examines Victorian literature and culture to expose the "representational taboos that restrict the depiction of women's hunger and work, both of which are associated with the body and with sexuality." Michie employs the figures of frame and mirror to explore the meanings ascribed to the female body in this period—and the various reflections and distortions of those meanings that are inscribed in literary and nonliterary texts. Michie also takes her argument beyond the Victorian period to demonstrate the extent to which contemporary feminist writers are caught up with questions that originate in the Victorian body.

Claire Kahane's "The Gothic Mirror" explores the genre of gothic fiction to argue that the gothic has always been attractive to women because it figures the female child's struggle for identity from the mother, with whom she shares "the female body and its symbolic place in our culture." Moving from the paradigmatic work of Ann Radcliffe to the fiction of Flannery O'Connor and Carson McCullers, Kahane unveils the powerful mother who frustrates the daughter's search for independent identity—"the uncanny mother of infancy" who dominates the infant's world while obtaining no power in the social sphere.

Using both readerly and writerly models, Susan Stanford Friedman compares the ways that men and women differently link artistic creativity and procreativity. She ultimately demonstrates that the childbirth metaphor, which emerges from the fact of female anatomy, begins

for men "in a fascination for the Other," but for women "in conflict with themselves as Other." This single metaphor illustrates the complex relationship gender has to the production of meaning in literary texts.

While these are only a few examples of the ways literary criticism has employed feminist theories of the body, it is clear that women's ambivalent relationship to their bodies and their negotiation of the cultural meanings ascribed to those bodies finds representation in literary texts that reflect and in turn reproduce the cultures from which the texts emerge.

Sheila Conboy

References

Adams, Parveen. "Versions of the Body." *m/f* 11/12 (1986): 26–37.

Bartky, Sandra Lee. *Femininity and Domination: Studies in the Phenomenology of Oppression*. New York: Routledge, 1990.

Beauvoir, Simone de. *The Second Sex*. New York: Bantam, 1961.

Benjamin, Jessica. "A Desire of One's Own: Psychoanalytic Feminism and Intersubjective Space." In *Feminist Studies/Critical Studies*, edited by Teresa de Lauretis, 78–101. Bloomington: Indiana University Press, 1986.

Berger, John. *Ways of Seeing*. Harmondsworth: Penguin, 1972.

Bordo, Susan. *Unbearable Weight: Feminism, Western Culture and the Body*. Berkeley: University of California Press, 1993.

Butler, Judith. *Bodies that Matter*. New York: Routledge, 1993.

Cixous, Hélène. "The Laugh of the Medusa." In *New French Feminisms*, edited by Elaine Marks and Isabelle de Courtivron, 245–264. New York: Schocken Books, 1981.

Foucault, Michel. *Discipline and Punish: The Birth of the Prison*. Translated by Alan Sheridan. New York: Random House, 1979.

Friedman, Susan Stanford. "Creativity and the Childbirth Metaphor." *Feminist Studies* 13, no. 1 (1987): 49–82.

Irigaray, Luce. "This Sex Which Is Not One." In *New French Feminisms*, edited by Elaine Marks and Isabelle de Courtivron, 99–106. New York: Schocken Books, 1981.

Jones, Ann Rosalind. "Writing the Body: Toward an Understanding of l'Ecriture

B

Feminine." *Feminist Studies* 7 (1981): 247–263.

Kahane, Claire. "The Gothic Mirror." In *The Mother Tongue: Essays in Feminist Psychoanalytic Interpretation*, edited by Shirley Nelson Garner, Claire Kahane, and Madelon Sprengnether, 334–351. Ithaca, N.Y.: Cornell University Press, 1985.

Kaplan, E. Ann. "Is the Gaze Male?" In *Powers of Desire: The Politics of Sexuality*, edited by Ann Snitow, Christine Stansell, and Sharon Thompson, 309–327. New York: Monthly Review, 1983.

Kristeva, Julia. *Revolution in Poetic Language*. Translated by Margaret Waller. New York: Columbia University Press, 1984.

Michie, Helena. *The Flesh Made Word: Female Figures and Women's Bodies*. New York: Oxford University Press, 1987.

Mulvey, Laura. "Visual Pleasure and Narrative Cinema." *Screen* 16 (1975): 6–19.

Scarry, Elaine, ed. *Literature and the Body: Populations and Persons*. Baltimore: Johns Hopkins University Press, 1988.

Smith, Barbara. "Introduction." In *Home Girls: A Black Feminist Anthology*, edited by Barbara Smith, xix–lvi. New York: Kitchen Table: Women of Color Press, 1983.

Stanbury, Sarah, and Linda Lomperis, eds. *Feminist Approaches to the Body in Medieval Literature*. Philadelphia: University of Pennsylvania Press, 1993.

Williamson, Judith. "Woman Is an Island: Femininity and Colonization." In *Studies in Entertainment: Critical Approaches to Mass Culture*, edited by Tania Modleski, 99–118. Bloomington: Indiana University Press, 1986.

Wolff, Janet. *Feminine Sentences: Essays on Women and Culture*. Berkeley: University of California Press, 1990.

Breast

A female organ associated at once with sexuality and maternity, the breast has functioned as a complex signifier of femininity in representations of sexual difference. Feminist critics have maintained that bodies and body parts cannot be understood simply as natural objects, but rather must be viewed in relation to the historical, social, and cultural forces that have shaped their representation. In the case of uniquely female organs, such as the breast or uterus, feminist theorists have focused upon their significance as sites for the sexual definition of women.

Mythic representations of the breast as a symbol of femininity include images of mother goddesses in ancient Sumer and ancient Egypt suckling infants; Greek legends of the Amazons, described as female warriors who burned off their right breasts in order to enhance their ability to draw their bows and who destroyed or sent away their male children; and Roman conceptions of the galaxy (from the Greek *galaktos,* for milk) as the spray of Juno's milk when she nursed Hercules. In the Christian tradition, the breast milk of the Virgin Mary served as an image of infinitely divisible grace. Literary representations of women's breasts, from the Renaissance on, frequently invoked metonymies, such as lilies, ivory, and snow, that eroticized the breast as an object of masculine desire while divorcing it from connotations of unstable flow and change.

Historically, women's breasts have been viewed in both maternal and erotic terms. In seventeenth-century England, breast milk was believed to be a purified form of menstrual blood, which changed color as it passed back and forth between the breast and the womb, bearing witness to the fluid materiality of women's bodies and their reproductive function. In the same period, the breast was subject to newly eroticized interest and signification, accompanied by increased exposure and decoration of women's breasts in clothing fashions. Treatises on breastfeeding that proliferated during the seventeenth and eighteenth centuries conveyed class tensions associated with the use of the breast; the hiring of lower-class women as wet nurses for infants from upper-class families was increasingly discouraged, due to perceived associations between the quality of breast milk and maternal social status. In the eighteenth century, the idealization of the maternal breast for purposes of infant nursing accompanied heightened social ambivalence about female sexual desire, constructing a seeming incompatibility between women's erotic and reproductive practices.

During the twentieth century, the importance of the maternal body to psychoanalysis was manifest in the image of the phallic mother, a grown woman with breasts and a penis, who was represented according to psychoanalytic doctrine as the archetypal object of desire. In the 1920s, British psychoanalyst Melanie Klein revised the Freudian emphasis on the phallus through her development of object-relations theory, identifying the mother as the central figure in the oedipal drama, and arguing that infants of both sexes identify most intensely with the prototypical object of the maternal breast. Klein theorized that the infant directs feelings of gratification and love toward the "good" breast, and destructive impulses toward the frustrating "bad" breast, and concluded that the deprivation of the breast, rather than the mother's lack of a penis, was the most fundamental cause of children's turning to the father.

More recently, the French feminists (1970s and 1980s) have revised the psychoanalytic theories of Freud and Lacan by referring to the maternal body as a locus for feminine discourse. Hélène Cixous in particular finds that there is always within woman "at least a little of that good mother's milk," so that "she writes in white ink." In feminist literary study, attention has been paid women writers' focal representations of the breast, in texts such as Sylvia Plath's *Ariel* (1961), Anne Sexton's *The Death Notebooks* (1974), and Toni Morrison's *Song of Solomon* (1977). Stephanie Demetrakopoulos finds, for example, that Morrison's description of the nursing Ruth, who felt "as if she were a cauldron issuing spinning gold" while her infant's lips pull from her "a thread of light," reflects the power of the female artist's production.

For other feminist critics, such as Iris Young, the experience of breasted existence in a sexist society can be seen to produce significantly different conceptualizations of breasts, whether viewed as solid objects by the male gaze or as indefinite and fluid by the female imagination. Advocating a "corporeal feminism," Elizabeth Grosz observes that women's corporeality has often been inscribed as a mode of seepage or liquidity, and analyzes the oppressive social consequences for women of masculine modes of representation that privilege the solid and the determinate over the fluid. At the same time, feminists have noted that the liquid flows associated with female organs such as the breast and the uterus can connote unbounded, unregulated, and renewable forces of reproduction and creation. Although the breast has served in the past as a site for dichotomous definitions of female sexuality that construct oppositions between the "good" breast and the "bad," or between maternal and erotic functions, the breast in contemporary feminist theory and criticism can also function as a locus for rethinking the cultural and corporeal constitution of female subjectivity.

Naomi J. Miller

References

Cixous, Hélène. "The Laugh of the Medusa." Reprinted in *New French Feminisms: An Anthology*, edited by Elaine Marks and Isabelle de Courtivron, 245–264. New York: Schocken Books, 1980.

Demetrakopoulos, Stephanie. "The Nursing Mother and Feminine Metaphysics: An Essay on Embodiment." *Soundings: An Interdisciplinary Journal* 65 (1982): 430–433.

Fildes, Valerie A. *Breasts, Bottles and Babies: A History of Infant Feeding.* Edinburgh: Edinburgh University Press, 1986.

Grosz, Elizabeth. *Volatile Bodies: Toward a Corporeal Feminism.* Bloomington: Indiana University Press, 1994.

Hollander, Anne. *Seeing through Clothes* [1978]. Harmondsworth: Penguin, 1988.

Ian, Marcia. *Remembering the Phallic Mother: Psychoanalysis, Modernism, and the Fetish.* Ithaca, N.Y.: Cornell University Press, 1993.

Klein, Melanie. *The Writings of Melanie Klein, 4 vols.* Vol. 1: *Love, Guilt and Reparation*; Vol. 2: *The Psycho-Analysis of Children*; Vol. 3: *Envy and Gratitude*; Vol. 4: *Narrative of a Child Analysis.* London: Hogarth, 1975.

Michie, Helena. *The Flesh Made Word: Female Figures and Women's Bodies.* Oxford: Oxford University Press, 1987.

Paster, Gail Kern. *The Body Embarrassed: Drama and the Disciplines of Shame in Early Modern England.* Ithaca, N.Y.: Cornell University Press, 1993.

Perry, Ruth. "Colonizing the Breast: Sexuality and Maternity in Eighteenth-Century England." *Journal of the History of Sexuality* 2 (1991): 204–234.

Van Buren, Jane Silverman. *The Modernist Madonna: Semiotics of the Maternal Metaphor.* Bloomington: Indiana University Press, 1989.

Young, Iris Marion. *Throwing like a Girl and*

Other Essays in Feminist Philosophy. Bloomington: Indiana University Press, 1990.

British Feminism

Since the publication of Mary Wollstonecraft's *Vindication of the Rights of Woman* in 1792, British feminism has been marked by two distinguishing features. First, it has emerged through a sustained, if often critical, dialogue with other radical political discourses (specifically, in the twentieth century, that of Marxism). Second, it has remained preoccupied with documenting and analyzing the determining effects of culture and ideology on women's experience. The British Women's Liberation Movement developed in the late 1960s from a combination of the involvement of workingclass and socialist-activist women in industrial disputes, the student movement, and New Left politics. The first national Women's Liberation Conference was held at Ruskin College, Oxford, in March 1970, organized by women from the History Workshop. Feminist debate in Britain has largely been conducted outside or on the margins of institutions of higher education, finding its outlets in radical politics, journalism, and publishing. Most of the formative theoretical writings of the feminist movement in the 1970s appeared in socialist journals such as *History Workshop* and *New Left Review*, registering left-wing women's dissatisfaction with British Marxism for its failure to consider women's political agency or to theorize their oppression in any other context than the family.

However, British feminist politics has always been closely aligned with cultural theory. The authors of a number of authoritative texts in feminist political theory are also literary and cultural theorists. Juliet Mitchell, author of *Woman's Estate*, which traces the emergence of the women's liberation movement in Britain and debates the causes of women's oppression, is also responsible for a number of essays on eighteenth- and nineteenth-century fiction. Rosalind Coward's *Patriarchal Precedents: Sexuality and Social Relations* explores the application of Marxist and Freudian theories to feminism, while her *Female Desire* investigates the ideological mechanisms of advertising, magazines, and popular journalism, assessing their effects on female subjectivity. Michèle Barrett provided an introduction to a selection of Virginia Woolf's writings on women in 1979, a year before the publication of her *Women's Oppression Today: Problems in Marxist Feminist Analysis.* The co-authors of *Beyond the Fragments: Feminism and the Making of Socialism*, Sheila Rowbotham, Lynne Segal, and Hilary Wainwright, detailed the traumatic emergence of feminism from Marxist-Leninist vanguardist movements in Britain in the 1970s.

In the 1980s, a number of British feminists turned from socialist politics toward psychoanalysis and poststructuralism as new modes of theorizing the ideological construction of women under patriarchy, at the same time as feminist methodologies and critiques began to be assimilated into departments of social sciences and humanities in British universities, polytechnics, and colleges. The tradition of historical criticism and a focus on the intersection of class and gender in literary texts can still be traced in the publications of feminist critics such as Janet Todd's *Women's Friendship in Literature* and Lisa Jardine's *Still Harping on Daughters,* while others, such as Jacqueline Rose's *Sexuality in the Field of Vision,* Catherine Belsey's *The Subject of Tragedy*, and Cora Kaplan's *Sea Changes* took a more explicitly psychoanalytic approach, stressing the importance of understanding the workings of unconscious desire in the construction of the ambiguous pleasures of literary and cultural texts in areas as diverse as Renaissance drama, Hollywood cinema, and nineteenth-century fiction and poetry.

In 1985, the Methuen "New Accents" series sponsored the publication of a formative text in British feminist criticism: Toril Moi's *Sexual/Textual Politics.* Moi's book registered and mediated the absorption of French poststructuralist "feminist" theories in feminist literary criticism in Britain, as well as launching a persuasive critique of humanist tendencies in the founding texts of Anglo American feminism. More recent work from young British feminist critics takes place in the context of this philosophical preoccupation with *écriture féminine* and the textual production of female subjectivity, but within the context of a longer tradition in British feminism of historicist and materialist approaches. Essay collections such as *New Feminist Discourses,* edited by Isobel Armstrong, and *Women, Texts and Histories*, edited by Clare Brant and Diane Purkiss, adopt a distinctive combination of poststructuralist and historical materialist insights to consider writings and representations by and about women from the medieval period to the twentieth century.

Despite the diversity in feminist literary criticism in Britain, there are significant trends and tendencies that indicate its difference from other European countries and from North America. Perhaps most significant is the continuing development of sociohistorical textual analysis, marked by an insistence on an attention to the institutional and political, as well as aesthetic or textual, processes that go into the production and consumption of literary and cultural texts.

Ros Ballaster

References

Armstrong, Isobel, ed. *New Feminist Discourses: Critical Essays on Theories and Texts*. London and New York: Routledge, 1992.

Barrett, Michèle. *Women's Oppression Today: Problems in Marxist Feminist Analysis*. London: Verso, 1980.

Belsey, Catherine. *The Subject of Tragedy: Identity and Difference in Renaissance Drama*. London and New York: Methuen, 1985.

Brant, Clare, and Diane Purkiss, eds. *Women, Texts and Histories 1575–1760*. London and New York: Routledge, 1992.

Coward, Rosalind. *Female Desire: Women's Sexuality Today*. London: Virago, 1984.

———. *Patriarchal Precedents: Sexuality and Social Relations*. London: Routledge and Kegan Paul, 1983.

Jardine, Lisa. *Still Harping on Daughters: Women and Drama in the Age of Shakespeare*. Brighton: Harvester, 1983.

Kaplan, Cora. *Sea Changes: Culture and Feminism*. London: Verso, 1986.

Mitchell, Juliet. *Women: The Longest Revolution*. London: Virago, 1984.

———. *Woman's Estate*. Harmondsworth: Penguin, 1971.

Moi, Toril. *Sexual/Textual Politics: Feminist Literary Theory*. London: Methuen, 1985.

Rose, Jacqueline. *Sexuality in the Field of Vision*. London: Verso, 1986.

Rowbotham, Sheila. "The Beginnings of Women's Liberation in Britain." *Dreams and Dilemmas: Collected Writings*. London: Virago, 1983.

———, Lynne Segal, and Hilary Wainwright. *Beyond the Fragments: Feminism and the Making of Socialism*. London: Merlin, 1979.

Todd, Janet. *Women's Friendship in Literature*. New York: Columbia University Press, 1980.

Brontë, Charlotte

Combining aspects of the traditional marriage plot with elements of the typically male-centered *Bildungsroman,* Charlotte Brontë's novels assert, both explicitly and implicitly, women's absolute need for, and right to, full expression of the self through autonomous action in the world beyond the domestic sphere. In the radically assertive voices of her heroines as well as the thematic implications of the novels, Brontë brought a new expression of feminist consciousness to the female literary tradition. In *Jane Eyre* (1847), *Shirley* (1849), and *Villette* (1853), Brontë's heroines challenge the Victorian norm of female self-abnegation, insisting on women's need for a wider sphere of action than that prescribed under the confining domesticity demanded by the Victorian ideology of womanhood. Jane Eyre struggles against powerful patriarchal figures in familial, institutional, and romantic contexts. The deep emotional cost of enforced female passivity is explored in *Shirley* and becomes the central theme of *Villette*, in which a conventional marriage plot conclusion is subverted and replaced by the heroine's ultimate fulfillment of self through the achievement of autonomous work. Challenging the Victorian code of male mastery and female submission, Brontë's novels explore the devastating emotional consequences of repression of self, whether imposed externally or from within.

Brontë's novels have become central texts in the development of Anglo American feminist literary criticism. The figures of Bertha Mason, the madwoman of *Jane Eyre*, and the secretive Lucy Snowe of *Villette*, a self-described "cypher," have led feminist critics to explore the multiple voices buried within texts which, themselves cyphers, both conceal and reveal powerful feminist rage. Sandra Gilbert and Susan Gubar have seen in the figure of Bertha Mason, the mad wife imprisoned in the attic, an expression of the suppressed rage Jane Eyre (and, by extension, the woman writer) experiences in response to the social and sexual oppression that threatens her survival. Similarly, in the ghostly nun of *Villette* critics have detected an image of the heroine's repressed rage and sexual passion, the explosive power of which the text must conceal. The figures of Vashti in *Villette* and the imagined mermaid in *Shirley* have likewise been seen as images of the dangerously subversive power of female sexuality, a power that can be expressed only indirectly in the text. Recent feminist critics have pursued the implications of such figures, as well as the novels' recurrent imagery of starvation and enclosure, as keys to a deep division concealed within the texts themselves, repressed material that disrupts the façade of traditional nineteenth-century realism.

While much Anglo American feminist critical practice has followed Gilbert's and Gubar's notion of women's texts as palimpsestic—concealing their radical critiques beneath a more acceptable surface pattern—Gayatri Spivak's influential deconstructionist reading of *Jane Eyre* inaugurated a new direction in feminist criticism. Spivak reads the figure of Bertha Mason as colonized Other whose erasure from the text makes way for the ascendance of the text's bourgeois white heroine. Spivak's discussion of the centrality of feminist individualism qua imperialism in the novel's plot extends to a critique of the analogous imperialism Spivak finds at the heart of much feminist practice. Spivak's critique of feminist hermeneutics has been pursued by later feminist critics such as Laura Donaldson. Thus Brontë's texts have remained central to the development of feminist criticism over the course of two decades.

Nancy Disenhaus

References

Abel, Elizabeth, Marianne Hirsch, and Elizabeth Langland, eds. *The Voyage In: Fictions of Female Development.* Hanover, N.H.: University Press of New England, 1983.

Chase, Karen. *Eros and Psyche: The Representation of Personality in Charlotte Brontë, Charles Dickens, and George Eliot.* London: Methuen, 1984.

Donaldson, Laura E. "The Miranda Complex: Colonialism and the Question of Feminist Reading." *Diacritics* 18 (1988): 65–77.

Foster, Shirley. *Victorian Women's Fiction: Marriage, Freedom and the Individual.* Totowa, N.J.: Barnes and Noble, 1985.

Gilbert, Sandra M., and Susan Gubar. *The Madwoman in the Attic: The Woman Writer and the Nineteenth-Century Literary Imagination.* New Haven: Yale University Press, 1979, 1984.

Jacobus, Mary. *Reading Woman: Essays in Feminist Criticism.* New York: Columbia University Press, 1986.

Lanser, Susan Sniader. *Fictions of Authority: Women Writers and Narrative Voice.* Ithaca, N.Y.: Cornell University Press, 1992.

Lawrence, Karen. "The Cypher: Disclosure and Reticence in *Villette*." In *Tradition and the Talents of Women,* edited by Florence Howe, 87–101. Urbana: University of Illinois Press, 1991.

Michie, Helena. *The Flesh Made Word: Female Figures and Women's Bodies.* New York: Oxford University Press, 1987.

Newton, Judith Lowder. *Women, Power, and Subversion: Social Strategies in British Fiction, 1778–1860.* Athens: University of Georgia Press, 1981.

Poovey, Mary. "The Anathematized Race: The Governess and Jane Eyre." In *Feminism and Psychoanalysis,* edited by Richard Feldstein and Judith Roof, 230–254. Ithaca, N.Y.: Cornell University Press, 1989.

Sadoff, Dianne F. *Monsters of Affection: Dickens, Eliot and Brontë on Fatherhood.* Baltimore: Johns Hopkins University Press, 1982.

Showalter, Elaine. *A Literature of Their Own: British Women Novelists from Brontë to Lessing.* Princeton: Princeton University Press, 1977.

Spivak, Gayatri. "Three Women's Texts and a Critique of Imperialism." *Critical Inquiry* 12 (1985): 243–261.

Brownmiller, Susan

Author of *Against Our Will: Men, Women and Rape* and *Femininity*, Susan Brownmiller examines the interface between biological and social gender differences. In doing so, she reveals how society uses biology to justify the relationship between men and women, as well as its definitions of masculinity and femininity.

In *Against Our Will*, Brownmiller documents a history of rape, arguing that feminists might better understand the current relationship between men, women, and rape by studying the history of the act. She locates the origins of rape in the fact that men are physically able to rape and women are physically able to be raped. Rape, she claims, or male recognition that the penis can be used as a weapon, has played a significant role in human social evolution. Primarily, rape is "man's basic weapon of force against woman. . . . [It is] nothing more or less than a conscious process of intimidation by which *all* men keep *all* women in a state of fear." Women can counteract this anatomical terrorism, Brownmiller states, by fighting back on the social, political, and personal levels.

In *Femininity*, Brownmiller returns to the significance of anatomy to explore its relationship to the social concept of femininity. She argues that femininity—or traits socially labeled feminine—has effectively been used to control women because it appears to be an inherently female characteristic. Entering early into the essentialist/constructionist debate, Brownmiller carefully separates traits that are truly biological from those that are actually cultural. In doing so, she reveals how cultural signs of femininity become "natural" clues to gender differences, especially distinguishing non–gender specific characteristics. The essence of femininity, Brownmiller writes, is its elusiveness, which keeps women in pursuit of what they can never achieve. In the process, femininity divides women among themselves in a competitive battle for male attention and prohibits them, by nature, from great accomplishments. Although Brownmiller does not ask that women give up the trappings of femininity completely, she does suggest that feminists pay attention to their own complicity in this social construct so that it does not become either a restricting or limiting force.

Sara E. Quay

References

Brownmiller, Susan. *Against Our Will: Men, Women and Rape*. New York: Simon and Schuster, 1976.

———. *Femininity*. New York: Simon and Schuster, 1984.

Bunch, Charlotte

Bunch's essay "Lesbians in Revolt" is an important statement of lesbian feminist separatism. Although she remains popularly associated with this controversial position, Bunch's subsequent writing emphasizes an integrative approach to political action, evolving by the mid 1980s, and Bunch's involvement with global feminism, to a concern with forging coalitions both between different feminist factions and across races and cultures.

Bunch's separatist manifesto theorizes that lesbianism is a necessary condition of women's liberation. While the heterosexual woman will always be held back by her complicity with patriarchal structures of oppression, the lesbian, free of such ties, will be able to act uncompromisingly against male supremacy.

Bunch's characteristic contribution to the women's movement of the 1970s and 1980s was the attempt to foster a fruitful negotiation between theory and action. The journal *Quest* (1974–1982), of which Bunch was a founder, provided a forum for analysis of feminist organizing. Activists were encouraged to consider the larger implications of their work, and to evolve strategies that served long-term goals. However, this model of theory requires that analytical speculation be closely tied to concrete action, a criterion of relevance that separates Bunch's call to theorize from much subsequent academic work in the field of women's studies.

Anna Wilson

References

Bunch, Charlotte. *Passionate Politics: Feminist Theory in Action*. New York: St. Martin's, 1987.

———, et al., eds. *Learning Our Way: Essays in Feminist Education*. Trumansburg, N.Y.: Crossing, 1983.

———, et al., eds. *The New Woman; a Motive Anthology on Women's Liberation*. Indianapolis, Ind.: Bobbs-Merrill, 1970.

Butler, Judith

Judith Butler, philosopher, feminist, and queer theorist, argues that categories that are often assumed to be "natural," like gender, sexuality, and the body, have always been defined to serve particular political agendas, such as the reinforcing of heterosexuality. In *Gender Trouble: Feminism and the Subversion of Identity*, Butler proposes that gender identity is not innate, but rather a set of behaviors that all members of a culture perform. Parodies of normative gender, such as drag, expose the artificiality of such categories by showing how easily they can be imitated.

Butler utilizes postmodern theories and methodologies to analyze the political effects of certain systems of representation and knowledge, especially within feminist theory. *Gender*

Trouble looks at the costs for feminism in adhering to notions of identity that reinforce binary categories and logic. While building on the ideas and theories of a wide range of contemporary intellectuals, Butler also points out the sexist and heterocentric assumptions within psychoanalytic, philosophical, and feminist thinking. In *Bodies that Matter*, Butler traces how conceptions of the body itself have been shaped by philosophical assumptions about gender, sexuality, and subjectivity.

Butler's work is a model of interdisciplinary scholarship, combining feminist, structuralist, psychoanalytic, and deconstructive methodologies. She has written about AIDS, pornography, film, queer identity, and literature. Her analyses of identity politics is of particular importance for lesbian, gay, and queer theorists, and her critical readings of feminist texts have been important for rethinking crucial problems in contemporary feminist theory.

Lorna J. Smedman

References
Butler, Judith. *Bodies that Matter: On the Discursive Limits of "Sex."* New York: Routledge, 1993.
———. *Gender Trouble: Feminism and the Subversion of Identity.* New York: Routledge, 1990.
———. "Imitation and Gender Insubordination." In *Inside/Out: Lesbian Theories, Gay Theories*, edited by Diana Fuss, 13–31. New York: Routledge, 1991.
———, and Joan W. Scott, eds. *Feminists Theorize the Political.* New York: Routledge, 1992.

C

Campbell, Beatrix

Journalist and author, Beatrix Campbell has been a vociferous critic of the traditional organizations of the British Left (the trade unions and the Labour Party) for their failure to address and serve women's interests. Her published work since *Sweet Freedom*, a founding text of the women's liberation movement (co-authored with Anna Coote), has consistently identified the crisis points of contemporary cultural politics in Britain. *Wigan Pier Revisited: Poverty and Politics in the 80s* retraced the steps of George Orwell's 1937 *The Road to Wigan Pier* to expose both the feminization of poverty in northern Britain and the poverty of imagination in traditional socialism that "hasn't and won't represent women." *The Iron Ladies: Why Do Women Vote Tory?* adopted similar techniques of ethnography and oral history to document women's involvement in British Tory party politics since the late nineteenth century. Campbell concludes that the Tory Party attracts women because, unlike the Labour Party, it addresses their concerns as women through policies on the family, law and order, sex and morality, but the price of this visibility is the requirement to conform to paternalism and political quietism. *Unofficial Secrets: Child Sexual Abuse—The Cleveland Case* is an account of the 1987 controversy surrounding a Middlesborough hospital where pediatricians diagnosed sexual abuse in a total of 165 children; the book highlights the failure of professionals in the health service and judiciary to offer viable solutions to the abuse endemic in parent/child and adult sexual relations. Campbell's communist politics and primary focus on the economic causes of women's oppression have prompted criticism from socialist-feminists who choose to privilege the development of theories of sexuality, representation, and ideology, but her robust populist feminism remains a vital force in contemporary cultural theory.

Ros Ballaster

References

Campbell, Beatrix. *The Iron Ladies: Why Do Women Vote Tory?* London: Virago, 1987.

———. *Unofficial Secrets: Child Sexual Abuse—The Cleveland Case*. London: Virago, 1988.

———. *Wigan Pier Revisited: Poverty and Politics in the 80s*. London: Virago, 1984.

———, and Anna Coote. *Sweet Freedom*. London: Virago, 1971.

Canon

The word "canon" has its origins in the Greek word *kanon*, a rod used for measurement, a ruler, and the concept of measuring or ruling still remains crucial to debates about the canon. Some writers see the canon as a way of measuring and preserving what is central or crucial to a culture; to these writers the canon represents those works, authors, and ideas accepted as major or essential. Yet the question feminist and other critics of the canon have asked repeatedly is, "major or essential to whom?" This second group of critics argue that the canon generally preserves the work of white, middle-class male writers, and calls for an "opening up" of the canon. Although in actuality the canon has never been a stable body of texts, its force as a cultural measurement or ruler of value remains.

According to George Kennedy, the concept

of the canon originates with scholars working in the Alexandrian library in the third and second centuries B.C. These scholars collected literary texts, but they also provided a guidepost to these texts by listing the best example of each literary genre. The canon also has a biblical antecedent; in the fourth century A.D., a "canon" of writing was established that included certain theological texts and excluded others; this canon of writing came to be known as the Bible. Texts were excluded from the Bible not for aesthetic but for doctrinal reasons; as John Guillory points out, the "Church Fathers" selected texts consistent with dominant ideas about the meaning of Christianity.

These early conceptions of the canon demonstrate two separate but related ideas: a canon preserves a culture's "best" works, and a canon preserves accepted and acceptable beliefs of a culture. In more current discussions of the canon, this first idea of the canon—the canon as a repository of aesthetic or literary value—has been dominant, but the idea of the canon as preservative of certain cultural ideas remains implicit. In "Sweetness and Light" (1869), for example, Matthew Arnold argues that certain literary works are worthy of study because they promote "culture" by making "the best that has been thought and known in the world current everywhere." T.S. Eliot similarly implies a canon of great works in "Tradition and the Individual Talent" (1917) when he states that "the existing monuments [of art] form an ideal order among themselves." Eliot, like Arnold, emphasizes that certain works are worthy of critical attention and preservation while others are not.

In the 1940s and 1950s the New Critical movement followed Arnold's and Eliot's lead and promoted a canon of works that preserved "culture" by elevating various works of art on aesthetic and formal grounds. As Paul Lauter has pointed out, although in theory this did not mean the canon had to be narrowed, in actuality works by women and ethnic minorities were seen as lacking New Critical ideals of complexity, ambiguity, tension, and irony. In anthologies edited by the New Critics, authors who did not create "masterpieces" were not included; these authors gradually became lesser known or dropped out of cultural circulation altogether.

Feminist and other critics began to notice in the 1970s that although the canon was supposed to represent masterpieces with "universal" aesthetic value, these works were almost exclusively written by white, middle-class males. Nina Baym notes that as late as 1977, the accepted canon of American literature did not include any female novelists, despite the fact that in the nineteenth century women writers dominated this genre. Baym and others began arguing that the canon, as it was constituted, failed to represent women's experience at all or presented a distorted representation of it; moreover, works in the canon reflected a tradition of sexism toward women and a failure to see women's experiences as important or valid in any way. Baym, Lauter, Lillian Robinson, Annette Kolodny, and many other critics began calling for a broadening of the canon to include more works by women and by writers from diverse ethnic, racial, and class backgrounds.

Beyond calling for an opening up of the canon, many critics in the 1970s and 1980s were also critical of the process of canonization and of the meaning of the canon itself. Some critics argued that texts excluded from the canon did have aesthetic value, but had simply been excluded because white male critics who created the canon could not understand the experiences described in these noncanonical texts. Another line of argument was that standards of aesthetic worth are not, in fact, value-neutral or universal; Eliot, for example, found texts that supported his idea of what literature should be, and then canonized them by calling them monuments of great art. A third critique of the canon argued that canonization has little to do with aesthetic value, but rather is tied into complex historical, ideological, and social realities. Writers such as Richard Ohmann and Barbara Herrnstein Smith, for example, argue that canons are relative, based on contingencies of value and on how well they perform "desired/able" functions. Many critics have also argued that since a culture such as the United States or England includes both men and women and many different races and classes, the culture's canon should reflect this diversity.

These various arguments led to an opening up of the canon in the 1980s. Separate traditions of women's writing, of African American writing, and of workingclass writings have been recovered, but writers from diverse backgrounds have also been included in anthologies and in the teaching of courses on "Western Civilization" or "Masterpieces of Literature." Yet some critics, hostile to this opening of the canon, argue that much has been lost. In the late 1980s educational fundamentalists such as E.D.

Hirsch, Allan Bloom, and William Bennett argued that today's students have not made contact with the great "masterpieces" of world literature, and that they are therefore culturally illiterate. For these writers, the real purpose of education should be acquainting students with the canon of "classics," works that have "universal" aesthetic value.

Yet as we have seen, the canon has never represented a consensus opinion about what is "classic" or "universal." The canon has changed over time, and it has been shaped and defined by principles that are at best idiosyncratic and at worst exclusionary. The "opening up" of the canon promoted by feminist and other literary critics reflects a refusal to see the canon as an unchanging, transcendent repository of value and culture, and an insistence that canons, like texts, are shaped by the political and cultural climate in which they are engendered.

Martha J. Cutter

References

Alberti, John, ed. *The Canon in the Classroom: Pedagogical Implications of Canon Revision in American Literature*. New York: Garland, 1995.

Baym, Nina. "Melodramas of Beset Manhood: How Theories of American Fiction Exclude Women Authors." In *The New Feminist Criticism,* edited by Elaine Showalter, 63–80. New York: Pantheon, 1985.

Bennett, William. "'To Reclaim a Legacy': Text of Report on Humanities in Education." *Chronicle of Higher Education* (November 28, 1984): 16–21.

Bloom, Allan. *The Closing of the American Mind*. New York: Simon and Schuster, 1987.

Guillory, John. "Canon." In *Critical Terms for Literary Study*, edited by Frank Lentricchia and Thomas McLaughlin, 233–249. Chicago: University of Chicago Press, 1990.

Hirsch, E.D. *Cultural Literacy: What Every American Needs to Know*. New York: Vintage Books, 1988.

Kennedy, George. "Classics and Canons." *South Atlantic Quarterly* 89 (1990): 217–225.

Kolodny, Annette. "Dancing through the Minefield: Some Observations on the Theory, Practice, and Politics of a Feminist Literary Criticism." In *The New Feminist Criticism*, edited by Elaine Showalter, 144–167. New York: Pantheon, 1985.

Lauter, Paul. *Canons and Contexts*. New York: Oxford, 1991.

Ohmann, Richard. "The Shaping of a Canon: U.S. Fiction, 1960–1975." In *Canons*, edited by Robert von Hallberg, 377–401. Chicago: University of Chicago Press, 1984.

Robinson, Lillian. "Treason Our Text: Feminist Challenges to the Literary Canon." In *The New Feminist Criticism*, edited by Elaine Showalter, 105–121. New York: Pantheon, 1985.

Smith, Barbara Herrnstein. "Contingencies of Value." In *Canons*, edited by Robert von Hallberg, 5–39. Chicago: University of Chicago Press, 1984.

C

Carby, Hazel V.

A British-born and educated black literary and cultural critic and scholar, Carby brings to contemporary feminist literary theory an interdisciplinary and international perspective. Her theoretical model, informed by British Marxist-based cultural studies and by black feminist theory, provides a richly concrete way to see black women's experience and writing as historical phenomena. Her early work is represented in *The Empire Strikes Back: Race and Racism in 70s Britain,* a historicized cultural critique of race and racism at a particular moment in British political and economic history. Her two essays in that collection, "Schooling in Babylon" and "White Woman Listen! Black Feminism and the Boundaries of Sisterhood," examine and critique, respectively, the failures of British multicultural educational projects for black students and the failures of white feminist theory and historical work for black women. Both essays earn their authority by means of the historical and textual specificity of Carby's analysis. *Reconstructing Womanhood: The Emergence of the Afro-American Woman Novelist* analyzes the work of black women writers from the late nineteenth and early twentieth centuries—Harriet Jacobs, Frances E.W. Harper, Anna Julia Cooper, Nella Larsen—establishing their writing as interventions in contemporary culture and politics on behalf of black people. The book lays down deep roots for the African American woman's intellectual tradition, as well as claiming and documenting a political and cultural role for African American women's fiction.

Carby continues to author essays and articles in which she historicizes black women's intellectual and artistic work. "Ideologies of Black Folk: The Historical Novel of Slavery" questions the critical tendency to see Zora Neale Hurston's version of the Southern rural black folk tradition as a dominant and originary site in African American literary history, arguing that the crucial urban novel and urban black experience can get lost in an "ideology of black folk." A 1988 essay examines the sexual politics of African American women's blues, continuing her focus on historicizing African American women's agency in reshaping and redefining their own sexuality. All of Carby's work is marked by her deep consciousness of the politics of human effort and of the material base of the production of knowledge. She consistently establishes the richness and usefulness of approaching the intersection of race, gender, and class with historical specificity.

Laura Quinn

References

Carby, Hazel V. "Ideologies of Black Folk: The Historical Novel of Slavery." In *Slavery and the Literary Imagination*, edited by Deborah E. McDowell and Arnold Rampersad, 125–143. Baltimore: Johns Hopkins University Press, 1989.

———. Introduction to *Iola Leroy*. Boston: Beacon, 1987.

———. "It Jus Be's Dat Way Sometime: The Sexual Politics of Women's Blues." In *Gender and Discourse: The Power of Talk*, edited by Alexander Dundas Todd and Sue Fisher, 227–242. Norwood, N.J.: Ablex, 1988.

———. "The Politics of Fiction, Anthropology, and the Folk: Zora Neale Hurston." In *New Essays on Their Eyes Were Watching God*, edited by Michael Awkward, 71–93. New York: Cambridge University Press, 1990.

———. *Reconstructing Womanhood: The Emergence of the Afro-American Woman Novelist*. New York: Oxford University Press, 1987.

———. "Schooling in Babylon" and "White Woman Listen! Black Feminism and the Boundaries of Sisterhood." In *The Empire Strikes Back: Race and Racism in 70s Britain*, 183–211, and 212–235. Center of Contemporary Cultural Studies, University of Birmingham. London: Hutchinson, 1982.

Care, Ethic of

See GILLIGAN, CAROL

Carnival

As it is used in feminist theory, this concept derives both from the theoretical writings of Mikhail Bakhtin and from women's historical involvement in carnivalesque social and political practices. It provides ways of analyzing problematic aspects of the representation of femininity as grotesque and hysterical; and also offers a set of textual and political strategies that women can deploy creatively in order to subvert patriarchal structures.

Following Bakhtin, accounts of carnival have focused on two issues: the grotesque body, and carnival as festive occasion, a time out of life when the normal rules are suspended, and—for a brief and clearly defined period—anything goes. The essential principle of carnival is embedded in the grotesque body, which is typified by events and activities—eating, defecation, birth, death, sex—in which the boundaries between bodies, and between bodies and the world, are obscured, displaced, and eroded. Descriptions of this grotesque body are replete with characteristics that have traditionally been coded as feminine. Feminist literary work has critiqued representations of the female body as grotesque and offered sensuous, pleasurable images of bodiliness, that turn the female grotesque into a positive sign. Such multifaceted uses of the grotesque recur, for example, in the fiction of Margaret Atwood and Angela Carter.

Historically, the assumption that women were the disorderly sex was similarly grounded in a perception of the female body as grotesque, linked to the belief that the possession of wombs made women prone to suffer from hysteria. Theorists have made connections between carnival and the Freudian account of hysteria, arguing that carnival can offer a way of reinscribing a historical dimension in universalizing, prescriptive discourses like psychoanalysis, and that the combination offers a powerful way of both inscribing and analyzing women's transgression. Examples might include the use of carnival and hysteria to construct the figure of the witch in Catherine Clement's contribution to *The Newly Born Woman* and the analysis of seventeenth-century prophetic and mystical writings by women in the work of Berg and Berry.

In an essay that has had a huge influence on literary criticism, social historian Natalie Zemon Davis argued that in early modern Europe, women used the carnivalesque figure of the unruly woman to legitimate their participation in political protest, and to widen the range of behavior available to them within marriage. But the power of the figure of the unruly woman lies precisely in its inversion of the familiar, accepted sexual and social order; and retribution enacted upon women who violated this order often took the form of carnivalesque punishments that involved the sexualized display of the female body and the violent public humiliation of the offending woman. Such rites were often associated with carnival under its aspect of liminal social space, the festive time out of life that celebrates the temporary suspension of the normal social order. Much scholarly work has shown a desire to locate these festive practices as a site of popular resistance, but historical evidence shows that carnival actually served a wide variety of purposes—oppositional and reactionary, progressive and conservative—and its political significance for feminism is equally ambivalent. Peter Stallybrass and Allon White argue that central to carnival is the tendency to abuse and demonize weaker social groups—women, ethnic and religious minorities, those who "don't belong." Thus carnival may be seen as being in a relation of mutual dependence with the dominant order; it is authority's way of producing subversion precisely in order to contain it. Significantly, perhaps, this aspect of carnival has been more important in feminist critique of male-authored texts—enabling reappraisals of the works of Rabelais and Ben Jonson, for example—rather than in women's writing.

It has been argued that the discourse of carnival allows women access to the public sphere only at the cost of inscribing their words and actions as symptoms of unruliness and hysteria. But it is in the nature of the carnivalesque to be contradictory and irreducible to a single, monolithic meaning; and it is clear that many women writers and theorists have found it an enabling way of inscribing bodily pleasure and subversive female subjectivity.

Kate Chedgzoy

References

Bakhtin, Mikhail. *Rabelais and His World.* Translated by Helen Iswolsky. Cambridge: MIT Press, 1968.

Berg, Christine, and Philippa Berry. "Spiritual Whoredom: An Essay on Seventeenth Century Women's Prophecy." In *1642: Literature and Power in the Seventeenth Century,* edited by Francis Barker et al, 37–54. Colchester: University of Essex, 1981.

Booth, Wayne C. "Freedom of Interpretation: Bakhtin and the Challenge of Feminist Criticism." *Critical Inquiry* 9, no. 1: 5–76.

Cixous, Hélène, and Catherine Clement. *The Newly Born Woman.* Translated by Betsy Wing. Minneapolis and Manchester: University of Minnesota Press, 1986.

Davis, Natalie Zemon. *Society and Culture in Early Modern France.* Stanford: Stanford University Press, 1975.

Newman, Karen. *Fashioning Femininity and English Renaissance Drama.* Chicago: University of Chicago Press, 1991.

Russo, Mary. "Female Grotesques: Carnival and Theory." In *Feminist Studies/Critical Studies,* edited by Teresa de Lauretis, 213–229. Bloomington: Indiana University Press, 1986.

Stallybrass, Peter, and Allon White. *The Politics and Poetics of Transgression.* London: Methuen, 1986.

Wills, Clair. "Upsetting the Public: Carnival, Hysteria and Women's Texts." In *Bakhtin and Cultural Theory,* edited by Ken Hirschkop and David Shepherd, 130–151. Manchester: Manchester University Press, 1989.

C

Carter, Angela

As a fiction writer, Angela Carter draws on history, myth, science fiction, fairy tale, pornography, Freudian psychology, and Marxist theory in order to create complex worlds that satirize patriarchy and capitalism. As a journalist, Carter writes materialist-feminist analyses of a wide range of cultural forms, from fashion to film and fiction. The best known of her nine novels include *The Passion of New Eve* and *Nights at the Circus,* which are both in some sense about the performance of gender. Carter has also written a feminist analysis of the "moral pornography" of the Marquis de Sade

(*The Sadeian Woman*) and has edited anthologies of fairy tales and "subversive" stories by
women. Throughout her work, she uses Freudian concepts as tools for the exploration of
sexuality (especially the female sexuality repressed by patriarchal culture), while simultaneously revealing that any system that purports
to analyze "human nature" in reality helps to
construct it.

In *The Sadeian Woman*, Carter argues
that, although most pornography supports the
sexist status quo, Sade's writings are protofeminist satires that both expose the violently unequal nature of relations between the sexes and
assert women's right to free sexuality. She uses
rape and sadomasochism in her novels (for example, *The Infernal Desire Machines of Doctor Hoffman*) to achieve similar ends, and to
illustrate the notion that gender is a violently
imposed category that oppresses women. Her
richly written novels envision worlds that seem
the logical and terrifying outcomes of the
battles between the sexes and the classes. Fairy
tales, which Carter appreciated for their encapsulation of both unconscious desires and
crystalline portraits of society, play a major
part in her writing. In the tales of *The Bloody
Chamber*, Carter explores the Freudian underpinnings of popular fairy tales, insisting on the
universality of human sexuality, while remaining aware that the tales both describe and inform concrete social situations; she therefore
foregrounds female heroism whenever possible. In her later stories (*Saints and Strangers*),
she reenvisions history to account for the material living conditions of such figures as Lizzie
Borden and Baudelaire's mistress, Jeanne
Duval.

Although she has been criticized for her
celebration of Sade and for failing to depict a
feminist utopia, Carter's eclectic work consistently raises key questions about the desires and
power of women and the oppressiveness of
hierarchies.

Debra Malina

References

Carter, Angela. *The Bloody Chamber*. New
    York and London: Penguin, 1979.
————. *The Infernal Desire Machines of Doc-
    tor Hoffman*. London: Penguin, 1972.
————. *Nights at the Circus*. New York and
    London: Penguin, 1984.
————. *Nothing Sacred: Selected Writings*.
    London: Virago, 1982.
————. *The Passion of New Eve*. London:
    Virago, 1977.
————. *The Sadeian Woman and the Ideol-
    ogy of Pornography*. New York: Pan-
    theon, 1978.
————. *Saints and Strangers*. London: Pen-
    guin, 1985.
————, ed. *Wayward Girls and Wicked
    Women: An Anthology of Subversive
    Stories*. London: Penguin, 1986.

Castellanos, Rosario

Mexican poet, novelist, essayist, teacher, playwright, and stateswoman, Rosario Castellanos
has been credited by fellow Mexican novelist
Elena Poniatowska as being "the one who
opened the door" for women writers in Mexico.
Castellanos produced a significant body of
work, both creative and critical, prior to her
untimely death in 1974—work that took as its
informing reality the "twofold condition of
being a woman and a Mexican."

Much of Castellanos's writing is characterized by a self-deprecating ironic humor and the
use of feminine and domestic metaphors that
she employs as a socially acceptable way of
criticizing Mexican social and cultural institutions that oppress women. Her use of domesticity as a discursive strategy—in stories such as
"Cooking Lesson," poems like "Self-Portrait,"
or essays such as "The Liberation of Love"—
is useful not only because it allows her to speak
as a woman to other women, but also because
it allows her to assert the legitimacy of feminine
discourse in the realm of poetic creativity—a
realm from which feminine experience historically has been excluded. Castellanos is a percep-
tive social observer who recognizes and records
the multiple and interlocking oppressions suffered by indigenous people—and particularly
non–Spanish speaking indigenous women—in
Mexico. In her novels *Balún Canan* and *Oficio
de Tinieblas*, as well as in her short story collection *Ciudad Real*, Castellanos depicts, and
makes an implicit critique of, the ways in which
violence, both literal and linguistic, supports a
cultural ideology that undergirds a rigid and
self-destructive caste system.

Both as a producer and an explicator of
texts, Castellanos has had a major influence on
Mexican women writers and critics, and on
their Chicana sisters in the United States. *A
Rosario Castellanos Reader*, edited by Maureen
Ahern, has begun the long-overdue task of in-

troducing Castellanos's work to the English-speaking world.

Paula Moya

References

Ahern, Maureen. "A Critical Bibliography of and about the Works of Rosario Castellanos." In *Homenaje a Rosario Castellanos,* edited by Maureen Ahern and Mary Seale Vásquez, 121–174. Valencia: Albatros-Hispanófila Ediciones, 1980.

———, and Mary Seale Vásquez, eds. *Homenaje a Rosario Castellanos.* Valencia: Albatros-Hispanófila Ediciones, 1980.

Castellanos, Rosario. *Another Way to Be: Selected Works of Rosario Castellanos.* Edited and translated by Myralyn Allgood. Athens: University of Georgia Press, 1990.

———. *A Rosario Castellanos Reader.* Edited by Maureen Ahern. Austin: University of Texas Press, 1988.

Censorship

The *Oxford English Dictionary* traces censorship back to ancient Rome and the actions of the magistrates who "had the supervision of public morals." Censorship traditionally excises material that might be considered morally offensive or that might pose a threat to the parties in power because of its commentary on politics or religion. Dictionaries generally do not consider gender as a component of censorship, but feminist critics have long acknowledged that gendered censorship is a powerful force against which women writers have struggled for years. Today, feminists explore gendered censorship in several areas, including canon formation and pornography.

The exclusion of women from the literary canon began before writers recognized a "canon" as such. Women in the Middle Ages and the Renaissance were frequently admonished to remain "chaste, silent, and obedient" on the basis of biblical exegesis that asserted that women were the "weaker vessel" morally, intellectually, and physically. Men's dismissal of women's work as inferior constituted a form of censorship, and, as Dale Spender has demonstrated, women who sought to publish their work were frequently labeled immoral, eccentric, or insane. This dismissal manifested itself in the exclusion of women's voices from the literary canon for hundreds of years. Adrienne Rich calls for a "re-vision" of cultural history as an act of survival for feminists, and Sandra Gilbert asserts that in order to overcome this censorship, feminists must "review, reimagine, rethink, rewrite, revise, and reinterpret the events and documents that constitute" history.

One of the early effects of a patriarchal culture's censorship of women's work is that many women writers internalized the modesty topos, believing that it was immodest for them to seek public expression, and demonstrating that belief through self-censorship. For women writers over the years, self-censorship manifested itself in several forms, including publishing works anonymously or pseudonymously, including disclaimers that stated that the work was published without their knowledge, or relying on "safe" genres or topics (such as closet dramas, conduct books, or religious translations). While many contemporary feminists feel that self-censorship is an abdication of power, other critics, such as Kate Flint, are beginning to explore self-censorship as an empowering experience, claiming that it can "allow the reader to merge her own desires, experiences, and imagination with those which are suggested but unvoiced within the text."

Another aspect of censorship that feminism explores, and one of the most controversial issues for feminists, is pornography. In 1983 Andrea Dworkin and Catharine MacKinnon introduced antipornography legislation that was "based on the premise that pornography is a form of discrimination against women" because it incites men to violent crimes like rape. Author Susan Brownmiller and some feminist organizations, such as Women against Pornography, Women against Violence against Women, and Women against Violence in Pornography and Media, support that position. These groups cite studies like Edward Donnerstein's 1987 *The Question of Pornography* which find that violent pornography increases aggression in men. Other feminists feel pornography should be censored because it includes racist, as well as sexist, depictions of women. Ironically, the procensorship feminists frequently find themselves linked by their critics to religious fundamentalists. Susan Griffin and Dworkin distinguish themselves from the Far Right by asserting that pornography itself is a form of censorship because it silences women's voices.

On the anticensorship side of the debate are feminists like Carol Clover and Sallie Tisdale, who feel that pornography can provide a means of expression for women's sexuality and that narrowly focusing on pornography ignores the sexism and oppression that exist in broader legitimized power structures. They argue that rather than censoring all pornography, feminists need to support production of pornography that is specifically designed for a female audience. Clover asserts that pornography is a "meaningful text about the sexual acts it represents" and refuses critics' charges that feminists like herself are "compliant with male domination."

Censorship continues to be a charged issue for feminist theorists, as the recent anthology *Sex Exposed: Sexuality and the Pornography Debate* demonstrates. While some feminists oppose censorship of any kind because of its history of oppressing women's voices, others support censorship of some materials (specifically pornography) because they feel those materials oppress women's voices by their very nature.

Sigrid King

References

Brownmiller, Susan. *Against Our Will: Men, Women, and Rape*. New York: Simon and Schuster, 1975.

Clover, Carol J. Introduction to *Dirty Looks: Women, Pornography, Power*, edited by Pamela Church Gibson and Roma Gibson. London: British Film Institute, 1993.

Donnerstein, Edward, Daniel Linz, and Steven Penrod, eds. *The Question of Pornography: Research Findings and Policy Implications*. New York: Free Press, 1987.

Dworkin, Andrea. *Pornography: Men Possessing Women*. New York: Perigee, 1979.

Flint, Kate. "'The Pools, the Depths, the Dark Places': Omen, Censorship and the Body 1894–1931." In *Literature and Censorship*, Essays and Studies Vol. 46, edited by Nigel Smith, 118–130. Cambridge: D.S. Brewer, 1993.

Gilbert, Sandra M. "What Do Feminist Critics Want." In *The New Feminist Criticism: Essays on Women, Literature, and Theory*, edited by Elaine Showalter, 29–45. New York: Pantheon, 1985.

Griffin, Susan. *Pornography and Silence: Culture's Revenge against Nature*. New York: Harper and Row, 1981.

MacKinnon, Catharine. *Feminism Unmodified: Discourses on Life and Law*. Cambridge: Harvard University Press, 1987.

Rich, Adrienne. *On Lies, Secrets, and Silence*. New York and London: W.W. Norton, 1979.

Segal, Lynne, and Mary McIntosh, eds. *Sex Exposed: Sexuality and the Pornography Debate*. New Brunswick, N.J.: Rutgers University Press, 1993.

Spender, Dale. *Women of Ideas and What Men Have Done to Them*. London: Pandora, 1982.

Tisdale, Sallie. *Talk Dirty to Me*. New York: Doubleday, 1994.

Chernin, Kim

Chiefly known for her work on anorexia, Kim Chernin could be categorized as a "difference feminist" with an interest in the psychoanalytic. She has employed autobiography, cultural criticism, fiction, and poetry to talk about subjects ranging from eating disorders and mother-daughter relationships to female sexuality.

Chernin became an important scholar for exposing anorexia as a disease inherently bound up in misogynist culture. Her first book, *The Obsession: Reflections on the Tyranny of Slenderness*, unearthed the injurious relationship between patriarchy and women's health. Her primary claim was that women have been conditioned to antagonize their instinctual physical needs and that they suffer from a "loss of the body as a source of pleasure." In *The Hungry Self: Women, Eating & Identity*, written in 1985, Chernin examines female rites of passage and mother-daughter relationships as they manifest in eating disorders. Her hypothesis suggests that a significant part of a young woman's identity formation pivots on her ability to differentiate herself from her parents in real and symbolic gestures—one of these gestures being a refusal to adhere to the specific food rituals of her parents' generation. Because young women identify more readily with their mothers, Chernin argues, their "coming of age" becomes a choice between repeating or surpassing their mothers' lives. Food obsessions represent the "turmoil and urgency" that modern young women are faced with in light of an increasing cultural pressure to surpass their mothers' generation while maintaining archaic notions of femininity.

Chernin often employs personal metaphors to relate her theories. In one book, *In My Mother's House*, she uses feminist analysis to inform her autobiography; in *Reinventing Eve: Modern Woman in Search of Herself*, Chernin reexamines traditional religious myths and goddess icons while narrating her experiences with depression and subsequent revelations about her own life and identity as a woman. *Sex and Other Sacred Games: Love, Desire, Power, and Possession* , co-written with Renate Stendhal, takes the form of a socratic dialogue between Alma Runau and Claire Heller, a French lesbian and a heterosexual American woman, who have to redefine traditional female sexuality to cultivate their three-year relationship.

Jenna Ivers

References

Chernin, Kim. *The Flame Bearers*. New York: Random House, 1986.

———. *The Hungry Self: Women, Eating & Identity*. New York: Times, 1985.

———. *In My Mother's House*. New York: Tiknor and Fields, 1983.

———. *The Obsession: Reflections on the Tyranny of Slenderness*. New York: Harper and Row, 1981.

———. *Reinventing Eve: Modern Woman in Search of Herself*. New York: Times, 1987.

———, and Renate Stendhal. *Sex and Other Sacred Games: Love, Desire, Power, and Possession*. New York: Times, 1989.

Chicana Theory

While U.S. women of color have joined together strategically for the purpose of political and social change and have proclaimed a collective voice in key anthologies such as *This Bridge Called My Back: Writings by Radical Women of Color*, they also continue to acknowledge their different races, histories, cultures, and experiences. The specific differences in history, cultural identity, and experience are combined to formulate a context and a theoretical framework for the understanding of the cultural productions of a given group. Chicana feminism is the name of a political movement or stance that takes as its point of departure the situation of workingclass women of Mexican descent living in the United States and identifies economic exploitation, racism, and sexism as factors that function to marginalize them. Chicana feminist literary criticism, then, has focused on the different ways that race, class, and gender are represented in the literature, and on the power struggles that Chicanas wage in the battle for self-determination. More recently, sexuality and sexual identity have been recognized as another perspective from which Chicana writings must be examined.

During the Chicano movement of the 1960s, the term "Chicano," a term that refers to people of Mexican descent living in the United States and derives from "oral usage of the term in working-class communities," (Alarcón) was taken up as a banner of protest that resonated with the Black Power, anti–Vietnam War, Civil Rights, Asian American, and Native American movements that were occurring at the time. At the first National Chicana Conference held in Houston, Texas, May 1971, women who had supported the Chicano movement, working "alongside the men" protested the sexism of the movement and insisted upon a self-designation as "Chicana feminist." While a number of women resisted what they saw as a separatist move, Chicana feminists persisted in forging a distinct perspective that implied not only a critique of Anglo and Chicano patriarchies, but also of Anglo feminist theory.

Out of the Chicana feminism inaugurated in the early 1970s emerged a group of scholars who turned to Chicana literature as a medium through which the Chicana creates a voice that resists domination, and that seeks not only to expose the social, economic, and political constraints placed upon Chicanas, but also to explore the complexity of their positioning within both a mainstream and a Chicano literary tradition that has silenced their voices.

The field is composed of a number of critical projects that take up the task of elaborating and revising the theoretical framework of Chicana feminism. One of these projects is concerned with the assessment of Chicana feminist literary theory in relation to Anglo and French feminisms. It seeks to show how such theories can be useful in analyzing Chicana literature, and explores the limits of such theories in producing interpretations that are attentive to contextual specificities. Another project argues for the development of a Chicana aesthetic that opposes a dominant aesthetic seeking to subsume Chicana literature into preexisting categories of literary study, as structured by either an

Anglo, patriarchal, and bourgeois academy, or by Chicano studies as institutionalized by a masculinist movement. Such an oppositional aesthetic gives rise to a new culture that represents the diversity of Chicana experiences. Yet another strand of Chicana literary criticism insists upon a return to oral tradition and to vernacular culture as a means of affirming the continuities between the recent upsurge in Chicana literary production and other cultural productions that may not be explicitly literary but that nevertheless are engaged in the process of telling the untold story of Mexican American women in the United States. Finally, a more recent turn in Chicana literary criticism engages with contemporary social theory, considerations of the political economy, testimonial narratives, and ethnographic studies as a means of pursuing a bridge between the situation of the "native" woman and that of the Chicana/critic intellectual.

Chicana theory is crucial to feminist literary theory because it necessarily interrogates the race, class, gender, and sexuality nexus in a manner that serves both as a critique of previous definitions of feminist theory that exclude women of color, and as a contribution to feminist theory that complicates current understandings of the position of women in society.

Dionne Espinoza

References

Alarcón, Norma. "Chicana Feminism: In the Tracks of 'the' Native Woman." *Cultural Studies* 4 (1990): 248–256.

Anzaldúa, Gloria, and Cherríe Moraga, eds. *This Bridge Called My Back: Writings by Radical Women of Color*. New York: Kitchen Table: Women of Color Press, 1981.

Cordova, Teresa, et al., eds. *Chicana Voices: Intersections of Class, Race, and Gender*. Austin, Tex.: Center for Mexican American Studies, 1990.

Del Castillo, Adelaida R., ed. *Between Borders: Essays on Chicana/Mexicana History*. Encino, Calif.: Floricanto, 1990.

García, Alma M. "The Development of Chicana Feminist Discourse, 1970–1980." *Gender and Society* 3 (1989): 217–238.

Herrera-Sobek, María, and Helena María Viramontes, eds. *Chicana Creativity and Criticism: Charting New Frontiers in American Literature*. Houston, Tex.: Arte Publico, 1987.

Mirande, Alfredo, and Evangelina Enriquez. *La Chicana: The Mexican American Woman*. Chicago: University of Chicago Press, 1979.

Quintana, Alvina. "Politics, Representation and the Emergence of a Chicana Aesthetic." *Cultural Studies* 4 (1990): 257–263.

Saldívar-Hull, Sonia. "Feminism on the Border: From Gender Politics to Geopolitics." In *Criticism in the Borderlands: Studies in Chicano Literature, Culture, and Ideology*, edited by Héctor Calderón and José David Saldívar, 203–220. Durham and London: Duke University Press, 1991.

Trujillo, Carla, ed. *Chicana Lesbians: The Girls Your Mother Warned You About*. Berkeley, Calif.: Third Woman, 1991.

Children

While feminism and children would seem to have a natural affinity from analogous positions on the margin, to date there is very little scholarship on the topic of children and feminist theory. Beverly Lyon Clark addresses this dearth of commentary in a recent article, and "calls feminists to account" for their "blindness" to or "dismissal" of anything juvenile.

Generally, the topic of children in feminist literary research is not separated from mothering. Adrienne Rich's *Of Woman Born*, for example, explores the pain and pleasure of experiencing motherhood within patriarchy, while Jane Silverman Van Buren's *The Modernist Madonna* offers a semiotic reading of the signs and symbols of the mother-infant relationship in literature and art. Fictional representations of motherhood—and thus childhood—include Tillie Olsen's *Tell Me a Riddle*.

There are strands of theoretical discussions about children or childhood development that are usefully employed by feminist literary theorists—including historical, sociological, anthropological, and materialist studies of the child and childhood. Psychological theory—in its varied incarnations (such as educational, developmental, and psychoanalytical)—is perhaps the most influential of these strands. The writings of Sigmund Freud, Melanie Klein, and Jacques Lacan have all been influential in constructing theories of psychosexual child behavior and development that are used in literary analysis. In terms of the female child in particular, Nancy Chodorow's *The Reproduction of Mothering* is a groundbreaking study that confronts the endless social cycle of women's mothering set up by a system of unequal parenting. Dovetailing with Chodorow's work is Carol Gilligan's *In a Different Voice*, which describes the differences between female and male moral development and personality, focusing on the adolescent girl.

The child as a victim of violence and abuse is another thematic feminist theorists have used to explore literature or literary figures. The theories developed by Judith Lewis Herman in *Father-Daughter Incest*, for example, have been applied by feminist critics such as Louise DeSalvo in evaluations of the lives and works of women writers.

The figure of the child in literature has always been a fascinating and powerful one, symbolically representing redemption, corrupted innocence, repressed potential or hope—for example, Little Eva in *Uncle Tom's Cabin*, Maggie Tulliver in *The Mill on the Floss*, Miles and Flora in James's *The Turn of the Screw*, and the child characters in Toni Morrison's *The Bluest Eye*. In their reevaluation of women writers, feminist literary critics have discussed the childhoods of heroines who grow up in the course of their fictions—such as Charlotte Brontë's *Jane Eyre*—as well as the iconography represented by dying children in works by writers such as Charles Dickens and Harriet Beecher Stowe.

While feminist discourse has not yet wholly separated children from either their adult selves or from their mothers, and although feminist literary theory has worked hard to place the woman in the position of the Subject rather than Object, children have only recently been afforded similar attention, particularly in current feminist/theoretical research in the field of children's literature.

Lynne Vallone

References

Chodorow, Nancy. *The Reproduction of Mothering: Psychoanalysis and the Sociology of Gender*. Berkeley: University of California Press, 1978.

Clark, Beverly Lyon. "Fairy Godmothers or Wicked Stepmothers? The Uneasy Relationship of Feminist Theory and Children's Criticism." *Children's Literature Association Quarterly* 18 (1993–1994): 171–176.

DeSalvo, Louise. *Virginia Woolf: The Impact of Childhood Sexual Abuse on Her Life and Work*. Boston: Beacon, 1989.

Doane, Janice L. *From Klein to Kristeva: Psychoanalytic Feminism and the Search for the "Good Enough" Mother*. Ann Arbor: University of Michigan Press, 1992.

Gilligan, Carol. *In a Different Voice: Psychological Theory and Women's Development*. Cambridge: Harvard University Press, 1982.

Herman, Judith Lewis, and Lisa Hirschman. *Father-Daughter Incest*. Cambridge: Harvard University Press, 1981.

Hirsch, Marianne. *The Mother/Daughter Plot: Narrative, Psychoanalysis, Feminism*. Bloomington: Indiana University Press, 1989.

Olsen, Tillie. *Tell Me a Riddle*. New York: Dell, 1961.

Rich, Adrienne. *Of Woman Born: Motherhood as Experience and Institution*. New York: W.W. Norton, 1976.

Van Buren, Jane Silverman. *The Modernist Madonna: Semiotics of the Maternal Metaphor*. Bloomington: Indiana University Press, 1989.

Children's Literature

In "Enigma Variations: What Feminist Theory Knows about Children's Literature," Lissa Paul states that "there is good reason for appropriating feminist theory to children's literature. Both women's literature and children's literature are devalued and regarded as marginal or peripheral by the literary and educational communities." Children's literature is pushed closer to the literary periphery because society places children in the domain and under the responsibility of already marginalized women. However, acting on Aidan Chambers's contention in *Introducing Books to Children* that "readers are made, not born" women stand in an enviable position to influence societal attitudes through bringing a feminist perspective and approach to reading, criticizing, and using children's literature.

Feminist literary theory charges one to "make" readers who consider the influence of gender in character and in plot; to retrieve forgotten or repressed women's texts and female authors; to note gender differences and gender controls in the use of language; and to attend to gender-specific ways of storytelling. In practice, feminist criticism in children's literature falls largely in three strands of inquiry, all of which Jack Zipes touches in *Don't Bet on the Prince: Contemporary Feminist Fairy Tales in North America and England*. A work "[c]reated out of the dissatisfaction with the dominant male discourse of traditional fairy tales," this volume of intentionally feminist fairy tales "challenge[s] conventional views of gender, socialization, and sex roles, . . . and map[s] out an alternative aesthetic terrain for the fairy tale as a genre to open up new horizons for readers and writers alike."

Aside from Zipes's comprehensive approach, feminist literary theory in children's literature most frequently addresses gender role stereotyping in traditional, award-winning, and contemporary texts. Feminist critics contrast the plot options available to male characters to those available to female characters. They study the depiction, visual and literary, of women and female children in texts from picture books to young adult novels. Mary J. Du Mont overlays a gender-role approach with attention to the works of female authors within a limited genre. She attributes an increase in the number of independent, thinking, and capable female protagonists to a growth in the numbers of women writing in the genre and to greater societal inclusion of women in varied professions and leadership roles.

Recent biocritical studies in children's and young adult literature, such as Mercier's and Bloom's *Presenting Zibby Oneal*, celebrate the artistic contributions by women authors. As they explore the intersections of an author's life and art, they examine the societal conditions in which the text was created, reflect on the psychological growth of a single female artist, and work toward understanding the development of a uniquely female aesthetic.

Because of its wide-ranging readership of maturing minds and evolving sensibilities, children's and young adult literature offers feminist literary theory fertile ground in which to effect social change. In the texts of childhood, a feminist reader can actively question sexist and racist beliefs; scrutinize role models and stereotypes; witness, monitor, and support the changing family; call for greater diversity, representation and inclusion; and celebrate women.

Cathryn M. Mercier

References

Chambers, Aidan. *Introducing Books to Children*. Boston: Horn Book, 1983.

Du Mont, Mary J. "Images of Women in Young Adult Science Fiction and Fantasy, 1970, 1980, and 1990: A Comparative Content Analysis." *Voice of Youth Advocates* (April 1993): 11–16.

Gersoni-Stavn, Diane. *Sexism and Youth*. New York: Bowker, 1974.

Gibson, Lois Rauch. "Beyond the Apron: Archetypes, Stereotypes, and Alternative Portrayals of Mothers in Children's Literature." *Children's Literature Association Quarterly* 13 (1988): 177–181.

Green, Carol Hurd, and Mary Mason, eds. *American Women Writers: Supplement*. New York: Continuum, in progress.

Harrison, Barbara, and Gregory Maguire, eds. *Innocence and Experience: Essays and Conversations in Children's Literature*. New York: Lothrop, 1985.

Hearne, Betsy, and Roger Sutton, eds. *Evaluating Children's Books: A Critical Look*. 34th Allerton Institute Conference Proceedings. Urbana-Champaign: University of Illinois, 1993.

Kortenhaus, Carole M., and Jack Demarest. "Gender Role Stereotyping in Children's Literature: An Update." *Sex Roles* 28 (1993): 219–232.

Mercier, Cathryn M., and Susan P. Bloom. *Presenting Zibby Oneal*. New York: Twayne, 1991.

Paul, Lissa. "Enigma Variations: What Feminist Theory Knows about Children's Literature." *Signal* 54 (1987): 186–201.

Sadler, Glenn E., ed. *Teaching Children's Literature: Issues, Pedagogy, Resources*. New York: Modern Language Association, 1992.

Vandergrift, Kay E. *Children's Literature: Theory, Research, and Teaching*. Englewood, Colo.: Libraries Unlimited, 1990.

Zipes, Jack. *Don't Bet on the Prince: Contemporary Feminist Fairy Tales in North America and England*. New York: Routledge, 1987.

Chodorow, Nancy

As the title and subtitle suggest, Nancy Chodorow's first book, *The Reproduction of Mothering: Psychoanalysis and the Sociology of*

Gender, uses principles of psychology and sociology to analyze the way women's mothering is "reproduced" across generations. Chodorow provided a compelling alternative account to Sigmund Freud's Oedipus complex and developmental theory by focusing on the mother and daughter relationship, rather than on the mother and son's. Her findings, suggesting that daughters do not turn away completely from their mothers but have an ongoing relationship with them, became the basis for questioning gender differences in social and moral attitudes. Literary critics use Chodorow's theories to argue for a distinction in women's reading, writing, and representation.

Chodorow's work follows that of object-relations theorists such as Alice and Michael Balint, W.R.D. Fairbairn, and D.W. Winnicott. She sees women's mothering as one of the few universal and enduring elements of the sexual division of labor and does not believe that the reproduction of mothering is based only on biology or role socialization. Combining Freud's explanations of pre-Oedipal and Oedipal development with her own clinical observations, Chodorow claims that a mother experiences a daughter as an "extension" or "double" of herself. She is more likely to emphasize "narcissistic" elements with cathexis of daughters, whereas, sons are more likely experienced by the mother as sexual others. The results of this differentiation are manifold. Because girls tend to identify with their mothers, they do not reject their mothers or experience penis envy the way sons do. Consequently, they do not simply "transfer" their affection from mother to father, but retain an external and internal relation to their mothers until at least adolescence. The love for the father is not a substitute for the mother, but is added to the primary relation as a third.

From this triangular or triadic structure, Chodorow contends that women have a more complex psyche than men. Women have "other resources" and a "certain distance" from their relationships to men. They have a "richer, ongoing inner world" to fall back on, and men do not represent an exclusive attachment for them, as women represent to men. Another implication of her study is that women "define" and experience themselves "relationally," while men both look for and fear "exclusivity." Throughout their development, men have tended to repress their "affective relational needs" and to develop ties based more on "categorical and abstract role expectations." Eventually, a heterosexual bond for men replicates the mother-infant exclusivity, while women require a "third person" on the level of psychic structure. For Chodorow, having a child completes the "relational triangle" for a woman.

Unlike Freud, Chodorow represents the mother, and the child's bonds to her, in a positive light. In traditional psychoanalytic theories, mothers represent dependence and regression. It is only by turning away from the mother that the individual is able to progress and participate in the real world. Chodorow's insistence that it is not necessary to reject the mother encourages women to valorize and pay attention to mother/daughter relations in their reading and writing. Her reformulations of the feminine Oedipus complex are also used to interpret differences in male and female behaviors both in literature and in life. For instance, according to Chodorow's model of female psychological development, women may tend to resolve difficult situations through accommodation rather than confrontation with authority figures. Women tend to preserve a stronger sense of connectedness to others and value affective ties more. They may appreciate friendships or personal bonds more, and take on the role of caretaking in the family. For Chodorow, in order to right the balance of the "unequal social organization of gender," primary parenting must be shared between men and women. Equal parenting would leave people of both genders with "positive capacities," without the current tendencies toward "destructive extremes."

Recent poststructuralist critics have been inclined to see Chodorow's theories as optimistic and overly simplistic. They believe that Chodorow reduces psychical reality to social reality, and that she does not fully take into account the role of the father, or repression in the construction of the subject. One critic, Patricia Elliot, thinks that Chodorow mistakenly believes that her work is free from "cultural and instinctual determinism," though it "incorporates" both. However, she does acknowledge that the focus on mother/daughter relationships in Chodorow is important.

Eleanor Ty

References

Chodorow, Nancy. *Feminism and Psychoanalytic Theory*. New Haven: Yale University Press, 1989.

———. *The Reproduction of Mothering: Psy-*

choanalysis and the Sociology of Gender. Berkeley: University of California Press, 1978.

Elliot, Patricia. *From Mastery to Analysis: Theories of Gender in Psychoanalytic Feminism*. Ithaca, N.Y.: Cornell University Press, 1991.

Chopin, Kate

Chopin was popular during her lifetime as a local colorist for her stories of Creole culture. Her work was retrieved from obscurity in the late 1960s and has become canonized as a significant part of the American literary tradition. Feminist scholars have found in Chopin's work a crucial transition between the nineteenth-century female traditions of sentimental and local color fiction and twentieth-century modernist literature. Many of Chopin's stories, such as "The Story of an Hour" (1894) and "Elizabeth Stock's One Story" (1898), as well as her novel, *The Awakening* (1899), explore the struggle of female characters to define and experience their own subjectivity in a society that insists upon woman's identity as object, defined by male desires.

Chopin's critics at the turn of the century were shocked not only by the frank depiction of female sexuality in *The Awakening*, but also by the "selfishness" of the novel's heroine, Edna Pontellier, whose awakening to consciousness of herself leads her to reject the world of conventional marriage, as well as the world of the "mother-women" valorized by nineteenth-century women writers. Female sexuality in the novel, neither spiritualized through maternity nor politely ignored, is the vehicle for the heroine's "awakening" to self-awareness. The novel's deeply ambivalent conclusion suggests the inability of women to pursue the Emersonian ideal of individuality, as men in American literature traditionally have: for women, there is no escape, ultimately, from their responsibilities to children, which are seen to conflict with responsibility to the self. Chopin's portrayal of Edna Pontellier marks a crucial development in the depiction of woman as subject in American literature, interrogating and resisting societal norms.

Nancy Disenhaus

References

Boren, Lynda S., and Sara deSaussure Davis. *Kate Chopin Reconsidered: Beyond the Bayou*. Baton Rouge: Louisiana State University Press, 1992.

Culley, Margaret, ed. *The Awakening: An Authoritative Text, Contexts, Criticism*. New York: W.W. Norton, 1976.

Gilbert, Sandra M. "The Second Coming of Aphrodite: Kate Chopin's Fantasy of Desire." *Kenyon Review* 5 (1983): 42–66.

Koloski, Bernard J., ed. *Approaches to Teaching Kate Chopin's The Awakening*. New York: Modern Language Association, 1988.

Martin, Wendy, ed. *New Essays on The Awakening*. Cambridge: Cambridge University Press, 1988.

Seyersted, Per. *Kate Chopin: A Critical Biography*. Baton Rouge: Louisiana State University Press, 1969.

———, ed. *The Complete Works of Kate Chopin*. Baton Rouge: Louisiana State University Press, 1969.

Stange, Margit. "Personal Property: Exchange Value and the Female Self in *The Awakening*." *Genders* 5 (1989): 106–119.

Toth, Emily. *Kate Chopin*. New York: William Morrow, 1990.

Christ, Carol P.

Feminist theologian and writer, Christ responded to the lack of writings on women's spirituality by creating one of the first collections of its kind, *Womanspirit Rising*, in 1979. The essays (written from 1960 to 1978) represent a wide range of authors and styles, from scholarly theological studies to passionate, well-reasoned opinion pieces. In *Diving Deep and Surfacing*, Christ argues that women readers gain access to their own spirituality in reading stories by (and about) other women. Examining the work of Kate Chopin, Doris Lessing, Adrienne Rich, Margaret Atwood, and Ntozake Shange, Christ finds a pattern to the protagonists' spiritual quest: from a sense of emptiness, the characters achieve a spiritual identification with nature or other women. This quest culminates in a "new naming" that transcends and transforms traditional cultural values. *Laughter of Aphrodite* is an autobiographical account of Christ's journey to a goddess-centered spirituality; her historical research documents the suppression of women-centered goddesses and rituals in Christianity and Judaism. *Weaving the Visions: New Patterns in Feminist Spirituality* represents a diverse selection of writers: the collection ranges from feminist critiques of Judaism to lesbian perspectives on goddesses to fictional essays. These theological writings demonstrate the various ways in which women are creating, revising, and renaming religion and spirituality.

Wendy C. Wahl

References

Christ, Carol P. *Diving Deep and Surfacing: Women Writers on a Spiritual Quest.* Boston: Beacon, 1980.

———. *Laughter of Aphrodite: Reflections on a Journey to the Goddess.* San Francisco: Harper and Row, 1987.

———, and Judith Plaskow, eds. *Weaving the Visions: New Patterns in Feminist Spirituality.* San Francisco: Harper and Row, 1989.

———, eds. *Womanspirit Rising: a Feminist Reader in Religion.* San Francisco: Harper and Row, 1979.

Cinema

See FILM

Cixous, Hélène

A prominent figure in the French women's movement since its inception in the years following the student uprising of May 1968, Hélène Cixous is known generally by Anglo American readers in conjunction with Luce Irigaray and Julia Kristeva. While the work of all three responds to Derridian deconstruction and Lacanian psychoanalysis, Cixous's particular contribution is her espousal of *écriture féminine* (feminine writing), a type of writing that subverts patriarchal discourse.

Born in 1937 in Algeria, of Austro-German Jewish descent, Cixous received her doctorate in 1968 and participated in founding the experimental University of Paris VIII at Vincennes. She became involved in the highly controversial group "Psych et Po" ("Psychanalyse et Politique") and published all of her works between 1976 and 1982 with its publishing house *des femmes.* (She eventually left the group to move away from official political affiliation.) Her work was largely unknown to Anglo American feminists until the 1979 publication of Elaine Marks's and Isabelle de Courtivron's *New French Feminisms*, an anthology that intro-duced the English reading public to a variety of French feminist writings, Cixous's included. The majority of her work, however, was not translated until the mid 1980s. This language barrier contributed, in Toril Moi's opinion, to the division between Anglo American and French feminists. While the former privileges women's empirical experience (for example, constructing a women's history, celebrating stories of previously silenced women) and maintains a wary relationship with theory, the latter, believing that the notion of "woman" does not have to be defined by anatomy, seemingly privileges theory over praxis. This theoretical bias of French feminists, however, is complicated by their participation in what Ann Rosalind Jones calls "the metaphysical and psychoanalytic frameworks, they attempt to dislodge." In other words, the scholarship of those patriarchal figures (for example, Derrida and Lacan) from which French feminists wish to distance their work actually informs a significant portion of French feminist theory.

Cixous has alienated some feminists (French as well as Anglo American) because of her claim that she is not a "feminist." Moi points out, however, that this statement results from Cixous's identification of "feminism" with bourgeois women's attempts to enter and participate in the patriarchal power structure. According to Jones, Cixous rejects "feminism" as a movement too similar to a male phallocentric search for power.

Cixous's work is known for its attacks on the system of binary oppositions that characterizes phallocentric society. Within this system, woman is always subordinate to man, the feminine to the masculine. Binaries that compose masculine or "marked" writing limit the writing process, stressing restraint and closure. These limiting tendencies are then challenged by *écriture féminine,* which appears in the margins or gaps of patriarchal discourse and emphasizes an "open-ended textuality." Feminine writing stems from the life drive; it is a site, writes Jones, of "resistance or liberation in this phallocentric universe."

Not all women's writing, however, is feminine writing. Cixous uses the term "feminine" reluctantly, not intending that it apply only to women, just as "masculine" does not refer solely to men. Rather, both these terms are derived from a Freudian language and refer to qualities that are traditionally ascribed to one sex or the other. Driven by a belief that we are all inherently bisexual, Cixous suggests that feminine writing can be produced by men as well as women. Bisexuality is conceived not in terms of neutrality, but rather as the presence of both sexes in an individual. The writing individual must contain some elements of the other sex within her/himself in order to produce feminine writing: as Cixous explains in "Sorties," "[T]here is no *invention* possible, whether it be philosophical or poetic, without the presence in the inventing subject of an abundance of the other, of the diverse." Because of their marginalized position in patriarchal culture, women appear to Cixous as particularly open to this bisexuality.

Cixous's "The Laugh of the Medusa" is considered the manifesto of *écriture féminine*. While stressing that men as well as women are capable of feminine writing, this essay also celebrates the female body and the manner in which feminine writing draws from its multitude of appetites. By conceiving of an "erotics of writing" grounded in what Jones describes as the "multiple physical capacities (gestation, birth, lactation)" of the female body, Cixous rejects Freudian and Lacanian ideas of woman as lack. The image of a laughing Medusa, now "beautiful," demonstrates, according to Verena Conley, a refusal to see women in terms of castration; Medusa's laughter "shatters the negative moment of death and brings women to life and movement."

Although she is particularly known for her essays, Cixous first wrote fiction. *Le Prenom de dieu*, a collection of short stories, was published in 1967, and *Dedans*, a 1969 fictionalized autobiography, won the Prix Medicis. Cixous, however, thinks of herself as a poet. Poetry subverts ordinary language and is, consequently, writes Conley, "necessary to social transformation." Cixous particularly privileges the powers of poetry because "poetry involves gaining strength through the unconscious and because the unconscious, that other limitless country, is the place where the repressed manage to survive." The lyricism of her essays defy linearity or phallocentric logic; these are texts that Moi believes resist analysis.

Cixous is often dismissed for her inconsistency and the woman-centered nature of her work. Conley suggests, however, that the reader need not become so obsessed with these charges of essentialism. Cixous's work still holds considerable relevance in a social climate that continues to violate and oppress a group of human beings our society has positioned as women. Conley suggests that the reader think of the feminine in terms of the life drive; Cixous's work is one that celebrates the living and the liberation of either sex.

Maria Jerinic

References

Baym, Nina. "The Madwoman and Her Languages: Why I Don't Do Feminist Criticism." In *Feminist Issues in Literary Scholarship*, edited by Shari Benstock, 45–61. Bloomington: Indiana University Press, 1987.

Benstock, Shari. "Beyond the Reaches of Feminist Criticism: A Letter from Paris." In *Feminist Issues in Literary Scholarship*, edited by Shari Benstock, 7–29. Bloomington: Indiana University Press, 1987.

Cixous, Hélène. "The Laugh of the Medusa." In *New French Feminisms: An Anthology*, edited by Elaine Marks and Isabelle de Courtivron, 245–264. New York: Schocken Books, 1980.

———. "Sorties." In *New French Feminisms: An Anthology*, edited by Elaine Marks and Isabelle de Courtivron, 90–98. New York: Schocken Books, 1980.

Conley, Verena Andermatt. *Hélène Cixous: Writing the Feminine*. Lincoln: University of Nebraska Press, 1991.

Jones, Ann Rosalind. "Inscribing Femininity: French Theories of the Feminine." In *Making a Difference*, edited by Gayle Greene and Coppélia Kahn, 80–112. London: Methuen, 1985.

Moi, Toril. *Sexual Textual Politics: Feminist Literary Theory*. London: Routledge, 1991.

———, ed. "Introduction." In *French Feminist Thought: A Reader*. New York: Basil Blackwell, 1987.

Showalter, Elaine. "Women Time, Women's Space: Writing the History of Feminist Criticism." *Feminist Issues in Literary Scholarship*, edited by Shari Benstock, 30–44. Bloomington: Indiana University Press, 1987.

Class

A basic definition of class is the grouping together of two or more individuals with the same economic or social status. Traditionally, class has been studied by political and economic theorists, as well as by other practitioners who emphasize a socioeconomic way of looking at the world. Class is important to feminist literary theory because both women and poor people, as well as individuals from other ethnic and minority groups, are routinely kept from positions of power and influence by ruling patriarchal structures.

Although primarily concerned with the workings of society and politics and not with literature, the most influential thinker in terms of class is Karl Marx. Orthodox Marxism studies the economic realities of society and class formation; however, today the term "Marxism" applies to any methodology concerned with the injustice of capitalism, the material relations of human beings, and the workings of real-life power. David Daiches's article "Jane Austen, Karl Marx, and the Aristocratic Dance" is an orthodox Marxist reading of how Jane Austen "exposes the economic basis of social behavior with an ironic smile."

With the rise of the women's movement during the 1960s, a number of women voiced their concern that orthodox Marxism did not attend to gender oppression with the same diligence that it did to class oppression. In an important study, Shulamith Firestone used biological differences between men and women to argue that gender conflict is the cause of all other human conflicts, including class conflict. Although her appeal to biology to explain women's oppression has been repeatedly, and convincingly, questioned as too simplistic, Firestone is important because of her insistence that gender oppression deserves as much attention as class oppression.

Although still under examination, the development of the dual systems theory is another important moment for the study of class by Marxist-feminist theorists. This theory explains that gender relations under patriarchy and economic relations under capitalism are separate, but interacting, systems of production. Catharine A. MacKinnon tries to balance class and gender by viewing production (work) and reproduction (sex) as similar activities. Joan Kelly attempts to break free from economic causality within the dual-systems theory, but most critics now agree that she is only partially successful because her work ends up endorsing what it sets out to dispute—economic determinism.

Building upon the work of Marx, and social theorists such as Pierre Machrey and Louis Althusser, in the 1970s and 1980s the analysis of class grew to include the ways that women could read the silences and gaps in their own texts and the ways that society indoctrinates people into certain ways of thinking and behaving. With the aid of psychoanalysis and poststructuralism, most Marxist-feminists now believe that, while important, economics cannot explain every facet of a woman's life or all of the reasons behind gender and class oppression.

Because the issue of class is so complex and intertwined with other social and economic structures, and because of theorists' varying methodologies and objects of studies, an exact definition of class and its specific relation to feminist literary theory remains elusive. Some theorists try to balance the competing claims of gender and class oppression. British materialist feminists, on the other hand, remain committed to a strictly materialist agenda as they try to transform the classic Marxist paradigm in their analysis of gender and class.

Within literary study, some practitioners explore the issue of class by focusing on the class of the reader (Radway), the class of the author (Lauter), or even the class of the material (popular versus elite forms of literature). There are also studies on the relationship of class to a woman's social and gendered identity, and on possible ways class can be reconciled with the competing claims of ethnicity, race, sexual orientation, and age (Spelman). Feminist theorists who focus upon class will continue to critique unjust socioeconomic systems of power while they explain and explore women's differing positions within those systems.

Pam Lieske

References

Althusser, Louis. "Ideology and Ideological State Apparatuses." In *Lenin and Philosophy and Other Essays,* translated by Ben Brewster, 127–186. New York: Monthly Review, 1971.

Daiches, David. "Jane Austen, Karl Marx, and the Aristocratic Dance." *American Scholar* 17 (1948): 289–296.

Firestone, Shulamith. *The Dialectic of Sex.* New York: Bantam, 1970.

Kaplan, Cora. "Pandora's Box: Subjectivity, Class, and Sexuality in Socialist Feminist Criticism." In *Making a Difference: Feminist Literary Criticism,* edited by Gayle Greene and Coppélia Kahn, 146–176. London: Metheun, 1985.

Kelly, Joan. "The Doubled Vision of Feminist Theory: A Postscript to the 'Woman and Power' Conference." *Feminist Studies* 5 (1979): 216–227.

Lauter, Paul. "Working-Class Women's Literature: An Introduction to Study." In *Women in Print: Opportunities for Women's Studies Research in Language and Literature, Vol. I*, edited by Joan Hartman and Ellen Messer-Davidow, 109–134. New York: MLA, 1982.

Machery, Pierre. *A Theory of Literary Production.* London: Routledge and Kegan Paul, 1978.

MacKinnon, Catharine A. "Feminism, Marxism, Method, and the State: An Agenda for Theory." *Signs: Journal of Women in Culture and Society* 7 (1982): 515–544.

Marx, Karl, and Frederick Engels. *Collected Works.* Translated by Richard Dixon and others. 47 vols. New York: International Publishers, 1975–[1995].

Newton, Judith, and Deborah Rosenfelt, eds. *Feminist Criticism and Social Change: Sex, Class and Race in Literature and Criticism.* London: Methuen, 1985.

Radway, Janice. *Reading the Romance: Women, Patriarchy, and Popular Literature.* Chapel Hill: University of North Carolina Press, 1984.

Sargent, Lydia, ed. *Women and Revolution: A Discussion of the Unhappy Marriage of Marxism and Feminism.* Boston: South End, 1981.

Spelman, Elizabeth V. *Inessential Woman: Problems of Exclusion in Feminist Thought.* Boston: Beacon, 1988.

Clément, Catherine

First introduced to English-speaking readers through her essay "Enslaved Enclave," which appeared in Elaine Marks's and Isabelle de Courtivron's *New French Feminisms*, Catherine Clément is best known for *The Newly Born Woman*, co-authored with Hélène Cixous. A pivotal text for American scholars new to French concepts of sexual difference and *écriture féminine*, *The Newly Born Woman* is a dialectical celebration of woman, women's writing, and the body. Clément's contribution, "The Guilty One," examines the figures of the hysteric and the sorceress and meditates on the roles of the mother and the daughter in the Freudian family romance. In "Exchange," the dialogue composing the book's final section, Clément and Cixous clash on whether Dora, the subject of the Freudian case history, is a revolutionary or a victim.

A participant in the seminars of Jacques Lacan, Clément has contributed to French feminism's ongoing interrogation of psychoanalysis in *The Weary Sons of Freud* and *The Lives and Legends of Jacques Lacan*. For Clément, psychoanalysis is an important tool because it recognizes that "men" and "women" are cultural categories that do not preexist the sociolinguistic order in which they are formed. *The Lives and Legends of Jacques Lacan* uses two events—Lacan's dissolution of his Ecole freudienne in 1980 and his death in 1981—to meditate on the mythologies surrounding the influential analyst and to translate the more difficult concepts of his *Écrits* (1977).

In *Opera or the Undoing of Women*, Clément presents a dazzling critique of the heroines in operas by Wagner, Puccini, Verdi, and Mozart. By examining the figure of the diva, and analyzing cultural expectations of her sexuality, temperament, body size, and physical attractiveness, she speculates on why the death of the heroine remains a powerful component of bourgeois romance.

Most recently, in *Syncope: The Philosophy of Rapture*, Clément traces instances of "syncope," or moments of "vanishing" manifest in behaviors such as fainting, swooning, laughing, sexual ecstasy, or epileptic seizure. For Clément, syncope produces "a creative discord" that is useful because it does not try to "control the rhythm of thought, its stops, its hesitations." Syncope has implications for feminism because it recuperates behaviors pathologized via their association with the feminine, such as depression, hysteria, and ecstasy.

Marti Hohmann

References

Clément, Catherine. "Enslaved Enclave." Translated by Marilyn R. Schuster. In *New French Feminisms*, edited by Elaine Marks and Isabelle de Courtivron, 130–136. Amherst: University of Massachusetts Press, 1980.

———. *The Lives and Legends of Jacques Lacan.* Translated by Arthur Goldhammer. New York: Columbia University Press, 1983.

———. *Opera or the Undoing of Women.*

Translated by Betsy Wing. Minneapolis: University of Minnesota Press, 1994.

———. *Syncope: The Philosophy of Rapture.* Translated by Sally O'Driscoll and Deirdre M. Mahoney. Minneapolis: University of Minnesota Press, 1988.

———. *The Weary Sons of Freud.* Translated by Nicole Ball. New York: Verso, 1987.

———, with Hélène Cixous. *The Newly Born Woman.* Translated by Betsy Wing. Minneapolis: University of Minnesota Press, 1986.

Lacan, Jacques. *Écrits.* Translated by Alan Sheridan. New York: W.W. Norton, 1977.

Cliff, Michelle

Jamaican-born novelist, essayist, and poet Michelle Cliff has integrated important but often neglected issues into women's literature and feminist thought. Since the publication of her first book, *Claiming an Identity They Taught Me to Despise*, Cliff's writing has addressed the politics of women's identity in a larger context by connecting gender to race, geographical place, sexuality, class, folklore, history, memory, and especially colonialism. Cliff's unique, nonlinear writing style collapses traditional barriers between genres to combine poetry, prose, folklore, letters, history, and autobiography into a single work.

Born in Jamaica, educated in London, and residing in the United States, Michelle Cliff has existed "between worlds." A light-skinned black woman, she has also been positioned between racial worlds. As a political feminist and out-lesbian, Cliff has been marginalized in both conservative Caribbean cultures and the rigidly defined Western intellectual and literary circles. "I feel that in almost every group I'm an outsider," Cliff remarked in a 1993 interview with Judith Raiskin, "and that's just the way it is, that's just the person I am." Nonetheless, Cliff's writing works to make connections between these worlds.

Cliff's writing is best described as "excavation," "recovery," or "re-vision." In her first two works, *Claiming an Identity They Taught Me to Despise* and *The Land of Look Behind*, Cliff recovers her personal historical past, her own identity and voice as a writer. Cliff's two semiautobiographical novels, *Abeng* and *No Telephone to Heaven,* tell of the light-skinned Jamaican girl Clare Savage who struggles to find an identity through a recovered history of folklore, memory, and tales of slave resistance in her native colonized country. Cliff's short-story collection, *Bodies of Water,* and her latest novel, *Free Enterprise*, an imaginative recovery of the life of African American revolutionary Mary Ellen Pleasant, are both set in the United States and extend the theme of personal and historical "excavation" into new territories.

Although frequently anthologized and analyzed as a Caribbean woman writer, Cliff considers herself more of a "political novelist." Her writing, like her life itself, reflects and struggles with the effects of existing in the "limbo" created by diaspora. In the past decade and a half, however, Cliff has pulled together these conflicting issues of identity, place, race, gender, class, politics, and sexuality to form a significant body of feminist resistance literature.

Anna Creadick

References

Adisa, Opal Palmer. "Journey into Speech—A Writer between Two Worlds: An Interview with Michelle Cliff." *African American Review* 28 (1994): 273–281.

Cliff, Michelle. *Abeng: A Novel.* Trumansburg, N.Y.: Crossing, 1984.

———. *Bodies of Water.* New York: Dutton, 1990.

———. *Claiming an Identity They Taught Me to Despise.* Watertown, Mass.: Persephone, 1981.

———. *Free Enterprise.* New York: Dutton, 1993.

———. *The Land of Look Behind: Prose and Poetry.* Ithaca, N.Y.: Firebrand, 1985.

———. *No Telephone to Heaven.* New York: Vintage Books, 1987.

Cudjoe, Selwyn. *Resistance and Caribbean Literature.* Athens: Ohio University Press, 1980.

———, ed. *Caribbean Women Writers: Essays from the First International Conference.* Wellesley, Mass.: Calaloux, and Amherst: University of Massachusetts Press, 1990.

Dance, Daryl Cumber, ed. *Fifty Caribbean Writers: A Bio-Bibliographical-Critical Sourcebook.* Westport, Conn.: Greenwood, 1986.

de Abruna, Laura Niesen. "Twentieth-century Women Writers from the English-speaking Caribbean." *Modern Fiction Studies* 34 (1988): 85–97.

Lima, Maria Helena. "Revolutionary Developments: Michelle Cliff's 'No Telephone to Heaven' and Merle Collins's 'Angel.'" *ARIEL* 24 (1993): 35–57.

Perera, Suvendrini. "Theories of Periphery, Politics of Place? Locating the Caribbean Fictions of Paule Marshall and Michelle Cliff." *Hecate* 17 (1991): 60–70.

Raiskin, Judith. "The Art of History: An Interview with Michelle Cliff." *Kenyon Review* 15 (1993): 53–71.

Schwartz, Meryl F. "An Interview with Michelle Cliff." *Contemporary Literature* 34 (1993): 594–619.

Clothes

See FASHION

Colonialism

In defining colonialism, one must necessarily articulate its intimate connection to imperialism. If imperialism is a concept that signifies any relationship of dominance and subordination, colonialism is the specific historical form of imperialism that involves direct military, economic, and political control. Before the intervention of feminist theory, theories about colonialism often overlooked the importance of gender necessary in any analysis of a structure based on unequal power, domination, and control. Feminist theorists in the field of history, anthropology, sociology, and literature have focused on the construction and manifestation of colonialism as a raced and gendered discourse perpetuating and reinforcing the racial and gender hierarchies of a patriarchal hegemony.

The term "colonialism," as it is currently used in literary scholarship, is not always associated with the condition of a subject people under the yoke of a foreign government. For example, for Marxists, colonialism expresses the changing character of the hegemony exercised by the capitalist West over the rest of the world. Marxist usage of "colonialism," however, fails to highlight the complex interplay of the dynamics of race, sex, and gender always imbricated in colonialism. However, even male critics such as Patrick Brantlinger, who in *Rule of Darkness: British Literature and Imperialism, 1830–1914* pointed out the erasure of racism in Marxist analyses of colonialism, fail to critically engage with colonialism, as a gendered discourse. A feminist focus has greatly challenged and altered general theories of colonialism, opened up important areas of exploration, such as the analyses of the complex roles played by white women in colonial history, and provided critical examinations of the literary representation of colonialism as a geography of rape in which the colonized space and its male inhabitants are repeatedly feminized. In the 1950s and 1960s Frantz Fanon, Albert Memmi, O. Manoni, and Aime Cesaire brilliantly analyzed the psychological dynamics of racism under colonialism. The 1978 publication of Edward Said's *Orientalism*, a study of the intimate connections between Orientalist scholarship and imperial policies, cogently argued that the desire for domination cannot be separated from the will to sexualize the dominated. In fact, though Said is not a feminist theorist per se, his analysis of the discourse of orientalism highlighted the epistemological urgency behind the desire to contain the cultural, geographical, and temporal difference of the Orient in "metaphors of depth, secrecy, and sexual promise: phrases like the 'veils of an Eastern bride' or 'the inscrutable Orient' passed into common language." *Orientalism* is now a standard book necessary for any in-depth study of the discourse of colonialism. Benita Parry's "Problems in Current Theories of Colonial Discourse," which critiques the works of Edward Said, Gayatri Spivak, Homi Bhabha, and Abdul Jan Mohammed, is the first essay to offer a systematic examination of the current trends in colonial discourse analysis.

Since Great Britain controlled the largest, most diverse Western Empire for more than seventy-five years, there is an immense body of criticism revolving around British policies, British literary representations of colonizer and colonized, and the various movements for independence in both conquered and settled colonies. In the last decade, the Subaltern Studies Group, intellectuals in India, Britain, and Australia, have, in their reevaluation of South Asian history, shifted the focus from the middle class to an examination of the contribution of peasant and other subaltern classes. Gayatri Chakravorty Spivak, a feminist-Marxist-deconstructionist critic of colonial and neocolonial discourses, sees in the work of the group a critique of Western humanism because they politicize the universal subject of history by reminding us of his collusion with imperialism. In one of her most famous formulations in *In Other Worlds*, Spivak terms the collective's restoration of the subaltern subject of history a "strategic use of positive essentialism." The collective is careful about recording how both men and women participate in rebellions. However, as Spivak points out in her ground-breaking essay "Can the Subaltern Speak?" the Subaltern Studies group produces a model of agency that cannot accommodate the sexed subaltern. Spivak argues that even as the group highlights the absence of peasant voices in elite historiography, it simultaneously manifests male indifference to sexual difference. The collective repeatedly ignores the erasure of female subaltern voices that results from a reduction of woman's subject position to one based solely on caste or class.

Emphasizing the complexities of women's exploitation under patriarchy and colonialism, Malek Alloula's *The Colonial Harem* analyzed the harem as a site of colonial pornography where the patriarchal gaze is at its harshest. In a different context, a special issue of the journal *Inscriptions* published a set of papers that questioned and critiqued the intersection of feminism and colonial discourses in a number of areas such as ethnography, literature, and Western feminist scholarship. Three very recent works continue to engage with gender issues in their examination of colonial and imperial discourses. A collection of essays edited by Kumkum Sangari and Sudesh Vaid titled *Recasting Women: Essays in Indian Colonial History* focuses "primarily on the regulation and reproduction of patriarchy in the different class-caste formations within [Indian] civil society." Mary Louise Pratt's *Imperial Eyes* offers a critique of travel writing as one of the ideological apparatuses of empire by focusing on nineteenth-century British and Latin American literature. In *Western Women and Imperialism: Complicity and Resistance* the essays focus on the complex involvement of Western women during an imperialist era "who used the . . . power of race and class to negotiate their own agenda within the colonial scene." Jenny Sharpe's recent book *Allegories of Empire: The Figure of Woman in the Colonial Text* addresses the complex and taboo subject of the rape of the white woman by the colored man. Sharpe analyzes various aspects of colonial discourse and the representations of the Sepoy Mutiny in British fiction. She demonstrates how the idea of Indian men raping colonial white women has implications for an understanding of contemporary theories of female agency.

I have outlined in very broad strokes some of the major contributions to the study of colonialism. Current literary scholarship in this field promises to provide needed work on the intersections of race, gender, and sexuality in the examination of colonialism in the Caribbean, Australia, Africa, the Indian subcontinent, and other parts of Asia. The current emphasis on postcolonial scholarship has helped produce a number of interesting works on the various aspects of postcolonial discourse. However, recent debates on the legitimacy of the term "postcolonial" suggest the importance of the critical examination of the various forms of colonialism to prevent an easy recuperation of all previously colonized spaces under a monolithic rubric.

Sangeeta Ray

References

Alloula, Malek. *The Colonial Harem*. Minneapolis: University of Minnesota Press, 1986.

Brantlinger, Patrick. *Rule of Darkness: British Literature and Imperialism, 1830–1914*. Ithaca, N.Y.: Cornell University Press, 1988.

Cesaire, Aime. *Discourse on Colonialism*. Translated by Joan Pinkham. New York: Monthly Review, 1972.

Chaudhuri, Nupur, and Margaret Strobel, eds. *Western Women and Imperialism: Complicity and Resistance*. Bloomington: Indiana University Press, 1992.

Fanon, Frantz. *Black Skin, White Masks: The Experiences of a Black Man in a White World*. Translated by Charles Lam Markmann. New York: Grove, 1967.

Inscriptions. Nos. 3/4 (1988).

Manoni, O. *Prospero and Caliban: The Psychology of Colonization*. New York: Praeger, 1964.

Memmi, Albert. *The Colonizer and the Colonized*. Translated by Howard Greenfield. Boston: Beacon, 1967.

Parry, Benita. "Problems in Current Theories of Colonial Discourse." *Oxford Literary Review* 9 (1987): 27–57.

Pratt, Mary Louise. *Imperial Eyes: Travel Writing and Transculturation*. New York: Routledge, 1992.

Said, Edward. *Orientalism*. New York: Vintage, 1979.

Sangari, Kumkum, and Sudesh Vaid, eds. *Recasting Women: Essays in Indian Colo-*

C

nial History. New Brunswick, N.J.:
Rutgers University Press, 1990.

Sharpe, Jenny. *Allegories of Empire: The Figure of Woman in the Colonial Text*. Minneapolis: University of Minnesota Press, 1993.

Spivak, Gayatri Chakravorty. "Can the Subaltern Speak?" In *Marxism and the Interpretation of Culture*, edited by Cary Nelson and Lawrence Grossberg, 271–313. Urbana: University of Illinois Press, 1988.

———. *In Other Worlds*. New York: Methuen, 1987.

References

Fanon, Frantz. *Black Skin White Masks* [1952]. New York: Grove, 1967.

Mohanty, Chandra T., et al., eds. *Third World Women and the Politics of Feminism*. Bloomington: Indiana University Press, 1991.

Spivak, Gayatri C. *In Other Worlds*. New York: Methuen, 1987.

Trinh, T. Minh-ha. *Woman, Native, Other: Writing Postcoloniality and Feminism*. Bloomington: Indiana University Press, 1989.

Colonization

Colonization refers not only to the act of being colonized but equally to the act of colonizing. The term encompasses the intricate connections existing in a power relationship between two sets of people—the colonizers and the colonized. Feminist theory has intervened in the analysis of the discourse of colonialism to examine the ways in which feminine and feminized images are incessantly used by the colonizers to justify their ravaging of foreign lands and to establish their inherently masculine superiority over other races. Feminist theory has also underscored how women are doubly marginalized and oppressed under colonialism.

The term "colonization" is also used by certain feminists in a metaphorical sense to depict their alienated and oppressed position in a patriarchal society. Both black and white feminists point out the political domination of women by men and underline the common experiences of oppression and repression that women share with colonized races and peoples. Like the latter, women too have been forced to articulate their experiences in the language of their oppressors. Women, like indigenous people under a foreign yoke, have had to construct a language of their own against the patriarchal language imposed on them by their colonizers—men. Black feminists and writers, even as they use the analogy, are careful to distinguish their double marginalization based on their gender and race. They insist that we pay close attention to the complicity of indigenous men with the colonizers in their desire to maintain the general status quo in a fundamentally patriarchal social system. Thus the intersection of theories of colonialism and feminist theory has proved mutually beneficial.

Sangeeta Ray

Comedy

Because of its wide range of applications—for example, to designate one half of human experience (tragedy, the other half)—comedy defies precise definition. Although some critics maintain that only dramatic works may be referred to as comedies, most feminist theories of comedy interpret the term "comedy" in its broadest sense as referring to a work written in a comic mode or to comic aspects within a particular work. (Along these lines, comedy is generally, but not always, taken to encompass the more specific term "humor.") By challenging the formal limitations of traditional theories of comedy and adopting an expansive view of comedy, critics have been able to discover and identify specifically feminist comic modes and to reclaim as comic many works by women that do not fit easily into traditional systems of classification.

Feminist comic theorists argue that previous theories of comedy have overlooked women's comic writing precisely because their definitions have been narrowly focused on what patriarchal males find funny or self-affirming. Theories of comedy that accept male domination as a given have emphasized conservative aspects of comedy, such as marriage or reunion as a unifying device. At most, they have but noted comedy's potential for disrupting the status quo. Feminist theories of comedy, by contrast, focus directly on the gender politics of comedy and investigate how comic strategies can question and destabilize patriarchal authority.

From the outset, feminist comic theory has had to grapple with a longstanding bias against women's comedy—the myth that women have no sense of humor. The notion that feminists are particularly humorless has raised additional stumbling blocks, obstacles that Nancy Walker sought to overcome in a 1981 essay entitled "Do Feminists Ever Laugh?: Women's Humor and Women's Rights." Pointing to the existence of feminist traditions of comedy, Walker and others have attributed the denial of women's sense of humor and the invisibility of women's comic efforts to the subversive nature and potential rebelliousness of comedy by women.

The earliest collection of critical essays on women and comedy, assembled in *Regionalism and the Female Imagination* in 1978, began to explore comic subversions in women's writing. This special issue on "Female Humor" includes landmark essays by Judy Little ("Satirizing the Norm: Comedy in Women's Fiction") and Gloria Kaufman ("Feminist Humor as a Survival Device"), as well as pieces by critics Zita Zatkin Dresner and Emily Toth, who have continued to map out the field of women's humor studies. Some common themes emerge from the *Regionalism and the Female Imagination* essays: first, that women's comedy can be an important form of resistance to patriarchal oppression; second, that women's comedy tends to operate covertly and to appeal to a female community with shared feminist values; and third, that in order to understand women's comedy we must attend to the social contexts in which it is produced.

Feminist comic theory initially worked to disprove the myth of female humorlessness and to set in motion the task of recovering comic works by women. In the 1980s, critics looked more closely at power dynamics and the historical contexts for women's comedy. The first systematic study of women's comedy, Judy Little's 1983 *Comedy and the Woman Writer: Woolf, Spark, and Feminism*, contends that whereas traditional comedy reverses the status quo only to reestablish order in the end, feminist comedy mocks the basic assumptions of a patriarchal worldview and denies the reestablishment of order. Because evaluations of order and disorder depend so much upon perspective, a main premise of feminist theories of comedy is that comedy cannot be adequately studied from a universalist position.

The most recent criticism recognizes that not just gender, but also race, class, sexual preference, and other factors affect the production and appreciation of comedy. While a central focus of feminist comic theory continues to be the resistance to patriarchy in women's comedy, an awareness of the connection between sexism

and other forms of oppression has implications for the study of comedy's liberatory potential. Two collections of essays—*Women's Comic Visions*, edited by June Sochen and *New Perspectives on Women and Comedy* edited by Regina Barreca—reflect the diversity of approaches possible within a feminist framework of comic theory: selections draw upon the methodologies of cultural studies, dialogic criticism, and gay studies, among others.

The study of comedy engages pivotal issues in feminist thought, for if comedy can be an empowering tool in the hands of the oppressed, it can also serve the ends of the dominant power structure by unifying group interests and mocking outsiders. Women have traditionally been the butts of patriarchal comedy; the history of a countertradition of feminist resistance comedy has yet to be fully recorded. A clearer understanding of comedy's ability to manipulate insider/outsider tensions is thus essential to the wider aims of feminist theory. By coming to terms with the workings of comedy in literature, feminist theory can offer greater insights into the persistence of patriarchy and might even provide a means of ensuring its end.

Audrey Bilger

References

Barreca, Regina. *They Used to Call Me Snow White . . . But I Drifted: Women's Strategic Use of Humor.* New York: Viking, 1991.

——, ed. *Last Laughs: Perspectives on Women and Comedy.* New York: Gordon and Breach, 1988.

——, ed. *New Perspectives on Women and Comedy.* New York: Gordon and Breach, 1992.

Carlson, Susan. *Women and Comedy: Rewriting the British Theatrical Tradition.* Ann Arbor: University of Michigan Press, 1991.

Little, Judy. *Comedy and the Woman Writer: Woolf, Spark, and Feminism.* Lincoln: University of Nebraska Press, 1983.

Mellencamp, Patricia. *High Anxiety: Catastrophe, Scandal, Age, and Comedy.* Bloomington and Indianapolis: Indiana University Press, 1992.

Regionalism and the Female Imagination 2–3 (1977–1978).

Sochen, June, ed. *Women's Comic Visions.* Detroit: Wayne State University Press, 1991.

C

Walker, Nancy. "Do Feminists Ever Laugh?: Women's Humor and Women's Rights." *International Journal of Women's Studies* 4 (1981): 1–9.

———. *A Very Serious Thing: Women's Humor and American Culture.* Minneapolis: University of Minnesota Press, 1988.

Wilt, Judith. "The Laughter of Maidens, the Cackle of Matriarchs: Notes on the Collision between Comedy and Feminism." In *Gender and Literary Voice*, edited by Janet Todd, 173–196. New York: Holmes and Meier, 1980.

Coming Out

"Coming out" is a term used by lesbians, gay men, and bisexuals to denote various processes or aspects of the development of their sexual identities or of making those identities known to others. The term is related to the metaphor of being "in the closet," that is, of hiding one's sexual identity from others and in some cases even oneself. Coming out of the closet means variously to acknowledge one's sexual identity to oneself; to claim as positive a label such as lesbian, dyke, gay, queer, homosexual, or bisexual; to enter a lesbian, gay, or bisexual relationship or community; to declare one's sexual identity to one's friends, family, co-workers, neighbors, or society at large. Integral to the process is what Penelope and Wolfe call "self-naming," confronting the dominant culture's negative definition of "lesbian" or "gay" or "bisexual" and then coming to define oneself on one's own terms.

The idea and the process of coming out require a culture in which the concept of sexual identity exists. Historians of sexuality in Western culture, for example, emphasize that the concepts of sexual identity, homosexuality, and heterosexuality did not exist prior to the latter half of the nineteenth century. Before the work of sexologists and psychoanalysts such as Havelock Ellis, Karl Ulrich, and Sigmund Freud was popularized, people thought in terms of sexual behaviors that were affirmed or stigmatized, but did not generally experience sexuality as a part of their self-identities. Various cultures may or may not have a social category for those who choose lovers from their own sex; therefore, coming out or some similar process may or may not be culturally relevant. Coming out as a homosexual phenomenon is also dependent on the assumption of one particular sexual identity (heterosexual) as normative and others as deviant, as Adrienne Rich has argued. Some lesbians hold that a true sexual revolution will have occurred when heterosexuals as well as homosexuals or bisexuals have to come out, when sexual development and identity are not assumed to be heterosexual.

Feminist literary critics such as Julia Penelope, Susan Wolfe, and Bonnie Zimmerman have recently named and started to delineate the history and characteristics of the genres of the coming out story and the coming out novel. Paying attention to these forms can tell us important truths about the patterns of female development in patriarchal culture and about the power of women writers both to adapt old forms such as the *bildungsroman* and to fashion new possibilities through language and story.

Diana L. Swanson

References

Maggiore, Dolores J. *Lesbianism: An Annotated Bibliography and Guide to the Literature, 1976–1991.* Metuchen, N.J.: Scarecrow, 1992.

Penelope, Julia, and Susan Wolfe. *The Original Coming Out Stories* [1980]. Freedom, Calif.: Crossing, 1989.

Rich, Adrienne. "Compulsory Heterosexuality and Lesbian Existence" [1980]. In *Blood, Bread, and Poetry: Selected Prose: 1979–1985*, 23–75. New York: W.W. Norton, 1986.

Sophie, Joan. "A Critical Examination of Stage Theories of Lesbian Identity Development." *Journal of Homosexuality* 12 (1986): 39–51.

Zimmerman, Bonnie. "Exiting from Patriarchy: The Lesbian Novel of Development." In *The Voyage In: Fictions of Female Development*, edited by Elizabeth Abel, Marianne Hirsch, and Elizabeth Langland, 244–257. Hanover, N.H.: University Press of New England for Dartmouth College, 1983.

Community

This term remains multivalent for feminism. It has three significant meanings today: (1) a "naturally–formed" body of people bound by common geography or ethnicity—such as New Yorkers; (2) a created body of people, organized by political or self-identified interests—such as lesbian feminists; and (3) an often utopic goal based on political consensus and inclusiveness. In the nineteenth century, notions of community shifted from emphasizing more tangible attributes like genealogy, locality, and custom, to stressing elements such as affective ties that might exist apart from fixed geographical or social bounds. That is, as Suzanne Graver argues, it moved from an understanding of community as a fact to community as a value.

Historically, the "community" has been used as a term that either excluded or censored women. In the Middle Ages, the second most common meaning was " the third estate of the commonwealth" (as opposed to the nobility or clergy); this points to the basic tripartite understanding of medieval society that leaves out women (who are sometimes relegated to a fourth class). Similarly, in the early seventeenth century, "community," as recorded in the *Oxford English Dictionary*, could also mean "a common prostitute." This meaning is of interest to modern feminism for its counterintuitive censoring of a type of woman. Today, within a political climate of backlash against feminism, "community" is used not just by feminists, but by antifeminists as well.

Many feminists value community and have it as a goal in a variety of guises. Indeed, some feminist organizations make decisions by consensus, thereby emphasizing group coherence. Similarly, liberal feminism often argues for a pluralism that strives for inclusivity. Radical feminism, in contrast, often advocates separatist women's communities—temporary or permanent—while the common trope of support groups attempts to create communal spaces that are "women-friendly." Finally, a strong thread of feminist writing concerns utopian feminist or women-only communities, from *Herland* to "The Laugh of the Medusa."

These forms of community share two items. First, they emphasize the community over the individual; this is in direct opposition to the dominant culture's "rule of individualism." Second, they simultaneously include and exclude, by virtue of the very act of defining communities; groups that operate by inclusion are at the same time defined by their exclusion of non-community.

A current related debate centers around the multiple communities—signified by multiple identities including various ethnicities, nationalities, and sexualities—that provide intersecting and sometimes conflicting bases for feminism. Gloria Anzaldúa's and Cherríe Moraga's work on *la communidad* has been important in this debate; they note that feminists of multiple identities—such as lesbian feminists with Anglo mothers and Latino fathers—are themselves at once within and without communities.

The multiple meanings of "community" and its attendant debates makes it an appealing yet problematic word. As well, they point to the common divisions between academic feminism and activism. Feminist literary theory and practice must answer the question: if community is not a natural phenomenon, but rather an actively organized entity, what propels its existence?

Nina Manasan Greenberg

References

Anzaldúa, Gloria. *Borderlands/La Frontera: The New Mestiza*. San Francisco: Spinsters/Aunt Lute, 1987.

———— and Cherríe Moraga, eds. *This Bridge Called My Back; Writings by Radical Women of Color*. Watertown, Mass.: Persephone, 1981. 2nd ed. New York: Kitchen Table: Women of Color Press, 1983.

Bennett, Judith, Elizabeth A. Clark, and Sarah Westphal-Wihl, eds. "Working Together in the Middle Ages: Perspectives on Women's Communities." *Signs* 12 (Special Issue, Winter 1989).

Graver, Suzanne. *George Eliot and Community: A Study in Social Theory and Fictional Form*. Berkeley: University of California Press, 1984.

Mellor, Anne K. "On Feminist Utopias." *Women's Studies* 9 (1982): 241–262.

Rooney, Ellen. *Seductive Reasoning; Pluralism as the Problematic of Contemporary Literary Theory*. Ithaca, N.Y.: Cornell University Press, 1989.

Shahar, Shulamith. *The Fourth Estate: A History of Women in the Middle Ages*. London: Routledge, 1983.

Compulsory Heterosexuality

"Compulsory heterosexuality" challenges the assumption that heterosexuality is the most innate or inherently satisfying sexual orientation; rather, sexual identity, desire, and practices are understood to be constructed by different forces and institutions in order to fulfill patriarchal social and political agendas. This concept be-

C

came widely known with the publication of Adrienne Rich's essay "Compulsory Heterosexuality and Lesbian Existence" in 1980. Rich argued that heterosexuality should be viewed as a "political institution" that keeps women from forming close bonds with each other by making them dependent upon and subservient to patriarchal power.

Rich analyzes the complex mechanisms by which heterosexuality becomes institutionalized by briefly summarizing some of the ways women's sexuality is constructed and regulated, from overt patterns of bodily harm to more subtle influences on women's consciousness. For instance, patriarchal control over women's sexuality is enforced through physically violent acts such as rape, wife beating, and incest, through an economic system that denies women equal status and dependence, and through representations of female sexuality in literature, popular culture, and pornography. At the same time, any alternative to heterosexual desire, such as lesbianism or other woman-identified relationships, is denigrated, punished, and erased from history.

Rich's criticism of contemporary feminist theorists for continuing this heterocentric bias spurred useful debate and challenged the heterocentric bias within some feminist thinking. Looking at gender and sexuality as socially constructed, in order to maintain the unequal power relationship between women and men, has been an important perspective in feminist and gender studies.

Lorna J. Smedman

References

Ferguson, Ann, Jacquelyn N. Zita, and Kathryn Pyre Addelson. "On 'Compulsory Heterosexuality and Lesbian Existence': Defining the Issues." *Signs: Journal of Women in Culture and Society* 7 (1981): 158–199.

Rich, Adrienne. "Compulsory Heterosexuality and Lesbian Existence." In *Blood, Bread, and Poetry*. New York, London: W.W. Norton, 1986.

Consumption

Narrowly conceptualized, the act of consumption involves an individual's purchase of a product. Feminist analyses of consumption study a wide range of topics—not just the marketing and buying of commodities, but also style, de-sire, the nature of choice, and the unpredictable ways in which commodities are endowed with new meanings via their active incorporation in people's lives—but they invariably begin by acknowledging that in a commercial society like that of the United States, where 85 percent of the clientele at malls is female, shopping is rarely imaged as the act of a gender-neutral individual. Charged with the major part of the labor of buying, constantly solicited by advertisers and retailers, women encounter in the marketplace a prime site for the reproduction of the inequities of a male-dominated society. Many feminist scholars study consumer practices and their representation in literature in order to reveal the profits that accrue to patriarchy and capitalism when women exercise their spending power. Since the 1980s, however, some scholars have become uncomfortable with the straightforward equation of consumerism and oppression: insisting that the implications of any particular consumer practice must be judged according to its historical context, they have begun to locate weak points in the fortress of consumer capitalism.

In *The Feminine Mystique* (1963), Betty Friedan offered the first sustained critique of the costs of women's consuming pleasures, contending that, manipulated by advertising and mass-circulation magazines, American women had lost the freedom won by the preceding generation of feminists. Friedan's account of the propagation of a false feminine consciousness was shaped by the pessimistic view of mass culture developed after the Second World War: as Mica Nava has argued, this influence may have been a liability. Marxist critics like Theodor Adorno (1947) and Herbert Marcuse (1963) sought to explain the political pacification of the working class in this period by showing how mass culture operated as "deception." Mass culture sold people the idea that they were free because they could freely choose among commodity-styles.

Feminist scholars of consumption have since borrowed the notion of "alienation" from that Marxist tradition—the notion that, within the capitalist market, where products are valued not according to their usefulness but according to their exchange value—workers do not experience their productive labor as an instance of self-expression, but as a loss of self. This dispossession is a motivating condition for consumer spending: we see in the commodity a means to our self-completion. As advertisers' appropriation of feminist themes suggests, consumer capitalism operates by channeling our social dissatisfaction into the desire for commodities. This means, then, that the commodity necessarily retains "utopian" traces of our desire for nonalienated social relations. The frantic pace of transformation in the fashion industry can thus be read in a "dialectical" manner—not just as guaranteeing a high rate of product obsolescence, but also as concealing the wish for social change despite social stasis.

However, the study of consumption has also been a site where feminists have discussed not only what should be preserved from the Marxist tradition but also what should be discarded. This sorting process has transpired in part as feminists have noted how, although the commodity seducing workers is described as a "prostitute" who "emasculates" her clients, real women are absent from Marxist analyses. Indeed, the imaginary femininity Marxism has invoked to devalue consumption has diverted critical attention from the historical processes positioning women as the preeminent consumers in consumer society. The woman in the mall is not so much enjoying "free time" and escaping from "real" problems; she is undertaking an obligation—(unsalaried) work that is as crucial to social reproduction as men's "productive" wage labor. Mass imagery has long cast susceptibility to the lures of commercial society as a stereotypically feminine trait, ridiculing women as passive slaves of fashion. Ironically, then, early feminist analyses like Friedan's actually confirmed that misogynist view of women's capacities by presenting the market as all too successful at persuading women to invest in an oppressive definition of femininity.

Alternatives to this view of the consumer as dupe give pleasure an edge by linking it to resistance. Since the 1980s, Foucauldian feminists and feminists in cultural studies have sought a more flexible model of oppression, one allowing for how protest can be found in, as Jane Gaines puts it, "the very practices which seem to most graphically implement . . . the patriarchal wish." Thus historians have noted how the department stores established in the 1840s were places where middle-class women could enjoy a public mobility previously denied them. Feminist theorists interested in the politics of style have argued that consumers are able to repossess and recode commodities in ways that make the very accouterments of fashionable femininity into instruments of subversion.

Thus, when African American women in the 1940s responded to mass culture's advocacy of a whitened appearance by sporting wigs in pointedly artificial colors, they were not buying into white femininity, but showing aesthetic convention to be just that—convention. In a kind of semiotic guerrilla warfare, they were using commodities as the raw material for new sorts of meanings.

Literary scholars unpack paradoxes of this kind while considering other topics, such as, the way that gendered binarisms like that of producer/consumer contribute to the notional separation of literature from commercial entertainment, or the way that, in the eighteenth and nineteenth centuries especially, woman author's entry into the literary marketplace as a producer rather than a consumer puts her in a position where at the same time that she menaced the doctrine of the separate spheres, she also risked being reduced to an object rather than a subject of exchange. The woman writer often found that women could sell themselves more easily than their products—much as the woman shopper continues to find that her purchase of clothing or cosmetics will be viewed (in implicitly misogynist and heterosexist terms) not as an exercise of agency, but as an attempt to render herself a more attractive commodity-object for masculine consumption. As Christina Rossetti's *Goblin Market* [1861] suggests, the examination of the female shopper's ambivalent relation to the market's public space—and of her occult resemblance to the prostitute—can double as an examination of the woman writer's uneasy position as producer and commodity at once.

Deidre Lynch

References

Abelson, Elaine S. *When Ladies Go A-Thieving: Middle-Class Shoplifters in the Victorian Department Store*. New York: Oxford University Press, 1989.

Bowlby, Rachel. *Just Looking: Consumer Culture in Dreiser, Gissing, and Zola*. New York: Methuen, 1985.

Clark, Danae. "Commodity Lesbianism." *Camera Obscura* 25–26 (1991): 180–201.

Gaines, Jane, and Charlotte Herzog, eds. *Fabrications: Costume and the Female Body*. New York: Routledge, 1990.

Helsinger, Elizabeth K. "Consumer Power and the Utopia of Desire: Christina

Rossetti's 'Goblin Market.'" *ELH* 58 (1991): 903–933.

Morris, Meaghan. "Things to Do with Shopping Centres." In *Grafts: Feminist Cultural Criticism*, edited by Susan Sheridan, 193–225. London: Verso, 1988.

Nava, Mica. "Consumerism and Its Contradictions." *Cultural Studies* 1 (1987): 204–210.

Newman, Karen. "City Talk: Women and Commodification." *ELH* 56 (1989): 503–518.

Spigel, Lynn, and Denise Mann. "Women and Consumer Culture: A Selective Bibliography." *Quarterly Review of Film and Video* 11 (1989): 85–105.

Williamson, Judith. *Consuming Passions: The Dynamics of Popular Culture*. London: Marion Boyars, 1986.

Willis, Susan. "I Shop Therefore I Am: Is There a Place for Afro-American Culture in Commodity Culture?" In *Changing Our Own Words: Essays on Criticism, Theory, and Writing by Black Women*, edited by Cheryl A. Wall, 173–195. New Brunswick, N.J.: Rutgers University Press, 1989.

Costume

Like many art media, theater has traditionally been gendered. Playwrighting, directing, managing, and dramaturgy have been traditionally male, costuming traditionally female. And like many traditionally female arts, costume has been largely overlooked for serious study, though recently some museums have begun to exhibit costume and couture collections. Feminist critics, though, have done valuable work on the history of costume in the theater (for example, the ways in which different cultures and periods have envisioned and "made up" Medea, Cleopatra, Juliet, and so on) and in the fashion world. Costume offers a rich and little-mined field for reading a culture's fashioning of gender roles and gender anxieties.

"Costume" has also been used extensively as a trope within feminist criticism. Often used in common parlance as a metaphor for falsity in opposition to a "true," ontologically prior identity underneath the false disguise, costume (like "performance" and "theatricality") has increasingly been thought of as a strategic pose and even as that which precedes and consti-

tutes whatever "reality" exists "underneath" the costume. "Transvestism" has been a particularly fraught trope. Women who tried to "pass" as men (for example, female authors who used a male pseudonym) were, in early feminist criticism, regretted as not being "true" to their womanhood. In the early 1980s, the terms "academic Tootsie" (Waller) or "critical cross-dressing" (Showalter) were used by some feminists to cast suspicion on men in feminism. By the late 1980s, the negative connotations of transvestism as an attempt to "pass" gave way to more positive connotations of the subversive mimicry of the dominant culture's sex and gender codes. "Transvestism" became a positive form of gender parody, and "butch-femme aesthetic" a major sign of the subversion of heterosexism and of other traditionally codified gender structures.

Deborah Thompson

References
Butler, Judith. *Gender Trouble: Feminism and the Subversion of Identity*. New York: Routledge, 1990.

———. "Gender Trouble, Feminist Theory, and Psychoanalytic Discourse." In *Feminism/Postmodernism*, edited by Linda J. Nicholson, 324–339. New York: Routledge, 1990.

———. "Performative Acts and Gender Constitution: An Essay in Phenomenology and Feminist Theory." In *Performing Feminism: Feminist Critical Theory and Theatre*, edited by Sue-Ellen Case, 270–282. Baltimore: Johns Hopkins University Press, 1990.

Case, Sue-Ellen. *Feminism and Theatre*. New York: Macmillan, 1988.

Gilbert, Sandra M. "Costumes of the Mind: Transvestism as Metaphor in Modern Literature." In *Writing and Sexual Difference*, edited by Elizabeth Abel, 193–220. Chicago: University of Chicago Press, 1982.

Showalter, Elaine. "Critical Cross-Dressing." In *Men in Feminism*, edited by Alice Jardine and Paul Smith, 116–132. New York: Methuen, 1987.

Waller, Marguerite. "Academic Tootsie: The Denial of Difference and the Difference It Makes." *Diacritics*, Spring (1987): 2–20.

Cott, Nancy F.

Cott has played a key role in rewriting U.S. history so as to reflect the coming to consciousness of women and the impact of this consciousness on the world around them. In *The Bonds of Womanhood: "Woman's Sphere" in New England, 1780–1835*, Cott examined the diaries and other writings of one hundred women in order to determine why the "cult" of domesticity appeared. She found that, although domestic ideology might seem the opposite of feminism insofar as it relegated women to the home, this "cult" was instrumental in gaining advances for women and in spurring the growth of feminism. The concept of "womanhood" and its source in women's supposedly inherent domestic expertise replaced the idea that women were "inferior" with the idea that they were simply "different." And because women could see themselves as a group classed by sex, they took the first necessary step in protesting their sexual fate. But Cott also emphasized that woman's sphere or domesticity led to problems as well. For as the concept opened up certain paths for women, it closed others down, namely roles in the public sphere. Hence Cott's title, taken from nineteenth-century reformer Sarah Grimké, refers both to the bonds that tie women together and those bonds that tie women down. Cott's work here aided literary critics in their reconsideration of literary texts by women writers, most notably their reevaluation of the political efficacy of domestic and sentimental novels.

In *The Grounding of Modern Feminism*, Cott traced the significance of the appearance of the word "feminism" in the 1910s. Whereas scholars had previously argued that feminism died out in the 1920s once suffrage for women was won, Cott found that the 1910s and 1920s mark the end of the woman movement and the beginning of a specifically modern agenda. According to this agenda, "individuality and heterogeneity among women" would be upheld while at the same time "holding these in abeyance by acting in sex solidarity."

Cott's scholarly articles include an investigation of eighteenth-century family life and an investigation of Victorian sexual ideology from 1790 to 1850, in which she disproved the traditional scholarly belief that men forced women to be passionless for their own ends.

As editor and co-editor of various anthologies, Cott has also been instrumental in making both primary source material and feminist scholarship readily available. Most notably, *A Heritage of Her Own: Toward a New Social History of American Women* collects texts of feminist social history from the 1970s, the first decade in which there was a significant increase in the amount of work done on women's history. Cott's work has provided a new and far more accurate context than had heretofore been available in which to situate literary texts by women writers.

Elise Lemire

References
Cott, Nancy F. *The Bonds of Womanhood: "Woman's Sphere" in New England, 1780–1835*. New Haven: Yale University Press, 1977.

———. "Eighteenth-Century Family and Social Life Revealed in Massachusetts Divorce Records." *Journal of Social History* 10 (1976): 20–43.

———. *The Grounding of Modern Feminism*. New Haven: Yale University Press, 1987.

———. "Passionless: An Interpretation of Victorian Sexual Ideology, 1790–1850." *Signs* 4 (1978): 219–236.

———, ed. *Root of Bitterness: Documents of the Social History of American Women*. New York: Dutton, 1972.

———, ed. *A Woman Making History: Mary Ritter Beard through Her Letters*. New Haven: Yale University Press, 1991.

———, and Elizabeth H. Pleck, eds. *A Heritage of Her Own: Toward a New Social History of American Women*. New York: Simon and Schuster, 1979.

Courtship

The *Oxford English Dictionary* traces the evolution of the word from its origins in the Renaissance court, when it meant the "behaviour or action befitting a court or courtier; courtliness of manners" or the "practice of the arts of a courtier," such as diplomacy or flattery, to the more current association of the word with "the action or process of paying court to a woman with a view to marriage; courting, wooing" and "the action of courting, soliciting, or enticing; endeavour to win over or gain." This definition raises an important question, which is essential for feminist critique of courtship ritual: why should the word for the flattering or solicitous behavior of Renaissance courtiers "gradually become assimilated into the language where it would be gentrified, or legitimized, by the bourgeois institution of marriage?"

In the fifteenth and sixteenth centuries, the term courtship was still strongly associated with the residence at court and the state "befitting a courtier." Around the 1570s, the political connotations became linked to the amorous ones—this is particularly significant because this was the period of Elizabeth I's reign, and her manipulation of courtship ritual for political ends made her a powerful ruler. Catherine Bates describes courtship in this period as having connotations of "predatory" or "opportunistic" behavior and embodying a "language of persuasion," but also under certain circumstances, expressing genuine admiration.

Elizabethan courtship rituals objectified young women, who frequently were described as their future husband's "chattel," or no better than property. Legally, women were defined in relation to the men in their lives, either as wives, widows, or daughters, and theologically, they are described as "the weaker vessel," a term Antonia Fraser describes as meaning morally, intellectually, and physically inferior. Thus, up through the seventeenth century, courtship rituals most frequently consisted of negotiations between parents, arranged marriages rather than companionate ones. Diane Dreher traces depictions of rebellious daughters in Shakespeare's plays and notes that in most cases, such as that of Juliet and Desdemona, disobedience to the patriarch's will ends in tragedy. However, in some of the plays, women (like Rosalind) successfully transgress the passive role assigned to them by society and become their own marriage brokers.

Rosalind prefigures the changes in courtship ritual that began in the seventeenth century. Lawrence Stone's 1977 monumental study of early English courtship claims that around the mid seventeenth century, a shift began from marriages of convenience to marriages that involved more affectionate relationships between spouses. Most historians attribute this shift to the Puritan influence, which gave women more freedom of speech and movement than their sixteenth-century predecessors.

Although the practice of arranged marriages had not died out completely by the eighteenth century, Ruth Yeazell argues that we can see a movement toward more involvement of women in their courtship rituals. Katherine Green specifically identifies the period between 1740 and 1820 as one in which the "heroine-centered courtship novels" flourished. These novels, which were frequently written for women by female authors such as Eliza Haywood, Charlotte Lennox, and Mary Brunton, stressed marriage for love and reflected the shift from arranged to companionate marriages. Green argues that these courtship novels "championed women's rights to choose marriage partners for personal, relational reasons rather than for familial, economic ones." Nancy Armstrong theorizes that the courtship narratives "offered their readers a way of indulging, with a kind of impunity, in fantasies of political power that were the more acceptable because they were played out within a domestic framework" that affirmed monogamy.

Feminists today frequently describe courtship rituals as part of a larger "homosocial exchange" between men. Eve Sedgwick provides a theoretical framework for the idea of the "traffic in women" and traces the development of that idea from the Renaissance into the twentieth century. Although arranged marriages are a thing of the past in Western cultures, they still exist in some cultures in which women are treated as objects of trade for substantial dowries.

Sigrid King

References

Armstrong, Nancy. *Desire and Domestic Fiction*. New York: Oxford University Press, 1987.

Bates, Catherine. *The Rhetoric of Courtship in Elizabethan Language and Literature*. Cambridge: Cambridge University Press, 1992.

Boone, Joseph Allen. *Tradition Counter Tradition: Love and the Form of Fiction*. Chicago: University of Chicago Press, 1987.

Dash, Irene. *Wooing, Wedding, and Power: Women in Shakespeare's Plays*. New York: Columbia University Press, 1981.

Dreher, Diane Elizabeth. *Domination and Defiance: Fathers and Daughters in Shakespeare*. Lexington: University Press of Kentucky, 1986.

Fraser, Antonia. *The Weaker Vessel: Woman's Lot in Seventeenth-Century England*. London: Methuen, 1989.

Green, Katherine Sobba. *The Courtship Novel, 1740–1820: A Feminized Genre*. Lexington: University Press of Kentucky, 1991.

Sedgwick, Eve Kosofsky. *Between Men: English Literature and Male Homosocial Desire*. New York: Columbia University Press, 1985.

Stone, Lawrence. *The Family, Sex and Marriage in England, 1500–1800*. New York: Harper and Row, 1977.

Yeazell, Ruth Bernard. *Fictions of Modesty: Women and Courtship in the English Novel*. Chicago: University of Chicago Press, 1991.

Creativity

Feminist literary theory has identified gendered value judgments hidden within the seemingly neutral term "creativity": historically, male critics have defined women as less creative than men and have judged women's creative output as less valuable than men's. Further, the concept of "creativity" has been used to imply that the artist is a solitary genius, creating ex nihilo (out of nothing). This view denies the crucial importance of material conditions, community, and tradition as factors in creative work. Denying these factors supports the false belief that women are "inherently" less creative when actually external forces have seriously impeded women's creativity. Women's creative output has been blocked by a lack of material resources, few or no chances for community with fellow artists, and an artistic tradition that excludes or trivializes women's interests and values.

The earliest definition of the verb "to create" is "to bring into being," an action attributed only to God (*Oxford English Dictionary*, first citation 1386). The adjective "creative" has been used since 1678, but the noun "creativity" did not appear until 1875, according to the *OED*; its use in the Victorian period built on the Romantic elevation of art into a divinity to be served by heroic, priestly (male) artists. In the definition of creativity that emerged then, men claimed "transcendent" power for themselves: according to the *Random House Dictionary*, "the ability to transcend traditional ideas, rules, patterns, relationships, or the like, and to create meaningful new ideas, forms, methods, interpretations, etc.; originality, progressiveness, or imagination."

This concept is tied to gender and power in ways that cause problems for women. To try to achieve a sense of superiority, men in positions of privilege and relative power have, as Virginia Woolf argues, historically conceived of women (and workers, "natives," children) as "inferior." They thus claimed that their own beliefs were universal, absolute values, while denying that their claims were motivated by a need to bolster their power in comparison with women and other "lesser" groups. For example, Romantic, Victorian, and Modernist artists claimed that only "geniuses" produced "great art" and only a man could be a "genius." However, in practice they defined "great art" in contrast with the art of women and others who were labeled "inferior." Further, they justified qualities such as depression, irritability, and irresponsibility as signs of "genius" and expected special consideration for their needs from the women around them, as Virginia Woolf points out in *A Room of One's Own*. Women's needs have never been so legitimated by the ideal of "genius" (Battersby), nor has women's depression been accorded value as a sign of "creativity" (Schiesari), nor have women's representations been highly valued as "creative work" (Carroll). It is only with active women's movements that a wide variety of women's creative output has gained in value, especially for other women.

Women who are motivated to create meet an array of obstacles, including lack of necessary social and material supports, as Woolf explains, a "room of one's own," and an income. The demands of husbands, children, and work use up time and energy needed for creation. However, even when women do manage to create, gender hierarchy affects the reception and evaluation of their work. Male critics have frequently judged "inferior" the literary genres that women have used most, such as letters, diaries, journals, memoirs. Women often chose such so-called "minor" genres because these would not require a classical education or extensive research or would fit the fragments of time women could find for their writing.

Women who did have the education, ambition, and time to allow them to tackle the "prestigious" genres such as lyric poetry or experimental fiction have frequently faced psychological blocks. Gilbert and Gubar point out the difficulties for women that follow from the traditional linkage of creativity with male sexuality (symbolically "pen = penis"). Further, social restrictions often impeded women's participation in the kinds of supportive and stimulating networks among fellow writers that have facilitated men's creativity in all periods.

When literary and aesthetic values change, male critics still tend to devalue or ignore women's creative output. For example, in the nineteenth century male critics granting new prestige to novels relegated women's novels to devalued subcategories like "sentimental" fiction. In the 1980s and 1990s, male critics establishing the new postmodern category "metafiction" usually ignored examples by women. These critics, as Molly Hite writes, see "female-created violations of convention or tradition" as "inadvertent shortcomings" rather than as "deliberate experiments" that are the signs of a postmodern creativity.

Two branches of feminist literary theory pose challenges to the very concept of creativity. Materialist feminists shift attention from creation (seen as an internal, individual act) to production (viewed as the result of external, social, and material forces). Poststructuralist feminists focus on texts as discourse, again shifting attention away from the subjectivity, agency, or identity of any individual "creator." Some feminist critics argue that poststructuralist theories devalue women artists' efforts to represent their own identities just when they are approaching success. However, these theories can be viewed as arguments against previous claims that creativity results from the efforts of a "solitary genius" and that identity is fixed and unified, rather than as arguments against women artists' efforts or against feminist re-evaluations of women's art. Most feminist re-evaluations do focus on the crucial importance of social, historical, cultural, and discursive contexts in artistic production and do not see identities as unitary or fixed. However, some feminist critics point out that arguments among feminists over these issues tend to drain energy away from efforts to challenge the dominant views.

Feminist canon revisions are underway. However, as Berenice A. Carroll argues, even feminists sometimes use the terms of masculine tradition to disparage women's creative work. Feminist literary critics can instead develop new criteria and strategies for praising women writers for satisfying women's needs and interests, as men have been doing for themselves for centuries, even if this means adopting a "strategic essentialism." In order to support and facilitate women's productivity and creativity, however defined, feminist literary theory and scholarship face major tasks: not only to combat the hostility toward women's creative output implicit in traditional judgments, but also to value highly its multiplicitous forms in the past, present, and future.

Deborah Weiner

References

Battersby, Christine. *Gender and Genius: Towards a Feminist Aesthetics*. Bloomington: Indiana University Press, 1989.

Carroll, Berenice A. "Originality and Creativity: Rituals of Inclusion and Exclusion." In *The Knowledge Explosion: Generations of Feminist Scholarship*, edited by Cheris Kramarae and Dale Spender, 353–361. New York and London: Athene Series, Teachers College Press, Columbia University, 1992.

Fuss, Diana. *Essentially Speaking: Feminism, Nature, and Difference*. New York: Routledge, 1989.

Gilbert, Sandra, and Susan Gubar. *The Madwoman in the Attic*. New Haven: Yale University Press, 1979.

Gubar, Susan. "'The Blank Page' and the Issues of Female Creativity." *Critical Inquiry* 8 (1981): 243–263.

Hartsock, Nancy. "Rethinking Modernism: Minority vs. Majority Theories." *Cultural Critique* 7 (1987): 187–206.

Hite, Molly. *The Other Side of the Story: Structures and Strategies of Contemporary Feminist Narrative*. Ithaca, N.Y.: Cornell University Press, 1989.

Olsen, Tillie. *Silences*. New York: Delacorte, 1978.

Schiesari, Julia. *The Gendering of Melancholia: Feminism, Psychoanalysis, and the Symbolics of Loss in Renaissance Literature*. Ithaca, N.Y.: Cornell University Press, 1992.

Spivak, Gayatri Chakravorty. *In Other Worlds: Essays in Cultural Politics*. New York: Methuen, 1987.

Woolf, Virginia. *A Room of One's Own*. New York: Harcourt Brace Jovanovich, 1929. 1989.

Cross-Dressing

Clothes make the man—or the woman; the real cultural significance of this cliché underlies the feminist interest in the practice and representation of cross-dressing. Making a choice to wear clothes that are normally assigned to the other gender exposes how the differences between male and female persons are socially constructed and maintained, and simultaneously enacts the blurring of such distinctions. The person who cross-dresses can thus be seen as embodying the "third term" that disrupts the binary logic of gender.

Historically and cross-culturally, transvestite behaviors have a very wide range of motives and meanings; for example, male-to-female cross-dressing often has a different cultural significance than the reverse. While it may be licensed in certain restricted situations—such as theatrical performance or shamanistic ritual—more generally, a man who cross-dresses is often perceived as perverse or ridiculous. Conversely, a woman who dresses as a man may either be seen as demonstrating commendable ambition and impatience with the restrictions imposed on her by her gender; or as transgressing improperly on the rights and privileges that men prefer to keep for themselves. Cross-dressing thus exposes the power differentials at stake in gender arrangements.

Although the two phenomena are by no means equivalent, in many cultures there is a long and complex association of cross-dressing with homosexuality, revealing the extent to which gendered and sexual identities are constructed with reference to each other. For example, lesbian butch-femme sexualities have recently provoked intense interest among feminist theorists, while canonical texts of lesbian fiction, such as Virginia Woolf's *Orlando* (1928) and Radclyffe Hall's *The Well of Loneliness* (1928), explore the relations between cross-dressing and sexual identities.

Cross-dressing is obviously of great interest to feminists who wish to theorize relations of gender and sexuality and the conditions under which they are represented. But it also offers a powerful explanatory metaphor for other cultural phenomena. Thus Marjorie Garber argues in *Vested Interests* that it is no coincidence that the same term—"passing"—is used to describe women who disguise themselves as men, and light-skinned black people who pretend to be white. This is not to collapse together diverse social experiences of racial and sexual difference, but to show that the analysis of cross-dressing in relation to other liminal social practices can be mutually illuminating.

In a literary context, interest in cross-dressing has centered on the early modern period, when the transvestite theater of Shakespeare's England, and the Restoration theater's taste for "breeches parts" (women disguised as men) coincided with an apparent proliferation of "real-life" cross-dressing; and the period from the late nineteenth century to the present, when the emergence of feminist movements and subcultural homosexual identities focused attention on the construction and destabilization of categories of gender and sexual identity.

Kate Chedgzoy

References

Bell-Metereau, Rebecca, *Hollywood Androgyny*. New York: Columbia University Press, 1985.

Dekker, Rudolf, and Lotte van de Pol. *The Tradition of Female Cross-Dressing in Early Modern Europe*. London: Macmillan, 1989.

Dugaw, Dianne. *Dangerous Examples: Warrior Women and Popular Balladry 1650–1850*. Cambridge: Cambridge University Press, 1989.

Garber, Marjorie. *Vested Interests: Cross-dressings and Cultural Anxiety*. New York and London: Routledge, 1992.

Gilbert, Sandra, and Susan Gubar. *Sexchanges*. Vol. 2 of *No Man's Land*. New Haven: Yale University Press, 1988.

Nestle, Joan, ed. *The Persistent Desire: The Femme-Butch Reader*. Boston: Alyson, 1992.

Newton, Esther. "The Mythic Mannish Lesbian." In *Hidden from History: Reclaiming the Gay and Lesbian Past*, edited by Martin Duberman, Martha Vicinus, and George Chauncey, Jr., 281–293. New York: New American Library, 1989.

Wheelwright, Julie. *Amazons and Military Maids*. London: Pandora, 1989.

Cultural Studies

As a scholarly enterprise whose intellectual history draws from a range of academic disciplines both in the United States and in Britain, including traditional humanities disciplines such as literary studies, English studies, and philosophy, and those in the social sciences such as sociology, anthropology, and political science, and more recently institutionalized "disciplines" such as media and film studies, cultural studies is now and has been historically a thoroughly interdisciplinary invention. The term was first used at the Centre for Contemporary Cultural Studies at the University of Birmingham in England in the 1960s and early 1970s. The intellectual project was defined, from early on, as an attempt to integrate the textual focus and interpretive methods of literary studies (borrowing also an understanding of the formal qualities of modes of cultural expression) with the analytical frameworks of sociology and critical theory and the field methods of anthropology, in the service of producing critical analyses of contemporary culture. In that it sought to combine the interpretive frameworks of textual studies with a political critique of the material conditions of the production and reception of cultural texts, cultural studies has been informed by the work of scholars trained in literary studies who were also attendant to the cultural context of the literature they studied.

Even as cultural studies emerged as a situated "invention" of a new form of academic work, it was also designed to be an "intervention" into the institutional dynamics of discipline formation. The organization of work at the center was structured around collaborative groups; one of the more interventionist working groups was the Women's Studies Group, whose early focus on the material conditions of women's access to literary culture and of women's writing inaugurated a multifaceted and multibranching program of research on the material conditions of women's lives under late capitalism. The book *Women Take Issue* (1978), the first edited collection of work by the Women's Studies Group, includes chapters on the various projects of group members: for example, Dorothy Hobson on the isolation and oppression of housewives and Janice Winship on the ideology of femininity. In the introduction to the book, the editorial group comments explicitly on the dynamics of doing feminist intellectual work at the center. Seeking to make visible women's invisibility in the work going on at the center at the time, these scholars outline a series of commitments that serve as the foundation for the development of a feminist politics of academic work. The importance of this book, in addition to the specific historical and institutional intervention it enacted, is that it lays the groundwork for the development of a specifically feminist framework of cultural analysis: namely the work that is now identified as feminist cultural studies.

The development of feminist cultural studies in the 1980s was influenced by a range of work by feminist scholars who theorize reading and writing as fundamentally cultural practices;

these will include those projects explicitly designed to examine what it means to "read" and "write" culture as a black feminist, a woman of color, a lesbian feminist, a workingclass woman, or sometimes as a white feminist. These projects include as well the feminist cultural criticism produced in the context of literary and film studies. For some the distinction between feminist literary criticism and feminist cultural studies may seem like a rather arbitrary demarcation, since many feminist literary critics (such as Balsamo, Ebert, and hooks) not only engage a broader cultural context in their discussion of literary works, but explicitly identify their work as making a contribution to the development of feminist cultural theory. Indeed as Catherine Belsey and Jane Moore describe in their introduction to *The Feminist Reader*, from the early 1970s whenever feminist writers discussed literature "they refused to isolate it from the cultural of which it forms a part" and in this sense offered an extremely radical critique of traditional literary criticism. Feminist cultural studies expands this critique to address the broader questions about the social and cultural determinations of reading practices and the material conditions of reading contexts. Nevertheless, feminist literary criticism and feminist cultural studies share a set of guiding commitments that could be specified in the following way: that writing be denaturalized as a solitary (individualist) act, that literature be understood as culturally and historically determined, and that art cannot be a retreat from politics. One of the consequences of the close connection between feminist literary criticism and feminist cultural studies is that by the late 1980s feminist literary critics are well advanced beyond their more androcentric colleagues in their apprehension of the expressly political aims of cultural studies more generally.

The affiliation between feminist literary criticism and feminist cultural studies is especially suggestive in the work that addresses the relationship between literary theory and feminist politics. Given that they share a critical focus on the relation between literature and the culture within which it is produced or consumed, feminist literary studies and feminist cultural studies are equally preoccupied with the discursive construction of identity and subjectivity, and what might be called the politics of representation. They diverge from one another in the amount of attention given to the circuit of production, exchange, and consumption of cultural products. This focus suggests certain questions for feminist cultural studies, not only about the cultural conditions of the production of given texts or other cultural forms, that is, music, body practices, geography, but also about the specific conditions of reading or consumption, which often requires the investigation of the everyday situations of lived cultures.

In these ways, the critical agenda of feminist cultural studies extends beyond the by-now familiar arguments for canon revision. It is probably fair to say that feminist cultural studies subsumes the study of literature under the broader study of culture, where textuality may be the medium of analysis, but the study of structures, institutions, and relations of power are the horizon of feminist scholarship. The struggle over the canon is understood to be a struggle about the politics of representation and the relations of power that organize knowledge. This not only concerns representation in books or films but more broadly in the university curriculum, social movements, and global economic relations (among other things). The point, of course, is to win the struggle for inclusion not only with respect to the list of required reading but, more important, in the social and political struggles outside of academe. For this reason, feminist cultural studies relies heavily on the analytical frameworks of contemporary feminist social and political theory. The divergence then between feminist literary criticism and feminist cultural studies can be identified by the notion of the "text" that grounds feminist criticism, the degree to which literature remains the privileged object of cultural criticism, and the extent to which each approach accounts for the network of relations (embodied and semiotic) within which any text makes sense.

Anne Balsamo

References

Balsamo, Anne. "Feminism and Cultural Studies." *Journal of the Midwest Modern Language Association* 24 (1991): 50–73.

Belsey, Catherine, and Jane Moore. *The Feminist Reader: Essays in Gender and the Politics of Literary Criticism.* New York: Basil Blackwell, 1989.

Brantlinger, Patrick. *Crusoe's Footprints: Cultural Studies in Britain and America.* New York: Routledge, 1990.

Ebert, Teresa L. "The Romance of Patriarchy: Ideology, Subjectivity, and Postmodern Feminist Cultural Theory." *Cultural Critique* 10 (1988): 19–57.

Franklin, Sarah, Celia Lury, and Jackie Stacey, eds. *Off-Centre: Feminism and Cultural Studies.* London: HarperCollins, 1991.

Grossberg, Lawrence, Cary Nelson, and Paula Treichler, eds. *Cultural Studies.* New York: Routledge, 1992.

Hall, Stuart. "Cultural Studies and the Centre: Some Problematics and Problems." In *Culture, Media, Language: Working Papers in Cultural Studies, 1972–1979,* edited by Stuart Hall, Dorothy Hobson, Andrew Lowe, and Paul Willis, 15–47. London: Unwin Hyman, 1980.

hooks, bell. *Yearning: Race, Gender and Cultural Politics.* Boston: South End, 1990.

Johnson, Richard. "What Is Cultural Studies Anyway?" *Social Text* 6 (1987): 38–80.

Turner, Graeme. *British Cultural Studies: An Introduction.* Boston: Unwin Hyman, 1990.

Women's Studies Group. *Women Take Issue: Aspects of Women's Subordination.* Centre for Contemporary Cultural Studies. London: Hutchinson, 1978.

Cyborg Feminism

A notion acquired from twentieth-century scientific discourse, the cyborg is a symbiotic being resulting from an interface between the cybernetic and the organic. The development of cybernetics—the science of self-regulating control processes in electronic, mechanical, and biological systems—was military-based, the paradigm of the post–World War II era. Cybernetic systems can include a wide array of machines and apparatuses, mechanisms that comprise systems described by Bill Nichols as having a "dynamic, even if limited" quotient of intelligence. And cybernetic organisms, in their "confusing" of mechanical and organic, the inner and outer realms, simulation and reality, have been considered by some contemporary feminists to hold tremendous potential for alternative subjectivities. Instead of the rigidity of subject positions structured by the stabilizing discourses of science and rationality, Oedipal subjectivity, or binary oppositions, cyborg subjectivity provides for multiple perspectives and the ongoing reinvention of positionings.

Donna Haraway is the feminist scholar who has most extensively developed ideas about the cyborg's potential as a destabilizing force within feminist theory. In *Primate Visions*, her 1989 study of gender, race, and nature in modern scientific discourse, she cites the monkeys involved in early space exploration as iconic cyborgs: "The spaceships, the recording and tracking technologies, animals, and human beings were joined to form a new kind of historical entity—cyborgs in a postmodern theater of war, science, and popular culture." Such creatures are, according to Haraway, important in their confusion or transgression of boundaries. They embody simultaneous statuses: human, animal, or machine; male or female; communication technology or writer; and so on. For Haraway, there is irony and blasphemy involved with the cyborg position, as its multiplicity instigates the breaking up of "masterful" subjectivity and its narratives. Such a breakup, with its resulting lack of a unified subject, has great potential for contemporary feminist studies and literature seeking to consider a range of differences. The refusal to become or to remain a "gendered" man or woman, can be considered, as Haraway states, an "eminently political insistence on emerging from the nightmare of the all-too-real imaginary narrative of sex and race." And the move toward more mobile figures, figures without an original unity, is being embraced by a variety of contemporary feminist theorists, including Trinh T. Minh-ha, Gloria Anzaldúa, Rey Chow, and Teresa de Lauretis, who reconceptualizes the subject as a shifting and multiply organized "eccentric" one.

These writers are creating subjects who occupy "a geography of elsewhere," a space that Allucquère Roseanne Stone links to the reworking of sociality's very structure and to the refiguring of links between bodies, selves, and communities. This elsewhere is shaped by information and communication technologies, by computer networks, and the virtual space of electronic "webs." It is, as Stone writes, an "(un)real estate, supporting a different mode of existence from face-to-face sociality." A variety of fiction, from the science fiction of Vonda McIntyre and Joanna Russ written in the 1960s and 1970s, to the cyber-texts of Sue Thomas in the 1990s, explores such possibilities for difference through the creation of various cyborgs. Russ, for example, creates in *The Female Man* four "characters" who are actually versions of the same genotype occurring at various points in a complex temporality. The extreme fragmentation frustrates any attempt at reading for

wholeness of identity, of gender, of time, or of place. In *Correspondence*, Thomas explores the limits of humanity, consciousness, and memory in the figure of a grieving woman who is turning herself into a machine. As the novel engages in role-play whereby audience and narrator are conflated, this character is herself in the process of becoming an extension of her computer. The effect is a richly ambiguous relationship between virtual reality and real life, a space in which the hybrid main character explores radically new emotional and creative choices.

The experimental mode of cyborg subjectivity, with its varied options for embodiment, holds for feminism the potential of mapping new territory for identity. Some feminist theorists choose to comment on the cyborg's utopian or idealistic character; others caution against the dangers of virtual reality and its decoupling of body from the subject. But many do so as they examine the complex interrelationships between human and machine and the new selves such interaction produces, such as Donna Haraway's promising monsters and Sherry Turkle's personality complex, the "second self." Simultaneously challenging and promising, cyborg feminism offers a consideration of how technology can be a strategy for literary, theoretical, and political intervention.

AnJanette Brush

References

de Lauretis, Teresa. "Eccentric Subjects: Feminist Theory and Historical Consciousness." *Feminist Studies* 16 (1990): 115–150.

Haraway, Donna. *Primate Visions: Gender, Race, and Nature in the World of Modern Science.* New York: Routledge, 1989.

———. "The Promises of Monsters." In *Cultural Studies*, edited by Lawrence Grossberg, Cary Nelson, and Paula Treichler, 295–337. New York: Routledge, 1992.

———. *Simians, Cyborgs, and Women: The Reinvention of Nature.* New York: Routledge, 1991.

Nichols, Bill. "The Work of Culture in the Age of Cybernetic Systems." *Screen* 29 (1988): 22–46.

Russ, Joanna. *The Female Man.* New York: Bantam, 1975.

Stone, Allucquère R. "Virtual Systems." In *Incorporations*, edited by Jonathan

Crary and Sanford Kwinter, 609–621. New York: Zone, 1992.

Thomas, Sue. *Correspondence.* Woodstock, N.Y.: Overlook, 1993.

Turkle, Sherry. The *Second Self: Computers and the Human Spirit.* New York: Simon and Schuster, 1984.

C

D

Daly, Mary

Radical feminist scholar, theologian, linguist, and philosopher, Mary Daly's 1978 book, *Gyn/ Ecology: The Meta-Ethics of Radical Feminism* influenced feminist discourse in many fields. Daly's brilliant wordplay, meticulous research, and interdisciplinary approach provided a new, and radical, type of feminist scholarship. Establishing herself as a feminist theologian with the publication of *The Church and the Second Sex* in 1968, Mary Daly continued her project of articulating the misogyny and sexism inherent in Christian mythology with *Beyond God the Father: Toward a Philosophy of Women's Liberation*. Daly's second book signaled an increasingly radical, rather than reformist, approach to patriarchal religions and societies, as she argued for a new "thealogy" and language to accompany women's transformation of human consciousness.

As women assume the power of naming, "New Words" emerge and are redefined. Daly's third book exemplifies this redefinition. *Gyn/ Ecology: The Meta-Ethics of Radical Feminism*, constructs a philosophy of radical feminism that subverts patriarchy at its root, through language. Daly's "gynomorphic" language enables women to realize radical change: because language constructs identity and reality, this new discourse makes possible a new reality. Daly redefines familiar terms (Gyn/Ecology, Preoccupation, Hag), invents new ones (Biophilic, Rapism, Fembot), and documents the deathly destruction of women in patriarchy (clitoridectomy, gynecology, war). Mapping out women's transcendent spirituality and elemental lifeforce (biophilic energy), Daly points to female friendship and ecstatic desire as forces through which women can reclaim themselves, and their own experience. The potential for this sisterhood to neglect the issue of racism is the subject of Audre Lorde's "An Open Letter to Mary Daly" (1979); Lorde questions the racism in Daly's presentation of nonwhite women's victimization when *Gyn/Ecology* offers images of women's strength exclusively through white, Judeo-Christian/Western-European images.

Daly's fourth book, *Pure Lust: Elemental Feminist Philosophy*, locates an ecstatic desire, where "active longing" propels a woman into her own, true self, her own "country." Furthering the description (and empowering force) of female friendship, Daly identifies the journey that women make in concert with one another. "Be-Longing: The Lust for Happiness," "Be-Friending: The Lust to Share Happiness," and "Be-Witching: The Lust for Metamorphosis" signal a desire that has moved beyond the maze of patriarchal "double-think." In 1987, Daly published a feminist dictionary of "gynomorphic" terms, titled *Webster's First New Intergalactic Wickedary of the English Language* (written with Jane Caputi); this collection features terms from her previous books, and a host of new and revised words and phrases.

Wendy C. Wahl

References

Daly, Mary. *Beyond God the Father: Toward a Philosophy of Women's Liberation*. Boston: Beacon, 1973.
———. *The Church and the Second Sex*. Boston: Beacon, 1968.
———. *Gyn/Ecology: The Meta-Ethics of Radical Feminism*. Boston: Beacon, 1978.
———. *Pure Lust: Elemental Feminist Philosophy*. Boston: Beacon, 1984.

————, and Jane Caputi. *Webster's First New Intergalactic Wickedary of the English Language*. Boston: Beacon, 1987.

Lorde, Audre. "An Open Letter to Mary Daly" [April, 1979]. Reprinted in *This Bridge Called My Back: Writings by Radical Women of Color*, edited by Gloria Anzaldúa and Cherríe Moraga, 94–97. Latham, N.Y.: Kitchen Table: Women of Color Press, 1981.

Daughter

While the father-daughter relationship has provided rich fodder for classic psychoanalytic thought, the mother-daughter relationship has been central to the revisionary efforts of psychoanalysts like Jessica Benjamin, Nancy Chodorow, and Carol Gilligan in America, and Luce Irigaray, Michele Montrelay, and Julia Kristeva in France, as a model of female subject-formation. Both object-relations and Lacanian theory—whether evolving around the presence or absence of the mother—seize the pre-Oedipal period as that which forges women's difference, and show how the daughter's deep sense of affiliation with the mother leads to a characteristically relational sense of self. Chodorow, for example, sees mother-daughter bonding, not phallic lack or shift of allegiance to the father, as characterizing female identity. Hélène Cixous sees in the fluidity of this connectedness the location of women's speech, which courses through the body in its menstrual blood, and is its mother's milk. Luce Irigaray, too, transforms female silence and evisceration in language to *parler-femme*, an other, specifically feminine speech. Kristeva sees women's psychosocial circumstances gravitating to a participation in the presymbolic, or the "semiotic," where abdication of signs leads to a tenuous hold over the mother Thing.

Adrienne Rich, in *Of Woman Born: Motherhood as Experience and Institution*, sees in the galvanic flow of energy between mother and daughter, the materials for "the deepest mutuality and the most painful estrangement." If, as Rich asserts, this relationship has been trivialized in the "annals of patriarchy," it has been reclaimed in the growth of the feminist consciousness in the 1970s, and has received considerable methodological attention as "the most private and the most formative of women's relationships." Whereas in the nineteenth-century novel, mothers had to be sidelined so that heroines could inflect the plot, in the texts of the 1970s, the marginalization or elimination of fathers has become necessary for fashioning what Marianne Hirsch calls "female plots."

The feminist daughter's cathexis with the maternal, however, is fraught with ambivalence and unease. Fran Scoble's essay, "Mothers and Daughters: Giving the Lie" outlines the mainspring of feminist "matrophobia" in the mother's acquiescence with the lopsided power dissemination of patriarchy; seen, in the words of Adrienne Rich, as "the victim in ourselves, the unfree women," we then individuate in quiet desperation by performing "radical surgery." Again, the mother's body reinvokes womblike claustrophobia, or what Elizabeth V. Spellman calls "somatophobia," the fear of the phallomorphic body. Finally, according to Kristeva, the woman's entry into language is predicated on mastering the mother's absences. Kristeva traces feminine melancholia to an ineradicable aspect of female sexuality, "its addiction to the maternal Thing and its lesser aptitude for restorative perversion." It is the absence of the Thing that allows signification, and disallowing that negation collapses the distinction between mother and daughter, swamping sign with affect, and eventually leading to psychosis and death. The mother thus catalyzes the female child's initiation into the symbolic by projecting herself as a vacancy, or as an "other," and it is in interlocution with that otherness that the daughter's selfhood is congealed.

Ankhi Mukherjee

References

Chodorow, Nancy. *The Reproduction of Mothering: Psychoanalysis and the Sociology of Gender*. Berkeley: University of California Press, 1978.

Cixous, Hélène, and Catherine Clément. *The Newly Born Woman*. Translated by Betsy Wing. Minneapolis: University of Minnesota Press, 1986.

Gallop, Jane. *The Daughter's Seduction: Feminism and Psychoanalysis*. Ithaca, N.Y.: Cornell University Press, 1982.

Hirsch, Marianne. *The Mother/Daughter Plot: Narrative, Psychoanalysis, Feminism*. Bloomington and Indianapolis: Indiana University Press, 1989.

Irigaray, Luce. *This Sex Which Is Not One*. Translated by Catherine Porter and Carolyn Burke. Ithaca, N.Y.: Cornell University Press, 1985.

Kristeva, Julia. *Black Sun: Depression and Melancholia*. New York: Columbia University Press, 1989.

Michie, Helena. "Mother, Sister, Other: The 'Other Woman' in Feminist Theory." *Literature and Psychology* 32 (1986): 1–10.

Rich, Adrienne. *Of Woman Born: Motherhood as Experience and Institution*. New York: W.W. Norton, 1979.

Scoble, Fran. "Mothers and Daughters: Giving the Lie." *Denver Quarterly* 18 (1984): 126–133.

Spellman, Elizabeth V. "Theories of Race and Gender: The Erasure of Black Women." *Quest: A Feminist Quarterly* 5 (1982): 36–62.

Davidson, Cathy N.

Davidson is most noted for her work on early-American novels (1789–1820) in *Revolution and the Word: The Rise of the Novel in America*. A large portion of this book is devoted to assessing the cultural role of the most popular form of early-American fiction, the sentimental novel. A form usually written by white women, about white women, and for white women, the sentimental novel has traditionally been ignored or denigrated by scholars of literature.

Scholars condemned sentimental novels for being overwrought fantasies. In *Revolution* and in her scholarly introductions to two editions of the most popular examples of early sentimental fiction, *The Coquette* (1797) and *Charlotte Temple* (first American edition, 1794), Davidson disproved such pronouncements. She noted that a white woman's chief goal during this period was to find a suitable husband. Her future welfare would be determined by her marriage, and yet marriage entailed the loss of most legal rights, the threat of abandonment by her husband, and the physical dangers of childbirth. Sentimental novels usually centered around a young female protagonist dominated by the larger social and economic forces that compelled her to submit to marriage and all of its attendant burdens or, alternatively, to a strong-willed seducer who often offered a far more attractive life yet one predicated on social ostracism. These novels thus allowed women readers to participate vicariously in a range of relationships whereby they could safely experience various outcomes. These novels also served as a feminist critique of early-American society insofar as they noted the forces that created such impossible choices for women and because they both implicitly and explicitly championed the cause of female education, believing it necessary if women were to make the informed choices that would lead to suitable marriage partners. Sentimental novels, then, played a central role in both mirroring and shaping early-American society.

Davidson also co-edited *The Oxford Companion to Women's Writing in the United States*, which attempts to "map out the contours of U.S. women's literary culture as a field." She has written extensively on Canadian Margaret Atwood and, in *The Lost Tradition: Mothers and Daughters in Literature*, has worked to recoup the portrayals of mothers and daughters in literature in a scholarly climate often concerned primarily with fathers and sons. She is currently the editor of *American Literature: A Journal of Literary History, Criticism, and Bibliography*. Her work *36 Views of Mount Fuji: On Finding Myself in Japan* is an account of her experiences teaching at Kansai Women's University in Japan, where she struggled to understand Japanese culture.

Elise Lemire

References

Davidson, Cathy N. Introduction to *Charlotte Temple*, by Susanna Rowson. Edited by Cathy N. Davidson. New York: Oxford University Press, 1986.

———. Introduction to *The Coquette*, by Hannah Webster Foster. Edited by Cathy N. Davidson. New York: Oxford University Press, 1986.

———. "The Life and Times of *Charlotte Temple*." In *Reading in America: Literature and Social History*, edited by Cathy N. Davidson, 157–179. Baltimore: Johns Hopkins University Press, 1989.

———. *Revolution and the Word: The Rise of the Novel in America*. New York: Oxford University Press, 1986.

———. *36 Views of Mount Fuji: On Finding Myself in Japan*. New York: Dutton, 1993.

———, and E.M. Broner, eds. *The Lost Tradition: Mothers and Daughters in Literature*. New York: Frederick Ungar, 1980.

———, and Arnold E. Davidson, eds. *The Art of Margaret Atwood: Essays in Criticism*. Toronto: Anansi, 1981.

D

———, and Linda Wagner-Martins, eds. *The Oxford Companion to Women's Writing in the United States.* New York: Oxford University Press, 1995.

Davis, Angela

Catapulted to fame because of her involvement in the Black Power movement of the late 1960s and early 1970s, African American Marxist feminist philosopher Angela Davis is known as much for her political activism as her scholarly writings. She has indirectly influenced feminist literary theory both through her insistence that gender is meaningful only with reference to other social determinants such as race, class, and sexuality, and through her belief that art can and should contribute to social transformation.

In 1969, political activities on behalf of imprisoned Black Power activists led to Davis's being charged in 1970 with murder, kidnaping, and conspiracy. By the time she was acquitted, after spending sixteen highly publicized months in prison, Davis had begun to study the history of the black family during slavery. Recognizing the "misogynist character of the prosecution's case," she developed a critique of the common perception that African American women were "dominating matriarchs" and "castrating females" who "oppressed their men." Her 1974 autobiography and subsequent writings demonstrate the evolution of her efforts to transcend the limitations of Marxism, black (cultural) nationalism, and white middle-class feminism in order to understand capitalism, racism, and heterosexism as forms of interlocking oppression.

The range of her concerns is amply illustrated by the essays collected in *Women, Race & Class* and *Women, Culture & Politics.* Davis explores issues as diverse as abolitionism, the campaign for women's suffrage, rape and lynching, birth control and sterilization abuse, disarmament, domestic labor, black women's health, apartheid in South Africa, and the institutionalization of ethnic studies. More recently, in *Women, Culture, & Politics,* she has begun to formulate a political philosophy of aesthetics, arguing that cultural practices such as literature, photography, and music should be understood as a "form of social consciousness that can potentially awaken an urge in those affected by it to creatively transform their oppressive environments." While believing that art can be a catalyst for the development of progressive revolutionary consciousness, Davis has continued to maintain that social change will occur only if cultural contestation is accompanied by political intervention.

Doris Witt

References
Ashman, Charles. *The People vs. Angela Davis.* New York: Pinnacle, 1972.
Bhavnani, Kum-Kum. "Complexity, Activism, Optimism: An Interview with Angela Y. Davis." *Feminist Review* 31 (1989): 66–81.
Davis, Angela. *Angela Davis: An Autobiography.* New York: Random House, 1974.
———. *If They Come in the Morning: Voices of Resistance.* New York: Third, 1971.
———. *Women, Culture & Politics.* New York: Random House, 1989.
———. *Women, Race & Class.* New York: Random House, 1981.

de Lauretis, Teresa

Teresa de Lauretis's *Alice Doesn't,* published in 1984, explores the ways in which semiotics, especially Italian semiotics, illuminate the discussion of the female subject in film theory and practice. De Lauretis accepts the general feminist premise that the cinema has been largely controlled by men and has been oppressive in its imaging of women; and yet she is not content with the opposition of narrative pleasure and political enlightenment adopted by feminist film criticism after Mulvey. In *Alice Doesn't,* de Lauretis notes that even avant-garde films require the spectator to accept the "the inner logic of play . . . the social contract by which external consistency is given up or traded against the internal coherence of the illusion." In other words, no matter what kind of film the spectator watches, he/she accedes to meaning that is illusory because it is constructed.

Drawing on her background in semiotics, de Lauretis is much more interested than other feminist film theorists in the context of a cinematic imaging. (Mary Ann Doane writes rather despairingly, in *The Desire to Desire,* of "the sheer multiplicity and dispersal of subject positions" in de Lauretis's description of cinematic representation.) The semiotic code cannot be separated from the occasion of the utterance, and so not only the films de Lauretis critiques but also the critiques themselves take the form of performances. De Lauretis quotes Pier Paolo Pasolini observing, "We represent ourselves, we perform ourselves. Human reality is this double representation in which we are at once actors and spectators."

Defining human reality in these terms, as a doubleness, allows de Lauretis to argue that a critical feminist reading of even the most oppressive film "changes the representation into a performance which exceeds the text." In a feminist critique a woman enacts the "irreducible contradiction" between the culturally constructed image of the woman and the real lives of women. De Lauretis provides examples, enacting the contradictions of gendered representation inherent in Michael Snow's *Presents* and Nicholas Roeg's *Bad Timing*. Although de Lauretis's chapter-long critiques of these films are detailed and thoughtful, in the end it is difficult to know what to do with *Alice Doesn't*. De Lauretis's invocation of double (and in some cases triple) layers of signification raise the specter of meaninglessness—not just as a political issue for women but in the case of the particular critiques underway. Like Lacan, de Lauretis regularly recognizes the slippage between her signifiers and the book's signified. The result is an exhilarating theoretical performance that seems to call for interpretation rather than application.

Given de Lauretis's interest in discourse as performance in excess of text, it is not surprising that she has gone on to study the ways in which the technology of the cinema can be understood to enact the crises of excess meaning brought on by the very process of engendering the image. In de Lauretis's most recent book, entitled *The Practice of Love: Lesbian Sexuality and Perverse Desire*, such a crisis takes the form of a consideration of lesbian sexuality: in the extremes of "perverse" desire, de Lauretis finds the examples she sought in *Alice Doesn't* of women living the contradiction between cultural codification and personal expression.

Ellen Draper

References

de Lauretis, Teresa. *Alice Doesn't: Feminism, Semiotics, Cinema*. Bloomington: Indiana University Press, 1984.
———. *The Practice of Love: Lesbian Sexuality and Perverse Desire*. Bloomington: Indiana University Press, 1994.
———. *Technologies of Gender: Essays on Theory, Film and Fiction*. Bloomington: Indiana University Press, 1987.
———, ed. *Feminist Studies, Critical Studies*. Bloomington: Indiana University Press, 1986.
———, and Stephen Heath, eds. *The Cinematic Apparatus*. New York: St. Martin's, 1980.
———, Andreas Huyssen, and Kathleen Woodward, eds. *The Technological Imagination: Theories and Fictions*. Madison, Wis.: Coda, 1980.
Doane, Mary Ann. *The Desire to Desire: The Woman's Film of the '40s*. Bloomington: Indiana University Press, 1987.

D

Death

In male representations, women have served both as muses and as threats, as the image of inspiration and as the femme fatale. Artists have attempted to understand, overcome, and "kill" enigmatic Woman, figured as Mother Nature or as the site of sexuality, absence, and the cause for castration anxiety. For women, death can signify the silence of women's voices and writing, or an escape from the constraints imposed by patriarchal society.

Images of dead women abound in literature: from Dido to Ophelia, from Emma Bovary to Anna Karenina. Sickly, weak, and anorexic women achieve "angelic" status through self-sacrifice in Victorian literature. Edgar Allan Poe wrote: "The death of a beautiful woman is, unquestionably, the most poetical topic in the world." Why are dead women so prominent?

Dead women often serve as muses for men, inspiring them toward love and beauty, like Dante's Beatrice, who leads him through *The Divine Comedy*. Elegies dedicated to women replace death with poetry. The dead woman makes the man seem strong; as Virginia Woolf said, women reflect men back at twice their natural size.

Women are perceived as the dangerous site of sexuality and death. The life-giving mother propels the child into mortality. Freud attributes castration and death anxieties to women's lack of a penis. Woman appears as the "dark continent," a Medusean creature who can kill the spectator. To conquer the threat of Woman and Nature, the artist attempts to reject biology and mortality and, in Pygmalionlike fashion, to breathe life into his own creation. Narrative structures often satisfy this desire to kill the threat of Woman. Traditional literary plots end with the woman's death (or safe marriage and return to Patriarchal structure). Many films allow the viewer (assumed male) to satisfy what Laura Mulvey calls his "scopophilic desires" and appease castration anxiety by killing the threatening woman on the screen. The woman's death grants the surviving artist immortality.

Where are the voices of these dead women? In *A Room of One's Own*, Woolf mourns the anonymity of writing by women and imagines what would have happened to Shakespeare's sister: she would have been betrothed rather than educated, run away from home and finally killed herself, impoverished and impregnated. There was no place for a mind of genius in a woman's body. The reality of women's silence and suicide unfortunately remains too prevalent.

In women's novels and poetry loom images of entrapment, silence, and death. Writers like Brontë and Eliot shift their focus from the woman as enigmatic object to active participant who faces the conflicts and pressures of patriarchy. References to death and to the enclosure created by societal expectations figure in the works of such poets as Dickinson, Plath, and Rich. In one Poem, Rich cites Dickinson's line "My Life has stood—Loaded Gun—" to represent repressed female power and anger. Writing involves defiance and self-assertion. Calls for rebirth and revision through poetry and fiction have refused the roles and the deaths traditionally prescribed to women.

The place of death remains a complex topic for feminist theory: What are women to make of the prominence of the image of beauty as a dead woman in society, art, and literature? Why does suicide, or even passivity, silence, and anorexia remain so prevalent among women today? How does this connection to a death drive in women relate to their creativity? The exploration of death leads women to explore how they are figured by men and how they figure themselves.

Judith Greenberg

References

Bassein, Beth Ann. *Women and Death: Linkages in Western Thought and Literature*. Westport, Conn.: Greenwood, 1984.

Bronfen, Elisabeth. *Over Her Dead Body. Death, Femininity and the Aesthetic*. New York: Routledge, 1992.

Brooks, Peter. *Reading for the Plot. Design and Intention in Narrative*. New York: Knopf, 1984.

Dijkstra, Bram. *Idols of Perversity. Fantasies of Feminine Evil in Fin-de-Siècle Culture*. Oxford: Oxford University Press, 1986.

DuPlessis, Rachel Blau. *Writing beyond the Ending. Narrative Strategies of Twentieth Century Women Writers*. Bloomington: Indiana University Press, 1985.

Freud, Sigmund. *Beyond the Pleasure Principle*. Standard Edition, 18. London: Hogarth, 1920.

Gilbert, Sandra M., and Susan Gubar. *The Madwoman in the Attic. The Woman Writer and the Nineteenth Century Literary Imagination*. New Haven: Yale University Press, 1979.

Mulvey, Laura. *Visual and Other Pleasures*. Bloomington: Indiana University Press, 1989.

Sacks, Peter. *The English Elegy*. Baltimore: Johns Hopkins University Press, 1988.

Woolf, Virginia. *A Room of One's Own*. New York: Harcourt Brace Jovanovich, 1929.

Decentering

If the "center" of a social, political, or theoretical system is the organizing principle or structure that determines how the system operates, then "decentering" a system involves repositioning that organizing principle, or understanding its relationship to the system in a different light. Jacques Derrida introduced the deconstructive practice of "decentering" to literary theory in "Structure, Sign, and Play in the Discourse of the Human Sciences." Derrida demonstrates that a center has "no natural site"; it holds its position as the center only by repressing "differences" within itself. Decentering is thus not a process of taking the center away, but rather an unveiling of repressions that previously had made something look and function like a center.

Feminists have politicized this technique, showing that patriarchal culture and the social, political, and theoretical systems within it are pervasively male-centered. This androcentrism is not natural, but instead reflects the repression of women. Joan W. Scott argues in *Gender and the Politics of History* that it is only through "exposing the illusion" of patriarchal assumptions about gender that change can be achieved.

Consequently, feminists seek to recover and emphasize the lives and works of women in order to decenter the male bias of fields ranging from history and social practice to science and the arts.

Especially in the 1980s and 1990s, the critical force of decentering has been used to address complex problems within feminism itself. For instance, Audre Lorde, Gayatri Spivak, and bell hooks (among many others) have critiqued feminist theory and practice as too centered upon white, middle-class issues, upon heterosexual experience, and upon Euro-American perspectives.

Terence Brunk

References

Butler, Judith. *Gender Trouble: Feminism and the Subversion of Identity.* New York: Routledge, 1990.

Derrida, Jacques. "Structure, Sign, and Play in the Discourse of the Human Sciences." In *Critical Theory since 1965,* edited by Hazard Adams and Leroy Searle, 83–94. Tallahassee: University Presses of Florida, 1986.

hooks, bell. *Feminist Theory: From Margin to Center.* Boston: South End, 1984.

Johnson, Barbara. *A World of Difference.* Baltimore: Johns Hopkins University Press, 1987.

Lorde, Audre. "The Uses of Anger: Women Responding to Racism." In *Women's Voices: Visions and Perspectives*, edited by Pat C. Hoy II, Esther H. Schor, and Robert DiYanni, 170–176. New York: McGraw-Hill, 1990.

Scott, Joan W. *Gender and the Politics of History.* New York: Columbia University Press, 1988.

Spivak, Gayatri. *In Other Worlds.* New York: Routledge, 1988.

Deconstruction

"Deconstruction," a term coined by Jacques Derrida, is an analysis showing that a particular metaphysical system relies not on the presence of an absolute essence centering the system (such as "God"), but on the linguistic opposition—the difference—between the presumed essence and its antitheses ("evil," "mortals," and so on). Gayatri Chakravorty Spivak, who translated Derrida's *Of Grammatology*, suggests that deconstruction is crucial to the feminist project of exposing masculine privilege as a human construct rather than a natural right. A deconstruction reveals that a given metaphysical system is a discourse, is linguistic rather than natural. The system is not held together by a center outside it (a transcendental signified) but actually creates its center.

Derrida typically critiques systems based on a single, totalizing concept, a *logos* or "God"-word. For example, all we predicate of God—infinite, omniscient, omnipotent, Creator—we predicate only in opposition to finite creatures with limited knowledge and power. Nor does the adjective "omniscient" describe God's essence, by definition beyond human description. Paradoxically, "God" is what language cannot describe, yet we can conceive of "God" only through language. The question of the absolute existence of God, or of any metaphysical center, is moot. Whether or not such centers exist, we conceive of them only within a specific discourse and only by means of what they oppose or exclude. The "reality" of any metaphysical center is thus always a discursive one.

"Discursive," however, does not mean "unreal." Because absolute centers remain inaccessible, our realities are constructed through discourse. Thus deconstruction proves useful to a necessarily political movement like feminism. It allows us to critique the logic through which we construct the putatively "natural" centers of our value systems, our ideologies, our cultures. A deconstruction displays the inherent contradiction (what Derrida terms *différance*) at the center of any center: the very attempt to assert any totality ("God") relies upon an opposing term that escapes and so establishes the boundaries of the totality ("evil") and defers its perfect self-reflection (in Christian theology, until the End of the World).

More important, because metaphysical centers sustain their illusion of totality only through exclusion, a deconstruction can undermine the logical bases of cultural hierarchies. For example, pychoanalytic feminists like Jane Gallop and Luce Irigaray argue that masculine identity is itself an illusion of totality. Because totality—identity—is illusory, men project their own divided psyches onto women. A culture sustains this projection on a grand scale by representing women as threatening to masculine identity and self-control. In his own exemplary deconstruction in *Literary Theory*, Terry Eagleton remarks that such representations of women are "intimately related to [man] as the image of what he is not, and therefore as an essential reminder of what he is." Hélène Cixous, particularly in *The Newly Born Woman*, deconstructs a literary and philosophical history of representing woman as merely man's other.

Nevertheless, many feminists remain skeptical about deconstruction's usefulness to feminism. Nancy Miller, for example, argues that the deconstruction of the authoritatively speaking subject "prematurely forecloses the question of agency for [women]." Miller's critique seems particularly appropriate to the work of "Yale School" critics like Paul De Man, Geoffrey Hartmann, and J. Hillis Miller, for whom deconstruction has remained an aesthetic practice marking a text's infinite repetition not of some truth, but of other, previous texts. A deconstruction's potential to question all absolutes makes political critics reluctant to embrace it. If a deconstruction can undermine the moral or philosophical or psychological or scientific bases for a group's oppression, it might also undermine similarly grounded claims that the group might make on its own behalf.

Yet to view a deconstruction as an end in itself—to proclaim triumphantly (again) "No truth in this text, either!"—is to ignore its political potential, as Eagleton describes it, "to dismantle the logic by which a particular system of thought, and beyond that a whole system of political structures and social institutions, maintains its force." A deconstruction need not deny the historical specificity of the way a certain group is oppressed at a certain time; in fact, it can show the way a representation is not only produced by, but produces in turn, an individual or group's consciousness of itself. As Spivak argues, "The people who produce literature, male and female, are also moved by ideas of world and consciousness to which they cannot give name." The ideology upon which a specific form of sexism is based may not be grounded in an absolute, but nevertheless has a reality-effect: it forms people's definitions of themselves. While a deconstruction cannot give anyone a vantage point outside the system of cultural texts producing them—the deconstructivist realizes that she cannot write from a God's-eye point of view—it can expose the assumptions informing her point of view and allow her to judge their usefulness to her goals.

In fact, feminists have used deconstructions to correct some exclusions of feminism itself.

Toril Moi's *Sexual/Textual Politics* and Elizabeth Meese's *(Ex)Tensions* critique feminists' attempts to define a female or feminist essence. Meese reveals that some feminists' push for a unified theoretical framework—absolute answers to the questions "what is woman?" or "what is feminism?"—has resulted in the exclusion of many women's perspectives from that unified framework.

In any case, deconstruction is already an important point of departure for much oppositional criticism, whether or not the theorist acknowledges its value. For example, in *Playing in the Dark*, Toni Morrison engages in a kind of deconstruction when she argues that the physical presence of an enslaved black population allowed American writers to conceive and represent an autonomous, radically free, male hero. Most feminists assume that masculine privilege is conventional, not natural. While relatively few follow the specific form of a deconstructive critique—that is, the unraveling of a philosophical argument by exposing the way it depends upon a hierarchical, binary opposition of a God-term to its excluded other— most start with the assumption that the transcendental signified "man" has already been deconstructed.

Colleen Kennedy

References

Belsey, Catherine. *Critical Practice*. London, Methuen, 1980.

Cixous, Hélène, and Catherine Clément. *The Newly Born Woman*. Translated by Betsy Wing. Minneapolis: University of Minnesota Press, 1982.

Derrida, Jacques. *Dissemination*. Translated by Barbara Johnson. Chicago: University of Chicago Press, 1981.

———. *Of Grammatology*. Translated by Gayatri Chakravorty Spivak. Baltimore: Johns Hopkins University Press, 1974.

Eagleton, Terry. *Literary Theory: An Introduction*. Minneapolis: University of Minnesota Press, 1983.

Gallop, Jane. *The Daughter's Seduction: Feminism and Psychoanalysis*. Ithaca, N.Y.: Cornell University Press, 1982.

Irigaray, Luce. *This Sex Which Is Not One*. Translated by Catherine Porter. Ithaca, N.Y.: Cornell University Press, 1985.

Johnson, Barbara. *The Critical Difference:*

Essays in the Contemporary Rhetoric of Reading. Baltimore: Johns Hopkins University Press, 1980.

Meese, Elizabeth A. (Ex)Tensions: Re-Figuring Feminist Criticism. Urbana: University of Illinois Press, 1990.

Miller, Nancy K. Subject to Change: Reading Feminist Writing. New York: Columbia University Press, 1988.

Moi, Toril. Sexual/Textual Politics: Feminist Literary Theory. London: Methuen, 1985.

Spivak, Gayatri Chakravorty. In Other Worlds: Essays in Cultural Politics. New York: Routledge, 1988.

Deleuze, Gilles and Felix Guattari

Although Gilles Deleuze and Felix Guattari, are, according to Alice Jardine, two of the rare male theorists in France who are publicly supportive of feminism and particularly of the feminist movement in France," their profeminist stance is not outspoken in their work, but articulated subtly and complexly. Before collaborating with Guattari, Deleuze developed in *Difference and Repetition* and *The Logic of Sense* a philosophy of difference that informs his work with Guattari as well as much poststructuralist feminist literary theory.

Deleuze subverts essentialist determinations and established certainties of Western rationality by positing an understanding of difference that is not dependent on negation or opposition. This entails an affirmative differentiating of difference that is antirational, beyond contradiction, and always in flux. It is to acknowledge and accept difference as a positive movement and actuality; difference is continually distinguished from itself without distinguishing itself. Thus there are no definitive origins, no natural hierarchies, no dialectics; there are only affirmative differences. For Deleuze, then, Hegelianism, structuralism, and psychoanalysis are problematic and politically and socially destructive.

To further combat the influence of these philosophies, Deleuze and Guattari wrote the two-volume *Capitalism and Schizophrenia*, which consisted of *Anti-Oedipus* and *A Thousand Plateaus*, and they wrote *Kafka: Toward a Minor Literature*, which applies many of the theories presented in *Capitalism and Schizophrenia*.

In *Anti-Oedipus*, Deleuze and Guattari argue that the pervasive imperialism of psychoanalytic theory is largely responsible for the exploitation and oppression caused by capitalism in the twentieth century. The faulty dependence of psychoanalysis on desire-as-lack (as in Freud's theory of penis envy) and fantasy-production (as in Freud's theory of wish-fulfillment) and Freud's own paramount tripartite formula—the Oedipal, neurotic one: daddy-mommy-me—makes psychoanalysis both implausible and the perfect dogma for championing patriarchy and furthering the negative ramifications of capitalism.

In *A Thousand Plateaus*, Deleuze and Guattari continue their poststructuralist attack Western metaphysics, and introduce their theory of "nomad" thought, which endeavors to synthesize everything without effacing the peculiarities of anything; it endeavors to realize a positive, free-flowing circulation and interaction of everything, of all ideological and cultural idiosyncrasies, even when something appears negative. Deleuze and Guattari attempt to shatter the constitutional structures of capitalism and patriarchy with an affirmative comprehension of desire and heterogeneity; and they insist that particular instances of literary discourse, such as the "political-immediate" literature of Kafka, and revolutionary investments of desire, as in masochism, will help to bring about such a demolition.

Deleuze and Guattari refer explicitly neither to feminist literature as politically immediate nor to woman's desire as revolutionary in either *Capitalism and Schizophrenia* or *Kafka: Toward a Minor Literature*, but their theories do support these realities, just as the gender and sexual neutrality in their work seeks to obviate all negatively informed social differentiations.

Bryan Reynolds

References

Bogue, Ronald. *Deleuze and Guattari*. London: Routledge, 1989.

Deleuze, Gilles. *The Logic of Sense*. Translated by Mark Lester with Charles Stivale. Edited by Constanin V. Boundas. New York: Columbia University Press, 1990.

———. *Nietzsche and Philosophy*. Translated by Hugh Tomlinson. New York: Columbia University Press, 1983.

———, and Felix Guattari. *Anti-Oedipus: Capitalism and Schizophrenia*. Translated by Robert Hurley, Mark Seem, and

Helen R. Lane. Minneapolis: University of Minnesota Press, 1983.

———. *Kafka: Toward a Minor Literature.* Translated by Dana Polan. Minneapolis: University of Minnesota Press, 1986.

———. *A Thousand Plateaus: Capitalism and Schizophrenia.* Translated by Brian Massumi. Minneapolis: University of Minnesota Press, 1987.

Jardine, Alice A. *Gynesis: Configurations of Woman and Modernity.* Ithaca, N.Y.: Cornell University Press, 1985.

Massumi, Brian. *A User's Guide to Capitalism and Schizophrenia: Deviations from Deleuze and Guattari.* Cambridge: MIT Press, 1992.

Derrida, Jacques

As the "founder" of deconstruction, Jacques Derrida is among the most influential theorists of the twentieth century. Nominally a philosopher, his numerous works have had a profound impact upon literary studies since the mid 1960s, especially in the United States. The radically progressive political implications of his ideas stand in contrast to the often quietist, some might say nihilistic tendencies of Paul de Man and the protodeconstructive "Yale School," and his work has been heavily appropriated by feminist theorists such as Luce Irigaray, Judith Butler, and Gayatri Chakravorty Spivak. But his relationship with feminism has been a troubled one, for two fundamental reasons. First, in spite of his repeated discussions of sexual difference, he rarely addresses concrete feminist concerns (such as the "glass ceiling") directly. Second, he adopts controversially playful and challenging stances in his discussions of sexual difference; consequently, the meanings of his work for feminism are difficult to discern.

Derrida's *Of Grammatology* established the grounds of his critique of "logocentrism." This term refers to the bias in Western metaphysical thinking in favor of the linguistic "presence" of speech ("logos") over the linguistic "absence" of writing: a bias carried over into the social structures grounded by metaphysics (for example, Judeo-Christianity, morality, political structure, patriarchy). Derrida deconstructs the traditional opposition between speech and writing (between presence and absence) by demonstrating how speech depends upon the same linguistic structures as writing,

thus "deconstructing" the difference between speech and writing. He extends his critique of logocentrism in a series of essays in *Dissemination* and *Margins of Philosophy* (both 1972). Coining the word "phallogocentrism," Derrida argues that logocentrism is intricately connected to phallocentrism, the privileging of the masculine ["phallus"] over the feminine. As with logocentrism, Derrida claims that phallogocentrism saturates both Western metaphysical thought and the social structures predicated on such thought. Derridean deconstruction thus provides theoretical grounds for feminism on two levels. It enables a critique of the symptoms of gender inequality as they appear in society. But it also offers an analysis of the deep-seated male bias woven into the fabric of patriarchal culture, and consequently opens the possibility of addressing gender inequality on more than a symptomatic front.

With his investigations of Hegel and Kant in *Glas*, Derrida began a more focused interrogation of sexual difference as a rhetorical trope and a structuring principle in Western thought. Hegel, for instance, argued that the gendered opposition "male-female" functioned dialectically, and achieved pure synthesis in copulation sanctioned by marriage. Kant, by contrast, claimed a fundamental incompatibility between men and women in marriage, because the cultural institution of marriage granted women an unnatural and therefore "perverse" power over men. Derrida critiques the phallogocentrism of Kant's argument by demonstrating its negation of women. He then deconstructs the opposition between Kant's and Hegel's perspectives to show how Hegel's synthesis depends upon an identical negation of women: Derrida unveils the male bias of purportedly neutral and nongendered synthetic terms such as "marriage" or "the subject." Derrida thus illustrates that gender inequality is not simply a matter of how individual men and women relate to each other, but rather a condition of social structure, especially those structures that claim to sidestep questions of gender.

Derrida continues his analysis of sexual difference in *Spurs: Nietzsche's Styles*. He reads Nietzsche's fragmentary and starkly misogynistic musings on "woman" as a (perhaps unconscious) effort to deessentialize "woman" as a category. Derrida traces the ways in which Nietzsche's statements about women participate in his larger critique of the Western philosophical tradition. Because so much of that tradition is predicated on the negation of women, Nietzsche's critique of the tradition inevitably criticizes its negation of women. As a result, Derrida claims to identify some feminist strands in Nietzsche's thought: feminist strands inseparable from the overall antifeminist timbre of Nietzsche's work. In effect, Derrida uses Nietzsche's texts to exemplify ways in which the category "woman" has no defining essence and is always already split against itself.

Spurs thus sets the stage for Derrida's deconstruction of sexual difference in "The Law of Genre" and "Geschlecht: Sexual Difference, Ontological Difference." "Geschlecht" is Derrida's examination of Heidegger's "failure" to discuss sexuality. He suggests that this failure results less from Heidegger's aversion to or discomfort with questions of gender, than from the ways Heidegger's language implies a problem with the concept of sexual difference itself. Derrida argues that, unlike Hegel's synthesis "beyond" sexual difference, Heidegger's concept of "dasein" ("being-there") is sexually neutral only to the extent that it avoids the notion of sexual opposition, the duality of "male" and "female." Just as phallogocentrism thrives on the artificial privileging of male presence over female absence, so the very opposition between "male" and "female" depends upon an artificial privileging of a dyadic concept of sexuality over the concept of sexuality as multiplicity. This deconstruction of sexual difference allows Derrida's claim in "The Law of Genre": "I am woman."

Such claims highlight Derrida's effort to think sexuality beyond binary opposition. As he stresses in "Choreographies" (1982), an interview with Christie McDonald, the deconstruction of sexual opposition is not the erasure of sexual difference, but an attempt to displace the phallogocentrism of sexuality understood as dualism. His argument is thus a critique of the "origin" of phallogocentrism itself. Yet many feminists are wary of the deconstruction of sexual difference. Some perceive it as a denial of sexual difference; others read it as a repudiation of women's experience. Feminists have also raised questions about the deconstruction of sexual difference at the precise historical moment in which feminists have begun to utilize theories of sexual difference to effect social change.

If Derrida's work has had a mixed reception in some feminist circles, his overall critique of phallogocentrism has become fundamental to many other feminist projects. His controversial deconstruction of sexual difference opens up new possibilities for further feminist investigations: to name only one, Derrida himself has linked gender-multiplicity to potential multiplicities in sexual preference beyond bisexuality (which he sees as governed by the same dualist logic of heterosexuality-homosexuality).

Terence Brunk

References

Bennington, Geoffrey, and Jacques Derrida. *Jacques Derrida*. Translated by Geoffrey Bennington. Chicago: University of Chicago Press, 1993.

Derrida, Jacques. "Choreographies: An Interview with Jacques Derrida." Edited and translated by Christie V. McDonald. *Diacritics* 12: 66–76.

———. *A Derrida Reader; Between the Blinds*. Edited with an introduction and notes by Peggy Kamuf. New York: Columbia University Press, 1991.

———. *Dissemination*. Translated with an introduction by Barbara Johnson. Chicago: University of Chicago Press, 1981.

———. "Geschlecht: Sexual Difference, Ontological Difference." Translated by Ruben Berezdivin. *Research in Phenomenology* 13 (1983): 65–83.

———. *Glas*. Translated by John P. Leavey, Jr., and Richard Rand. Lincoln: University of Nebraska Press, 1986.

———. "The Law of Genre." Translated by Avital Ronell. *Glyph* 7 (1980): 176–232. Reprinted in *Critical Inquiry* 7 (1980): 55–81.

———. *Margins of Philosophy*. Translated by Alan Bass. Chicago: University of Chicago Press, 1982.

———. *Of Grammatology*. Translated with an introduction by Gayatri Chakravorty Spivak. Baltimore: Johns Hopkins University Press, 1976.

———. *Spurs: Nietzsche's Styles*. Translated by Barbara Harlow. Chicago: University of Chicago Press, 1979.

Desire

A term utilized by French psychoanalytic theorist Jacques Lacan to explain the development of the individual as a social and symbolic being. Although the notion of "desire" can be and often is thought of as having to do primarily with relations between the sexes, Lacan traces the function of this fundamental concept to the very beginnings of an individual's identity formation as the result of the subject's entrance into the symbolic world of language. Lacan explains the development of individual identity in a child as movement from an "imaginary" realm of seamless union with its surroundings to a "symbolic" realm characterized by a sense of separation and thus the necessity to articulate needs. Prior to her entrance into language, the child does not perceive herself to be separate from her world or the things which meet her needs; there is only a continuous presence. When the child begins to realize her independent existence from the mother (a realization brought on in part through the insertion of the father into the mother-child dyad), there opens up for the child a gap or discontinuity, a lack where there had been wholeness. From this point on, the child must articulate her needs, must represent them in language. Without that seamless wholeness in which all needs were met, there will always be something missing. Because the child is now a symbolizing subject, inscribed in the realm of language, and because there is by virtue of the representational nature of language an incommensurability between the signifier (the word) and the signified (the thing represented), there will always be for symbolic subjects this gap between what we need and what we demand. This difference between need and demand, which can neither be named nor satisfied, is desire.

Because at its core desire is a longing for that imaginary prelinguistic wholeness and unity, we are destined to be continually desiring. We will seek to satisfy desire in the place of the other, sure that the other has the thing that will make us whole. But in this we fail to see that there is desire or lack in the place of the other as well. This is important for feminism because of the way sexuality plays into this search to satisfy desire. To see "male" and "female" as absolute and complementary categories that satisfy and make each other whole is to mask the complexities of sexuality. This is an important consideration for feminism because of the way historically women have been made the objects of men's desire. This has taken the form both of casting them as unknowable and mystical and of elevating them to the position of supreme goodness or truth (both the literary phenomena of courtly love and romantic poetry are pertinent here). For Lacan psychoanalysis teaches us to explode this mythi-

cal reduction of women by recognizing the lack that exists in the other.

Because the ultimate aim of desire is to regain that lost union with the mother, which was interrupted by the father, Lacan claims that our primary desire is to engender the desire of the other (the mother), to be the object of the other's desire. Lacan asserts that we express this desire to be desired most obviously in such areas as gender construction and in relations between men and women. For example, Lacan argues that femininity is one such expression: women construct feminine behavior as a masquerade designed to engender the desire of the other.

The Lacanian notion of desire is extremely important for feminist theory because of the connection it articulates between issues of sexuality and the inscription of the historical subject. However, feminists have also argued that this formulation of desire, with its basis in the Oedipal conflict and resulting binary logic, is oppressive for women. Feminists have looked for ways around the binary equation of subject/object either by embracing the position of lack (expressed as silence and diffuse multiplicity or in the margins or interstices of literature and social institutions [Irigaray, de Lauretis]) or by exaggerating the objectifying trappings of femininity into mimicry that undercuts the subject's authority (expressed, for example, in the dangerous woman of *film noire* [Doane, Mulvey]). However, both of these options are problematic for feminists—the first because it treads dangerously close to essentialism and the second because of the danger that mimicry can collapse into simple objectification. Ultimately, feminists have been aided in their attempt to move beyond the limitations of this formulation of desire by the advent of the notion of a deconstructed, nonauthoritative subject. The challenge for feminists remains in utilizing the very helpful aspects of the concept of desire, such as its highlighting of the constructed nature of femininity, while avoiding its more problematic tendency to reduce women to mere representations of unconscious desire.

Anna Geronimo

References

de Lauretis, Teresa. *Alice Doesn't: Feminism, Semiotics, and Cinema.* Bloomington: Indiana University Press, 1984.

Doane, Mary Ann. *The Desire to Desire: The Woman's Film of the 1940's.* Bloomington: Indiana University Press, 1987.

Irigaray, Luce. *This Sex Which Is Not One.* Translated by Catherine Porter. Ithaca, N.Y.: Cornell University Press, 1985.

Lacan, Jacques. *Feminine Sexuality: Jacques Lacan and the école freudienne.* Edited by Juliet Mitchell and Jacqueline Rose. Translated by Jacqueline Rose. New York: W.W. Norton, 1982.

———. "The Mirror Stage as Formative of the Function of the I." In *Écrits*, 1–7. Translated by Alan Sheridan. New York: W.W. Norton, 1977.

Mulvey, Laura. "Visual Pleasure and Narrative Cinema." In *Feminism and Film Theory*, edited by Constance Penley, 57–68. New York: Routledge, 1988.

Determinism

See BIOLOGICAL DETERMINISM

Dickinson, Emily

Emily Dickinson has been the subject of much feminist criticism; she is often read as a writer of distinctly feminine texts, sometimes interpreted as overtly feminist, and frequently seen as a central figure in the debate over gender roles and relations in the nineteenth century. Dickinson's place in feminist theory, however, has not been as pronounced. She was not the author of any theoretical texts—at least none that have survived—but her life and poetry have served as the starting points for many feminist theoretical texts. Dickinson is most often used in feminist literary theory as a model of the female writer; despite her acknowledged uniqueness, many theorists see her as the type of the female poet and use her as the basis for a theory of feminist poetics. But there the resemblances among theorists end. She was most often seen, in the late 1970s and early 1980s, as the oppressed but resisting woman; her oddities of dress and isolation came to represent the toll that the psychic cruelty of nineteenth-century America exacted from talented women. In the late 1980s and early 1990s, though, another, more self-assertive and healthy Emily Dickinson has emerged—the lesbian or woman-centered writer whose oddities were simply differences and a sign of her healthy resistance to the patriarchal, heterosexual norm. In other essays, especially on Adrienne Rich's relationship to her, Dickinson has been seen as a model of how women writers affect one another and of how female readers approach the texts of other women writers.

Probably the most important feminist essay on Dickinson is Adrienne Rich's "Vesuvius at Home: The Power of Emily Dickinson" (which appears in *On Lies, Secrets, and Silence*, but which has been widely reprinted). In this essay, Rich uses Dickinson as a figure for the dilemmas of being a woman poet and as a starting point for developing a specifically feminine poetics. She raises the difficulty of being both a woman and a poet in a culture that has traditionally figured the poet as male. (As we'll see shortly, Gilbert and Gubar do the same, but they extend the danger to writing fiction, which Rich does not.) Rich posits that "the nineteenth-century woman poet . . . felt the medium of poetry as dangerous" and that the danger of poetry itself comes to shape much of women's poetry. But she also concludes that Emily Dickinson's efforts to confront, resist, and use that danger offer us the key to begin reading female poets' undoing of patriarchy.

In *Madwoman in the Attic*, Sandra Gilbert and Susan Gubar see Emily Dickinson as suffering the same "anxieties of authorship" they trace in the work of nineteenth-century women writers. (The "anxiety of authorship" is the strain female writers felt from writing within and against a male tradition; Gilbert and Gubar see it expressed in women's texts as "fantasies of guilt and anger.") But whereas other writers expressed their "fantasies of guilt and anger" in their fictional and poetic texts, Emily Dickinson, they argue, enacted them. They see her as a *poseur*, a woman who made herself into a madwoman, who played a fictional role; "this inventive poet enacted and eventually resolved both her anxieties about her art and her anger at female subordination" through this role-playing.

In an essay that focuses on the relationship between Dickinson and Rich, Betsy Erkilla rewrites the theory of influence from a feminist perspective. In "Dickinson and Rich: Toward a Theory of Female Poetic Influence," Erkilla suggests a connection between female writers that is independent of male writers. Unlike Harold Bloom's "anxiety of influence" (in which poets must struggle against and overthrow their poetic forefathers) or Gilbert's and Gubar's "anxiety of authorship" (in which women writers must struggle against a male tradition that leaves them out), the paradigm that Erkilla sees is one of kinship. She argues that "[w]hile the family romance between women poets has some of the same ambivalence as the relationship between mothers and daughters, there is a primary sense of identification and mutuality between women poets that sets them apart from the more agonistic relationship between precursor and ephebe in the Bloomian model." For Erkilla, this relationship allows the woman poet, like Dickinson, to "become her own heroine," a role she sees as positive, in contrast to Gilbert's and Gubar's madwoman.

In another essay that examines the Dickinson/Rich connection, "Reading Ourselves: Toward a Feminist Theory of Reading" (from *Gender and Reading*, 1986), Patricinio Schweikart turns to the question of feminist reading rather than feminist writing. Using Rich's essay as a model of feminist readers reading female writers, Schweikart suggests that such readers are "motivated by the need 'to connect,' to recuperate, or to formulate . . . the context, the tradition, that would link women writers to one another, to women readers and critics, and to the larger community of women." She argues that Rich's reading of Dickinson becomes a "weaving" of reader and writer, a weaving that she sees as the basis for all feminist reading.

Two fairly recent criticisms of Dickinson participate in significant ways to recent debates in feminist theory. Joanne Dobson, in *Dickinson and the Strategies of Reticence: The Woman Writer in Nineteenth-Century America* (1989), interprets Dickinson's work in terms of her female contemporaries. In re-placing Dickinson in this context, Dobson raises questions generated by Rich, Gilbert, and Gubar about "the" response of a woman writer to her own talent and poetic efforts. Dobson further obliquely challenges the formalist bent of much of feminist criticism of Emily Dickinson by so rigorously historicizing and contextualizing Dickinson's work (a critique of feminist criticism's use of formalism made eloquently by Paul Lauter in "Caste, Class, and Canon" [1987]).

Paula Bennett's *Emily Dickinson: Woman Poet* (1990) rejects another early tenet of feminist theory, the supposition that the woman writer felt a conflict between her roles as woman and as writer. Rather than seeing Dickinson as a conflicted bourgeois female poet, who found it difficult to deal with both patriarchy and the feminist challenge to it, Bennett views Dickinson as a figure of the strong, homoerotic poet who outright challenges phallocentrism and urges instead a "cliterocentrism." Perhaps even more important to feminist theory is Bennett's essay on Dickinson criticism, "The Pea that Duty Locks: Lesbian and Feminist-Heterosexual Readings of Emily Dickinson's Poetry" (from *Lesbian Texts and Contexts*, 1990). In this essay Bennett uses writing about Dickinson as an example of the "splitting of feminist criticism along sexual orientation lines"; she suggests that for feminist-heterosexual critics, Dickinson's relation to patriarchy is most significant, while for lesbian-feminist critics, her more confident homoeroticism is stressed. In this, Bennett outlines one of the conflicts within feminist theory, which is especially evident in Dickinson criticism—seeing the woman writer as victimized and seeing her as courageous and resisting.

Diana Price Herndl

References

Bennett, Paula. *Emily Dickinson: Woman Poet*. Iowa City: Iowa University Press, 1990.

———. "The Pea that Duty Locks: Lesbian and Feminist-Heterosexual Readings of Emily Dickinson's Poetry." In *Lesbian Texts and Contexts: Radical Revisions*, edited by Karla Jay and Joanne Glasgow, 104–125. New York: New York University Press, 1990.

Dobson, Joanne. *Dickinson and the Strategies of Reticence: The Woman Writer in Nineteenth-Century America*. Bloomington: Indiana University Press, 1989.

Erkilla, Betsy. "Dickinson and Rich: Toward a Theory of Female Poetic Influence." *American Literature* 56 (1984): 541–559.

Gilbert, Sandra, and Susan Gubar. *The Madwoman in the Attic: The Woman Writer and the Nineteenth-Century Literary Imagination*. New Haven: Yale University Press, 1979.

Lauter, Paul. "Caste, Class, and Canon." In *Feminisms: An Anthology of Literary Theory and Criticism*, edited by Robyn Warhol and Diane Price Herndl, 227–248. New Brunswick, N.J.: Rutgers University Press, 1991.

Rich, Adrienne. "Vesuvius at Home: The Power of Emily Dickinson." In *On Lies, Secrets, and Silence*, 157–183. New York: W.W. Norton, 1979.

Schweikart, Patricinio. "Reading Ourselves: Toward a Feminist Theory of Reading." In *Gender and Reading: Essays on Readers, Texts, and Contexts*, edited by Elizabeth A. Flynn and Patricinio P. Schweikart, 31–62. Baltimore: Johns Hopkins University Press, 1986.

Différance

Jacques Derrida argues that this term encapsulates language's operations. *Différance*, a play on the French verb *différer* (to differ and to defer) suggests that language creates meaning through both difference and deferral. Derrida traces his notion of *différance* to Ferdinand de Saussure's language theories. Saussure argued that the words (signifiers) of a given language are arbitrarily assigned to particular objects and concepts (signifieds) to create the sign—the complex of word and meaning. According to Saussure, the sign's arbitrariness is illustrated by the fact that different languages refer to the same object with different words: "dog" in English is *chien* in French, for example. Were there an inherent connection between the word and the object, different languages would not be possible. In this arbitrary system of meanings, signs are intelligible only because they are different from one another: "dog" is understood because it is not "human" or "cat."

Derrida emphasizes that in this system of differences, there are no positive terms, no signs that can be understood without being placed in relation to the other signs of the system. In other words, signs are understood by what they are not as much as by what they are. There is no "transcendental signified" or meaning that can be known in and of itself, independent of this system of differences. In this system of differences, meaning is always doubly deferred, by the sign itself and by the system. As Derrida explains, a "sign is put in place of the thing itself, the present thing—'thing' holding here for the sense as well as the referent." In other words, the sign indicates a mediated understanding or indirectness since the sign stands in for the thing itself. The meaning of the sign is further deferred by the system of differences in which meaning occurs.

What are the significances of this notion of differing and deferring for feminist literary critics? One important implication of *différance* is its role in deconstruction: *différance* demon-strates the way meaning is constructed by the system of differences, and can therefore be broken down and analyzed. In particular, the binary oppositions (subject/object, male/female, European/Non-European) that many feminist critics are interested in interrogating can be shown to be part of a "multivalent" system of meaning. For example, the primacy accorded by Western metaphysics to the concept of the subject or self (first-person identity), modeled on the white, male bourgeois, can be questioned, since with *différance* there is no signified with more strength than another. Derrida extends his discussion of *différance* to include the concept of the subject, and deconstructs the "self-presence" that subjects assume, and thus the status of their "others" as objects. By showing how the concept of the subject has been constructed by language, Derrida deconstructs the assumptions that enable the subject to think of itself as present, solid, unwavering, and independent. Because humans refer to themselves and others through language, subjectivity itself is implicated in the differing and deferring of *différance*.

Some feminist literary critics find Derrida's deconstruction of the binary opposition and the subject a liberating move, one that enables them to explore the ways various "others" are constructed in literature. Others find *différance* a useful model for analyzing structures of meaning different from that assumed by phallocentric language, and use *différance* to explore fluidity, multivalency, and silences in literature or in women's writing. However, some feminist literary critics question, as does Linda Kintz, whether deconstructing the "universal" subject means the "disappearance of women as active subjects yet again, only more subtly this time?" That is, some critics argue that there might be some use in constructing a model of feminine subjectivity, even as the model of masculine subjectivity is deconstructed.

Susan B. Taylor

References

Derrida, Jacques. "Différance." In *Speech, Phenomena and Other Essays*, translated by David B. Allison. Evanston, Ill.: Northwestern University Press, 1973.

Irigaray, Luce. *Speculum of the Other Woman*. Translated by Gillian C. Gill. Ithaca, N.Y.: Cornell University Press, 1985.

Kintz, Linda. "In-Different Criticism: The

Deconstructive Parole." In *The Thinking Muse: Feminism and Modern French Philosophy*, edited by Jeffner Allen and Iris Marion Young, 113–135. Bloomington and Indianapolis: Indiana University Press, 1989.

Marks, Elaine, and Isabelle de Courtivron. *New French Feminisms: An Anthology.* New York: Schocken Books, 1981.

Spivak, Gayatri Chakravorty. *In Other Worlds: Essays in Cultural Politics.* New York and London: Routledge, 1988.

Difference

The many uses of this term in feminist criticism reflect the variety of concerns feminist critics address. The *Oxford English Dictionary* defines "difference" most generally as the "condition, quality, or fact of being different, or not the same in quality or essence" and for many feminists, gender has been the most important quality of being different. The distinction between female and male or feminine and masculine has been feminism's primary ground (especially since gender forms the basis for much of the marginalization and oppression of the female in patriarchal culture). However, feminist critics diverge considerably in their uses of gender difference as a category for feminist thought and interpretation. In addition to gender differences, feminist literary critics have explored and invoked several other categories of difference, including culture, race, sexuality, and class. In all of these various categories, feminists may use difference as a tool for analyzing literature, or they may in turn analyze difference itself as a cultural practice or concept.

One ramification of theories of gender difference is the idea that writing by women deserves to be explored as a distinct literary field, one of the earlier subjects of feminist criticism in the 1970s. Sandra Gilbert's and Susan Gubar's *The Madwoman in the Attic: The Woman Writer and the Nineteenth-Century Literary Imagination* suggested that women writers share a "uniquely female" set of literary symbols and imaginative strategies for circumventing the limitations placed on their gender in the nineteenth century. Feminist literary studies such as Gilbert's and Gubar's also argue for the establishment of a tradition of women writers, based on the notion that women's writing has a different focus and imagistic vocabulary than that of men.

The question of gender difference is also explored by feminist critics who focus on women's bodies as distinct from men's, and extrapolate from these physical differences to differences in women's experience of sexuality and creativity. French feminists such as Julia Kristeva, Hélène Cixous, and Luce Irigaray suggest a model for feminine sexuality that focuses on *jouissance* instead of the phallocentric model of masculine sexuality. In varied ways, these writers also connect women's physical experiences to their writing, and explore the ways *écriture féminine* may call into question the primacy assumed by masculine writing and phallocentric discourse. Indirectness, playfulness, and nonlinearity are some of the qualities of women's writing posited by these writers. These notions of a distinctly feminine style of writing have been criticized by some feminist, who argue that they create dangerously essentialized concepts of gender and are thus potentially limiting.

Theories of gender difference based in women's experiences have also been criticized by feminists who draw attention to the ways cultural or racial differences are ignored by a monolithic concept of women's experience. Barbara Smith, in "Toward a Black Feminist Criticism," counters the tendency of feminist criticism in the 1970s to ignore questions of race, class, and sexuality while it focused on creating a canon of white women writers. Smith argues that the "politics of sex as well as the politics of race and class are crucially interlocking factors in the works of Black women writers" and need to be included in black feminist criticism. She also calls for recognition that "Black women writers constitute an identifiable literary tradition." Gayatri Chakravorty Spivak and other postcolonial feminist critics analyze the ways cultural differences have been used and ignored in literature and in feminist criticism, arguing readings of characters, for example, who have previously been obscured by models of white women's development.

Bonnie Zimmerman in "What Has Never Been: An Overview of Lesbian Feminist Literary Criticism" writes of the need to create the "lesbian literary tradition" that has been left out of attempts by feminists to create a tradition of women writers. Additionally, she argues that "lesbian criticism and cultural theory in general" need to acknowledge the differences among lesbians, to avoid the tendency "to write and act as if lesbian experience—which is perceived as that of a contemporary, white middle-class feminist—is universal and unchanging." Similarly, Barbara Smith calls attention to the position of the black lesbian in feminism, as well as lesbians in black writing and criticism.

These various invocations and analyses of difference themselves point to differences between feminist literary critics: even though these theorists may write about literature, they do not simply share the same concerns because they are feminists. This reflects another layer of the *Oxford English Dictionary*'s definition of difference: "dissimilarity, distinction, diversity; the relation of non-agreement or non-identity *between* two or more things, disagreement." While all of these critics may call themselves feminists, they do not necessarily agree on the definition of feminism. Many of the critics' interests may combine several of these categories of difference. Yet many of the different uses of difference in feminist literary criticism share similar issues: about canon formation; whether there is an "essential" quality to the lesbian novel, to woman's writing, to African American women's poetry, and so on; and whether to assert differences or call them into question.

Finally, differences cannot be spoken of without considering the ways they are also construed hierarchically in binary oppositions. One thing these various explorations of difference may share is an interest in challenging the way differences in Western metaphysics and cultures have traditionally been organized into hierarchical pairs, into binary oppositions (such as male/female) in which one term is seen as the dominant original and against which the other is seen as derivative, inferior, secondary. Challenging this use of difference by asserting differences in positive terms is one feminist response to such hierarchies; questioning the fundamental functions and construction of difference is another.

Susan B. Taylor

References

Belsey, Catherine, and Jane Moore, eds. *The Feminist Reader: Essays in Gender and the Politics of Literary Criticism.* London: Macmillan Education, 1989.

Christian, Barbara. "The Race for Theory." *Cultural Critique* 6 (1987): 51–63.

Cixous, Hélène. "The Laugh of the Medusa." Translated by Keith Cohen and Paula Cohen. *Signs* 1 (1976): 875–893.

Gilbert, Sandra, and Susan Gubar. *The Mad-woman in the Attic: The Woman Writer and the Nineteenth-Century Literary Imagination.* New Haven and London: Yale University Press, 1979.

Greene, Gayle, and Coppélia Kahn, eds. *Making a Difference: Feminist Literary Criticism.* London and New York: Routledge, 1985.

Irigaray, Luce. *Speculum of the Other Woman.* Translated by Gillian C. Gill. Ithaca, N.Y.: Cornell University Press, 1985.

Marks, Elaine, and Isabelle de Courtivron, eds. *New French Feminisms: An Anthology.* New York: Schocken Books, 1981.

Smith, Barbara. "Toward a Black Feminist Criticism." Reprinted in *All the Women are White, All the Blacks are Men, but Some of Us Are Brave: Black Women's Studies*, edited by Barbara Smith, 157–175. Old Westbury, N.Y.: Feminist, 1982.

Spivak, Gayatri Chakravorty. In *Other Worlds: Essays in Cultural Politics.* New York and London: Routledge, 1988.

Zimmerman, Bonnie. "What Has Never Been: An Overview of Lesbian Feminist Literary Criticism." *Feminist Studies* 7 (1981): 451–476.

Dinnerstein, Dorothy

Author of *The Mermaid and the Minotaur: Sexual Arrangements and Human Malaise*, Dinnerstein locates the roots of misogyny—antifemale sentiment—in the fact that early child care is carried out primarily by women. The effect of this gender role division, she argues, is twofold. It enables us to fend off our most profound anxieties about being human and, at the same time, perpetuates a communal neurosis that threatens our very existence. In order to forge a healthier humanity, and to become more fully human ourselves, Dinnerstein urges men and women to recognize and act upon the need for shared parenting in early childhood.

The mermaid and minotaur figures in Dinnerstein's title refer to the half-human state in which she believes we currently exist, and which is played out in our "sexual arrangements" and "human malaise." "Sexual arrangements" are defined as our current male-female role divisions, especially woman's role as primary caregiver. Such arrangements, Dinnerstein claims, help us to cope with our "human malaise," or communal psychopathology, which ambivalently faces the human condition of lost infant oneness, bodily vulnerability, and mortality. Although such strategies are superficially successful at allaying the pain of our humanity, they also maintain the very pain they seek to soothe because they prevent us from fully confronting these basic human truths. Why we continue to adhere to them—despite the fact that they are essentially uncomfortable to us and, given our technological advances, perhaps no longer even necessary—is the crucial question we must consider if we are to continue to develop as a species in healthy ways.

For Dinnerstein, the answer to this question lies in the fact that women are responsible for early child care. Turning to psychoanalytic theories of development, she argues that because woman is the primary caretaker, she is also the primary love object of both boys and girls. This early bond, which must be disrupted in order for children to become adults, leaves boys and girls—and men and women—desperately attempting to repress the pain that such separation forces them to face. Yet such loss— essential to who we are—cannot be permanently denied and inevitably resurfaces in unhealthy forms that superficially allow us to avoid its reality. Our uniquely human capacity for invention, creation, and mastery, for example, counteracts our inability to control aspects of the world. Our relationship to "woman" provides another route. Primarily responsible for early care, woman becomes the first and only sex associated with the essential aspects of our humanity: isolation, physical vulnerability, and mortality. In our attempt to defend against what she reminds us of, she is on the one hand idolized and on the other debased: idolized in an attempt by both men and women to regain the mother-infant bond that she alone represents, and debased because she can never adequately do so and is a constant reminder of what is forever beyond our reach. This intersection of defense mechanisms impacts our social structure in several ways. It creates a male-based, patriarchal world that leaves women out of the creation/history-making process altogether. It also impacts our creative impulses, which, potentially healthy tools for coping with our primary loss, become fraught with aggression that is dangerous and lead to ends that alienate us from each other, our history, and the natural world for which we are responsible.

Despite the fact that at some level men and women alike feel uncomfortable with these sexual arrangements and their consequences, until we are willing to face the core of our human malaise these familiar social structures remain both necessary and destructive.

Dinnerstein's work contributes to feminist theory in several significant ways. It moves the feminist argument beyond its focus on woman's child-bearing status—which cannot be changed—to an analysis of woman's child-rearing status, which can and must be altered by way of shared early parenting. It also complicates feminist analyses of patriarchy and misogyny, viewing their cultural presence not as choices made by power-hungry men, but as crutches men and women together rely on to cope with the pain and ambivalence they feel about the realities of being human. Finally, Dinnerstein makes the feminist project of liberation and equality between the sexes an urgent concern of both men and women, one that impacts not only human beings but the world in which they exist.

Sara E. Quay

References

Dinnerstein, Dorothy. *The Mermaid and the Minotaur: Sexual Arrangements and Human Malaise.* New York: Harper and Row, 1976.

Discourse

See LANGUAGE

Doane, Mary Ann

In "Women's Stake: Filming the Female Body" (reprinted in *Femmes Fatales*), Doane articulates her understanding of the relation of the body to feminist film theory; she examines the impasse that essentialist and antiessentialist feminist film critics have reached; and she briefly suggests ways in which avant-garde feminist films may move beyond this theoretical impasse. Regarding Hollywood cinema, in *Femmes Fatales* and *The Desire to Desire: The Woman's Film of the 1940's*, Doane accepts the broad premise of feminist film critics after Mulvey, that the classical cinema's camera's gaze is male. *The Desire to Desire* looks for redeeming value in "women's films" made specifically for a female audience: maternal melodramas, romances, *noir* films centered around paranoid female protagonists, and films that utilize a "medical discourse" to discuss female hysteria. These women's films, Doane argues, offer the female spectator a female protagonist, but a female protagonist who is inherently unstable in a cinema defined by patriarchal psychological and semiotic systems of representation. Doane traces, in film after film, the dissolution of the female protagonist as the organizing agent of the narrative; and suggests that this collapse of female subjectivity requires that the female spectator surrender not only her sexual identity, but also her very "access to sexuality." The female spectator of a woman's film can ultimately claim nothing more than "the desire to desire."

The Desire to Desire intimates that women's films of the forties offer only fleeting critiques of patriarchal power. In *Femmes Fatales,* Doane uses the femme fatale as "a kind of signpost or emblem" to center a collection of essays heavily informed by psychoanalytic theory. Doane considers half a dozen films and in a lengthy exposition on veils and masks, proposes that the representation of a female on film must be a masquerade of femininity. Regarding *femmes fatales,* Doane extends the concept of femininity as a masquerade to *noir* female protagonists who embody mysterious, and often fatal, otherness. Yet it is only in an avant-garde film such as Leslie Thornton's *Adynata* that Doane finds real resistance to the classical cinema's oppression of women. As she explains at the end of *The Desire to Desire,* Doane believes that Hollywood cinema is politically beyond redemption and that "it is now possible to *look elsewhere*" for a cinema that offers true female subjectivity to the female spectator.

Ellen Draper

References

Doane, Mary Ann. *The Desire to Desire: The Woman's Film of the 1940's.* Bloomington: Indiana University Press, 1987.

———. *Femmes Fatales: Feminism, Film Theory, Psychoanalysis.* New York: Routledge, 1991.

———. *Revision: Essays in Feminist Film Criticism.* Edited by Mary Ann Doane, Patricia Mellencamp, and Linda Williams. Los Angeles: University Publications of America, in association with the American Film Institute, 1984.

Domesticity

Domesticity refers to those qualities and traits that relate to the family and the household. However, within academic settings, and especially feminist circles, this definition has been broadened to include those ideas and issues related to the organization of men and women into two distinct spheres of activity: the masculine public sphere of politics and the marketplace, and the feminine private sphere of home and family life. Domesticity is an important topic for feminist literary theory because it explores a neglected subject: the domestic lives of women. By studying the meaning and value of women's behavior within the home, domesticity encourages, among other things, a reassessment of gender roles, both within and outside the home, as well as an exploration of the symbolic and material functions of the home during different times and in different settings.

Twenty years ago, if domesticity was mentioned at all, it was usually in terms of how it functioned in relation to the needs of men and male power structures. In the late 1960s and 1970s, however, feminists in a number of disciplines realized that social and literary history needed to focus on and address the needs of women. Accordingly, the topic of domesticity grew out of the efforts of feminist historians and anthropologists to rewrite history from a feminine point of view by focusing on women's personal experiences and accomplishments. The anthropologist Michelle Zimbalist Rosaldo was one of the first feminists to address the topic of domesticity and the notion of separate spheres. She claimed that the separation of men and women into public and domestic spheres—and the related perception that women's power is inferior to that of men—is a universal occurrence.

Placed within the private setting of the home, women are associated with activities such as the bearing and raising of children, cooking, housekeeping, and nurturing and supporting men and children. Men, on the other hand, are positioned within the workplace where they are actively involved in economic life and participate in political, social, and economic decision-making. For feminists, an investigation of the domestic economy and women's domestic roles strengthened the argument that, though they were not paid, women's lives within the home were just as important as men's lives in the public sphere.

Detailed descriptions of the public/private

D

split, and women's and men's roles within their respective spheres, were common in the 1970s. In addition, a number of psychoanalytic feminists have examined women's unique traits and abilities and their association with home and family life. Nancy Chodorow, for instance, studies the cross-cultural activity of mothering, while other feminists examine female sexuality, reproduction, lactation, and menstruation. Within literary study, Myra Jehlen's influential article "Archimedes and the Paradox of Feminist Criticism" (1981) compares Samuel Richardson's novels with American sentimental novels in her investigation of what it means to be a woman. Jehlen argues, among other things, that whether the person is male or female, the interior life is uniquely feminine. She sees this pattern occurring both in fiction and in real life.

While they admit that the study of women's private lives is important, many poststructuralist feminists believe that cross-cultural ways of investigating domesticity often try to do too much. They feel that universal statements about the home and women's private lives tend to neglect differences among women living in different cultures and at different times. In addition, it is felt that differences between men and women are often reinforced and not questioned or explored in any real depth. As men are aligned with the workplace and women with the home and family, characteristics are assigned to each sex, and discussions often focus upon the behavior of men and women within their respective spheres of influence.

To account for these perceived weaknesses, poststructuralist feminists took the issue of domesticity in a new direction, and as a result, universal narratives about the essential nature of women, men, and the domestic sphere have declined. There are now less romantic and utopian views about women's position within the home and an increased recognition that the public and private spheres are not so distinct and separate after all. For instance, theorists like Gillian Brown now admit that the marketplace has already been domesticated, to a certain extent, by women's contact with their husbands and other male family members. Others, like Elizabeth Langland and Linda Nicholson, point out that the domestic setting is not immune from the forces of the marketplace.

Within literary study, this recognition of the domestic sphere's influence has prompted a number of studies on romances, sentimental fiction, and domestic novels—all works associated with women's private domestic lives, and works primarily written and read by women. These more popular forms of fiction have historically been ignored or degraded by the literary establishment. Yet, as Jane Tompkins argues in her study of popular American sentimental fiction, these texts do cultural work as they try "to reorganize culture from the woman's point of view." Nancy Armstrong builds upon this idea in her investigation of domesticity. She posits that British conduct books and domestic novels between the late seventeenth and mid nineteenth centuries, works that centered on an idealized domestic woman, helped to create and define the middle-class and the domestic woman. While Tompkins focuses more on the subtle and broad influence of domestic novels within American culture, Armstrong grants the domesticated woman—both inside and outside of fiction—the power to transform her culture and shape class consciousness.

Some feminist literary theorists examine what has been called literary domesticity or the relationship between the domestic sphere and women's efforts as professional writers. Feminists such as Judith Lowder Newton and Annette Kolodny study the relationship between domesticity in literature and in history, and whether or not certain texts subvert or reinforce a culture's beliefs about separate spheres. In a fascinating study of key intersections between domestic ideology and nineteenth-century American individualism, Gillian Brown examines work by Stowe, Hawthorne, Melville, Fern, and Gilman as she discusses such diverse topics as health, work, housekeeping, marketplace practices, and property.

As Brown's work illustrates, current scholarship on domesticity tends to examine the complex interplay between domesticity as a cultural force and as a literary object of study. Moreover, critics such as Hazel Carby help us to realize that the traditional domestic sphere argument centers upon white, middle-class, heterosexual women and that this way of thinking is not wholly relevant to lesbians, women of color, and women from different ethnic and socioeconomic groups. By uncovering hidden biases and assumptions about women's place within the home and by examining how discourses on domesticity participate in other cultural codes and practices, literary theorists continue to challenge our views about the roles of men and women both within and outside of the home.

Pam Lieske

References

Armstrong, Nancy. *Desire and Domestic Fiction: A Political History of the Novel.* New York: Oxford University Press, 1987.

Brown, Gillian. *Domestic Individualism: Imagining Self in Nineteenth-Century America.* Berkeley: University of California Press, 1990.

Carby, Hazel. *Reconstructing Womanhood.* New York: Oxford University Press, 1987.

Chodorow, Nancy. *The Reproduction of Mothering: Psychoanalysis and the Sociology of Gender.* Berkeley: University of California Press, 1978.

Jehlen, Myra. "Archimedes and the Paradox of Feminist Criticism." *Signs: Journal of Women in Culture and Society* 6 (1981): 575–601.

Kerber, Linda K. "Separate Spheres, Female Worlds, Woman's Place: The Rhetoric of Women's History." *Journal of American History* 75 (1988): 9–39.

Kolodny, Annette. *The Land before Her: Fantasy and Experience of the American Frontier, 1630–1860.* Chapel Hill: University of North Carolina Press, 1984.

Langland, Elizabeth. "Nobody's Angel: Domestic Ideology and Middle-Class Women in the Victorian Novel." *PMLA* 107 (1992): 290–304.

Newton, Judith Lowder. *Women, Power, and Subversion: Social Strategies in British Fiction 1778–1860.* Athens: University of Georgia Press, 1981.

Nicholson, Linda. *Gender and History: The Limits of Social Theory in the Age of the Family.* New York: Columbia University Press, 1986.

Rosaldo, Michelle Zimbalist. "Woman, Culture and Society: A Theoretical Overview." In *Woman, Culture, and Society,* edited by Michelle Zimbalist Rosaldo and Louise Lamphere, 17–42. Stanford: Stanford University Press, 1974.

Tompkins, Jane. *Sensational Designs: The Cultural Work of American Fiction 1790–1860.* New York: Oxford University Press, 1985.

D

Dora

The subject of Sigmund Freud's *Dora: An Analysis of a Case of Hysteria,* "Dora" is the pseudonym for Ida Bauer, a nineteenth-century Viennese woman who was treated by Freud for symptoms of hysteria. Feminist literary theorists have viewed Dora's case as a text, focusing on the way it illustrates issues of narrative authority, textual interpretation, and sexual difference.

Suffering from symptoms of hysteria—migraine, coughing, difficulty breathing, and periodic loss of voice—eighteen-year-old Ida Bauer entered treatment with Sigmund Freud at the insistence of her father. During her analysis, the young woman told Freud the story of her family, a somewhat scandalous, if typical, Victorian drama. Unhappily married, her mother was a compulsive cleaner and her father was engaged in an adulterous affair with the wife of a family friend. Ida's role in this liaison was complex. She had been an intimate companion of her father's mistress, Frau K., for several years and had cared for the older woman's children. In addition, at two points during Ida's adolescence Frau K.'s husband, Herr K., had made sexual advances toward the young woman that she firmly rebuked. In response to Ida's story, Freud claimed that she was bisexually attracted to Frau K. and that her reports of Herr K.'s sexual advances were part of a fantasy of seduction. Ida abruptly terminated her psychoanalytic sessions after only three months. Freud concluded that his treatment had been unsuccessful and blamed the failure on his inability to prevent his patient's transference.

Feminist literary theorists have responded to Dora's case in a variety of ways. Confronting Freud's assertion that the primary symptom of hysteria is the inability to tell a coherent story, they have analyzed Freud's attempt to impose his own story onto Dora in an attempt to "cure" her, an approach they argue patriarchy holds toward women in general. In this light, Dora becomes a victim whose hysteria and hysterical symptoms represent woman's position in an oppressive society. Conversely, those symptoms have also been interpreted as heroic and Dora as a heroine, a woman who found a way to circumvent patriarchy through a literal body language that expressed rather than contained her story. Turning Freud's therapeutic strategy on its head, some feminists claim that it is Freud's narrative, not Dora's, that is hysterical. They have also balked at Freud's insistence that Dora's description of sexual violation was purely fantasy and have recuperated his original seduction theory, which recognizes that children can be and are (as Dora may have been) sexually seduced or violated. Still other feminist theorists have focused on Freud's assertion that Dora held a bisexual love for Frau K., a claim he makes but never pursues. In response to the surge of interest in Dora's case, Ellie Ragland-Sullivan warns that feminist attempts to "master" Dora may reproduce the same sort of narrative violence enacted by Freud on his patient's story. Whatever the critical stance, in *Dora* Freud left a richly woven text not only of psychoanalytic and patriarchal "readings" of woman, but of his reading of himself as well.

Sara E. Quay

References

Appleby, Robin S. "Dracula and Dora: The Diagnosis and Treatment of Alternative Narratives." *Literature and Psychology* 39 (1993): 16–37.

Bernheimer, Charles, and Claire Kahane, eds. *In Dora's Case: Freud-Hysteria-Feminism.* New York: Columbia University Press, 1985.

Frank, Lawrence. "Freud and Dora: Blindness and Insight." In *Seduction & Theory: Readings of Gender, Representation, and Rhetoric,* edited by Dianne Hunter, 110–132. Urbana: University of Illinois Press, 1989.

Freud, Sigmund. *Dora: An Analysis of a Case of Hysteria.* Edited by Philip Rieff. New York: Collier, 1963.

Harries, Elizabeth W. "Fragments and Mastery: Dora and Clarissa." *Eighteenth-Century Fiction* 5 (1993): 217–238.

Hertz, Neil, ed. "A Fine Romance: Freud and Dora." Special issue. *Diacritics: A Review of Contemporary Criticism* 13 (1983).

Lopez, Donna Bentolila. "Frau K and Dora." In *Criticism and Lacan: Essays and Dialogue on Language, Structure, and the Unconscious,* edited by Patrick Colm Hogan and Lalita Pandit, 180–184. Athens: University of Georgia Press, 1990.

Ragland-Sullivan, Ellie. "Dora and the Name-of-the-Father: The Structure of Hysteria." In *Discontented Discourses: Feminism/Textual Intervention/Psychoanalysis,* edited by Marleen S. Barr and Richard Feldstein, 208–240. Urbana: University of Illinois Press, 1989.

Suleiman, Susan Rubin. "Mastery and Transference: The Significance of Dora." In *The Comparative Perspective on Literature: Approaches to Theory and Practice,* edited by Claton Koelb and Susan Noakes, 213–223. Ithaca, N.Y.: Cornell University Press, 1988.

Van den Berg, Sara. "Reading Dora Reading: Freud's 'Fragment of an Analysis of a Case of Hysteria.'" *Literature and Psychology* 32 (1986): 27–35.

Douglas, Ann

In her groundbreaking study *The Feminization of American Culture*, Ann Douglas considered the previously neglected work of antebellum American women writers and ministers. Douglas was the first to argue that the sentimental fiction white women wrote was central to nineteenth-century culture and thus a deciding element in the shaping of the twentieth century. In *Terrible Honesty: Mongrel Manhattan in the 1920s*, Douglas argued that the 1920s in the United States were characterized by the shared assault in black and white culture against the figure that had dominated nineteenth-century American culture: the matriarch of white, middle-class society. In this regard, *Terrible Honesty* is a sequel to *Feminization*.

In *Feminization*, Douglas defined the sentimental as "the manipulation of nostalgia" by women and ministers who, because they lacked any real power to change society, used sentimental literature to exert "influence." Douglas argued that this literature led, not to reforms, but to the decline of America's great intellectual tradition, once fostered by Calvinism, and to the rationalization of an unjust economic order. Despite the efforts of Melville, Hawthorne, and other more "serious" writers to continue the older, more "rigorous" traditions, the twentieth century is left with an antiintellectual consumer society as opposed to an intellectually rigorous producer society. For Douglas, then, women's literature failed to replace the male-dominated Calvinist tradition with a "comprehensive feminism." In her new preface to *Feminization*, Douglas responded to subsequent feminist scholarship, much of which has argued, conversely, that sentimental literature by women made important feminist criticisms of society. She noted that she "underrated" antebellum women writers because she didn't adequately consider the "long-term efficacy of their social goals and methods."

Douglas's scholarship was particularly concerned with the many ways in which patriarchal stipulations have impoverished women's writing and, by extension, society as a whole. Although *Feminization* is decidedly antisentimental and thus not celebratory of much of the literature by women, its conclusion that sentimentality was a central component of nineteenth-century American culture has paved the way for the reassessment of American literature written by white women.

Elise Lemire

References
[Early publications under Ann D. Wood]
Douglas, Ann. *The Feminization of American Culture*. New York: Knopf, 1977. New York: Doubleday, 1988.
———. "The 'Scribbling Women' and Fanny Fern: Why Women Wrote." *American Quarterly* 23 (1971): 3–24.
———. *Terrible Honesty: Mongrel Manhattan in the 1920s*. New York: Farrar, Straus and Giroux, 1995.
———. "Willa Cather: A Problematic Ideal." In *Women, the Arts, and the 1920s in Paris and New York*, edited by Kenneth W. Wheeler and Virginia Lee Lussier, 14–26. New Brunswick, N.J.: Transaction, 1982.
Wood, Ann D. "The Literature of Impoverishment: The Women Local Colorists in America, 1865–1914." *Women's Studies* 1 (1972): 3–46.

Drabble, Margaret

Margaret Drabble, who published her first novel, *A Summer Bird-Cage*, in 1963, has herself lived through, participated in, and chronicled the impact of the second wave of feminism on the lives of British women during the past three decades. Drabble's earliest novels are not consciously feminist, but their subjects and stories, particularly their representations of motherhood, expanded the novel's territory. Drabble achieved a new level of aesthetic and political sophistication in her fifth work, *The Waterfall* (1975), which initiates an intertextual critique of European novelistic tradition that has only intensified in Drabble's later work. *The Waterfall* is also noteworthy as the novel in which Drabble begins an ongoing project of recovering the repressed female body by speaking the previously silenced truths of the sexuality of maternity and orgasmic genital sexuality.

In her subsequent novels Drabble has continued to explore the subtle ways in which ideology becomes inscribed in traditional narrative and literary techniques and to search for new narrative forms adequate to the realities of women's changing lives. Her four most recent novels—*The Middle Ground* (1980) and the trilogy comprising *The Radiant Way* (1987), *A Natural Curiosity* (1989), and *The Gates of Ivory* (1991)—all employ multiple protagonists to depict broad visions of contemporary British society. Drabble employs the techniques of feminist metafiction, including intrusive narrators, intertextuality, unresolved endings, and plots that chart the complex interrelations of community and friendship. Her protagonists are primarily women in mid life, whose stories cannot be contained within traditional plots of courtship or feminist revisions of the quest plot. In her most recent work Drabble has also focused on the power of social class to determine lives and their stories.

Pamela Starr Bromberg

References
Bromberg, Pamela. "Margaret Drabble's *The Radiant Way*: Feminist Metafiction." *Novel* 24 (1990): 5–25.
Creighton, Joanne. *Margaret Drabble*. London: Methuen, 1985.
Drabble, Margaret, "Mimesis: The Representation of Reality in the Post-War British Novel." *Mosaic* 20 (1987): 1–14.
Greene, Gayle. *Changing the Story: Feminist Fiction and the Tradition*. Bloomington: Indiana University Press, 1991.
Rose, Ellen Cronan, ed. *Critical Essays on Margaret Drabble*. Boston: G.K. Hall, 1985.
———. *The Novels of Margaret Drabble: Equivocal Figures*. Totowa, N.J.: Barnes and Noble, 1980.
Rubinstein, Roberta. "Sexuality and Intertextuality: Margaret Drabble's *The Radiant Way*." *Contemporary Literature* 30 (1989): 95–112.
Sadler, Lynn Veach. *Margaret Drabble*. Boston: Twayne, 1986.
Schmidt, Dorey, ed. *Margaret Drabble: Golden Realms*. Living Author Series No. 4. Edinburg, Tex.: Pan American University Press, 1982.
Wyatt, Jean. *Reconstructing Desire: The Role*

D

of the Unconscious in Women's Reading and Writing. Chapel Hill: University of North Carolina Press, 1990.

Dualism

Feminist theory has pointed out the connections between dualism—the structuring of thought as opposing pairs, hierarchically ranked—and domination. Domination is often signaled by clear separation between "opposites" such as "man/woman" and "self/other," with man ranked as "superior" to woman and self as "superior" to other. One strategy of second-wave feminist activism has been to celebrate woman over man, reversing old hierarchies. In the 1980s, poststructuralist feminist theory challenged this strategy, focusing on problems inherent in retaining dualisms of any kind, even those favoring women.

Poststructuralist theory argues that Western philosophical and literary traditions are built on pairs of opposites, in which the first term, aligned with "man," is hierarchically ranked as superior to the second term, which is aligned with "woman." These pairs, called "hierarchized binary oppositions," include, for example, man/woman, self/other, reason/emotion, active/passive, culture/nature, mind/body, spirit/matter, order/chaos. Mainstream thinkers have generally found oppositions useful for creating order, simplifying complex problems or ideas, and preserving the status quo; from a feminist viewpoint, such thought structured by binary oppositions is orderly, oversimplified, conservative, and, what is even worse, oppressive to groups labeled inferior. As bell hooks argues, we need to challenge "the kind of dualistic thinking that helps reinforce and maintain all forms of domination." Feminist critics like Elizabeth Grosz find that dualities can be seen as markers; looking for dualities can uncover hidden points of conflict and attempts at domination in texts.

Dualism is fundamental to classical logic, which uses the form "A/Not A," where the second concept loses its own identity and exists only as a negation of the first. From Aristotle to Freud, male thinkers have taken "men" as their standard and, employing the duality "men/not-men," have defined women as "not-men," that is, as defective or mutilated (castrated) men. This way of thinking causes thinkers to focus on a few points of difference and thus lose sight of the wide range of similarities between the two

terms. As Nancy Jay explains, a further problem is that classical Aristotelian logic depends on three principles, all of which limit thinking processes in dualist ways. The "Principle of the Excluded Middle" forbids finding a third term or a continuum between the two terms ("anything and everything must be either A or Not-A"). The "Principle of Contradiction" forbids a term that refers to both other terms ("nothing can be both A and not A"). The "Principle of Identity" forbids a term that refers to neither of them ("if anything is A, it is A"). Jay points out that a rigid "A/Not A" dichotomy reinforces gender distinctions and the established social order. The "A/Not A" form of dualism also carries the problem of "infinitude of the negation," as in the opposition "order/not-order," where "not-order" or chaos, aligned with "not-men," is infinite, and women are thus perceived as infinitely threatening to the limited, established order of men.

These dualities in turn probably derive from the most basic duality, the perceived opposition between self and others, which grows out of attempts to separate and differentiate self from other. The politically most dangerous forms of dualism have arisen as people try to make the separation absolute, portraying themselves as wholly good and projecting all their own weaknesses and badness onto others portrayed as the source or embodiment of evil or other negative qualities, as, for example, racists portray groups stereotyped as inferior or as sexists portray women.

Some feminist theorists (for instance, Nancy Chodorow) have proposed that the close bonding between mother and daughter allows women in later life to remain relatively interconnected with others, whereas men struggle to separate from the mother to achieve an autonomous masculine identity. This model aims to explain why men so often maintain polarized dualistic thinking.

However, men may strive to separate from their mothers not because of gender difference but in order to take on a dominant role: to be able to dominate they must learn to see themselves as separate, different, and superior. From this viewpoint, dualism in identity-formation is a sign of a difference not in gender but in power. People who hold positions of power and privilege tend to promote dualisms of all kinds to maintain their domination and control. Therefore, one basic method for fighting domination is to challenge dualistic thinking, in others or in ourselves, especially thinking that uniformly labels groups or individuals with the implicit duality "superior/inferior."

Some feminist theorists, in particular Julia Kristeva and Hélène Cixous, have looked for writing that avoids dualistic thinking. Other feminist thinkers, also aware of the connections between domination and dualism, have proposed a variety of strategies to avoid dualism. For example, as Deborah Weiner argues, the poet and novelist Margaret Atwood's strategies include challenging expected hierarchies, refusing to see the self as unified and separate, finding a range of positive and negative qualities within the self and within the other, seeing the self as both autonomous and connected with others, looking for possibilities in a range or continuum rather than a simple dualism, and judging differences as good for some purposes, less good for others, rather than accepting a single or "universal" standard of judgment. Eve Tavor Bannet contributes further ways to leave behind oppositional thinking in an article that describes an alternative "both/and" logic, drawing especially on texts by Luce Irigaray.

Trends in feminist literary theory since the 1980s (new historicism, cultural studies) have deemphasized the analysis of dualism, focusing instead on historical and cultural processes of gender construction and social change. However, if feminist theorists thereby neglect to analyze dualisms, they will lose a powerful tool for recognizing and overcoming domination.

Deborah Weiner

References

Bannet, Eve Tavor. "The Feminist Logic of Both/And." *Genders* 15 (1992): 1–20.

Chodorow, Nancy. *Feminism and Psychoanalytic Theory*. New Haven: Yale University Press, 1989.

Cixous, Hélène. "Sorties." In *The Newly Born Woman*, edited by Hélène Cixous and Catherine Clément, translated by Betsy Wing, 63–132. Minneapolis: University of Minnesota Press, 1986.

Derrida, Jacques. *Dissemination*. Chicago: University of Chicago Press, 1981.

Grosz, Elizabeth. *Sexual Subversions: Three French Feminists*. Sydney: Allen and Unwin, 1989.

hooks, bell. *Yearning: Race, Gender, and Cultural Politics*. Boston: South End, 1990.

Jay, Nancy. "Gender and Dichotomy," *Feminist Studies* 7 (1981): 38–56.

Johnson, Barbara. "Translator's Introduction." In *Dissemination* by Jacques Derrida, vii–xxxiii. Chicago: University of Chicago Press, 1981.

Weiner, Deborah. "'Difference that Kills'/ Difference that Heals: Representing Latin America in the Poetry of Elizabeth Bishop and Margaret Atwood." In *Comparative Literature East and West: Traditions and Trends*, edited by Cornelia Moore and Raymond Moody, 208–219. Honolulu: College of Language, Linguistics, and Literature, University of Hawaii, and East-West Center, 1989.

DuPlessis, Rachel Blau

As a modernist, artist, and feminist critic, DuPlessis has contributed significantly to the development of a feminist literary history and aesthetics by recovering and including in her own works the works of marginalized or forgotten women writers such as Schreiner, Doolittle, Richardson, Woolf, Lessing, and Rich, who have used "difference" to create a feminist language and criticism to rewrite a history that includes women's experience and meaning.

By including these critics' strategies in her own work, DuPlessis has demonstrated the importance of continuously rewriting an empowered, female self into history and interrogating the entire field of representation by: (1) mixing literary genres and using nonconventional narratives, textual, and syntactical strategies; (2) depicting alternative representations of power relations between women and men such as contradictory gender positions, male violence, compulsory heterosexuality, racism, classism, bisexuality, lesbianism, androgyny, and a nonpatriarchal world with a women-centered morality; and (3) questioning the notion of a "pure" criticism, the claim that language is neutral, claims of objectivity, normative writing conventions, and dominant representations of gender, sexuality, race, and class.

"For the Etruscans," an essay that DuPlessis has rewritten several times, is an excellent example of a feminist practice that disrupts the entire field of representation with its juxtaposition of diverse writing forms and topics including excerpts from her diary, Freud, literary criticism about Woolf, and a summary of Etruscan history (signifying the canon's exclusion of women's meaning).

Kay Hawkins

References

DuPlessis, Rachel Blau. "For the Etruscans." In *The Pink Guitar: Writing as Feminist Practice,* 157–174. New York: Routledge, 1990.

———. *H.D. The Career of that Struggle.* Bloomington: Indiana University Press, 1986.

———. *Writing beyond the Ending. Narrative Strategies of Twentieth-Century Women Writers.* Bloomington: Indiana University Press, 1985.

Duras, Marguerite

One of France's most prolific and well-respected writers and filmmakers. Duras's novels, plays, film scripts, and essays address the effects of political and psychological violence, pain, and marginalization, especially upon women. Many of her texts resist categorization because they blur literary genres. Duras began publishing novels in 1943 and making films in 1959 with Alain Renais's production of *Hiroshima mon amour.* Like much of Duras's work, this film about a tabooed affair explores the relations between love and war, passion and death. In 1984 Duras won the Prix Goncourt for her first best-seller, *L'Amant.*

Duras confuses the distinction between the real and the fictitious by creating scenarios that parallel her biography. Born Marguerite Donnadieu in 1914 in French Indochina (Vietnam), Duras grew up in conditions resembling those in *L'Amant de la Chine du Nord* (1991): her father died when she was four, leaving her and her two older brothers to live in poverty with their mother, who suffered from madness and depression. At eighteen, Duras left for France.

Sadness, loneliness, and alienation define Duras's female characters. They are ravished and compelling, hovering around the border of madness and rationality. Many are haunted by maternal figures. In place of a language of logical description and mastery, Duras uses the repetition of themes, silences, and bodily gestures to narrate these women's stories.

Duras's contribution to feminism extends from the writing of essays and interviews, to nontraditional filmmaking that problematizes scopophilic pleasure, to the introduction of poignant female characters. While her reputation has long been established in France, it continues to grow in the United States. Duras demonstrates the complexity of remembering, narrating, and interpreting stories of trauma and desire.

Judith Ann Greenberg

References

Hill, Leslie. *Marguerite Duras: Apocalyptic Desires.* London: Routledge, 1993.

Kristeva, Julia. "The Malady of Brief Duras." In *Black Sun: Depression and Melancholia,* translated by Leon S. Roudiez, 221–259. New York: Columbia University Press, 1989.

Willis, Sharon. *Marguerite Duras: Writing on the Body.* Urbana: University of Illinois Press, 1987.

Dworkin, Andrea

One of the more controversial figures in contemporary feminism, Andrea Dworkin unabashedly describes herself as a "radical feminist" and has become one of the key theorists in the continuing debate over pornography. With her friend and co-activist Catharine MacKinnon, Dworkin has campaigned strenuously against the pornography industry, most notably in her 1981 book *Pornography: Men Possessing Women.* However, Dworkin's antipornography stance is also closely woven into her broader theoretical analysis of the place of women within modern Western society.

For Dworkin, the relationship between pornography and the status of women in society as a whole is critical and reciprocal. Pornography, she argues, is a political problem to which power and the omnipresent lack of female empowerment are fundamental. The nature of patriarchal society is such that men are endowed with intrinsic authority, the capacity for self-determination, while "women must, by definition, lack it." This message is communicated and reinforced through cultural representations of women, since "[t]he culture predetermines who we are, how we behave, what we are willing to know, what we are able to feel." Thus, the roles set out for women in materials as seemingly innocuous as fairy tales are polarized (good princess versus evil witch or stepmother), and emphasize that "happiness for a woman is to be passive, victimized, destroyed, or asleep." Pornography, she continues, is an extension of this process. It is "the cultural scenario of male/female," containing "men and women, grown now out of the fairy-tale landscape into the castles of erotic desire," but with the same conclusion for women: "death or complete submission."

This "complete submission" is neatly encapsulated in the sexual objectification of women, not only in pornography, but endemic to the central institutions of Western society. Using the legal tenets of marriage as an example, Dworkin demonstrates the "ongoing reality of women as sexual property." In effect, she argues that since the law defends the right for a man to have sex with his wife, women live inside a system of forced sex: "[h]is sex act, intercourse, explicitly announces his power over her." Women are therefore brought up in accordance with a barrage of "feminine" propaganda to make them want to be these ideal objects of male desire: "[t]he right attitude is to want intercourse because men want it." And once this objectification of women has been legally enshrined and culturally accepted, it is but a short step to the literal objectification of women in pornography or in the mind of the rapist: "[s]he is then a provocation. The object provokes its use." This enforced system of limitations on women and female sexuality through powerful cultural representations denies women the opportunity to express their natural desires, actual bodies, and real sexuality. In contrast to this oppressive system, Dworkin proposes a reformulation of the nature of female, and indeed human, sexuality with androgyny as the embodiment of "a vast fluid continuum where the elements called male and female are not discrete."

As ideal as this solution sounds, Dworkin is not content to simply formulate her theories, but is passionately committed to the practical applications of her feminism. As she writes in *Woman Hating*, "I want writers to write books that can make a difference in how, and even why, people live." Her own works, along with those of Catharine MacKinnon, have been influential in the formulation of recent antipornography legislation in Canada, mirroring her and MacKinnon's currently unsuccessful efforts to enact similar civil legislation in the United States. Though many feminists object to Dworkin's conception of heterosexuality as inevitably forced upon women and view her as a dangerous proponent of censorship under the guise of feminism, Dworkin continues to have a profound effect upon current debates over pornography and the meanings of cultural representations of women.

Alexandra Bennett

References

Dworkin, Andrea. *Letters from a War Zone.* New York: Dutton, 1989.
———. *Pornography: Men Possessing Women.* New York: Putnam, 1981.
———. *Right-Wing Women.* New York: Putnam, 1983.
———. *Woman Hating.* New York: Dutton, 1974.
Hawkins, Gordon, and Franklin E. Zimring. *Pornography in a Free Society.* Cambridge: Cambridge University Press, 1988.

E

Eating

Eating and food have for centuries been a primary female concern in Western culture and thus figure prominently in feminist literary and cultural theory. Even if the Women's Movement of the 1960s challenged a woman's traditional role as housekeeper and cook, eating and food in many ways remain central to women's lives and identities, as the current epidemic of eating disorders—and the feminist concern with this problem—makes evident.

From Eve onwards, female archetypes manifest a close association between the concept of "woman" and that of food, an association encompassing both eating and feeding. Thus we have the dichotomy of the nurturing, nourishing maternal body—whose synecdoche is the lactating breast—versus the devouring female—metonymized by mouth and genitals. This duality is epitomized by the Eve/Mary paradigm and all its literary manifestations. Because patriarchal thought equates woman with flesh, it follows that the fleshly appetites for food and coitus are viewed as typical female vices. Thus female eating—a sexualized activity—shows up in many texts as something that must be controlled. Female gustatory appetite and female sexual appetite are closely linked, not only symbolically but often causally, in the literary, religious, and medical texts produced by a misogynist culture.

Given the profound meaning of food in women's lives, a woman's decision to renounce food carries grave and complex social implications. These implications, of course, vary depending upon the historical and social context, and the topic of female self-starvation as a culturally inscribed gesture has recently generated some groundbreaking feminist scholarship.

Caroline Walker Bynum explores medieval female asceticism in her work *Holy Feast and Holy Fast*, framing a phenomenon often equated with current-day anorexia nervosa in a context that makes clear its distinct historicity. Bynum analyzes the writings of women mystics in order to highlight their intimate relationship to a maternal Christ-figure who nourishes the faithful with his body and blood. Helena Michie, in the first chapter of *The Flesh Made Word*, conducts a similar study of female starvation but focuses on the Victorian novel. Michie's analysis points up the Victorian connection between female sexual purity and anorectic self-denial, as embodied in the romantic heroine.

Turning to current-day attitudes toward women and eating, Susan Bordo's recent work, *Unbearable Weight*, offers a feminist critique of the strictures placed upon women's bodies. Of particular interest is the chapter entitled "Reading the Slender Body," in which Bordo decodes "the contemporary slenderness ideal so as to reveal the psychic anxieties contained within it." Bordo makes use of advertising images and slogans in order to locate the source of eating disorders in the contradictory forces driving advanced consumer capitalism—with its dialectic of indulgence and control—and to explore the way these contradictory messages are played out along gender lines. Other useful studies of women and eating disorders are Kim Chernin's *The Obsession* and *The Hungry Self*, as well as Susie Orbach's *Hunger Strike*.

A more unusual critical approach to the topic of women and food is provided by Carol J. Adams in *The Sexual Politics of Meat*. Adams's groundbreaking work draws together feminist theory and animal rights politics, highlighting these as intrinsically related causes.

Adams argues that "meat's recognizable message includes association with the male role; its meaning recurs within a fixed gender system; the coherence it achieves as a meaningful item of food arises from patriarchal attitudes including the idea that the end justifies the means, that the objectification of other beings is a necessary part of life, and that violence can and should be masked." Adams underscores the sexist association between women and animals as objects of consumption—whether sexual or alimentary—an association made clear by comtemporary obscenities that describe a woman as "a piece of meat." Pointing out that in fact many feminists are also vegetarians, Adams calls upon both groups to join forces against the patriarchal exploitation of living things. As radical as some may find her message, it nonetheless complements other scholarly efforts to analyze "eating" as not merely a metaphor but a socially significant act in a world of real bodies, both animal and human.

Celia R. Daileader

References

Adams, Carol J. *The Sexual Politics of Meat: A Feminist-Vegetarian Critical Theory.* New York: Continuum, 1990.

Bordo, Susan. *Unbearable Weight: Feminism, Western Culture, and the Body.* Berkeley: University of California Press, 1993.

Bynum, Caroline Walker. *Holy Feast and Holy Fast: The Religious Significance of Food to Medieval Women.* Berkeley: University of California Press, 1982.

Caskey, Noelle. "Interpreting Anorexia Nervosa." In *The Female Body in Western Culture: Contemporary Perspectives,* edited by Susan Rubin Suleiman, 174–189. Cambridge: Harvard University Press, 1986.

Chernin, Kim. *The Hungry Self: Women, Eating, and Identity.* New York: Harper and Row, 1986.

———. *The Obsession: Reflections on the Tyranny of Slenderness.* New York: Harper and Row, 1981.

Michie, Helena. *The Flesh Made Word: Female Figures and Women's Bodies.* New York: Oxford University Press, 1987.

Orbach, Susie. *Hunger Strike: The Anorectic's Struggle as a Metaphor for Our Age.* London: Farber, 1986.

Écriture Féminine

Since the French word *féminin* designates both "female" and "feminine," *écriture féminine* can mean both writing by women and writing that is feminine. The lack of distinction between the cultural construction of gender and the anatomical essence of woman makes the term rather ambiguous and contributes to its appeal, but also presents problems. One of the most influential of the Anglo American interpretations of the term is Ann Rosalind Jones's essay published in the mid eighties called "Writing the Body: Toward an Understanding of l'écriture féminine." Jones reads four French women—Julia Kristeva, Luce Irigaray, Hélène Cixous, and Monique Wittig—within a materialist feminist framework congenial to English-speaking readers. The "common ground" among the four writers, according to Jones, is an analysis of Western culture as fundamentally "oppressive," as "phallogocentric." These women agree that resistance to institutions and signifying practices that include myths, language, and rituals takes the form of *jouissance. Jouissance* has been defined as women's physical, bodily pleasures linked with infancy, with fluidity and diffusion, without the authority of the Law of the Father.

The term the "Law of the Father" has been borrowed from Jacques Lacan whose ideas influenced these writers. For Lacan, a subject's entry into the symbolic order, where one acquires language, necessarily entails giving up or repressing the desire for the lost mother, and accepting the phallus as the representation of the law. Religion, philosophy, literature, and language all support the notion that the man/father, possessor of the phallus, is the center of meaning, and the rest of the world, particularly woman, becomes defined as the "Other." Kristeva, Irigaray, Cixous, and Wittig all challenge and attempt to redefine this marginalized "Other" in their works in different ways. However, they do not represent a single movement or collective organization, and they have not all used the term "l'écriture féminine" specifically in their argument.

For Kristeva, the repressed or unconscious manifests itself in what she calls the "semiotic." The "semiotic" is associated with preverbal, pre-Oedipal drives and energies, discontinuity, the maternal body, pulsions and rhythm, and plurality. The notion is appealing to feminists because the semiotic is potentially subversive. It can disrupt the unity, order, and stability of symbolic language that is linked to the Law of the Father. While Kristeva has rejected the idea of an inherently feminine form of writing, her theories of marginality and dissidence, her belief that an identity is constantly in flux rather than stable, have been useful for feminists who attempt to read the writings of women who are defined as marginal by patriarchy. Kristeva's psycholinguistic theories provide a way of approaching experimental, poetic, discontinuous, and allusive writings of women writers who do not or are unable to conform to conventional styles. In an essay called "Women's Time," Kristeva suggests that radical feminists refuse "linear temporality" in order to "give a language to the intrasubjective and corporeal experiences left mute by culture in the past."

The terms Luce Irigaray uses to discuss writing and women are "parler-femme" (speaking as a woman) and "la sexuation du discours" (the sexualization of discourse). At one point, Irigaray talks about women's language as "contradictory" and inexact, always in the process of "weaving itself." The difficulty of woman's speech or writing stems from what Irigaray sees as the absence of a female symbolic, or a place from which women can speak, since women are always predicated as object. Irigaray believes that in order for *écriture féminine* to occur, women have to stop functioning mainly as a mirror or a specularized Other for man in Western culture. Because of her exclusion, she becomes silent or speaks in the inadequate language of "mimicry" and "hysteria." Irigaray contests psychoanalytic and philosophical conceptions of women that tend to equate them with lack, and writes of the "two lips" women possess that empower them to write or speak. Her metaphor of the "two lips," which could stand for the mother and daughter, or two lovers of the same sex, suggests that she is seeking to find new words, images, and a different language to express female subjectivity. Writing by women is possible only after a repositioning of the female in the imaginary.

Like Irigaray, Hélène Cixous rejects Freudian and Lacanian models of sexual difference and the privileging of the phallus, and instead creates her own images to talk about the feminine. In "The Laugh of the Medusa" Cixous locates difference in the representation of the body and in *jouissance*. In a lyrical, poetic, and passionate style, she encourages woman to "write her self," and to "put herself into the text." For Cixous, "feminine" writing is linked to the "white ink" of the mother's milk. The desire to write is connected to the "gestation drive," a desire for the "swollen belly, for language, for blood." In "Sorties," she challenges the patriarchal binary system that sets up oppositions such as sun/moon, man/woman, head/heart because it privileges the first term and tends to associate the female with the negative second term. Disputing these oppositions, Cixous believes in the bisexual nature of all human beings, and particularly women. Writing that is feminine is variable, multiple, associative, outside traditional structures, and nonhierarchical.

Characteristics of *écriture féminine* can be seen in Monique Wittig's *Les Guérillères,* which deliberately defies narrative conventions. Wittig evokes the symbol 0, the circumference, the ring, the sphere, and identifies it with women. The book gives lists of female names and heroines, valorizing aspects of culture and history that the male-dominated society customarily suppresses. Through lines such as "ACTION OVERTHROW" which are repeated as if in an incantation, Wittig calls for a revolution.

Some other writers who explore the experimental possibilities of female writing are Annie Leclerc, who praises female difference in *Parole de femme,* and postcolonial critic and filmmaker Trinh T. Minh-ha, who examines displacement and marginality in the context of race and gender in a hybrid language. Works such as *The Hour of the Star* by Brazilian novelist Clarice Lispector and *Ana Historic* by Canadian poet and novelist Daphne Marlatt are other examples of "l'écriture féminine."

Eleanor Ty

References

Cixous, Hélène. "The Laugh of the Medusa." In *New French Feminisms: An Anthology,* edited by Elaine Marks and Isabelle de Courtivron, 245–263. New York: Schocken Books, 1980.

———, and Catherine Clément. *The Newly Born Woman.* Translated by Betsy Wing. Minnesota: University of Minnesota Press, 1986.

Irigaray, Luce. *Speculum of the Other Woman.* Translated by Gillian C. Gill. Ithaca, N.Y.: Cornell University Press, 1985.

———. *This Sex which Is Not One.* Translated by Catherine Porter. Ithaca, N.Y.: Cornell University Press, 1985.

Jones, Ann Rosalind. "Writing the Body: Toward an Understanding of l'écriture féminine." In *The New Feminist Criticism: Essays on Women, Literature, & Theory*, edited by Elaine Showalter, 361–377. New York: Pantheon, 1985.

Kristeva, Julia. *Revolution in Poetic Language*. Translated by Margaret Waller. New York: Columbia University Press, 1984.

———. "Women's Time." Translated by Alice Jardine and Harry Blake. In *The Kristeva Reader*, edited by Toril Moi. 188–213. New York: Columbia University Press, 1986.

Lispector, Clarice. *The Hour of the Star*. Translated by Giovanni Pontiero. New York: New Directions, 1992.

Marlatt, Daphne. *Ana Historic: A Novel*. Toronto: Coach House, 1988.

Minh-ha, Trinh, T. *Woman, Native, Other: Writing Postcoloniality and Feminism*. Bloomington: Indiana University Press, 1989.

Moi, Toril, ed. *French Feminist Thought: A Reader*. London: Basil Blackwell, 1987.

Wittig, Monique. *Les Guérillères*. Translated by David le Vay. New York: Avon, 1971.

Éditions des Femmes

The publishing house initiated by the French women's liberation group "Politique et Psychanalyse ("Psyche et Po") in 1973 under the title *des femmes* [of women/some women]. In 1974 *éditions des femmes* began publishing the newspaper *Le Quotidienne des femmes*, reflecting *Psych et Po*'s emphasis on the psychosexual dimension to women's oppression. *Psych et Po* became one of the most visible radical women's groups formed in the wake of the May 1968 student demonstrations in Paris, but distinguished itself from the "bourgeois" efforts of other feminist groups (known collectively as the MLF, or Mouvement de Libération des Femmes).

Psych et Po focused on the symbolic nature of women's oppression, and *éditions des femmes* provided the textual space for women to develop the repressed feminine element in themselves. While the books published by *éditions des femmes* did not necessarily represent the political ideology of the group, the journal *des femmes en mouvements* [women in movement/women on the move], published in 1979, reflected *Psych et Po*'s preoccupation with language and the unconscious. The unsigned editorials, repetitive prose, and deliberately difficult style were presented in a glossy, picture-filled format. While their considerable financial resources benefited all women, giving voice to an audience that was overlooked by mainstream publishers, *des femmes* renamed and reprinted the work of other groups in the MLF, appropriating these texts for their own benefit. By 1984, however, *Psych et Po* was less powerful, and *éditions des femmes* was no longer a political alliance, but a commercial enterprise.

Wendy C. Wahl

References

Duchen, Claire. *Feminism in France: From May '68 to Mitterand*. London: Routledge and Kegan Paul, 1986.

Gelfand, Elissa D., and Virginia T. Hules. *French Feminist Criticism: Women, Language, and Literature: an Annotated Bibliography*. New York: Garland, 1985.

Marks, Elaine, and Isabelle de Courtivron, eds. *New French Feminisms: An Anthology*. Amherst: University of Massachusetts Press, 1979.

Sellers, Susan. *Language and Sexual Difference: Feminist Writing in France*. New York: St. Martin's, 1991.

Eighteenth-Century Studies

The field of eighteenth-century studies has seen a rapid expansion of feminist theory and criticism within its domain in the last decade. One of the most significant issues for feminists working in eighteenth-century studies has been canon revision and the restoration of women writers to the traditionally male literary canon of the eighteenth century. Within the work of canon revision, the decision of which women writers to recuperate has been tempered by questions of "feminist value" versus "historical value" versus "aesthetic value," as feminist scholars work to establish criteria for the inclusion of texts that have long been considered subliterary within critical discourse. The gradual development of an eighteenth-century countercanon has been accomplished by a variety of methodological and theoretical approaches.

The overriding material concern of making women's texts available in modern editions and compiling textual and biographical information has been usefully addressed by a number of critics. New editions of eighteenth-century women's texts with accompanying critical apparatus have appeared, although unfortunately some have also disappeared with rapidity. Several anthologies of women's writing have recently been published, including Roger Lonsdale's *Eighteenth-Century Women Poets*, Katharine Rogers's and William McCarthy's *The Meridian Anthology of Early Women Writers: British Literary Women from Aphra Behn to Maria Edgeworth 1660–1800* and Moira Ferguson's *First Feminists: British Women Writers 1578–1799*. Important reference works, most notably Janet Todd's *A Dictionary of British and American Women Writers 1660–1800,* which has more than five hundred entries, have contributed to the development of the countercanon of women's writing. Finally, historiographical critical texts that posit a new literary history of women's writing within the period, such as Jane Spencer's *The Rise of the Woman Novelist: From Aphra Behn to Jane Austen* and Janet Todd's *The Sign of Angellica: Women, Writing and Fiction, 1660–1800*, have significantly altered the critical understanding of women's role in eighteenth-century literature.

In addition to canon revision, feminist scholars of the eighteenth century have isolated significant feminist concerns within women's writing of the period. They have examined such issues as women's self-identity, the mother-child dyad, women's education, the importance of so-called subliterary genres of romance, scandal chronicles, journals and familiar letters, the emergence of a dominant ideology of domesticity, and a new ideology of femininity and of patriarchy in the eighteenth century. Early autobiographical and feminist psychoanalytic study by Patricia Meyer Spacks in *Imagining a Self: Autobiography and Novel in Eighteenth-Century England* and her later *Desire and Truth: Functions of Plot in Eighteenth-Century English Novels* focus on issues of female identity and sexuality. Materialist feminist work by Donna Landry (*The Muses of Resistance: Laboring-Class Women's Poetry in Britain 1739–1796*) and Terry Castle (*Masquerade and Civilization: The Carnivalesque in Eighteenth-Century English Culture and Fiction*) has brought issues of class to the forefront; while new historical studies like Ruth Perry's early *Women, Letters, and the Novel*, Elizabeth Bergen Brophy's *Women's Lives and the Eighteenth-Century English Novel*, and Elizabeth

Kowaleski-Wallace's *Their Fathers' Daughters: Hannah More, Maria Edgeworth and Patriarchal Complicity* emphasize women's role in the daily life and transforming ideologies of the period. With Nancy Armstrong's important Marxist critique *Desire and Domestic Fiction: A Political History of the Novel*, which argues a causal relationship between the new bourgeois female subject of domestic fiction and the rise of the middle class, laying the groundwork for subsequent studies, this critical reassessment of women's writing has been incorporated into an enlarged understanding of emergent political and social systems of the period.

Feminist scholars have also examined canonic (mostly male) writing from a feminist perspective, thereby opening new levels of understanding of eighteenth-century life and culture. Two important textual studies that offer feminist rereadings of the canon are Felicity Nussbaum's *The Brink of All We Hate: English Satires on Women 1660–1750*, which thoroughly scrutinizes the misogyny of Augustan satire, and Ellen Pollack's *The Poetics of Sexual Myth: Gender and Ideology in the Verse of Swift and Pope*, which offers a feminist critique of the sexual ideologies of Swift and Pope and an analysis of the dominant gender myths of the eighteenth century. Biographical studies like Valerie Rumbold's *Women's Place in Pope's World* have also helped to increase the complexity of understanding concerning men's writing about women in the eighteenth century.

Finally, women's social and historical position within the eighteenth century has been explored, enabling a revision of historical, as well as literary historical understanding of the period. *Family Fortunes: Men and Women of the English Middle Class, 1780–1850* by Leonore Davidoff and Catherine Hall emphasizes women's role in the formation of the middle-class economy, and Susan Staves's *Married Women's Separate Property in England, 1660–1833* analyzes women's contractual rights within marriage and the general position of married women in the eighteenth century. Kathryn Shevelow combines many critical methodologies in *Women and Print Culture: The Construction of Femininity in the Early Periodical*, as she investigates the cultural work of early periodicals in producing women readers as physical embodiments of a new, increasingly domestic ideology of femininity.

Eighteenth-century studies has undoubtedly been transformed by the recent work of

E

feminist scholars, making it now almost unheard of to undertake a literary or historical study of the eighteenth century without taking women's role and women's writing into account. Feminist eighteenth-century studies have moved from an initial focus on the writings and concerns of the bourgeois or emergent middle-class woman, to issues and texts of working-class women, to recent postcolonial studies of slavewomen's texts and work of, or concerning, women of color. The critical work has been most influenced by theories of Marxist feminism, materialist feminism, and new historicism, but has been marked not by one theory but by a growing montage of feminist work.

Kathleen B. Grathwol

References

Armstrong, Nancy. *Desire and Domestic Fiction: A Political History of the Novel.* New York: Oxford University Press, 1987.

Bergen Brophy, Elizabeth. *Women's Lives and the Eighteenth-Century English Novel.* Tampa: University of South Florida Press, 1991.

Castle, Terry. *Masquerade and Civilization: The Carnivalesque in Eighteenth-Century English Culture and Fiction.* Stanford: Stanford University Press, 1986.

Davidoff, Leonore, and Catherine Hall. *Family Fortunes: Men and Women of the English Middle Class, 1780–1850.* London: Hutchinson, 1987.

Ferguson, Moira, ed. *First Feminists: British Women Writers, 1578–1799.* Bloomington, Ind., and Old Westbury, N.Y.: Indiana University Press/Feminist Press, 1985.

———, ed. *Subject to Others: British Women Writers and Colonial Slavery, 1670–1834.* New York: Routledge, 1992.

Kowaleski-Wallace, Elizabeth. *Their Fathers' Daughters: Hannah More, Maria Edgeworth, and Patriarchal Complicity.* New York: Oxford University Press, 1991.

Landry, Donna. *The Muses of Resistance: Laboring-Class Women's Poetry in Britain, 1739–1796.* New York: Cambridge University Press, 1990.

Lonsdale, Roger, ed. *Eighteenth-Century Women Poets.* New York: Oxford University Press, 1990.

Nussbaum, Felicity. *The Brink of All We Hate: English Satires on Women 1660–1750.* Lexington: University Press of Kentucky, 1984.

Perry, Ruth. *Women, Letters, and the Novel.* New York: AMS, 1980.

Pollack, Ellen. *The Poetics of Sexual Myth: Gender and Ideology in the Verse of Swift and Pope.* Chicago: University of Chicago Press, 1985.

Poovey, Mary. *The Proper Lady and the Woman Writer: Ideology as Style in the Works of Mary Wollstonecraft, Mary Shelley, and Jane Austen.* Chicago: University of Chicago Press, 1984.

Rogers, Katharine M., and William McCarthy, eds. *The Meridian Anthology of Early Women Writers: British Literary Women from Aphra Behn to Maria Edgeworth 1660–1800.* New York: Meridian, 1987.

Rumbold, Valerie. *Women's Place in Pope's World.* Cambridge: Cambridge University Press, 1989.

Shevelow, Kathryn. *Women and Print Culture: The Construction of Femininity in the Early Periodical.* New York: Routledge, 1989.

Spacks, Patricia Ann Meyer. *Imagining a Self: Autobiography and Novel in Eighteenth-Century England.* Cambridge: Harvard University Press, 1976.

———. *Desire and Truth: Function of Plot in Eighteenth-Century Novels.* Chicago: University of Chicago Press, 1990.

Spencer, Jane. *The Rise of the Woman Novelist: From Aphra Behn to Jane Austen.* New York: Basil Blackwell, 1986.

Staves, Susan. *Married Women's Separate Property in England, 1660–1833.* Cambridge: Harvard University Press, 1990.

Todd, Janet. *The Sign of Angellica: Women, Writing and Fiction, 1660–1800.* New York: Columbia University Press, 1989.

———, ed. *A Dictionary of British and American Women Writers 1660–1800.* London: Methuen, 1987.

Eliot, George

George Eliot (1819–1880) is the pseudonym of Mary Ann Evans, one of the most celebrated writers of Victorian England. Eliot has been a paradoxical figure for feminist literary criticism. From her iconoclastic decision to live with

George Henry Lewes, which resulted in the censure of polite London society, to her use of a male pseudonym, from her complex and sympathetic exploration of female characters to her denunciation of "Silly Novels by Lady Novelists," Eliot has been both criticized for assuming masculine superiority and celebrated for her achievements and vision. Referring to her unconventional relationship with Lewes, Kate Millett writes of Eliot that she "lived the revolution . . . but she did not write of it." According to Ellen Moers, "George Eliot was no feminist." While it is undeniable that Eliot has been viewed largely in terms of male literary history, nevertheless, Gillian Beer argues, "She persistently worked at the central dilemmas of feminism in her time without setting out to write feminist novels." She was reluctant to see herself as an activist in women's rights, writing to a friend "there is no subject on which I am more inclined to hold my peace and learn, than on the 'Woman Question.'" However, Eliot can be seen working in a tradition of feminist writings, such as Mary Wollstonecraft's *A Vindication of the Rights of Women* (which Eliot read and admired), which address the ways in which women's educational opportunities keep them in states of ignorance and dependence. Eliot's 1856 article in the *Westminster Review*, "Silly Novels by Lady Novelists," while harshly criticizing contemporary popular writing by women, extends some of Wollstonecraft's idea's such as her disparagement of the current reading habits of women, suggesting that addiction to romances seemed to perpetuate female ignorance and dependency. Eliot argues in her essay that writing "silly novels" is as harmful as reading them for "it tends to confirm the popular prejudice against the more solid education of women." Women, according to Eliot, need to show their general humanity and learning, but they need to show it in a subdued and modest manner: "A really cultured woman, like a really cultured man, is all the simpler and the less obtrusive for her knowledge."

"Great writers," Eliot argues, "have modestly contented themselves with putting their experience into fiction, and have thought it quite a sufficient task to exhibit men and things as they are." As the subtitle of her arguably greatest achievement, *Middlemarch: A Study of Provincial Life*, reveals, George Eliot followed her belief as to what made a "great writer." The detailed rendering of "provincial life" as well as the scope and breadth of her analysis resulted

in many compelling and complex explorations of what it meant to be a woman in the nineteenth century; however, the confining circumstances (circumstances, it could be argued, Eliot herself transcended) and renunciation of power by her women characters have often drawn fire from feminist critics. While the question of her feminism remains a debate for feminists, her writings stage many of the central debates within feminism.

Caroline Reitz

References

Beer, Gillian. *George Eliot*. Bloomington: Indiana University Press, 1986.

Gilbert, Sandra M., and Susan Gubar. *The Madwoman in the Attic*. New Haven: Yale University Press, 1979.

Haight, Gordon S. *George Eliot*. New York: Oxford University Press, 1968.

Millett, Kate. *Sexual Politics*. Garden City, N.Y.: Doubleday, 1970.

Moers, Ellen. *Literary Women*. Garden City, N.Y.: Doubleday, 1976.

Sadoff, Dianne F. *Monsters of Affection*. Baltimore: Johns Hopkins University Press, 1982.

Showalter, Elaine. *A Literature of Their Own*. Princeton: Princeton University Press, 1977.

Spacks, Patricia Meyers. *The Female Imagination*. New York: Knopf, 1975.

Epistemology of the Closet

See SEDGWICK, EVE

Erasure

This is a key concept (and term) to feminist literary theory as well as feminist methodology overall. Generally, "erasure" articulates a link between visibility and power by referring to absences as conspicuous or political. To the extent that women have been erased from or do not appear in dominant historical accounts, the literary canon, and critical inquiries into literature and literary history, feminist literary theory responds by calling attention to and theorizing this absence, and by paying close attention to women in literature and literary history.

Earlier feminist literary theory is especially characterized by the need to "mine" and establish visible presence through critical historical research. By discovering (and championing)

E

women writers who have been devalued and buried by a male literary establishment, feminist theorists reveal and affirm a female literary tradition, a history of women's writing erased by or not represented in the institutionalized literary canon. It was in the 1960s that more concentrated numbers of feminist literary critics began to emerge and focus on the absence or invisibility of women in the literary canon. In *Silences*, Tillie Olsen discusses many "absorbing" and "enduring" female writers who are often invisible in literary history and criticism, and asks us to consider how even female writers of "acknowledged stature" are "comparatively unread, untaught." Olsen's book exemplifies the interest in "erasure" that made early feminist literary theory largely a historical enterprise of excavation and revisionary reading.

Adrienne Rich also addresses the problem of erasure in her landmark essay "When We Dead Awaken: Writing as Revision." In an introduction to this essay, Rich points out that "some feminist scholars, teachers, and graduate students, joined by feminist writers, editors, and publishers, have for a decade been creating more subversive occasions, challenging the sacredness of the gentlemanly canon, sharing the rediscovery of buried works by women, asking women's questions, bringing literary history and criticism back to life."

As Rich notes, however, the erasure that feminist theoretical scholarship sought to challenge on "women's" behalf became typified in that very scholarship, for "feminist literary criticism itself has overlooked or held back from examining the work of black women and lesbians." A different brand of erasure has then been enacted within the discourse of feminist theory itself, to the extent that it remains a discourse for and about white, heterosexual, middle-class women. Yet feminist theory, both literary and otherwise, has recently exhibited a consciousness regarding its "internal" problems. Feminist criticism, to the extent that it responds to those voices that need visibility and appreciation, continues to make progress toward a more diverse, more inclusive, more plural conversation.

Kim Savelson

References

Crenshaw, Kimberle. "Demarginalizing the Intersection of Race and Sex." In *Feminist Legal Theory*, edited by Katharine T. Bartlett and Rosanne Kennedy, 57–80. Boulder, Colo.: West View, 1991.

Gilbert, Sandra M., and Susan Gubar. *No Man's Land*. Vols. 1 and 2. New Haven: Yale University Press, 1988, 1989.

Morrison, Toni. *Playing in the Dark*. Cambridge: Harvard University Press, 1992.

Olsen, Tillie. *Silences*. New York: Dell, 1965.

Rich, Adrienne. *On Lies, Secrets and Silence*. New York: W.W. Norton, 1979.

Eroticism

Eroticism is hard to define because it is not an exclusively emotional, spiritual, or even physical aspect of life. In an effort to provide a definition of eroticism that rings true for women generally, feminist theorists have offered a picture of sensuality involving all three aspects. The understanding of eroticism, and female eroticism in particular, has shifted throughout Western history, changing the most during times of profound transformation in both cultural attitudes toward women's autonomy and the social significance ascribed to their bodies.

In her book *Sexual Politics*, Kate Millett outlines how the rules governing social behavior fluctuated significantly between 1830 and 1960, consequently revising gender and sexual conventions. Although the Victorian period imposed strict standards of prudery and morality, Millett documents this as the first moment in history in which the ethical and sexual double standard as well as the institution of prostitution were challenged in a way that illuminated the issues of female inequality and suffering. An increased erotic freedom followed the Victorian age, as Freud ushered in the twentieth century with a view of sexuality as the basic instinct underlying almost every human motive. However, because the substructure of society—the patriarchal, heterosexual family—remained intact, conventions concerning female economic, psychological, and erotic equality never underwent any authentic transformation. For instance, Freud's sexual rhetoric still defined women as creatures of "lack," beings constructed around the absence and "envy" of a penis, while substantial improvements in women's lives concerning issues such as "venereal disease, coercive marital unions, and involuntary parenthood" were never made. After 1930 women did gain some measure of sexual autonomy as technological improvements increased the accessibility of birth control, but their social equality was held in check by increasingly denigrating attitudes toward the female body. Meanwhile, the nuclear family stood firm as a cultural standard of normalcy, fostering an intolerance for homosexuality or any alternative lifestyle incorporating new definitions of eroticism.

The Civil Rights Movement of the 1960s regenerated discussions on the problems of inequality. Although first published in 1953, Simone de Beauvoir's *The Second Sex* gained popularity about ten years later, arguing that women's social emancipation depended fundamentally on their erotic freedom. The late 1960s and early 1970s saw an increased interest in the actual physiology of women's eroticism, validating the clitoral orgasm as well as—or even instead of—vaginal climax. From here, feminist groups could highlight the possibility for women to achieve satisfaction and sexual pleasure outside of traditional heterosexual intercourse, roles, and practices. Ann Snitow, Christine Stansell, and Sharon Thompson, in their anthology *Powers of Desire: The Politics of Sexuality*, describe how the emergence of consciousness-raising groups in the 1970s encouraged women to talk together about their erotic lives, while feminist criticism began publicly to deconstruct the oppressive values placed on women's bodies in our literature, laws, and social customs.

Snitow et al. also outline how the 1970s and 1980s brought renewed dissent within feminism, as lesbian, workingclass, and non-Caucasian women demanded that the feminist movement make amends for its own conventional, upper-middle class, white, heterosexual biases toward issues such as leadership, birth control, and sexual preference. These debates continue into the 1990s, as we tackle not only questions of sexual "difference," but also whether there is a viable intersection between the erotic and the pornographic, or the pleasurable and the psychologically—and even physically—dangerous. Contemporary theorists generally stress the importance of sexual tolerance and variety.

Throughout the last few decades, feminist literary theory has both shaped and been influenced by these historical changes, thereby producing widely fluctuating definitions of eroticism. Feminist literary critics strive to understand or modify attitudes toward women's sensuality by analyzing texts that portray the body and thus help to construct its cultural role. Some revise traditional readings of canonical sex, extracting empowering messages

about women's sensuality out of works typically considered misogynist. For instance, Angela Carter urges a reconsideration of the novels written by Marquis de Sade in the late eighteenth and early nineteenth centuries. Although his work is conventionally viewed as violent and degrading toward his female characters, Carter describes Sade's pornography as sexually progressive because of "his refusal to see female sexuality in relation to its reproductive function," his declaration of the "right of women to fuck," and his "descriptive and diagnostic" connection of erotic with political oppression.

Other theorists explore texts written by women authors living in extremely conservative climates and find female eroticism embedded in culturally "appropriate" patriarchal religious and political desire. For instance, Donald Wehrs reads Aphra Behn's *Love Letters between a Nobleman and His Sister* (1684–1687) as an example of a book by a seventeenth-century female author who explicitly discusses the powerful centrality of human passion and pleasure. He shows how Behn simultaneously conforms to cultural mores about female modesty by contextualizing Eros as a personal and political threat capable of "depriv[ing]" respectable citizens of their "selfhood." Walter Hughes also finds blatant sensual images in the seventeenth-century poetry of Anne Bradstreet, who connects erotic lust with religious yearning, and portrays heterosexual sex as a "foretast[e]" of spiritual union with the Judeo-Christian god.

Other feminist critics analyze textual representations of eroticism in order to dissect the cultural construction of sex as male prowess and aggression toward "the other." In *Sexual Politics*, Millett focuses on twentieth-century fiction, highlighting D.H. Lawrence's use of "the words 'sexual' and 'phallic' interchangeably" and Henry Miller's portrayal of sex as a practice where "men fuck women and discard them." She also exposes Norman Mailer's alignment of male virility with power and violence against female vulnerability, and Jean Genet's conflation of homoeroticism with shame.

In order to rebut these denigrating images, feminist literary theorists strive to articulate alternative representations of female eroticism. *Écriture féminine*, a school of French feminist linguistics that emerged in the 1970s, reaches beyond the limitations of standard logical discourse in an effort to produce accurate descriptions of women's "non-rational" experiences based in the body rather than the mind. Pursuing a similar project, Elizabeth Meese considers how lesbian authors such as Virginia Woolf and Olga Broumas express desire in words, asking "How is it that lesbian : writing speaks (our) textual/sexual pleasure to us?" *[sic]*, and arriving at an analogy matching the space between words and their meanings to the desire one woman feels to touch another's body and soul. Other critics, such as Jane Gallop and Susan Winnett, analyze both resistance to and reflections of feminist thought in conventional, psychoanalytic models of narrative pleasure. Gallop lauds Roland Barthes's *The Pleasure of the Text* for privileging the sensual enjoyment of reading over literal meaning, relating this "valoriz[ation]" of a "'different physiology'" to the feminist argument that women's pleasure should not be "subjugated to any function, such as reproduction." Winnett, meanwhile, challenges the Freudian model of desire—and the analogy critics such as Peter Brooks have drawn "between Freud's plotting of the life trajectory in *Beyond the Pleasure Principle* and the dynamics of beginnings, middles, and ends in traditional narratives"—highlighting their linearity, their ignorance of female patterns of pleasure, and their implication that the male heterosexual orgasm represents what the erotic looks and feels like for all human beings.

Literary theorists also revise or clarify existing notions of sexuality by exploring other feminist writers' definitions of eroticism. Jo Ann Pilardi finds that de Beauvoir's work, while unabashedly bringing female sexuality into the forefront, still upholds patriarchal myths of the phallus as biologically superior: as more visible, straightforward, and powerful than woman's hidden and supposedly mysterious erogenous zones. Cora Kaplan compares Mary Wollstonecraft's "A Vindication of the Rights of Women" from 1792 to Adrienne Rich's 1980 essay "Compulsory Heterosexuality." She objects to both arguments' essentialist portrayals of sex as inherently polarized by gender. Kaplan charges the former as being both "suffused with" and "severe about" women's sexual desire—which is cast as errant, vulnerable, and in need of careful monitoring—while questioning the latter's simplification of lesbianism as the "reformed libidinal economy" which will liberate women from oppressive, patriarchal conventions of eroticism. In another essay, Kaplan criticizes Millett's *Sexual Politics* as having "rigid notions of sexual health" and "an extreme distaste for the recrudescent sado-masochistic elements of sexuality." Lisa Henderson complains about a similar phenomenon in feminist interpretations of lesbian pornography, defending its sado-masochism as an appropriate, "unambiguous distinction between rape, as sexual violence, and dominance and submission, as consensual sexual forms." Meanwhile, in the novel *Sex and Other Sacred Games* by Kim Chernin and Renate Stendhal, critic Lisa Weil finds both a representation of variety in women's sexual lives and the possibility for "straight" and "queer" women to find interconnections by joining together.

Ultimately, a review of the history of feminist literary definitions of eroticism leads us back to the initial problem concerning the difficulty of pinning down one explanation for what the word signifies. Just as an erotic experience—whether it involves two people, two parts of the same body touching, or one mind fantasizing about another—requires a merging of more than one entity, so the meanings of the term proliferate and overlap. Fittingly, feminists have mainly tried to loosen eroticism from its harshly categorized, polarized reputation as a force existing between people defined by an opposition in role, gender, or power. An even more expansive understanding can be achieved by future exploration of contemporary anthologies of erotica, and especially by considering erotic narratives written by, for instance, older, non-Western, or physically disabled women.

Tracy Slater

References

Carter, Angela. *The Sadeian Woman*. New York: Pantheon, 1978.

Gallop, Jane. *Thinking through the Body*. New York: Columbia University Press, 1988.

Henderson, Lisa. "Lesbian Pornography: Cultural Transgression and Sexual Demystification." In *New Lesbian Criticism*, edited by Sally Munt. New York: Simon and Schuster, 1992.

Hughes, Walter. "'Meat out of the Eater': Panic and Desire in American Puritan Poetry." In *Engendering Mean: The Question of Male Feminist Criticism*, edited by Joseph Boone and Michael Cadden. New York: Routledge, 1990.

Kaplan, Cora. *Sea Changes: Essays on Culture and Feminism*. London: Verso, 1986.

Meese, Elizabeth. *(SEM) erotics: Theorizing Lesbian : Writing*. New York: New York University Press, 1992.

Millett, Kate. *Sexual Politics*. New York: Doubleday, 1970.

Pilardi, Jo Ann. "Female Eroticism in the Works of Simone de Beauvoir." In *The Thinking Muse*, edited by Jeffner Allen and Iris Marion Young, 18–34. Bloomington: Indiana University Press, 1989.

Reynolds, Margaret, ed. *Erotica: Women's Writings from Sappho to Margaret Atwood*. New York: Ballantine, 1990.

Slung, Michele, ed. *Slow Hand: Women Writing Erotica*. New York: HarperCollins, 1992.

Snitow, Ann, Christine Stansell, and Sharon Thompson, eds. *Powers of Desire: The Politics of Sexuality*. New York: Monthly Review Press, 1983.

Taylor, Dena, and Amber Coverdale Sumrall, eds. *The Time of Our Lives: Women Write on Sex after Forty*. Freedom: Crossing, 1993.

Wehrs, Donald. "Eros, Ethics, Identity: Royalist Feminism and the Politics of Desire in Aphra Behn's Love Letters." *Selected Studies in English Literature* 32 (1992): 461–478.

Weil, Lisa. "Lowering the Case: An After-Reading of *Sex and Other Sacred Games*." In *An Intimate Wilderness: Lesbian Writers on Sexuality*, edited by Judith Barrington, 240–249. Portland: Eighth Mountain, 1991.

Winnett, Susan. "Coming Unstrung: Women, Men, Narrative, and Principles of Pleasure." *PMLA* (May 1990): 505–518.

Essentialism

Although discussions of essence may be found in the writings of Aristotle, Plato, Locke, and Hegel, the term "essentialism" has taken on more specific meanings in recent feminist discourses. To make matters more confusing, the term is a contested one among feminists. No one, in other words, has captured the definitive "essence" of feminist essentialism.

"Essentialism" is most often a pejorative term, invoked to dismiss those feminists whose work conceives of the category "women" in limiting ways. Elizabeth Grosz defines four interrelated words: essentialism, biologism (bio-logical determinism), naturalism, and universalism. Essentialism is the attribution of a fixed essence to women, whether through women's supposedly shared biology, nature, or psychology (such as empathy, nurturance, or noncompetitiveness). Naturalism is similar to biologism, but women's differences may be seen as God-given or as a fact of existence, rather than as purely physical. Universalism, however, does not have to involve biologism or naturalism. Indeed, some feminists who see women's differences arising from social factors nevertheless adhere to universalist explanations. Such feminists, often called "social constructionists," generally identify themselves as antiessentialists. But some social constructionist feminists assert that all women have a certain trait, as Grosz points out. Universalism overlooks differences of ethnicity, class, culture, sexual practices, or historical contexts to talk about "common oppression." In so doing, differences between women are erased, thus making all women appear to be the same. Different feminisms use many kinds of essentialisms—often unwittingly—according to Grosz.

The label "essentialist" includes those who think women must stick to the traditional roles of good wife and mother, such as Phyllis Schlafly. The label also includes radical feminists who write about creating a separate woman's culture or a "gynomorphic language," as do Mary Daly and Adrienne Rich. Nancy Chodorow's *Reproduction of Mothering* (1978) and Carol Gilligan's *In a Different Voice* (1982) were hailed as groundbreaking for their explanations of women's ways of thinking, relating, and parenting in a world where these ways are frequently devalued. At the same time, however, these works were criticized for being psychologically essentializing; both theorized women's "superior" capacity for caring and nurturance. Those who criticized Gilligan and Chodorow claimed that work of this kind did not explain traits of all women and privileged, in fact, a white, middle-class, heterosexual worldview.

Literary critical essentialisms include theories that attempt to describe a "women's tradition" of literary development. These traditions often chart a continuous line of heritage linking women-authored texts, seeing them as distinct from "men's books." "Gynocritics" is one such critical project, where women's writings are recovered and revalued in a tradition of female specificity. This model often suggests that women learned how to be writers through reading the works of their foremothers. Elaine Showalter's *A Literature of Their Own* (1977) pioneered work in this mode. In a related way, some have seen women's writings as similar because of the anxious reactions female authors must have had to writing in a "male" world. Works such as Sandra Gilbert's and Susan Gubar's *Madwoman in the Attic* (1979) described social and psychological hurdles that all women authors supposedly faced and dealt with in a like manner in their writings.

If it now seems uncomplicated to label the above works essentialist, it is not so simple with French psychoanalytic feminisms. Perceived to be aligned and dubbed "the French feminists," theorists Julia Kristeva, Hélène Cixous, and Luce Irigaray were said to endorse projects for re-visioning (or, more accurately, deconstructing) cultural understandings of femininity. Anglo American scholarship engaging "the French feminists" often called them essentialist. Irigaray's work theorized women's speaking and writing with analogies to the "two lips" of mouths and labia, characterizing the female sex as "not one" but as multiple. Kristeva and Cixous used models of womblike languages or of mother's milk as ink. Such simple descriptions do not do justice to the complexities and differences of their theories, but "the French feminists" were criticized by some for suggesting that women's speech and writing could be explained or described by using analogies to their bodies.

Other factors shedding a different light on feminist "essentialism" during the 1980s were critiques of feminist elitism, racism, or homophobia. Many Anglo American feminisms were criticized as inordinately focused on heterosexual white Western bourgeois issues. Gendered essentialisms or universalisms were increasingly cited as exclusionary by those who were situated outside of a white, Western, middle-class background. bell hooks's article on black women's experience and essentialism in the classroom provides one example of such a critique.

Currently, "essentialism" is being rethought for the ways it has been used to legitimate various feminist projects. Investigating how the works of Irigaray, Cixous, or Kristeva do or do not fall under the rubric "essentialism" is an ongoing feminist project. Judith Butler and Drucilla Cornell have written important reconsiderations of these questions. Diana Fuss's *Essentially Speaking*, the first full-length study of feminist essentialism, laid the groundwork for many of these reconsiderations. Fuss's book concludes that there is constructionism in essentialism as well as essentialism in constructionism. Fuss doesn't interrogate whether essentialisms are good or bad. Asking where, how, and why essentialism is invoked and what its political and textual effects are provides the more interesting and difficult questions, according to Fuss.

An issue that continually crops up in these discussions about "essentialism" is, "Can there be a thing called 'feminism' without a presupposed category of 'women' who share certain concerns?" Denise Riley and others would keep the unity of feminism by answering with a theory/practice split. In theory, "women" is a fiction or a socially constructed category; in practice, women activists must continue to organize as if they are all the same. Gayatri Spivak has similarly theorized "strategic essentialism," in which feminists struggle against sexism but at the same time appeal to "the feminine" as a strategy to meet their goals. Fuss and Spivak argue that in varying degrees one can't avoid rhetorical or strategic essentialisms and that it may be counterproductive for feminisms to repudiate them.

The implications of these strategies continue to provide pressing questions. Should or must an understanding of women's identity or common experience be in force to have a "feminism"? To what degree or when should feminism involve an ad hoc unity, particularly if we see that describing "common experience" leaves out some women? These questions lay out the terrains on which essentialisms and feminisms will continue to intersect.

Devoney Looser

References

Alcoff, Linda. "Cultural Feminism Versus Post-Structuralism: The Identity Crisis in Feminist Theory." In *Feminist Theory in Practice and Process*, edited by Micheline R. Malson et al., 295–326. Chicago: University of Chicago Press, 1989.

Allen, Jeffner, and Iris Marion Young, eds. *The Thinking Muse: Feminism and Modern French Philosophy*. Bloomington: University of Indiana Press, 1989.

Butler, Judith. *Gender Trouble: Feminism and the Subversion of Identity*. New York: Routledge, 1990.

———, and Joan W. Scott, eds. *Feminists Theorize the Political*. New York: Routledge, 1992.

Cornell, Drucilla. *Beyond Accommodation: Ethical Feminism, Deconstruction, and the Law*. New York: Routledge, 1991.

de Lauretis, Teresa. "Upping the Anti (sic) in Feminist Theory." In *Conflicts in Feminism*, edited by Marianne Hirsch and Evelyn Fox Keller, 255–270. New York: Routledge, 1990.

Fuss, Diana. *Essentially Speaking: Feminism, Nature and Difference*. New York: Routledge, 1989.

Grosz, Elizabeth. "Conclusion: A Note on Essentialism and Difference." In *Feminist Knowledge: Critique and Construct*, edited by Sneja Gunew, 332–344. New York: Routledge, 1990.

hooks, bell. "Essentialism and Experience." *American Literary History* 3 (1991): 172–183.

Kirby, Vicki. "Corporeal Habits: Addressing Essentialism Differently." *Hypatia* 6 (1991): 4–24.

Riley, Denise. *'Am I that Name?' Feminism and the Category of "Women" in History*. Minneapolis: University of Minnesota Press, 1988.

Spivak, Gayatri Chakravorty, with Ellen Rooney. "In a Word: Interview." *differences* 1.2 (1989) [special issue on essentialism].

Ethnicity

Originating from the Greek root *ethnos*, ethnicity was once used to identify heathendom (*Oxford English Dictionary*). As early as the nineteenth century, however, ethnicity has referred to any group of people classed according to common traits based on tribal, linguistic, religious, national, or racial affiliation. The term "ethnic," once referring to the non-Christian, non-Jew, has now come to signify the nonwhite. From government documents to college applications, sections entitled "ethnicity" divide certain groups according to signifiers such as African American, Hispanic, Asian American, and white (with the usual qualifier of 'non Hispanic'), or, more specifically, Chicano, Latino, Pacific Islander, and so on. These ethnic identifiers are often ambiguous, inconsistent, and contested. These complicated issues of ethnicity have often problematically intersected with feminist literary discourse and the white feminist movement.

Despite a historical overlapping of the women's movement and the Civil Rights movement of the 1960s and 1970s, theoretical and creative writings by feminists of color have, during the last three decades, challenged, confronted, and critiqued racism within the women's movement and the academic establishment. Two anthologies, *The Bridge Called My Back: Writings by Radical Women of Color* and *Making Face, Making Soul = Haciendo Caras: Creative and Critical Perspectives by Women of Color* have been especially influential in exposing how the women's movement has treated race as secondary to feminine oppression and therefore as a less pressing problem. Feminists of color demand and work toward a more inclusive feminist discourse, which analyzes class, gender, and ethnicity, and which represents the diversity of female experience.

Other feminist scholars have also critiqued what sociologist Lynn Uttal calls "the problem of inclusion without influence." As writers and scholars, women (and men) of color have traditionally been marginalized and tokenized. In their essay entitled "The Costs of Exclusionary Practices in Women's Studies," Maxine Baca Zinn, Lynn Weber Cannon, Elizabeth Higginbotham, and Bonnie Thorton Dill reveal the token representation of women of color at *Signs* and *Feminist Studies*, two highly influential journals of feminist theory. According to their study, there were no black, Hispanic, Native American or Chinese American women in the top editorial positions at the journals in 1983–1984.

Not surprisingly, many feminist critics of color have felt estranged from the predominantly white academy and have explored new avenues of theoretical discourse. In the early 1970s, for example, Chicana feminists developed a "resistance" theory, a Chicana feminist theory that challenged the traditional Anglo and French feminisms and sought to redefine and challenge the theoretical framework that often excluded women of color. Current work by filmmaker and theorist Trinh T. Minh-ha has explored questions of language and identity in relation to notions of ethnicity and femininity. In *Woman, Native, Other*, she analyzes issues of postcoloniality and feminism, especially in relation to writings and art by women of color.

To assume that all members of an ethnic group think alike or are unified in their theoretical perspectives would be reductive. It is imperative, then, that feminist literary critics continue to challenge unidimensional approaches to feminist studies and constantly examine the racial hierarchies that exist within feminist studies.

Monica A. Brown

References

Anzaldúa, Gloria, ed. *Making Face, Making Soul = Haciendo Caras: Creative and Critical Perspectives by Women of Color.* San Francisco: Aunt Lute Foundation, 1990.

———, and Cherríe Moraga, eds. *This Bridge Called My Back: Writings by Radical Women of Color.* New York: Kitchen Table: Women of Color Press, 1981.

Lentricchia, Frank, and Thomas McLaughlin, eds. *Criticial Terms for Literary Study.* Chicago and London: University of Chicago Press, 1990.

Lester-Massman, Elli, Susan Searing, and Linda Shult, eds. *Women, Race, and Ethnicity: A Bibliography.* Wisconsin: University of Wisconsin System Women's Studies Librarian, 1991.

Minh-ha, Trinh T. *Woman, Native, Other: Writing Postcoloniality and Feminism.* Bloomington and Indianapolis: Indiana University Press, 1989.

Zinn, Maxine Baca, Lynn Weber Cannon, Elizabeth Higginbotham, and Bonnie Dill. "The Costs of Exclusionary Practices in Women's Studies." *Signs* 11 (1986): 290–303.

Eurocentric

Literally meaning centered on Europe and the Europeans, this term has become an abbreviated way to refer to the central position given to European culture, history, and thought by academic institutions and American culture. Many feminist literary theorists have argued that the Eurocentric tradition further centers on works by male, white writers, and thus excludes many women writers and women's issues.

In addition to questioning the exclusion of women writers from the Eurocentric canon, feminist critiques of Eurocentrism focus on the ways European culture and experience become held as the model for all other cultures. Feminist literary theorists working against Eurocentric approaches argue that European culture is just one among many, and that its inherent worth is no greater or less than any other culture. Some counter Eurocentrism by studying work by writers whose cultural experiences are not based in Europe, such as African American, Latina, or Chinese American writers. By studying works by "ethnic" writers, feminist literary theorists raise questions of ethnicity and race often ignored by Eurocentric writers.

Emphasizing multicultural rather than Eurocentric notions of culture, literature, and history also decenters and "deconstructs the borders erected by Eurocentric feminism," as Sonia Saldivar-Hull writes of the Chicana feminism practiced by Alma Gómez, Cherríe Moraga, and Mariana Romo-Carmona (294). In other words, for many feminist theorists, it is not enough to address the gender bias of Eurocentrism; feminism needs to examine its own Eurocentric attitudes and recognize that other issues, such as oppression and the experiences of specific cultural groups, need to be included in literary studies.

Susan B. Taylor

References

Anzaldúa, Gloria. *Borderlands/La Frontera: The New Mestiza.* San Francisco: Spinsters/Aunt Lute, 1987.

Johnson, Barbara. *A World of Difference.* Baltimore: Johns Hopkins University Press, 1987.

Moraga, Cherríe. *Loving in the War Years: lo que nunca pasó por sus labios.* Boston: South End, 1983.

Saldivar-Hull, Sonia. "Feminism on the Border: From Gender Politics to Geopolitics." In *Tradition and the Talents of Women,* edited by Florence Howe, 292–307. Urbana: University of Illinois Press, 1991.

Simonson, Rick, and Scott Walker, eds. *The Graywolf Annual Five: Multicultural Literacy.* Saint Paul, Minn: Graywolf, 1988.

Exchange of Women

See Traffic in Women

F

Faderman, Lillian

Best known for her *Surpassing the Love of Men: Romantic Friendship and Love between Women from the Renaissance to the Present*, Faderman was one of the first feminist literary scholars to examine representations of women's same-sex intimacy and lesbianism in both literature and culture. Reading canonical works by authors such as Emily Dickinson and Henry James, Faderman points to homoeroticism in literature and connects such themes to larger cultural and political forces.

In *Surpassing the Love of Men*, Faderman traces women's same-sex intimacy throughout history, noting the shifts in cultural attitudes toward such connections. Until the nineteenth century, she argues, a woman's intimacy with another woman—known then as a "romantic friendship"—was equivalent to a heterosexual love relationship in every sense except the sexual. Unlike twentieth-century attitudes toward women's same-sex relationships, however, which consider them "abnormal" and threatening, romantic friendships were not only socially accepted, but encouraged and admired as well. Furthermore, the women involved in them expressed no concern, guilt, or anxiety about their deep ties to someone of the same sex. Rather, especially in their written correspondence, women stated their love and desire for one another with great openness. Faderman explores this contrast, marking the late-nineteenth/early-twentieth century as a period of dramatic change. With the rise of new medical "knowledge," Faderman claims, romantic love and sexual desire, which were once considered separate impulses, become inextricably related. The result is the categorization of female-female relationships as lesbian, and, therefore, threat-ening and wrong. This belief system, Faderman suggests, is internalized in some lesbian writers of the twentieth century. Using texts both by and about women in relationships with other women, Faderman's work expands the field of feminist literary theory to include women's romantic and lesbian relationships as they are represented throughout the history of literature.

Sara E. Quay

References

Faderman, Lillian. "Emily Dickinson's Homoerotic Poetry." *Higginson Journal* 18 (1978): 19–27.

———. "Emily Dickinson's Letters to Sue Gilbert." *Massachusetts Review* 28 (1977): 197–225.

———. "Female Same-sex Relationships in Novels by Henry Wadsworth Longfellow, Oliver Wendell Holmes, and Henry James." *New England Quarterly* 16 (1978): 309–332.

———. *Odd Girls and Twilight Lovers: A History of Lesbian Life in Twentieth-century America.* New York: Columbia University Press, 1991.

———. *Surpassing the Love of Men: Romantic Friendship and Love between Women from the Renaissance to the Present.* New York: William Morrow, 1981.

Fairy Tales

Short prose narratives of unknown origin passed on by means of oral transmission, fairy-tales traditionally developed in illiterate or semi-literate cultures, and express the beliefs and concerns of common people. The term is generally applied to Western European folk tales, which were widely disseminated beginning in the seventeenth century. In the nineteenth century, folklore from England, Germany, Norway, and other European cultures was gathered in a flurry of activity by middle-class intellectuals anxious to preserve a rustic culture threatened by industrialization and urbanization.

Charles Perrault's collection of fairy tales, translated as *Mother Goose Tales*, was among the first to be published (1697). The first serious collection of authentically recorded tales that stressed the importance of tracing origin was Jacob and Wilhelm Grimms's *Children's and Household Tales*, published in 1812. At about the same time, collections of Norwegian and Celtic lore were being gathered and printed in Scandinavia and in England. Most works in the genre follow the structure of the German folk tale, which involves various marvelous acts and the theme of quest or heroic journey with final rewards for goodness and the defeat of evil. But recently feminists and other critics, along with scholars from other disciplines, have examined the constructions of good and evil in such stories in order to uncover patterns of racist or sexist bias. Drawing on a large corpus of folklore and legend from England, France, Norway, and other European nations, feminists like Ethel Johnston Phelps have looked at the heroine in fable and myth. John Phillips, for instance, examines the implications for the idea of womanhood in French adaptations of the genre in his *Nathalie Sarraute: Metaphor, Fairy Tale, and the Feminine of the Text*.

Despite their culturally and geographically diverse origins, fairy tales often share common themes and characteristics. Since the 1960s, critics have considered the feminist implications of leitmotifs inherent in the fairy tale form. The messages contained in much of fairy tale literature are seen as antipathetic by a number of feminist writers and critics. The praise for demure heroines and the privileging of feminine beauty are interpreted as delightful but mindless illusions that reward passive and submissive behavior, or that foster disappointment at trying to meet unrealistic standards of womanhood. Other tales portray women as opportunistic or cruel.

Recently, feminist critics have reexamined the fairy tale and critiqued its restrictive narrowing of positive roles for females outside of marriage and motherhood. Such critics react against proscribed roles that deprive women of contact with external reality. The sexually un-

available woman or the woman deemed unmarriageable according to the standards of the culture is portrayed in fairy tale literature as an outcast with no options for a rewarding life. In some feminist readings, furthermore, helplessness, docility, and passivity are seen as harmful negative stereotypes that reinforce the standards by which women must aspire to subordinate roles, or which preclude entry to other venues of fulfillment. Happily-ever-after scenarios in fairy tale literature are seen as attempts to mask what was in reality a difficult and unrewarding feminine existence by dressing it with romance and glamour. Jack Zipes has recently commented on the fairy tale as an instrument of socialization. Along with Ruth Bottigheimer and others, he has examined fairy tale morphologies and debunked the universal meaning and mythic significance previously thought to exist in their tropes, viewing such readings as culturally determined and ultimately illusory.

In *Transforming the Cinderella Dream*, Huang Mei argues that until the late nineteenth century, English novelists followed the lead of Richardson, drawing on fairy tale metaphor and structure patterned after the Cinderella story. The strong-willed heroines of Charlotte Brontë and George Eliot later overturned such expectations of model behavior, and dismissed the conventions of domestic culture in which decorativeness, marriage, and motherhood are the only appropriate roles for women. A group of more militant feminist critics has come out of Dublin to address the association in fairy tale literature of beauty and sexuality with goodness and worth, and to react against the theme of domesticity through fairy tale spoof. Zoe Fairbairns and others in *Cinderella on the Ball* rewrite the archetypal fairy tale under such titles as "No More Embroidery!" (Celia De Freine) "Happy Ever After and Other Obsessions" (Mairide Woods), and "The Ugly Sisters Strike Back" (Linda Kavanaugh). *Ride on Rapunzel* (Maeve Binchy et al.) is another collection of fairy tale satire that burlesques the traditional form.

Canadian novelist and poet Margaret Atwood tailors the fiction of Hans Christian Andersen and the brothers Grimm in works such as *Power Politics*, *Surfacing*, and *The Handmaid's Tale*, deconstructing fairy tale narrative in order to comment on themes of sexual "power politics." Through her creation of metafairy tales Atwood reenvisions the traditional folk images that constrict gender roles, then leads beyond them in a movement toward imagery of liberation, metamorphosis, and healing. Critics have explored, for example, the intertextual relationship between the Grimms' "Robber Bridegroom" and Atwood's *The Edible Woman*, (1969) and the influence of "Rapunzel" and Andersen's "Snow Queen" on her 1988 novel *Cat's Eye*. *The Robber Bride* carries forward her themes of gender and power in a postfeminist reexamination of sexual politics in the face of changing cultural dynamics.

Susan P. Reilly

References

Atwood, Margaret. *Cat's Eye*. Toronto: McClelland and Stewart, 1988.

———. *The Edible Woman*. Boston: Little, Brown, 1969. New York: Popular Library, 1976.

———. *The Handmaid's Tale*. Toronto: McClelland and Stewart, 1985. Boston: Houghton Mifflin, 1986.

———. *The Robber Bride*. Toronto: McClelland and Stewart. London: Bloomsbury, 1993.

———. *Surfacing*. New York: Popular Library, 1976.

Barzilai, Shuli. "Snow White: The Mother's Story," *Signs* 15 (1990): 515–534.

Binchy, Maeve, et al. *Ride on Rapunzel*. Dublin: Attic, 1992.

Bottigheimer, Ruth. *Fairy Tales and Society: Illusion, Allusion, and Paradigm*. Philadelphia: University of Pennsylvania Press, 1986.

———. *Grimms' Bad Girls and Bold Boys: The Moral and Social Vision of the Tales*. New Haven: Yale University Press, 1987.

Bryant, Sylvia. "Re-constructing Oedipus through Beauty and the Beast." *Criticism* 31 (1989): 439–539.

Fairbairns, Zoe, et al. *Cinderella on the Ball*. Dublin: Attic, 1991.

Franz, Marie-Louise von. *The Feminine in Fairy Tales*. Rev. ed. Boston: Shambhala, 1993. Originally published as *The Problem of the Feminine in Fairy Tales*.

Granofsky, Ronald. "Fairy-tale Morphology in Margaret Atwood's *Surfacing*." *Mosaic* 23 (1990): 51–65.

Huang, Mei. *Transforming the Cinderella Dream: From Frances Burney to Charlotte Brontë*. New Brunswick, N.J.: Rutgers University Press, 1990.

Irons, Glenwood, ed. *Essays on Popular Narrative*. Toronto: University of Toronto Press, 1992.

McGlathery, James M. *Fairy-tale Romance: The Grimms, Basile, and Perrault*. Urbana: University of Illinois Press, 1991.

Nolan, Barbara. *Sweeping Beauties: Fairy Tales for Feminists*. Dublin: Attic, 1989.

Phelps, Ethel Johnston. *The Maid of the North: Feminist Folk Tales from around the World*. New York: Holt, Reinhart, and Winston, 1981.

Phillips, John. *Nathalie Sarraute: Metaphor, Fairy-tale, and the Feminine of the Text*. New York: Peter Lang, 1994.

Rifelj, Carol deDobay. "Cendrillon and the Ogre: Women in Fairy Tales and Sade." *Romantic Review* 81 (1990): 11–24.

Rowe, Karen. "Feminism and Fairy Tales." *Women's Studies: An Interdisciplinary Journal* 6 (1979): 237–257.

Warner, Marina. "The Absent Mother: Women against Women in Old Wives' Tales." *History Today* 41 (1991): 22–28.

———. *From the Beast to the Blonde: On Fairy Tales and Their Tellers*. London: Chatto, 1994.

———. "Mother Goose Tales: Female Fiction, Female Fact?" *Folklore* 101 (1990): 3–25.

Wilson, Sharon Rose. *Margaret Atwood's Fairy-Tale Sexual Politics*. Jackson: University Press of Mississippi, 1993.

Zipes, Jack, ed. *Don't Bet on the Prince: Contemporary Feminist Fairy Tales in North America and England*. New York: Methuen, 1986.

———, ed. *Fairy Tales and the Art of Subversion: The Classical Genre for Children and the Process of Civilization*. New York: Methuen, 1988.

Family Systems Theory

Family systems theory defines the family as an emotional system consisting of a network of interlocking relationships. Rather than explaining an individual's behavior as emanating from within an autonomous individual, family systems theory considers an individual's behavior as part of the pattern of the family system. Family systems theory is important for feminist theory particularly because it suggests that a woman's debilitating behavior or illness may be functioning to maintain homeostasis in the patriarchal nuclear family.

Family systems theory developed out of the studies of schizophrenics and their families in the 1940s and 1950s, and was influenced by general systems theory. Therapists including Murray Bowen, Theodore Lidz, and Lyman Wynne, and anthropologist Gregory Bateson, gradually stopped treating schizophrenia as an individual illness, and started treating schizophrenia as a family-wide process. Ludwig von Bertalanffy's work in organismic biology in the 1920s produced the founding principles of general systems theory, which considers a system to consist of interacting subsystems while simultaneously interacting with its environment. Thus, family systems thinking considers individuals, dyads, and triads to be interacting subsystems of the family system, which must maintain stability. Bowen, in *Family Evaluation*, further claims that dyads—marriages, for example—are the most unstable systems, requiring a third person under stress, and that family systems consist of interlocking triangles. Family systems theory differentiates itself from psychoanalysis in that it takes a synchronic, circular approach to individual behavior, seeing the behavior as part of the current family process, rather than taking a diachronic, linear approach that sees individual symptoms as the result of past, traumatic events.

Paula Marantz Cohen's *The Daughter's Dilemma* is the first feminist literary study to include a family systems approach. Cohen examines the daughter's function in the family, defining the heroines in the novels she examines as "regulating daughters" whose virtues are metaphorically or literally symptoms that function to maintain family stability. Family systems theory suggests that the ideology of family homeostasis may be as coercive an influence on novelistic form as the ideology of marriage. Finally, family systems theory helps demystify women's complicity in maintaining the patriarchal family.

Emily Koch

References

Bateson, Gregory. *Steps to an Ecology of Mind: Collected Essays in Anthropology, Psychiatry, Evolution, and Epistemology.* San Francisco: Chandler, 1972.

Bowen, Murray, and Michael Kerr. *Family Evaluation: An Approach Based on Bowen Theory.* New York: W.W. Norton, 1988.

Cohen, Paula Marantz. *The Daughter's Dilemma: Family Process and the Nineteenth-Century Novel.* Ann Arbor: University of Michigan Press, 1991.

Hoffman, Lynn. *Foundations of Family Therapy: A Conceptual Framework for Systems Change.* New York: Basic, 1981.

Schultz, Stephen J. *Family Systems Therapy: An Integration.* New York: Jason Aronson, 1984.

Fashion

Conventionally connected with women and feminine concerns, fashion has suffered from these associations. As a feminine concern, fashion has been denigrated as trivial. As a feminist concern, fashion has been seen as an instrument of sexual subjugation, or, at best, a great waste of time, money, and energy. To its harshest critics, fashion may seem contaminated with the toxins of patriarchy and capitalism. But fashion may be used to imagine alternatives as well as to manufacture consent. Intimately connected with the body and sexuality, fashion defines and disrupts gender identifications. The product of corporate and media enterprise, fashion plugs the body into consumer culture, announcing acceptance, challenge, or revision of the limits that culture offers. Work on fashion always talks about women, but its concerns have not always been feminist. This is changing. In the 1980s and 1990s feminist work on fashion has gotten underway. These studies may be categorized: revisionist historical studies; psychoanalytic formulations of the masculine and feminine gaze; and cultural studies work on the politics of consumption and taste.

The conventional identification of women with fashion is a historical one not fully institutionalized until the eighteenth century with the formation of separate gendered spheres: arenas of production are masculine, arenas of consumption, feminine. Men dress soberly for business; women dress prettily for men: not only for men's sexual gratification, but also for men's social prestige. In *The Theory of the Leisure Class*, Thorstein Veblen defines fashion as luxurious waste and discusses its use in bourgeois status competition—"conspicuous consumption." Men make money; women spend it to produce themselves as status objects. In "Fashion," Georg Simmel explains women's investment in fashion as compensation for lack of a professional identity. Women construct their identities through fashion because few other channels are available.

Echoing some of Veblen's and Simmel's principles, in *The Second Sex*, Simone de Beauvoir defines issues subsequent feminists take up: women's roles as status and erotic objects self-constructed to satisfy dictates of social convention and masculine desire; the split subjectivity this construction entails; the tragic "enslavement" of women to fashion. Beauvoir says that women are always masquerading in fashion. They fashion "unreal" characters, presenting these rather than their "true" selves to the world. Beauvoir assumes that the "true" self continues to exist, but stifled under fashion's masquerade.

Drawing on poststructuralism, more recent work on gender, like that of Judith Butler, has gone far to erode the distinction between "authentic" and "constructed" selves. Is there an "authentic" self obscured by fashion or is fashion a cultural code for constructing selves inconceivable outside this codification? As Janet Radcliffe Richards points out, even antifashion feminists devoted to representing "authentic" selves do so in an (anti-)fashion system more prescriptive and exclusive than the fashion of femininity they oppose.

Recent critics question as well women's "enslavement" to fashion. They unsettle the assumption that fashion works unilaterally to sexually exploit and oppress women. Who is to say, for instance, that women are always dressing for men? In *Fashion and Eroticism*, Valerie Steele argues that women, even Victorian "house angels," dress for their own pleasure and power. Fashion is never a one-way street.

Any approach to fashion proceeds through erotic and commodified visual perception. Not only men, but also women consume images of women-on-display. But how does their consumption of media images inform women's production of self-images? This process is rarely one of symmetrical imitation. In "Film and the Masquerade," Mary Anne Doane uses the idea of "masquerade" to explain women's relation to media images. Masquerade produces a distance from the image, a space where women spectators may manipulate and produce female images. Women are not caught in the grip of complete identification with the images they consume. Following Doane, Silvia Kolbowski's "Playing with Dolls" denies that fashion photography effects any "simple transmission of socially coded femininity."

What happens instead? Answers cover a spectrum of issues. Feminist critics concentrate in locally focused ways on a wide range of topics: marketing and consumption, style resistance and subcultures, designers and the ideological cut of their clothes, historical inquiries that particularize and complicate the ways that women have practiced fashion from early- to postmodern times.

This is not to say that the principled critique of fashion is silenced by the muzzle of poststructuralist ambiguity. Feminist work in cultural studies has broadened the critique by looking at workingclass fashion practices and at the relationship between the corporate/media production of fashion and its consumption. Most new fashions are found, if not in the gutter, then at least on the street. Women produce fashion through selective consumption; the fashion industry produces its designs by selectively consuming street-style. No clear line between the production and consumption of fashion exists. The fashion system is a complex network; its effects may be readable only in local and momentary contexts. Once read, its messages have broad implications for a culture far from just and for subjects far from empowered.

Fashion's inequities are most clearly written not on the bodies of those who wear stylish clothes, but of those who produce them. Staffed by an 80 percent female underclass, sweatshops thrive. Manufacturing clothing through subcontracts often in the Third and Fourth Worlds, in extremely short runs with predominantly unskilled labor, often through female home workers, the fashion industry thrives on modes of production possible only in a world where lines of race, class, and gender define the map of privilege and oppression.

Erin Mackie

References

Ash, Juliet, and Elizabeth Wilson, eds. *Chic Thrills: A Fashion Reader*. Berkeley: University of California Press, 1992.

Beauvoir, Simone de. *The Second Sex*. Translated by H.M. Parshley. New York: Knopf, 1952.

Butler, Judith. *Gender Trouble: Feminism and the Subversion of Identity*. New York: Routledge, 1990.

Carter, Erica. "Alice in Consumer Wonderland." In *Gender and Generation*, edited by Angela McRobbie and Mica Nava, 185–214. London: Macmillan, 1984.

F

Doane, Mary Ann. "Film and the Masquerade: Theorizing the Female Spectator" [1982]. In *The Sexual Subject: A Screen Reader in Sexuality*, 227–243. London and New York: Screen/Routledge, 1992.

Gaines, Jane, and Charlotte Herzog, eds. *Fabrications: Costume and the Female Body*. New York and London: Routledge, 1990.

Kolbowski, Silvia. "Playing with Dolls." In *The Critical Image: Essays on Contemporary Photography*, 139–154. Seattle: Bay, 1990.

Phizacklea, Annie. *Unpacking the Fashion Industry: Gender, Racism, and Class in Production*. London and New York: Routledge, 1990.

Radcliffe Richards, Janet. *The Sceptical Feminist*. London: Routledge and Kegan Paul, 1980.

Simmel, Georg. "Fashion." Reprinted in *The American Journal of Sociology* 62 (1957): 541–558.

Steele, Valerie. *Fashion and Eroticism*. New York and Oxford: Oxford University Press, 1985.

Williamson, Judith. "A Piece of the Action: Images of 'Women' in the Photography of Cindy Sherman." In *Consuming Passions: The Dynamics of Popular Culture*, 91–113. London and New York: Marion Boyars, 1986.

Wilson, Elizabeth. *Adorned in Dreams: Fashion and Modernity*. London: Virago, 1985.

Father

For feminists the father is literally and symbolically the heart of patriarchy. Etymologically, the root of "patriarchy" is *pater*, and almost every feminist theory of psychosexual development of human identity privileges the father's role. As Dorothy van Ghent wrote in *The English Novel* (1953), "Under our anciently inherited patriarchal organization of the family . . . our 'fathers' are not only individual fathers but all of those who have come before us—society as it has determined our conditions of existence, and the problems we have to confront." Yet if the father is found at the heart of patriarchy, he is not himself the same thing as patriarchy. The feminist struggle to understand the relationship between the father and patriarchy has entailed the gradual recognition of how patriarchy works on and through all of us, regardless of our place within the family.

First wave feminist literary criticism, in the process of rediscovering and celebrating the mother-daughter relationship, tended to see the father as the negative figure in a Freudian drama of separation and individuation. For example, Jane Flax explained the daughter's identification with the father as a self-division: the father represents "autonomy," and he appears as gatekeeper to the outside world. Yet in order to move closer to the father—and to the privileges of his authority—"the daughter must give up her own pre-Oedipal tie to the mother, and often take on the father's devaluation of and contemptuous attitude for the mother and, by extension, for women as a group." Working on biographical and autobiographical materials, feminist literary scholars scrutinized women's stories to discover the psychodynamics of the father-daughter relationship. Women writers in particular were thought to have paid a tragic price for identifying with their fathers rather than their mothers. In the meantime, the father himself was often cast as both patriarch and patriarchy. In other words, individual fathers tended to be read as if they embodied patriarchy in human form.

With the entrance of Lacan onto the critical scene, some feminists subsequently argued that the real, individual, biological father mattered less than had been assumed. Lacan's concept of the "paternal metaphor" led to the notion that, even if "fathers" did not exist at all, patriarchy as a principle might nonetheless prevail. As Juliet Mitchell wrote, "For whether or not the actual father is there does not affect the perpetuation of the patriarchal culture within the psychology of the individual; absent or present, 'the father' always has his place." The work of Lacanian critics Juliet Mitchell and Jacqueline Rose led Beth Kowaleski-Wallace to suggest that father ought not to be read as a metaphor but rather as a synecdoche for patriarchy. That is, she urged feminist critics to read the individual father not as a human substitute for patriarchy, but rather as a marker for a larger and more complex process of patriarchal formation and learning. In her book entitled *Their Fathers' Daughters* she similarly argued that patriarchy is not a monolithic force, but a psychological process that positions the daughter, mother, and father. The daughter's gravitation toward the father and the political position he represents is necessitated by the cultural devaluation of the maternal body. Women thus become identified with patriarchy within a larger social and psychological context.

In a similar vein, in *Monsters of Affection*, Dianne Sadoff deals with the connection between fatherhood and structures of desire in the work of Charles Dickens, George Eliot, and Charlotte Brontë. She explores the figurative father around whom configurations of desire organize themselves. She reads George Eliot, for example, as a writer who experiences a profound discontinuity between her masculine personae and her female self. Her fictional fathers play a key role in her attempt to address that discontinuity.

Covering a range of texts, a range of geographical and historical locations, as well as a range of cultural settings, *Daughters and Fathers* brings the father-daughter relationship to the fore. The collection is divided into three sections: "Cultural Filialogy," which examines "the theoretical ideas through which the daughter-father relationship has been culturally understood"; "In Nomine Patris: The Daughter in Her Father's House," which investigates the control that the literary or familial patriarch exerts over the daughter in the family; and In Nomine Filiae: The Artist as Her Father's Daughter," which explores the "logic of patronymics," that is, the daughter's attempt to find authority outside her father. In this most comprehensive collection, a number of daughter-father relationships are seen from many angles; the "father" may be literal (as in the case of Anne Thackeray Ritchie), or figurative or symbolic (as for Christina Rossetti or Emily Dickinson). In either case, he is the figure who precipitates a clearer understanding of the daughter's creativity.

Like several of the contributors to *Daughters and Fathers*, Lynda Zwinger is also interested in the dynamics of desire between the father and daughter. In *Daughters, Fathers, and the Novel: The Sentimental Romance of Heterosexuality*, she posits that the father "always has a question he will neither articulate nor take responsibility for"; namely, the question of his daughter's response to his desire for her. Zwinger explores a range of fictional texts, from Samuel Richardson's *Clarissa* to Alcott's *Little Women*, to Réage's *Story of O*, that "bind" and "tame" the daughter. Her interest lies in the way that sentimentalized representations of desiring daughters, occurring in the presence of a fictional father who is represented as not desiring her, grounds "the system of cultural constructs and prescription that we have learned to think of as heterosexual desire."

Finally, the collection entitled *Refiguring the Father: New Feminist Readings of Patriarchy* takes as its subject the father himself. Rather than viewing the father as if he were an unhistorical, univocal function, contributors to this collection seek to embody the father, to view him as a desiring and somatic figure. For example, Nancy Sorkin Rabinowitz investigates the father-son eroticism in Euripides's *Hippolytus*, while Heather Hathaway focuses on mulatto fathers to explore how miscegenation exacerbates the Oedipal motivation. Thus, the essays in the collection renegotiate the Oedipal paradigm by considering the father's own psychological investments. In the end, they show how the father's authority "can be subverted, disembodied, or dissipated" in a variety of ways. The father who emerges from this collection is, the editors explain, "plural, shattered, amorphous, and contradictory."

In conclusion, feminist literary analysis of the father has concentrated on explaining the relationship between the father and patriarchy. Working both within and against psychoanalytic paradigms, it has explored the meaning of the father in the daughter's life, and it has offered fruitful interpretations of the father himself as someone who receives his essence from the structure that names him.

Beth Kowaleski-Wallace

References

Boose, Lynda E., and Betty S. Flowers. *Daughters and Fathers*. Baltimore: Johns Hopkins University Press, 1989.

Flax, Jane. "Mother-Daughter Relationships: Psychodynamics, Politics, and Philosophy." In *The Future of Difference*, edited by Hester Eisenstein and Alice Jardine, 20–40. New Brunswick, N.J.: Rutgers University Press, 1980.

Kowaleski-Wallace, Beth. "Reading the Father Metaphorically." In *Refiguring the Father: New Feminist Readings of Patriarchy*, edited by Patricia Yaeger and Beth Kowaleski-Wallace, 296–311. Carbondale: Southern Illinois University Press, 1989.

———. *Their Fathers' Daughters: Hannah More, Maria Edgeworth, and Patriarchal Complicity*. New York: Oxford University Press, 1991.

Mitchell, Juliet. *Women: The Longest Revolution*. New York: Pantheon, 1984.

Sadoff, Dianne. *Monsters of Affection: Dickens, Eliot, and Brontë on Fatherhood*. Baltimore: Johns Hopkins University Press, 1982.

Yaeger, Patricia, and Beth Kowaleski-Wallace, eds. *Refiguring the Father: New Feminist Readings of Patriarchy*. Carbondale: Southern Illinois University Press, 1989.

Zwinger, Lynda. *Daughters, Fathers, and the Novel; The Sentimental Romance of Heterosexuality*. Madison: University of Wisconsin Press, 1991.

Felman, Shoshana

Since the 1970s, the American critic Shoshana Felman has provided a link between Anglo American and French feminists by bringing French and European psychoanalytical theory into dialogue with Anglo American literary criticism. An early proponent of the deconstructive reading practices of Jacques Derrida, Felman has been instrumental in interrogating the work of Jacques Lacan, whose psychoanalytical theories have described and often seemed to endorse women's inferior position in Western culture.

Felman opened "Women and Madness: The Critical Phallacy" by connecting Phyllis Chesler's sociohistorical study *Women and Madness* to Luce Irigaray's meditation on cultural definitions of femininity, *Speculum of the Other Woman*. Felman revealed that women's historical tendency to be labeled "hysterical" or "insane" by male culture arises from the binary logic that characterizes Western thought, a logic that persistently privileges masculine subjectivity and silences and marginalizes women. Enlisting a short story by Balzac, Felman illustrated that women's madness may actually express their exclusion from the linguistic systems male speakers use to define and reinforce their superior position.

Like French feminists, Felman has critiqued canonical literary and psychoanalytical theories of sexual difference, arguing that "masculinity" and "femininity" are not fixed attributes but merely concepts that serve to buttress patriarchal power. Noting that male culture has traditionally defined "woman" as "Other" and even as insane in order to silence and marginalize her, Felman has investigated textual and psychoanalytical strategies that would allow women to create a language—an *écriture féminine*—that would enable them to speak authentically.

Lisa Jadwin

References

Felman, Shoshana. *What Does a Woman Want? Reading and Sexual Difference*. Baltimore: Johns Hopkins University Press, 1993.

———. "Women and Madness: The Critical Phallacy." In *Feminisms: An Anthology of Literary Theory and Criticism*, edited by Robyn R. Warhol and Dianne Price Herndl, 6–19. New Jersey: Rutgers University Press, 1991.

———. *Writing and Madness: Literature/Philosophy/Psychoanalysis*. Translated by Martha Noel Evans and Shoshana Felman, with Brian Massumi. Ithaca, N.Y.: Cornell University Press, 1985.

———, ed. *Literature and Psychoanalysis: The Question of Reading, Otherwise* [1977]. Baltimore: Johns Hopkins University Press, 1982.

———, and Dori Laub. *Testimony: Crises of Witnessing in Literature, Psychoanalysis, and History*. New York: Routledge, 1991.

Female Eunuch

The title of Germaine Greer's widely popular 1970 book that challenged women to rethink prevailing sexual stereotypes underlying patriarchal structures of society, economy, marriage, and the family. The title refers to the "castration" of women that results from the action of male oppression in contemporary society, and that serves in effect to deprive women of contact with external reality. Greer argues that the images perpetuated in commercial advertising of vapid, passive females uphold unnatural standards of femininity, and promote the image of woman as an object of male fantasy. Claiming that woman's essential quality in the current culture must be "castratedness," Greer identifies a "gynolatry" in Western culture that is inscribed in film, television, newspapers, and other media forms. In order to fit the male-centered myth of ideal womanhood, Greer claims, women must belie their own intelligence, and function so as to increase their "market value" by taking on the role of submissive and dependent marriage partner. The book advocates a "rebellion" by women against their prescribed role in society. The work is now seen in certain circles as something of an oddity having little to do with recent feminist theory, but its effects on popular thinking influenced the women's movement, and introduced readers to a new ideal of womanhood.

Susan P. Reilly

References

Greer, Germaine. *The Female Eunuch* [1970]. New York: McGraw-Hill, 1971.

Feminine

Pretty, dainty, fragile, soft, nurturing, caring, healing, passive, narcissistic, duplicitous, irrational, powerless—in its most traditional sense, the term "feminine" summons up these qualities. Feminists have appropriated various of these traditional attributes to describe a uniquely female power, to characterize writing and other forms of female creativity, and to work toward various other political ends. In more recent years, the question of whether or not feminine attributes are biologically determined has fueled heated debates between essentialists (who argue that femininity resides in the female body), and constructionists (who argue that femininity is socially constructed and hence detachable from the body). Interestingly, both positions generate powerful arguments for the empowerment of those of us with female bodies.

The principles of deconstruction and the psychoanalytic theories of Jacques Lacan provide the groundwork for much recent scholarship on femininity. Deconstructionists such as Jacques Derrida have analyzed Western metaphysical thought to reveal the oppositional logic upon which it is based. This logic, which aligns masculinity with rationality and power, relies upon the suppression of its opposite, the feminine, which it links with multivocality, uncertainty, and undecidability. The feminine, then, is threatening in that its empowerment has the potential to unsettle this opposition and so to overturn the system of patriarchal logic. Similarly, Lacan sees femininity relegated to the realm of the Other, so that "woman" in patriarchy is silent, unspeakable, and unable to articulate herself because the symbolic order that constitutes her characterizes her as a negative term. Lacan's distinction between the "phallus" (the master signifier of the Symbolic) and the penis has also been useful in that it suggests a similar distinction between the characteristic

assessment of femininity and the female bodies upon which that assessment operates.

If "masculine" language is rational, linear, and univocal, "feminine" language is irrational, circular, and polyvocal. In the 1970s, French feminists Hélène Cixous, Luce Irigaray, and Julia Kristeva, among others, began to explore the potential for a uniquely feminine style of writing that might collapse the gendered opposition between articulate, masculine mind and inarticulate, feminine body. Called *l'écriture féminine*, this style is based in what Kristeva terms the "semiotic," and draws upon a language of the body that references the preverbal relationship between infant and mother. These theorists argue that feminine language is composed of rhythms, sounds, and repetitions, and is more fluid and open-ended than its masculine counterpart. In its refusal to remain silent, feminine writing has the potential to unsettle patriarchal logocentric thought; "writing the body" offers a way to shake up the existing order. Interestingly, feminine writing is not restricted to those with female bodies. Writers such as Jean Genet, James Joyce, and Antonin Artaud have been credited with the ability to "write like a woman."

Many feminists have launched sophisticated arguments for the reassessment of femininity, which is frequently defined on the basis of women's reproductive capabilities. Many in this camp suggest that, rather than trying to access "masculine" power, women need to fight for the valuation of such traditionally feminine strengths as caring and nurturing. This strategy echoes across the feminist canon, finding voice in the work of Nancy Chodorow, who suggests that our culture might benefit were men and women to share more equitably the responsibilities and traits of mothering, and of Carol Gilligan, who has argued that the basis of women's moral judgments differs from that of men due to women's more interpersonal concerns. Some feminist theologians write about a feminine spirituality that valorizes women's natural fecundity, healing powers, and connection to the earth. In less academic arenas, many women who argue that our society would be a better place if women were in power do so with reference to a set of uniquely feminine attributes such as connectedness, caring, and nonviolence. Many feminist utopias are based on the more positive attributes of the set that opened this entry.

Much of this work has met with radical

critiques from constructivist feminists who find such theories perilously close to denigrating, stereotypical views of women. As critics of both the *écriture* group and of more overtly essentialist theorists note, linking the female body with irrationality, maternity, and nurturing comes dangerously close to replicating the arguments of conservative groups who argue that women belong in the home because their bodies are made to bear children.

Constructivist feminists argue that sexuality is socially produced, not biologically determined. Much recent work in this field has focused on transsexuals and transvestites because they present the most radical challenge to the concept of biological destiny. Marjorie Garber, for example, explores the ways in which cross-dressing appropriates, mimics, and represents gender codes in such a way as to trouble deeply the very category of gender. Transsexuals push this "category crisis" to its limit: if the body itself is reducible to a series of "spare parts" that can be added or subtracted as the subject desires, if the body itself is malleable in this way, the absolute determination of gender identity crumbles accordingly. Lillian Faderman's research on butch and femme roles within the lesbian community destabilizes the coherence of essentialized gender categories by pointing to women who cover the spectrum of gendered behavior and only one side of the biology. Judith Butler takes perhaps the most extreme stance on this issue. In *Gender Trouble*, she argues that sexuality is performed, that what we read as femininity is reducible to a series of costumes, gestures, and acts. Butler calls for the subversion of gender roles through the process of making these acts visible as acts through such strategies as camp, repetition, and parody. By "putting on the feminine," Butler argues, women may be able to denaturalize femininity and thus to open up other potential categories of identity that might allow for a more complex understanding of gender.

Both essentialist and constructivist arguments have their strengths and their weaknesses. Some of the most recent work in contemporary feminism integrates these two positions so as to move beyond the essentialist/constructivist binary. Diana Fuss's 1989 book *Essentially Speaking*, for example, offers a sophisticated evaluation of the strategic uses of essentialism, of the ways in which linking femininity with biological femaleness can be politically efficacious.

Rebecca F. Stern

References

Beauvoir, Simone de. *The Second Sex*. New York: Vintage, 1952.

Butler, Judith. *Gender Trouble*. New York: Routledge, 1990.

Chodorow, Nancy. *The Reproduction of Mothering*. Berkeley: University of California Press, 1978.

Cixous, Hélène. "The Laugh of the Medusa." *Signs* 1 (1975): 875–893.

Derrida, Jacques. *Spurs*. Translated by Barbara Harlow. Chicago: University of Chicago Press, 1978.

Faderman, Lillian. *Odd Girls and Twilight Lovers*. New York: Columbia University Press, 1991.

———. *Surpassing the Love of Men*. New York: William Morrow, 1981.

Fuss, Diana. *Essentially Speaking*. New York: Routledge, 1989.

Garber, Marjorie. *Vested Interests*. New York: Routledge, 1992.

Gilligan, Carol. *In a Different Voice*. Cambridge: Harvard University Press, 1982.

Irigaray, Luce. *Speculum of the Other Woman*. Translated by Gillian C. Porter. Ithaca, N.Y.: Cornell University Press, 1985.

———. *This Sex Which Is Not One*. Translated by Catherine Gill. Ithaca, N.Y.: Cornell University Press, 1985.

Jones, Ann Rosalind. "Writing the Body: Toward an Understanding of L'Écriture Féminine." In *Feminisms*, edited by Diana Price Herndl and Robyn R. Warhol, 357–370. New Brunswick, N.J.: Rutgers University Press, 1991.

Kristeva, Julia. *Desire in Language: A Semiotic Approach to Literature and Art*. Edited by Leon Roudiez. New York: Columbia University Press, 1980.

———. *Revolution in Poetic Language*. Translated by Margaret Walker. New York: Columbia University Press, 1980.

Lacan, Jacques, and the école freudienne. *Feminine Sexuality*. Edited by Juliet Mitchell and Jacqueline Rose. Translated by Jacqueline Rose. New York: W.W. Norton, 1982.

Feminine Mystique

A phrase coined by Betty Friedan, in the book

by the same name, to describe the idealization of the feminine woman whose self-definition is based exclusively on her role as wife and mother. The feminine mystique names the restrictive and oppressive definitions of woman that dominated the 1950s and Friedan's cogent analysis was a catalyst to the first wave feminism of the women's movement. Her analysis of the way in which the mystique was created and perpetuated by fiction published in women's magazines underscores literature's ability to influence—and critique—cultural values and norms.

First published in 1963, *The Feminine Mystique* articulated the growing dissatisfaction American women felt with their exclusive role as housewife and mother. A cultural belief system that naturalizes characteristics thought to be "feminine," the feminine mystique emphasizes "sexual passivity, male domination, and nurturing female love." In doing so, it reifies these traditionally undervalued traits, claiming that they make women different from—and probably even superior to—men. Women's unhappiness, the mystique asserts, is a result of rejecting this privileged position and trying to be too much like men. True female fulfillment, on the other hand, comes from completely embracing the "mysterious and intuitive" feminine role. Friedan asserts that once the false consciousness of the feminine mystique is lifted—the goal of first wave feminism—women can discover their true selves, finding satisfaction in their careers, families, and relationships.

In *The Second Stage*, Friedan discusses what must happen once the feminine mystique has been revealed as an oppressive construct. The challenge of second-wave feminism, she argues, is to negotiate the complications that arise once women are no longer confined to the home. Balancing two-income families, negotiating child care, and achieving equal rights are all important issues if feminism is to continue to evolve. Although Friedan's concept of the feminine mystique as a type of false consciousness risks, in its own way, essentializing gender roles, the idea was nothing short of revolutionary in its time. Naming the feminine mystique validated the presence of feminists within the academy, paved the way for women's and gender studies departments, and exposed the ways in which popular culture, including literature, constructs and limits human behavior.

Sara E. Quay

References

Friedan, Betty. *The Feminine Mystique*. New York: W.W. Norton, 1963.
———. *The Second Stage*. New York: Summit, 1981.

Feminist Aesthetics

Aesthetics denotes the philosophy of art or of a specific medium. Feminist interventions in aesthetics account for the historical absence of women from the canons of creative disciplines; recover and revalue the work of women artists; critique theoretical structures that devalue the feminine or exclude female producers; and propose alternative aesthetics that centralize female subjectivity or highlight the role of gender in art.

Arising alongside bourgeois culture in the eighteenth century, the field of aesthetics served to organize meanings neglected by scientific rationalism. Historically, aesthetics concerns theories of sensory perception, taste, value, and response to the perception of beauty. Positing taste free of any interest other than the evaluation of beauty, aesthetics describes the artist as a solitary genius and the work of art as an independent, self-referential object. The artist is an exemplary consumer, elevating matter into form by sublimating desire through contemplation. The female body, central to the visual arts, tests the artist's ability to sublimate; representations of nudes signify the artist's mastery of psychic and social order while also signaling anxieties about dissolution and incoherence. Feminists have described this identification of visual perception with maleness and of the object of perception with femaleness as a "heterosexual representational economy." Artistic creation has been equated with male sexuality since Antiquity; with the rise of expressive aesthetics, the suffering associated with childbirth was appropriated for the male artist. Eighteenth-century philosophers identified the beautiful with women as objects, with small details, with sympathetic emotions, with pleasure, play, and sociability. The sublime was the sphere of isolated male genius, where the inhibition of physical drives for the sake of abstract principles leads to violent experiences of grandeur accompanied by intense emotion, and to recognition of a power beyond the perceiver's control.

Feminist discourse on aesthetics arose in the 1970s out of the women's movement. Far-reaching early propositions were that women's artistic productions do not fit into the existing categories of art history; that art history as traditionally constituted applies mainly to male experience; and that aesthetics needs to be set in a social history of gender. Feminists sketched out a progress of women's art from household crafts to artworks with liberatory social messages. Feminist artists and critics have worked in popular media such as science fiction and rock music as well as in the fine arts. In visual art, feminist artists have transformed the American and European art worlds since 1970. Working with established art institutions or forming alternative exhibition sites, producing personal expressions and large collaborative statements, feminist artists developed new, socially conscious models of artworks and provided new public venues for collective political expression. Associating their concerns with those of others marginalized by the art world, feminist artists have mounted exhibitions, performances, media actions, and poster campaigns to call attention to racism, classism, and sexism. Performance and video art rose from feminist self-representations confronting the gendered structure of the aesthetic gaze; photography, painting, and sculpture, too, have been used to provoke crises in the representational regime that fixes on an objectified other. Feminist artists also use the materials and techniques of traditional women's decorative and practical crafts (such as fibers, fabrics, and food), mounted at exhibition scale, to break the historically sexist distinction between art and craft, as W. Chadwick explains.

No single definition of "feminist aesthetics" has developed, though several have been proposed. Cixous and Irigaray proposed an experimental writing based on the forms and sensations of women's bodies ("*écriture féminine*"). DuPlessis and others proposed a "female aesthetic" defined as the creative strategies (that is, contextual judgment, inclusiveness, open and decentered form) that women have shared in struggling with the gendered imbalance of social power. These proposals have inspired women working in various creative media, but have been critiqued as narrowly prescriptive and as reflecting rather than challenging oppressive social structures. Feminists have not all agreed that feminist aesthetics is a possible or desirable category. For example, Kappeler finds aesthetics incompatible with feminist politics because of the gendered subject-object dualism endemic to representa-

tion. In contrast, Ecker and others assert that aesthetics is important to feminism because gaps and contradictions in the social and symbolic order surface in artistic production, opening meanings and values to the potential of political change. By 1990 many feminist critics had cautioned against aesthetics that were gendered "feminine" without regard for the artist's gender or for the social impact of artworks. Increasingly the debate on feminist aesthetics became directed toward critical practices taking a pragmatic approach to political and social change. Defining feminist aesthetics as any theory of a necessary or privileged relationship between female gender and a particular style or form, Felski argues that there is no basis for classifying any style as feminine. Instead of a style-centered approach to artworks, Felski advocates addressing their social meanings and functions in relation to women producers and audiences. Aesthetic representations of shared experiences can help affirm a collective political identity and thus create an alternative public sphere where feminist ideas circulate. For Battersby, feminist aesthetics is a creative project of the critical consumer whose tasks are to render visible, interpret, and evaluate the achievements of women artists. Through shared aesthetic value judgments, women can form alternative collectives capable of reshaping the past and future of a society.

That creative strategies drawn from the historical practices of women are congruent with postmodern aesthetics has stirred much discussion about whether feminism is allied with postmodernism or whether liberatory politics require a unified selfhood antithetical to postmodernism. Schor explores the development of the congruence between femininity and postmodernism by focusing on the history of the aesthetic detail. Formerly devalued as "feminine," in the nineteenth century the detail gained the role of signifying material truth and repressed meaning. The postmodern privileging of the detail suggests the breakdown of sexual difference and of the misogynist idealism reflected in the heterosexual representational economy, but it may represent simply a revision of the category of masculinity rather than a gain for the feminine. Schor suggests that, rather than showing a special affinity for detail, women's art may reflect an effort to transcend the large structures of masculinist violence. Schor urges feminists to continue reevaluating historically feminine attributes while at the same time engaging in the postmodern project of dismantling gender categories.

Janet Gray

References

Battersby, Christine. *Gender and Genius: Towards a Feminist Aesthetic*. Bloomington: Indiana University Press, 1989.

Bronfen, Elisabeth. *Over Her Dead Body: Death, Femininity and the Aesthetic*. New York: Routledge, 1992.

Chadwick, Whitney. *Women, Art, and Society*. London: Thames and Hudson, 1990.

DuPlessis, Rachel. *The Pink Guitar: Writing as Feminist Practice*. New York: Routledge, 1992.

Ecker, Gisela, ed. *Feminist Aesthetics*. London: Women's, 1985.

Felski, Rita. *Beyond Feminist Aesthetics: Feminist Literature and Social Change*. Cambridge: Harvard University Press, 1989.

Hedges, Elaine, and Ingrid Wendt, eds. *In Her Own Image: Women Working in the Arts*. Old Westbury, N.Y.: Feminist, 1980.

Hein, Hilda, and Carolyn Korsmeyer, eds. *Aesthetics in Feminist Perspective*. Bloomington: Indiana University Press, 1993.

Jones, Suzanne W., ed. *Writing the Woman Artist: Essays on Poetics, Politics, and Portraiture*. Philadelphia: University of Pennsylvania Press, 1991.

Kappeler, Susanne. *The Pornography of Representation*. Minneapolis: University of Minnesota Press, 1986.

Marcus, Laura. "Feminist Aesthetics and the New Realism." In *New Feminist Discourses: Critical Essays on Theories and Texts*, edited by Isobel Armstrong, 11–25. New York: Routledge, 1992.

Schor, Naomi. *Reading in Detail: Aesthetics and the Feminine*. New York: Routledge, 1989.

Wolff, Janet. *Feminine Sentences: Essays on Women and Culture*. Berkeley: University of California Press, 1990.

Feminist Jurisprudence

Feminist jurisprudence, sometimes called feminist legal theory, challenges conventional legal theory from a feminist perspective, its adherents arguing that traditional jurisprudential claims to objectivity conceal an androcentric foundation. Feminist legal theorists ground their work in feminist theory and deconstruction, as well as in the feminist practice of storytelling. Thus their methodology has much in common with that of literary theory. While demonstrating how sexual discrimination undermines the American legal system's claims to equality, they simultaneously try to imagine a jurisprudential system based in feminist practice and principle.

Although the term's first recorded use did not occur until the late 1970s and found common acceptance only in the early 1980s, the field of feminist jurisprudence developed out of the concerns of the feminist movement of the 1960s as well as those of the critical legal studies movement of the 1970s. The first "Women and the Law" course was taught at New York University Law School in 1969, spreading from there to the Yale and Georgetown law schools. Meanwhile, women drawn together at critical legal studies conferences joined to form groups to study feminist issues in law. Not surprisingly, these feminist legal theorists drew on the critique of rights discourse and the deconstructionist approach favored by the critical legal studies movement, yet insisted on critiquing both from a feminist perspective. Feminist jurisprudence gained enormous vitality when female law students of the late 1960s and early 1970s achieved positions of power and, simultaneously, pressure began to be exerted by the rising number of women who attended law schools in the 1980s. The field has carved out a space of its own in law school course offerings, while feminist revisions of traditional law school courses, if not exactly welcomed by the male-dominated legal establishment, have gained a foothold in the curriculum. The most telling indicia of the field's acceptance is the development of curricular materials both for teaching feminist jurisprudence as a designated course and for incorporating feminist approaches into traditional law school courses like torts and property.

Far from a coherent or unified movement, feminist jurisprudence has been typified by debate and division. Typical of the field are recent debates that call into question the very use of the words "feminist" and "jurisprudence," the first because of its tendency to reinscribe essentialism, and the second because of what is seen as an oxymoronic relationship between feminism and the patriarchal juridical system. Feminist jurisprudence draws upon feminist theorists as varied as Carol Gilligan, Adrienne Rich, bell hooks, Andrea Dworkin, and Luce Irigaray, as well as on Marxist theory. Perhaps in no other area have the practical consequences of theoretical paradigms been so quickly and publicly tested.

The division between what feminist legal theorists call "sameness" feminism and "difference" feminism dominated feminist jurisprudence throughout the 1980s. Sameness feminists of the 1970s were driven by claims to equality and thus focused largely on women's efforts to gain access to various male-dominated public spheres. Drawing on equal protection doctrine, feminist legal scholars argued that all persons have equal rights under the law and thus that similarly situated men and women should be treated alike. Although the sameness argument—which implies a constructivist approach to gender as well as what has been termed a "formal equality" or "equal treatment" approach to the law—resulted in huge gains in women's access to male-dominated institutions, it created a complex set of problems in areas in which men and women do differ: those involving pregnancy and childbirth. The case law created in *Geduldig v. Aiello* 417 U.S. 484 (1974) and *General Electric Co. v. Gilbert* 429 U.S. 125 (1976) ignored feminist goals and carried equality doctrine to absurd lengths by holding that employer disability programs that refused to cover pregnant women were not discriminating against women but were rather treating all nonpregnant persons alike. Although the Pregnancy Discrimination Act of 1982 prohibited such policies, the problems raised by issues of pregnancy have persisted.

Difference feminists, those favoring "special" or "preferential" treatment, especially for pregnant and child-bearing women, have taken an essentialist approach to gender. Perhaps their most influential extradisciplinary scholar has been Carol Gilligan, whose 1982 *In a Different Voice* elicited as large a legal following as it did an oppositional, even hostile, response. Used by feminist legal scholars in ways she could not have imagined, Gilligan has been a primary influence on important scholars like Robin West, who in her "connection thesis" makes the leap from culture to nature by asserting that women's "relational" emphasis derives from female physical characteristics that connect their bodies to the bodies of others.

The sameness-difference debate came to a head in *EEOC v. Sears, Roebuck & Co.*, 628 F.Supp. 1264 (N.D. Ill. 1986), a much-discussed case that provided a crucible for the study of the impact of feminist theory on employment discrimination law. The case pitched two expert witnesses—both well-known female historians of women's labor history—against each other. In her testimony, Rosalind Rosenberg took a difference position, testifying that women have fundamentally different attitudes toward work. Alice Kessler-Harris, on the other hand, supported a sameness position, testifying that to the extent that women's employment interests seem different, these differences are constructed by employer-controlled opportunities and prejudices. Although the relatively insignificant finding of the District Court—upholding Sears's exclusion of women from the sale of high-commission items like tires and washing machines—has had little influence on the law, the ensuing debate on whether difference feminism inevitably hurts women when it appears in the legal arena crystallized the problems associated with the sameness-difference dichotomy. As many feminist legal scholars concluded, the debate itself tended to obscure the issue of whether people who may or may not be different are to be treated equally in American society. Moreover, it tended to accept male structurings of societal relations as normative.

Most recently, feminist jurisprudence has attempted to transcend the dichotomous thinking encouraged by the sameness-difference debate. In 1987, radical feminist Catharine MacKinnon shifted the grounds of the debate from issues of gender to issues of power by arguing that inequality results not from sameness or difference but from dominance and subordination. In 1989, Joan Williams, in *Feminist Legal Theory*, suggested that "a systematic refusal to institutionalize gender in any form" can overcome the limitations of the sameness position. Numerous other scholars, including Patricia Cain, Angela Harris, Patricia Williams, and Judy Scales-Trent, have insisted on a return to the feminist practice of attending to women's stories, not only disrupting the already-institutionalized discourse of feminist jurisprudence, but also challenging fundamental assumptions about the foundational nature and universalizing processes of law. Offering a highly theorized alternative to previous work, Drucilla Cornell's philosophically informed yet story-based challenge to the grounds of Western identity both builds upon and calls into question earlier approaches. In arguing for a guarantee that all people receive equivalent rights to an equality that promotes well-being, Cornell redefines feminist jurisprudence as capable of reconceptualizing not only the ways both men and women define themselves but also what it means to live under a democratic system.

Despite its continuing debates, feminist jurisprudence has significantly altered both the law itself—especially laws regarding pornography, spousal battering, and rape—and the study of the law. As Cornell's work demonstrates, its range has extended beyond its vital impact on every area of law to reorder our conceptions—both personal and political—of identity itself.

Kathryn Temple

References

Bartlett, Katharine T., and Rosanne Kennedy, eds. *Feminist Legal Theory: Readings in Law and Gender.* Boulder, Colo., San Francisco, and Oxford: Westview, 1991.

Becker, Mary, and Cynthia Grant Bowman, et al. *Cases and Materials on Feminist Jurisprudence: Taking Women Seriously.* St. Paul, Minn.: West, 1994.

Cornell, Drucilla. *Transformations: Recollective Imagination and Sexual Difference.* New York: Routledge, 1993.

Fineman, Martha Albertson, and Nancy Sweet Thomadsen, eds. *At the Boundaries of Law: Feminism and Legal Theory.* Routledge: New York and London, 1991.

Heinzelman, Susan Sage, and Zipporah Batshaw Wiseman, eds. *Representing Women: Law, Literature and Feminism.* Durham and London: Duke University Press, 1994.

MacKinnon, Catharine A. *Feminism Unmodified: Discourses on Life and Law.* Cambridge, Mass., and London: Harvard University Press, 1987.

Pruitt, Lisa A. "A Survey of Feminist Jurisprudence." *University of Arkansas at Little Rock Law Journal* 16 (1994): 183–210.

Rhode, Deborah L. *Justice and Gender: Sex Discrimination and the Law.* Cambridge: Harvard University Press, 1989.

Scales-Trent, Judy. "Commonalities: On Being Black and White, Different, and the Same." *Yale Journal of Law and Feminism* 2 (1990): 305–326.

Smith, Patricia, ed. *Feminist Jurisprudence.* New York and Oxford: Oxford University Press, 1993.

Weisberg, D. Kelly, ed. *Feminist Legal Theory: Foundations.* Philadelphia: Temple University Press, 1993.

Williams, Patricia. *The Alchemy of Race and Rights.* Cambridge: Harvard University Press, 1991.

Feminist Poetics

Poetics derives from *poiein*, to make; feminist poetics are feminist theories about making, creating, constructing. Historical and current usages of poetics suggest definitions ranging from the specific (theory of poetry) to the general (implicit principles of any discipline of knowledge). Treatises on poetics define and rank kinds of literary making, describing the relations of literary making to the political sphere, setting standards of cultural highness and lowness, and justifying innovation in relation to material and philosophical change. The relative placements of audience and author, form and substance, pleasure and instruction, representation and expression are matters of recurrent debate. Like other theoretical domains, poetics historically casts women as lesser beings, restricted in their capacity to act and speak. Aristotle's ranking tragedy over other poetic genres, and *Oedipus Rex* as the perfect tragedy, situates classical poetics at the source of the intellectual tradition on which psychoanalysis founds its description of enculturation into a patrilineal legal structure. For this tradition, maleness creates knowledge, transcending physicality by learning the limits of what can be rationally known, while femaleness is the passive medium through which male transformation takes place.

Feminist poetics includes feminist interventions with poetics anywhere in its range of meanings and, in its broadest sense, is roughly equivalent to feminist theory, or to terms and relations that link feminist literary study to feminist practice in other disciplines, everyday life, and social movements. In the sense of a feminist theory of poetry, feminist poetics has been shaped both by the writings of feminist poets (such as Gloria Anzaldúa, Rachel Blau DuPlessis, Susan Howe, June Jordan, Audre Lorde, Cherríe Moraga, Marge Piercy, and Adrienne Rich) and by the history of feminist critics' efforts to constitute an intellectual field related to political efforts to change the status of women. This history concerns how feminist

F

poetics responded to the requirements of academic disciplines (canonicity, evaluation, research, specialized vocabulary) as it gained legitimacy and influence. While no single systematic definition has sustained widespread consensus, an influential, enduring proposition associated with feminist poetics is that poetics must be placed in the context of history, since ahistorical valuations give "universal" works the highest rank while obscuring differences among social groups' life experiences, particularly access to literacy and learning. Reconsiderations of devalued modes (such as sentimentality and popular verse) have assisted in the recovery of women poets. The assignment of value remains a practical concern of feminist poetics: What works do we study? On what basis do we make these choices? What do our criteria of value invisibly exclude?

Feminist discussions of poetics began to consolidate in the 1970s as literary publishing and scholarship absorbed the impact of the women's movement, then reached into the past to incorporate earlier feminist thought and recover earlier women's poetry. A poetics of women's experience formed around the model of consciousness-raising and around feminist critics' calls for poetics to be contextualized in the social history of gender. Consciousness-raising validated and politicized personal life by urging rejection of patriarchal representations of women and redefinition of women through authentic speech about our lives, bodies, and relationships. Feminist critics recognized that the recovery of earlier women poets could encourage contemporary women's self-exploration and radically critiqued the traditions of poetic value as impediments. Scholarly projects such as anthologies made women, the symbolic field associated with femininity (such as nature and love), and resistance to sexism the objects of study. Critics proposed that the newly recovered literature be read with the understanding that the sexist division of gender roles historically made "woman" and "poet" contradictory identities, and for a woman to write was subversive and risky. A progressive narrative grew out of the poetics of women's experience, in which contemporary feminist poets fulfilled the wholeness and autonomy toward which earlier poets struggled. Gilbert and Gubar built on this narrative in describing women's poetic culture as an evolutionary struggle through which the poet learns to recover a priestly, aristocratic "I," her creative self. This narrative, often situating

women poets at different stages of feminist development, maintained a hold on Anglo American feminist poetry criticism in the 1980s.

By 1980 the poetics of women's experience encountered criticisms that it overlooked difference: differences among women's experiences because of race, class, and sexuality; the difference between language and what it represents; differences between essences and socially constructed categories; differences internal to the self. Various studies aimed to define the "women's tradition" and date its beginning, but accumulated scholarship showed women's poetic production to fluctuate in relation to multiple social factors, booming with the rise of women's literacy and the market economy, and periodically being purged from cultural memory by male critical devaluation. As the emphasis shifted from unifying projects (women's experience, the female tradition) to explorations of difference and the textual politics of women's writing, anthologies increasingly focused on sexual, ethnic, national, and historic groupings. Discussions of difference drawing on new theoretical thinking (such as *écriture féminine*) modulated toward a complex poetics of gender. Homans argued that women's marginality as other to a dominant masculine self should place women poets in a position to recognize the fictiveness of language and thereby oppose phallogocentrism. DuPlessis described gender's embeddedness in language as central to feminist poetics and affirmed the critical potential of women's speaking from a position that is both within and against the dominant social narratives. Montefiore described poetics as an area of perpetual interpretive and political struggle; the strength of women's poetry, therefore, is not progress toward autonomy but continuing engagement to transform inherited meanings.

In the 1990s poetics has served as a model of the fictiveness of social constructions such as gender. Increasingly feminist poetics concerns strategies for managing complexity and inclusiveness rather than efforts to define a systematic theory of making. Freedman argued that the traditions of female creativity—making do with limited time and resources, patching together multiple voices—are especially suited to the postmodern project of mediating specific situations from an interested rather than detached point of view, using dialogue instead of individual authority. Finke proposed a poetics of complexity to describe the relations of competing meanings in local instances. Such a poetics would situate the act of writing in relation to other aspects of daily life, examine how power relations fix and destabilize meaning, attend to echoes from other disciplines and texts, position women as both cultural workers and works of culture, explore reading as an act of consumption, and analyze the erotics of reading.

Janet Gray

References

Abel, Elizabeth, ed. *Writing and Sexual Difference*. Chicago: University of Chicago Press, 1982.

Bennett, Paula. *My Life a Loaded Gun: Dickinson, Plath, Rich, and Female Creativity*. Boston: Beacon, 1986.

Berg, Temma F., ed. *Engendering the Word: Feminist Essays in Psychosexual Poetics*. Urbana: University of Illinois Press, 1989.

DuPlessis, Rachel Blau. *The Pink Guitar: Writing as Feminist Practice*. New York: Routledge, 1990.

Finke, Laurie A. *Feminist Theory, Women's Writing*. Ithaca, N.Y.: Cornell University Press, 1992.

Freedman, Diane. *An Alchemy of Genres: Cross-Genre Writing by American Feminist Poet-Critics*. Charlottesville: University Press of Virginia, 1992.

Gilbert, Sandra M., and Susan Gubar. *The Madwoman in the Attic: The Woman Writer and the Nineteenth-Century Literary Imagination*. New Haven: Yale University Press, 1979.

———, eds. *Shakespeare's Sisters: Feminist Essays on Women Poets*. Bloomington: Indiana University Press, 1979.

Homans, Margaret. *Women Writers and Poetic Identity: Dorothy Wordsworth, Emily Brontë, and Emily Dickinson*. Princeton: Princeton University Press, 1980.

Juhasz, Susanne. *Naked and Fiery Forms: Modern American Poetry by Women, a New Tradition*. New York: Octagon, 1976.

Kintz, Linda. *The Subject's Tragedy: Political Poetics, Feminist Theory, and Drama*. Ann Arbor: University of Michigan Press, 1992.

McEwen, C., ed. *Naming the Waves: Contemporary Lesbian Poetry*. London: Virago, 1988.

Marks, Elaine, and Isabelle de Courtivron, eds. *New French Feminisms*. Amherst: University of Massachusetts Press, 1980.

Miller, Nancy, ed. *The Poetics of Gender*. New York: Columbia University Press, 1986.

Montefiore, Jan. *Feminism and Poetry: Language, Experience, and Identity in Women's Writing*. London: Pandora, 1987.

Ostriker, Alicia S. *Stealing the Language: The Emergence of Women's Poetry in America*. Boston: Beacon, 1986.

Rich, Adrienne. *Blood, Bread, Poetry*. New York: W.W. Norton, 1986.

———. *Of Woman Born*. New York: W.W. Norton, 1976.

———. *On Lies, Secrets, and Silence*. New York: W.W. Norton 1978.

Ross, Marlon B. *The Contours of Masculine Desire: Romanticism and the Rise of Women's Poetry*. New York: Oxford University Press, 1989.

Feminist Review

This British journal is published three times a year by a collective based in London. Started in 1979 with the aim of servicing the development of women's studies in institutions of higher education and intervening in the political debate within the women's liberation movement, the first issue denied the journal was a vehicle for socialist feminism, but issue no. 8 announced a commitment to this political perspective. The membership of the collective has been largely drawn from feminists teaching in higher education with an emphasis on the social sciences. A special issue in Summer 1986 on *Cultural Politics* (no. 23) signaled a policy shift to better representation of the humanities (history, literature, film and media, in particular), as well as initiating the publication of creative/imaginative writing. The journal also carries announcements of and reports on international feminist events, reviews of recent publications and letters responding to previous numbers. The history of the journal charts the development of feminist preoccupations in Britain—from the women's liberation movement's split with Marxist-Leninism in the late 1970s, to an attention to theories of representation and culture in the mid 1980s, to international feminism, black politics, and debates around lesbian sexuality in

F

the late 1980s and 1990s. Influential articles that first appeared in *Feminist Review* include Rebecca O'Rourke, "Summer Reading" (no. 2); Ros Coward, "Women's Novels" (no. 5); Jacqueline Rose, "Femininity and Its Discontents" (no. 14); Sheila Rowbotham, "What Do Women Want?" (no. 20); Susan Ardill and Sue O'Sullivan, "Difference, Desire and Lesbian Sadomasochism" (no. 23).

Ros Ballaster

Fetishism

The term "fetishism" is generally defined as the act of paying excessive attention, or attributing mystical ability, to an inanimate thing. Originally used in reference to religious objects believed to have magical or spiritual powers, fetishism has been central to Western theories of aesthetics, economics, and psychology. Feminist literary theorists have used the concept of fetishism to analyze representations of female characters in literary texts, to challenge the structure of the literary canon, and to name the visual preoccupation with women's bodies.

Although various definitions of fetishism make up the word's history, its most common interpretations are found in the work of Karl Marx and Sigmund Freud. In *Capital*, Marx discusses fetishism in economic terms, arguing that the "fetishism of commodities" must be resisted if capitalism is to be overcome. Marx locates the origin of fetishism in the "peculiar social character" of the labor that produces commodities. For while laborers interact only in terms of the material exchange of the objects they produce, those objects—or commodities—take on a social life of their own in which they appear to interact with one another. Hence, the relationship between people is expressed as a relationship between things, and commodities begin to rule people rather than being ruled by them. As a result, objects become invested with mystified power—are fetishized—and workers are alienated not only from each other but from the product of their labor.

While Marx used the concept of fetishism to describe people's relationship to things in economic terms, Freud adopted the word to name a psychological phenomenon. In "Fetishism," he defines the concept as a primarily male condition in which an object or nonsexual body part becomes a significant, if not the only, source of sexual arousal and gratification. Freud claims that fetishism originates in a boy's refusal to acknowledge that his mother has no penis. Such refusal results from the boy's unwillingness to recognize the threat of his own castration. Rather than acknowledge—through sexual interest in—the "castrated" female genitals, the boy adopts a substitute sexual object-choice in the form of a nonsexual thing or body part: the foot or shoe, a piece of velvet or fur.

Feminist literary theorists have used the concept of fetishism to analyze literary representations of women, interrogating, for instance, the portrayal of women as fetishized objects. Conversely, critics like Emily Apter and Naomi Schor have challenged whether the term refers only to male behavior, and have used literature to locate a specifically female fetishism. In turn, critics have asked whether the desire to locate a female fetishism is something akin to "penis envy" in which women want what they do not have. Marjorie Garber responded to this concern, arguing that female fetishism is invisible because it has been naturalized in heterosexual desire for the male body, a body that holds the phallus, the object of female fetishistic impulses.

Fetishism has also been used to analyze the visual representation of women in both popular and pornographic films. This particular form of fetishism—"fetishistic scopophilia" as Laura Mulvey calls it—occurs when the image of the woman on the screen becomes erotically charged. The fetishized image is meant to disavow the possibility of castration by transforming the woman into a reassuring presence, manageable under the male gaze, protagonist and spectator alike. Paradoxically, however, because the nature of a fetish lies in its ability to fixate its viewer, that image breaks the illusion that film fosters, leaving the spectator "in direct erotic rapport" with the very image that threatens him.

Finally, fetishism has been a useful category of analysis for feminists because of its deconstructive potential. For the very concept behind fetishism collapses the boundaries upon which sexual difference rests; where fetishism aims to hide the woman's "castration," it in effect hides her sexual difference, ultimately denying the possibility or reality of that difference. Moreover, the very definition of fetishism reveals the constructedness of patriarchy since it highlights—and thereby fetishizes—the privileged status of the phallus and the absolute fear of its loss. In a similar way, fetishism can also be used to undermine the traditional structure of the canon. By arguing that canonical texts are fetishized objects, and that there is nothing inherently more "valuable" about them than other works of literature, feminists have attempted to demystify the idea that there is such a thing as "great" books.

Sara E. Quay

References

Apter, Emily. *Feminizing the Fetish: Psychoanalysis and Narrative Obsession in Turn-of-the-Century France*. Ithaca, N.Y.: Cornell University Press, 1991.

Freud, Sigmund. "Fetishism." In *The Standard Edition of the Complete Psychological Works of Sigmund Freud*, 24 vols., translated by James Strachey et al., 21: 152–157. London: Hogarth, 1953–1974.

Garber, Marjorie. "Fetish Envy." *October* 54 (1990): 45–56.

Ian, Marcia. *Remembering the Phallic Mother: Psychoanalysis, Modernism, and the Fetish*. Ithaca, N.Y.: Cornell University Press, 1993.

Kofman, Sarah. *The Enigma of Woman*. Translated by Catherine Porter. Ithaca, N.Y.: Cornell University Press, 1985.

Marcus, Jane. "The Asylums of Antaeus: Women, Ware and Madness—Is There a Feminist Fetishism?" In *The New Historicism*, edited by H. Aram Veeser, 132–151. New York: Routledge, 1989.

Marx, Karl. *Capital: A Critique of Political Economy*. Translated by Ben Fowkes. New York: Vintage, 1976.

Mulvey, Laura. "Visual Pleasure and Narrative Cinema." *Screen* 16 (1975): 6–18.

Schor, Naomi. "Female Fetishism: The Case of George Sand." In *The Female Body in Western Culture*, edited by Susan Suleiman, 363–372. Cambridge: Harvard University Press, 1986.

———. *Reading in Detail: Aesthetics and the Feminine*. New York and London: Methuen, 1987.

Wardley, Lynn. "Relic, Fetish, Femmage: The Aesthetics of Sentiment in the Work of Stowe." In *The Culture of Sentiment*, edited by Shirley Samuels, 203–220. New York and Oxford: Oxford University Press, 1992.

Fetterley, Judith

The Resisting Reader demonstrated the power of reading as a feminist. Working from the basic principle that literature is a shaping force in the world, Fetterley focused on the power relations between men and women in eight "classic" American texts, and uncovered a consistent pattern of male dominance. The central insight of the book was Fetterley's discussion of how women learn to think like men, a process she called "immasculation." The woman reader encounters negative images of herself created by male writers, and is confronted with two choices: to identify against women, with the more appealing male characters and narrative voice, or to identify with the female characters, and make herself into this despised, limited figure from the masculine imagination. The aim of *The Resisting Reader* was to uncover the workings of this dynamic and help women resist it.

The Resisting Reader was an important example of how literary criticism as practiced by feminists could be political, by helping women understand how their experiences were shaped by the political and social power held by men. The book was important, too, in bringing a feminist perspective to "reader-response" criticism, a school of criticism that replaces the traditional focus on the author or the text with an examination of the reader. By focusing on the feminist reader's response to traditional "Great Works," Fetterley exposed the hidden masculine bias in literature and literary criticism.

Julia Willis

References

Fetterley, Judith. "*A Farewell to Arms*: Hemingway's Resentful Cryptogram." *Journal of Popular Culture* 10 (1976): 203–214.

———. "*My Antonia*, Jim Burden, and the Dilemma of the Lesbian Writer." In *Lesbian Texts and Contexts*, edited by Joanne Glasgow, Karla Jay, and Catherine Stimpson, 369–383. New York: New York University Press, 1990.

———. "Reading about Reading." In *Gender and Reading*, edited by Elizabeth Flynn and Patrocinio Schweickart, 147–164. Baltimore: Johns Hopkins University Press, 1986.

———. *The Resisting Reader*. Bloomington: Indiana University Press, 1978.

———. "The Temptation to Be a Beautiful Object: Double Standard and Double Bind in *The House of Mirth*." *Studies in American Fiction* 5 (1977): 199–211.

Film

The relation between feminism and film being large, this discussion will highlight, on the one hand, direct connections between women's narratives and the cinema, and, on the other hand, reading strategies and analytical approaches developed within feminist film theory.

The film industry was relatively open to women through the 1910s and 1920s, and scriptwriters like Frances Marion and Anita Loos were influential through the 1930s. Also, novels by women have provided some of Hollywood's most characteristic and successful fantasies, such as *The Sheik* (1921; E.M. Hull), *Stella Dallas* 1925, 1937, and 1990; Olive Higgins Prouty), *Gone with the Wind* (1936; Margaret Mitchell), and *Rebecca* (1940; Daphne du Maurier). Alice Guy-Blache arguably deserves credit as not just the first woman but the first person to direct a fiction film; she was the first woman to own her own film production studio. Lois Weber, who also had her own production facilities, directed films often dealing with morally uplifting if not explicitly feminist messages; like Weber, Ida Lupino produced and directed films in the 1940s and 1950s dealing with issues like bigamy and rape that Hollywood usually ignored.

Many of these early directors and producers, like their counterparts from 1970 on, have declined to identify themselves as feminists; that no direct correlation exists between their gender and the politics of their work became an early debating point. The films of Dorothy Arzner served as a catalyst for developing new feminist reading strategies. Pam Cook and Claire Johnston, for example, developed the rupture thesis with reference to Arzner films like *Christopher Strong* (1933) and *Dance, Girl, Dance* (1940), in which "pregnant moments" and other disruptive aspects challenge the dominant patriarchal discourse and engage the spectator in an active, critical reading. Closely related to the rupture thesis is the rescue reading, which focuses on those moments in generally conservative films that present strong, independent women or that otherwise challenge the patriarchal status quo. The rescue reading can help explain and justify the emotional pleasure feminists derive from films they must, on an intellectual level, reject or condemn. Authors like Annette Kuhn and Mary Ann Doane further redeemed some of Hollywood's worst offenders, the "weepies" or "woman's film," by pointing to the gendered address of this genre;

Molly Haskell had already noted that these films consistently place a woman "at the center of the universe."

If the establishment in 1966 of the National Organization for Women (NOW) and its committee to study the media's sexist representation of women can be taken as a germinal point, then the feminist study of women and film, at least in the United States, originates outside academia, in a practical and political desire to change the social status quo. Feminist film theory within the academy works for such change but it is often criticized for being too esoteric and abstract. Feminist filmmakers, beginning in the late 1960s, produced a number of avant-garde and documentary films that functioned as texts for discussion at feminist consciousness-raising sessions. Works like Jean Kilbourne's *Killing Us Softly* (1978) and its sequel, *Still Killing Us Softly: Advertising's Image of Women* (1987), exemplify the "images of women" branch of early feminist film studies, while Connie Field's *The Life and Times of Rosie the Riveter* (1980) represents a highpoint of feminist filmmaking that documents the lives of ordinary women whose successes may inspire other women.

By the early 1970s academic feminist film studies was engaged in the rediscovery of such "lost" figures as Guy-Blache and Weber, whose work often appeared problematic from a feminist point of view. When film studies generally was dominated by the *auteur* theory and its emphasis on a single director's *oeuvre*, feminist film studies could do little more than call for women's increased access to the means of production, point to the work of Arzner (the lone female director to produce a significant body of work from within the Hollywood studio system), and study the work of male directors in search of progressive elements in their representation of women.

The publication in 1975 of Laura Mulvey's "Visual Pleasures and Narrative Cinema" changed this picture; furthermore, its influence extends across the disciplines. Mulvey's essay argues against the pleasure Hollywood cinema provides as detrimental to women because that pleasure rests on woman's role as "bearer of meaning, not maker of meaning" in narratives whose action stops when the woman's image appears "to be looked at," to pick up again only with the appearance of the male protagonist. Mulvey's essay calls for the use of psychoanalysis as a methodological tool in the feminist struggle against Hollywood's misrepresentation of women. Woman's image, she argues, functions simultaneously as a threat of castration and a reassurance against that threat, in narratives that punish or fetishize their female characters.

Criticized for presuming a male spectator, Mulvey wrote a follow-up article that posits the female spectator as positioned either as a masochist identifying with the female protagonist's subordinate role or, though "restless in . . . transvestite clothes," as identifying with the male protagonist. Doane suggests that female identity always involves a masquerade; Janet Bergstrom notes that male images have also been fetishized. Over the years these and other responses to Mulvey's essay have been extensively considered.

"Visual Pleasure and Narrative Cinema" is most important for opening up the area of film studies known as spectator studies, a field that simultaneously insists on the specificity of the cinematic medium while incorporating theoretical and methodological insights from sources such as reception and cultural studies. Recent examples of spectator studies include Jacqueline Bobo's work on black women's responses to *The Color Purple* (1985) and Elizabeth Ellsworth's study of lesbian community reactions to *Personal Best* (1982). Writing in a 1990 issue of the feminist film theory journal *Camera Obscura* devoted to the current state of spectator studies, Meaghan Morris notes that once a reading position is identified, it can be used by nonmembers of the group originating the reading.

"Visual Pleasures and Narrative Cinema" and the work that followed it either in adopting psychoanalytical perspectives or in eschewing the pleasure offered by Hollywood cinema have generated two other debates, one on methodology and the other essentially a continuation of the high-art/low-art debate that has preoccupied aesthetic studies throughout this century. Psychoanalysis has been criticized for theorizing about people outside historical and cultural contexts, a perspective that suggests that problems are eternal and insolvable. Categorically rejecting Hollywood's pleasures is also problematic. While Adorno spoke disparagingly of popular culture, the *auteur* theory functioned to legitimate Hollywood films as art. The films Mulvey championed as a feminist challenge to Hollywood pose the sort of problems Godard recognized in the 1960s when he desired to make Marxist films: the language of narrative cinema is itself permeated with the ideological values of the status quo, so that politically progressive films must either compromise themselves through the use of an "impure" medium or accept the fact that they may limit their political effectiveness through their inaccessibility to mainstream audiences. Either the popular must be at least potentially politically effective or else politically effective art, feminist or otherwise, speaks only to the cultural elite.

Harriet E. Margolis

References

Acker, Ally. *Reel Women: Pioneers of the Cinema 1896 to the Present.* New York: Continuum, 1991.

Camera Obscura: A Journal of Feminism and Film Theory 1 (1976).

de Lauretis, Teresa. *Alice Doesn't: Feminism Semiotics Cinema.* Bloomington: Indiana University Press, 1984.

Doane, Mary Ann. *The Desire to Desire: The Woman's Film of the 1940s.* Bloomington: Indiana University Press, 1987.

Erens, Patricia. *Issues in Feminist Film Criticism.* Bloomington: Indiana University Press, 1990.

Haskell, Molly. *From Reverence to Rape: The Treatment of Women in the Movies.* 2nd ed. Chicago: University of Chicago Press, 1987.

Kaplan, E. Ann. *Women and Film: Both Sides of the Camera.* New York: Methuen, 1983.

Kuhn, Annette. *Women's Pictures: Feminism and Cinema.* London: Routledge, 1982.

Mulvey, Laura. "Visual Pleasures and Narrative Cinema." In *Feminism and Film,* edited by Constance Penley, 57–68. New York: Routledge, 1988.

Penley, Constance, ed. *Feminism and Film Theory.* New York: Routledge, 1988.

Pribram, E. Deidre, ed. *Female Spectators: Looking at Film and Television.* London: Verso, 1988.

Quart, Barbara Koenig. *Women Directors: The Emergence of a New Cinema.* New York: Praeger, 1988.

First Wave Feminists

This term is generally used to describe those feminist critics who were at work in the years preceding the early 1980s. The definition given here will go beyond what is conventionally thought of as "first wave" feminist criticism. First wave feminist criticism traditionally has been regarded as straight, white feminist work, which places the criticism and theory of black and lesbian feminists as an afterthought to white straight feminists, rather than to see that these branches of criticism were developing alongside all along. Certainly, some work by black feminist critics and lesbian feminist critics provides "corrective" measures to a mainstream feminist criticism. However, to see all of this work only as reactionary continues to place white straight feminist work at the center, while marginalizing work by those who do not fit into the conventional critical definitions. By expanding the definition to be more inclusive, a broader range of material comes into view that provides a truer portrait of the work of all feminist critics during this period.

Feminist literary theory and criticism grew directly out of the women's movement, the growth of feminist presses, and the development of women's studies programs in the academy. As such, it was in a unique position to critique patriarchal notions about women and literature, reexamine the grounds of literary study, recover noncanonical women writers to establish a female literary history, and generate new insights into the theory and practice of literary criticism.

Most early work of conventional feminist literary criticism took the form of examining images of women in literature, usually written by men. Katharine A. Rogers's *The Troublesome Helpmate: A History of Misogyny in Literature* (1966) and Mary Ellman's *Thinking about Women* (1968) are but two examples. Perhaps the best-known of these is Kate Millett's *Sexual Politics* (1969), which argues that a connection exists between the images of women in literature by men and the real attitudes toward women in society. Some feminist critics also began to explore ways in which feminist criticism could put to good use contextual, archetypal, bibliographic, and textual criticism, while others believed that feminist criticism, to remain revolutionary, was necessarily estranged from these traditional modes. The first anthology of feminist literary criticism was published in 1972. Edited by Susan Koppelman Cornillon, *Images of Women in Fiction: Feminist Perspectives* contains "new forms of analysis growing out of the new consciousness" that range from the highly academic to the highly experimental, written by contributors whose educational backgrounds range from high school graduates to Ph.D.s. The collection speaks to the power literature, especially fiction, for feminists who were searching for realism in the authority of personal experience and rejecting formalist New Criticism and its attendant emphasis on universal values and inviolable aesthetics.

By the mid 1970s, feminist critics turned their attention toward examining the works of women writers and formulating theory. Elaine Showalter's *A Literature of Their Own: British Women Novelists from Brontë to Lessing*, Nina Auerbach's *Communities of Women: An Idea in Fiction* (1978), and Sandra Gilbert's and Susan Gubar's *The Madwoman in the Attic: The Woman Writer and the Nineteenth-Century Literary Imagination* (1979) all examine literature by women and work to explore female subcultures and to establish a Eurocentric female literary tradition. Lillian S. Robinson, a Marxist-feminist who feared the growing institutionalization of women's studies would only serve to mitigate its revolutionary potential, insisted that feminist analysis include class as well as gender in *Sex, Class and Culture* (1978). Feminist critics' own training as literary scholars soon predisposed them to look more carefully at issues of structure, imagery, and style, and the question "Is there a female aesthetics?" produced some highly speculative research, while often ignoring or conflating what might be the differences between female, feminine, and feminist. Prescriptive criticism, setting standards for what could be perceived as good literature from a feminist standpoint, came briefly to the fore, only to be rejected as feminist critics sought acceptance within the academy. As the decade progressed, multiple readings of texts began to be recognized, and open-ended questions began to be valued.

The mid 1970s also brought the beginnings of French feminism to an Anglo American audience with Hélène Cixous's "The Laugh of the Medusa" (1976). By the late 1970s, American feminists had to deal with what certainly must have seemed an invasion of French feminism. While the French feminists theoretically differed from one another, on the whole they focused on the force of the unconscious and *écriture féminine* or feminine writing from the body as the place where discourse could disrupt the phallic order of logic, history, and culture. In 1980, Elaine Marks and Isabelle de Courtivron compiled their collection, *New French Femi-*

nisms, which finally brought a wide variety of French feminist thought to an American audience. While a number of American feminist critics responded enthusiastically to the new theoretical models (such as Mary Jacobus, Jane Gallop, and Shoshana Felman), still others remained suspicious of the high theory, the unproblematized experience of the female body, and the practical implications of depending on a male-centered and reductive psychoanalysis. Nonetheless, while the introduction of French feminist theory is not generally seen as part of the first wave, these early French feminist critics stimulated many American feminists throughout the 1980s.

Black feminist theory arose out of the need to explicitly address the stereotyping of African American women, the exploration of a black female literary tradition, and the ignorance of white feminist critics in regard to women of color. Alice Walker's "In Search of Our Mothers' Gardens" (1974) addresses the importance of examining the creative outlets of cooking, storytelling, gardening, and other domestic activities to discover the creativity of black foremothers whose lives silenced their ability to create in recognized cultural modes. Barbara Smith's pioneering work "Toward a Black Feminist Criticism" (1977) led the way to a groundswell of work by feminists of color in the 1980s. Smith proposes the theoretical principles that would provide the basis for a "highly innovative" black feminist criticism: a commitment to examining the racial and sexual politics of black female identity and their connection to black women's writing, the assumption that black women writers constitute a black female literary tradition that grows out of their shared experiences as black women, and the interpretation of black women's work within the context of black women's thought. *Sturdy Black Bridges: Visions of Black Women in Literature* (1979), edited by Roseann P. Bell, Bettye J. Parker, and Beverly Guy-Sheftall, continued the work in a collection that contained critical essays about African and African American women writers.

The same kinds of concerns that contributed to the emergence of black feminist theory also contributed to the birth of lesbian feminist theory. In "Toward a Feminist Aesthetic" (1978), Julia Penelope and Susan Wolfe examine the syntax, punctuation, and imagery of lesbian writers and propose that a lesbian feminist consciousness contributes to an explicitly rebellious feminist aesthetic. Bonnie Zimmerman's groundbreaking article "What Has Never Been: An Overview of Lesbian Feminist Criticism" (1981) posits a lesbian literary criticism that rests in the lesbian's perspective as resistant to patriarchal culture. Zimmerman grapples with the problems of definition and self-identification that are primary to lesbian feminist theory, outlines a lesbian literary tradition, considers the questions of lesbian stylistics, and suggests future directions for further developing lesbian literary theory. Catharine R. Stimpson, Lillian Faderman, and Bertha Harris all contributed work that focused on images of lesbians in literature and reclaiming a lesbian literary past. Barbara Smith effectively illustrated the strength of a black lesbian feminist criticism in revealing new understandings of a literary work not explicitly lesbian.

The plethora of works that came about in the 1970s gave way to often conflicting impulses in feminist literary theory. Myra Jehlen's "Archimedes and the Paradox of Feminist Criticism" (1981) explores these very points of contradiction as fruitful sites upon which to practice feminist criticism. Jehlen articulates the contradiction as lying between feminist politics and transcendent aesthetics, where works may be politically pleasing but aesthetically distasteful, or conversely, politically distasteful but aesthetically pleasing. Jehlen proposes that by recognizing this paradox, feminist critics can move toward a "new epistemology" that embraces the contradictions and provides a truly fresh perspective. Ultimately, of course, it is just this very outlook that first wave feminist critics began to provide for literary studies.

Linnea A. Stenson

References

Bell, Roseann P., Bettye J. Parker, and Beverly Guy-Sheftall, eds. *Sturdy Black Bridges: Visions of Black Women in Literature.* Garden City, N.Y.: Anchor-Doubleday, 1979.

Donovan, Josephine, ed. *Feminist Literary Criticism: Explorations in Theory.* Lexington: University Press of Kentucky, 1975.

Gallop, Jane. *Around 1981.* New York: Routledge, 1992.

Jehlen, Myra. "Archimedes and the Paradox of Feminist Criticism." *Signs* 6 (1981): 575–601.

Kolodny, Annette. "Dancing through the

Minefield: Some Observations on the Theory, Practice and Politics of a Feminist Literary Criticism." *Feminist Studies* 6 (Spring 1980): 1–25.

Koppelman Cornillion, Susan, ed. *Images of Women in Fiction: Feminist Perspectives*. Bowling Green, Ohio: Bowling Green University Popular Press, 1972.

Register, Cheri. "Literary Criticism." *Signs* 6 (1980): 268–282.

Showalter, Elaine. "Literary Criticism." *Signs* 1 (1975): 435–460.

Smith, Barbara. "Toward a Black Feminist Criticism." *Conditions* 2 (October 1977): 25–44.

Todd, Janet. *Feminist Literary History*. New York: Routledge, 1988.

Zimmerman, Bonnie. "What Has Never Been: An Overview of Lesbian Feminist Criticism." *Feminist Studies* 7 (1981): 451–476.

Flax, Jane

Thinking Fragments represents a significant contribution to the study of psychoanalysis, feminism, and postmodernism; Flax pushes the meaning and effectiveness of these theories as they intersect and diverge with respect to gender, knowledge, self, power, and justice. As a teacher of political theory and a practicing psychotherapist, Flax rigorously examines the use of feminist theory (in a postmodern context) as it applies to and reveals the "human experience."

Flax's ideas often center in negotiating gender inequity and gender biases by arguing that feminist theory is useful in exposing the harsh realities of a dominant patriarchal society while simultaneously acknowledging society's need to impose order and structure. In other words, Flax interrogates the idea that domination is a gender-based notion of society in which difference exists as a problematic subtext. Flax's more recent work focuses directly on a postmodernist-feminist approach to the idea of justice in contemporary Western culture.

Manju Kurian

References

Flax, Jane. "Beyond Equality: Gender, Justice and Difference." In *Beyond Equality and Difference*, edited by Gisela Brock and Susan James, 193–210. London: Routledge, 1992.

———. *Thinking Fragments: Psychoanalysis, Feminism, and Postmodernism in the Contemporary West*. Berkeley: University of California Press, 1990.

Food

See EATING

Formalism

See NEW CRITICISM

Foucault, Michel

The investigations of French philosopher, historian, and literary critic Michel Foucault have been instrumental in the revision of the premises of contemporary sociophilosophical understanding. A controversial, although undeniably influential, figure among both feminist and nonfeminist scholars, Foucault aimed not so much to produce theories as to create tools for critiquing theories. His work is concerned with power and the historical structures through which it is created and transmitted in our culture. As this work progresses, it deals increasingly with the overlap between the "personal" and the "political." Because of this focus, it has generated lively discussion among, especially, Anglo American feminists. Theorists have applied his writings to a variety of feminist-related subjects, including the social construction of femininity, forms of sexual desire, and analyses of anorexia nervosa. His works often focus on the body as a key site of modern disciplinary practices and explore, as Jana Sawicki writes, the "power of internalized oppression, and the seeming intractability of gender as a key to personal identity." Foucault suggests that the loosening of boundaries of selfness might enable one to recast questions of subjectivity in a fresh light. He urges us, as Kathy Ferguson explains, "to promote new forms of subjectivity through the refusal of (the) kind of individuality which has been imposed upon us for several centuries." Despite an apparent compatibility between these themes and the emancipatory agenda of mainstream Anglo American feminism, there is much in the work of Foucault that has come under intense scrutiny from feminist theorists.

Foremost of the feminist criticisms of Foucault are charges of Eurocentrism and androcentrism. He has been accused of being blind to feminists and to other writers facing oppression, exclusion, and domination. *The History of Sexuality*, for instance, focuses on issues of power, discipline, and knowledge and yet never speaks of male domination per se, speaking instead of power as if everyone were equally subjugated. As an advocate of specific and not generalizing theories, Foucault cannot be forgiven in the eyes of many feminists for overlooking the specific struggles of women and the persistently patriarchal nature of power. Foucault believed that history is not a continuous, progressive concept, but rather discontinuous and accidental. His work, therefore, serves not only to destabilize history but also to demonstrate the inherently unstable nature of human subjectivity itself. Although the destabilization of subjectivity has been a useful concept to some feminists, to many others his insistent opposition to the notion of "continuous history" undermines the ability of women to speak of their historical oppression. Psychoanalytic feminist theorists in particular are critical of this aspect of Foucault's work, and believe that Foucault would have dismissed feminism as yet another "contemporary true discourse" or even as another "disciplinary" institution—had he addressed the subject at all. Furthermore, to psychoanalytic scholars who view certain types of therapeutic "confessions" as being vital steps toward women's finding both voice and self-awareness, Foucault's repeated warnings, found especially in *The History of Sexuality*, of the "dangers of confession" are further proof to some feminist theorists that the term "Foucaldian feminism" is an inherently oxymoronic one. His advocation of the destabilization of identity and his valorization of critique over vision would be disastrous stands for women to take, they claim, just at the point in history when women's voices are beginning to be heard and their visions to be seen.

Also problematic for many feminist theorists is Foucault's definition of power as a phenomenon necessarily constituted through discourses. He insists that there neither is nor can be an all-powerful subject that manipulates discourse and that, therefore, power cannot be possessed by any individual or group. These claims make problematic any concepts of a "pre-discursive reality," such as the existence of the human body before it is socially constructed or of feelings that are nonexpressible, both concepts that many feminist theorists insist can and do exist. Foucault's body of work moves increasingly to a position that denies that power is a repressive force, or comes from a dominating class. While feminists define men's power as repressive and illegitimate, Foucault defines all power as productive—that is, as producing knowledge rather than repression. Moreover, his vision of power as all-pervasive and nondiscriminating makes it difficult if not impossible to distinguish between malign and benign forms of power as Ramazanoglu explains. Theorists who see the development of methods of resistance to malignant forms of power as a crucial, concrete step have been harshly critical of this "egalitarian" view as antithetical to a productive feminist agenda.

Other feminists, however, believe that much in Foucault's writings, lectures, and interviews has been and can be useful to a feminist project. His critiques of humanism and biological determinism, for example, as well as his arguments against an inherently direct link between specific forms of knowledge (such as hegemonic, masculine forms of knowledge) and "progress" have much in common with feminist beliefs. Because his work supports the theory that loosening the boundaries of the self can and should enable us to recast questions of subjectivity in a new light, say supportive feminists, Foucault has in fact opened up new avenues of resistance, and should not be accused of contributing to the blind oppression of women. Foucaldian feminists can and do exist, says Sawicki, and their aim should be to "stress the sheer variety of ways in which effects of male domination are produced and gendered identities are constituted."

Foucault's unique method of revelation of the concept of sociological and historical constructionism has been extremely useful to many scholars, both feminist and nonfeminist. To prove his theories of a discontinuous, non-linear history, Foucault began tracing the descent of the histories of ideas, backward in time, and not forward in an ascending manner, as had been the traditional method of historical investigations prior to the poststructuralist era. He believed that the traditional ascending model of historical investigation begged the question of the natural "progression" of Western culture. For this reason, Foucault's works are referred to as "archaeologies" and "genealogies." Many feminist theorists who believe that to view the body as natural is to create a trap for feminism, for example, believe that Foucault's genealogical method of tracing the descent of the history of ideas is invaluable for showing us that, although there may be no universal, natural category of woman, "women" can still discover common interests via their overlapping locations within culturally constructed networks of power relations. These feminists maintain that, despite the varied interpretations of his work, Foucault has enabled us to circumvent ideological biases by granting us the tools with which to consciously question the sociological and historical paradigms hampering us from resisting the forms of power that have for so long informed our identities.

Few argue that Foucault paved the way for poststructuralist theorists through his demonstration that both truth and the human subject that "knows" truth are not unchanging givens but rather are phenomena that are produced—and reproduced—within a constantly changing, complex network of power relations. And although much disagreement remains over the extent to which his work has helped or hindered the ongoing projects of feminist theorists, his philosophies, writes Jana Sawicki, embrace the "theoretical tensions that result when one acknowledges that we are both victims and agents within systems of domination, that our discourses can extend relations of domination at the same time that they are critical of them, and that any emancipatory theory bears the traces of its origins in specific historical relations to power/knowledge." Widely considered the father of poststructuralism, Foucault saw his role as an exposer of the contradictions of the history of ideas. It is little wonder, then, that his own work is itself characterized by internal inconsistencies, gaps, and aporias, much to the dismay of those who have attempted to discern a consistent Foucaldian agenda. Even those who disagree with his claims, however, do not deny Foucault's impact on postmodern thinking. As Jonathan Arac has written, "Even to defend a subject against Foucault requires redefining the subject." While many feminist scholars have found Foucault's productive methods of deconstructing power relations useful and have noted the fertility of the contradictions in his thought, however, most are wary of a wholesale purchase of a Foucaldian philosophy and believe that feminists must, at the very least, in the words of Caroline Ramazanoglu, "go beyond Foucault in theorising feelings that have no discourses and in exploring the unspeakable." While Foucault's discourse may not be a solution to the problems confronted by feminist scholars or to the problems of oppression in general, it has raised radical new questions and has prompted scholars in every field of humanistic study, whether offended by or in defense of Foucault, to reevaluate both their assumptions and their methodologies.

J. Nicole Cosentino

References

Arac, Jonathan, ed. *After Foucault: Humanistic Knowledge, Postmodern Challenges.* New Brunswick, N.J.: Rutgers University Press, 1988.

Bartky, Sandra. *Femininity and Domination.* London: Routledge, 1990.

Cooper, Barry. *Michel Foucault: An Introduction to the Study of His Thought.* New York: Edwin Mellen, 1981.

Diamond, Irene, and Lee Quinby, eds. *Feminism and Foucault: Reflections on Resistance.* Boston: Northeastern University Press, 1988.

Ferguson, Kathy E. *The Man Question: Visions of Subjectivity in Feminist Theory.* Berkeley: University of California Press, 1993.

Harstock, Nancy. "Foucault on Power: A Theory for Women?" In *Feminism/Postmodernism,* edited by Linda J. Nicholson, 157–175. New York: Routledge, 1990.

McNay, Lois. *Foucault and Feminism: Power, Gender and the Self.* Boston: Northeastern University Press, 1993.

Martin, Biddy. "Feminism, Criticism, Foucault." *New German Critique* 27 (1982): 3–30

Miller, Jim. *The Passion of Michel Foucault.* New York: Simon and Schuster, 1993.

Rabinow, Paul, ed. *The Foucault Reader.* New York: Pantheon, 1984.

Ramazanoglu, Caroline, ed. *Up against Foucault: Explorations of Some Tensions between Foucault and Feminism.* London: Routledge, 1993.

Sawicki, Jana. *Disciplining Foucault: Feminism, Power, and the Body.* New York: Routledge, 1991.

French Feminism

A body of writings whose philosophical underpinnings fundamentally challenged the Anglo American style of criticism. French feminism has been the single most important theoretical influence on contemporary feminist literary criticism. It is inextricably bound up with debates surrounding the methods and politics of a feminist critical practice.

While neglecting the diversity of the French scene that includes various critical strands oppositional to "French Feminism," such as Marxism, the term has come to denote the work of the three most famous protagonists: Hélène Cixous, Luce Irigaray, and Julia Kristeva. Like most of the leading American feminist critics, these women have their origins in the activist political movement of 1968. Unlike most American feminists, however, these French thinkers are steeped in the tradition of philosophy and psychoanalysis. And, since the European tradition ascribes the role of the revolutionary to the intellectual, the French feminists aim at inserting themselves into the discursive tradition.

French feminism has taken on the larger questions that permeate the Western canon and reexamined them from the standpoint of woman: What are the conditions of subjectivity, identity, and representation? of politics or aesthetics? How do space and time—the framework that enables experience, relate to sex and gender? What are the links between patriarchal politics and aesthetics? between the speaking subject and language? What is the nature of thought and writing? What are the assumptions governing the process of (feminist) theory itself? How does one represent woman, when she has been traditionally relegated to the register of silence and the unrepresentable?

Toril Moi explains that "in American colleges in the early 1970s, the great majority of courses on women in literature centered on the study of female stereotypes in male writing." Concomitantly, the American focus shifted toward female writers and aimed at broadening the canon to include the voices of women. The American predilection of the era was for bourgeois realism, not poetry. Underpinned by a naturalized concept of experience, feminist criticism relied on an identification with characters or their rejection according to preordained aesthetic ideals of integrity and totality as well as on certain models of behavior exemplified by the plot or the characters' speech in the text.

Entering the American scene in the seventies, French feminists exposed the major flaw of this approach, namely, that a supposedly feminist politics still unknowingly subscribed to a patriarchal aesthetics. As philosophers, they furthered the work of Lacan and Derrida. As literary critics, they privileged the canon of great male writers (mostly of French modernity) as the locus of écriture féminine. However, if feminism is defined as the struggle for women's equality, whose equality does such male writing further? Where is woman's difference or identity anchored: in the texts? in her body? in social practices?

French feminists argue that because Anglo American feminists make the phenomenal Other an extension of the self, they benefit the patriarchal oppressors. Woman is conceptualized as man's Other in a dichotomy that privileges man as the One that sets the standards for comparison and subsequently denotes woman as the lesser sex. In response, the French have revalorized the predicates ascribed to women: formlessness, darkness, hysteria, uncertainty, and so on, and most of all perhaps woman's link with the physical. Because of the insistence on the body, French feminists have often been accused of biologism and essentialism by Anglo American critics. For the French, however, the body serves as a locus of resistance to patriarchal thinking.

Given that the position of individual thinkers changes with time and that French feminism does not present a homogenous body of writing, the political and professional implications of the works classified under this rubric are complex. French feminists make a point of distinguishing themselves from liberal feminism, that is, from a mode of thought that leaves the system of binary oppositions intact and thus supports its collateral power structures, such as capitalism. Aesthetics is politics. Therefore, the French discourse tends to be poetic and innovative.

Beginning in the eighties, feminist critics extended the model of sameness and Otherness to all so-called marginal people and start to either analyze patriarchy as a multifaceted system of oppression that uses predicates such as class, race, and sexual orientation to identify and denigrate the respective social others or relate patriarchy to these forms of oppression. *Woman, Native, Other* by Trinh T. Minh-ha represents an example of the impact of French feminism on postcolonial criticism. Some of the essays in the reader *Lesbian Texts and Contexts: Radical Revisions,* edited by Karla Jay and Joanne Glasgow, are indebted to French feminist theory. The eighties also saw a plethora of critical writings by women who go directly back to the forefathers of French feminism, thus often reworking French critical problems under the auspices of a politicized multicultural and American feminist practice (for example, Jane Gallop, and Gayatri Spivak). Readings of literary critics have often centered around an analysis of the figurative impact of woman and the effects of uncertainty she has on language, such as Barbara Johnson's *A World of Difference*.

French feminism continues to challenge our epistemological legacy, conceptions of language, the role of the unconscious, models of the subject, and the ideological and political premises of discussions about identity and justice. Dialectically factoring back onto each other, French feminism has largely been assimilated into American discursive practices. However, French feminism, as Alice Jardine writes, "does not enjoy a valorized position in the vast majority of French and American circles, while feminism, especially as linked to women's studies in the United States, is one of the few viable critical discourses around."

Nina Zimnik

References

Cixous, Hélène. *The Newly Born Woman.* Translated by Betsy Wing. Minneapolis: University of Minnesota Press, 1986.

Irigaray, Luce. *Speculum of the Other Woman.* Gillian C. Gill. Ithaca, N.Y.: Cornell University Press, 1985.

———. This *Sex Which Is Not One.* Translated by Catherine Porter. Ithaca, N.Y.: Cornell University Press, 1985.

Jardine, Alice. *Gynesis: Configurations of Woman and Modernity.* Ithaca, N.Y.: Cornell University Press, 1985.

Kristeva, Julia. *Desire in Language: A Semiotic Approach to Literature and Art.* Translated by Thomas Gora. New York: Columbia University Press, 1980.

———. "Women's Time." Translated by Alice Jardine and Harry Blake. *Signs* 7 (1981): 13–35.

Marks, Elaine, and Isabelle de Courtivron, eds. *New French Feminisms: An Anthology.* Amherst: University of Massachusetts Press, 1979.

Moi, Toril, ed. *French Feminist Thought: A Reader.* Oxford and New York, Blackwell, 1987.

French became a household name upon publication of *The Women's Room*, a chronicle of woman's war to know herself. Told through a compendium of female voices, the novel angrily catalogues the endless betrayals that were women's lot, the drabness of women's lives, as well as women's ability to cope with, what French refers to as "the shit and the string beans." Through the course of the novel, French's acquiescent and eager-to-please repressed protagonist leaves a conventional marriage, becomes liberated and independent, but in the end, is alone, painfully attempting to adjust to the isolation that her new life has brought her.

The theme of liberation at the expense of loneliness receives further treatment in *Her Mother's Daughter*, a novel depicting the lives of four generations of women, each determined to seek happiness and freedom, and not to make the same mistakes and sacrifices that her mother made. In doing so, however, each becomes estranged from her children, exhausted, depressed and alone—just as her mother was one generation earlier.

French gives her most glaring indictment of society in her nonfiction. In *Beyond Power: On Women, Men, and Morals* and *The War against Women*, French argues that society was originally maticentral, matrifocal, and matrilineal, and that peace reigned between the sexes. This idyllic era came to an end with the rise of patriarchy. According to French, male self-identity depends on the ability to control women and nature, and the history of fatherhood is a long chronicle of a tyranny that has distorted human culture with its obsession for power. "The major problem facing feminists," she writes, "can be easily summed up: there is no clear way to move."

J.S. Postol

References

French, Marilyn. *Beyond Power: On Women. Men, and Morals.* New York: Summit, 1986.

———. *Her Mother's Daughter.* New York: Summit, 1987.

———. *The War against Women.* New York: Summit, 1987.

———. *The Women's Room.* New York: Summit, 1977.

French, Marilyn
Scholar, essayist, social critic, and fiction writer,

Friedan, Betty
See FEMININE MYSTIQUE

Friendship

Studies of women's friendships are crucial to our understanding of how women's identities, particularly our feminist identities, are constructed in connection with others. Sociological and literary interpretations suggest that women's friendships variously subvert, elide, influence, and are influenced by heterosexual romances and traditional family structures.

In *A Room of One's Own*, Virginia Woolf expresses her frustration with the difficulty of finding literary representations of female friendships that might define women other than by their relationships with men. In the late 1970s and early 1980s, feminist critics began to address this problem. Early studies of women's friendships helped lay the groundwork for new, women-focused, literary, psychological, and historical insights. Carroll Smith-Rosenberg examines female friendships of the nineteenth century as expressed in diaries and letters and observes that, contrary to popular opinion, a high level of intimacy was "accepted" between women at this time; she argues that by comparison twentieth-century cultural norms are more restrictive, simultaneously sexualizing all forms of same sex love while condemning them. Like Smith-Rosenberg, Adrienne Rich celebrates a "lesbian continuum" of women's affection for women; however in analyzing the position of twentieth-century women, she adds that "compulsory heterosexuality" weakens the bonds women share. Janet Todd paves the groundwork for a literary history of women's friendships, studying male and female authored fictional friendships of the eighteenth century, and examining gender-related differences in these representations. She shows how sentimental, erotic, manipulative, political, and social friendships in eighteenth-century texts/contexts intersected with and at times challenged other dominant ideologies. Lillian Faderman contributes further to making visible the strong history of woman to woman relationships. She rereads women's friendships as represented in diverse texts from the sixteenth century to the 1970s, arguing that women of the past participated in same sex friendships which, in terms of commitment and intensity, were similar to lesbian relationships today. Faderman asserts that woman to woman relationships of previous centuries, even when they took the place of marriage, were "accepted" because women did not yet have the economic or social power to replace men.

Writing in 1986, Janice Raymond coined the term "Gyn/affection" to describe the love and caring that she suggests women have always shown toward each other. Other feminist critics of the mid 1980s began additionally to explore more difficult aspects of women's friendships and our understanding of them. Some problems are imposed on women's friendships from without. For example, Lillian Rubin argues that the normative, heterosexual family trivializes friendships, as in the term "just friends." Luise Eichenbaum and Susie Orbach suggest that competition and envy are by-products of a patriarchal, capitalist society that damage women's friendships.

Some problems within women's friendships occur as a result of internalized patriarchal values. For example, rather than encouraging one another's increased independence, the women friends Stacey Oliker interviews seem to "enforce marital accommodation." In other instances, women must work through differences to become friends. Letty Cottin Pogrebin examines the "checkpoints" and bridges that must be negotiated for friendships to cross "boundaries of color, culture, sexual preference, disability, and age." Helena Michie uses the term "sororophobia" to suggest the negotiations of personal sameness and difference that occur even between familial sisters.

Many feminists see in the complexity of women's friendships, including women's largely unexamined friendships with men, a potential paradigm for larger feminist communities. As Mary E. Hunt describes it, in their "fierce tenderness" friendships have a great deal to teach us about the spiritual-political ethics of justice, nurture, and accountability.

Karen Sosnoski

References

Eichenbaum, Luise, and Susie Orbach. *Between Women*. New York: Viking, 1987.

Faderman, Lillian. *Surpassing the Love of Men: Romantic Friendships and Love between Women from the Renaissance to the Present*. New York: William Morrow, 1981.

Hunt, Mary E. *Fierce Tenderness: A Feminist Theology of Friendship*. New York: Crossroads, 1991.

Michie, Helena. *Sororophobia: Differences among Women in Literature and Culture*. New York and Oxford: Oxford University Press, 1992.

Oliker, Stacey J. *Best Friends and Marriage: Exchange among Women*. Berkeley, Los Angeles, and London: University of California Press, 1989.

Pogrebin, Letty Cottin. *Among Friends: Who We Like, Why We Like Them, and What We Do with Them*. New York: McGraw-Hill, 1987.

Raymond, Janice G. *A Passion for Friends: Toward a Philosophy of Female Affection*. Boston: Beacon, 1986.

Rich, Adrienne. "Compulsory Heterosexuality and Lesbian Existence." *Signs: Journal of Women in Culture and Society* 5, no. 4 (1980): 158–199.

Rubin, Lillian Breslow. *Just Friends*. New York: Harper and Row, 1985.

Smith-Rosenberg, Carroll. "The Female World of Love and Ritual: Relations between Women in Nineteenth-Century America." In *A Heritage of Her Own*, edited by Nancy F. Cott and Elizabeth H. Pleck, 311–342. New York: Simon and Schuster, Touchstone, 1979.

Todd, Janet. *Women's Friendship in Literature*. New York: Columbia University Press, 1980.

Woolf, Virginia. *A Room of One's Own*. New York: Harcourt, Brace, 1929.

Fuller, Margaret

American author, critic, and social reformer, Fuller is best known for her pioneering book *Woman in the Nineteenth Century*, which, like Mary Wollstonecraft's *Vindication of the Rights of Woman*, is one of the classic early feminist texts. In *Woman*, Fuller argues for complete equality and freedom for women, both at home and in the workplace. Additionally, she explores images of woman in literature, history, the Bible, poetry, and myth. The ideas Fuller presents here served as inspiration for the Declaration of Sentiments at the Seneca Falls Convention of 1848, and also as the intellectual basis of the subsequent women's movement in America.

While feminist literary critics are familiar with Fuller primarily through *Woman in the Nineteenth Century*, she also helped advance the women's movement through her role as translator, editor, and conversationalist. In 1839 Fuller originated "Conversations," a highly successful series of discussions in Boston that were open to women only. Focusing on a variety of intellectual and aesthetic topics, these discussions initiated many of the ideas Fuller developed in *Woman*. She also edited the Transcendentalist magazine the *Dial* from 1840 to 1842, and from 1844 to 1846 she served as literary critic for *The New York Tribune*. Like *Woman*, the essays, reviews, and poetry that Fuller contributed to these publications frequently stirred controversy; ahead of her time, Fuller confronted issues of gender and power that are still relevant today.

Melissa Tedrowe

References
Allen, Margaret Vanderhaar. *The Achievement of Margaret Fuller*. University Park: Pennsylvania University Press, 1979.

Dickenson, Donna. *Margaret Fuller: Writing a Woman's Life*. New York: St. Martin's, 1993.

Fuller, Margaret. *Woman in the Nineteenth Century*. New York: Greenwood, 1968.

Myerson, Joel. *Critical Essays on Margaret Fuller*. Boston: G.K. Hall, 1980.

Fuss, Diana

Employing a variety of theoretical perspectives, such as deconstruction and psychoanalysis, Fuss explores questions of identity, difference, sexuality, and subjectivity in a wide range of texts and spaces, from theoretical texts and film to popular culture and the classroom. In her work in feminist and lesbian and gay theory, Fuss interrogates what are often considered to be philosophical oppositions or conventional binaries, such as inside/outside, essentialism/constructionism, heterosexuality/homosexuality. Fuss suggests that one of the difficulties in examining binary oppositions such as these is "the tendency of hierarchical relations to reestablish themselves." For example, homosexuality, read as a transgression of heterosexuality, can reconfirm the centrality of heterosexuality. However, Fuss writes in the introduction to *Inside/Out: Lesbian Theories, Gay Theories*, "That hierarchical oppositions always *tend toward* reestablishing themselves does not mean that they can never be invaded, interfered with, and critically impaired." By revealing the hidden dependencies of each term in the binary on the other, Fuss's work provides just this interference in order "to erode and to reorganize the conceptual ground of identity."

In *Essentially Speaking: Feminism, Nature*

and Difference, Fuss examines what she terms a "structuring debate for feminism," the debate between essentialism (the position that differences are innate) and constructionism (the position that differences are constructed, not innate). Fuss identifies her own position as that of an antiessentialist "who wants to preserve (in both senses of the term: to maintain and to embalm) the category of essence." Fuss reads such issues as race, homosexuality, and pedagogy as well as the theories of individual feminist theorists, such as Monique Wittig, an antiessentialist materialist, and Luce Irigaray, an essentialist psychoanalytic philosopher, in terms of the essentialism/constructionism debate. The essentialism/constructionism opposition, Fuss contends, is a largely artificial, though powerful, antagonism. Her analysis illustrates how essentialism can be used strategically and how constructionism can operate as a form of essentialism.

Inside/Out, a collection of essays edited by Fuss, represents the variety of work currently being done in gay and lesbian scholarship. Fuss's recent work, exploring identification and desire across a range of texts from films to Freud, shows a continuing inquiry into questions of identity and difference and a continuing deconstruction of binary oppositions. The need to deconstruct binaries such as inside/outside, Fuss argues, "is that such polemics disguise the fact that most of us are both inside and outside at the same time."

Caroline Reitz

References

Fuss, Diana. *Essentially Speaking: Feminism, Nature and Difference*. New York: Routledge, 1989.

———. "Fashion and the Homospectatorial Look." *Critical Inquiry* 18 (1992): 713–737.

———. "Freud's Fallen Women: Identification, Desire and 'A Case of Homosexuality in a Woman.'" *Yale Journal of Criticism* 6 (1993): 1–23.

———. "Monsters of Perversion: Jeffrey Dahmer and *The Silence of the Lambs*." In *Media Spectacles*, edited by Marjorie Garber, Jann Matlock, and Rebecca Walkowitz, 181–205. New York: Routledge, 1993.

———, ed. *Inside/Out: Lesbian Theories, Gay Theories*. New York: Routledge, 1991.

F

G

Gallop, Jane

In *The Daughter's Seduction*, Jane Gallop proposed an alliance between contemporary feminist theory and Lacanian psychoanalysis. It is difficult now to separate its theoretical from its historical importance, since it wore even at that time a double aspect; it offered a self-sufficient interpretation of Freud, Lacan, Irigaray, and Cixous, even while it entered a longstanding debate within feminism about the usefulness of psychoanalysis for feminist thought. Viewed historically, Gallop's work responded to feminist discussions of Freud from the 1960s and 1970s that had harshly criticized him for his personal biases and questioned the scientific pretensions of psychoanalysis. Without abandoning these concerns, Gallop demonstrated a different approach to Freud; following Lacan, she reconceptualized Freud's intellectual authority, treating him not as the "founding father" of a science but as a peculiarly susceptible interpreter of other people's language. Gallop's unmasking of Freud's authority is the most striking instance of her vision of women's studies, a feminist criticism not limited to women's texts or representations of women, but capable of "revolutioniz[ing] the very structures of knowledge."

Throughout her career, Gallop's interests have shifted from theoretical discussion to institutional history, though she has consistently maintained a commitment to close textual analysis. Her first book, *Intersections*, was an extended reading of Sade; her second, *The Daughter's Seduction*, as mentioned above, mapped out the possible relations between psychoanalysis and feminism; her third, *Reading Lacan,* used Lacan to discuss the problems of interpretation and interpretive authority. Not the least of her accomplishments in these books is a style which, in its sensitivity, lucidity, and directness, sets her books apart from most other theoretical commentaries. Her readings are "strong" readings, not in the polemic sense of annihilating potential opposition, but in her self-professedly "psychoanalytic" sense of strength as resilience, flexibility, and a capacity for self-revision.

Gallop's next two books, *Thinking through the Body* and *Around 1981*, extended her "demystifying, even aggressive" style of interpretation to the institutional history of feminism. *Thinking through the Body* expanded essays from different stages of her career, revealing the autobiographical and historical displacements within those interpretations, and noting her occasionally vexed relations with an increasingly successful, increasingly institutionalized academic feminism. *Around 1981* reads like a series of feminist anthologies of literary criticism to reveal the insights and blind spots shared by their collective authors.

Gallop's most important contribution to feminism may well be as an intellectual mediator, someone capable of working between theoretical discourses that once seemed too antagonistic for productive interchange. Closely connected with this mediating role is her ability to move certain polemical oppositions (such as feminism versus psychoanalysis, French versus American feminism, heterosexual versus homosexual, male versus female) out of their rigid antagonism and into a dialectical "exchange between the terms." Her unique rapprochement of psychoanalysis and feminism, most evident in her theory and practice of interpretation, helped make possible many of the analyses of sexual desire, sexual difference, and constitution of identity now offered by feminist social theory and literary criticism.

David Mazella

References

Gallop, Jane. *Around 1981: Academic Feminist Literary Theory.* New York: Routledge, 1992.

———. *The Daughter's Seduction: Feminism and Psychoanalysis.* Ithaca, N.Y.: Cornell University Press, 1982.

———. *Intersections: A Reading of Sade with Bataille, Blanchot, and Klossowski.* Lincoln: University of Nebraska Press, 1981.

———. *Reading Lacan.* Ithaca, N.Y.: Cornell University Press, 1985.

———. *Thinking through the Body.* New York: Columbia University Press, 1988.

Gates, Henry Louis, Jr.

A prominent African American academic literary critic since the early 1980s, Gates is known for his textual editing and his theoretical work, which claims to transfuse postmodern literary theory with African (specifically Yoruba) and African American interpretative systems, thereby creating a literary criticism that can confront the complexities of the African American literary tradition. This project has drawn his attention to African American women writers as he uncovers and edits previously unavailable texts, such as Harriet Wilson's privately printed *Our Nig; or Sketches from the Life of a Free Black.* Additionally and relatedly, he makes use of and publicizes feminist literary theory, that generated by black feminist and womanist thinkers in particular; he edited and introduces the important collection *Reading Black, Reading Feminist: A Critical Anthology,* which brings together some of the contemporary classics of critical/theoretical discourse on black women writers and the tradition they create. Gates continues to use his prominence and power in the American Academy to promote and facilitate serious study of African American women's writing.

After the success of the discovery and republication of *Our Nig,* Gates initiated an expanded project of reprinting the lost work of black women writers in the forty-volume Oxford–Schomburg Library of Nineteenth-Century Black Women's Writings. Works by figures such as Pauline Hopkins, Anna Julia Cooper, Emma Dunham Kelley, and Frances Harper are now available for teaching and research through this effort. In his forward to each volume in the series (entitled "In Her Own Write") Gates articulates both his commitment to women's writing and his own critical emphasis on intertextuality and revision: "That the progenitor of the black literary tradition was a woman [Phillis Wheatley] means, in the most strictly literal sense, that all subsequent black writers have evolved in a matrilinear line of descent, and that each, consciously or unconsciously, has extended and revised a canon whose foundation was the poetry of a black woman."

Gates is as prolific a writer as he is an editor. In addition to his best known books, *Figures in Black* and *The Signifying Monkey,* his *Loose Canons: Notes on the Culture Wars* devotes space to the subject of women's writing and to feminist issues in contemporary culture.

Laura Quinn

References

Gates, Henry Louis, Jr. *Loose Canons: Notes on the Culture Wars.* New York: Oxford University Press, 1992.

———. *The Signifying Monkey: Towards a Theory of Afro-American Literary Criticism.* New York: Oxford University Press, 1988.

———, ed. *Our Nig; or, Sketches from the Life of a Free Black* by Harriet E. Wilson. New York: Random House, 1983.

———, ed. *Race, Writing, and Difference.* Chicago: University of Chicago Press, 1986.

———, with Charles T. Davis, eds. *The Slave's Narrative: Texts and Contexts.* New York: Oxford University Press, 1983.

Gaze

Psychoanalysis and semiotics intersected film studies in the mid seventies and resulted in the concept of the gaze, a characterization of the film camera's gaze as inescapably masculine. The concept of looking as a form of institutionalized violence to women has also been adopted for use in literary studies and art history.

In 1975 Laura Mulvey's "Visual Pleasure and Narrative Cinema" argued that the cinema was a symbolic order akin to language, and that the camera's gaze routinely reenacted the Freudian/Lacanian scenario of castration anxiety in the process of making meaning. Thus Hollywood cinema's objectification and fetishization of women was not accidental, nor even simply ideologically determined, but was rather a necessary condition of the way in which the classical cinema makes meaning. The only alternative, Mulvey suggested, was a feminist cinema that forswore narrative pleasure in order to create a new process of signification, an alternative to the symbolic order.

Other feminist film theorists have largely accepted the parameters of Mulvey's proposition: that classical Hollywood cinema is a system of representation akin to language; that a Lacanian psychoanalytic model with an emphasis on Oedipal crisis, sadomasochism, and fetishization is the appropriate model for cinematic signification; and that lapses from dominating male subjectivity in the cinema actually tend to reinforce patriarchal oppression because they allow women the illusion of subjectivity in a system that by definition cannot give the controlling power of the camera to a female gaze.

Mulvey's assertion—that cinematic articulation (camera distance, angle, movement, composition, and film editing) is inseparable from the cinema's phallocentric modes of production and processes of representation—has been appealing because it conjoins some basic tenets of Marxist, feminist, psychoanalytical, and semiotic theory. Applied in the most general terms, Mulvey's analysis of the gaze seems corroborated by many classical films: men are more likely to move freely in deep space in Hollywood movies, and women are more likely to appear in shallow focus, constrained by the frame of the film. As a tool for reading specific films, however, the proposition that the gaze is male has proved problematic.

Specifically, feminist theorists and critics have struggled with the idea that the female viewer must either identify with the sadistically phallocentric gaze of the camera or take a masochistic pleasure in identifying with the confinement and humiliation of women in classical films. Most feminists seem willing to relegate the female viewer to some form of ironic distance. Mulvey went on to characterize the female viewer as a transvestite, and Mary Ann Doane has suggested that the female viewer takes up, as a masquerade, both the masculine position of viewing and the feminine position of being viewed. Linda Williams argues for mul-

tiple identifications on the part of the viewer, and Teresa de Lauretis has demonstrated ways in which individual films allow the female viewer to reconcile, however conditionally, the mutually exclusive positions of masculine gaze and female objectivity. Tania Modleski has gone the farthest to validate the pleasure a female viewer takes in viewing a classical film, arguing that spectatorial empathy is an essentially feminine trait that may challenge, and even mitigate, the phallocentric symbolic order of the film text.

Mulvey's insistence that the viewer's pleasure in watching classical films derives from the camera's fetishization or sadistic violation of women has also proved difficult for feminists writing about alternative films made by women filmmakers. In order to theorize the female viewer's bond with the camera's gaze as active rather than passive, and to describe an alternative cinema that allows a female viewer both sexual subjectivity and pleasure, Kaja Silverman insists that the infant's identification with the mother be included in the discussion of Oedipal struggle as it gives rise to the symbolic order. In another move to valorize the bond between women, Judith Mayne explicitly invokes the figure of the lesbian to characterize the countercinema's feminine gaze as "a chain of female-to-female desire."

Gaylyn Studlar defends the pleasure that a viewer takes in watching classical Hollywood films and offers an interesting account of spectatorial identification by rejecting the Freudian concept of sadomasochism that Mulvey and other feminists have used to negotiate the opposition of active, controlling male gaze and passive, objectified female image. Turning to the writings of Gilles Deleuze and Leopold von Sacher-Masoch, Studlar argues that the camera's gaze is male, but masochistic. A masochistic male gaze may be passive, interested in deferred pleasure, eager to surrender control, effectively bisexual, and motivated by an ambivalent, pre-Oedipal desire for a mother figure in the realm of the Lacanian "Imaginary," Studlar proposes. Thus Studlar challenges the premises of Mulvey while retaining a concept of the gendered gaze.

Other critics have returned to Freud for a more sophisticated reading of "masculine" and "feminine" psychological development to complicate the discussion of the gaze. David Rodowick focuses intently on Freud to provide complex descriptions of sexual difference that are not as restrictive as Mulvey's adaptation of Freudian/Lacanian theory. Marian Keane turns to Freud to contest Mulvey's theorization of the camera's gaze, specifically in terms of Mulvey's reading of "Vertigo." Keane argues that Mulvey distorts Freud's descriptions of active and passive instincts and his use of "masculine" and "feminine" to reduce the camera's role to a monolithically masculine oppressor. Mulvey's insistence that the camera's gaze is a male gaze fails to acknowledge the camera's central representation of female subjectivity in "Vertigo," Keane suggests. By implication Keane aligns feminist theories of the gaze with the villainy of the men in "Vertigo," as both deny the humanity of the female protagonist.

Keane's essay serves as a reminder that any broad characterization of the camera's gaze as oppressively gendered may limit a critic's response to a film even as it exposes the film's participation in patriarchal systems of representation. The proposition that the gaze is male (or lesbian, or masochistic) derives from the traditions of philosophical skepticism, importing Cartesian doubts about whether the world and other people can ever be adequately known into the relation between viewer, camera, and subject. The idea that in the classical cinema the camera's gaze necessarily denies the subjectivity of women has its roots in three centuries of philosophical argument: proponents of the gendered gaze take upon themselves an enormous intellectual burden, one not yet fully discharged.

Ellen Draper

References

Berger, John. *Ways of Seeing.* New York: Viking, 1973.
de Lauretis, Teresa. *Alice Doesn't: Feminism, Semiotics, Cinema.* Bloomington: Indiana University Press, 1984.
————. *Technologies of Gender: Essays on Theory, Film, and Fiction.* Bloomington: Indiana University Press, 1987.
Doane, Mary Ann. *The Desire to Desire: The Woman's Film in the 1940's.* Bloomington: Indiana University Press, 1987.
————. *Femmes Fatales: Feminism, Film Theory, Psychoanalysis.* New York: Routledge, 1991.
————. "Film and the Masquerade: Theorising the Female Spectator." *Screen* 23, no. 3–4 (September–October 1982): 74–87.
————, Patricia Mellencamp, and Linda Williams, eds. *Revision: Essays in Feminist Film Criticism.* Los Angeles: University Publications of America, in association with the American Film Institute, 1984.
Keane, Marian. "A Closer Look at Scopophilia: Mulvey, Hitchcock, and *Vertigo.*" In *A Hitchcock Reader,* edited by Marshall Deutelbaum and Leland Poague, 231–248. Ames: Iowa State University Press, 1988.
Mayne, Judith. *The Woman at the Keyhole.* Bloomington: Indiana University Press, 1990.
Modleski, Tania. *The Women Who Knew Too Much: Hitchcock and Feminist Theory.* New York: Methuen, 1988.
Mulvey, Laura. *Visual and Other Pleasures.* Bloomington: Indiana University Press, 1989.
Penley, Constance, ed. *Feminism and Film Theory.* New York: Routledge, 1988.
Rodowick, David. *The Difficulty of Difference.* New York: Routledge, 1991.
Silverman, Kaja. *The Acoustic Mirror: The Female Voice in Psychoanalysis and Cinema.* Bloomington: Indiana University Press, 1988.
Studlar, Gaylyn. *In the Realm of Pleasure: Von Sternberg, Dietrich, and the Masochistic Aesthetic.* Chicago: University of Illinois Press, 1988.
————. "Masochistic Performance and Female Subjectivity in *Letter from an Unknown Woman.*" *Cinema Journal* 33, no. 3 (Spring 1994): 35–57.
Williams, Linda. "'Something Else Besides a Mother': *Stella Dallas* and the Maternal Melodrama." *Cinema Journal* 24, no. 1 (Fall 1984): 2–27.

Gender

The original definition of gender is two or more subclasses within a grammatical category, though this meaning does not hold true in all languages and cultures. Up until the mid to late 1980s, most feminists used gender descriptively as a term synonymous with women, sexual difference, or sex roles. However, within the last decade, gender, like class, has been seen less as a descriptive term and more as a complex category of analysis.

Within feminist theory, gender is now commonly defined as what Joan Scott calls "knowledge of sexual difference." However, gender is more than a single piece of empirical data—a piece of clothing, a glance, a gesture—whereby we distinguish between people on the basis of their sex. Gender is also, writes Teresa de Lauretis, "the product and the process of a number of social technologies" through which men and women learn to think of themselves as gendered beings—as men and women—and not merely (generic) human beings. What this means is that gender has moved out of the realm of nature and into the realm of culture, where it is viewed as a socially constructed and historically specific object of study with important implications not only for feminist literary theory, but also for disciplines as diverse as history, science, philosophy, psychology, and anthropology. Gender is important because before the sex/gender system can be changed, people need to understand their position within it, how their gendered identities are constructed, and how gender is inscribed in a number of discourses and disciplines.

The development of gender as a category of analysis parallels the history and development of feminist theory because, until the last decade, the terms gender and women were used interchangeably. In the 1970s Marxists and feminists from the social sciences began to question all-inclusive ways of looking at women and women's lives. Gayle Rubin wrote an influential article critiquing the sex-gender system and the need to study diverse social constructions of men and women. At this same time, literary theory as a whole began to move away from largely celebratory and exclusionary ways of looking at women, and into more complex theorizations about the relationship between gender and literature. Led by Elaine Showalter, American gynocriticism turned to such topics as "the history of styles, themes, genres, and structures of writing by women" and "the psychodynamics of female creativity," while French feminists, such as Hélène Cixous, Luce Irigaray, and Julia Kristeva relied more heavily on deconstruction and psychoanalysis in their explorations of feminine textuality and discourse.

The historian Joan Wallach Scott, and the film and social theorist Teresa de Lauretis, have done important work in the development of gender as a category of analysis. Because gender theory is still such a new and developing field there are dangers that the term might come to signify either too much or too little. Without

scrupulous theorization and an awareness of how the concept is being used, gender could revert back to its descriptive stance as a synonym for women or femininity. On the other hand, gender could also become so amorphous and unwieldy that people will not know what is meant by its use. In addition, some feminists are uncomfortable with the introduction of masculinity into feminist circles; however, viewing men and women as relational beings tends to necessitate that both male and female gendered identities come under study.

The study of gender in literature continues to grow and develop. Critics study, among other things, the relationship between sexuality and gender, the inscription of gender biases within texts, the construction of characters' gendered identities at particular moments, and the ways that reading and writing are gendered acts. With an increased sensitivity to the cultural construction of gender, feminist theorists will continue to gain new insights into how and why men and women experience gender in the many and particular ways that they do.

Pam Lieske

References

de Lauretis, Teresa. "The Technology of Gender." In *Technologies of Gender: Essays on Theory, Film, and Fiction*, 1–30. Bloomington: Indiana University Press, 1987.

Greene, Gayle, and Coppélia Kahn. "Feminist Scholarship and the Social Construction of Woman." In *Making a Difference: Feminist Literary Criticism*, edited by Gayle Greene and Coppélia Kahn, 1–37. London: Routledge, 1985.

Jehlen, Myra. "Gender." In *Critical Terms for Literary Study*, edited by Frank Lentricchia and Thomas McLaughlin, 263–273. Chicago: University of Chicago Press, 1990.

Miller, Nancy K., ed. *The Poetics of Gender.* New York: Columbia University Press, 1986.

Poovey, Mary. *Uneven Developments: The Ideological Work of Gender in Mid-Victorian England*. Chicago: University of Chicago Press, 1988.

Riley, Denise. "Does a Sex Have a History? 'Women' and Feminism." *New Formations* 1 (1987): 35–45.

Rubin, Gayle. "The Traffic in Women: Notes toward a Political Economy of Sex." In

Toward an Anthropology of Women, edited by Rayna Reiter, 157–210. New York: Monthly Review, 1975.

Salvaggio, Ruth. *Enlightened Absence: Neoclassical Configurations of the Feminine.* Urbana: University of Illinois Press, 1988.

Scott, Joan Wallach. "Gender: A Useful Category of Historical Analysis." *American Historical Review* 91 (1986): 1053–1075.

———. *Gender and the Politics of History.* New York: Columbia University Press, 1988.

Spector, Judith. "Gender Studies: New Directions for Feminist Criticism." *College English* 43 (1981): 374–378.

Showalter, Elaine, ed. *The New Feminist Criticism.* New York: Pantheon, 1985.

Gilbert, Sandra, and Susan Gubar

With the publication of the groundbreaking work *Madwoman in the Attic,* the authors suggest that the natural anxiety of authorship experienced by any writer was compounded for women writers of the nineteenth century by societal attitudes that either characterized them as unfeminine interlopers into the realm of men, or dismissed them as inferior "lady novelists." Compelled to write in an alien landscape, physically and mentally confined by a patriarchal culture, authors such as the Brontës, George Eliot, Mary Shelley, and even Jane Austen produced texts that worked within accepted literary bounds while at the same time enabling their authors to express their rage and sense of otherness. *Jane Eyre,* for example, had long been considered merely a competent example of the Gothic, and the characterization of Bertha Rochester essentially a staple of that genre. Gilbert and Gubar, however, see this figure both as Jane's adversary, foil, and double, and as a manifestation of Charlotte Brontë's own "ire," an anger so terrifying it must be repressed, but yet so great it must have life. While none of the other writers examined in this volume have literal madwomen in their attics, they have all employed unique literary tactics to express their repressed anxieties. As the authors examine other texts, they dismember the idea of mere "lady novelists," and demonstrate how these writers worked the male formula to their own ends, subverting and remaking texts to give voice to their own concerns.

The three-volume study, *No Man's Land* (Vol. 1, *The War of the Words,* 1988; Vol. 2 *Sexchanges,* 1989; Vol. 3, *Letters from the Front,* 1994), continues this critical exploration into the twentieth century. As the title suggests, in this century the suppressed friction between men an women erupts into verbal battle and in these volumes Gilbert and Gubar explore modernism and the ways in which it is differently inflected for male and female writers. In the authors' view, this "battle of the sexes," fueled by the changing definition of post-Victorian femininity and rising feminism, is responsible for much of what we term modernism, as well as many avant-garde responses to male-inflected language, such as the work of Gertrude Stein.

For years literature produced by female writers has been belittled or at best grudgingly accepted as anomalous. Gilbert's and Gubar's works dismantle the theory that equates the pen only with masculinity, and compel us to examine women's texts as legitimate, free-standing pieces, rather than as pale imitations of previous masculine "masterpieces." In addition, acknowledging the sexual tensions inherent in society, they invite us to consider the effect of gender on the creation of literature. Far from measuring women by a patriarchal rule, Gilbert's and Gubar's insights help us to mine a rich literary mother lode.

Sarah Amyes Hanselman

References

Gilbert, Sandra, and Susan Gubar. *The Madwoman in the Attic: The Woman Writer and the Nineteenth-Century Literary Imagination.* New Haven: Yale University Press, 1979.

———. *No Man's Land: The Place of the Woman Writer in the Twentieth Century.* Vol. 1, *The War of the Words.* New Haven: Yale University Press, 1988.

———. *No Man's Land: The Place of the Woman Writer in the Twentieth Century.* Vol. 2, *Sexchanges.* New Haven: Yale University Press, 1989.

———. *No Man's Land: The Place of the Woman Writer in the Twentieth Century.* Vol. 3, *Letters from the Front.* New Haven: Yale University Press, 1994.

———, eds. *The Female Imagination and the Modernist Aesthetic.* Vol. 1 of *Studies in*

Gender and Culture. New York: Gordon and Breach Science Publishers, 1986.

———, eds. *The Norton Anthology of Literature by Women.* New York: W.W. Norton, 1985.

———, eds. *Shakespeare's Sisters: Feminist Essays on Women Poets.* Bloomington: Indiana University Press, 1979.

Gilligan, Carol

With the publication of her book *In a Different Voice,* Carol Gilligan revolutionized the understanding of female psychological and moral development. By exploring the disparity between women's reported experience and the representations of that experience in psychological literature, Gilligan popularized the idea that women speak with a unique "voice." In doing so she posited a fundamental difference between how men and women communicate with both the world and one another. Most important, Gilligan reframed the traditional views of women as developmental "failures," asserting instead that their "inadequacies" are actually strengths that help to sustain the human life cycle.

Gilligan's work originated in the field of psychological and moral development, areas dominated by male theorists whose research relied primarily on male subjects. At the time of Gilligan's groundbreaking research, the established routes to adulthood mapped out by theorists such as Sigmund Freud, Erik Erikson, and Lawrence Kohlberg had consistently marked separation as the key to the formation of both a healthy identity and a mature moral sense. Because women do not usually define themselves in terms of separation, but rather establish a sense of identity through connection, these models frequently labeled women as developmentally deviant or inadequate. In a similar way, because they have difficulty making decisions based on basic rights and rules, and are concerned instead with the responsibility toward others that their choices place on them, women were also judged as unable to reach the highest level of moral maturity.

Like other psychologists before her, Gilligan too found that, against the traditional psychological background, women frequently stand out as different. While researching morality and moral development, Gilligan identified what she called two distinct "voices" in her subjects' descriptions of moral conflict: women expressed consideration for relationship and connection while men paid attention to a sense of justice based on established rules. Unlike her predecessors, however, Gilligan did not assume that because her female subjects were different they were also deviant. Rather, she began to question the theories themselves and concluded that the problem lay not in women, but in asking women to follow what were essentially male models of moral and psychological development. In response to this recognition, Gilligan coined the terms "ethic of care" and "ethic of responsibility," which emphasize the central role that connection and relationship play in women's morality.

For literary theorists, Gilligan's ideas substantiate the importance of studying women authors, their texts, and female characters in literature. Gilligan's more recent work has focused on how, beginning in adolescence, girls' knowledge and articulation of that knowledge is suppressed. This research offers the study of female authority and authorship an understanding of the ways in which the female voice has been subverted and disempowered in the patriarchal world. Gilligan has been questioned about her essentialist approach to women's development, which posits identity in exclusively gendered terms, and for overlooking the risks inherent in the ethics of care and responsibility, which conflict with and therefore repress and conceal women's anger. Despite such criticism, however, Gilligan's documentation of a "different voice" has emphasized the fact that when a woman speaks—as author, character, or critic—what is said is worth listening to.

Sara E. Quay

References

Gilligan, Carol. *In a Different Voice: Psychological Theory and Women's Development.* Cambridge: Harvard University Press, 1982.

———, et al., eds. *Making Connections: The Relational Worlds of Adolescent Girls at Emma Willard School.* Cambridge: Harvard University Press, 1990.

———, et al., eds. *Mapping the Moral Domain: A Contribution of Women's Thinking to Psychological Theory and Education.* Cambridge: Harvard University Press, 1988.

Hayles, N. Katherine. "Anger in Different

Voices: Carol Gilligan and *The Mill on the Floss.*" *Signs* 12 (1986): 23–29.

Gilman, Charlotte Perkins

Now celebrated in feminist circles, Charlotte Perkins Gilman developed an extensive and complex social theory combining feminism and socialism. Deemed a leading feminist in her own time (along with Olive Schreiner and Ellen Key), this internationally recognized theorist and lecturer, ironically, repudiated the term "feminist" when it came into use in her later years. Rather, she called herself a humanist. Her world was masculinist, men having usurped human traits as their own, and Gilman wanted to restore an equal gender balance, to emancipate women to promote the best development of society. Unencumbered by domestic servitude, women could benefit the world. *Women and Economics* established Gilman's worldwide reputation. She is best known today for her fiction, *Herland* (1915) and "The Yellow Wallpaper."

In *Women and Economics*, Gilman argues that women's "sexuo-economic" dependence on men creates an unhealthy imbalance, demeaning half the human race. This subordination will end only when women's struggle for autonomy frees women as well as men. The short story "The Yellow Wallpaper" graphically depicts a patriarchal society's crippling limitations, which drive the female protagonist to madness. In contrast, her utopian novel *Herland* envisions a socialized motherhood, children raised by a genuine community of women.

Today, Gilman's prodigious output (novels, stories, poetry, and theoretical works) stands as a major theoretical contribution to modern feminist thought. Her work subverts patriarchal ideologies, challenges female subjugation, and argues for equal rights—gender issues with which we are still grappling today.

Catherine Golden

References

Gilman, Charlotte Perkins. *Herland*. With an introduction by Ann J. Lane. New York: Pantheon, 1979.
———. *Women and Economics: A Study of the Economic Relation between Men and Women as a Factor in Social Evolution.* Boston: Small, Maynard, 1898. Reprint, edited and with an introduction by Carl N. Degler. New York: Harper and Row, 1966. Source Book, 1970.
Golden, Catherine, ed. *The Captive Imagination: A Casebook on "The Yellow Wallpaper."* New York: Feminist, 1992.
Hill, Mary Armfield. *Charlotte Perkins Gilman: The Making of a Radical Feminist, 1860–1896.* Philadelphia: Temple University Press, 1980.
Lane, Ann J. *To "Herland" and Beyond: The Life and Works of Charlotte Perkins Gilman.* New York: Pantheon, 1990.

Goddess

A female, especially maternal divinity or divine principle; archetype of female power; a symbol of or focus for women's spirituality; object of historical rediscovery in feminist scholarship and philosophy.

The women's movement of the 1960s and 1970s not surprisingly led to a rethinking of the Judeo-Christian belief system with its foundation in a supreme father god. This critique of the patriarchal Western religions, as put forth by feminist thinkers such as Mary Daly, was accompanied by renewed interest in prehistoric matriarchal cultures based on reverence for a female generative principle or "Great Goddess" immanent within nature. The "Great Mother" as archetype was explored in depth by Erich Neumann, a student of Carl C. Jung, in 1955; Neumann bases his claim for an archetypal "Earth Mother" or "Primordial Goddess" on artifacts gathered from several continents and dating as far back as the Stone Age. Perhaps the most frequently cited archaeological evidence for prehistoric Goddess-worship is an abundance of stone amulets featuring female figures with vastly exaggerated reproductive organs—traces of a lost culture in which fertility as embodied in the feminine was the basis of ritualistic celebration and religious awe.

Feminist scholars such as Merlin Stone—whose pivotal work, *When God Was a Woman*, defined the terms of the feminist discussion of religion—argue for the prior existence of a widespread matriarchal belief system that endured for thousands of years until the rise of the Western patriarchal religions. From this time forth, the female divine principal was either repressed or incorporated into male-dominated systems in such forms as the classical goddesses or the Virgin Mother of Christianity. Elinor W. Gadon defines the contrast between Goddess worship and the Judeo-Christian heritage as follows: "Goddess religion was earth-centered, not heaven-centered, of this world not otherworldly, body-affirming not body-denying, holistic not dualistic. The Goddess was immanent, within every human being, not transcendent, and humanity was viewed as part of nature, death as a part of life."

Feminist philosophy's recovery of the Goddess can be linked to trends in feminist literary theory and criticism. Julia Kristeva presents a fascinating exploration of the relationship between the Christian tradition and the mother goddess principle in her essay "Stabat Mater," and feminist readings of literary works often focus on goddess figures in order to highlight similar issues.

Celia R. Daileader

References

Christ, Carol. *Laughter of Aphrodite: Reflections on a Journey to the Goddess.* San Francisco: Harper and Row, 1987.

Daly, Mary. *Beyond God the Father: Toward a Philosophy of Women's Liberation.* Boston: Beacon, 1973.

———. *The Church and the Second Sex.* New York: Harper and Row, 1968.

Eisler, Riane. *The Chalice and the Blade: Our History, Our Future.* San Francisco: Harper and Row, 1987.

Gadon, Elinor W. *The Once and Future Goddess.* New York: Harper and Row, 1989.

Griffin, Susan. *Woman and Nature: The Roaring Inside Her.* New York: Harper and Row, 1978.

Kristeva, Julia. "Stabat Mater." In *The Female Body in Western Culture,* edited by Susan Suleiman, 99–118. Cambridge: Harvard University Press, 1986.

Neumann, Erich. *The Great Mother* [1955]. Princeton: Princeton University Press, 1963.

Olson, Carl. *The Book of the Goddess Past and Present: An Introduction to Her Religion.* New York: Crossroads, 1983.

Stone, Merlin. *Ancient Mirrors of Womanhood: A Treasury of Goddess and Heroine Lore from Around the World.* Boston: Beacon, 1991.

———. *When God Was a Woman.* New York: Dial, 1976.

Whitmont, Edward. *Return of the Goddess.* New York: Crossroads, 1982.

Gothic

In literary studies, a term applied, usually pejoratively and with gender biases, to horror fiction most popular from 1780 to 1820. Anthologies and companions to literature characterize the gothic novel as a romantic story whose primary aim is to invoke terror by describing mysterious and horrific incidents. Given that gothic's popularity arose during the Enlightenment, it is not surprising that gothic authors locate horror in unenlightened settings, usually choosing medieval settings replete with wild landscapes, decayed castles, ghosts and mysterious incidents, and the idealized heroes, heroines, and villains of romance. Traditionally, literary critics identify Horace Walpole, William Beckford, Anne Radcliffe, Matthew G. Lewis, Charles Brockden Brown, Charles Maturin, Thomas De Quincey, Mary Shelley, and Edgar Allan Poe as practitioners of gothic fiction, and name Walpole as the inventor of the genre. Such a critical lineage, however, ignores the vast majority of gothic novels written by women, among them Clara Reeve, Mary Robinson, Charlotte Smith, and Charlotte Dacre. More important, it elides that gothic novels were "feminized"—criticized in gender-specific ways—both in the time in which they were written, and also in the 160 years of critical history that have followed the gothic novel's greatest popularity.

Gothic fiction has become important in the last two decades to feminist critics because its marginal status in critical histories epitomizes the gender biases present in processes of literary canonization. Changes in the definition of the word "gothic" itself reflect the depreciation of gothic fiction's status from dominant narrative form to embarrassing period piece. Because the term "gothic" derives itself from the Goths, it originally meant at once "medieval," "Germanic," and "barbarous"; both Walpole in *The Castle of Otranto* (1764) and Reeve in *The Old English Baron* (1778) described their stories as gothic because of their medieval subject matter. When gothic fiction first gained extraordinary popularity in the 1780s and 1790s, British reviewers lumped it with other "modern romances" and "historical novels"—classes of fiction perceived at the time as "female" in spite of large male readerships—and, in aggressive and openly misogynist language, joined with Anglican and government officials in condemning all such publications as pernicious. Consequently, "gothic" became a term for this body of prose fiction only in retrospect, coined to dismiss a group of novels written primarily by women as tasteless and barbarously medieval. The gothic novel's decline in status in the face of unanimous opposition from predominantly male cultural institutions was complete by the early 1820s, when it diffused itself into pirated chapbooks, "penny dreadfuls," and high metrical romances.

While most critical writing on gothic novels still focuses primarily on Walpole, Radcliffe, Lewis, and Mary Shelley, feminist critics in the last two decades have begun to rediscover forgotten gothic novelists and to reassess their importance in our understanding of the English Romantic period. Dorothy Blakey's *The Minerva Press* remains an excellent source for information on lesser-known gothic novelists, their distributors, and their readers. Bibliographical and critical guides to gothic fiction are plentiful; at least five separate ones have been published since 1970. Since 1981, feminist critics have published over forty articles and at least eight full-length studies on gothic fiction and its influence on nineteenth- and twentieth-century women writers. Among the most influential are Eve Kosofsky Sedgwick's *The Coherence of Gothic Conventions* and *Between Men: English Literature and Male Homosocial Desire*, and Kate Ferguson Ellis's *The Contested Castle: Gothic Novels and the Subversion of Domestic Ideology*. Sedgwick's *The Coherence of Gothic Conventions* proposes a twofold argument: first, that the "surfaces" (architecture, settings, language, and narrative structure) of gothic fiction hold in common a set of metaphors of enclosure and live burial; second, that these "surfaces" are in themselves worthy of study, without requiring that corresponding "depths" (psychological structures of consciousness, for instance) exist where critics locate meaning. In *Between Men*, Sedgwick argues that gothic romance explores systems of symbolic exchange between men governed by what she calls male homosocial desire; she asserts that the breakdown of such systems in "the Gothic novel crystallized for English audiences the terms of a dialectic between male homosexuality and homophobia." The book's absence of sustained analysis of gothic fiction by women, however, suggests that Sedgwick is unable to accommodate female gothic novelists into the masculinist thematics by which she defines the genre. In opposition to Sedgwick, Ellis, in *The Contested Castle*, attempts to define gothic fiction as a feminist genre that reinvents domestic space by dramatizing the struggles of female characters who must negotiate that space successfully in response to the threat of a menacing and powerful male figure. Ellis's Marxist-feminist analysis is especially powerful where it examines the subversive roles that servants—the traditional runners of interference and communicators of messages—play in gothic fiction by women. Ellis and other feminist critics have found such approaches to gothic fiction to be useful in revealing not only the cultural ambivalences of the English Romantic period, but also the sexist assumptions inherent in the romantic canon.

Michael Crews Gamer

References

Blakey, Dorothy. *The Minerva Press, 1790–1820*. London: Oxford University Press, 1939.

Ellis, Kate Ferguson. *The Contested Castle: Gothic Novels and the Subversion of Domestic Ideology*. Urbana: University of Illinois Press, 1989.

Langbauer, Laurie. *Women and Romance: The Consolations of Gender in the English Novel*. Ithaca, N.Y.: Cornell University Press, 1990.

McAndrew, Elizabeth. *The Gothic Tradition in Fiction*. New York: Columbia University Press, 1979.

Milbank, Alison. *Daughters of the House: Modes of the Gothic in Victorian Fiction*. New York: St. Martin's, 1992.

Poovey, Mary. *The Proper Lady and the Woman Writer*. Chicago: University of Chicago Press, 1984.

Sedgwick, Eve Kosofsky. *Between Men: English Literature and Male Homosocial Desire*. New York: Columbia University Press, 1985.

———. *The Coherence of Gothic Conventions*. New York: Methuen, 1986.

Winter, Kari J. *Subjects of Slavery, Agents of Change: Women and Power in Gothic Novels and Slave Narratives, 1790–1865*. Athens: University of Georgia Press, 1992.

Great Books Tradition

See CANON

Great Mother

A female divinity or archetype, embodying a sacred maternal principle immanent within nature and its generative force and characterized by qualities on the one hand nurturing, life-giving, and life-sustaining, but on the other hand potentially destructive. Some manifestations of the archetype are the prehistoric mother goddesses surviving in clay amulets; the classical goddess Ceres or Demeter; the Christian Virgin Mother and her prototypes in literature; and the popular myth of "Mother Nature."

The rise of feminist thought in the 1960s and 1970s led to a general critique of patriarchal religions and hence to a rediscovery of the prehistoric, matriarchal belief systems documented by scholars such as Erich Neumann. In particular, the French feminist theorists of the 1970s urged women to reclaim a prepatriarchal, essential mode of existence grounded in the body; this produced revolutionary works on the meaning of maternity and the maternal principle in religion, such as Julia Kristeva's essay "Stabat Mater," and in America, Marina Warner's *Alone of All Her Sex*. Recently, theorists have questioned the concept of an "essential," transhistorical, female or maternal experience in ways that complicate discussion of the Great Mother as archetype or center of feminist philosophy. Yet feminist readings of literary works often focus on characters embodying the principal, as reflecting cultural views toward women.

Celia R. Daileader

See also GODDESS

References

Daly, Mary. *Beyond God the Father: Toward a Philosophy of Women's Liberation*. Boston: Beacon, 1973.

Griffin, Susan. *Woman and Nature: The Roaring Inside Her*. New York: Harper and Row, 1978.

Kristeva, Julia. "Stabat Mater." In *The Female Body in Western Culture*, edited by Susan Rubin Suleiman, 99–118. Cambridge: Harvard University Press, 1986.

Neumann, Erich. *The Great Mother*. Princeton: Princeton University Press, 1955, 1963.

Rich, Adrienne. *Of Woman Born: Motherhood as Experience and Institution*. New York: W.W. Norton, 1986.

Warner, Marina. *Alone of All Her Sex: The Myth and Cult of the Virgin Mary*. New York: Knopf, 1976.

Greene, Gayle

Literary critics often situate their scholarship within one dominant critical approach. By contrast, Gayle Greene successfully reads from multiple perspectives. Greene has applied her pluralist approach in studies of twentieth-century women's novels, particularly contemporary feminist metafictions, that is, fictions that narrate the acts of reading and writing fiction.

Along with Coppélia Kahn, Greene co-edited *Making a Difference: Feminist Literary Criticism*, an enormously influential collection of feminist criticism taken from a range of perspectives, including lesbian, black feminist, psychoanalytic, and Marxist criticism. For literary critics interested in feminist criticism, this text provides an extensive overview of work done through the mid 1980s. In *Changing the Story: Feminist Fiction and the Tradition*, Greene brings literary critics' attention to women's metafiction. Here Greene suggests that unlike former images of the mad housewife, metafictional protagonists learn to substantiate the self and reconsider their world through the acts of reading or writing. Her book especially focuses on the 1970s metafictions of Doris Lessing, Margaret Drabble, Margaret Laurence, and Margaret Atwood, offering feminist-Marxist, -deconstructionist, -psychoanalytic, and other readings. Another collection of essays Greene edited with Coppélia Kahn, *Changing Subjects: The Making of Feminist Literary Criticism*, chronicles American feminist literary scholars' introduction to feminist theory and criticism since the 1960s, documenting a history of second-wave feminism told from personal and professional autobiographical experiences.

Greene's research plays an influential role in reconstructing the history of feminist literary theory and criticism and in rediscovering twentieth-century women's metafictions.

Michelle L. Deal

References

Greene, Gayle. *Changing the Story: Feminist Fiction and the Tradition*. Bloomington: Indiana University Press, 1991.

———, and Coppélia Kahn, eds. *Changing Subjects: The Making of Feminist Literary Criticism*. New York: Routledge, 1993.

———, eds. *Making a Difference: Feminist*

Literary Criticism. New York: Methuen, 1985.

Greer, Germaine

Germaine Greer's *The Female Eunuch* is one of the earliest and most influential works in late twentieth-century feminism, a provocative blend of literary and cultural criticism, social commentary, historical assessment and political activism. Greer argues powerfully for change in women's lives, for resistance to the "castration" of women, the deliberate suppression of women's sexuality, physical strength, mental acuity, anger, independence, and "completeness." In her 1980 introduction to the paperback edition, Greer claims that she wrote the book with the hope that her "disgust with the traditional feminine postures and procedures would be added to the spurs which were forcing women to rise up and smash the mold made for them."

In 1980, Greer established the now defunct Center for the Study of Women's Literature at the University of Tulsa and founded *Tulsa Studies in Women's Literature*, the longest-running academic journal focusing exclusively on women's writing. As the founding editor of TSWL, Greer reinforced the newly formed "gynocritical" approach in feminist literary criticism by calling for, publishing, and herself contributing original research on hitherto little known women writers. Her opening editorial essay for the new journal proclaimed, "If we can bring the face of one of our foremothers clearly out of the shadow we shall have made a [great] change."

Though her loyalty to feminist literary excavation, an insistence on the primary importance of scholarly studies of women's work, and a seeming lack of interest in current feminist theory (and jargon) have all provoked criticism, Greer continues to include canon reformation among her widespread feminist activities (which include hosting televised women's talk shows in the U.K., making frequent radio presentations, and contributing regular columns to the English press). *Kissing the Rod: An Anthology of Seventeenth-Century Women's Verse*, edited by Greer and three of her American graduate students, made a significant contribution to the inclusion of women in the literary canon by publishing long-neglected poems with extensive commentary, supported by original research. Greer continues this work as the founder and general editor of Stump Cross Books, a small press dedicated to issuing scholarly editions of the work of early modern English women poets.

Jeslyn Medoff

References

Greer, Germaine. *The Change: Women, Aging and the Menopause.* New York: Knopf, 1992.

———. *The Madwoman's Underclothes: Essays and Occasional Writings.* New York: Atlantic Monthly, 1987.

———. *The Obstacle Race: The Fortunes of Women Painters and Their Work.* New York: Farrar, Straus, and Giroux, 1979.

———. *Sex and Destiny: The Politics of Human Fertility.* New York: Harper and Row, 1984.

———. *Shakespeare. Past Masters Series.* New York: Oxford University Press, 1986.

———, et al., eds. *Kissing the Rod: An Anthology of Seventeenth-Century Women's Verse.* New York: Farrar, Straus, and Giroux, 1989.

Griffin, Susan

Griffin's emphasis in much of her writing on the connections between the body and nature has made her thoughts crucially important to the ecofeminist movement and to others seeking a women's culture more aligned with the natural world. By rebelling against a patriarchal society that strives to maintain a separation between intellect/body and civilization/nature, Griffin reenvisions an entirely new social structure, most recently in her work *A Chorus of Stones: The Private Life of War.*

Griffin's writing was vital to the development of the feminist movement in the 1970s. Two texts in particular, *RAPE: The Power of Consciousness*, which first appeared as a shorter essay in 1971, and *Pornography and Silence: Culture's Revenge against Nature*, were essential building blocks in feminist discussions of both rape and pornography. In both of these pieces, Griffin argued that the patriarchal system as it was constructed operated to make pornography and rape attractive to men.

Griffin's poetry and plays have not received as much critical attention as her work on rape and pornography, but her plays and poems are still an important part of her oeuvre, since she believes that poetry is a central form of feminist expression. Griffin's most significant poem has been her long prose poem, *Woman and Nature: The Roaring inside Her*. Dense and multidimensional, this piece provides a radical critique of the entire structure of Western civilization. Griffin creates a world in which women and nature infiltrate and, ultimately, alter patriarchal society. Widely praised by critics, this complex work is foundational for ecofeminists and other feminists interested in creating a world in which a distinctly feminine nature has a greater importance than in our current society.

Griffin has also published a number of different poetry collections: *Dear Sky*, *Let Them Be Said*, *Letter*, *The Sink*, *Like the Iris of an Eye*, and *Unremembered Country*. In her collected poems Griffin gives a voice to women's many different concerns, such as motherhood and rape. In her last collection, Griffin has begun to develop an increasingly global perspective, writing poems on ecological disasters and hunger in Africa.

Throughout her long career, Griffin has been a strong voice in articulating woman's relationship to nature. In addition, her experimentation with combining poetry and prose, breaking away from more standard academic writing, positions her as a key figure in the ongoing feminist discussion of what style most accurately represents women's thoughts.

Sherrie A. Inness

References

Freedman, Diane P. "Living on the Borderland: The Poetic Prose of Gloria Anzaldúa and Susan Griffin." *Women and Language* 12 (1989): 1–4.
Griffin, Susan. *A Chorus of Stones: The Private Life of War*. New York: Doubleday, 1992.
———. *Made from This Earth: An Anthology of Writings*. New York: Harper and Row, 1982.
———. *Pornography and Silence: Culture's Revenge against Nature*. New York: Harper and Row, 1981.
———. *RAPE: The Power of Consciousness* [1979]. San Francisco: Harper and Row, 1986.
———. *Unremembered Country*. Port Townsend, Wash.: Copper Canyon, 1987.
———. *Woman and Nature: The Roaring inside Her*. New York: Harper and Row, 1978.

Grosz, Elizabeth

Elizabeth Grosz reinterprets prominent psychoanalytic theories, including those of male theorists such as Lacan and Freud and feminists such as Kristeva and Irigaray. For literary theorists, Grosz's ideas further confirm the importance of rereading women's texts from a feminist psychoanalytic critical approach to reconstruct female identities.

In *Sexual Subversions: Three French Feminists*, Grosz clarifies for English speakers current French feminist philosophical critical texts by Kristeva, Irigaray, and Le Doeuff. Grosz compares and contrasts their theoretical development, showing correspondences and differences among them so that feminist literary critics, for instance, can better synthesize modern French feminist thought. In *Jacques Lacan: A Feminist Introduction*, Grosz critiques Lacan's theories of psychoanalysis. She finds his ideas to be inimical to women's equality and misleading for feminist theorists and critics, literary or otherwise. Her most recent book, *Volatile Bodies: Toward a Corporeal Feminism*, addresses the failures of the mind/body opposition in Western philosophy. This dichotomy glorifies the mind over the body and connects masculinity to intellect and femininity to the corporeal. Like other feminist philosophers, she theorizes about sexual difference as a plural existence and sees the body as a culturally crafted product.

Grosz's research has played a valuable role in disputing the psychoanalytic assumption that women's psychological processes are somehow less important than men's. For literary theory, Grosz's synthesis of French psychoanalytic philosophy has emphasized the feminist view that identity is plural and not generalizable.

Michelle L. Deal

References

Grosz, Elizabeth. *Jacques Lacan: A Feminist Introduction*. New York: Routledge, 1990.
———. *Sexual Subversion: Three French Feminists*. Boston: Allen and Unwin, 1989.
———. *Volatile Bodies: Toward a Corporeal Feminism*. Bloomington: Indiana University Press, 1994.

Grotesque

Feminist critics have examined the grotesque in order to critique various representations of the female body and challenge traditional notions of beauty. As opposed to the sleek, proportionate, and hermetic classical body, the grotesque body overflows, protrudes, ruptures, and secretes; it is a body of transgression and change, always unfinished. Such protean, bodily images resist not only traditional images of classical beauty, but also the assumed permanency of established social orders—two recurrent subjects that feminism itself tries to dispute.

The word "grotesque" originated as a technical term to describe the murals found in Roman chambers (grotte) excavated in early-sixteenth-century Italy. These murals resisted "natural" form by blurring the anatomical boundaries between humans, animals, and plants. Initially defined as a composite or collage, the grotesque body can also be anatomically uniform yet disproportionate, as in caricature. When applied to literature and other styles of art, the grotesque denotes that which is nonconventional, disordered, transgressive, or heavily embellished. It has been both praised and condemned by artists and critics although it lacks, as a descriptive term, any intrinsic positive or pejorative meaning. The most common criticisms of the grotesque have been levied by proponents of a classical style that represents a monolithic "Truth" and singular "Nature."

One recent advocate of the grotesque is Mikhail Bakhtin. In his book *Rabelais and His World*, Bakhtin examines the sociopolitical implications of "grotesque realism," which he argues is central to the literature and culture of the Middle Ages. For example, during carnival celebrations, the populace expresses through grotesque realism a production of knowledge antithetical to the prevailing secular and religious truths. These images and statements of carnival serve to dissect, recombine, and redeploy the truths of church and state in different contexts, rather than simply effacing them. The exaggerated and polymorphous grotesque body—as exemplified, for Bakhtin, in the Kerch terracotta figurines of decaying, deformed, senile, pregnant hags—is emblematic of grotesque realism's recombinant epistemology.

In a recent reading of Bakhtin, "Female Grotesques: Carnival and Theory," Mary Russo recognizes Bakhtin's invocation of the hags as a further illustration of men exploiting the Female Grotesque for their own critical ends. Specifically, she reminds us that men masqueraded as women during carnivals or riots to fight for political change. Russo juxtaposes this spectacular, male-produced, "female" body of cultural resistance against the cultural imperative that women not make spectacles of themselves in order to ask "in what sense can women really produce or make spectacles out of themselves?" In search for a feminist use of grotesque realism, Russo offers readings of both masquerade and *écriture féminine* as possible ways in which women can perform their bodies as texts that challenge social and literary conventions.

Jon Hodge

References

Bakhtin, Mikhail. *Rabelais and His World*. Translated by Helen Iswolsky. Cambridge: MIT Press, 1968.

Clayborough, Arthur. *The Grotesque in English Literature*. Oxford: Clarendon, 1965.

Kayser, Wolfgang. *The Grotesque in Art and Literature*. New York: Columbia University Press, 1981.

Kuryluk, Ewa. *Salome and Judas in the Cave of Sex: The Grotesque: Origins, Iconography, Techniques*. Chicago: Northwestern University Press, 1987.

Russo, Mary. *The Female Grotesque*. New York: Routledge, 1995.

———. "Female Grotesques: Carnival and Theory." In *Feminist Studies, Critical Studies*, edited by Teresa de Lauretis, 213–229. Bloomington: Indiana University Press, 1986.

Stallybrass, Peter, and Allon White. *The Politics and Poetics of Transgression*. Ithaca, N.Y.: Cornell University Press, 1986.

Gyn/Ecology

The title of Mary Daly's 1978 book (subtitled "The Meta-Ethics of Radical Feminism"), Gyn/Ecology was conceived by this feminist scholar and theologian as a way of "wrenching back some word power" from a patriarchal language. Daly uses the term to reveal the process of breaking down artificial barriers between fields of knowledge, of which Daly's own work is a provocative example. Combining history, etymology, and dazzling wordplay to re-vision this term and others, Daly demonstrates the Gyn/Ecological process of changing "the nouns of knowledge into verbs of know-ing." A visual and aural pun on gynecology, a profession that is an example of "male control over women and over language," Gyn/Ecology is reconstructed by Daly to denote a science in which women choose to be the subjects, not the objects, of inquiry. This science affirms the interconnected web of relationships between organisms and their environment, providing a holistic contrast to gynecology, which depends upon the "fixation and dismemberment" of women. This "web" of relationships serves as the functioning metaphor for practitioners of Gyn/Ecology: by "weaving world tapestries," women are "developing the complex web of living/loving relationships." As a consequence, Gyn/Ecology works against the life-threatening "material pollution" generated by phallic myths and language. Daly continued re-visioning and inventing words, collecting them in her 1986 feminist dictionary, *Webster's New First Intergalactic Wickedary* (co-authored with Jane Caputi).

Wendy C. Wahl

See also DALY, MARY

References
Daly, Mary, and Jane Caputi. *Gyn/Ecology: The Meta-Ethics of Radical Feminism.* Boston: Beacon, 1978.
———. *Webster's First New Intergalactic Wickedary of the English Language.* Boston: Beacon, 1987.

Gynesis

A term coined by Alice Jardine to theorize the relationship between poststructuralism and feminism and to bridge the gap between French and American feminist thought. Jardine asserts that the sign of "woman" has become a significant focus of the twentieth century's rethinking of literature, philosophy, history, and religion. In reconceptualizing and exploring traditional Western works, postmodern theorists have paid particular attention to instances where the text seems to lose control of itself or what it appears to know, as well as to moments when a woman suddenly appears or speaks where she was previously absent or silent. Jardine is particularly interested in how poststructuralist thought has encoded these moments as "feminine" and how, in doing so, "woman" has become a metaphor for the disruption of patriarchy. Gynesis is the process by which the sign of "woman" is put into postmodern discourse and how she becomes essential to new ways of speaking, writing, and thinking about Western symbolic structures. Authors in whose work gynesis can be

seen include Jacques Derrida, Jacques Lacan, and Gilles Deleuze.

Jardine's work raises important questions for feminist literary theory: can woman be the symbol of process and change in Western thought and still continue to exist as a sexual identity? Once the concept of "woman" has been set into motion and becomes a prominent category of literary analysis, how does the light of real women find expression? Does one preclude the other? For American feminists in particular, Jardine's work emphasizes the importance of seeing "woman" not just as a biological being, but as a powerful sign in the context of poststructuralist thought.

Sara E. Quay

References
Jardine, Alice. *Gynesis: Configurations of Woman & Modernity.* Ithaca, N.Y.: Cornell University Press, 1985.

Gynocritics

Elaine Showalter first used this term in 1979 in an essay entitled "Toward a Feminist Poetics" to describe the "study of women's writing, including readings of women's texts and analyses of the intertextual relations both between women writers, and between women and men." Showalter's own work began with a study of nineteenth- and twentieth-century English women novelists in *A Literature of Their Own.* This work is an example of gynocritics as it investigates literature written by women with the assumption that writing is marked by gender. In American literary criticism, gynocritics signaled a movement away from criticism that usually consisted of "close readings" of texts by predominantly male writers, and a step beyond "feminist critique," which discussed the stereotypes found in these works. Showalter attempted to explore the questions, how can we constitute women as a distinct literary group? and what is the difference of women's writing? She locates difference in four possible areas: biological, linguistic, psychoanalytic, and cultural.

In recent years, poststructuralist critics have disparaged gynocriticism for its humanist view that the study of women's writings can reveal what women have "experienced," for its lack of theoretical sophistication, and for its focus on nineteenth-century realist texts. However, gynocritics appeared at a crucial historical moment in Anglo American criticism, and inspired many feminists to restore or rediscover texts by women that were not included in the traditional literary canon.

Eleanor Ty

References

Showalter, Elaine. "Feminist Criticism in the Wilderness." *Critical Inquiry* 8 (1981): 179–205. Reprinted in *The New Feminist Criticism: Essays on Women, Literature, & Theory*, edited by Elaine Showalter, 243–270. New York: Pantheon, 1985.

———. *A Literature of Their Own: British Women Novelists from Brontë to Lessing*. Princeton: Princeton University Press, 1977.

———. "Toward a Feminist Poetics." In *The New Feminist Criticism: Essays on Women, Literature, & Theory*, edited by Elaine Showalter, 125–143. New York: Pantheon, 1985.

———, ed. *Speaking of Gender*. New York: Routledge, Chapman and Hall, 1989.

H

H.D.

Twentieth-century American poet, novelist, translator, memoirist, Hilda Doolittle reflects in her life and work central concerns of literary modernism: reaction to the violence of two world wars, the impact of feminism upon conventional gender roles, the breakup of racial and class hegemonies, and the myth-making quest for new meanings. Writing as "H.D." she is known chiefly as a poet: first, as a founding member, in the second decade, of the Imagist movement (with friends Ezra Pound and Amy Lowell), and for her Greek translations; later, as the author of lyric epics in the forties and fifties (*Trilogy* and *Helen in Egypt*). The first woman to receive the Award of Merit medal in poetry from the American Academy of Arts and Letters (1960), she also wrote experimental, autobiographical novels and memoirs, many of which were privately circulated or left unpublished during her lifetime. The recent publication or reprinting of the novels *Palimpsest*, *HERmione*, *Bid Me to Live*, *Paint It Today*, and *Asphodel* and the memoirs *Tribute to Freud*, *The Gift*, and *End to Torment*, written in the twenties, thirties, and forties, has resulted in increasing critical recognition of her place in the avant-garde of modernist fiction, beside Virginia Woolf, Gertrude Stein, James Joyce, and William Faulkner. Like them, she experiments with language, syntax, and narrative perspective to capture the shifting subjectivities of consciousness and the eruptions of the unconscious.

Like the long poems of her fellow expatriates, T.S. Eliot and Ezra Pound, H.D.'s lyric epics feature the poet as a prophet in the wasteland of a war-torn world, who calls upon the resources of many cultures to forge new myths and meanings. Unlike those of male modernists, however, H.D.'s poems center on the consciousness of female speakers who simultaneously critique the nihilism of cultures imbued with masculinist values and find potential for healing in the presence of reinvoked female deities. The web of allusions she invokes grows out of her extensive involvement with classical Greece and ancient Egypt, psychoanalysis, cinema, Moravian protestantism, and occult mysticism. The impetus and emotional intensity of these poems derives from H.D.'s attempt to integrate and comprehend the meaning of the trauma she suffered during World War I, a nexus of death and birth that she came to call her "personal hieroglyph."

Although H.D. grew up in Pennsylvania, and always considered herself an American, her literary identity blossomed after she went abroad in 1911 to join the circle of writers around Ezra Pound, W.B. Yeats, Ford Madox Ford, and May Sinclair. She lived from then on mainly in England and Switzerland. Bisexually oriented, she became engaged to Pound, loved Frances Gregg, married Richard Aldington in 1913, and after her separation from him, in 1919, lived with Bryher (Winifred Ellerman) until 1946. Her first book of poems (*Sea Garden*, 1916) appeared shortly after the still-birth of her first child, during the same year that her British husband joined the army. After almost dying of pneumonia herself during her second pregnancy (1918–1919), at which time her brother and father died, she had a daughter, Perdita, by Cecil Gray, crediting her survival to Bryher's devotion. In her prose fiction and memoirs, H.D. engages this personal story more directly, reweaving it to come to terms with the catastrophes she identified with World War I. These avant-garde texts explore heterosexual and lesbian love, the conflicts around mother-hood and creativity, the transformations of the female self from the object of man's desire to the subject of her own, and the intersections of race, class, and gender.

Although critics and poets like Norman Holmes Pearson, Robert Duncan, and Denise Levertov did their best to keep her reputation alive after her death, H.D. did not receive the critical acclaim her work merited until the 1980s, when the publication of Louis Martz's edition of her *Collected Poems* (1983), and the advent of feminist criticism, illuminated the later work of this major modernist.

Donna Krolick Hollenberg

References

Bloom, Harold, ed. *Modern Critical Views: H.D.* New York: Chelsea House, 1989.

Boughn, Michael. *H.D. A Bibliography 1905–1990.* Charlottesville: University Press of Virginia, 1993.

Buck, Claire. *H.D. and Freud: Bisexuality and Feminine Discourse.* New York: St. Martin's, 1991.

Burnett, Gary. *H.D. Between Image and Epic: The Mysteries of H.D.'s Poetics.* Ann Arbor, Mich.: UMI Research, 1990.

Chisholm, Diane. *H.D.'s Freudian Poetics: Psychoanalysis in Translation.* Ithaca, N.Y.: Cornell University Press, 1992.

DuPlessis, Rachel Blau. *H.D.: The Career of that Struggle.* Brighton: Harvester, 1986.

Friedman, Susan Stanford. *Penelope's Web: Gender, Modernity, H.D.'s Fiction.* New York: Cambridge University Press, 1990.

———. *Psyche Reborn: The Emergence of H.D.* Bloomington: Indiana University Press, 1981.

———, and Rachel Blau DuPlessis, eds. *Signets: Reading H.D.* Madison: University of Wisconsin Press, 1990.

Guest, Barbara. *Herself Defined: The Poet H.D. and Her World.* New York: Doubleday, 1984.

Hollenberg, Donna Krolik. *H.D.: The Poetics of Childbirth and Creativity.* Boston: Northeastern University Press, 1991.

Heath, Stephen

A longtime member of the editorial board of the British journal *Screen*, which pioneered feminist film theory in the 1970s, Heath is known primarily for his work on cinema and on the role of sexuality in cultural production. In a 1978 essay for *Screen*, Heath offered a theory of how sexual difference is constructed and contained through representation in cinema. Responding to the work of Laura Mulvey and Jacques Lacan, Heath argues that the function of the production of representation is directly related to a "fixing" of female difference. By containing difference, Heath goes on to argue, the dominant order reveals its assumption of sameness, an assumption that always works to the disadvantage of women.

In *The Sexual Fix*, Heath critiqued the history of ideas about sexuality in cultural production, in which sexuality is dichotomized as either repressed or liberated. Heath maintains that "liberated" sexuality, as a result of increased knowledge, does not yield more pleasure, but merely the need to know ever more (the "sexual fix"). This in turn fuels the commodification of sexuality and leads to increased social control and regulation.

Jenifer K. Ward

References

Heath, Stephen. "Difference." *Screen* 19, no. 3 (1978): 51–112.

———. "Joan Riviere and the Masquerade." In *Formations of Fantasy*, edited by Victor Burgin, James Donald, and Cora Kaplan, 45–61. London and New York: Methuen, 1986.

———. "Male Feminism." In *Men in Feminism*, edited by Alice Jardine and Paul Smith, 1–33. London and New York: Methuen, 1987.

———. *The Sexual Fix.* London: Macmillan, 1982.

Heilbrun, Carolyn

In her work as literary critic, professor of English at Columbia University, MLA president, and prolific writer, Heilbrun consistently defines herself as a woman in opposition to the expectations of a dominant, male culture. Heilbrun's career illustrates a continuous commitment to release women from the "prison of gender." She sees an urgent need for more satisfactory female models, asking us to reexamine existing literature, to write honest biographies and autobiographies of women, and to create more complete female characters in fiction.

Heilbrun's early work, *Toward a Recognition of Androgyny*, shows the notion of androgyny to be an old idea, firmly, yet often obscurely, grounded in the "vast world of myth and literature." Heilbrun traces the cultural denial of androgyny while she urges the "reconciliation between the sexes" in life and literary thought. This new understanding, Heilbrun believes, will offer new choices to both women and men; it will diminish the popularity of the "too-manly man" who ultimately wages war, as well as the too-womanly woman, who remains marginalized by her cultural definition.

In *Writing a Woman's Life*, Heilbrun continues to question gender division as she records and examines the lives of several "ambiguous" women who, like herself, have chosen to live "beyond the labyrinth" of the patriarchal plot of courtship, marriage, and motherhood. As she insists on the need for authentic female narratives, Heilbrun offers several biographies of women, from George Sand to Virginia Woolf, who have voyaged out into the public, "masculine" sphere of power and control. Heilbrun continues her work in her subsequent book, *Hamlet's Mother and Other Women*, in which she presents new biographies and confronts the rendering of women in literature always pushing beyond the conventional gender interpretations.

Heilbrun's work shows evidence of the strong connection between "the written life" and lived experience. She calls for new scripts in which the lives of women are written not as objects, but as complete subjects who place their work, not man, at their centers. These new models experience both anger and personal satisfaction and who, like men, are able to act and choose. Heilbrun believes that these stories can give encouragement, support, and validity to women who have felt isolated. Heilbrun also encourages women to write in genres previously reserved for men; quest and confessional modes give more accurate form to the lives of many women.

As Heilbrun's life moves forward, she reaches for new models, examining marriage, friendship, and the relationship between mothers and daughters. She plunges bravely into the absence of plot, identifying middle age as a time of freedom and dramatic risk taking; it is a time when women are no longer burdened by the need to be "female impersonators." Heilbrun illustrates these challenges in her detective fiction, published under the pseudonym Amanda Cross. The main character, detective Kate Fansler, reflects her author's energy as she pushes against external boundaries in her quest for truth.

Beth Dacey

References

Heilbrun, Carolyn. *Hamlet's Mother and Other Women.* New York: Ballantine, 1990.

———. *Toward a Recognition of Androgyny.* New York: Harper Colophon, 1973.

———. *Writing a Woman's Life.* New York: Ballantine, 1988.

Henderson, Mae Gwendolyn

Much of Henderson's writing develops a black feminist theory of reading that privileges difference. Her work focuses on the doubly marginalized position of African American women in society—not white, not male—and the relation of their writing to the canonic literary tradition. The clearest articulation of her theory can be found in her essay "Speaking in Tongues: Dialogics, Dialectics, and the Black Woman Writer's Literary Tradition."

Drawing from Michel Foucault, Hans-Georg Gadamer, and Mikhail Bakhtin, Henderson picks up where Barbara Smith and Audre Lorde began, asserting that black women speak and write with multiple voices, as gendered and racial subjects. In Henderson's formulation, though, gender and race are not discrete categories of analysis; rather, she proposes a model of reading that "seeks to account for racial difference within gender identity and gender difference within racial identity." This approach foregrounds the "deconstructive function" of black women's literature and feminist literary criticism: the writing of black women's lives disrupts the discourse of universalism that excludes considerations of race, class, and gender. Therefore, Henderson argues, with its emphasis on difference, black women's writing remaps the boundaries that have defined Western white male literature and criticism. Yet, Henderson also maintains that black women writers are not trying to move from the margin to the center, but rather wish to remain at the margins, speaking in a multivocal fashion as both insiders and outsiders.

The value of Henderson's work for feminist literary theory is its emphasis on dialogue within critical practice. In advocating debate among competing critical camps, Henderson offers a productive model for feminist exchange: rather than seeking consensus, feminists can find empowerment through rival critical paradigms that attend to the diversity of women's experience.

Kimberley Roberts

References

Henderson, Mae G. "Speaking in Tongues: Dialogics, Dialectics, and the Black Woman Writer's Literary Tradition." In *Changing Our Own Words: Essays on Criticism, Theory, and Writing by Black Women,* edited by Cheryl Wall, 16–37. New Brunswick, N.J.: Rutgers University Press, 1989.

———. "Toni Morrison's Beloved: Remembering the Body as Historical Text." In *Comparative American Identities: Race, Sex, and Nationality in the Modern Text,* edited by Hortense Spillers, 62–86. New York: Routledge, 1991.

———, ed. *Borders, Boundaries and Frameworks.* New York: Routledge, 1994.

———, et al., eds. *Antislavery Newspapers and Periodicals: An Annotated Index of Letters, 1817–1891.* 5 vols. Boston: G.K. Hall, 1980–.

Heroine

Signifying everything from the feminine-gender version of the masculine-gender term "hero" to a strong female role model, the "heroine" is a subject of much debate for feminists in both literary studies and society. The question for feminists is not only which term, hero or heroine, to use when referring to a woman sharing the qualities generally attributed to a "hero" or the principal female character in a literary or dramatic work, but whether the figure of the heroine can be recovered from its derivative implications (that a heroine is a female hero) or dependent status. The hero, some literary theorists suggest, is a leader; the heroine follows, and takes second place. In her preface to *Maria,* Mary Wollstonecraft provides this definition: "The hero is allowed to be mortal, and to become wise and virtuous as well as happy, by a train of events and circumstances. The heroines, on the contrary, are to be born immaculate." Rejecting the inferior associations of "heroine," some feminist theorists choose hero when referring to women or female characters. The choice of hero, however, raises the question of whether or not it is possible or even desirable to recuper-

ate the figure of the heroic individual from its masculinist associations with the "Great Man."

The debate spans from the terminological to the philosophical. M.H. Abrams's *A Glossary of Literary Terms* defines "heroine" simply as "the chief character in a work, on whom our interest centers." "Heroine" is treated as a synonym for the protagonist: "Elizabeth Bennett is the protagonist, or heroine, of Jane Austen's *Pride and Prejudice.*" The term "heroine," however, has often been spurned by feminists who see the term as "sex-limited" or see the suffix "ine" as derivative and dependent. According to *The Handbook of Nonsexist Writing,* "the word hero applies to males and females alike; the word heroine, although it has a long and honorable history going back to the Greek heroine (counterpart of the masculine-gender heros), is anomalous." The use of the term heroine make females "nonstandard."

Beyond the terminological dilemma, the debate over the figure of the heroine encompasses larger philosophical questions within feminism. With the women's movement's focus on the everyday struggles of all women, many feminist theorists see the figure of the heroine, an exceptional individual, as problematic. The creation of a heroine or heroine-worshiping is seen as antithetical to the movement's goals of sisterhood. However, this antiheroine position contradicts some of the main objectives articulated in the early days of the women's movement: to provide role models and promote positive images of women. The contradictory positions on the figure of the heroine in the women's movement highlight the paradoxical nature of the heroine. In her feminist exploration of the literary heroine, *Becoming A Heroine,* Rachel Brownstein suggests that the figure of the heroine encompasses contradictions: "[The heroine] is unlike all other women, being important and unique, but she is also quintessentially feminine, therefore rightly representative of her sex." The paradox of the heroine—being at once unique and representative—illustrates the paradoxical position of the heroine within feminism as well. The heroine is at once a consciousness-raising role model and a unique individual, a focus on which can be seen as detrimental to the collective aims of the women's movement.

One of the problems the "exceptional individual" presents for feminism is that the figure of the heroic individual has historically been male. Thomas Carlyle, Victorian essayist and critic, gendered the term irrevocably in his series of lectures in the late 1830s, "On Heroes, Hero-Worship and the Heroic in History." Statements such as the "History of the world is but the Biography of Great Men" illustrate that the hero is a great individual but significantly that he is a great man. In the literary tradition, the same assumption that "individual" silently implies a male character is evident in discussions of the *bildungsroman*, German for the "novel of formation." The *bildungsroman* focuses on the hero's development in the passage from childhood through varied experiences into his mature identity. Recognizing the gendered implications of this genre, Sandra Gilbert and Susan Gubar provide a reading of the "female bildungsroman" in their influential *The Madwoman in the Attic*. Gilbert and Gubar describe Charlotte Brontë's *Jane Eyre* as a "distinctly female bildungsroman in which the problems encountered by the protagonist as she struggles from the imprisonment of her childhood toward an almost unthinkable goal of mature freedom are symptomatic of difficulties Everywoman in a patriarchal society must meet and overcome."

The paradox of the figure of the heroine, as both an exceptional individual and an "Everywoman," raises a question, outside the specifically literary treatments of the hero/heroine, as to whether the heroine can ever be a feminist figure, sharing, as it must, in the masculinist history of the "hero." The creation of heroines, some feminists argue, goes against the movement's basic philosophy. In *Sex, Class, and Culture*, Lillian Robinson writes, "It is not role models we need so much as a mass movement, not celebration of individual struggle . . . so much as recognition that we are all heroes." However the reality, according to feminist theorist Jane Gallop in *Around 1981*, is that there are heroes in feminism: "Whether in some ideal, superior version of feminism, 'serious' feminists would completely shun 'hero-worshipping,' in the real 'popular' form that feminism is usually found, we tend to celebrate exceptional individual women." The debate surrounding the figure of the heroine often calls for a new theory of individuality, one that recognizes the importance of the individual in social movements but also understands the history and ideology of the term.

Most feminist literary theorists agree that one of the ways literature functions in society is in providing role models. Brownstein writes

that this is one of the central reasons why women read: "The operative fantasy dominating both reader and novel . . . is becoming a heroine." Becoming a heroine, however, is a contradictory process. "The idea of becoming a heroine, which can organize the self," Brownstein suggests, "can also enclose it. . . . The image of the heroine . . . makes multiple contradictory suggestions about the illusion of an ideal feminine self." The heroine represents many of the contradictions surrounding women in society. The paradox of the heroine, a paradoxical figure for feminism, can be seen as a challenge to social roles, a figure for questioning the very assumptions that gendered the term "hero" in the first place.

Caroline Reitz

References

Brownstein, Rachel M. *Becoming a Heroine.* New York: Viking, 1982.
Edwards, Lee R. *Psyche as Hero.* Middletown, Conn.: Wesleyan University Press, 1984.
Gallop, Jane. *Around 1981.* New York: Routledge, 1992.
Miller, Casey, and Kate Swift. *The Handbook of Nonsexist Writing.* New York: Harper and Row, 1988.
Robinson, Lillian. *Sex, Class, and Culture.* Bloomington: Indiana University Press, 1978.

Hirsch, Marianne

With the publication of *The Mother/Daughter Plot*, Marianne Hirsch expands the psychoanalytic discussion of the female narrative that she had begun in *The Voyage In* (a collaboration with Elizabeth Abel and Elizabeth Langland). With *The Mother/Daughter Plot*, Hirsch also continues to develop the discussion undertaken by other feminists, such as Nancy Chodorow's *The Reproduction of Mothering* (1978). Hirsch establishes her position within the historical framework of psychoanalysis (and is indebted to Freud), but her location as a critic also remains firmly within the growing field of psychoanalytic feminist theory. In *The Mother/Daughter Plot* Hirsch challenges the existing framework in order to illustrate the need for a new theoretical vantage point. In particular, Hirsch responds to those aspects (such as the Oedipus complex) that limit psychoanalytic description; she seeks ways to escape those aspects of psychoanalytic theory that have resulted in the marginalization of mothers and daughters, the characters she sees as forgotten by both traditional plot structures and by psychoanalytic theory. Hirsch makes use of psychoanalytic methodology to reexamine those neglected characters and theories in relation to the dominant patriarchal tradition within which female plots are written. The text itself is organized chronologically so that Hirsch might examine the historical and social progress in her analysis. After a prelude on "origins and paradigms," Hirsch divides the work into three sections, organized chronologically. This allows Hirsch to examine what she sees as the "silence" of the nineteenth-century mothers and daughters, the contradictions inherent in the post–World War I changes in the mother/daughter relationship and "compulsory heterosexuality," and the ways postmodern theories and fictions of the 1970s and 1980s offer the opportunity of going beyond the limitations of the Oedipal patterns.

Hirsch's more recent work, *Conflicts in Feminism*, which she edited with Evelyn Fox Keller, clarifies how discussions of feminist theory are beset by conflicts. This work, a compilation of essays, examines the problems of difference by exploring critically divisive feminist issues in the United States. The work here attempts to create a new discourse, one that accepts and allows for difference.

Patricia LaRose Pallis

References
Abel, Elizabeth. Marianne Hirsch, and Elizabeth Langland, eds. *The Voyage In: Fictions of Female Development.* Hanover, N.H.: New England University Press, 1983.

Hirsch, Marianne. *The Mother/Daughter Plot: Narratives, Psychoanalysis, Feminism.* Bloomington: Indiana University Press, 1989.

———, and Evelyn Fox Keller, eds. *Conflicts in Feminism.* New York: Routledge, 1990.

HIV Disease
See ACQUIRED IMMUNE DEFICIENCY SYNDROME

Homans, Margaret
Homans's work consistently addresses the problem of the woman writer's search for an adequate language. How can women achieve subjectivity within a language that reproduces their own status as object? Drawing from Anglo American and French feminist theory, Homans argues that these apparently contradictory systems of analysis need to be integrated in order that we may read fully woman's complex relations with language.

In *Bearing the Word*, Homans proposes that women writers necessarily both inhabit and revise the symbolic order: in order to speak they must enter into language, but to speak as women they must refuse its assumptions. Simply "bearing the word" of a male tradition would be to reiterate woman's systemic exclusion from linguistic authority. Working with a Lacanian model of language acquisition in which the maternal must be abandoned, but introducing a revalued mother/daughter relation based on the theories of Nancy Chodorow, Homans identifies a return to literal language and mother-daughter communication as women writers' strategies.

Homans's projected reconciliation of two conflicting feminist theories of language has provided critics with a flexible conceptual model. Her emphasis on women's systemic linguistic alienation has been an important intervention in American feminist criticism.

Anna Wilson

References
Homans, Margaret. *Bearing the Word: Language and Female Experience in Nineteenth-Century Women's Writing.* Chicago: University of Chicago Press, 1986.

———. "Feminist Criticism and Theory: The Ghost of Creusa." *Yale Journal of Criticism* 1 (1987): 153–182.

———. "Feminist Fictions and Feminist Theories of Narrative." *Narrative* 2 (1994): 3–16.

———. "'Her Very Own Howl': The Ambiguities of Representation in Recent Women's Fiction." *Signs* 9 (1983): 186–205.

———. *Women Writers and Poetic Identity: Dorothy Wordsworth, Emily Brontë, and Emily Dickinson.* Princeton: Princeton University Press, 1980.

Home
See DOMESTICITY

Homophobia

Many feminist and antihomophobic agendas share similar goals, in part because they react against the same loci of oppression. For example, feminist and queer theories have examined the misogynistic element of homophobic attacks against lesbians, gay men, and bisexuals. Furthermore, both men and women have had to address the assumption that his/her sexuality or masculinity/femininity is in question if he or she supports feminism. The need to insist on the possibility of a heterosexual female feminist gives cause for many lesbians to note a form of institutional homophobia emanating from within the woman's movement. For a discussion of the overlap between feminist and antihomophobic theories see Eve Kosofsky-Sedgwick's "Introduction: Axiomatic" in *Epistemology of the Closet.*

In many respects the term "homophobia" is an etymological and semantic conundrum. "Homo" does not refer to the greek *homo* meaning "same," but instead it synecdochically refers to "homosexual." Therefore, homophobia is most broadly conceived of as a fear of (phobia), or negative attitude toward, homosexuals or homosexuality. Antihomophobic activists and theorists have taken issue with the word's second half, "phobia," because it suggests a pathological, psychic condition beyond the homophobic person's control; instead, it should be remembered that homophobia is culturally learned as is sexism, racism, and anti-Semitism, and therefore a person is responsible for her or his homophobia. Typical expressions of homophobia are "hate crimes" (violent, physical assaults on people perceived to be homosexual) and institutional homophobia (antihomosexual policies and legislation as well as a simple disregard for issues concerning homosexuals, all of which work to secure the homosexual's cultural invisibility).

Since homophobic logic strongly relies on the assumption that from anatomy follows gender, sex, and sexuality, both feminist and queer literary theory confront homophobia as they problematize the above assumption and renounce "heterosexism," the conviction that all desire is structured heterosexually. Specifically, Adrienne Rich's "Compulsory Heterosexuality and the Lesbian Existence" and Monique Wittig's "The Straight Mind" both explore how heterosexism structures contemporary culture and theory. In addition, Judith Butler's *Gender Trouble* discusses the homophobic and misogynistic cultural presumptions about the sex-gender matrix.

Jon Hodge

References

Butler, Judith. *Gender Trouble: Feminism and the Subversion of Identity.* New York: Routledge, 1990.

———. "Imitation and Gender Insubordination." In *Inside/Out: Lesbian Theories, Gay Theories,* edited by Diana Fuss, 13–31. New York: Routledge, 1991.

Dynes, Wayne, ed. *Encyclopedia of Homosexuality.* New York: Garland, 1990.

Rich, Adrienne. "Compulsory Heterosexuality and Lesbian Existence." *Signs: Journal of Women in Culture and Society* 5 (1980): 631–660.

Sedgwick, Eve Kosofsky. *Epistemology of the Closet.* Berkeley: University of California Press, 1990.

Wittig, Monique. "The Straight Mind." *Feminist Issues* (1980): 103–111.

Homosexuality

Feminism and queer studies have extensively theorized how the semantic boundaries of homosexuality take shape on a lexical map of "related" terms such as homoeroticism, male bonding, gay, lesbian, transvestite, transsexual, heterosexual, homosocial, Boston marriage, sodomite, molly, dandy, dyke, bisexual, and tom boy, just to name a few. Indeed, much influential criticism has worked to expose homosexuality where dominant culture denies its presence (for example in female friendships or male bonding) and challenge the cultural assumptions that all gender-bending and nonnormative sexual activity are bodily expressions of homosexuality. Such a definitional crisis makes apparent that this volume can present only a representative, not an exhaustive, cross-section of criticism concerning homosexuality.

Etymologically, the term predates its antonym, "heterosexual," and is a composite of Greek (*homo,* or "same") and (late) Latin (*sexualis*). *Homosexualität* appeared in German antisodomy pamphlets around 1869 and was quickly adopted by the German sexologists, though it does not appear in English until some twenty-three years later. Michel Foucault argues, in *The History of Sexuality, Volume I: An Introduction,* that as medical discourse appropriated the term, it came to denote a species with an identity, not simply a temporary aberration as its predecessors, like "sodomite," had done. The 1969 Stonewall riots mark the moment when "gay" came into circulation, thus displacing "homosexual." Although both terms are used today, they are not equivalent and a writer may often meditate, in her/his introduction, on the usage of these terms within her/his argument.

Feminist critics have theorized how male and female homosexuality each either advance or resist feminist projects. Lesbian-feminism argues that lesbianism is the only form of liberated sexuality for feminists because it renounces men, and subsequently patriarchy. Material feminists perceive women as commodities which, through their exchange, serve to strengthen the homosocial bonds between men, bonds that have been read as homoerotic. For example, Luce Irigaray argues, in *This Sex Which Is Not One*, that all sexuality in phallogocentric culture is always already male homosexuality—or "ho(m)mo-sexuality," to use her orthographic play in French—and heterosexual exchange serves only to further promote this structuring homosexuality. Eve Kosofsky Sedgwick similarly argues, in *Between Men*, that the rivalry between men for a woman produces a desire for each other that equals the desire for the woman. Some feminist approaches to psychoanalysis, such as the work of Julia Kristeva or Diana Fuss, have returned to the tension between the Freudian notions of "identity" and "desire" to suggest, in part, that the pre-Oedipal, to-be-gendered-female child can erotically cathect her mother. Other feminist readings of psychoanalysis, such as *Male Subjectivity at the Margins* by Kaja Silverman, primarily center on male homosexuality yet touch on feminist issues as well.

Jon Hodge

References

Dynes, Wayne, ed. *Encyclopedia of Homosexuality*. New York: Garland, 1990.

Foucault, Michel. *The History of Sexuality, Volume I: An Introduction*. New York: Vintage Books, 1978.

Fuss, Diana. "Fashion and the Homospectatorial Look." *Critical Inquiry* 18 (1992): 713–737.

———. "Freud's Fallen Women: Identification, Desire, and 'A Case of Homosexuality in a Woman.'" *Yale Journal of Criticism* 6 (1993): 1–23.

Irigaray, Luce. *This Sex Which Is Not One*. Translated by Catherine Porter. Ithaca, N.Y.: Cornell University Press, 1985.

———. *Epistemology of the Closet*. Berkeley: University of California Press, 1990.

Kristeva, Julia. *Desire in Language: A Semiotic Approach to Literature and Art*. Translated by Thomas Gora, Alice Jardine, and Leon S. Roudiez. Edited by Leon S. Roudiez. New York: Columbia University Press, 1980.

Sedgwick, Eve Kosofsky. *Between Men: English Literature and Male Homosocial Desire*. New York: Columbia University Press, 1985.

Silverman, Kaja. *Male Subjectivity at the Margins*. New York: Routledge, 1992.

Homosociality

Homosociality refers to the broad range of socially structured interactions between people of the same sex. Such interactions include but are not limited to gay and lesbian sexuality. The concept of homosociality emerged in the wake of the explosion of gay and lesbian theory in the early 1980s, and has been used primarily to investigate same-sex interactions that are not overtly sexual. These investigations are crucial to feminism because they unveil structures of power, knowledge, and oppression not immediately available to interrogations of relationships between the sexes.

In the work of the most significant feminist theorist of homosociality, Eve Kosofsky Sedgwick, homosocial relationships function as structures of exchange. Sedgwick's *Between Men: English Literature and Male Homosocial Desire* examines a wide spectrum of mostly British texts from the Renaissance to the Victorian era. She evaluates the ways men in these texts foster and consolidate their bonds with other men by literally or symbolically exchanging women, frequently as sexual objects. These male bonds take a variety of forms, and serve a variety of functions: the establishment of a normative nuclear family, the construction of the bourgeois male as the representative modern subject, and the drawing of lines of power, especially economic power, as Britain hurtled toward the industrial revolution and empire.

To the extent that patriarchal society is structured around male-male relationships, investigations of male homosociality allow for new critques of patriarchy that are not based on simple models of female oppression. The study of female homosocial relationships holds similar potential. bell hooks, for instance, discusses the need for female "sisterhood" to move beyond an uncritical support for women as women, and toward a structured relationship between women that is geared toward social change.

Terence Brunk

References

Rousseau, G.S. "The Sorrows of Priapus: Anticlericalism, Homosocial Desire, and Richard Payne Knight." In *Sexual Underworlds of the Enlightenment*, edited by G.S. Rousseau and Roy Porter, 101–153. Chapel Hill: University of North Carolina Press, 1988.

Schleiner, Winifred. "La feu cache: Homosocial Bonds between Women in a Renaissance Romance." *Renaissance Quarterly* 45 (1992): 293–311.

Sedgwick, Eve Kosofsky. *Between Men: English Literature and Male Homosocial Desire*. New York: Columbia University Press, 1985.

Van Leer, David. "The Beast of the Closet: Homosociality and the Pathology of Manhood." *Critical Inquiry* 15 (1989): 587–605.

hooks, bell

Since the publication of *Ain't I a Woman: Black Women and Feminism* in 1981, hooks (also Gloria Watkins; bell hooks is her great grandmother's name, which she chose to adopt) has occupied a complex position in American letters. A professional academic, she chooses to write for a wider audience. She consistently advocates a radical and anticapitalist politics in her writing while at the same time critiquing what she sees to be the failures, shortfalls, and blind spots in contemporary political movements such as feminism, black nationalism, and New Left politics. Self-described as a black woman advocating feminism, her work has been consistent in its focus on black women and its refusal to dodge difficult racial and gendered issues, such as the controversy over the representations of black male figures in African American women's writing. As indicated in the title of her second book *Feminist Theory: From Margin to Center*, hooks, is interested in how women position themselves in relation to au-

thority and dominant structures. The vantage point of the margin as a site of resistance (as well as repression) is a theme in her work that serves to explain her construction of herself as a populist academic, a purposefully marginalized critic. The accessibility and forcefulness of her writing have made her widely read, especially in women's studies courses.

hooks is a prolific writer and a wide-ranging cultural critic who does not limit herself to her disciplinary base in English and women's studies. She published a book a year between 1989 and 1993, including a collaboration with black intellectual and religious leader Cornel West called *Breaking Bread: Insurgent Black Intellectual Life*. Increasingly, her politicized critique addresses issues of popular culture, contemporary representations of blacks in film and television, and consumerism. *Sisters of the Yam: Black Women and Self-Recovery* is an African Americanized self-help book that draws heavily on hooks's own experiences rooted in Southern black community. As in all of her work, its popular appeal is leavened with passionate political commitment to effective struggle against racist, sexist, and capitalist oppression.

Laura Quinn

References

hooks, bell. *Ain't I a Woman: Black Women and Feminism*. Boston: South End, 1981.

———. *Black Looks: Race and Representation*. Boston: South End, 1992.

———. *Breaking Bread: Insurgent Black Intellectual Life*. Boston: South End, 1991.

———. *Feminist Theory: From Margin to Center*. Boston: South End, 1984.

———. *Sisters of the Yam: Black Women and Self-Recovery*. Boston: South End, 1993.

———. *Talking Back: Thinking Feminist, Thinking Black*. Boston: South End, 1989.

———. *Yearning: Race, Gender and Cultural Politics*. Boston: South End, 1990.

Howe, Florence

A literary scholar, historian, and feminist teacher, Howe is also the director (and one of the founders) of the Feminist Press. An early practitioner of women's studies and a professor of English at the City University of New York, Howe was one of the first scholars to write about the gender politics of education, identi-

H

fying education as an act that "controls destinies." To this end, much of her work has focused on removing legal, social, and economic obstacles to women in the American educational system. In her role as the first chair of the Modern Language Association's Commission of the Status of Women (1969–1971), Howe challenged the legality of discriminatory employment practices in higher education.

Her books include *No More Masks! An Anthology of American Women Poets*, with Ellen Bass, and *Myths of Coeducation*, a collection of Howe's classic feminist essays, written from 1964 to 1983. The essays address many topics, including the images of women in American literature, feminist teaching methods, and the future of women's colleges; the essays are accessible and impassioned, combining research, autobiography, and literary references. In 1979, Howe edited a collection of essays that celebrate women working; *Women Working* treats both paid and unpaid labor, and demonstrates the goal-oriented, pragmatic approach used in women's studies classrooms. *Women and Higher Education in American History* concentrates on the history of women college students.

Wendy C. Wahl

References

Howe, Florence. *Myths of Coeducation: Selected Essays. 1964–1983*. Bloomington: Indiana University Press, 1984.
———. *Women and the Power to Change*. New York: McGraw-Hill, 1975.
———, ed. *Tradition and the Talents of Women*. Urbana: University of Illinois Press, 1991.
———, ed. *Women and Higher Education in American History: Essays from the Mount Holyoke College Sesquicentennial Symposia*. New York: W.W. Norton, 1988.
———, et al., eds. *Mother to Daughter, Daughter to Mother: Mothers on Mothering: A Daybook and Reader*. New York: Feminist, 1984.
———, et. al., eds. *No More Masks! An Anthology of American Women Poets*. New York: Doubleday, 1973.
———, et al., eds. *With Wings: An Anthology of Literature by and about Women with Disabilities*. Westbury, N.Y.: Feminist, 1987.
———, et al., eds. *Women Working: An Anthology of Stories and Poems*. Westbury, N.Y.: Feminist, 1979.

Hull, Gloria T.

As one of the pioneers in the field of African American feminist studies, Gloria Hull has devoted the last twenty years of her professional life to teaching and studying African American women's texts, as well as promoting black women's studies as an academic discipline. Hull's landmark, award-winning work (edited with Patricia Bell Scott and Barbara Smith), *All the Women Are White, All the Blacks Are Men, but Some of Us Are Brave: Black Women's Studies*, represented the first interdisciplinary reference text and pedagogical tool published for black feminist studies. The lack of resources on black women's experiences, both within and outside the academy, led Hull and her co-editors to compile a collection of essays, bibliographies, and sample course syllabi focusing on a range of issues affecting African American women. Thus one of Hull's primary contributions to literary theory has been to foster the study of African American women's literature, a now thriving field of academic inquiry.

A scholar and educator whose mission is to integrate her class-conscious, anticapitalist, feminist political stance into every enterprise, Hull, in *All the Women Are White*, views research and literary criticism not as "an academic/intellectual game, but [as] a pursuit with social meanings rooted in the 'real world.'" As a professor of English and women's studies, Hull has focused her frequently biographically based scholarship primarily on the recovery of little-known black women poets from the Harlem Renaissance. Her work has also filled gaps in the study of African American women writers by focusing both on lesser-known literary figures and on less traditional literary genres—diaries and professional journalistic writing, for example. She has also produced critical work on the poetry and fiction of more contemporary writers such as Audre Lorde and Toni Cade Bambara.

Hull is important to feminist literary theory for her recovery of "lost" women authors, for her groundbreaking work in teaching and writing about the texts of black women, and for recognizing the need for a specifically race- and class-conscious feminist approach to literature.

Kimberley Roberts

References

Hull, Gloria. *Color, Sex, and Poetry: Three Women Writers of the Harlem Renaissance.* Bloomington: Indiana University Press, 1987.

———. *Healing Heart: Poems 1973–1988.* Latham, N.Y.: Kitchen Table: Women of Color Press, 1989.

———, ed. *Give Us Each Day: The Diary of Alice Dunbar-Nelson.* New York: W.W. Norton, 1984.

———, ed. *The Works of Alice Dunbar-Nelson.* 3 vols. New York: Oxford University Press, 1988.

———, et al., eds. *All the Women Are White, All the Blacks Are Men, but Some of Us Are Brave: Black Women's Studies.* Old Westbury, N.Y.: Feminist, 1982.

Hurston, Zora Neale

A major twentieth-century African American woman writer, Hurston authored prize-winning short stories, plays, essays, four published novels including the classic *Their Eyes Were Watching God*, two anthropological narratives/collections of African American and African Caribbean folklore and voodoo practices, and her autobiography, *Dust Tracks on a Road*. A key figure of the period labeled the Harlem Renaissance, Hurston was important for creative and anthropological work on Southern black folk culture and for her spirited and often controversial presence in the rich cultural milieu of Harlem in the twenties. Her work, her life, and her critical history have all entered into late-twentieth-century thinking on a range of issues, including the representation of race and gender in literature to canon formation, gendered and racialized linguistic practices, black feminist (or womanist) identity and spirituality, and the relationship between ethnographer and informant in social science research.

Led by the efforts of contemporary writer Alice Walker, Hurston has been canonized within an African American women's literary tradition and claimed as a crucial forebear of writers like Alice Walker, Toni Morrison, Toni Cade Bambara, Gloria Naylor, and Paule Marshall. These efforts represent a claim to literary and critical authority on the part of black women writers—the authority to determine one's literary lineage and to participate in the formation of a canon. Hurston's writing is often read as being about the empowerment of women. While her best known novel, *Their Eyes Were Watching God,* is the most frequently invoked narrative of empowerment, some readings of her other works—including the anthropological *Mules and Men*—find evidence of successfully negotiated female empowerment, resistance, and agency in very traditional rural Southern settings. The complexity and cultural richness of Hurston's work and life story continue to generate critical interest on the part of African American and feminist scholars.

Laura Quinn

References

Hemenway, Robert. *Zora Neale Hurston: A Literary Biography.* Urbana: University of Illinois Press, 1977.

Holloway, Karla F.C. *The Character of the Word: The Texts of Zora Neale Hurston.* Westport, Conn.: Greenwood, 1987.

Hurston, Zora Neale. *Dust Tracks on a Road.* Philadelphia: J.B. Lippincott, 1942. 2nd ed. Urbana: University of Illinois Press, 1984.

———. *I Love Myself When I Am Laughing . . . and Then Again When I Am Looking Mean and Impressive: A Zora Neale Hurston Reader.* Edited by Alice Walker. Old Westbury, N.Y.: Feminist, 1979.

———. *Jonah's Gourd Vine.* Philadelphia: J.B. Lippincott, 1934. Reprinted with introduction by Larry P. Neal, 1971. Reprinted with foreword by Rita Dove. New York: Harper and Row, 1990.

———. *Moses, Man of the Mountain.* Philadelphia: J.B. Lippincott, 1939. Urbana: University of Illinois Press, 1984.

———. *Mules and Men.* Philadelphia: J.B. Lippincott, 1935. New York: Harper and Row, 1990.

———. *Seraph on the Suwanee.* New York: Scribners', 1948.

———. *Tell My Horse.* Philadelphia: J.B. Lippincott, 1938. New York: Harper and Row, 1990.

——— *Their Eyes Were Watching God.* Philadelphia: J.B. Lippincott, 1937. Urbana: University of Illinois Press, 1978. Reprinted with a foreword by Mary Helen Washington. New York: Harper and Row, 1990.

Newson, Adele S. *Zora Neale Hurston: A Reference Guide.* Boston: G.K. Hall, 1987.

Walker, Alice. *In Search of Our Mother's Gardens: Womanist Prose.* New York: Harcourt Brace Jovanovich, 1983.

Hysteria

Hysteria shows itself in bodily symptoms for which there is no apparent organic cause. The disorder has a long history in the annals of medicine and psychiatry, having been the subject of the earliest known medical document, the Egyptian *Kahun Papyrus*, circa 1900 B.C., which describes a series of morbid states attributed to displacement of the uterus, so-called "wandering womb" diseases. This theory of displacement, further developed by Hippocratic writings, gave hysteria its name, after the Greek word for womb. Plato's *Timaeus* describes the womb as an animal that longs to generate children, and claims that when a woman remains barren too long after puberty, her womb becomes distressed and strays around in her body, cutting off the breath and provoking extreme anguish until it is appeased by passion and love.

This idea was revised in Freud's early commentaries on hysteria, in which he traced disturbances in the erotic sphere as the origin of hysterical symptoms, which he saw as signs of a story repressed by the psyche. Freud seems to have put Timaeus's notions together with the concept of "hysteresis" in physics, where it refers to the time lag exhibited by a body in reacting to changes in forces affecting it. In hysteresis, the reaction of a system to changes is dependent on its past reactions to change. Thus, in Freud's first theory of hysteria, the theory Ernest Jones named "the seduction theory," Freud postulated that hysterical symptoms were a delayed response to having suffered sexual invasion in infancy or early childhood, and having repressed the memory of that unpleasant experience. Freud later altered this theory, redefining hysteria as a delayed response to fantasies of infantile sexual experiences revived during adolescence upon the reawakening of strong sexual urges and the development of mature genitality. Now that the person has become sexually mature, he or she grasps the significance and affects associated with childhood sexual scenes, and abreacts, in repressed form, emotions appropriate to those earlier scenes. These scenes remain, however, warded off by the hysteric's consciousness.

This latter explanation of hysteria has generally not been well received by feminists.

Catherine Clément, in *The Newly Born Woman*, scoffs at Freud's displacements of guilt in his various rewritings of the narrative of the production of hysteria. Examining how Freud's altered views made the guilt of fathers ultimately fictional, Clément points out that Freud's first theory in 1896 blamed the father as the guilty one: hysterics are victims of (usually paternal) sexual aggression. In Freud's altered, Oedipal narrative, which Clément titles "The Lying Daughters," he proposes that the hysteric's traumatic scenes were not real but based on something heard, bits of family legend perhaps. The guilt in this explanation is the daughter's: the hysteric, projecting her own repressed desires to sleep with her father, fantasizes she has been seduced. According to Clément, Freud's final theory of seduction, as articulated in "Femininity" in 1933, makes the mother guilty. In this essay, Freud writes that the fantasy of seduction by the father is an effect of the child's Oedipus complex, whereas it is through the mother's (or nursemaid's) bodily contacts with the child that this fantasy touches the ground of reality. Thus, indicates Clément, the guilt associated with the onset of the hysteric's sexuality has wandered from father to daughter to mother, where, in Freud's view, it touches ground.

This displacement of guilt was reversed in the 1970s by the Parisian women's liberation group Psychanalyse et Politique, whose revival of the lost narrative of incestuous child abuse Freud had dropped from his official theorization helped to open the way for the voluminous accounts by victims of incest that continue to be made public in France, the United Kingdom, the United States, and elsewhere. Indeed, Freud himself had vacillated throughout his career between his contradictory narratives and never stopped believing in the harmful psychological consequences of the sexual abuse of children. Mary Jacobus has pointed out that in *Studies on Hysteria*, where the incest narrative of hysteria was suppressed as a result of Breuer's influence on Freud at the time of the book's composition, incest as a theme nevertheless appears in the form of footnotes to the text and in subplots to the main narratives of Freud's case histories.

As a result of Lacan's French commentaries on and French revival of the early works of Freud, hysteria has become a hot topic again. The current wave of fascination with hysteria encompasses historians of medicine and psychiatry, social historians, historians of consciousness, dramatists and performers, psycho-analytic writers, and literary critics, both feminist and nonfeminist. More specifically, thanks to the resurgence of women's movements, among other factors, hysteria, traditionally pejoratively associated with femininity, has received a massive, complex, and extremely ambivalent reworking. Since hysteria is perceived as emotion in excess of the facts as they appear, and women's emotional expressivity has traditionally been more acceptable than states of lost control in men, hysteria has been interpreted by some feminists as a strong and legitimate form of femininity. Juliet Mitchell has gone as far as to claim that "feminism is the demand *for* the right to be hysterical." Similarly, in tracing from hysteric to feminist the career of Bertha Pappenheim (Breuer's famous patient, a.k.a. Anna O.), both Hunter and Herndl argue that Pappenheim's hysteria was cured by writing. Hunter and Herndl, like Elaine Showalter, see hysteria as protofeminist expression, a protocreativity otherwise lacking an outlet in patriarchal society. Among those feminists who valorize hysteria (Irigaray, Cixous, Hunter, Showalter, and Herndl), a prevailing idea is that hysteria is a repudiated form of discourse, a feminine body language addressed to patriarchal thought. In this light, nineteenth-century sufferers of "big hysteria" can be seen as threshold figures for the spectacular gains in theory and practice worked out by the twentieth-century women's movements in writing, the performing arts, and other arenas where power is on display.

French influence on contemporary feminist thinking about hysteria has taken the form of application of psychoanalysis to the understanding of social interactions, especially as they involve power and gender. Thus Lacanian thinkers see hysterics as wanting to be at the center of the generation of knowledge. A hysteric seeks a master to baffle so the hysteric can undermine the master's authority and perhaps supersede it; alternatively, the hysteric poses the question, "Am I a man? Am I a woman?" and looks to the master to supply an answer to this uncertainty. Clinically, the hysteric's narrative usually involves these elements: (a) a father who failed—he either died, was incestuous, went bankrupt, or failed in some other or combination of ways to embody patriarchal law or authority; (b) idealization of a woman outside the hysteric's immediate biological family circle; (c) a love/hate relationship to the body of the mother; and (d) the posing of an enigma that generates new insight in the domain of cultural authority. Beyond these scenarios, one can also see hysteria as a negotiation of creativity separate from childbirth, a way of giving birth to new knowledge, or a new way of perceiving reality, as Dianne Hunter argues.

For some feminists, hysteria's "cure" lies in the social transformation attendant on critique of patriarchal ideologies, including psychoanalysis, the chief domain, along with literary criticism, in which hysteria remains a topic of discourse. In *Fits and Starts,* Evans concludes, "As a manifestation of what is unacceptable to consciousness, hysteria has consistently evoked counterreactions of denial, isolation, confinement, and control. As long as gender difference continues to carry the ideological weight it has been assigned, femininity will continue to be construed as a disorder, and hysteria will continue to return, like the repressed, as a mystifying, uncanny neurosis." That is, as long as our social institutions are dominated by the idea that men are sturdy pillars of rationality and control, while women are idealized as loving mothers without the aggression, desire, or talent required for other achievements, hysteria will exist to give that idea the lie.

Feminist studies of hysteria have exploded its exclusive assignment to women, as had Freud, and Charcot before him. Male hysteria has been studied by Showalter, Jacobus, Kahane, and Micale. Appignanesi and Forrester, and Gilman, have illuminated Freud's own hysteria, as well as his feminine identifications. In literary criticism, hysteria has been used as an interpretive category for unpacking narratives characterized by internal contradictoriness (Jacobus and Hunter in 1993); preoccupation with castration and displacement (Hertz, reprinted in Bernheimer and Kahane); gaps, incoherencies, multiple perspectives, and a repressed feminine identification in the narrator (Sprengnether, reprinted in Bernheimer and Kahane; Evans, reprinted in Bernheimer and Kahane).

Dianne Hunter

References

Appignanesi, L., and J. Forrester. *Freud's Women.* London: Weidenfeld and Nicolson, 1992.

Bernheimer, Charles, and Claire Kahane, eds. *In Dora's Case.* New York: Columbia University Press, 1985.

Cixous, Hélène. *Benmussa Directs: Portrait of Dora.* Translated by A. Barrows. Dallas: Riverrun, 1979.

Clément, Catherine, and Hélène Cixous. *The Newly Born Woman.* Translated by B. Wing. Minneapolis: University of Minnesota Press, 1986.

Evans, Martha Noel. *Fits and Starts: A Genealogy of Hysteria in Modern France.* Ithaca, N.Y.: Cornell University Press, 1991.

———. "Hysteria and the Seduction of Theory." *Seduction and Theory,* edited by Dianne Hunter, 73–85. Urbana: University. of Illinois Press, 1989.

———. *"Portrait de Dora:* Freud's Case History as Reviewed by Hélène Cixous." *Sub-stance* 36 (1982): 64–71.

Gilman, Sander, H. King, R. Porter, G.S. Rousseau, and E. Showalter. *Hysteria beyond Freud.* Berkeley: University of California Press, 1993.

Goldstein, Jan. "The Hysteria Diagnosis and the Politics of Anticlericalism in Late Nineteenth-Century France." *Journal of Modern History* 54 (1982): 209–239.

Herndl, Diane Price. "The Writing Cure: Charlotte Perkins Gilman, Anna O., and 'Hysterical' Writing." *NWSA Journal 1* (1988): 52–74.

Hunter, Dianne. "Hysteria, Psychoanalysis, and Feminism: The Case of Anna O." In *The (M)other Tongue,* edited by Shirley Garner, M. Sprengnether, and C. Kahane, 89–115. Ithaca, N.Y.: Cornell University Press, 1985.

———. "Representing Mad Contradictoriness in *Dr. Charcot's Hysteria Shows."* In *Themes in Drama 15: Madness,* edited by J. Redmon, 93–118. Cambridge University Press, 1993.

Irigaray, Luce. *Speculum of the Other Woman.* Translated by G. Gill. Ithaca, N.Y.: Cornell University Press, 1985.

Jacobus, Mary. *Reading Woman.* New York: Columbia University Press, 1986.

Kahane, Claire. "*The Bostonians* and the Figure of the Speaking Woman." In *Psychoanalysis and . . . ,* edited by Richard Feldstein and H. Sussman, 163–174. New York: Routledge, 1990.

McCall, A., C. Pajaczkowska, A. Tyndall, and J. Weinstock. "Dora Script." *Framework* 15–17 (1981): 75–81.

Micale, Mark S. "Hysteria and Its Historiography: The Future Perspective." *History of Psychiatry* 1 (March 1990): 33–124.

———. "Hysteria and Its Historiography: A Review Past and Present Writings (I & II)." *History of Science* 27 (1989): 223–261, 319–351.

Mitchell, Juliet. *Women: The Longest Revolution.* New York: Pantheon, 1984.

Ragland-Sullivan, Ellie. "Hysteria." In *Feminism and Psychoanalysis: A Critical Dictionary,* edited by E. Wright, 163–166. Oxford: Basil Blackwell, 1992.

Showalter, Elaine. *The Female Malady.* New York: Pantheon, 1985.

———. "Representing Ophelia." In *Shakespeare and the Question of Theory,* edited by Patricia Parker and G. Hartman, 77–94. New York: Methuen, 1985.

Smith-Rosenberg, Carroll. "The Hysterical Woman: Sex Roles and Role Conflict in Nineteenth-Century America." In *Disorderly Conduct,* edited by Carroll Smith-Rosenberg, 197–216. New York: Oxford University Press, 1985.

Willis, Sharon. "A Symptomatic Narrative." *Diacritics* 13 (1983): 46–60.

I

Identity

Identity is understood both in terms of a sameness that is shared within a given system and the differences that deviate from that sameness. For feminism these junctures and fissures are relevant because they point to the desired equality of women and the needs of women as different.

Simone de Beauvoir, in *The Second Sex* (1949), defines women as the absolute Other of men. There are no biological, psychological, or economic destinies that define women, rather social and political forces that influence their relationship to each other and to men. While some feminists still accept Beauvoir's notion of women's identity, Luce Irigaray maintains that Beauvoir's entire structure of representation is inadequate because both the subject and the Other are part of "a closed phallogocentric signifying economy that achieves its totalizing goal through the exclusion of the feminine altogether."

For the feminism of the 1960s and 1970s, identity is defined in terms of all women's common oppression and the belief that women may join across all national and cultural boundaries to create a society free of domination. Arguments for an essentialist notion of identity in which all women share common goals are articulated. These ideas echo Virginia Woolf's ideals put forth in *Three Guineas* (1939): "As a woman I have no country. As a woman I want no country. As a woman my country is the whole world." It is also a time when feminists celebrate the geographical location within, the female body, as do the French feminists who articulate the theory of *écriture féminine*. Breasts, the uterus, and the clitoris become symbols of a new source of authority, debunking the patriarchal, morphological inscriptions of a lacking, incomplete, or inadequate body. For Julia Kristeva, women's bodies accent "process" and "differentiation," thus deflating the notion of a fixed, unchanging identity.

In the 1980s and 1990s, the focus of identity shifts to its differences. The essentialist view is contrasted with the social-constructionist view, which argues more for a social basis that constructs identity rather than an ahistorical essence. White feminist studies are criticized for their self-aggrandizement and for their disregard of race, ethnicity, class, nationality, able-bodiedness, and other locations. Barbara Smith, Trinh T. Minh-ha, and others reexamine identity and locate its shortcomings. Minh-ha, in *Woman, Native, Other*, explains that identity—the pattern of sameness in a human life—denies the differences or deviations that simultaneously form the "I." Judith Butler also suggests that the feminist "we" is a "phantasmagoric construction." She urges that identity no longer be thought of in epistemological terms, that is, as an inert substance, but be relocated within practices of signification. Identity needs to be defined in terms of its effects, not its foundational restrictions. This rethinking of the category of identity lends itself to other configurations of genders, bodies, and politics itself.

Feminist writing on identity has given and continues to give a rich and complex picture of the intersections between the personal and the political and, as Diana Fuss maintains in *Essentially Speaking*, cannot be summed up as a binary opposition between essentialist and constructionist perspectives. Deciphering the interplay of female identity requires a variety of critical approaches from political to sociological to philosophical and more. The definition of identity will continue to evolve with changes in social, political, and individual institutions.

Carolyn A. Nadeau

References

Butler, Judith. *Gender Trouble. Feminism and the Subversion of Identity.* New York: Routledge, 1990.

Díaz-Diocaretz, Myriam, and Iris M. Zavala, eds. *Women, Feminist Identity and Society in the 1980's: Selected Papers.* Philadelphia: John Benjamins, 1985.

Fuss, Diana. *Essentially Speaking; Feminism, Nature & Difference.* New York: Routledge, 1989.

Hull, Gloria T., Patricia Bell Scott, and Barbara Smith, eds. *All the Women Are White, All the Men Are Black, But Some of Us Are Brave.* Old Westbury, N.Y.: Feminist, 1982.

Irigaray, Luce. *The Sex Which Is Not One.* Translated by Catherine Porter and Carolyn Burke. Ithaca, N.Y.: Cornell University Press, 1985.

Kristeva, Julia. "Woman Can Never Be Defined." Translated by Marilyn A. August. In *New French Feminisms. An Anthology,* edited by Elaine Marks and Isabelle de Courtivron, 137–140. Amherst: University of Massachusetts Press, 1980.

Minh-ha, Trinh T. *Woman, Native, Other. Writing Postcoloniality and Feminism.* Bloomington: Indiana University Press, 1989.

Nicholson, Linda, ed. *Feminism/Postmodernism.* New York: Routledge, 1990.

Riley, Denise. *"Am I That Name?" Feminism and the Category of "Women" in History.* Minneapolis: University of Minnesota Press, 1988.

Identity Politics

In current usage, as Diana Fuss explains, the term "refers to the tendency to base one's politics on a sense of personal identity." This "personal identity" can be multivalent; perhaps the most common identity politics today are those centered around identities involving race, gender, sexuality, religion, and ability. The groups these common identity politics represent include women of color, black feminists, gays and lesbians, Jews, and the disabled. (Notably, for feminism, questions of identity are rooted in feminist revisions of psychoanalysis.) The issues that the term "identity politics" raises for feminism are similar to those for other social movements. The two main debates center on the conflict between essentialists and social constructionists, and the opposition of identity politics to coalition politics.

On one hand, identity politics often depend on a belief in an essentialist—a stable, universal, and definable—notion of identity. For example, feminist essentialists argue that all women naturally share the same interests and traits because of their very natures. Often feminist essentialists such as Luce Irigaray speak of the theoretical "woman," as opposed to discrete "women," to indicate this universal nature. This construction is often found in radical feminism, and is also associated with French feminists who subscribe to the theory of *écriture féminine*. For essentialists, then, there is a universal sameness among women, and a basic, innate difference between men and women.

On the other hand, feminist social constructionists such as Judith Butler argue that the notion of an ahistorical essence should not be the foundation of feminism or feminist inquiry. Rather, they believe that one's gender/identity is a production of one's social surroundings—of culture and of language. That is to say, gender differs in various contexts, and that gender intersects at all times with one's other defining (and socially constructed) characteristics, such as race, sexuality, class, ethnicity, ability, and nationality. According to this argument, then, difference is not innate but is, rather, constructed. Often, social constructionists speak of "women" rather than woman, though even this term is problematic for many of them. Diana Fuss's *Essentially Speaking* has figured most prominently in this debate insofar as it argues that the essentialism/constructionism opposition is an "overvalued binarism." *Essentially Speaking* argues that, rather than being simply opposed to each other, the two notions are theoretically dependent upon one another.

The conflict between identity politics and coalition politics is parallel to the conflict between essentialism and social constructionism. There is a sense with identity politics that women will naturally band together and find a sort of "home" in feminism. But, as Bernice Johnson Reagon declares, "Coalition work is not done in your home." Donna Haraway's figure of the cyborg lends rhetorical power to the notion of feminist coalition—feminists linked by "affinity, not identity." For coalition politics, chosen political interests are at the forefront of the collective, not essential identity. Haraway's and Reagon's readings of identity politics underscore one of the critical questions for feminism: Is feminist literary theory at base an academic, a political, or a personal practice?

Nina Manasan Greenberg

References

Anzaldúa, Gloria. *Borderlands/La Frontera: The New Mestiza*. San Francisco: Spinsters/Aunt Lute, 1987.

Butler, Judith. *Gender Trouble; Feminism and the Subversion of Identity*. New York: Routledge, 1990.

Fuss, Diana. *Essentially Speaking; Feminism, Nature & Difference*. New York: Routledge, 1989.

Haraway, Donna. "A Manifesto for Cyborgs: Science, Technology, and Socialist Feminism in the 1980s." In *Coming to Terms; Feminism, Theory, Politics*, edited by Elizabeth Weed, 173–204. New York: Routledge, 1989.

Moraga, Cherríe, and Gloria Anzaldúa, eds. *This Bridge Called My Back; Writings by Radical Women of Color*. Watertown, Mass.: Persephone, 1981. 2nd ed. New York: Kitchen Table: Women of Color Press, 1983.

Reagon, Bernice Johnson. "Coalition Politics: Turning the Century." In *HOME GIRLS: A Black Feminist Anthology*, edited by Barbara Smith, 356–368. New York: Kitchen Table: Women of Color Press, 1983.

Riley, Denise. *"Am I That Name?" Feminism and the Category of "Women" in History*. Minneapolis: University of Minnesota Press, 1988.

Ideology

This highly contested term is most often defined as a system of ideas that determines how we conceive of ourselves and culture. For many feminist theorists the term has come to mean specifically a system of ideas that creates an oppressive, false vision of femininity and female experience. Using such feminist paradigms, ideology may be detected in contemporary and historical social formations by examining what qualities and characteristics have been associated with the biological sex we call female. The social meaning of "woman," how women live their daily lives, to what ideals they are expected to conform, and how their experience is defined and delimited—all form the core of a feminist understanding of ideology.

Originally coined in late-eighteenth-century France, the term "ideology" was later defined by Karl Marx in his preface to *A Contribution to the Critique of Political Economy* as "the definite forms of social consciousness" that legitimate the ruling class. According to Marx, this consciousness was determined by the material conditions the worker was subject to, which thus affected the worker's conception of life. Ideology, then, has been traditionally associated with a system of class, class consciousness, and power. Because much of the work of Marx and Frederick Engels sidesteps the special status of women in a capitalist society, many feminist theorists have substituted "gender" for "class" as the source of the primary form of consciousness. Other feminist theorists believe that such a substitution simply reduces the issues of gender to those of class and cannot account for the many differences between those two categories. Yet the term ideology is very often appropriated in feminist analyses of structures that oppress women.

In a classical Marxist sense, social meaning depends on prevailing economic structures. The "superstructure" is made up of political, legal, and religious institutions, as well as ideas about ethics and aesthetics, literature, and art. The "base" or "infrastructure" consists of the economic system. It includes the production, distribution, and consumption of goods. The base accounts for the organization of labor into those who own the means of production and those who must sell their labor to function within such a system. The base cannot be said to determine the superstructure, or vice versa, but both may participate in how the other is conceived, structured, or transformed. This more or less reciprocal relationship reveals, in the words of Louis Althusser, that "ideology has a material existence." That is, ideology adheres to such "material" structures as the church and the state. While a base/superstructure formulation is very useful for looking at matters of class, because it assumes that a worker may exchange labor for cash, it may well prove unsatisfactory when examining matters of gender and relations among men and women, in part because women are most often not paid for domestic labor and were not until this century active in the public work force. In many ways, "sex" as the biological designation of male and female has come to have an analytical function similar to "base" in Marxist theory. Meanwhile, "gender" represents the system of meaning in which so-called feminine qualities have come to be associated with being female. This system of signification forms a fairly cohesive ideology that constructs an ideal that may not conform to women's actual experience or to their actions.

While one may see that many qualities of femininity have been lined up under the designation female, such qualities do not remain fixed or transcendent; in other words, what it means to be female and feminine now is quite different, for example, from what it meant to be female in the nineteenth century. Ideology is not static as the production of meaning in society; ideology is historically specific. In *Marxism and Literature*, Raymond Williams reveals how ideologies, or ruling ideas of a ruling class, shift across time, so that at any one cultural moment one may detect bits of old forms that may be said to be nearly outmoded (which he calls residual); emerging or new ideas, some of which have not yet been institutionalized or recognized (designated emergent); and dominant patterns of consciousness and social relations. The purpose of such analytical categories is not to draw neat lines in historical formations, but to give historians and literary and cultural critics tools for understanding the complex nature of history and ideology and to reveal how contradictory modes may be present simultaneously.

One can see such shifts, for example, in American culture. A fairly cohesive ideology of domesticity emerged in the early nineteenth century, which has come to be called "the cult of true womanhood." This ideology measured the good woman as a domestic, pious and religious, selfless, dependent being who was morally superior to men. What we might now call the repressive aspects of this ideology were that women were expected to remain in the home, which meant, among other things, that they could not gain economic parity with men; that they were best married so as to be seen as chaste as well as to have someone to support them because they could not work; and that they should not vote and that they should raise the next generation of citizens. This repressive ideology, embedded in state apparatus that did not allow women to hold property or to vote, was not only part of public institutions, but also simply a code of ethics—in many ways invisible and apparently natural—against which European-American women were measured by their fathers, brothers, friends, and, in short, the whole of society. Although it may be clear to us now that these women's lives were closely circumscribed by patriarchal structures, to say that nineteenth-century European-American women were resolutely innocent and passive, victims of a concept called "false consciousness," implies that women were unable to form ideas about the circumstances of their existence and also avoids the question of how women were able to work within structures and gain a certain measure of power. For early suffragettes this ideology also provided women with a basis to agitate for the right to vote, for property and other civil rights, and gave rise to the first feminist movement. For example, from the dictate that women were pious, religious, morally superior to men, and charged with the duty of raising the next generation of citizens, came the argument that women should then be able to use these qualities to domesticate the public sphere so rife with intemperate men; that, in fact, women should be allowed to vote and make the world safe. A counterattack, however, would cite that women should channel such energies from the private sphere through their husbands, fathers, or other male guardians, because they were too delicate to stand the rigors of analytical thinking and public life.

A century later, by the 1970s and 1980s, the second feminist movement had earned women many rights and had seen an influx of women into the public sphere. During this time, a popular television commercial for a woman's fragrance advertised that a woman should be able to "fry up the bacon, bring it home in a pan, and never, ever, let you forget you're a man"; in the tag line the woman vamped, "'Cuz I'm a woman." Such a representation reveals the ideological expectations of the working woman, while, at the same time, summoning a new vision of the woman who can do it all. This cultural text, like literature, while not a transparent means to understanding social relations and modes of production, represents the relationship between the economic base and the ideological superstructure. At the same time it creates an entirely new idea of what it means to be a woman. The representation becomes a place to negotiate ideology, and it can provide the historian or literary or cultural critic with information about the social formation.

Lisa Blansett

References

Althusser, Louis. "Ideology and the Ideological State Apparatus." In *Lenin and Philosophy*, translated by Ben Brewster, 127–186. New York: Monthly Review, 1971.

Barrett, Michèle. "Ideology and the Cultural Production of Gender." In *Feminist Criticism and Social Change*, edited by Judith Newton and Deborah Rosenfelt, 65–85. New York: Methuen, 1985.

Eagleton, Terry. *Ideology*. New York: Verso, 1991.

———. *Marxism and Literary Criticism*. Berkeley: University of California Press, 1976.

Haraway, Donna J. "'Gender' for a Marxist Dictionary: The Sexual Politics of a Word." In *Simians, Cyborgs, and Women: The Reinvention of Nature*, 127–148. New York: Routledge, 1991.

Jameson, Fredric. *The Political Unconscious*. Ithaca, N.Y.: Cornell University Press, 1981.

McLellan, David. *Ideology*. Minneapolis: University of Minnesota Press, 1986.

Marx, Karl, and Frederick Engels. *The German Ideology*. Edited by C.J. Arthur. New York: International, 1988.

Williams, Raymond. *Marxism and Literature*. Oxford: Oxford University Press, 1977.

Images of Women

As Laura Mulvey puts it, "Consumer society moulds woman's image so that it conforms to a given concept of female sexual appeal." Feminist theorists in the visual and linguistic arts are working to expose and critique sexist imagery "created out of male needs and desires" (Nochlin), while formulating alternatives. While feminist artists and writers are working to produce "more viable, less one-sided imagery" that reflects women's realities rather than male fantasies, feminist critics are calling attention to the ideological content of images of women.

As Linda Nochlin points out, Marxist and materialist critiques of art images, which began in the 1970s, paved the way for feminist ones. Critics such as Nochlin and John Berger were among the first to "analyze women's position in, and relation to, the history of art and representations" (Parker and Pollock). While women are produced as images, their marginal status in the culture as a whole has hampered them from producing images of their own. As Berger puts it, "The 'ideal' spectator is always assumed to be male and the image of the woman is designed to flatter him," hence, these images depict women as passive, sexual, and subservient to men. Art forms such as the nude are particularly problematic for women since they depict women as little more than "an appearance to be enjoyed" (Mulvey); while male viewers may be titillated, female ones are likely to experience an uncomfortable identification with the model that prevents them from seeing the image in the same, appreciative way. Andrea Dworkin believes that pornography, which often depicts women as masochistic, passive, sexually available objects of male violence, contributes to and promotes actual violence against women. She believes that images must be controlled in order to reform sexist practices. While not all feminists condone censorship, all agree that "women's struggles to gain rights over their bodies [cannot] be divorced from questions of image and representation" (Mulvey).

More recent feminist critics, such as de Lauretis and Caws are striving to get beyond debating "good" versus "bad" images of women. While it is important to identify prevailing sexist imagery, most critics agree that it is equally important for women to analyze how historical factors and material social practices have made these images possible. Our culture is so full of imagery that depicts women as merely a "spectacle, object to be looked at, vision of beauty" (de Lauretis) that one must ask "whether any positive visual representation of women is possible at all" (Nochlin). While Nochlin writing in 1972 saw some "signs of change," contemporary popular media such as television, advertising, and film remind us that this change is far from complete. Though the 1970s inaugurated a new willingness to discuss the previously neglected topic of sexist images of women, much more feminist critique of received images, and feminist remaking and recreation of alternative images will be necessary before the culture reflects the experience of both genders.

Lisa Nakamura

References

Berger, John. *Ways of Seeing*. London: British Broadcasting Corporation and Penguin, 1972.

Caws, Mary Ann. "Ladies Shot and Painted:

Female Embodiment in Surrealist Art." In *The Female Body in Western Culture: Contemporary Perspectives*, edited by Susan Rubin Suleiman, 265–287. Cambridge: Harvard University Press, 1986.

de Lauretis, Teresa. *Alice Doesn't: Feminism, Semiotics, Cinema*. Bloomington: Indiana University Press, 1984.

Doane, Mary Ann. *Femmes Fatales: Feminism, Film Theory, Psychoanalysis*. London and New York: Routledge, 1991.

Dworkin, Andrea. *Pornography: Men Possessing Women*. New York: Perigee, 1981.

Mulvey, Laura. *Visual and Other Pleasures*. Bloomington: Indiana University Press, 1989.

Nochlin, Linda. *Women, Art, and Power and Other Essays*. New York: Harper and Row, 1988.

Parker, Rozsika, and Griselda Pollock. *Framing Feminism: Art and the Women's Movement 1970–1985*. London: Pandora (Routledge and Kegan Paul), 1987.

Imperialism

See COLONIALISM

Incest

Representations of incestuous desire and its prohibition have played a major role in the literary, theological, and scientific discourses of the West. Feminist literary theory seeks to understand the connections between the alarming incidence of incestuous abuse in contemporary Western societies and the patriarchal discursive traditions that form the cultural context in which that abuse occurs.

Traditional literary approaches to the representation of incest are of roughly three main types: rhetorical, historicist, and psychoanalytic. Traditional rhetorical criticism looks at how incest functions as a metaphor in literary texts—at how, for example, Satan's incest with Sin in *Paradise Lost* serves as a trope for his narcissistic quest for self-sufficiency, or at how in the Romantic period incest becomes a symbol for the creative self-reflection and isolation of the individual. Traditional historicist critics examine fictional texts in terms of the way they incorporate historical debates surrounding incest; they look at the relationship of the plot of

Hamlet, for example, to Elizabethan controversies regarding a man's marriage to his deceased brother's widow (sometimes called the Levirate marriage). And traditional psychoanalytic criticism approaches literary incest as a projection of universally repressed human drives or of individual authors' unresolved inner conflicts. Feminist literary approaches to incest distinguish themselves from these earlier approaches by their interest in how the multiple dimensions of literary incest—its figurative function, its deployment in historical discourses (be they forensic, medical, moral, or theological), and its assumptions about universal human desire—work together as diverse but interrelated aspects of a system of representation that protects the sexual rights of men over their female relatives.

Incest became a sustained object of feminist analysis in the social sciences in the early 1980s with the publication of Florence Rush's *The Best-Kept Secret* and Judith Lewis Herman's and Lisa Hirschman's *Father-Daughter Incest*, a trend that culminated in 1986 in Diana E.H. Russell's *The Secret Trauma*, a major empirical study of the prevalence of incest in the lives of American girls and women. While the standard dictionary definition of incest as "sexual relations between persons who are so closely related that their marriage is illegal or forbidden by custom" tends to assume that incest involves the mutual consent of two people in an illicit sexual act, these studies argue that the meaning of incest cannot be properly understood outside an analysis of the gender and power inequities that structure the social context in which it occurs. Uncovering an alarming and apparently growing incidence of incestuous abuse in contemporary American families, and demonstrating that the overwhelming majority of these cases involve adult men and female children, these studies initiate a major redefinition of incest; rejecting traditional views of incest as an act of demonic or natural passion, they identify it as a form of violence against children and an abuse of familial power. Analyzing cultural attitudes toward incest from the beginnings of the Judeo-Christian and Greco-Roman traditions and tracing the development of these attitudes into contemporary media representations and proincest lobbies, Rush shows how our culture has tacitly sanctioned the incestuous abuse of (primarily female) children for centuries. For Herman and Hirschman, father-daughter incest becomes "a paradigm of female sexual victimization, . . . an exaggeration of patriarchal family norms, but not a departure from them."

Rush was the first to look at how the development of Freudian psychoanalytic theory has participated in the cultural "conspiracy of silence" surrounding the subject of childhood sexual abuse. On the basis of his clinical experience with hysterical patients, mostly women, Sigmund Freud theorized that hysteria had its roots in childhood sexual trauma. He later repudiated this "seduction theory" of neurosis in favor of the conclusion that his female patients' reports of childhood incestuous experiences, in most cases with their fathers, were not memories of actual events but outgrowths of their own infantile erotic fantasies. His patients' symptoms, he decided, were not caused by real incest but by their own unresolved Oedipal desires. As in the later studies of Alice Miller and Jeffrey Moussaieff Masson, this "Freudian cover-up" emerges for Rush as an exemplary instance of how cultural pressure to protect fathers operates to maintain incest as our society's "most muted crime."

While feminist critics have been exploring representations of rape since at least the early 1980s, only a few feminist literary analyses of incest (by Lynda Boose, Sandra Gilbert, and Jane Gallop) appeared before 1989. That year saw a burgeoning of literary studies concerned with incest or incestuous relations. Among them were Louise DeSalvo's revisionary critical biography of Virginia Woolf—which rereads Woolf's life and work in light of her childhood experience of molestation by her older half-brother, George Duckworth—and two important anthologies of essays: *Daughters and Fathers* and *Refiguring the Father: New Feminist Readings of Patriarchy*. These essays offer theoretical discussions as well as feminist interpretations of representations of incestuous desire in classic and contemporary texts. They consider literary texts as sites for the reinscription of traditional patriarchal plots as well as for resistant reading and revisionary writing. Using a variety of critical methodologies, traditional as well as poststructuralist and Lacanian, they raise questions about how to renegotiate the Oedipal structures of traditional narrative and about how the father-daughter dyad opens out onto and helps to define representations of other intrafamilial relationships (mother-daughter, father-son, father-mother, mother-son, sister-brother, niece-uncle, and so forth). Finally, they explore the operative relationships between incest and the pervasive cultural silencing of women. More recent work by Paula Marantz Cohen and Linda Zwinger seeks to extend and refine these efforts.

While practical studies in the social sciences have focused mainly on the meaning of incestuous acts, one profoundly influential theoretical essay in the field of feminist anthropology approaches the issue of incest in terms of the meaning of its prohibition. This is Gayle Rubin's "The Traffic in Women," which engendered developments in feminist thinking about the problem of incest that both differ from and run parallel to those represented by the work of Rush, Herman and Hirschman, and Russell. Through her critique of the overlapping theories of Freud and the structural anthropologist Claude Lévi-Strauss, Rubin showed how the incest taboo functions as a key factor in the social construction of gender by ensuring the circulation of women among men. By identifying the prohibition against incest with the founding moment of culture, she observed, both psychoanalysis and structural anthropology inscribe the exchange of woman-as-sign as a cultural necessity. Although Rubin's aim was to show that the exchange of women was a historical phenomenon and not a cultural inevitability, her line of reasoning has led some feminists to regard women's violation of the incest prohibition as a potential site of resistance to patriarchy, a refusal of the imperatives of exchange. Gallop, reading French feminist psychoanalyst Luce Irigaray's *Speculum of the Other Woman*, raises this theoretical possibility; and Judith Kegan Gardiner positively valorizes sibling incest in her reading of Aphra Behn's *Love Letters between a Nobleman and His Sister*. As feminist philosopher Judith Butler has suggested in her critique of Rubin's work, however, the notion of a natural sexuality into which women can be freed from patriarchy (a notion implicit in Rubin's famous concept of the "sex/gender" system) oversimplifies the mechanisms by which power operates. With Michel Foucault in *The History of Sexuality*, Butler argues that the notion that sexuality has a "natural" ground outside its social construction is an illusion power creates to sustain and justify itself. Feminist theorists need to think not simply beyond incest but beyond the legal prohibitions that produce it as an object of desire (and thus constitute the sexual abuse of children as attractive). They need, in Irigaray's words, to consider "*the seduction function of the law it-*

self." Ellen Pollak considers the importance of this imperative for literary interpretation in a counterreading to Gardiner's.

The feminist project of unraveling the cultural significances of incest is an ambitious one in which much is at stake and much remains to be done. Historical gaps need filling so that incest texts can be mined for their historical specificities and sociocultural nuances. Literary theorists also need to look more closely at the writings of incest survivors, such as those collected by Ellen Bass and Louise Thornton in 1983. Understanding the multiple discourses that constitute incest—fictional, autobiographical, and theoretical—is one way to work toward eradicating this damaging social syndrome.

Ellen Pollak

References

Bagley, C. *Child Sexual Abuse within the Family: An Account of Studies 1978–84.* Calgary, Canada: University of Calgary Press, 1985.

Bass, Ellen, and Louise Thornton, eds. *I Never Told Anyone: Writings by Women Survivors of Child Sexual Abuse.* New York: Harper and Row, 1983.

Boose, Lynda E. "The Father and the Bride in Shakespeare." *PMLA* 97 (1982): 325–347.

———, and Betty Flowers, eds. *Daughters and Fathers.* Baltimore and London: Johns Hopkins University Press, 1989.

Butler, Judith. *Gender Trouble: Feminism and the Subversion of Identity.* New York: Routledge, 1990.

Cohen, Paula Marantz. *The Daughter's Dilemma.* Ann Arbor: University of Michigan Press, 1991.

DeSalvo, Louise. *Virginia Woolf: The Impact of Childhood Sexual Abuse on Her Life and Work.* Boston: Beacon, 1989.

de Young, M. *Incest: An Annotated Bibliography.* Jefferson, N.C.: McFarland, 1985.

Gallop, Jane. *The Daughter's Seduction.* Ithaca, N.Y.: Cornell University Press, 1982.

Gardiner, Judith Kegan. "The First English Novel: Aphra Behn's *Love Letters*, The Canon, and Women's Tastes." *Tulsa Studies in Women's Literature* 8 (1989): 201–222.

Gilbert, Sandra M. "Life's Empty Pack: Notes toward a Literary Daughteronomy." *Critical Inquiry* 11 (1985): 355–384.

Herman, Judith Lewis, and Lisa Hirschman. *Father-Daughter Incest.* Cambridge: Harvard University Press, 1981.

Masson, Jeffrey Moussaieff. *The Assault on Truth: Freud's Suppression of the Seduction Theory.* New York: Farrar, Straus, 1984. 3rd ed. New York: Harper, 1992.

Meiselman, Karin C. *Resolving the Trauma of Incest.* San Francisco and Oxford: Jossey-Bass, 1990.

Miller, Alice. *Thou Shalt Not Be Aware.* Translated by Hildegarde and Hunter Hannum. New York: Meridian, 1984.

Pollak, Ellen. "Beyond Incest: Gender and the Politics of Transgression in Aphra Behn's *Love Letters between a Nobleman and His Sister*." In *Rereading Aphra Behn: History, Theory, and Criticism,* edited by Heidi Hutner, 151–186. Charlottesville: University Press of Virginia, 1993.

Rubin, Gayle. "The Traffic in Women: Notes on the 'Political Economy' of Sex." In *Toward an Anthropology of Women,* edited by Rayna R. Reiter, 157–210. New York: Monthly Review, 1975.

Rush, Florence. *The Best-Kept Secret: Sexual Abuse of Children.* Englewood Cliffs, N.J.: Prentice-Hall, 1980.

Russell, Diana E.H. *The Secret Trauma: Incest in the Lives of Girls and Women.* New York: Basic, 1986.

Yaeger, Patricia, and Beth Kowaleski-Wallace, eds. *Refiguring the Father: New Feminist Readings of Patriarchy.* Carbondale and Edwardsville: Southern Illinois University Press, 1989.

Zwinger, Linda. *Daughters, Fathers, and the Novel: The Sentimental Romance of Heterosexuality.* Madison: University of Wisconsin Press, 1991.

Insanity

Commonly used to refer to "mental derangement" or "unsound mind," insanity has been used to describe women in three distinct ways: to designate the female body—and therefore mind—as a site of instability; to define female behavior that stands outside of that accepted by patriarchy as "normal"; and to label women who resist patriarchal socialization. Feminist literary criticism uses literature to reveal how these connections between women and insanity can be challenged, coopted, and subverted in service of women in general and women writers in particular.

Early definitions claimed that insanity was a physical problem, specifically the result of an unstable balance between body and mind, particularly in women. The word "hysteria," for instance, derives from the word "womb," an organ that was thought to wander around the female body producing symptoms of madness in the process. The idea that the female body is an unstable site prone to insanity entered the discourse as a metaphor for the general instability of women, creating a deeply rooted association between women and madness. In *The Female Malady*, Elaine Showalter inverts this traditional view of insanity by claiming that it is not women's bodies that lead to unstable mental health, but rather patriarchy's oppression of women that prevents women from functioning as normal, healthy individuals and leads them to retreat to broken and poorly adapted ways of life defined as "insane."

Insanity has also been used to describe behavior that exists outside of, or cannot be defined by, patriarchy. Feminists have recuperated such behavior, seeing it not as instances of female madness, but as ways that women can escape the system that dominates them and access their essential femaleness. Hélène Cixous for instance sees behavior defined by patriarchy as "insane" to be the repressed zone of true womanhood. The image of the insane woman, she suggests, is exemplary of what women are and should be, the way women must be if they are to stand outside of the false, because male-dominated world. Writing, from this perspective, can be an avenue through which the restrictions of culture can be escaped and a uniquely female literature can emerge. From another angle, Sandra Gilbert and Susan Gubar use Charlotte Brontë's *Jane Eyre* to claim that women authors hide their real, "insane," creative self in the attic, and present the world with their socially acceptable "sane" double. In a similar way, Freud's Dora has been seen as a woman who uses the definition of insanity placed upon her to escape the hegemony. By using the label of insanity for their own purposes, women are able to escape the patriarchal bonds that restrict them, moving beyond those bonds into a "saner," because essentially female, place.

Finally, insanity has been used to define—and thereby control—women who resist or oppose patriarchy. Feminists have responded to this particular silencing of women by recovering and recognizing those women who, although labeled insane, were actually activists for, or believers in, women's freedom and rights. In *Women and Madness*, Phyllis Chesler claims that women placed in insane asylums were often those whose beliefs—frequently identifiable as feminist—went against the patriarchal construction of women as passive, submissive, maternal figures. Literary critics have similarly reinterpreted "insane" female characters as women who were labeled insane because they were a threat to the dominant culture. The nameless main character of Charlotte Perkins Gilman's *The Yellow Wallpaper*, for instance, is defined as insane by both her physician and her family because she denies the traditional female domestic role by her desire to write and by her less than enthusiastic attachment to her newborn infant. As a "treatment" for her illness, the narrator is prevented from writing and confined to her room. Feminists have seen Gilman's story as an example of what happens, literally and figuratively, to women who do not conform to, or actively oppose, patriarchal society. They also see mental illness as itself a subversive act, one that disrupts the dominant culture and asserts its own voice.

Traditionally used to contain and silence women, definitions and labels of insanity have been recuperated by feminists to reveal rich and complex analyses of women's relationship to the patriarchal world. Women writers have used their characters to challenge the problematic connections typically established between women and insanity, using such connections to form their own style of writing, to validate their own experience, and to subvert the culture that oppresses them.

Sara E. Quay

See also HYSTERIA; NEUROSIS

References

Chesler, Phyllis. *Women and Madness*. New York: Doubleday, 1972.
Cixous, Hélène. "The Laugh of the Medusa." *Signs* 1 (1975): 875–893.
———, and Catherine Clément. *The Newly Born Woman*. Translated by Betsy Wing. Minneapolis: University of Minnesota Press, 1975.

Felman, Shoshana. "Woman and Madness: The Critical Phallacy." *Diacritics 5* (1975): 2–10.

Freud, Sigmund. *Dora: An Analysis of a Case of Hysteria.* Edited by Philip Rieff. New York: Collier, 1963.

Gilbert, Sandra M., and Susan Gubar. *The Madwoman in the Attic: The Woman Writer and the Nineteenth-Century Literary Imagination.* New Haven: Yale University Press, 1979.

Gilman, Charlotte Perkins. *The Yellow Wallpaper.* New York: Feminist, 1973.

Rigney, Barbara Hill. *Madness and Sexual Politics in the Feminist Novel: Studies in Brontë, Woolf, Lessing and Atwood.* Madison: University of Wisconsin Press, 1978.

Ripa, Vannick. *Women and Madness: The Incarceration of Women in Nineteenth-Century France.* Minneapolis: University of Minnesota Press, 1990.

Russell, Denise. *Women, Madness, and Medicine.* Cambridge, Mass.: Polity, 1995.

Showalter, Elaine. *The Female Malady.* New York: Penguin, 1985.

Invalidism

In the nineteenth century, invalidism was defined as weakness and a tendency to illness, not (as it is today) being bedridden; nor was there a clear distinction between mental and physical ailments. In the last several years, feminist theorists in history, psychoanalysis, and literature have examined the prevalence of female illness and invalidism in the nineteenth century as representative of the sickness of gender roles. Much of this work has made its way into feminist literary theory. In these analyses of historical invalidism, women's illness has been seen largely as a result of the oppressive use of male power, as the resistance to oppressive power, or as the means to a kind of artistic, political, or "sentimental" power. These three views of invalidism sometimes overlap and are sometimes mutually exclusive; they sometimes focus on only one kind of illness and are sometimes more wide-ranging, but most agree that female invalidism has been and remains an important field of investigation for scholars of women's literature and culture.

The most influential school of thought about female invalidism holds that nineteenth-century ailments were most often the result of "cultural conditioning," patriarchal oppression, and the masculine power to define and control women's bodies. These arguments usually take one of two forms—maintaining either that oppression actually caused the illness or that oppressive norms caused women to be defined as ill, no matter their actual physical condition. Sandra Gilbert and Susan Gubar argue in *Madwoman in the Attic* that norms for women's behavior—selflessness and submissiveness—were themselves the causes of ill health. Historian Carroll Smith-Rosenberg argues in *Disorderly Conduct* that much illness from that time can be understood as an exaggeration of Victorian feminine norms. Elaine Showalter and Mary Poovey focus on how medical thought was able to solidify masculine privilege by defining women as ill and how literature helps to enforce that definition.

A second group of feminist theorists speaks of illness not as the result of oppression, but as either a resistance to it, or as a form of artistic expression and feminine power. Elaine Showalter, for instance, raises the question of whether hysteria was a mode a protest, concluding that "hysteria and feminism do exist on a kind of continuum." In essays on Charlotte Perkins Gilman, Paula Treichler argues that the narrator and the writer use the description of a woman's illness to develop a language of resistance, healing, and female community. Critics like Phyllis Chesler see insanity as a label applied to the woman who rebels. In her critical play "Portrait of Dora," for example, Hélène Cixous sees Freud's patient Dora as a courageous figure refusing masculine norms, while Luce Irigaray in *Speculum of the Other Woman* sees the invalid as a woman whose artistic and self-expressive attempts to redefine her relation to language are, because different, defined as mad. Again, this school is not separate from others—Gilbert and Gubar see Emily Dickinson's madness as an expression of her anger at masculine norms for women.

In a third approach to women's invalidism, illness is seen expressly as a form of power gained either through exploitation and manipulation or through a type of Christian sacrifice. In "The Fashionable Diseases," Ann Douglas Wood argues that women often exploited their position as invalids to achieve personal ends; in *Feminization of American Culture*, Ann Douglas further argues that literary and religious texts that depicted illness became the means for "ministers and women" to assert their own importance. In a reading very different from Douglas's, Jane Tompkins asserts that illness in nineteenth-century texts often allowed the woman writer to demonstrate or use the power of the deathbed to propagate morals that were both Christian and woman-centered. In these interpretations, the representation of invalidism is understood as a means to an end.

In the most recent feminist exploration of invalidism, *Invalid Women*, Diane Price Herndl incorporates a Foucaultian notion of power into these three analyses of female illness to focus on the issue of representation and its political work. She argues that these three views of invalidism are not necessarily at odds, if one reads the representations historically and in relation to issues of female power. Invalidism can, of course, be invalidating to women, but it need not be, if we situate it in a larger context of women's struggle for equal treatment.

Diane Price Herndl

References

Chesler, Phyllis. *Woman and Madness*. Garden City, N.Y.: Doubleday, 1972.

Cixous, Hélène. "Portrait of Dora." *Diacritics* 13 (1983): 2–32.

Douglas, Ann. *The Feminization of American Culture*. New York: Knopf, 1977.

Gilbert, Sandra, and Susan Gubar. *Madwoman in the Attic: The Woman Writer and the Nineteenth-Century Literary Imagination*. New Haven: Yale University Press, 1979.

Irigaray, Luce. *Speculum of the Other Woman*. Translated by Gillian C. Gill. Ithaca, N.Y.: Cornell University Press, 1985.

Poovey, Mary. *Uneven Developments: The Ideological Work of Gender in Mid-Victorian England*. Chicago: University of Chicago Press, 1988.

Price Herndl, Diane. *Invalid Women: Figuring Feminine Illness in American Fiction and Culture, 1840–1940*. Chapel Hill: University of North Carolina Press, 1993.

Showalter, Elaine. *The Female Malady: Women, Madness, and English Culture, 1830–1980*. New York: Pantheon, 1985.

Smith-Rosenberg, Carroll. *Disorderly Conduct: Visions of Gender in Victorian America*. New York: Oxford University Press, 1985.

Tompkins, Jane. *Sensational Designs: The Cultural Work of American Fiction*. New York: Oxford University Press, 1985.

Treichler, Paula. "Escaping the Sentence: Diagnosis and Discourse in 'The Yellow Wallpaper.'" *Tulsa Studies in Women and Literature* 3 (1984): 61–77.

Wood, Ann Douglas. "'The Fashionable Diseases': Women's Complaints and Their Treatment in Nineteenth-Century America." *Journal of Interdisciplinary History* 4 (1973): 25–52.

Irigaray, Luce

In her two early texts translated as *Speculum of the Other Woman* and *This Sex Which Is Not One*, Luce Irigaray explores the notion of woman as "Other." Both works are philosophical critiques of the ideas of influential male thinkers such as Freud, Hegel, Kant, and Plato. Irigaray argues that in Western patriarchal culture, women function as mirrors for men. The title of the first work is suggestive: speculum is an instrument gynecologists use to examine the cavities of the female body, an instrument of power that makes women the object of interest. The world centers on "man" as subject. Everyone else is marginalized or rendered an object for his use. Irigaray says that woman "does not exist yet" because our discourse is incapable of representing woman other than as a negative reflection of man. Concerned with the discursive constructions of "feminine sexuality," she would like to discuss it without using terms prescribed by a male way of thinking. Women have to free themselves from their "expropriation" within patriarchal culture.

Irigaray's work originated in linguistics and psychoanalysis and is influenced by the ideas of the French theorist Jacques Lacan, whom she criticizes. It engages in philosophic debates about the realities of women's lives and raises concerns about ethics and the social contract. Irigaray reworks Lacan's notions of the "imaginary" and the "symbolic" because she finds that his theories are applicable only to a male subject. When Lacan provides explanations for the development of women and men, he is in fact offering a "representation" that identifies woman with the mother, the original lost object that creates desire. Although he claims that human identity is constructed in discourse, he relegates the woman's body to biological reproduction that lies outside of culture or the symbolic. Irigaray points out that, in the history of thought or symbolic organiza- tion, women are given the unwanted aspects of men. They are associated with waste, scraps, and death drives. Woman is at once "decay" and "growth." So long as she is seen through the eyes of men, she remains in "unrealized potentiality." As a way of countering this sym- bolism, Irigaray advocates and adopts a strat- egy of "mimesis," which is to assume the "femi- nine role" deliberately in order to call into question woman's exploitation by phallic dis- course.

One of Irigaray's most important contribu- tions to feminist literary criticism is her valori- zation of women's bonds and female experi- ences. Irigaray notes that the theories of the unconscious articulated by men have barely touched on the relation of woman to the mother, and the relation of women among themselves. She believes that the "murder" of the mother results in the "nonpunishment" of the son and the burial of women "in madness." According to Irigaray, mothers, and the woman within them, have been "trapped" in the role of she who "satisfies need" but has no access to desire. Hence women become paralyzed or be- come hysterical because they have no means, no metaphors for expressing desire. In her writing, Irigaray often uses puns to suggest the fluidity and plurality of woman's sexuality and expres- sion. Thus her metaphor for the female style is the "two lips," which suggest being in touch with one's body, self-sufficient *jouissance*, ex- change, and an alternate discourse. She uses vaginal lips rather than the phallus as the model for textual/sexual subjectivity. "Parler-femme" or "speaking as a woman" will become possible only when women are able to find a female imaginary experience in which to situate their desires and lived experiences.

Eleanor Ty

References

Burke, Carolyn, Naomi Schor, and Margaret Whitford, eds. *Engaging with Irigaray: Feminist Philosophy and Modern Euro- pean Thought.* New York: Columbia University Press, 1994.

Fuss, Diana. *Essentially Speaking: Feminism, Nature, and Difference.* New York: Routledge, 1989.

Grosz, Elizabeth. *Jacques Lacan: A Feminist Introduction.* London: Routledge, 1990.

Irigaray, Luce. *The Irigaray Reader.* Edited by Margaret Whitford. Oxford: Blackwell, 1991.

———. *Speculum of the Other Woman.* Translated by Gillian C. Gill. Ithaca, N.Y.: Cornell University Press, 1985.

———. *This Sex Which Is Not One.* Trans- lated by Catherine Porter. Ithaca, N.Y.: Cornell University Press, 1985.

Whitford, Margaret. *Luce Irigaray: Philoso- phy in the Feminine.* New York: Routledge, 1991.

J

Jacobus, Mary

A British feminist literary critic and a critic of romanticism, Mary Jacobus came to the United States from Oxford in 1980. She described the move as ironically bringing her "closer to France" and to an affinity for French theory. Advocating "a psychoanalytically and theoretically informed feminism," Jacobus challenged feminist assumptions about gender identity and guided feminist literary criticism from its atheoretical, experiential origins toward engagement with contemporary theories of language and representation.

Influenced by feminism, poststructuralism, and psychoanalysis, Jacobus's *Reading Women* challenged Anglo American feminist hostility to theory, particularly Freudian theory. In a pivotal essay entitled "The Difference of View," Jacobus argued that sexual difference, and the "woman reader/writer," are produced by language. The feminist critic's task is thus to interrogate, not privilege, "women's writing." The critic must examine the repressions in a text that produce and sustain particular constructions of gender. Here Jacobus reclaimed Freud for feminism, reading his work as a history of the production of sexual difference.

Jacobus brought together her background in romanticism with her work on feminist literary criticism and theory in her book entitled *Romanticism, Writing, and Sexual Difference: Essays on the Prelude*. Her new book entitled *First Things* pursues the uses of psychoanalytic theory for feminism with a focus on issues of "maternal imaginary," a phrase Jacobus coins to cover a range of topics related to maternal themes.

Jacobus helped broaden the scope of feminist literary criticism from the recovery of women writers to an appreciation of the textual production of gender, a focus on "not the sexuality of the text but the textuality of sex." In forcing a confrontation between Anglo American feminism and French theory, Jacobus produced fresh insights into both the production of gender and the process of reading itself.

Diane Helene Miller

References

Jacobus, Mary. *First Things*. New York: Routledge, 1995.

———. *Reading Women: Essays in Feminist Criticism*. New York: Columbia University Press, 1986.

———. *Romanticism, Writing, and Sexual Difference: Essays on the Prelude*. New York: Oxford University Press, 1989.

———, ed. *Women Writing and Writing about Women*. London: Croom Helm, 1979.

Jehlen, Myra

In the controversial essay "Archimedes and the Paradox of Feminist Criticism," Myra Jehlen voiced her concern that the separatist philosophy of feminism had caused women's studies programs, research interests, and feminist literary criticism to be largely inconsequential within the still male-dominated academy. Because of this concern, Jehlen called for a reconceptualization of feminist criticism and for a "radical comparativism," a feminist analysis that would juxtapose texts written by women with those written by men.

Drawing upon formalist theory, Jehlen argued that feminist critics should not privilege political concerns, but should address the aesthetic questions raised by literary works, even if those works are ideologically offensive. From this theoretical base, Jehlen critiqued such contemporaneous feminist texts as Ellen Moers's *Literary Women*, Elaine Showalter's *A Literature of Their Own*, and Sandra Gilbert's and Susan Gubar's *The Madwoman in the Attic* for focusing solely on women. Jehlen claimed that because of this narrow focus, which she called a "territorial approach to feminist criticism," feminists could not fully and legitimately support assertions about female artistic conceptions or achievements. To validate their assertions, Jehlen contended, feminists needed to ground their research in "relatedness and historicity"; that is, they should examine women's works with men's in the context of specifics about cultural-historical-political dynamics and then discuss the relative literary merit of the works.

By questioning feminist premises and practices, Jehlen offered an important critique of gynocriticism and raised the possibility of a more expansive feminist literary enterprise— one using feminist criticism to read texts written by men as well as by women.

Phyllis Surrency Dallas

See also GILBERT, SANDRA, AND SUSAN GUBAR

References

Jehlen, Myra. "Archimedes and the Paradox of Feminist Criticism." *Signs* 6 (1981): 575–601.
———. "Gender." In *Critical Terms for Literary Study*, edited by Frank Lentricchia and Thomas McLaughlin. Chicago: University of Chicago Press, 1990.
———, and Rachel Blau DuPlessis. "'The Tongue of Power.'" Review of *The Madwoman in the Attic* by Sandra Gilbert and Susan Gubar. *Feminist Studies* 7 (1981): 539–546.

Johnson, Barbara

A former student of Paul de Man and a translator and critic of Derrida, Johnson has worked primarily within the context of deconstructionist theory. And indeed, her concept of binary oppositions and how they allow certain entities to be seen as central and meaningful, while others are devalued and marginalized, draws directly upon the work of Derrida. What most distinguishes Johnson from her male precursors, however, is her attempt to show the political relevance of deconstruction, particularly in issues of race and gender. Feminists must recognize, Johnson believes, that simple reversals of the devalued terms in binary oppositions will leave the structures of our social institutions intact.

Johnson explores binary oppositions or "difference" primarily at the textual level in her earlier writings. In *The Critical Difference*, the exploration of textual difference involves two movements. First, Johnson discovers a series of binary oppositions in the writings of male writers and theorists such as Stéphane Mallarmé, Herman Melville, Jacques Derrida, and Jacques Lacan. Second, Johnson demonstrates how these oppositions between categories such as prose/poetry and masculine/feminine are "illusions." Furthermore, she shows that these illusory differences between entities are "based on a repression of difference within entities."

But while binary oppositions may be spurious and based on a repression of difference within, they have, Johnson notes, consequences in the real world such as the exclusion of women from the canon. Thus in *A World of Difference*, she turns her attention to the political effects of binary oppositions and to texts by writers such as Zora Neale Hurston who have been marginalized because of their biological sex or color. However, even as Johnson shifts to subject matter in which the differences between entities appear to have "real world" consequences, her focus remains on "texts," and her strategy continues to be one of close, deconstructive reading. And in fact Johnson shows that the difference between reality and the world of the text may be another opposition to be discarded as she examines how political issues can be inhabited by textual and linguistic forces, how texts can be imploded by the violence of the political.

Johnson asserts that to effect real social and political change we must first examine the patterns of thinking; otherwise it is likely that any marginalized group that attempts to challenge the dominant institution or tradition will find itself relying on the central concepts of the very structure it wishes to dismantle.

Elisabeth Sheffield

References

Johnson, Barbara. *The Critical Difference: Essays in the Contemporary Rhetoric of*

Reading. Baltimore, Md.: Johns Hopkins University Press, 1980.

———. *The Wake of Deconstruction*. Bucknell Lectures in Literary Theory 11. Cambridge, Mass.: Blackwell, 1994.

———. *A World of Difference*. Baltimore, Md.: Johns Hopkins University Press, 1987.

Jouissance

A term initially used by French psychoanalytic theorists that has now gained popular acceptance as an encapsulation of female sexual desire, pleasure, and power. Although this word once existed in English with many of the meanings it now retains in French, according to the *Oxford English Dictionary*, it fell out of use around 1750. *Jouissance* has variously been translated as "bliss," "sexual pleasure," and "enjoyment," but it also involves possession (of property and of rights), total ecstasy, and a surpassing (and thus the implicit presence) of meaning. Clearly, there is no adequate English equivalent of this word, and it is thus often left untranslated. Roland Barthes, in his transposition of the written text onto the physical body in *The Pleasure of the Text*, was the first writer to distinguish between comfortable, canonical "pleasure" and the radical, unsettling, "precocious" realm of *jouissance*. It is this power to disrupt established ideologies that feminists have seized upon and claimed for women. Unlike male *jouissance*, which Jacques Lacan links indissolubly to ideas of profit and the fear of castration, female *jouissance* is unbounded, fluid, unlimited, omnipresent. Its simplest (metaphorical) sense suggests that a woman's ability to have multiple orgasms means that she has the potential to reach beyond the fixed to-

tality of ordinary experience, that she has a literal and figurative abundance that transcends her physicality.

The transformative power of female *jouissance* enables feminists to question many previously unchallenged ideological dictates and patriarchal definitions of femininity. As the editors of *New French Feminisms* explain, it provides both pleasure and power "which women know and which men fear." Theorists that have explored the possibilities opened up by this concept include Luce Irigaray, Hélène Cixous, and Julia Kristeva.

Alexandra Bennett

References

Barthes, Roland. *The Pleasure of the Text*. Translated by Richard Miller. New York: Hill and Wang, 1975.

Cixous, Hélène, and Catherine Clément. *The Newly Born Woman*. Translated by Betsy Wing. Minneapolis: University of Minnesota Press, 1986.

Gallop, Jane. "Beyond the *Jouissance* Principle." *Representations* 7 (1984): 110–115.

Irigaray, Luce. *This Sex Which Is Not One*. Translated by Catherine Porter. Ithaca, N.Y.: Cornell University Press, 1985.

Kristeva, Julia. *Desire in Language*. Edited by Leon S. Roudiez. Translated by Thomas Gora, Alice Jardine, and Leon S. Roudiez. New York: Columbia University Press, 1980.

Lacan, Jacques. *Écrits: A Selection*. Translated by Alan Sheridan. New York: W.W. Norton, 1977.

Marks, Elaine, and Isabelle de Courtivron, eds. *New French Feminisms*. Amherst: University of Massachusetts Press, 1980.

J

K

Kahane, Claire

Kahane is best known for her contribution to psychoanalytic literary criticism: in 1985 she assembled (with Shirley Nelson Garner and Madelon Sprengnether) one of the first collections of literary criticism informed both by psychoanalysis and feminism. The introduction to *The (M)other Tongue: Essays in Feminist Psychoanalytic Interpretation* is useful for its overview of feminism and psychoanalytic theory; the authors chart the influence of French feminists and theorists (Cixous, Derrida, Irigaray, Lacan) on American psychoanalytic theory, and the importance of Nancy Chodorow's 1978 theory of the maternal to American feminist theorists. The first section of *The (M)other Tongue* features essays that subject Freud's texts to his own psychoanalytic method; Part II explores the pre-Oedipal aspects of patriarchal texts, while Part III trains the feminist psychoanalytic lens on texts by women authors.

Also in 1985, Kahane co-edited *In Dora's Case: Freud—Hysteria—Feminism* with Charles Bernheimer. The collection reexamines a text that was the subject of many interpretations in the mid 1970s and early 1980s: Freud's *Dora: Fragment of an Analysis of a Case of Hysteria.* Kahane's introduction notes the continuing interest in the case, which she attributes to its central contradiction: Freud constructed his theory of hysteria and the psychoanalytic method of treatment on this case study, yet the "Fragment of an Analysis" represents his failure to finish the case and treat the patient. For feminists, Dora's case is situated in the middle of a reexamination of cultural beliefs about femininity, and thus Freud's narrative is a "rich gift," a window through which the construction of those beliefs can be viewed.

Kahane's work supports her claim that the "radical promise" of psychoanalysis can be recovered in the intersection between psychoanalysis and feminism. Kahane has also written on the maternal voice, gothic fiction and feminine identity, and the comic-grotesque.

Wendy C. Wahl

References

Kahane, Claire. "Hysteria, Feminism, and the Case of *The Bostonians.*" In *Feminism and Psychoanalysis*, edited by Richard Feldstein and Judith Roof, 280–297. Ithaca, N.Y.: Cornell University Press, 1989.

———, et al., eds. *In Dora's Case: Freud—Hysteria—Feminism.* New York: Columbia University Press, 1985.

———, et al., eds. *The (M)other Tongue: Essays in Feminist Psychoanalytic Interpretation.* Ithaca, N.Y.: Cornell University Press, 1985.

Kaplan, Cora

From her earliest publications in the 1970s, to the influential *Sea Changes*, and her more recent work on nineteenth-century ideologies of gender and race, Kaplan has made a selective rereading of Marx, Freud, and Lacan to posit literature as the psychic representation of social meaning—and to offer women's texts, in particular, as important registers of female subjectivity as it has been inflected by ideologies of class and race.

Kaplan's critical range is broad, with the essays of *Sea Changes* alone considering writers as diverse as Emily Dickinson and Alice Walker, Christina Rossetti and Colleen

McCullough, and more recent articles discussing detective fiction and film. It is the early, proto- and paradigmatic texts of modern feminism, however—Mary Wollstonecraft's *A Vindication of the Rights of Women*, for example, Brontë's *Jane Eyre*, the essays and fiction of Virginia Woolf—that particularly fascinate her, and to which her work has returned again and again. Typically she uses such texts as the starting points for insightful meditations on the limits and exclusions, as well as the successes, of modern feminism: thus "Pandora's box" (*Sea Changes*) exposes the inadequacies of feminist humanist and radical feminist criticism via a reading of Wollstonecraft and Charlotte Brontë. "Like a Housemaid's Fancies" takes its title from *Orlando*, and reveals hostile representations of black and workingclass femininity as the repressed underside of the bourgeois feminist project. With such essays Kaplan has established herself as both an eloquent practitioner of Anglo American feminist criticism, and one of its own most astute genealogists and critics.

Sarah Waters

References

Kaplan, Cora. "Dirty Harriet/*Blue Steel*: Feminist Theory Goes to Hollywood." *Discourse* 16 (1993): 50–70.

———. Introduction to Browning, Elizabeth Barrett. In *Aurora Leigh and Other Poems*. London: Women's, 1978.

———. "'Like a Housemaid's Fancies': The Representation of Working-class Women in Nineteenth-century Writing." In *Grafts: Feminist Cultural Criticism*, edited by Susan Sheridan, 55–76. London: Verso, 1988.

———. *Salt and Bitter and Good: Three Centuries of English and American Women Poets*. New York: Paddington, 1975.

———. *Sea Changes: Essays on Culture and Feminism*. London: Verso, 1986.

———. "'What We Have Again to Say': Raymond Williams, Feminism and the 1840s." In *Cultural Materialism: On the Work of Raymond Williams*, edited by Chris Prendergast, 211–236. Minneapolis: University of Minnesota Press, 1995.

Keller, Evelyn Fox

Keller's work has substantiated the social construction of scientific knowledge, making it subject to discourse analysis, as well as opening the way to a consideration of the role played by class and racial ideologies in the production of scientific worldviews. Her first book, *A Feeling for the Organism*, was a biography of Barbara McClintock, a marginalized geneticist whose discoveries eventually earned her a Nobel prize. Keller's groundbreaking study *Reflections on Gender and Science* challenged the belief that science is a neutral, objective, gender-free process. Arguing that gender and science are both socially constructed, Keller employed a psychoanalytic approach and feminist methodologies to analyze the development of science in political and social contexts, and to identify the function of gender ideology in the production of scientific knowledge.

Keller co-edited *Conflicts in Feminism*, essays attempting the mediation of opposing theoretical and philosophical perspectives in contemporary feminism. She also co-edited *Body/Politics*, essays that critiqued the use of women as substance and subject of science, and examined intersections of scientific, literary, and social discourses concerning the female body to reveal their material effects. In *Secrets of Life, Secrets of Death*, Keller pursued questions of gender and science, analyzing deployments of language in the production of scientific knowledge, and addressing the ways in which particular linguistic conventions make possible certain kinds of scientific discoveries while forestalling others.

Ronna C. Johnson

References

Keller, Evelyn Fox. *A Feeling for the Organism: The Life and Work of Barbara McClintock*. New York: Freeman, 1983.

———. *Reflections on Gender and Science*. New Haven: Yale University Press, 1985.

———. *Secrets of Life, Secrets of Death: Essays on Language, Gender, and Science*. New York: Routledge, 1992.

———, et al., eds. *Body/Politics: Women and the Discourse of Science*. New York: Routledge, 1990.

———, et al., eds. *Conflicts in Feminism*. New York: Routledge, 1990.

Kelly, Joan

With the publication of her essay "Did Women Have a Renaissance?" in 1977, Joan Kelly (who also published under the name Joan Kelly-Gadol) changed the way history is studied by contesting the widely accepted belief that the

Renaissance was a time of economic rebirth and liberation. While this may have been true for men, she argues that this new birth came at the expense of women's freedom. Thus Kelly encouraged historical scholars to include gender issues in their discussions. Her research offers a study of women as a distinct social grouping—and not just as "different." She argues that class, gender, and race are terms produced within a power struggle and she believes that women's history should be viewed as a component of history, not as something outside of male history.

Kelly's work combines Renaissance studies with Marxist and feminist theories. Her article "The Doubled Vision of Feminist Theory" emphasizes (1) that the division between "female sphere" as "private" and "male sphere" as "public" is an ideological split and is not based on biological difference; (2) that the breakdown between subjective and objective knowledge is arbitrary; (3) that combining theoretical approaches to feminism and practical solutions is important and necessary. Also significant is Kelly's essay "Family Life: A Historical Perspective" in which she traces the history of the relationship between family roles in the household and the places where it collides with gender and class. Kelly's significance as a historian and feminist lies in her awareness that men's and women's histories are neither identical, nor separate, but interrelated.

Heidi N. Kaufman

References

Kelly, Joan. *Women, History & Theory: The Essays of Joan Kelly*. Edited by Catherine R. Stimpson. Chicago: University of Chicago Press, 1984.

Kingston, Maxine Hong

Kingston's *The Woman Warrior: Memoirs of a Girlhood among Ghosts* has been a significant text in women's studies, literary studies, and Asian and ethnic studies since its inception. Writing an autobiography infused with some revisions of Chinese mythology, Kingston tests the boundary between fiction and nonfiction. Furthermore, the use of ghosts as metaphors for many of the figures in her American life and her Chinese ancestry articulates the kind of "otherworldliness" experienced by a woman who is also a minority in American culture. It seems clear that Kingston both attempts to revive and revise the Chinese woman within herself while negotiating the manifestations that same self has experienced as a first generation Chinese American. Her conscious alterations of Chinese history reveal what America can do to one's sense of culture and may represent a kind of linguistic cultural survival.

In *China Men*, Kingston's second book, stories of the oppression of Chinese men during the nineteenth century in America seem to serve as a parallel to her representations of women in Chinese culture from *The Woman Warrior*. Kingston has been criticized by some Chinese readers for some implicit admonishments of Chinese culture that suggest a pervasive misogyny. *China Men*, however, makes many attempts to answer such critics.

By persistently fusing fiction and nonfiction, Kingston brings close the worlds of imagination and fact, ultimately obscuring the boundaries between language and body, thought and experience. Kingston's only novel, *Tripmaster Monkey: His Fake Book*, uses such themes to articulate the modern experience of these cultural dualities and identity politics for Chinese Americans. The reconciliation of such dichotomies in her mythological autobiographies and historical fictions are indirectly related to the topic of "gendered writing" in feminist literary theory. Kingston successfully debunks the myth that logic and instinct (mind and body) are gendered and separate, and thus she puts pressure on the essentialist notion that men and women have mutually exclusive relationships to language or intellect. Her lesson to feminist literary theorists seems to be an absolute insistence on putting culture and gender into the same discussions and representations while privileging neither. Finally, by restoring a sense of oral tradition and underscoring the personalization of myth- and story-telling, Kingston proves not only that language is always fluid, but that history is often flexible.

Jenna Ivers

References

Kingston, Maxine Hong. *China Men*. New York: Random House, 1980.
———. "Cultural Mis-readings by American Reviewers." In *Asian and Western Writers in Dialogue: New Cultural Identities*, edited by Guy Amirthanayagam, 55–65. London: Macmillan, 1982.
———. *Hawai'i One Summer*. San Francisco: Meadow, 1987.

———. "Imagined Life." *Michigan Quarterly Review* 22 (1983): 561–570.

———. "San Francisco's Chinatown: A View from the Other Side of Arnold Genthe's Camera." *American Heritage* (1978): 35–47.

———. *Tripmaster Monkey: His Fake Book.* New York: Random House, 1989/1990.

———. *The Woman Warrior: Memoirs of a Girlhood among Ghosts.* New York: Random House, 1976.

Kolodny, Annette

A powerful critic of mainstream academic literary institutions, Annette Kolodny helped define feminist criticism in the 1970s and 1980s, especially through two influential essays, "Dancing through the Minefield" and "Dancing between Left and Right." She also authored two books that provided a feminist perspective on the American frontier: *The Lay of the Land* focused on Euro-American men, and *The Land before Her* examined the way Euro-American women imagined and experienced the frontier. She found that while men saw the land as a feminine Eden, a kind of body with which they joined in varying degrees of violence—from the gentle love between mother and son to the violent rape of a peaceful paradise—women saw the land as a garden to be cultivated. Kolodny demonstrated the importance of including women's perspective on the frontier, emphasizing the fact that women offer a less violent way to imagine and inhabit our ecological environment.

Kolodny focused in her criticism both on women as writers, readers, and characters, and on the symbolic, psychological, and linguistic forces of gender. This allowed her to see, for example, that the American land was imagined as female by Euro-American men, and that literature is shaped by gender even when no women are present. This insight considerably extended the scope and power of feminist analysis.

Kolodny has contributed to some of the central debates in American literary criticism, from defining feminist criticism itself, to refining Harold Bloom's ideas about the "anxiety of influence." As critic, teacher, and administrator, Kolodny helped make feminist criticism one of the most important schools in the American university.

Julia Willis

References

Kolodny, Annette. "Dancing between Left and Right: Feminism and the Academic Minefield in the 1980s." In *Literature, Language, and Politics*, edited by Betty Jean Craige, 27–38. Athens: University of Georgia Press, 1988.

———. "Dancing through the Minefield: Some Observations on the Theory, Practice, and Politics of a Feminist Literary Criticism." *Feminist Studies* 6 (1980): 1–25.

———. *The Land before Her.* Chapel Hill: University of North Carolina Press, 1984.

———. *The Lay of the Land.* Chapel Hill: University of North Carolina Press, 1975.

———. "Letting Go Our Grand Obsessions: Notes toward a New Literary History of the American Frontiers." *American Literature* 64 (1992): 1–18.

———. "A Map for Rereading: On Gender and the Interpretation of Literary Texts." *New Literary History* 2 (1980): 451–467.

———. "Turning the Lens on 'The Panther Captivity.'" *Critical Inquiry* 8 (1981): 329–345.

Kristeva, Julia

A product of the intellectual, political, and social milieu of the radical 1960s, French linguist, psychoanalyst, semiotician, literary critic, and novelist, Julia Kristeva is celebrated for her revolutionary ideas about communication, the human psyche, and Western societies. Her first important work, *La Révolution du langage poétique* (translated as *Revolution in Poetic Language*), investigates the workings of "poetic language" or "signifying practice" generated by a speaking subject within a social, historical field. Influenced by the theories of the linguist Ferdinand de Saussure, the psychoanalyst Jacques Lacan, and the Russian philosopher and literary theorist Mikhail Bakhtin, Kristeva presents the notion of the "subject-in-process" in this work. She attempts to construct a dialectical view of subjectivity, one that takes into account specific situations of language, history, and politics. Two important terms introduced by Kristeva are the "semiotic" and the "symbolic," which are components of the signifying process that constitutes language. "Semiotic" refers to the pre-Oedipal, primary processes, the drives and energies located in the *chora*, which she links to the body of the mother. The "semiotic" is associated with rupture, with "vocal or kinetic rhythm," with excess, with the preverbal, while the "symbolic" is tied to order, identity, consciousness, and the Name of the Father. The "symbolic" occurs when the Father intervenes in the mother-child dyad.

Kristeva believes in the possibilities of the "semiotic," which does not manifest itself in our everyday world, except in dreams, and in certain types of poetic language, for example in the texts of Mallarmé and James Joyce. Kristeva highlights the suppressed and the marginalized aspects of discourse. Her notion of the subject-in-process emphasizes the heterogeneity and flux, rather than the stability and coherence, of the individual, and her concept of the "semiotic" is potentially exciting for its valorization of writing that is not rigidly ordered, teleological, and patriarchal.

Kristeva has also published on cultural and literary attitudes to subjects ranging from motherhood to "women's time," from love to depression and melancholia. Her style is at times lyrical, at times philosophical and learned, at times quasi-scientific. In "Stabat Mater," for instance, Kristeva undermines the conventions of the essay by breaking up her text into two columns: one side explores the historical development of the cult of the Virgin Mary in traditional academic discourse, while the side printed in bold face records her own experience and observations of maternity in a poetic style. Kristeva believes that there is a need for a "post-virginal" discourse on maternity, a new antireligious ethics, or "herethics," encompassing reproduction, as well as loss, separation, and death.

Another important book is *Pouvoirs de l'horreur* (translated as *Powers of Horror*), which explores horror and abjection. In Western cultures, abjection, which Kristeva defines as the "improper," the "unclean," the "immoral, sinister, scheming," remains as a kind of background support for the symbolic. Our society is founded upon a rigorous imposition of symbolic law that banishes the abject. In certain religions, abjection persists as "exclusion" or "taboo." Women are related to the abject because their bodies, their menstrual blood, are constant reminders of the state before the ego gives up the abject. Abjection preserves what existed in "pre-objectal relationship," in the violence with which a body becomes separated from another body in order to be. In contrast to Freud, who views the mother-child bond idealistically, Kristeva sees this bond with ambivalence. Objects and people who remind one of the abject, of abomination and horror, are repulsive, but they are paradoxically closely linked with the fascinating, ecstasy, and power. There is nothing like the "abjection of self" to show that all abjection is in fact recognition of the want on which any being, meaning, language, or desire is founded. Her observations about the powers of horror, and in particular, society's association of abjection with femininity, are useful for explaining many literary and cultural fears and stereotypes.

Although Kristeva remains somewhat skeptical of liberal feminism, her interest in the disruptive powers of the unnameable, the marginal, the heterogeneous, and the feminine makes her theories appealing to those who are seeking literary, social, and political change.

Eleanor Ty

References

Kristeva, Julia. *About Chinese Women.* Translated by Anita Barrows. London: Marion Boyars, 1977.

———. *Black Sun: Depression and Melancholia.* Translated by Leon S. Roudiez. New York: Columbia University Press, 1989.

———. *Desire in Language: A Semiotic Approach to Literature and Art.* Edited by Leon S. Roudiez. New York: Columbia, 1980.

———. *The Kristeva Reader.* Edited by Toril Moi. New York: Columbia University Press, 1986.

———. *Powers of Horror: An Essay on Abjection.* Translated by Leon S. Roudiez. New York: Columbia University Press, 1982.

———, Julia. *Revolution in Poetic Language.* Translated Margaret Waller. New York: Columbia University Press, 1984.

L

Labor
See WORK

Lacan, Jacques

As the major successor to Freudian psycho-analysis, Jacques Lacan's theories of the development of human subjectivity and human sexuality have been profoundly influential not only for psychoanalysis, but also for postmodernism and poststructuralist theory as well as for literary theory and feminism. Lacan was a practicing psychoanalyst and lecturer, giving weekly lectures for twenty years at his "école freudienne" in which he advocated a return to Freud's writings. Lacan emphasized what he felt were pyschoanalysis's most important insights: the fundamentally divided nature of the subject and the importance of the unconscious. Lacan's theory of subjectivity is based on the fundamental notion that the human subject is formed through the radical division caused by her entrance into language. To be constituted through this division is to be constituted as divided. Lacan's notion of the subject differs widely from the other general interpretation of Freud's work, ego psychology, which holds that the goal for psychoanalysis is to work toward the formation of a whole, complete, integrated identity. Lacan's teachings have been extremely important for feminist theory because of his emphasis on the role played by sexual difference and sexuality in the story of the formation of the subject. Feminists have both leaned heavily on Lacan's theories and forcefully rejected them; in all cases, Lacanian psychoanalysis has been one of the most important influences on feminist theory in this century.

In founding his work on Freud, Lacan situates his theories in a context that lacks any sense of teleology or of an autonomous subject. Because subjectivity is formed through language the subject is defined by her place in language, not by a set of historically specific conditions. This perspective sets up a fundamental distinction between Lacanian psychoanalytic feminism and Anglo American feminism, which focuses on the social conditions that create the self as an autonomous individual, and thus create sexuality. For Lacan, sexuality is not developed; it is, as Jacqueline Rose explains in her introduction to *Feminine Sexuality*, "enjoined on the subject like a law." The seeming inevitability of this concept of sexuality has led many feminists to reject the psychoanalytic perspective as essentialist in the sense, as Freud says, that "anatomy is destiny." Lacan would respond, however, that such a critique fails to take into consideration psychoanalysis's major insight, which is that the subject itself is not a whole, complete, autonomous subject but rather is fundamentally split. For Lacan, the divided and precarious nature of the speaking subject must call into question its authority to oppress others.

The main feminist critique of psychoanalysis centers on the primacy accorded to the phallus. Lacan, following Freud, asserts that the phallus is the primary signifier of lack: the phallus stands for the father, who stands for the law of separation from the mother, that initial loss through which the subject is constituted as divided. This sets up a model of signification based on and derived from the phallus as the primary signifier of lack. Feminist theorists have rejected this as "phallocentrism," the privileging of the phallus. They charge that Lacan, like Freud, is producing a theory which, in describing social and sexual relations that are patriarchal, replicates that patriarchal power dynamic. These French feminists, typified by Luce Irigaray, have elaborated theories of subjectivity not based on the phallus as primary signifier but based rather on a "multiplicity" of feminine sexuality—in the sense of the multiplicity of lips and breasts—to counter the "monosexuality" of what Irigaray calls the "phallic economy."

But such a critique is a far too literal reading of Lacan's theory of the signification of the phallus and ignores two crucial points. The first is that it fails to account for Lacan's insistence that the phallus itself is a symbol of the lack that constitutes all subjects and therefore is itself vacant. As such, it functions to place sexuality in the realm of the symbolic. That is, although having or not having the phallus determines sexual difference, having the phallus does not mean one is whole or complete or without the constitutive lack. It only means that one has the means to represent that lack. Thus though a person's subjectivity is formed through sexuality, sexuality is symbolic, not biologically determined.

The second problem with the theories of a multiple feminine sexuality is that in rejecting the division represented by the phallus, such theories reproduce an essentialist definition of woman. In asserting a multiple sexuality that is outside the phallic division, Irigaray and others also theorize a relationship to expression for women that is outside of the symbolization of language, or rather, prior to language. This emphasis on a prelinguistic point of origin serves to identify woman with drives and impulses, with the body, raising the problematic issue of a special or distinct essence for women, which brings us squarely back to the realm of biology as destiny.

The key intersection of Lacan's theories with feminism has occurred around this notion of placing sexuality in the realm of the symbolic. This symbolic nature of sexuality allows Lacan to say two potentially contradictory things about feminine sexuality. First, if sexuality is symbolic, then it is not essential. There is no essential or normative sexuality; sexuality is merely one representation of the fundamental desire that constitutes us as subjects. In this sense, Lacan sees femininity as "masquerade," as the constructed representation of the desire to be the object of the other's desire. At the same time, though, if sexuality is in the realm of the symbolic, then it is prey to the very fantasies of wholeness that characterize our symbolic identities. That is, as symbolic subjects we are continually searching for that which will complete us. In the same way that we erect the illusion of a confident, competent speaking subject, the enlightenment "I," we also erect fantasies around the notion that sexuality can provide fulfillment. Lacan's pronouncements that "there is no sexual relation" and that "the Woman does not exist" refer to the need to debunk myths of completion, of fulfillment, of a place of essential wholeness and goodness in the Other.

These theories have proven to be both helpful and controversial for feminist theory. One of the most provocative aspects of Lacan's theories is that he has underscored the distinction between women as social beings and femininity as a construct or category. Some feminists have seen the notion of femininity as a symbolic construction as providing an opening for feminism, a way around the idea of anatomy as destiny. Such theorists see room for ironic manipulation within the construction of femininity as a means of unsettling its social value. Other feminists have rejected this distinction as not addressing the pressing problem of real women in society existing within and under the weight of these constructs. Lacan's response, again, would be to point out that the authority that accrues to the phallic position is no less symbolic, no less constructed, than the limiting category of femininity. Lacan and his advocates would assert that this understanding is helpful for feminism because it undercuts the teleological drive to authority and unity and reveals the fraudulence of the phallic position. The continuing question for feminist theory, however, seems to be how to assimilate such a theoretical knowledge with the very real effects that nevertheless flow from these symbolic constructs.

Anna Geronimo

References

Clark, Michael. *Jacques Lacan: An Annotated Bibliography*. New York: Garland, 1988.

Gallop, Jane. *The Daughter's Seduction: Feminism and Psychoanalysis*. Ithaca, N.Y.: Cornell University Press, 1982.

Irigaray, Luce. *This Sex Which Is Not One*. Translated by Catherine Porter. Ithaca, N.Y.: Cornell University Press, 1985.

Lacan, Jacques. *Ecrits*. Edited by Jacques-Alain Miller. Translated by Alan

Sheridan. New York: W.W. Norton, 1978.

———. *Feminine Sexuality: Jacques Lacan and the école freudienne.* Edited by Juliet Mitchell and Jacqueline Rose. Translated by Jacqueline Rose. New York: W.W. Norton, 1982.

———. *The Four Fundamental Concepts of Psychoanalysis.* Translated by Alan Sheridan. New York: W.W. Norton, 1978.

Language

"Why is language a feminist issue?" asks Deborah Cameron in *The Feminist Critique of Language.* Cameron's question is most obviously rhetorical, in light of the last twenty years of debate about precisely why language is a feminist issue. Language has been and continues to remain an extremely crucial focus of feminist analysis. Although they have approached language from many different origins, Anglo American, French, Marxist, and deconstructive feminist critics have all argued that language oppresses women, that women do not have the same power within language that men do, that language serves the interests of men in a male-dominated society. Also fundamental to these diverse traditions is the idea that language and identity are connected, that the power to name, to say, to write, to speak is in some way fundamental to the power to define an individual self or an individual life. And yet, although there has been a great deal of debate about why language is an important feminist issue, few feminist theorists have actually attempted to define language itself. In the end, whether one sees language as oppressive to women has very much to do with what "language" itself is understood to mean.

Anglo American feminists have approached the topic of language from two distinct points of view: linguistic and literary. Linguists such as Barrie Thorne, Cheris Kramarae, and Nancy Henley have devoted extensive attention to the study of sex differences in language usage. Their writings and the writings in the collections they have edited ask whether men and women use language differently, whether language is sexist, whether the use of generic terms such as "mankind" to represent all humanity has a detrimental effect on women. Although some view the insistence on gender-neutral terms like "s/he" or "chairperson" as trivial, these authors have done a good deal to challenge "traditional" linguistic practices both within and outside the academy. These critics also go beyond examination of sexist language to discuss a variety of situations in which language is used against women to deny them power. Language is even seen by some authors as "man-made"; Dale Spender, for example, argues that men make the rules of language and that men's monopoly over language is one of the ways they ensure their own primacy and women's invisibility. Unfortunately, as numerous critics have pointed out, Spender's ideas lack theoretical and empirical support.

From the point of view of American literary critics such as Sandra Gilbert and Susan Gubar, language is not so much "man-made" as governed or controlled by men. Gilbert's and Gubar's study of nineteenth-century English and American women writers, *The Madwoman in the Attic,* argues that creativity and writing are viewed as fundamentally masculine activities; the author "fathers" his text, using the pen/penis to penetrate or inscribe the blank page. Women writers confront and undermine this male tradition by producing works with encoded messages, works with surface designs that conceal deeper and more subversive messages. As Toril Moi notes, then, for Gilbert and Gubar "the female voice is a duplicitous, but nevertheless true, and truly female voice."

A concern with the "female voice" is also present in French feminist writers, although their approach is much more theoretical than the empirical and literary approaches of Anglo American feminists. Writers such as Luce Irigaray, Hélène Cixous, and Julia Kristeva have in the last twenty years begun a critique of "phallocentric" discourses—theoretical models in which women are regarded as absent, silent, Other. Through their examinations of psychoanalysts like Sigmund Freud and Jacques Lacan and structuralist/linguists like Ferdinand de Saussure, French feminists have focused attention on how theories of psychological and linguistic development systematically place women outside of, or in an oppositional relationship to, language. In Lacan's theory of development, for example, the phallus is the symbol of power that determines all order and meaning, including language. The phallus is not a piece of flesh (the penis), but rather the cultural sign of masculinity and power, the cultural sign of sexual difference. Since women usually perceive themselves as lacking the phallus, they remain marginal to both culture and language.

Against these totalizing and monolithic masculine theories, writers such as Irigaray and Cixous assert the presence of feminine *difference*, of a feminine language that struggles to undermine the dominant phallogocentric logic. For Cixous and Irigaray, this *écriture féminine* is connected to women's body and, more particularly, women's sexuality, which is plural and multiple and which undermines monolithic phallocentric language. Julia Kristeva, on the other hand, locates feminine discourse not in the female body, but in marginality and subversion. Like Irigaray and Cixous, she argues that the "feminine" is always repressed in culture, yet unlike Irigaray and Cixous, explains Toril Moi, she defines femininity not biologically, but relationally, as "that which is marginalized by the patriarchal symbolic order." For Kristeva, the "feminine" in language constitutes not so much a stable essence but a disruptive presence—a disruptive presence that both male and female writers can utilize.

Thus numerous feminist critics have approached the topic of language from radically different fields of study and points of view. One reason for the diversity of work on this subject is that, as Cameron notes, the word "language" is used differently by different writers; its meaning varies from the most specific usage (language as pronunciation, lexis, and syntax), to the most broad (language as art or mythology). Some feminist critics interested in language have also worked to redefine what linguists, psychoanalysts, or literary critics mean when they examine "language." Kristeva, for example, suggests that we shift our attention from language as a monolithic system, to language as a heterogeneous signifying process. Cameron similarly calls for an "integrational" approach to women and language, an approach that acknowledges that language is always changing, always being redefined by situation, context, and usage. Only theories that define language as flexible and radically indeterminate can take account of the way language can both oppress and liberate women. When feminist critics move toward a redefinition of language, they move toward liberation from the silence and passivity imposed upon women by a patriarchal culture.

Martha J. Cutter

References

Cameron, Deborah. *Feminism and Linguistic Theory*. New York: St. Martin's, 1992.
———, ed. *The Feminist Critique of Language: A Reader*. London: Routledge, 1990.
Cixous, Hélène. "The Laugh of the Medusa." In *New French Feminisms*, edited by Elaine Marks and Isabelle de Courtivron, 245–264. New York: Schocken Books, 1981.
Coward, Rosalind, and John Ellis. *Language and Materialism: Developments in Semiology and the Theory of the Subject*. London: Routledge and Kegan Paul, 1977.
Gilbert, Sandra, and Susan Gubar. *The Madwoman in the Attic: The Woman Writer and the Nineteenth-Century Literary Imagination*. New Haven: Yale University Press, 1979.
Irigaray, Luce. "The Sex Which Is Not One" and "When the Goods Get Together." In *New French Feminisms*, edited by Elaine Marks and Isabelle de Courtivron, 99-110. New York: Schocken Books, 1981.
Kristeva, Julia. "The Ethics of Linguistics." In *Desire in Language: A Semiotic Approach to Literature and Art*. New York: Columbia University Press, 1980.
Lakoff, Robin. *Language and Woman's Place* [1975]. New York: Harper, 1989.
Moi, Toril. *Sexual/Textual Politics: Feminist Literary Theory*. London: Methuen, 1985.
Sellers, Susan. *Language and Sexual Difference: Feminist Writing in France*. New York: St. Martin's, 1991.
Spender, Dale. *Man Made Language*. London: Routledge and Kegan Paul, 1980.
Thorne, Barrie, and Nancy Henley, eds. *Language and Sex: Difference and Dominance*. Rowley, Mass.: Newbury House, 1975.
———, Cheris Kramarae, and Nancy Henley, eds. *Language, Gender and Society*. Rowley, Mass.: Newbury House, 1983.

Laughter

Women, feminists in particular, are popularly represented as lacking a sense of humor; uptight, they are incapable of laughter. Regina Barreca points to William Congreve for the origins of this stigma, while other feminist scholars (Flieger, Modleski, Reincke) look to the silenced position of women in Sigmund Freud's joke triangle. Whatever the origin, this motif of humorlessness has resulted in traditional literary criticism's neglect of women's textual humor. Critical disregard for this area, however, reveals a discomfort with just what women's laughter does signify: a subversion and rejection of male hegemony.

Feminists have found laughter's subversive quality particularly useful in resisting patriarchal power structures. Hélène Cixous, in her essay "The Laugh of the Medusa," employs the motif of laughter to reject Freudian ideas of a castrating femininity and in her work with Catherine Clément, *The Newly Born Woman*: "All laughter is allied with the monstrous." It "breaks up, breaks out, and splashes over." Clarissa Pinkola Estés and Nancy Reincke identify laughter as forging a bond between women that serves to subvert masculine power.

Feminist literary scholarship has not fully explored issues of women's comedy, perhaps in an effort, as Regina Barreca suggests, to gain credibility in a patriarchal establishment. Recently, however, feminist scholars and critics have sought out women's use of laughter, as a sign of pleasure and a physical manifestation of humor, in literature. For example, Reincke's article "Antidote to Dominance: Women's Laughter as Counteraction" is a self-avowed "search for signs of women's sense of humor in the universe of critical theory," while Patricia Meyer Spacks focuses specifically on the use of laughter within Jane Austen's texts. Alicia Suskin Ostriker identifies humor as an important element in American woman's poetry because "[l]aughter is the most subversive agent in literature."

Maria Jerinic

References

Barr, Marleen S. "'Laughing in a Liberating Defiance': *Egalia's Daughters* and Feminist Tendentious Humor." In *Discontented Discourses,* edited by Marleen S. Barr and Richard Feldstein, 87–99. Urbana: University of Illinois Press, 1989.

Barreca, Regina. "Introduction." *Women's Studies* 15 (1988): 3–22.

Cixous, Hélène. "The Laugh of the Medusa." In *New French Feminisms,* edited by Elaine Marks and Isabelle de Courtivron, 245–264. New York: Schocken Books, 1981.

———, and Catherine Clément. *The Newly Born Woman.* Translated by Betsy Wing. Minneapolis: University of Minnesota Press, 1986.

Estés, Clarissa Pinkola. *Women who Run with the Wolves.* New York: Ballantine, 1992.

Flieger, Jerry Aline. "The Purloined Punchline: Joke as Textual Paradigm." *Modern Language Notes* 98 (1983): 943–967.

Modleski, Tania. "Rape versus Mans/laughter: Hitchcock's *Blackmail* and Feminist Interpretation." *PMLA* 102 (1987): 304–315.

Ostriker, Alicia Suskin. *Stealing the Language: The Emergence of Women's Poetry in America.* Boston: Beacon, 1986.

Reincke, Nancy. "Antidote to Dominance: Women's Laughter as Counteraction." *Journal of Popular Culture* 24 (1991): 27–37.

Spacks, Patricia Meyer. "Austen's Laughter." *Women's Studies* 15 (1988): 71–85.

L

Lerner, Gerda

A women's historian, Gerda Lerner has played a pivotal role in that field's creation, practice, and theory. Lerner's work documents all women's oppression while pointing out that discourse on "women" as a whole hides unequal oppression based on race and class. Lerner has enabled historians to bring all women into history by publishing several collections of women's voices, beginning in 1972 with the early and influential *Black Women in White America*.

In her two-volume *Women and History,* Lerner presents an overarching theory of how History has shaped women. Differentiating history (past events) from History (the process of recording and interpreting these events), Lerner argues that women's relation to History has been one of exclusion. A "cultural product," History has "obliterated and marginalized" women. Women have been excluded from education and writing, and thus from the power to define and name themselves and their world. This exclusion is the primary factor in their oppression, keeping women from coming to a feminist consciousness of themselves as an oppressed "Other."

The patriarchal exclusion of women has profoundly shaped their literature. Feminist literary theory must recognize that women's intellectual endeavors focused on counteracting the "pervasive patriarchal assumptions" of women as inferior and less than fully human. Echoing Virginia Woolf, Lerner points out that women had no access to their foremothers' traditions of thought and writing and had to struggle to higher consciousness as individuals, repeating efforts made by women in previous centuries. Women's writings illustrate this repeated struggle, and ultimately women's slow path to feminist consciousness.

Lynn L. Sharp

References

Lerner, Gerda. *Black Women in White America: A Documentary History*. New York: Pantheon, 1972.
———. *The Creation of Feminist Consciousness from the Middle Ages to 1870* (*Women and History*, Vol. 2). New York: Oxford University Press, 1993.
———. *The Creation of Patriarchy* (*Women and History*, Vol. 1). New York: Oxford University Press, 1986.
———. *The Female Experience: An American Documentary*. Indianapolis: Bobbs-Merrill Educational, 1977.

Lesbianism

Lesbianism as a concept opposed to female heterosexuality has existed only since the mid nineteenth century. Nonetheless female homosexual desire has a long and complicated historical and political presence that makes it problematic to define. Historically, in many periods, intense romantic friendships and passionate, public declarations of romantic love between women have been socially permissible. Although explicitly sexual texts and claims are rare, Lillian Faderman, among others, has made an excellent case for the claim that a whole continuum of lesbian desire and relationships has existed over time. Feminist scholars and literary theorists have taken up this claim, and since the 1970s, lesbianism has existed in a broad sense to define those who may choose to identify themselves with the love of women, regardless of the primary direction of their desire. Indeed, in 1970s feminist parlance, lesbianism was taken by some to be the logical extension of feminism.

Eve Kosofsky Sedgwick has said, in her volume *The Epistemology of the Closet,* "To alienate conclusively, definitionally, from anyone on any theoretical ground the authority to describe and name their own desire is a terribly consequential seizure. In this century, in which sexuality has been made expressive of the essence of both identity and knowledge, it may represent the most intimate violence possible." Because the stakes of defining desire are so great, recent criticism has avoided defining the terms of lesbianism. Diana Fuss articulates the scope of the problem of naming a lesbian identity, saying, "The lack of consensus and the continued disputes among feminists over the definition of 'lesbian' pivot centrally around the question of essentialism. Exactly who is a lesbian? Is there such a thing as a lesbian essence? Does 'woman' include lesbian?"

Can we speak of a "lesbian mind" as distinct from what Wittig calls "the straight mind"? The definitions of lesbian in feminist discourse are various and inventive. The historical understanding of lesbianism has suffered historically from both the failure of history to acknowledge women, and also from its rejection of homosexuality. John Boswell, one of the primary scholars of homosexual history, lists all the available texts on lesbian women for late Antiquity and the Middle Ages, and yet is able to locate less than a page of references. While there is an ongoing concerted effort to locate and reclaim the historical lesbian, and to contextualize lesbianism historically, both in the realm of literary theory and other disciplines, it is a slow and troubled process, troubled not only by lack of available material, but also by the fact of lesbianism's conflicted place in the disciplines that overlap it.

For periods later than the Middle Ages, lesbianism becomes a more available topic. Judith Brown, in an article on lesbianism in the latter Middle Ages and Renaissance, documents that in the seventeenth century, women frequently professed romantic love for one another, and claimed that relationships between women exceeded and improved upon those involving men. The eighteenth century had its own renaissance of romantic friendship and of passionate poetry and letters written from woman to woman that are just now being explored.

The nineteenth and twentieth centuries have developed a pluralism of critical understandings that make lesbianism as a historical notion even more complicated. Romantic friendship was still common, until in nineteenth-century America, the "Boston marriage" had become almost conventional, but explicit expressions of lesbian desire were still taboo. Joan Nestle, in her history of modern lesbianism, has shown that whole cultural aesthetics of lesbianism developed in the twentieth century, where "butch" and "femme" shaped an understanding of lesbian sexuality whose implications still linger in the community. Later feminism, as has been carefully documented, added still another dimension, with its simultaneous homophobia and requirement that feminist-identified women come out as lesbians. Adrienne Rich pioneered the notion of the "lesbian continuum," taking into account the myriad possible identities of lesbianism while trying to avoid the slighting of the real experiences of women's lives. Black lesbianism and minority discourse created further permutations that are only beginning to be properly taken into account.

Critical understanding of lesbianism has developed largely from feminist criticism, although more recently queer theory has added a significant contribution. Lesbianism has been frequently read as subverting the status quo, but also as supporting it. The unnamed desire of the Victorian period has become, on some level, the desire that cannot speak its name because of the complexity of that name.

Psychoanalysis has been concerned with female homosexuality since Freud's two cases, the famous "Dora" case, and, much less examined, his "Case of Homosexuality in a Woman," both of which struggle to place female homosexual desire on his continuum of bisexuality and account psychologically for female sexual desire. Although Freud can be said never to have entirely succeeded in making a place for female homosexuality, later scholars have taken female homosexual desire to be integral to any understanding of the female psyche. Irigaray understands female desire for the feminine as the door into a feminine language, and presents the metaphor of the two lips of the labia speaking together. For Wittig, lesbians are so outside of the realm of desire that they are literally not women, but constitute another sex because they are not subject to the same economies of masculinity that heterosexual women are.

Lesbians of color have left profound marks upon understandings of lesbianism. Scholars like bell hooks have made evident the dangers defining the margins of lesbianism, and the essential homophobia of a position that does not take into account the problematic intersections of color and gender. Postcolonial theory has also expanded an understanding of the issues of lesbianism, with scholars like Chandra Talpade Mohanty and Gayatri Spivak, who have drawn close parallels between the colonization of female desire and the colonization of nation.

Postcolonial and race theory exist in a complicated relationship with feminist criticism and with other understandings of lesbianism, in a complex triangle that includes queer theory as well, as they act in consortion and in opposition to creating a space for the marginal that neither trivializes nor demeans.

Other theorists have concentrated in placing lesbianism historically, or within poststructuralist and deconstructive critical frameworks. Bonnie Zimmerman has noted that much of the lesbian feminist criticism of the 1980s and early 1990s has been interested in the reconstruction of the lesbian as metaphor or subject position. This shift in emphasis is reflected in the tropes we now use; they refer less to the act of seeing than to the place from which one sees. Another way of putting this is that we are less focused on essential "deep" *knowledge* than on historically situated knowing.

Sharon Astyk

References

Boswell, John. *Christianity, Social Tolerance and Homosexuality: Gay People in Western Europe from the Beginning of the Christian Era to the Fourteenth Century*. Chicago: University of Chicago Press, 1980.

Brown, Judith. "Renaissance Sexuality: An Exchange." *Renaissance Quarterly* 40 (1987): 485–511.

Butler, Judith. *Gender Trouble: Feminism and the Subversion of Identity*. New York: Routledge, 1990.

Duberman, Martin B., Martha Vicinus, and George Chauncey, Jr., eds., *Hidden from History: Reclaiming the Gay and Lesbian Past*. New York: New American Library, 1989.

Faderman, Lillian. *Surpassing the Love of Men: Romantic Friendship and Love between Women from the Renaissance to the Present*. New York: William Morrow, 1981.

Fuss, Diana. *Essentially Speaking: Feminism, Nature, and Difference*. New York: Routledge, 1989.

hooks, bell. *Yearning: Race, Gender and Cultural Politics*. Boston: South End, 1990.

Irigaray, Luce. *This Sex Which Is Not One*. Ithaca, N.Y.: Cornell University Press, 1985.

Mohanty, Chandra T., et al., eds. *Third World Women and the Politics of Femi-*

L

nism. Bloomington: Indiana University Press, 1991.

Munt, Sally, ed. *New Lesbian Criticism: Literary and Cultural Readings.* New York: Columbia University Press, 1992.

Nestle, Joan. *A Restricted Country.* Ithaca, N.Y.: Firebrand, 1987.

Sedgwick, Eve Kosofsky. *Between Men: English Literature and Male Homosocial Desire.* New York: Columbia University Press, 1985.

Shaktini, Namascar. "A Revolutionary Signifier: The Lesbian Body" in *Lesbian Texts and Contexts,* edited by Joanne Glasgow and Catharine Stimpson, 291–303. New York: New York University Press.

Wittig, Monique. *The Straight Mind and Other Essays.* Boston: Beacon, 1992.

Lesbian Studies

The burgeoning of lesbian and gay literature in the twenty-five years since the formation of the gay rights and feminist movements would have been impossible without the creation of alternative presses, bookstores, and journals devoted to lesbian and gay writing and writers and the political commitment and persistence of lesbian and gay activists. Lesbian studies is itself an outgrowth of lesbian feminism and the production of lesbian literature. Simply put, we may claim lesbian literary studies as the ongoing critical interrogation of lesbian writing, writers, and readers. A backwards glance at two decades of lesbian literary studies, however, reveals all this and much more—a rich discursive field, employing a variety of theoretical approaches, flourishing both inside and outside the academy, and increasingly concerned with the limits and possibilities of lesbian representation.

In the March 1957 issue of *The Ladder,* the Daughters of Bilitis (DOB) began a regular feature entitled "Lesbiana": a bibliography of lesbian literature. *The Ladder,* the monthly publication of DOB, America's first lesbian organization, is an extraordinary source of "forgotten" lesbian texts; for example, in May 1957, Jeannette Forster's *Sex Variant Women in Literature* was favorably reviewed by Marion Zimmer Bradley. Included in "Lesbiana" were many of the very popular lesbian paperbacks of the 1950s and 1960s. For isolated lesbians, these pulp romances were often the only sign that there were others like themselves.

Responding to an outpouring of lesbian literature during the 1970s, lesbian feminist literary scholars articulated a political agenda for lesbian literary studies. In an essay first published in 1972, Adrienne Rich calls on students of literature to engage literary texts "from a new critical direction." This act of radical revision—the reworking of a text's dominant meanings—is for women, she suggests, a matter of survival: a clue to how women have lived in the past and a map for the "imaginative transformation of reality." Although not overtly "lesbian," Rich's call for a language to match women's dawning feminist consciousness was adopted by lesbian critics for their own inquiries into the intersections of lesbian writing, the ideas and forms of newly emerging feminist criticism, and the imperatives of the dominant literary culture.

When, in 1981, Bonnie Zimmerman posed the question: "What is a lesbian-focused literary criticism?" ("What Has Never Been: An Overview of Lesbian Feminist Criticism"), she began by indicting feminist journals for their inattention to lesbian literary commentary. She charges lesbians with the double task of unmasking heterosexist assumptions and of uncovering "a unique lesbian feminist perspective." Zimmerman's intervention into the specificity of lesbian literary criticism set the tone for the 1980s. Insisting that lesbianism is a meaningful category, that is, a unified identity based in woman-identification or love between women, Zimmerman endowed the lesbian subject with a specific vantage point for questioning heterosexual "norms" and with a critical perspective or aesthetic; furthermore, she claimed that lesbian identity encouraged identification between author, character, and reader. In keeping with her example, other critics, such as Catharine Stimpson ("Zero Degree Deviancy: The Lesbian Novel in English," 1981) and Jean Kennard ("Ourself behind Ourselves: A Theory for Lesbian Readers," 1984), likewise depend upon a definition of "lesbian" as the ground for their respective explorations of lesbian texts and lesbian readers.

In the late 1970s, Anglo American feminism experienced a crisis of meaning: a belief in common experiences among women, a view rehearsed in the "lesbian consciousness" approach of some lesbian literary scholars, was increasingly contested as activists and theorists (foremost among whom were lesbians of color) began to explore the overlapping systems of power that shape women's lives. Recognizing the ethnocentrism of much gender theory, feminist scholarship was reinvigorated by a perspective gradually more attuned to the interlocking forces of gender, race, sexuality, and class.

In 1977, Barbara Smith authored "Toward a Black Feminist Criticism," in which she accused white feminists and black male critics of ignoring literature by black women and all literary scholars of the ongoing suppression of black lesbian creativity. Throughout her essay, Smith draws connections between politics and the literary imagination, arguing that the literary contributions of black women, and especially of black lesbians, will remain relatively unknown without the sustaining presence and authorization of an autonomous black feminist movement. Prioritizing identification and the referentiality of race and sexuality, Smith calls for a rereading of (white) feminism to reflect the reality of black lesbian experience. In so doing, she enhances questions of identity posed by white lesbian critics to ask in what ways being both black and lesbian contributes to a writer's understanding.

If, initially, lesbian feminist literary studies were characterized by efforts to consolidate a unified set of meanings for the term "lesbian"—a project as compelling among lesbians of color as among white lesbians—more recently, lesbian criticism has been influenced by lesbian and gay studies. While not monolithic, lesbian and gay studies often take an antiessentialist approach to identity, contesting any precise correlation between text and experience. Exposing the terms by which binaries of sex and gender are secured, lesbian and gay scholars interrogate gender imperatives in order to denaturalize identity categories.

Writer and literary critic Monique Wittig views lesbianism as exceeding the categories of sex, that is, the political regime that divides society into male and female, men and women: lesbians, she writes, are not women. In her writing, which breaks down boundaries between fiction and theory, Wittig radically destabilizes sex as a category, preempting the position of the speaking subject to invoke "lesbianism" as a universal point of view. Similarly, Teresa de Lauretis, in a wide ranging discussion of lesbian subjectivity ("Sexual Indifference and Lesbian Representation," 1988), surveys literature, theater, film, political and cultural theory to conclude that sexual difference preserves the tyranny of gender binaries, casting "woman" in terms of "man." In order for lesbians to escape heterosexualization, what she calls "sexual (in)difference," feminists, de Lauretis argues, will have to interrupt the trajectory of sex, gender, and sexuality and reimagine (or reinvent) lesbian identities as heterogeneous, fractured, and socially contingent.

In less than twenty-five years, lesbian literary studies have gone from trying to uncover a lost lesbian tradition, premised upon an uninterrupted lesbian identity, to scrutinizing identity categories as sites of "trouble": as Judith Butler writes, to define "lesbian" is to control or limit sexuality. Once marginalized within the classroom, professional conferences, and anthologies of literary criticism, lesbian theory has become an established component of feminist literary studies, moving expertly among a variety of disciplines to articulate new theoretical frameworks for a range of lesbian identifications and pleasures.

Cheryl Kader

References

Butler, Judith. *Bodies That Matter: On the Discursive Limits of "Sex."* New York: Routledge, 1993.

———. *Gender Trouble: Feminism and the Subversion of Identity.* New York: Routledge, 1990.

de Lauretis, Teresa. "Sexual Indifference and Lesbian Representation." *Theatre Journal* (Spring 1988): 155–177.

Grier, Barbara. *The Lesbian in Literature.* 3rd ed. Tallahassee, Fla.: Naiad, 1981.

Jay, Karla, and Joanne Glasgow, eds. *Lesbian Texts and Contexts.* New York: New York University Press, 1990.

Kennard, Jean E. "Ourself behind Ourselves: A Theory for Lesbian Readers." *Signs* 9 (1984): 647–662.

Martin, Biddy. "Lesbian Identity and Autobiographical Difference(s)." In *Life/Lines: Theorizing Women's Autobiography,* edited by Bella Brodzki and Celeste Schenck, 77–103. Ithaca, N.Y.: Cornell University Press, 1988.

Nelson, Emmanuel, ed. *Critical Essays: Gay and Lesbian Writers of Color.* New York: Haworth, 1993.

Newton, Esther. "The Mythic Mannish Lesbian: Radclyffe Hall and the New Woman." In *The Lesbian Issue: Essays from SIGNS,* edited by Estelle B. Freedman, et al., 1–26. Chicago: University of Chicago Press, 1985.

Rich, Adrienne. "When We Dead Awaken: Writing as Re-Vision." *On Lies, Secrets, and Silence: Selected Prose, 1966–1978,* 33–49. New York: W.W. Norton, 1979.

Roberts, J.R. *Black Lesbians: An Annotated Bibliography.* Tallahassee, Fla.: Naiad, 1981.

Rule, Jane. *Lesbian Images.* Trumansburg, N.Y.: Crossing, 1982.

Smith, Barbara. "Toward a Black Feminist Criticism." In *All the Women Are White, All the Blacks Are Men, But Some of Us Are Brave: Black Women's Studies,* edited by Gloria T. Hull, Patricia Bell Scott, and Barbara Smith, 157–175. Old Westbury, N.Y.: Feminist, 1982.

Stimpson, Catharine R. "Zero Degree Deviancy: The Lesbian Novel in English." *Critical Inquiry* 8 (1981): 363–379.

Wittig, Monique. *The Straight Mind.* Boston: Beacon, 1992.

Zimmerman, Bonnie. "What Has Never Been: An Overview of Lesbian Feminist Criticism." In *The New Feminist Criticism: Essays on Women. Literature & Theory,* edited by Elaine Showalter, 200–224. New York: Pantheon, 1985.

Lessing, Doris

Throughout a writing career that spans more than forty years and includes numerous novels, short stories, and essays, Doris Lessing has courageously explored the patterns that connect the individual to the group, particularly in the lives of women. Her breakthrough novel *The Golden Notebook* portrays the relationship between the personal and the political through interlaced diaries and sections of a novel by a blocked woman writer. For many women, this novel provided their first encounter with an uncompromisingly honest portrayal of a woman's view of sexual relationships with men, disillusionment with Marxism, and mental breakdown.

Lessing began her writing career with a five-volume series of mainly realistic novels, *Children of Violence,* centering on her experience of marginality as a white woman growing up in the British colony of Southern Rhodesia (now Zimbabwe). By volume five, *The Four-Gated City,* however, Lessing had begun to explore the realm of inner space, especially that of middle-aged women, through dreams, fantasies, and the descent into madness. In her visionary five-volume space-fiction series *Canopus in*

Argos: Archives, the psychological and political are now set in the context of the cosmic. However, the second volume, *The Marriages between Zones Three, Four, and Five,* again investigates the sexual and emotional relationships between men and women, this time through a parable about marriage and spiritual growth.

Lessing's more recent writing is again realistic, but it continues to stimulate readers to question their assumptions about gender, race, politics, and spirituality.

Phyllis Sternberg Perrakis

References

Lessing, Doris. *The Four-Gated City.* Vol. 5 of *Children of Violence.* London: MacGibbon and Kee, 1969. New York: Knopf, 1969.

———. *The Golden Notebook.* London: Michael Joseph, 1962. New York: Simon and Schuster, 1962.

———. *The Marriages between Zones Three, Four, and Five.* Vol. 2 of *Canopus in Argos: Archives.* London: Jonathan Cape, 1980. New York: Knopf, 1980.

Pickering, Jean. *Understanding Doris Lessing,* 197–210. Columbia: University of South Carolina Press, 1990.

Lorde, Audre

Describing herself as a "black lesbian feminist warrior poet," Audre Lorde represented the lives of poor women of color and of lesbians. Her work focused on intersections of race, gender, and class in women's oppression, which placed her at the forefront of emerging feminist thought of the 1970s. Lorde's expressly political literary forms merged theory and activism, and art, offering feminist theory alternative epistemological paradigms.

Nominated for the National Book Award for poetry in 1974 for *From a Land Where Other People Live,* Lorde received wider recognition for *The Black Unicorn,* poems of African maternal cosmology, love between women, and outrage over racism and sexism. She chronicled her experience of breast cancer and mastectomy in *The Cancer Journals,* using her refusal to wear a prosthesis to expose a medical profession and economic system that value profit above human well-being. *Zami,* a prose fusion of history, autobiography, and myth, recounts Lorde's development of identity as an African American lesbian poet in the 1940s and 1950s in New York, and its roots in her mother's Caribbean homeland. *Sister Outsider* collects Lorde's essays on the uses of difference and of the erotic, which anticipated important directions in feminist thought. She theorized that difference may undermine an "easy sameness" promoted to control people through racism, sexism, and homophobia, and that the erotic is one means by which differences among people can become a source of creative dialogue rather than threat.

Lorde's work powerfully conveys that women of color and lesbians are not marginal but central to the empowerment of all women, and that their reality and imagination must be comprehended by feminist theory and strategies for social change.

Ronna C. Johnson

References

Lorde, Audre. *Between Our Selves*. Point Reyes, Calif.: Eidolon, 1976.
———. *The Black Unicorn*. New York: W.W. Norton, 1978.
———. *Cables to Rage*. London: Paul Bremen, 1970.
———. *The Cancer Journals*. Argyle, N.Y.: Spinsters, Ink, 1980.
———. *Chosen Poems*. New York: W.W. Norton, 1982.
———. *Coal*. New York: W.W. Norton, 1976.
———. *The First Cities*. New York: Poets, 1968.
———. *From a Land Where Other People Live*. Detroit: Broadside, 1973.
———. *New York Head Shop and Museum*. Detroit: Broadside, 1975.
———. *Our Dead behind Us: Poems*. New York: W.W. Norton, 1986.
———. *Sister Outsider*. Freedom, Calif.: Crossing, 1984.
———. *Zami: A New Spelling of My Name*. Freedom, Calif.: Crossing, 1982.

L

M

McDowell, Deborah

McDowell's contributions in the field of African American and American literature include important projects in publishing and incisive essays on literary theory and the politics of intellectual inquiry. In 1989, she co-edited *Slavery and the Literary Imagination* with Arnold Rampersad; in 1985 and 1986, she edited and wrote introductions for newly reprinted novels by Jessie Fauset and Nella Larsen, respectively.

In essays on African American fiction and critical works on slavery, novels of the Harlem Renaissance, and black feminist criticism, McDowell employs feminist, poststructuralist, and reader-response theories to explore issues such as agency, identity, and desire. McDowell's essays on Harlem Renaissance writers Nella Larsen and Jessie Fauset contain some of her most innovative work on African American women's writing and issues of sexuality. During her tenure as general editor for Beacon Press's Black Women Writer Series, McDowell oversaw the release of twelve titles, among them Jessie Fauset's out-of-print 1929 novel *Plum Bun,* and novels by Frances Harper, Octavia Butler, Gayl Jones, Alice Childress, and Ann Petry.

McDowell and scholars such as Barbara Christian, Ann duCille, and Valerie Smith have been actively debating feminist issues in African-American studies and the academy. In her 1980 essay "New Directions for Black Feminist Criticism," McDowell offers an extensive response to Barbara Smith's historic "Toward A Black Feminist Criticism" (1977). McDowell defines black feminist criticism as work done by "black female critics who analyze the works of Black female writers from a feminist or political perspective." According to McDowell, black feminist critics, regardless of their theoretical positions, can generate a more complete scholarship only by performing intensive textual analysis that is informed by historical, social, and political contexts.

Lois Brown

References

McDowell, Deborah. "Boundaries: Or Distant Relations and Close Kin." In *Afro-American Literary Study in the 1990's,* edited by Houston A. Baker, Jr., and Patricia Redmond, 51–77. Chicago: University of Chicago Press, 1989.

———. "The Changing Same: Generational Connections and Black Women Novelists." *New Literary History* 18 (1987): 281–302.

———. "'The Nameless . . . Shameful Impulse': Sexuality in Nella Larsen's *Quicksand* and *Passing.*" In *Studies in Black American Literature,* Vol. 3, edited by Houston A. Baker, Jr., 139–167. Greenwood, Fla.: Penkevill, 1988.

———. "Negotiating between Tenses: Witnessing Slavery after Freedom—*Dessa Rose.*" In *Slavery and the Literary Imagination,* edited by Deborah McDowell and Arnold Rampersad, 144–163. Baltimore, Md.: Johns Hopkins University Press, 1989.

———. "New Directions for Black Feminist Criticism." *Black American Literature Forum* 14 (1980): 153–159.

———. "The Self and the Other: Reading Toni Morrison's *Sula* and the Black Female Text." In *Toni Morrison: Collected Essays,* edited by Nellie McKay, 77–90. Boston: G.K. Hall, 1988.

———, and Arnold Rampersad, eds. *Slavery*

and the Literary Imagination. Baltimore, Md.: Johns Hopkins University Press, 1989.

McKay, Nellie

McKay's most influential work has been in the recovery and reexamination of black women's writing. McKay's work reveals the diversity and richness of black women's literary history. Analyzing black women's writing from the nineteenth century to the present, McKay shows how black women writers have consistently debunked the negative stereotypes propagated by the dominant culture and have conveyed with authenticity the complexity of the black American female experience. McKay has also written eloquently about the status of black women academics in the white academy. Despite the widespread complaints of these scholars that they often find themselves isolated, overworked, and embattled due to racial and sexual bias, black women academics have nonetheless made considerable inroads in transforming the administrative policies of predominantly white universities, as well as significant contributions to the reconstruction of the American canon.

McKay has written that "black women writers project a dynamic 'I' into the canon, one that makes more complete the reality of the multi-faceted American experience." As one of the first-generation black feminist scholars to emerge from the civil rights and women's liberation movements, McKay has done no less for the study of literature through her assiduous efforts as a feminist scholar and teacher.

Kimberley Roberts

References

McKay, Nellie. "The Girls who Became the Women: Childhood Memories in the Autobiographies of Harriet Jacobs, Mary Church Terrell, and Anne Moody." In *Tradition and the Talents of Women,* edited by Florence Howe, 105–124. Urbana: University of Illinois Press, 1991.

———. *Jean Toomer, Artist: A Study of His Literary Life and Work, 1894–1936.* Chapel Hill: University of North Carolina Press, 1984.

———. "Reflections on Black Women Writers: Revising the Literary Canon." In *The Impact of Feminist Research in the Academy,* edited by Christie Farnham, 174–189. Bloomington: Indiana University Press, 1987.

———. "A Troubled Peace: Black Women in the Halls of the White Academy." In *"Turning the Century": Feminist Theory in the 1990s,* edited by Glynis Carr, 21–37. Lewisburg, Pa.: Bucknell University Press, 1992.

———, ed. *Critical Essays on Toni Morrison.* Boston: G.K. Hall, 1988.

MacKinnon, Catharine A.

To describe lawyer and antipornography activist Catharine MacKinnon as a controversial figure would both assert the obvious and be a major understatement. Through the publication of several of her speeches in *Feminism Unmodified* and in later works such as *Towards a Feminist Theory of the State* and *Only Words,* she established a comprehensive theoretical framework for the feminist analysis of pornography and American law. In so doing, MacKinnon has polarized opinions on this problematic issue among lawyers, academics, and feminists alike.

Her stance on the essentially anti-Constitutional nature of pornography rests on three elements: what pornography is, what it does, and the broader social effects of its use and distribution. But these elements cannot be easily separated, for they are all inextricably linked and equally fundamental to the nature of pornography as she sees it. For MacKinnon, pornography both is and means what it does: its epistemological standing is dependent on its status and function as an act. It is crucial, she argues, for pornography to be understood "as constructing and performative rather than as merely referential or connotative." Whatever else it might be, pornography is not an image or a fantasy of something that does not exist—since "it takes a real person doing each act to make what you see," it is more than an idea, goes beyond expression, and transcends symbolism.

In this framework, pornography is not even a representation of sexual reality—it is sexual reality. By casting men (the primary consumers of pornography) in the role of perpetual and aroused viewers and women (the primary group represented in pornography) as those perpetually and erotically viewed, pornography implicitly creates powerful hierarchies of gender and sexuality that are then normalized within Western society. The refusal of American legal bodies to define pornography, she argues, appears to stem from "the inability to draw a line between pornography and everything else." In this paradigm, pornography both creates and relies upon a culture of male domination constitutive of sexuality, and consequently has the power to "invent women" to fulfill any role it chooses to create. And if this is the case, then the harm that pornography does in shaping female subjectivity to its own purposes, in promoting the objectification of women in mass culture, and in justifying or inciting rape and sexual assault by showing women smiling as they are beaten, becomes normalized and undetectable. Hence, she insists, to dismiss or defend pornography on the grounds of free speech, as "only words," is to ignore its vast performative and constitutive power.

The radicalism on which MacKinnon's theory is based also forms the foundation of her legal work against pornography. Dissatisfied with the current legislative options of federal and state obscenity laws, and insisting that she has "no particular interest in increasing the power of the state over sexuality or speech," MacKinnon, in conjunction with her friend and co-activist Andrea Dworkin, crafted a civil law defining pornography and providing the opportunity for those who have been harmed by pornography to seek legal redress. In 1986, the United States Supreme Court struck the law down as a violation of the First Amendment, but MacKinnon's legal work has since had a strong influence in shaping the antipornography decisions reached by the Supreme Court of Canada in 1992. However, this success has not diminished the controversy surrounding her theories, nor has it silenced her vehement critics. Her feminist opponents see her as not only a controversial figure, but as a dangerous one. Her theories fly in the face of First Amendment rights, they believe, and deprive women of any constitutive agency outside of that granted to them by law, even as these theories are promoted by a woman who sees herself as a feminist. Moreover, the difficulties inherent in determining which materials are pornographic remain despite MacKinnon's detailed definition of the term. Others note that MacKinnon's encapsulation of the problem of pornography is far too rigid, leaving no room for discussion of any erotic materials intended for viewers other than heterosexual men. Nevertheless, by challenging previous conceptions of and reactions to pornography, MacKinnon continues to strive toward her ultimate aim of a society where "[s]ex between people and things, human beings and pieces of paper, real men and unreal women, will be a turn-off."

Alexandra Bennett

References

Bottomley, Anne, and Joanne Conaghan, eds. *Feminist Theory and Legal Strategy.* Cambridge, Mass.: Blackwell, 1993.

MacKinnon, Catharine. *Feminism Unmodified: Discourses on Life and Law.* Cambridge: Harvard University Press, 1987.

———. *Only Words.* Cambridge: Harvard University Press, 1993.

———. *Towards a Feminist Theory of the State.* Cambridge: Harvard University Press, 1989.

Madness

See INSANITY

Marcus, Jane

Jane Marcus is an eminent Virginia Woolf scholar and literary critic of British Modernism. Marcus combines the gynocritical project of recovering women's literary texts with a commitment to reevaluating cultural and political histories in light of women's experiences of class, sexuality, and race. Her Woolf scholarship has highlighted aspects of Virginia Woolf's life and work ignored by previous critics, particularly her socialist politics and lesbian sexuality. Woolf is Marcus's touchstone in essays such as "Storming the Toolshed," and "Thinking Back through Our Mothers," where she urges feminist critics to aggressively make use of contemporary critical theories in the service of a "socialist feminist criticism," a cooperative, collective project of studying women's writing that would combine materialist politics with a feminist aesthetics and practice.

Marcus's revisionary scholarship on Woolf, including the three volumes of critical essays she has edited in 1981 and 1987, used biographical and cultural research to give a more complete context for the literary texts; in doing so, Marcus revealed information about Woolf's important relationships to other women and her actual involvement in socialist political movements, allowing for new readings of Woolf's novels and essays. This kind of historical research has informed her recent writing about gender issues and the contributions of women activists and novelists during the world wars.

Marcus urges feminist scholars to account for the material circumstances of women's writing, celebrating their own connections with women writers and scholars, without taking for granted the important differences of race, class, and sexual orientation.

Lorna J. Smedman

References

Marcus, Jane. *Art and Anger: Reading like a Woman.* Columbus: Ohio State University Press, 1988.

————. "The Asylums of Antaeus: Women, War, and Madness—Is There a Feminist Fetishism?" In *The New Historicism,* edited by Aram Veeser, 132–151. New York: Routledge, 1989.

————. "Sapphistory: The Woolf and the Well." In *Lesbian Texts and Contexts,* edited by Karla Jay and Joanne Glasgow, 164–179. New York: New York University Press, 1990.

————, ed. *New Feminist Essays on Virginia Woolf.* Lincoln: University of Nebraska Press, 1981.

————, ed. *Virginia Woolf and Bloomsbury: A Centenary Celebration.* Bloomington: Indiana University Press, 1987.

————, ed. *Virginia Woolf and the Languages of Patriarchy.* Bloomington: Indiana University Press, 1987.

Marginality

Few terms in the oeuvre of feminist theory have simultaneously afforded new opportunities for women and expanded the very parameters of feminist theory itself. "Marginality" is one of these terms. Although in her influential book *Feminist Theory: From Margin to Center,* bell hooks notes that "to be in the margin is to be part of the whole but outside the main body," others resist codifying the term and urge instead a reconsideration of the margin/center dichotomy. The problem of definition notwithstanding, however, feminist literary scholars in particular have used the term to question those excluded from the (literary) canon and academic disciplines because of their race, class, ethnicity, gender, or sexuality; furthermore, they have suggested that to pay attention to the margins is to examine how knowledge is produced and for whom. Yet attention to the margins—to who or what has been excluded or marginalized—necessitates an examination of the very confines of feminist theory itself: who has defined feminist theory, and who has been excluded by this definition?

First, the literary canon. In the last decade, scholars have begun to question how the study of literature is conducted. In *Canons and Contexts,* Paul Lauter defines the canon as a set of literary works; a grouping of religious, philosophical, or political texts; and the story of a history. He adds that the construction of the canon is one way in which culture validates social power and maintains that works excluded from it are invariably produced by those with less power than the dominant group. Women, he insists, have been excluded because of their gender and sexuality and race and workingclass status. In order to redress this problem, he advocates a move from literature as the study of "classics" (a term that is itself politically charged) to a recognition of difference—the difference of race, gender, sexuality, and class. Women have much at stake in this project.

If Lauter's work has been helpful in its attempt to define both the canon and the current academic/institutional constraints surrounding it, feminists have long sought to interrogate traditional definitions of literature itself. Although there is a healthy list of women engaged in such work, two prominent examples emerge from 1984 and 1987 respectively. In her study of nineteenth-century women writers, entitled "Rewriting the Scribbling Women," Nina Baym maintains that those she calls the "guardians of culture," have used the method of literary analysis as a process of cultural indoctrination; in response, she urges women not merely to defend women's texts (for this would be to engage in the strategy of our forefathers), but rather to expose the contradictions inherent in the way in which literature has been defined. Nellie McKay's "Reflections on Black Women Writers: Revising the Literary Canon," extends Baym's analysis and demonstrates how black women writers have forced a recognition of the many voices of America; additionally, she suggests that those outside dominant culture continue to assert their own individualism and experience, what she calls their own "dynamic 'I,'" into the writing of drama, fiction, and slave narratives.

McKay's work on canon formation is related to a larger agenda of black and Third-

World feminists that seeks to reformulate feminist theory itself. *Making Face, Making Soul= Haciendo Caras: Creative and Critical Perspectives by Women of Color,* edited by Gloria Anzaldúa and published in 1990; *Home Girls: A Black Feminist Anthology,* edited by Barbara Smith, published in 1983; and *This Bridge Called My Back: Writings By Radical Women of Color,* edited by Cherríe Moraga and Gloria Anzaldúa, published in 1981, are three of the most influential texts in and for this project. While in *Making Face, Making Soul=Haciendo Caras,* Gloria Anzaldúa highlights how the identities—the bodies and faces—of women of color have been inscribed by social structures, the foreword to the second edition of *This Bridge Called My Back* most succinctly expresses the marginalized status of Third-World women and women of color. Querying the particular concerns of women of color as they have been overlooked by Third-World movements, solidarity groups, and international and white feminist coalitions, this foreword suggests what the collection contends: the oppression of women of color is manifold and simultaneous and often is manifested in racism, sexism, classism, and homophobia. A single version of feminist theory, then, will never be an adequate solution.

Many of the concerns of all three texts are articulated in an essay in *This Bridge Called My Back.* In "A Black Feminist Statement," the words of the Combahee River Collective, a group of women who began meeting in 1974, are reprinted. These words articulate the thoughts of many women of color who have been marginalized from the canon, literary studies, and hegemonic definitions of feminist theory: "It was our experience and disillusionment within these liberation movements [civil rights, black nationalism, and so on], as well as experience on the periphery of the white male left, that led to the need to develop a politics that was antiracist, unlike those of white women, and antisexist, unlike those of black and white men." Yet this confrontation with a dominant feminist theory has not been brought to a close with women of color, but has continued as lesbian theorists assert both the specificity of their experiences and the concomitant need for any theory of women's oppression to recognize its limitations. In "Thinking Sex: Notes for a Radical Theory of the Politics of Sexuality," Gayle Rubin asks us to recognize the political dimension of erotic life, especially an erotic life that differs from what is sanctioned by the center. She also contends that

feminism is the theory of gender oppression and to conflate this with the theory of sexual oppression is to negate the difference between gender and desire. Rubin's essay explicitly disrupts dominant notions of feminist theory and insists on the specific political implications of gay and lesbian sexuality. Her work allows for the possibility of later lesbian theorists such as Biddy Martin. In her essay "Sexual Practice and Changing Lesbian Identities," Martin cautions lesbian theorists themselves against maintaining a fixed norm of erotic life and, perhaps more urgently, from failing to recognize that any theory of sexuality necessarily has the potential to obscure issues of race and class. Contending that in 1992 "sexuality is in the process of being *centered* in ways that make it not only autonomous, but independent of other variables," she maintains that gender and sexuality are never performed outside of a complex web of variables. While highlighting what has been marginalized—here lesbian sexuality—Martin cautions against a too easy shift toward centrality.

Gayatri Chakravorty Spivak, too, working within theories of deconstruction, Marxism, and postcoloniality, recognizes what gets elided when one term—marginality for example—becomes central. Spivak is keenly aware that the center selects and accepts certain inhabitants of the margin in order to better exclude this site, and she speaks convincingly about the precarious relationship between the center and margin. In "Explanation and Culture: Marginalia," published in her collection *In Other Worlds: Essays in Cultural Politics,* she effects a change that will be important for future postcolonial critics; here Spivak deconstructs our understanding of the margin (domestic/private) and center (economic/ public) binary. She engages in this deconstruction to examine imperialism, sexism, and the humanities and to insist that the relationship between the margin and center is "intricate and interanimating." For Spivak, there is no easy distinction between the margin and center; what is marginal is also sometimes central. Therefore, she calls for a shifting—a displacement rather than a reversal—of preconceived definitions of the margin and marginality.

Whether it is signaled in connection with canon formation, racial, sexual, or gender identification, or as that which allows for an exploration of feminist theory, marginality is one of the operative terms in any examination of those practices and persons that have long remained outside dominant constructions. To explore its

M

meanings and implications is to begin to order a more inclusive domain for women.

Megan Sullivan

See also CANON

References

Anzaldúa, Gloria, ed. *Making Face, Making Soul=Haciendo Caras: Creative and Critical Perspectives by Women of Color*. New York: Kitchen Table: Women of Color Press, 1990.

Baym, Nina. "Rewriting the Scribbling Women." *Legacy* 1985 (2): 3–12.

Combahee River Collective. "A Black Feminist Statement." *This Bridge Called My Back: Writings By Radical Women of Color*. Edited by Gloria Anzaldua and Cherríe Moraga, 210–218. New York: Kitchen Table: Women of Color Press, 1981.

hooks, bell. *Feminist Theory: From Margin to Center*. Boston: South End, 1984.

Lauter, Paul. *Canons and Contexts*. New York and Oxford: Oxford University Press, 1991.

McKay, Nellie. "Reflections on Black Women Writers: Revising the Literary Canon." In *Feminisms: An Anthology of Literary Theory and Criticism*, edited by Diane Prince-Herndl and Robyn Warhol, 249–261. New Brunswick, N.J.: Rutgers University Press, 1991.

Martin, Biddy. "Sexual Practice and Changing Lesbian Identities." In *Destabilizing Theory: Contemporary Feminist Debates*, edited by Michele Barrett and Anne Phillips, 93–119. Stanford: Stanford University Press, 1992.

Rubin, Gayle, "Thinking Sex: Notes for a Radical Theory of the Politics of Sexuality." In *Pleasure and Danger*, edited by Carol Vance, 267–319. Boston: Routledge and Kegan Paul, 1984.

Smith, Barbara, ed. *Home Girls: A Black Feminist Anthology*. New York: Kitchen Table: Women of Color Press, 1983.

Spivak, Gayatri Chakravorty. *In Other Worlds: Essays in Cultural Politics*. New York and London: Routledge, 1988.

Marks, Elaine

Well known for her edition of *New French Feminisms* (with Isabelle de Courtivron), Elaine Marks has been an instrumental contributor to feminist theory through her work with French feminisms and lesbian literary criticism. She has written and edited works on Simone de Beauvoir and Sidonie Gabrielle Colette.

Her work *Homosexualities and French Literature* (edited with George Stambolian) incites the discovery of homosexuality within texts, and then, proposes using that sexuality as a point for critical analysis. Marks argues that French writers have written, consistently and clearly, on similarities and differences within homosexual experience(s). Further, Marks states that because homosexuality disrupts the "social order," it can be defined as a literary "other." Her work on "Lesbian Intertextuality" opens new possibilities for reading lesbian texts, as she uses various lesbian literary models to illuminate works of Sappho, Colette, and contemporary French writer Monique Wittig. Her current work interrogates (and complicates) the arising problematic question of dividing and separating French national, French women's, and Western lesbian literature(s).

Manju Kurian

References

Marks, Elaine. "Lesbian Intertextuality." In *Homosexualities and French Literature*, edited by George Stambolian and Elaine Marks, 353–377. Ithaca, N.Y.: Cornell University Press, 1979.

———. "'Sapho 1900': Imaginary Renee Viviens and the Rear of the Belle Epoque." In *Displacements*, edited by Joan DeJean and Nancy K. Miller, 211–227. Baltimore, Md.: Johns Hopkins University Press, 1991.

———, and Isabelle de Courtivron, eds. *New French Feminisms*. Amherst: University of Massachusetts Press, 1980.

Marxism

If feminism can be described in the most abstract terms as a concern with gender inequality, Marxism is similarly concerned with class and economic inequality. That is, Marxism is a form of socialism—a historically specific, mid-nineteenth-century response originating with Karl Marx to earlier forms of utopian socialism in Charles Fourier, Saint-Simon, Robert Owen, and Pierre Joseph Proudhon. And of course Marxism is intimately bound up with subsequent international socialist and communist movements. Marxism differs from earlier forms of utopian socialism by rejecting liberal egalitarianism; it does not simply argue for a redistribution of property or for the abolition of private property ("property is theft," as Proudhon put it), but it differs in its analysis of the inherent structural imbalance of capitalism that invariably concentrates economic wealth and social power in the hands of a few as the many must work for the few who own the corporations and factories, the means of production. Marxism as socialism stands for a radical collectivism, the collective ownership of the means of production: from each according to his or her ability and to each according to his or her needs. Or, in the words of the early English communist William Morris, "Competition is bestial, cooperation only is human." Thus Marxism comes to insist not only on an abstract doctrine of fairness and justice, but also on the historically specific imbalance and inequality within capitalism; and further, in the writings of Marx and Engels and on through Lenin and Western Marxism (Georg Lukács and on up through Louis Althusser), Marxists analyze capitalism as a total system, offering an elaborate theory of the social whole, in an analysis that crosses traditional disciplines and discourses, drawing together economics, political theory, philosophy, sociology, and anthropology.

However many variants there are, as practice Marxism is always a political struggle against economic inequality, disentitlement, dispossession, and consequent oppression. As a struggle against inequality and oppression, Marxism would appear to be the natural ally of feminism. Catharine MacKinnon writes, "Sexuality is to feminism what work is to Marxism: that which is most one's own, yet most taken away." Both Marxism and feminism are then both struggles against oppression and both entail theories of oppression. It is often on the level of theory that Marxism seems most useful to feminism. For, as theory, Marxism constitutes an elaborate model for explaining oppression synchronically and diachronically—how power works and how it changes.

Marxism is first and foremost materialist: in the *German Ideology*, Marx argued, "Life is not determined by consciousness, but consciousness by life." A culture's conception of itself and its whole system of beliefs, its ideology, is a function of material circumstances, or, as in the *Grundrisse,* "Human beings become individuals only through the process of history." Under capitalism individual subjects come to be defined by their relation to things, for "capital is not a thing but a social relation between persons, established by the instrumentality of things." This social relation is the basis of Marx's famous theory in *Capital* of the Fetish of the Commodity, which "conceals the social character of private labor and the social relations between the individual workers, by making those relations appear as relations between material objects." It appears as if we exchange dollars for a tomato, rather than exchange our own paid labor for the labor of a migrant worker: "There is a definite social relation between men [and women], that assumes, in their eyes, the fantastic form of a relation between things."

The key to Marxist method, deriving from Hegel's dialectic, is the concept of contradiction, that in order for ideology to assert one thing, it must deny another, and so as a system of beliefs ideology is riddled with negations and contradictions. A dialectical concept of history presumes that something is always changing into something else, thus cultural phenomena are always transforming, always negating what they were; in Raymond Williams's model, any given historical formation consists of a dominant or hegemonic ideology, the residual elements of an older ideology, and the seeds of a newer or emergent ideology, and the residual, hegemonic, and emergent all exist in contradiction to one another.

However natural and desirable an alliance between Marxism and feminism might seem, in practice, the relations, both on the level of theory and practice, have been anything but smooth. Indeed the history of socialist feminism/feminist socialism has been more antagonistic than cooperative. In a classic study, Heidi Hartmann captures the relationship in her title: "The Unhappy Marriage of Marxism and Feminism." This is such a revelatory title because it raises the issue of the Doctrine of Separate Spheres. Marxists have had a tendency to subsume gender problems within a Marxist paradigm, seeing gender inequality as secondary to class oppression and class conflict, and presuming that, along with the withering away of the state, once private ownership of the means of production is abolished, male and female will be equally free. Many, including Engels, acknowledge that gender inequality appears more universal than class inequality, and that there can be patriarchal oppression before and perhaps even after capitalism. Feminists argue that, because Marxism relies on hierarchy (deal with class oppression first, and gender oppression will wither away), it perpetuates the problem of gender inequality. As poststructuralism has taught us, dichotomy (male/female; class/gender) is always hierarchy in disguise, and the outside/inside, public/private dichotomy is no exception. It is finally Marxism's drive to totalize that lies at the heart of the problem: from the Hegelian wing of Marxism, with its assumption that "the true is the whole," from Marx and Engels to Fredric Jameson, Marxists present their theory as the master discourse of liberation, and other struggles from feminism to gay and lesbian rights must be arrayed beneath its banner.

Much socialist feminism has argued, on the contrary, for a dual systems theory, that patriarchy and capitalism, though mutually reinforcing, are separable systems: see Gayle Rubin, "Traffic in Women," for an anthropological focus on kinship systems and an exchange system in which females are traded by males; alternately, analyzing housework, Christine Delphy offers a theory of a domestic mode of production in which women's work is devalued. Instead of arguing that Marxism remains the master discourse or that feminism has superseded Marxism, or even that they must be reconciled, Gayatri Spivak argues that they should serve as interruptions, regularly exposing each other's limitations and illuminating their blind spots.

James Thompson

References

Barrett, Michèle. *Women's Oppression Today*. London: Verso, 1980.

Coward, Rosalind. *Patriarchal Precedents: Sexuality and Social Relations*. London: Methuen, 1983.

Delphy, Christine. *Close to Home: A Materialist Analysis of Women's Oppression*. Amherst: University of Massachusetts Press, 1984.

Engels, Frederick. *The Origins of the Family, Private Property, and the State*. Harmondsworth: Penguin, 1985.

Haraway, Donna. "Gender for a Marxist Dictionary." In *Simians, Cyborgs and Women*, 127–148. London: Routledge, 1991.

Hartmann, Heidi. "The Unhappy Marriage of Marxism and Feminism." In *Women and Revolution*, edited by Lydia Sargent, 1–42. Boston: South End, 1981.

Kuhn, Annette, and AnnMarie Wolpe, eds. *Feminism and Materialism: Women and Modes of Production*. London: Routledge and Kegan Paul, 1978.

MacKinnon, Catharine A. *Towards a Feminist Theory of the State*. Cambridge: Harvard University Press, 1989.

Marx, Karl, and Frederick Engels. *Collected Works*. Translated by Richard Dixon et al. 47 vols. New York: International Publishers, 1975–1995.

Newton, Judith Lowder, and Deborah Rosenfelt, ed. *Feminist Criticism and Social Change: Sex, Class, and Race in Literature and Culture*. London: Methuen, 1985.

Rubin, Gayle. "The Traffic in Women: Notes on the 'Political Economy' of Sex." In *Towards an Anthropology of Women*, edited by Rayna R. Reiter, 157–210. New York: Monthly Review, 1975.

Spivak, Gayatri. *The Post–Colonial Critic*. New York: Routledge, 1990.

Vogel, Lise. *Marxism and the Oppression of Women: Toward a Unitary Theory*. New Brunswick, N.J.: Rutgers University Press, 1983.

Masquerade

A ball or party at which all the participants are in disguise—a masquerade—is a recurring topos of eighteenth- and nineteenth-century fiction, to which powerful symbolic meanings have been attributed. In her influential account, Terry Castle identifies the masquerade as a carnivalesque social form, releasing participants from the cultural categories that govern everyday life while providing an ironic commentary on them. The central interest of masquerade lies in the way disguise problematizes the relationship between self and other, and thus it offers a fruitful way of exploring how identity is constructed in literary texts.

Masquerade is also an important concept for the psychoanalytic account of feminine identity, deriving from the work of English psychoanalyst Joan Riviere. It equates feminine social identity with the wearing of a disguise, implying that conventional femininity is a performance that masks the essential lack that characterizes the state of being a woman in patriarchal culture. In women's writing and feminist literary criticism, the notion of masquerade has been used both to critique the processes by which women are compelled to submit to men's desire for a certain presentation of femininity, and, by insisting on the perception that femininity is itself a performance, to create a space in which alternative constructions of femininity can be put into play. The psychoanalytic account of masquerade has been most extensively used in film theory, but also offers a productive way of analyzing how women can intervene in male-defined literary forms.

Kate Chedgzoy

See also BUTLER, JUDITH

References

Castle, Terry. *Masquerade and Civilization: The Carnivalesque in Eighteenth-Century English Culture and Fiction.* London: Methuen, 1986.

Doane, Mary Ann. "Masquerade Reconsidered: Further Thoughts on the Female Spectator." In *Femmes Fatales: Feminism, Psychoanalysis, Cinema,* 33–43. New York and London: Routledge, 1992.

Heath, Stephen. "Joan Riviere and the Masquerade." In *Formations of Fantasy,* edited by Victor Burgin et al., 45–61. London: Methuen, 1986.

Riviere, Joan. "Womanliness as a Masquerade." Reprinted in *Formations of Fantasy,* edited by Victor Burgin, James Donald, and Cora Kaplan, 35–44. London: Methuen, 1986.

Schofield, Mary Anne. *Masking and Unmasking the Female Mind: Disguising Romances in Feminine Fiction, 1713–1799.* Delaware, Md.: University of Delaware Press, 1990.

Materialist Feminism

The term "materialist feminism" emerged in Great Britain and the United States during the late 1960s and indicates an explicit or implicit engagement with Marxism. Arguing the multivocality evident in the works of Marx and Engels, materialist feminists approach Marxism as a collection of texts that defy both reductive and totalizing readings. With a view to analysis of social structures, a materialist feminist critique examines the ways in which ideologies of history, class, race, and the economic are implicated—individually or collectively—in the construction of gender identity and subjectivity. Materialist feminists demonstrate the relation between capitalism and patriarchal configurations of oppression, while problematizing the orthodox Marxist notion that class analysis alone is capable of adequately addressing the interests of women. Consequently, materialist feminists argue that to link women's historical oppression exclusively to male domination and class affiliation is to ignore the web of cultural factors and ideological structures that inform lived experience.

British socialist feminists of the 1970s, who debated the connection between capitalism and patriarchy, often worked with the Labor Party, the Communist Party, or the Marxist-Feminist Literary Collective. Their agenda called for a radical transformation of state and social apparatuses that had contributed to or created women's oppression. Materialist feminism in the United States has, however, no explicit political party affiliation. Its putative origins have been traced to the second wave of the women's movements, with connections to the various 1960s civil rights organizations—(the first wave having as its tentative starting point the suffrage movements of the late nineteenth century). In effect, British and American feminists engaging in a materialist critique challenge received notions about structures of knowledge within capitalist modes of production.

Because of the family's position of influence in the instruction and construction of gender and sexual identities, Marxists-Feminists began to critically reexamine both Marxist and Freudian texts in an attempt to articulate questions concerning familial configurations. Such critiques of the psychic became tools to examine the social. One early such example is *The Dialectic of Sex,* in which Shulamith Firestone calls for a construction of a "materialist view of history based on sex." Firestone argues that women's seizure of control of the means of reproduction would precipitate the final revolution. While specifics were never provided, Firestone perceived the dismantling of traditional concepts of motherhood and family as the revolution's ultimate goal. Juliet Mitchell counters Firestone's argument in *Woman's Estate,* contending that Firestone reduced women's oppression to a function of biology and failed to account for the shifting historical significance of womanhood, sexuality, and family. Mitchell calls for an analysis of all structures influencing women's subordination. She emphasizes both the economic and psychological realities of women's participation in the labor force—that is, women as a reserve army of labor, the kinds of work for which women do and do not receive payment, and the historical changes in what has been considered "women's work." Mitchell's project continued with *Psychoanalysis and Feminism,* in which she produces a compelling rereading of Lacan, Marx, and Freud, that problematizes the received notions of women's subjectivity both within psychic and social theories of sexual development. In *The Daughter's Seduction,* a work influenced by Lacan, Jane Gallop takes *Psychoanalysis and Feminism* as her "point of departure" to argue the instability of identity. For Gallop, multipositionality is the catalyst capable of disrupting the hegemony of patriarchal power structures.

While psychoanalytical and socialist feminists struggled to demystify Marx and Freud, they had failed to engage effectively with the connected issues of racial and sexual difference, and the politics of postcolonialism. As early as 1970, Cellestine Ware's *Woman Power* was offering an analysis of capital that included an antiracist position within a Marxist critique of the social. Ware called for a historical understanding of race relations within capitalism that would acknowledge both the race blindness of Anglo feminists and the lived experiences of black and workingclass women. By 1977, Ware's antiracist positions were being reiterated by the Combahee River Collective in "A Black Feminist Statement." While acknowledging Marxism as an important tool for understanding "very specific" economic relations, the Collective argued for critical inquiry to include the economic situations of black women and lesbians. This position was then taken up in *This Bridge Called My Back,* a collection of essays denouncing the negation or homogenization of "women of color" by white feminists, and calling to attention the impact of heterosexism, capitalism, classism, and racism on women excluded from Anglo feminist analysis. In *Women, Race and Class,* Angela Y. Davis posits race and class as central when accounting for the differing experiences of oppression within capitalism.

Hortense Spillers builds upon and provocatively expands earlier antiracist projects as she challenges the authority and ethnocentrism of master-narratives that reinscribe patriarchal myths. Providing a critique of African American subjectivity within slavery and capitalism, Spillers questions the ability of Freudian analyses to account for the experiences of the family whose roots are found in slavery and whose bodies were exchanged as capital. For Spillers, the formation of gender identity within a family structure permeated with historical violence explodes the identity myths of Freud's theories. Both in "Mama's Baby, Papa's Maybe" and "'The Permanent Obliquity of an In(pha)llibily Straight,'" Spillers convincingly contends that the violent intervention imposed on the body of the captive erases the rights of consanguinity experienced by a free community. When the slave woman and her children are considered property, "the various inflections of patriarchalized female gender—'mother,' 'daughter,' 'sister,' 'wife'—are not available in the historical instance."

If we are to understand how the psychic is embedded within the social, sociologist Michele Barrett argues in *Women's Oppression Today: Problems in Marxist Feminist Analysis,* Marxist ideological and class analyses must be directly and transformatively engaged. Finding orthodox Marxist analysis of the division of labor inadequate for the understanding of women's subordination, Barrett turns for explanations to the examination of the histories of gender ideologies in relation to their deployment within capitalist and precapitalist cultures. Her 1988 revision of *Women's Oppression* appears with the new subtitle *The Marxist/ Feminist Encounter* and indicates Barrett's frustration toward an "attempt to bring together two world-views that have continued to go their separate ways." The second edition includes a revised introduction addressing the 1980 edition's "ethnocentricity." Barrett emphasizes that oppression is not a prerequisite of capitalism, but rather historically embedded in social relations. Although Barrett has maintained that literary questions are not central to her analysis, her approach to ideology has made her work especially valuable to literary critics.

Women's Oppression Today provoked charged debates among materialist feminists in Britain and America, which played themselves out in the pages of the *Feminist Review* and *m/f.* In an effort to problematize sexual dif-ference, Parveen Adams and Elizabeth Cowie (editors of the now-defunct socialist-feminist journal *m/f* (1978–1986), reject Barrett's Althusserian-based theories of ideology in favor of Foucault's discourse theory. For Adams and Cowie, women's oppression is contained within discursive practices and not, as Barrett contends, a by-product of ideology with its relative autonomy in regard to the economic structure.

Gayatri Chakravorty Spivak—alternately labeled a Derridean deconstructivist, Marxist, materialist, postcolonial critic, or feminist—utilizes a Marxist intervention in the reading of literary and cultural texts so as to uncover the webbed social and discursive structures that have stripped agency from the marginalized and oppressed. In *In Other Worlds,* Spivak produces a deconstructivist rereading of Marx that negotiates global politics and destabilizes capitalist ideologies. She cautions that, because of our complicity with the structure we attempt to critique, any antiimperialist analysis of culture or literature is bound to repeat the imperialist gesture. Her understanding of epistemic violence (or, our violated ways of knowing), complicity, and colonial hybridity are valuable tools for a materialist critique.

While materialist feminists articulate the consequences of our multiple positions and fractured identities within capitalism, Donna Haraway, a U.S. biologist and historian of science, argues instead for an understanding of our "mobile positioning" and our "situated knowledge." In *Primate Visions* and *Simians, Cyborgs, and Women,* Haraway articulates a postindustrial subjectivity intimately influenced both by technology and biology, or culture and nature. The cyborg, a construction of the information-producing era of global capitalism, displaces the boundaries between human and nonhuman. Haraway, in an engagingly irreverent manner, underscores that, in an era where technology permeates contemporary existence, one must acknowledge it as intricate to identity.

In "Materialist Feminisms," an entry in the *Johns Hopkins Guide to Literary Theory and Criticism,* Donna Landry and Gerald MacLean supply a clear account of the recent shifts in materialist feminist criticism along with a useful bibliography. Landry's and MacLean's *Materialist Feminisms,* one of the first full-length studies of the subject, combines materialist feminist theory with praxis. They recognize a "call to active political struggle in the everyday" and "a struggle with and within social institutions." Beginning with the Marxist-feminist encounter and materialist feminism's putative origins in the U.K. and the United States, *Materialist Feminisms* develops a "deconstructivist materialist perspective." While showing a commitment to theory, Landry and MacLean engage with projects of antiracism, antiimperialism, lesbian and gay issues, and what they consider the problematic stance of ecofeminists. Materialist feminists often take their lead from a Marxist analysis of class as central, and then extend this to include class contradictions and the ideologies of race, sexuality, and colonialism. In various fashions, these theorists posit subjectivity as a consequence of material shifts in theories of womanhood, family, femininity/masculinity, complicity, oppression, and modes of production.

Jo Dulan

References

Adams, Parveen. "Family Affairs." *m/f* 7 (1982): 3–14.

———, Beverly Brown, and Elizabeth Cowie. "Introduction." *m/f* 4 (1980): 2–4.

Barrett, Michele. *Women's Oppression Today: Problems in Marxist Feminist Analysis.* London: Verso, 1980.

Combahee River Collective. "A Black Feminist Statement." In *Capitalist Patriarchy and the Case for Socialist Feminism,* edited by Eisenstein R. Zillah, 362–372. New York: Monthly Review, 1979.

Davis, Angela Y. *Women, Race and Class.* New York: Random House, 1981.

Firestone, Shulamith. *The Dialectic of Sex: The Case for Feminist Revolution.* New York: Bantam, 1970.

Gallop, Jane. *The Daughter's Seduction: Feminism and Psychoanalysis.* Ithaca, N.Y.: Cornell University Press, 1982.

Haraway, Donna. *Primate Visions: Gender, Race, and Nature in the World of Modern Science.* New York: Routledge, 1989.

———. *Simians, Cyborgs, and Women: The Reinvention of Nature.* New York: Routledge, 1991.

Landry, Donna, and Gerald MacLean. "Materialist Feminisms." In *Johns Hopkins Guide to Literary Theory and Criticism,* edited by Michael Groden and Martin Kreiswirth, 247–252. Baltimore, Md.: Johns Hopkins University Press, 1993.

———. *Materialist Feminisms.* Oxford and New York: Basil Blackwell, 1993.

Mitchell, Juliet. *Psychoanalysis and Feminism.* New York: Pantheon, 1974.

———. *Woman's Estate.* New York: Random House, 1971.

Moraga, Cherríe, and Gloria Anzaldúa, eds. *This Bridge Called My Back: Writings by Radical Women of Color.* 2nd ed. New York: Kitchen Table: Women of Color Press, 1983.

M

Spillers, Hortense. "Mama's Baby, Papa's Maybe: An American Grammar Book." *Diacritics* 17 (1987): 65–81.

———. "'The Permanent Obliquity of an In(pha)llibly Straight': In the Time of the Daughters and the Fathers." In *Changing Our Own Words: Essays on Criticism, Theory, and Writing by Black Women,* edited by Cheryl A. Wall, 127–149. New Brunswick, N.J. and London: Rutgers University Press, 1989.

Spivak, Gayatri Chakravorty. *In Other Worlds: Essays in Cultural Politics.* New York and London: Routledge, 1988.

Ware, Cellestine. *Woman Power: The Movement for Women's Liberation.* New York: Tower, 1970.

Maternal

Contrary to the centuries-old dominant view established in patriarchal literature, theology, and political and economic theory, current feminist theory holds that the maternal is not "natural," "essential," or "universal." Twentieth-century feminist theorists, most influentially Simone de Beauvoir, Adrienne Rich, Nancy Chodorow, Julia Kristeva, Luce Irigaray, and Hélène Cixous, have called into question the antifemale rationalist claim, articulated in Classical Antiquity by Aristotle, that woman is relegated to the interior bodily role of reproduction while man is destined to superior rational mental activity. Feminists have also critiqued the historical perpetuation of this reductive theme in the Christian patristic argument of Aquinas and Augustine that woman's body is the sole reason for her creation because of its usefulness in the preservation of the species; in Martin Luther's Protestant Reformation doctrine for women—"Let them bear children to death; they are created for that"; and in Sigmund Freud's psychoanalytic construction of the eroticized, threatening, but ultimately dispensable mother who satisfies her envy of the male's penis by giving birth to a child.

Beauvoir sees pregnancy as an unenviable ordeal, part of the abject role a woman as wife is called on to play. She accepts some patriarchal stereotypes of the maternal, but argues that women are forced into a possessive, sometimes angry, stance as mothers because society denies them control and independence in their lives. Rich also underlines the social construction and male appropriation of the maternal; referring to her own experience and to examples from literature, she emphasizes the tedium, the violence, and the destructive power, especially passed from mothers to daughters, at the heart of the so-called "sacred calling."

Nancy Chodorow and the three French theorists turn to psychoanalysis as a means of understanding the misconstruction of the maternal. Chodorow's object-relations theory offers an alternative feminist construction of the ways in which, because, as she says bluntly, "women mother," they also determine, in gender-specific ways, the socialization and psychological development of their daughters and sons. Irigaray and Cixous draw on Jacques Lacan's deconstructive reading of Freud to show the inescapable power of patriarchal language as a constitutive factor in the empowering subjective construction of men and the linguistic marginalization of women. They both suggest the value of female-female relations, especially in a prolonged "narcissistic" mother-daughter connection, as a means to a future language for women. As Cixous says, women, "never far from 'mother,'" are compelled to "write through their bodies." Kristeva pursues the question of the mother's satisfaction in motherhood, questioning standard biological, scientific, and psychoanalytic accounts of the maternal. Although these French theorists have been charged by some feminist readers, for example Judith Butler and Toril Moi, with essentializing the maternal, recent close readings by Elizabeth Grosz and Kelly Oliver have disputed this judgment. In any case, as Madelon Sprengnether, for example, has made clear, psychoanalytic and poststructuralist theories have formed an important bridge between maternal and literary/linguistic realms.

The maternal is complex, even elusive. As a repository of social and literary meaning, it contains physical but also attitudinal and symbolic dimensions. It embraces perhaps the most powerful and provocative matrix of value in Western culture and literature. The maternal operates in the ambiguous borderland between the biology of birthing and the psychology of nurturing emotion. It is an area where public and private intersect and reveal the falsity of their dichotomy, as society fights for control over the bodies and the reproductive mechanisms that women claim as their own. From the point of view of feminist theory, the maternal body (necessarily female) is a territory where issues of linguistic, social, political, and religious power are engaged.

Because women are the only bearers of children, feminists argue, women's procreative bodies have been held hostage by the patriarchy to protect the economic power and privilege of men, so that maternal reproduction merges with economic production. Similarly, the nurturing element of the maternal, the caring, protectively emotional role women are called upon to play is also open to cultural debate as well as literary interpretation. Is the maternal, as cultural concept or personal feeling, constructed or innate? Are women agents of their maternal experiences or are they victims of social expectations placed upon their maternity? Do women need the maternal experience for their own self-esteem and for the sake of social esteem? Is there a way in which women can resist—or fall short of—the maternal without incurring society's disapprobation—and their own? Do women have access to the language that constructs the maternal. All of these questions come into political play in literary readings as well as in social forums.

Consideration of the biologically creative aspects of the maternal has led to critical discussions such as those by Nina Auerbach, Elaine Showalter, and Susan Stanford Friedman, about literary creativity as sublimation for, or complement to, maternity. Questions about the inhibiting or enhancing connections between maternal and literary production have been debated by writers as diverse as Mary Astell, Katherine Philips, Jane Austen, Mary Shelley, Elizabeth Barrett Browning, Charlotte Perkins Gilman, Virginia Woolf, Erica Jong, Muriel Rukeyser, Lucille Clifton, Sylvia Plath, Alice Walker, and Margaret Drabble.

Simone de Beauvoir is apprehensive about the connection of the writerly with the maternal; this way of thinking, she argues, simply relies on a "counter-penis." Viewing herself as maternal, however, a woman writer may elide her literary creativity with the metaphor of childbirth. Hélène Cixous says the gestation drive is "just like the desire to write: a desire . . . for a swollen belly, for language." And a literary tradition in which a woman writer can place herself may well be seen as a maternal tradition. Elizabeth Barrett Browning commented that, as a writer, she unavailingly looked for her literary foremothers. Virginia Woolf said that women writers need to think back through their mothers. And Alice Walker, in searching for a creative tradition and artistic models among black women, suggests that we should search in "our mothers'

gardens." Audre Lorde and Judy Grahn have explored the maternal from a lesbian point of view, depicting in their poetry past matriarchies.

The impact on literary theory of the feminist concern with the maternal has been apparent not only in the exploration of women's writing history, but also in feminist readings or maternal images in literature. Feminist readers have called for a reconsideration and critique of the multiple and (self-contradictory) literary depictions and interpretations of maternal women influenced by male-constructed theories—as, on the one hand, voraciously maternal, body- and earth-bound neurosis-inducing, suffocatingly co-dependent; and, on the other hand, infinitely self-sacrificing, devoted, ideally loving and nurturing; or simply absent, not on the scene at all. (See Margaret Homans's reading of *Wuthering Heights*.)

A short list of recent scholarly work will indicate the very wide-ranging critical engagement with representations of the maternal: Monica Sjoo, Barbara Mor, and Susan Griffin reread earth-mother stereotypes employing ecofeminist, mythic, and anthropological feminist insights; Marianne Hirsch employs psychoanalytic theory to read mother-daughter relations in her own biography as well as in a series of literary texts; Janet Adelman explores the negotiations with maternal power in Shakespeare's plays; and Ann Kaplan analyzes the paradigms of mother as "Angel" and "Witch" in nineteenth-century women's writing and in twentieth-century cinema. The maternal as "real" or as sociolinguistic construction, as comforting or as fearsome, as object of desire or repulsion, pervasively inhabits literary texts and title imagination of the feminist reader.

Lynette McGrath

See also BIRTH

References

Adelman, Janet. *Suffocating Mothers: Fantasies of Maternal Origin in Shakespeare's Plays, Hamlet to the Tempest.* New York: Routledge, 1991.

Auerbach, Nina. "Artists and Mothers: A False Alliance." *Women in Literature* 6 (1978): 3–15.

Beauvoir, Simone de. *The Second Sex.* Translated by H.M. Parshley. New York: Random House, 1952

Butler, Judith. *Gender Trouble: Feminism and the Subversion of Identity.* New York: Routledge, 1990.

M

Chodorow, Nancy. *The Reproduction of Mothering: Psychoanalysis and the Sociology of Gender.* Berkeley: University of California Press, 1978.

Cixous, Hélène. "The Laugh of the Medusa." In *New French Feminisms,* edited by Elaine Marks and Isabelle de Courtivron, 245–267. New York: Schocken Books, 1980.

————, and Catherine Clément. *The Newly Born Woman.* Translated by Betsy Wing. Minneapolis, Minn.: University of Minneapolis Press, 1975.

Friedman, Susan Stanford. "Creativity and the Childbirth Metaphor: Gender Difference in Literary Discourse." In *Speaking of Gender,* edited by Elaine Showalter, 73–100. New York: Routledge, 1989.

Griffin, Susan. *Woman and Nature: The Roaring Inside.* New York: Harper and Row, 1980.

Grosz, Elizabeth. *Sexual Subversions. Three French Feminists.* London: Allen and Unwin, 1989.

Hirsch, Marianne. *The Mother/Daughter Plot.* Bloomington: Indiana University Press, 1989.

Homans, Margaret. "The Name of the Mother in *Wuthering Heights.*" In *Emily Brontë: Wuthering Heights. Case Studies in Contemporary Criticism,* edited by Linda H. Peterson, 341–358. Boston: Bedford, 1992.

Irigaray, Luce. *Speculum of the Other Woman.* Translated by Lillian C. Gill. Ithaca, N.Y.: Cornell University Press, 1985.

————. *This Sex Which Is Not One.* Translated by Catherine Porter. Ithaca, N.Y.: Cornell University Press, 1985.

Kaplan, E. Ann. *Motherhood and Representation.* New York: Routledge, 1992.

Kristeva, Julia. *Desire in Language*, edited by Leon S. Roudiez. New York: Columbia University Press, 1980.

————. "Stabat Mater." In *Tales of Love.* Translated by Leon Roudiez. New York: Columbia University Press, 1987.

Moi, Toril. *Sexual/Textual Politics: Feminist Literary Theory.* New York: Methuen, 1985.

Oliver, Kelly. *Reading Kristeva.* Bloomington: Indiana University Press, 1993.

Rich, Adrienne. *Of Woman Born: Motherhood, Experience and Institution.* New York: W.W. Norton, 1976.

Showalter, Elaine. "Feminist Criticism in the Wilderness." *Critical Inquiry* 8 (1981): 179–205.

Sjoo, Monica, and Barbara Mor. *The Great Cosmic Mother: Rediscovery of the Religion of the Earth.* San Francisco: Harper Collins, 1987.

Sprengnether, Madelon. *The Spectral Mother: Freud, Feminisms and Psychoanalysis.* Ithaca, N.Y.: Cornell University Press, 1990.

Maternal Thinking

This phrase is most closely associated with Sara Ruddick, who used it as the title of an essay and of a subsequent book; the concept has also entered feminist thinking through the work of Carol Gilligan, Nel Noddings, and Jean Bethke Elshtain, as well as other feminist theorists concerned with drafting what may be loosely termed an "ethic of care."

Ruddick suggests that most women, in response to the demands of their mothering tasks, have learned to think and behave in ways that are distinctive, manifesting qualities she describes as responsiveness to growth, resilient good humor, and cheerfulness, attentive love, and humility. Ruddick argues further that social advocacy of these attitudes and of "maternal thinking" in men as well as in women, will diminish prospects of war and enhance prospects of peace. This association of "peace-keeping" with women's "maternal thinking" is also developed by Elshtain and Noddings. Carol Gilligan's research, while not directly focused on maternal thinking, interestingly showed that a group or women, facing the possibility of an abortion, typically based their ethical decisions on caring, affiliative considerations rather than on adherence to abstract principles of what is right. Like Ruddick, Elshtain, and Noddings, Gilligan suggests that society as a whole may benefit from encouraging in all of its members, male and female, those attitudes of caring and attention that have often, in patriarchal culture, been associated derisively with women and dismissed as "emotional" and "irrational."

Some concern has been expressed among feminist critics of "maternal thinking" that to designate certain moral virtues as deriving from maternal experience essentializes these virtues as female and therefore leaves women solely responsible for their continuance. Furthermore, not all women are mothers and not all mothers behave in an ideal way. Some women wish to reject the maternal experience; some wish to participate in competitive, aggressive behavior of the kind that has been culturally socialized as male; some mothers abuse their children; and crossculturally and historically, motherly behavior has not always comprehended the virtues listed by Ruddick. This kind of criticism, though it raises valid considerations, almost certainly overgeneralizes the particular arguments of Ruddick, Elshtain, Noddings, and Gilligan.

Lynette McGrath

See also BIRTH

References

Elshtain, Jean Bethke. *Women and War*. New York: Basic, 1987.
Gilligan, Carol. *In a Different Voice: Psychological Theory and Women's Development*. Cambridge: Harvard University Press, 1982.
Larrabee, Mary Jeanne, ed. *An Ethic of Care: Feminist Interdisciplinary Perspectives*. New York: Routledge, 1992.
Noddings, Nel. *Caring*. Berkeley: University of California Press, 1984.
Ruddick, Sara. *Maternal Thinking: Towards a Politics of Peace*. Boston: Beacon, 1989.

Maternity

Unlike the verb "to father," the verb "to mother" refers to relationships neither strictly biological nor restricted to one's offspring. The nurturing attitudes and behaviors associated with maternity, often regarded as natural or timeless, actually reflect relatively recent shifts in cultural understandings of privacy, selfhood, and work. Arguing that women's subordinate position in society is largely attributable to maternity as both biological fact and cultural construct, feminists from Mary Wollstonecraft to Shulamith Firestone, from Charlotte Perkins Gilman to Adrienne Rich, have focused on the effects on social and individual well-being of the gendered division of labor that has been the correlate of modern maternity. Sharing the desire to differentiate social norms and expectations of maternity from the "maternal instinct" or "feminine nature" invoked to explain or justify them, their diagnoses nonetheless differ markedly in ways that are best indicated by a brief survey of the entwined histories of maternity and feminist views of it.

Before the eighteenth century, throughout Europe and America, maternal duties received little specific attention in religious and didactic literature, and specialized mothering was not assumed the primary occupation of women. Upon mothers fell near total responsibility for child-rearing (itself newly redefined) only with the advent of industrial capitalism. The resulting separation of fathers from family and mothers from productive labor, combined with the weakening of extended kinship systems by urbanization, a sharp decline in childhood mortality, and Locke's highly influential emphasis upon the susceptibility of young children to influence brought about what could be called the professionalization of maternity, the view that mother's work could be performed by mothers only and required their full attention. This emergent maternal ideal can be seen in such seemingly disparate phenomena as the return to fashion of breast-feeding among the middle and upper classes in late-eighteenth-century Britain, in the spate of sermons and pamphlets offering "Advice to Mothers," and in the decline in midwifery.

It was only in the nineteenth century that maternity—narrowly, the biological capacity to become pregnant and bear children—came to be identified with motherliness and presumed definitive of female "nature." As "natural" custodians of a private, familial realm, mothers were held to exert a purifying moral influence upon those in their direct care and, by extension, upon society. Alfred Lord Tennyson's encomium to this moral mother in "The Princess" as "all dipt In angel instincts, breathing Paradise, Interpreter between the gods and men" typifies the cultural romanticization of maternity to which feminist literary scholars have devoted much attention. Motherliness thus epitomized the self-sacrificing domesticity expected of women that led Virginia Woolf, considering "Professions for Women," to urge the would-be woman writer to "kill the angel in the house," to overcome internalized equations of femininity with service. Feminist literary critics have followed Woolf's lead in exploring the ways maternity as institution, symbol, and experience has silenced women artists and channeled women's productivity into an exclusively domestic realm. Susan Moller Okin, for example, notes the centrality of the mother-centered sentimental family to the political philosophies most influential in shaping of the modern notion of the state. By contrasting a standard of citizenly rationality to allegedly natural maternal sentiment, political philosophers from Hobbes to Bentham categorically excluded women from participation in civic or political life.

Feminist views of maternity have not, however, unambiguously rejected the allegedly communitarian familial realm so long deemed the province of an idealized maternity. Over the past two centuries, the institution of motherhood has offered women both expanded and restricted possibilities for personal satisfaction and social activity, a paradox already evident in Mary Wollstonecraft's *Vindication of the Rights of Woman,* where her insistence upon women's participation in civic society is inseparable from her unquestioned assumption that their first responsibilities are maternal. Wollstonecraft advocated female education not from the conviction that women were as entitled as men to such privileges but from the belief that women had social duties equal to men's that cultural norms prevented them from fulfilling: "If children are to be educated to understand the true principle of patriotism," she wrote, "their mother must be a patriot." Through the early twentieth century, women's advances into the public realm—to teach, vote, advocate labor reform, practice medicine—often built upon and were explained as extensions of maternal duties outward from the home. Indeed, it could be argued that it was only when mothers had come to be regarded as custodians of moral and religious values that feminism could arise: early feminists urged women's rights to enable women to influence more effectively the men and children for whom they were deemed morally responsible. Thus the early-twentieth-century feminist lecturer and writer Charlotte Perkins Gilman saw in "The New Mothers of a New World" the standard for American virtue: "This new motherhood shines before us like a sunrise," she wrote, anticipating the dawn of a world in which mothers would be "world-builders."

Recent feminist attention to the centrality of maternity to the ideological separation of "public" from "private" has taken two broad directions, both of which reflect the related centrality of maternity to widely differing conceptions of gender equality. One line, of which Betty Friedan's *The Feminine Mystique* is an early representative, focuses on the ways the institution of motherhood has stunted women's human capabilities by restricting them to the domestic realm. Friedan's call to women to look for personal fulfillment beyond their roles as caretakers arose in response to a specific context, the idealized isolation of many middle-class mothers with children deemed by post-Freudian psychologists essential to children's emotional health. Shulamith Firestone's *The Dialectic of Sex,* sharing with Friedan the desire to free women from motherhood into public achievement, goes so far as to argue that women's subordination to men will not end until technological reproduction has replaced biological reproduction. Both views indicate the goal, women's fuller participation in the public realm, toward which much feminist reform (including reproductive control, maternity and paternity leaves, day care, and flexible worktime arrangements) was directed through the 1970s, reforms that sought to ensure that women's lives would be no more constrained by maternity than are men's lives.

A later group of feminists questioned the allegiance to competitive individualism they found implicit in such views. Adrienne Rich's influential *Of Woman Born: Motherhood as Experience and Institution* turned feminist attention from the functions of maternity in social structures to the experience of mothering and being mothered, closely linking maternity with female sexuality and damning the ideological and material damage wrought by male-dominant society upon mothers' relationships to their bodies and their experiences of mothering. Rich's argument for the eradication of the institution of motherhood differs from earlier criticism in its celebration of the unique power she associates with maternal bodies and relationships. In the same era, Nancy Chodorow focused on boys' and girls' differing experience of being mothered by women, arguing in *The Reproduction of Mothering* that the greater identification of mothers and daughters and the lesser identification of mothers and sons typically results in adult females with the capacities and the desire to mother and adult males who are more comfortable with the self-sufficient autonomy believed appropriate to the competitive public realm. Chodorow thus explains the increased psychological and ideological significance invested in maternity over the past two centuries, a period in which the physical requirements of child-bearing and child care have decreased, by relating such gender-specific effects of mothering to "the construction and reproduction of male dominance itself."

Specifically literary feminist study of maternity in a sense replays this same conflict between advocacy of extending "male" privileges to women allegedly barred from full participation in public life by their mothering roles and celebration of social ideals of nurture associated with maternity. Alice Walker has urged attention to maternal legacies as an elided source of identity and power for women writers. Similarly desirous of the recovery of metaphoric and literal foremothers, long legally subsumed within husbands upon marriage by coverture and between fathers and sons by primogeniture, feminist literary scholars have scrutinized texts by canonical literary "forefathers" for absent or elided mothers. Recent feminist literary study has also focused on the use of maternity to separate public from private realms by investigating the metaphoric uses of "mother" so often invoked in relation to nationalism, such as "motherland" and "mother tongue," and the rhetoric of queens as mothers, challenging both the idealization of maternity by subjecting it to historical analysis.

French feminist attention to maternity of the past twenty years, driven more by psychological than by historical concerns, has criticized the masculinist bias they see in language and Western logic, focusing on the mother-child harmony that allegedly precedes the infant's acquisition of language and fall in patriarchy. Thus Hélène Cixous imagines a utopian feminine language that privileges "voice," the pre-Oedipal mother she believes all women deeply remember: "Voice: inexhaustible milk. She has been found again. The lost mother." Julia Kristeva's analysis of the role of women in the symbolic order similarly emphasizes "maternal rhythms" as the site of a valued pre-Oedipal relationship to language.

Jennifer Thorn

See also BIRTH

References

Badinter, Elisabeth. *Mother Love: Myth and Reality.* New York: Macmillan, 1981.

Bassin, Donna, Margaret Honey, and Meryle Mahrer Kaplan, eds. *Representations of Motherhood.* New Haven: Yale University Press, 1994.

Bernard, Jessie. *The Future of Motherhood.* New York: Dial, 1974.

Bloch, Ruth H. "American Feminine Ideals in Transition: The Rise of the Moral Mother, 1785–1815." *Feminist Studies* 4 (1978): 101–126.

Burke, Carolyn G. "Rethinking the Maternal." In *The Future of Difference,* edited by Hester Eisenstein and Alice Jardine, 107–113. Boston: G.K. Hall, 1980.

Chodorow, Nancy. *The Reproduction of Mothering: Psychoanalysis and the Sociology of Gender.* Berkeley: University of California Press, 1978.

———, and Susan Contratto. "The Fantasy of the Perfect Mother." In *Rethinking the Family: Some Feminist Questions,* edited by Barrie Thorne and Marilyn Yalom, 54–75. New York: Longmans, 1982.

Cixous, Hélène. "Sorties." In *New French Feminisms,* edited by Elaine Marks and Isabelle de Courtivron, 245–264. Amherst: University of Massachusetts Press, 1980.

Dally, Ann. *Inventing Motherhood: The Consequences of an Ideal.* New York: Schocken Books, 1982.

Davidson, Cathy N., and E.M. Broner, eds. *The Lost Tradition: Mothers and Daughters in Literature.* New York: Frederick Ungar, 1980.

Friedan, Betty. *The Feminine Mystique.* New York: W.W. Norton, 1963.

Hunt, Lynn. *The Family Romance of the French Revolution.* Berkeley: University of California Press, 1992.

Kittay, Eva. "Womb Envy: An Explanatory Concept." In *Mothering: Essays in Feminist Theory,* edited by Joyce Trebilcot, 94–128. Totowa, N.J.: Rowman and Allanheld, 1984.

Kristeva, Julia. "The Maternal Body." Translated by C. Pajaczkowski. *m/f* 5, 6 (1981): 158–163.

Okin, Susan Moller. "Women and the Making of the Sentimental Family." *Philosophy and Public Affairs* 10 (1981): 65–88.

Pagels, Elaine. "What Became of God the Mother? Conflicting Images of God in Early Christianity." In *The Signs Reader: Women, Gender, and Scholarship,* edited by Elizabeth Abel and Emily K. Abel, 97–107. Chicago: University of Chicago Press, 1983.

Rich, Adrienne. *Of Woman Born: Motherhood as Experience and Institution.* New York: W.W. Norton, 1976, 1986.

Walker, Alice. *In Search of Our Mothers' Gardens: Womanist Prose.* New York: Harcourt Brace Jovanovich, 1983.

M

Matriarchy

A society ruled by women. Nineteenth-century social theorists speculated that the first societies were matriarchal. Further anthropological research has found patriarchy universal. Nevertheless, myth critics, Jungians, many writers, and some feminists including Adrienne Rich in her groundbreaking analysis of motherhood, *Of Woman Born,* use matriarchy as a powerful literary icon representing nurturing and creativity.

Champions of matriarchy envision an egalitarian society that does not simply reverse patriarchy, but creates new social relations between the sexes. Literary works making political critiques sometimes invoke matriarchal themes to symbolize an alternative social order. In John Steinbeck's *The Grapes of Wrath,* for example, the nurturing matriarch, Ma Joad, represents socialism's potential strengths.

The popular use of matriarchal concepts raises serious questions for feminists. Anthropologists show that patriarchal cultures legitimize women's subjugation through matriarchal myths stating that when women held power, they abused it. Such African American feminists as bell hooks demonstrate that white sociologists' depiction of lopsided, supposedly "matriarchal" communities blames women of color for their socioeconomic subjection. Many feminists agree with Simone de Beauvoir's view that ultimately the concept of matriarchy valorizes women primarily for bearing children, and thus contributes to female oppression.

Lisa Cody

See also MATROCENTRIC

References

Bamberger, Joan. "The Myth of Matriarchy: Why Men Rule in Primitive Society." In *Woman, Culture, and Society,* edited by Michelle Zimbalist Rosaldo and Louise Lamphere, 263–280. Stanford: Stanford University Press, 1974.

Barrett, Eileen. "Matriarchal Myth on Patriarchal Stage: Virginia Woolf's *Between the Acts*." *Twentieth-Century Literature* 33 (1987): 18–37.

hooks, bell. *Ain't I a Woman. Black Women and Feminism.* Boston: South End, 1981.

Motley, Warren. "From Patriarchy to Matriarchy: Ma Joad's Role in *The Grapes of Wrath*." *American Literature* 54 (1982): 397–412.

Rich, Adrienne. *Of Woman Born.* New York: W.W. Norton, 1976, 1986.

Matrocentric

Literally, "centered upon the mother." In anthropology, matricentric (or "matrifocal") describes cultures where women are valued as mothers but also possess relative socioeconomic authority. Matricentric communities exist, for example, among the Javanese, the Navajo, African Americans, and the British workingclass. In literature, many authors portray matricentric communities as sources of resistance and creativity. African American poet Audre Lorde explains: "The white fathers told us: I think, therefore I am. The Black mother within each of us—the poet—whispers in our dreams: I feel, therefore I can be free."

Matrocentric defines two additional aspects of feminist studies. First, matrocentric describes feminism's historical search for foremothers. Second, in feminist psychoanalysis it describes the emotional, linguistic state between mother and child during the pre-Oedipal period, and later when an adult daughter wishes to replicate that bond. Melanie Klein and Nancy Chodorow revise Freudian theory by focusing on the mother's central role in the development of subjectivity. French feminist Julia Kristeva analyzes the integration between mother and child before the child enters the symbolic order of the father, calling the language of this mother-centered period "semiotic." Fellow French feminists Hélène Cixous and Chantal Chawaf experimentally write in a semiotic, or matrocentric style. Matrocentric criticism includes *The (M)other Tongue* (1985), an analysis of these psychoanalytic theories and mother-centered literature.

Lisa Cody

References

Chodorow, Nancy. *The Reproduction of Mothering.* Berkeley: University of California Press, 1978.

Garner, Shirley Nelson, Claire Kahane, and Madelon Sprengnether, eds. *The (M)other Tongue.* Ithaca, N.Y.: Cornell University Press, 1985.

Klein, Melanie. *Envy and Gratitude and Other Works, 1946–1963.* New York: Free Press, 1984.

Kristeva, Julia. *Desire in Language.* New York: Columbia University Press, 1980.

Lorde, Audre. *Sister Outsider*. Trumansburg N.Y.: Crossing, 1984.

Tanner, Nancy. "Matrifocality in Indonesia and Africa and among Black Americans." In *Woman, Culture, and Society*, edited by Michelle Rosaldo and Louise Lamphere, 129–156. Stanford: Stanford University Press, 1974.

Matrophobia

Not simply fear of mothers, but rather fear of becoming one's mother. Lynn Sukenick coined the term in her 1973 article on novelist Doris Lessing's central female characters, who are stereotypically "masculine" in their rationality and emotional restraint. Sukenick interprets women's aversion to the emotional and feminine in themselves because such qualities replicate the stifling life of their mothers.

"Matrophobia" helps explain why some women identify more with men rather than women. Though feminist scholars search for inspiring foremothers like Mary Wollstonecraft, they sometimes ignore distinctly nonfeminist women of the past. Matrophobia allows literary critics including Elizabeth Kowaleski-Wallace to analyze how, for example, novelist and antifeminist Hannah More is important to feminist criticism. Through "patriarchal complicity," More sought a public role among male literati by identifying with and seeking favor from father figures rather than aligning herself with the maternal and feminine.

Feminist criticism asks why women, universally subject to patriarchy, do not identify with each other or share a feminist vision. Matrophobia suggests that in patriarchy, some women seek liberation not by identifying with their (oppressed and perhaps oppressive) mothers and their feminine selves, but by seeking the approval from those in control of the symbolic order: fathers.

Lisa Cody

References

Kowaleski-Wallace, Elizabeth. *Their Fathers' Daughters: Hannah More, Maria Edgeworth, and Patriarchal Complicity*. New York: Oxford University Press, 1991.

Rich, Adrienne. *Of Woman Born*. New York: W.W. Norton, 1976, 1986.

Sukenick, Lynn. "Feeling and Reason in Doris Lessing's Fiction." *Contemporary Literature* 14 (1973): 515–535.

Medieval Studies

Feminist literary theorists writing about medieval texts have had their work shaped by enduring mythic narratives about medieval women. Chief among these, a Victorian back formation, sketches the nameless lady of romance, trapped passive, helpless, and virginal in a resolutely patriarchal tower. The enchanting of the medieval past, the perennial fiction of its profound otherness, has contributed to a long-standing dominance of philological and historical criticism in studies of medieval texts, a critical optic that has also tended to eclipse feminist theory. It is only in the late 1980s and 1990s that feminist scholars have begun to find terms with which to suture the "pastness" of the Middle Ages with current theory.

A dominant question in medieval feminist scholarship, and one that responds to the mystification of the Middle Ages, concerns the absence of women, both as producers of texts and as subjects within texts written by men. Whereas work in the 1970s focused chiefly on images of women, metaphorized and type-cast as courtly lady, heroic warrior/saint, virgin, or hag, later works have looked more directly at the articulation of female agency through the very space of her absence, as in studies of Old English poetry, especially by Overing, which argue that the heroic binarisms of *Beowulf* nevertheless allow women a space of ambiguity that challenges the very dualities of the heroic ideal. Fisher's and Halley's essay collection, *Seeking the Woman in Late Medieval and Early Renaissance Writings*, even more directly explores the empty metaphorization of woman, particularly as she is fictionalized through chivalric tropes of the Lady. The volume also points, as in Fisher's essay on *Sir Gawain and the Green Knight*, "Leaving Morgan Aside," to the empty stage from which women nevertheless exert formidable control.

In Chaucer studies, the question of female absence has been nuanced by Chaucer's ventriloquism of women's voices. Studies of Chaucer have returned again and again to question Gavin Douglas's fifteenth-century assertion that Chaucer was always a friend to women. Dinshaw's *Chaucer's Sexual Poetics* argues that Chaucer borrows from patristic exegesis the trope of a text as a feminized body, and accordingly represents women as texts to be inscribed by male subjects. A similar uneasiness with Chaucer's portrayal of the feminine is articulated in Hansen's *Chaucer and the Fictions of Gender*, which chiefly explores Chaucer's feminization of the male hero, a characterizing impulse that masks both an anxiety about masculinity as well as the texts' repression of women as subjects. While agreeing that the male hero is a feminized hero, Jill Mann offers an entirely different take on the matter of Chaucer as a friend to women, claiming that Chaucer confronted the problem of how to represent woman for herself, and not just as a male stereotype, bringing her from the periphery to the center as "the norm against which all human behavior is to be measured." Feminist studies of Chaucer in the mid 1990s, influenced by work on the social constructions of gender, have increasingly looked at Chaucer's transvestic play with gender. Applying Fowler's definition of genre to gender as well—"less a pigeonhole than a pigeon, mobile, organic, and subject to time"— Crane, *Gender and Romance in Chaucer's Canterbury Tales,* shifts the terms of the debate from Chaucer's allegiances to his manipulation of romance through a protean staging of gender.

Some of the most important new work in medieval feminist studies addresses devotional writing, and especially religious texts by women. Fueled by studies on the embodied spirituality of medieval religious women, the production of editions and translations of primary texts has burgeoned into a minor industry. Interest in the writings and lives of medieval religious women has focused in part on the process Finke, in essays on the courtly lyric and on female mysticism, calls "poaching," the expression of subjectivity through the reconstruction of oppression into power through visionary experiences. The mystics' metaphorization of body and of food is central to this transformation, giving graphic shape to the meditations of Julian of Norwich and to the autobiography of Margery Kempe, as Lochrie argues, claiming that Margery exploited taboos against female speech through her own express carnality.

The overlapping of bodiliness and female identity, both as evoked in female devotional expression and also in antifeminist clerical writing that equated women with fallen carnality, has made medieval literature a particularly rich subject for feminist discourses on the body, a topic of increasing importance. The essay collection by Lomperis and Stanbury offers a range of methodological approaches to body questions in English and Continental texts. Burns's *Bodytalk,* an excellent study of the speaking body in Old French literature, is also of value for studies of English texts through its exami-

nation of the ways that female speech, even in texts by men, operates as a "resistant doubled discourse." The body is also a focus of psychoanalytic criticism by Margherita and others, work that uses psychoanalytic narratives of origins and repression to explore patriarchal appropriations and erasures of the past. The modern mystification of the Middle Ages as a site of romance and of otherness derives from a set of feminine erasures performed by the modern historical (male) critic and by the medieval (male) poet. In Margherita's study, as in much of medieval feminist criticism, the project rests on the archaeological premise of recoverability: however absent in body or voice, the feminine is a presence in the text.

Sarah Stanbury

References

Burns, E. Jane. *Bodytalk: When Women Speak in Old French Literature.* Philadelphia: University of Pennsylvania Press, 1993.

Crane, Susan. *Gender and Romance in Chaucer's Canterbury Tales.* Princeton: Princeton University Press, 1994.

Dinshaw, Carolyn. *Chaucer's Sexual Poetics.* Madison: University of Wisconsin Press, 1989.

Finke, Laurie. *Feminist Theory, Women's Writing.* Ithaca, N.Y.: Cornell University Press, 1992.

Fisher, Sheila, and Janet E. Halley, eds. *Seeking the Woman in Late Medieval and Early Renaissance Writings: Essays in Feminist Contextual Criticism.* Knoxville: University of Tennessee Press, 1989.

Hansen, Elaine Tuttle. *Chaucer and the Fictions of Gender.* Berkeley: University of California Press, 1992.

Lochrie, Karma. *Margery Kempe and Translations of the Flesh.* Philadelphia: University of Pennsylvania Press, 1991.

Lomperis, Linda, and Sarah Stanbury, eds. *Feminist Approaches to the Body in Medieval Literature.* Philadelphia: University of Pennsylvania Press, 1993.

Mann, Jill. *Geoffrey Chaucer. Feminist Reading Series.* Atlantic Highlands, N.J.: Humanities Press International, 1991.

Margherita, Gayle. *The Romance of Origins: Language and Sexual Difference in Middle English Literature.* Philadelphia: University of Pennsylvania Press, 1994.

Overing, Gillian R. *Language, Sign, and Gender in Beowulf*. Carbondale: Southern Illinois University Press, 1990.

Medusa

Traditional representations of this female figure from Classical Greek mythology emphasize her head of serpents and her power to immobilize those who meet her gaze. Twentieth-century feminist literature and criticism, however, reclaims Medusa from this stigmatized position by eradicating her horrifying image and positing her as a liberatory icon.

In considering the following account, one must be aware that there are many conflicting representations and versions of the Medusa myth. The origins of some can be traced to long before the Classical period. For a detailed account of the evolution of these numerous images, see Judith Suther's scholarly account as well as that of Joseph Campbell.

The classical myth presents Medusa as a beautiful young woman—endowed with an exceptionally lovely head of hair—who is raped by Poseidon in Athena's temple. Jealous of Medusa's beauty and enraged by the sexual desecration of her temple, Athena subsequently turns Medusa's hair into a mass of snakes, curses her with a petrifying stare, and banishes her to the earth's end with her two sisters. These three Gorgons are then surprised by Perseus, who manages to chop off Medusa's head while she sleeps, avoiding her dangerous eyes by watching her reflection in his shield. Perseus then escapes with the severed head that Athena eventually puts upon her shield to stun her enemies. From Medusa's severed neck, Pegasus bursts forth. Her blood is taken by the god of healing, Asclepius, who uses the blood of her left side to kill and that from her right side to cure and resurrect.

Beginning with the late Middle Ages, literary representations of Medusa focused on the conquering of her monstrosity by a virtuous hero, explained Joan Coldwell. Romanticism cultivated this motif by seizing upon the Medusa as the "embodiment of the dark lady, the contaminated and irresistible beauty whose real name was Death," writes Judith Suther, of which Coleridge's Geraldine and Keats's Lamia are examples. See Mario Praz's *The Romantic Agony* for a discussion of the place of the Medusa myth in the nineteenth-century's eroticization of horror.

Many feminist critics, such as Coldwell, attribute the persistence of a negative Medusa motif in the twentieth century to Sigmund Freud's reading of the figure as a castrating female. Twentieth-century feminist literary interpretations, however, have done much to celebrate and redeem the Medusa. Hélène Cixous, in her manifesto "The Laugh of the Medusa," sees the Medusa as a "beautiful" "laughing" figure, a woman who rejects Freud's notions of castration. And Coldwell points out that poets such as Sylvia Plath and May Sarton have identified with the Medusa figure or positioned her as a Muse. Adrienne Munich's *Andromeda's Chains: Gender and Interpretation in Victorian Literature and Art* reexamines traditional patriarchal representations by studying British nineteenth-century fluctuations in Medusa imagery as they appear in relation to the Perseus and Andromeda legend.

Feminist literary revisions of the Medusa myth have succeeded in destabilizing its male-centeredness. In many feminist circles, Medusa has become a vehicle for expressing the position of women battling patriarchal subjugation.

Maria Jerinic

References

Campbell, Joseph. *The Masks of God: Occidental Mythology*. New York: Viking, 1976.

Cixous, Hélène. "The Laugh of the Medusa." In *New French Feminisms: An Anthology*, edited by Elaine Marks and Isabelle de Courtivron, 245–264. New York: Schocken Books, 1980.

Coldwell, Joan. "The Beauty of the Medusa: Twentieth Century." *English Studies in Canada* 4 (1985): 422–437.

Freud, Sigmund. "Medusa's Head." In *The Standard Edition of the Complete Psychological Works of Sigmund Freud*, Vol. 18, 273. Translated and edited by James Strachey. London: Hogarth, 1961.

Munich, Adrienne Auslander. *Andromeda's Chains: Gender and Interpretation in Victorian Literature and Art*. New York: Columbia University Press, 1989.

Plath, Sylvia. "Medusa." In *The Collected Poems*, edited by Ted Hughes, 82–84. New York: Harper and Row, 1981.

———. "Perseus: The Triumph of Wit over Suffering." In *The Collected Poems*, edited by Ted Hughes, 224–226. New York: Harper and Row, 1981.

Praz, Mario. *The Romantic Agony*. London: Oxford University Press, 1970.

Sarton, May. "The Muse as Medusa." In *Collected Poems, 1930–1973*, 332. New York: W.W. Norton, 1974.

Suther, Judith D. "The Gorgon Medusa." In *Mythical and Fabulous Creatures: A Source Book and Research Guide*, edited by Malcolm South, 163–178. New York: Bedrick, 1987.

Men in Feminism

This controversial phrase was coined in the 1980s debates about the relationship of men, particularly male literary critics, to feminism. For feminist critics, the question of men's relation to feminism is necessarily a difficult one. On the one hand, that male feminist criticism is an issue underscores the impact feminism has had on men; masculinity, like femininity, is constructed and heterogeneous. On the other hand, there is always the risk that male critics engaged in feminist criticism will repeat the patriarchal structure of male homosocial exchange that excludes women.

The status of men in feminism in the early 1980s depended on the importance assigned to the sex of the reader: does the experience of one's sex determine how one reads or writes? Elaine Showalter's "Critical Cross-Dressing: Male Feminists and the Woman of the Year" claimed that male critics are female impersonators who use feminism to further their own (nonfeminist) projects. In contrast to Showalter's focus on the importance of woman's experience, Mary Jacobus stresses the construction of gender in discourse, emphasizing the textual play of differences that displace the fixity of gender binarisms. Positions like that of K.K. Ruthven in *Feminist Literary Studies* exemplify the possible problems of men in feminism; despite its profeminist stance, Ruthven's argument positions male critics as outsiders with the objectivity to judge feminism as merely another way of reading.

More self-aware in its positioning, Stephen Heath's essay "Male Feminism" became the cornerstone for the first stages of the debate, culminating in *Men in Feminism*. Heath claims that "men's relation to feminism is an impossible one": feminism gives men against women's oppression a new position, but it also implies their exclusion. He argues that men, as objects and agents of patriarchal privilege, risk colonizing feminism. With the exception of a few essays, *Men in Feminism* reiterates the impossibility of men in feminism.

Literary criticism in the 1990s seeks alternatives to the essentializing problems of the 1980s debates, in part in response to important work in gay and lesbian studies, like that of Craig Owens and Eve Sedgwick. Two collections of essays, *Engendering Men* and *Out of Bounds*, both published in 1990, have begun to redress the question of men and feminism through alternative readings of men's relations to patriarchy. *Engendering Men*, a group of essays by a new generation of male critics educated by "first generation" feminist critics, contests the oppositionality (feminists versus men) of the 1980s debate. Focusing on the specificity and diversity of their positions as men, editors Boone and Cadden posit a male feminist practice that is contiguous with but not the same as feminism. In order to disrupt the tradition of male privilege, these essays shift attention to the possibilities of joining men and feminism by stressing the differences among men as well as their multiple identifications. Despite the dangers of male feminist criticism, the questions it poses continue to emphasize the transformative possibilities of feminism, its ability to turn Man into something other.

Ashley J. Cross

References

Boone, Joseph, and Michael Cadden, eds. *Engendering Men: The Question of Male Feminist Criticism*. New York: Routledge, 1990.

Claridge, Laura, and Elizabeth Langland, eds. *Out of Bounds: Male Writers and Gender(ed) Criticism*. Amherst: University of Massachusetts Press, 1990.

Culler, Jonathan. "Reading as a Woman." In *On Deconstruction: Theory and Criticism after Structuralism*, 43–64. Ithaca, N.Y.: Cornell University Press, 1982.

Fuss, Diana. "Reading like a Feminist." In *Essentially Speaking: Feminism, Nature, and Difference*, 23–37. New York: Routledge, 1989.

Heath, Stephen, "Male Feminism." In *Men in Feminism*, edited by Alice Jardine and Paul Smith, 41–46. New York: Methuen, 1987.

Jacobus, Mary. *Reading Woman: Essays in Feminist Criticism*. New York: Columbia University Press, 1986.

Jardine, Alice, and Paul Smith, eds. *Men in Feminism.* New York: Methuen, 1987.

Lipking, Lawrence. "Aristotle's Sister: A Poetics of Abandonment." *Critical Inquiry* 10 (1983): 61–81.

Ruthven, K.K. *Feminist Literary Studies.* Cambridge: Cambridge University Press, 1984.

Showalter, Elaine. "Critical Cross-Dressing: Male Feminists and the Woman of the Year." *Raritan* 3 (1983): 130–149.

Todd, Janet. *Feminist Literary History.* New York: Routledge, 1988.

Mill, John Stuart

A well-known essayist, Mill is referred to by some as a nineteenth-century male feminist. As the "apostle" for sexual equality, he argued for the recognition of women. In 1833 he wrote that "first rate people" are gifted with both feminine and masculine qualities, while second rate people unfortunately occupy the "peculiar" position of one or the other qualities. Further, Mill advocated woman's suffrage during a much-publicized speech in 1867. One of Mill's most popular works, *The Subjection of Women,* directly confronts the subject of sexuality, exposing the patriarchal bias of language and revealing how it silences women. Mill makes a plea for equality and incites women to write with their own voice. He not only argues for women to be recognized in writing, but also for their equal consideration in all occupations. He depicts the institution of marriage as a contract binding women into slavery. Mill's own part in the writing of *The Subjection of Women* has been questioned, since his wife, Harriet, collaborated with him on the project. Some say that Mill wrote the essay out of "worship" for his wife; nonetheless, references to sexual equality in his speeches, letters, and other writings undeniably support Mill's concern for the rights of women.

Ron May

References
Mill, John Stuart, and Harriet Taylor Mill. *Essays on Sex Equality.* Edited by Alice S. Rossi. Chicago: University of Chicago Press, 1970.

Miller, Nancy K.

Nancy K. Miller is a literary critic who came to feminism from French literary studies in the late 1970s. In her writings, from *The Heroine's Text* in 1980 to *French Dressing* in 1995, she uses French and Anglo American feminist and postmodernist theories to discuss French and British authors writing between the seventeenth and twentieth centuries.

Throughout her work, Miller addresses the relationship between author, literary work, and gender. In *The Heroine's Text,* Miller reads eighteenth-century French and British novels written by male authors about female heroines. This study of what Miller calls "feminocentric" novels addresses women writers only in passing. In her later writings, Miller then foregrounds women writing from the 1700s to today, and challenges the traditionally male novel canon—especially in *Subject to Change.* This collection of essays written between 1980 and 1988 focuses on women's fiction, while her next essay collection, *Getting Personal,* explores autobiography and links literary criticism to the feminist tradition of the confessional narrative. Miller returns to eighteenth-century fiction in her most recent book, *French Dressing.*

Miller's call for rethinking the novel canon places her in the feminist tradition of speaking for forgotten women artists. She contributes most significantly to literary studies through her exploration of gendered authorship. Throughout her work, Miller is skeptical of essentialist definitions of the "female" in authors, texts, and writing styles, and gradually comes to see authorship and gender as constructed. She is thus also among the first feminist critics to emphasize the uncertainties of gender in authorship (for example in discussing anonymous authors, women authors with male pseudonyms, and male authors writing in the female voice).

Antje Schaum Anderson

References
Miller, Nancy K. "Cultural Memory and the Art of the Novel: Gender and Narrative in Eighteenth-Century France." In *Textuality and Sexuality: Reading Theories and Practices,* edited by Judith Still and Michael Worton, 87–99. Manchester and New York: Manchester University Press, 1993.

———. "Feminist Writing and the History of the Novel." *Novel: A Forum on Fiction* 21 (1988): 310–321.

———. *French Dressing: Women, Men, and*

Ancien Regime Fiction. New York and London: Routledge, 1995.

———. *Getting Personal: Feminist Occasions and Other Autobiographical Acts.* New York and London: Routledge, 1991.

———. *The Heroine's Text: Readings in the French and English Novel, 1722–1782.* New York: Columbia University Press, 1980.

———. "'I's" in Drag: The Sex of Recollection." *Eighteenth-Century: Theory and Interpretation* 22 (1981): 45–57.

———. *Subject to Change: Reading Feminist Writing.* New York: Columbia University Press, 1988.

———, ed. *The Poetics of Gender.* New York: Columbia University Press, 1986.

Millett, Kate

Millett is usually considered a radical feminist who spoke openly about her bisexuality amid the gay-straight split within the American women's liberation movement of the early 1970s. Her *Sexual Politics,* published in 1970, is one of the earliest major theoretical works of early feminism. In this work she proposes that the relationship between women and men should be viewed as a power relationship and as the most basic and pervasive model for all political relationships. Partly literary criticism and partly cultural critique, *Sexual Politics* places Millett among "first wave feminists." Like other works from that time, *Sexual Politics* analyzes representations of women in the works of canonical male authors. Millett's goal is to investigate the works of modern male writers; her purpose is to reveal that power and domination, not love or passion, are the real issues at stake.

In keeping with her belief that the personal is the political, Millett's later works often use events from her own life to highlight and explore public problems and issues of power and control. Examples include *Sita,* which illustrates that power dynamics are not limited to heterosexual relationships; *The Basement: Meditations on a Human Sacrifice,* which explores how and why women can be capable of destructive behaviors usually connected with men; and *The Looney-Bin Trip,* in which Millett argues that socially constructed labels such as insanity are used to control people who deviate from the norm.

Michele Mizejewski

References

Humm, Maggie, ed. *Modern Feminisms: Political, Literary, Cultural.* New York: Columbia University Press, 1992.

Malinowski, Sharon, ed. *Gay and Lesbian Literature.* Detroit: St. James, 1994.

Millett, Kate. *The Looney-Bin Trip.* New York: Simon and Schuster, 1990.

———. *Sexual Politics.* New York: Avon, 1970.

———. *Sita.* New York: Farrar, Straus and Giroux, 1977.

———. *The Basement: Meditations on a Human Sacrifice.* New York: Simon and Schuster, 1979.

Mimesis

The concept of mimesis was formalized in Aristotle's *Poetics* as an imitation of reality that occurs through the types of speech and action characters employ in drama or that authors create from poetry. For many students of literature, Eric Auerbach's *Mimesis: The Representation of Reality in Western Literature* is the standard text used to examine mimesis in literature from *Oedipus Rex* to *To the Lighthouse.* If mimesis means an imitation of reality, feminist theorists ask upon whose reality is mimesis based. Feminist literary theorists use mimesis to investigate how literary treatments of women may reflect or reveal unarticulated ideas about women held by the authors of those works. Feminist theorists may also contemplate the influence of mimesis on women's literary reputations and productions. If the reader is a Marxist feminist or a gynocritic, it would be important to assert a different view of "reality" (in particular a nonpatriarchal view) for women writers to distance themselves from male writers. Mimesis appears to have previously been a gendered term that is now being rethought and modified to encompass a more pluralistic conception of the reality it intends to imitate.

Beverly Schneller

References

Aristotle, *Poetics.* New York: Random House, 1964.

Auerbach, Eric. *Mimesis: The Representation of Reality in Western Literature.* Translated by Willard Trask. Princeton: Princeton University Press, 1953.

Heilbrun, Carolyn. *Reinventing Womanhood.* New York: W.W. Norton, 1979.

Minh-ha, Trinh T.

Influenced by both Zen and deconstruction, Trinh T. Minh-ha is a writer, composer, and film-maker who uses poststructuralist theory to question or decenter stifling categories, especially those of woman, artist, and Third World. In her book *Woman, Native, Other,* which established her as one of the first "postcolonialist" critics, Minh-ha illustrates how such categories are made with the dominant group as the point of reference. She responds to colonialists' assertion of rights and progress by asking "progress for whom?" Minh-ha also suggests that the First World, which identifies itself as homogenous, is threatened by the diversity of the Third World and therefore marginalizes people of color. As a result, she views people of color as being challenged to escape the marginal status of "other," while still retaining their cultural pride.

For Minh-ha, women of color are particularly subject to categorization that fails to allow for individual identity. For instance, the categories "women," "Third World," and "writer" are made to exclude each other in Western academic discourse since "woman" implies white, and "Third-World person" implies man. Minh-ha suggests that early feminists excluded Third-World women in the same way that men have historically excluded women. When feminism excludes women of color, she warns, it becomes a tool for individual advancement instead of a movement for the advancement of all women. Minh-ha asserts that the issues of sexism and racism are therefore inseparably interrelated issues.

Minh-ha also criticizes language and the linearity of rational thought for supporting the established structures of authority. To write, she claims, is to exert power over others, and to write "well" (according to Western liberalism) means to objectify the mind, artifically separating the author from the subject. For women, Minh-ha suggests, achieving distance from their subjects means alienation, and being objective means forgetting yourself. She acknowledges that using language is unavoidable but, in her own work, defies traditional rules, writing from the body rather than the mind, with all the messiness and physicality that entails. As a result, her writing gives meaning to difference: she rejects linearity and bases her prose on the story as a never-ending, circulating gift that can never be possessed but is constantly being replenished. The style of her writing and films also reflects her rejection of classification, for neither her books nor her films fit into even the broadest of traditional categories, "fiction" or "nonfiction." Rather, Minh-ha's writing is both analytic and poetic, and her films document the way real people, both herself and her subjects, have distorted views of the world that are influenced by their personal experiences. In effect, she shows the way the "real" world is made fiction.

Finally, Minh-ha suggests that consciousness is not an accumulation of knowledge or truth but an unsettling. She claims that she writes not just to destroy what she considers to be destructive categories, as in divide and conquer, but tries to fragment in order to decenter, an act that she believes allows for more diversity.

Clare E. Conry

References

Minh-ha, Trinh T. "From a Hybrid Place: An Interview with Trinh T. Minh-ha." *Afterimage* 18 (1990): 6–9.
———. *When the Moon Waxes Red.* New York: Routledge, 1991.
———. *Woman, Native, Other: Writing Postcoloniality and Feminism.* Bloomington: Indiana University Press, 1989.

Mirror Stage

French psychoanalyst Jacques Lacan describes the "mirror stage" as a developmental phase that lays the foundation for the child's initiation into language by awarding her the image of the "I" to which her later speech will refer. Because Lacan believes that the subject is constituted through language, this moment of acquiring an "I" is instrumental to his theory of identity. Instituted the moment at which a child first recognizes its own image, the mirror stage occurs during a period in which the child still has relatively little motor coordination and its consciousness is composed of incoherent drives, desires, and sensations. Lacan writes that the mirror offers a deceptive image of an idealized, coherent self that, rather than corresponding to the child's current abilities, "anticipates in a mirage the maturation of his power." This first self-identification, then, is in fact a misrecognition *(méconnaissance)* that points to a gap at the very foundation of subjectivity. This gap will enable and mediate the subject's passage out of the Imaginary and into the Symbolic register.

M

Characterized by dyadic relationships and blurred boundaries between self and other, the mirror stage has been read by some theorists as a brief, "edenic" period in which consciousness is untroubled as yet by the recognition of sexual difference and the cultural baggage that accompanies that difference. Because the mirror stage begins the process of identification with images outside of the self, it is instrumental in reading how representations of women affect the formation of female subjectivity. Lacan's schema closely links vision with both power and self-image; hence, many feminist theorists of film, art, literature, and popular culture draw upon Lacanian theory to formulate their analyses.

Rebecca F. Stern

References

Erens, Patricia, ed. *Issues in Feminist Film Criticism*. Bloomington: Indiana University Press, 1990.

Gallop, Jane. *Reading Lacan*. Ithaca, N.Y.: Cornell University Press, 1985.

Lacan, Jacques. "The Mirror Stage as Formative of the Function of the I as Revealed in Psychoanalytic Experience." In *Écrits*, translated by Alan Sheridan, 1–7. New York: W.W. Norton, 1977.

Miscegenation

Broadly defined as the interbreeding of peoples of diverse races, the term is believed to have been first used in an 1864 eponymous pamphlet by David Goodman Croly that purported to champion the concept of intermarriage between blacks and whites but was, in fact, a cynical attempt to scandalize Northern white voters about the prospect of an interracial American society.

In the last decade there has been an upsurge of interest among feminist critics in what can be called a tradition of miscegenation fiction, from its beginnings in the work of such nineteenth-century reform writers as Lydia Maria Child and Catherine Maria Sedgwick, to the early twentieth-century novels of "passing" published by such African American writers as Nella Larsen and Pauline Hopkins.

One notable example is a critical study by Susan Gillman entitled "The Mulatto, Tragic or Triumphant? The Nineteenth-Century American Race Melodrama," which argues that many works of melodrama—both black and white authored—written during this period offer an

"erotics of politics" that combine narratives of familial love disrupted and restored with the political project of "imagining a viable bi-racial community." Such imaginative sociopolitical resolutions, she avers, range along a continuum from separatism to assimilation.

We can see from this single example the important implications of the study of the literary representations of miscegenation for a more inclusive feminist theory and practice that recognizes the mutually constitutive and interdependent nature of the American and African American literary traditions of women's writing. Indeed, in the broadest sense, such an enterprise is vital for feminists engaged in furthering the scholarly, pedagogical, and social goals of multiculturalism.

Eve Allegra Raimon

References

Berzon, Judith R. *Neither White nor Black*. New York: New York University Press, 1978.

Bloch, J.M. *Miscegenation, Melaleukation, and Mr. Lincoln's Dog*. New York: Schaum, 1958.

Carby, Hazel V. *Reconstructing Womanhood: The Emergence of the Afro-American Woman Novelist*. New York: Oxford University Press, 1987.

Croly, David Goodman, and George Wakeman. *Miscegenation: The Theory of the Blending of the Races, Applied to the American White Man and Negro*. New York: H. Dexter, Hamilton, 1864.

Davis, F. James. *Who Is Black? One Nation's Definition*. University Park: Pennsylvania State University Press, 1991.

Gillman, Susan. "The Mulatto, Tragic or Triumphant? The Nineteenth-Century American Race Melodrama." In *The Culture of Sentiment*, edited by Shirley Samuels, 221–243. New York: Oxford University Press, 1992.

Nelson, Dana D. *The Word in Black and White: Reading "Race" in American Literature, 1638–1867*. New York: Oxford University Press, 1992.

Williamson, Joel. *New People: Miscegenation and Mulattoes in the United States*. New York: New York University Press, 1984.

Mitchell, Juliet

A psychoanalyst and a Marxist, Mitchell explores in her work the connections among feminism, literature, and psychoanalysis. Written in 1966, her essay "Women: The Longest Revolution" grew out of Mitchell's dissatisfaction with the absence of women in the practices and theories of Marxism. In it, she traces the original weaknesses in classic socialist theory that made women as a distinct social group invisible and "a normative ideal, an adjunct to socialist theory, not structurally integrated into it." The emancipation of women that Fourier claimed would be human nature's triumph over brutality became in Marx's early writings simply an indicator of the progress of the cultural over the natural. In later Marxist thoery, the problem of women is a subsidiary to an analysis of the family as precondition of private property and the maternal function is seen as one of the fundamental conditions that made woman economically dependent on man. Mitchell argues that even Simone de Beauvoir's *The Second Sex*, the first explicitly feminist analysis, in its combination of idealist psychological explanation with more orthodox economic approach, leaves women's liberation divorced from any historical development. Rather than a derivative of the economy or a symbol of society, Mitchell posits, woman's condition is a specific structure, a complex unity of four elements: production, reproduction, socialization, and sexuality. The slow progress of women's liberation is due to the fact that gains in one area can be offset by losses in another.

In *Psychoanalysis and Feminism*, Mitchell challenged the then-popular feminist valorization of Reich and Laing and concurrent villification of Freud by arguing that Freud's analysis of patriarchal society was more significant for feminism. Arguing that the dismissal of Freud arose more from the post-Freudian reduction of his psychological distinctions to biological ones, she returns to Freud's concept of psychological bisexuality and its initial confrontation with patriarchal society, in which the dilemma for each person is to determine "the place he occupies in the world, in terms of his (and her) wish for it not to be the feminine place, which is the only, and ever-present, alternative to where anyone really wants to be—in the male position within the patriarchal human order." In her restoration of the psychological emphasis of Freudian theory, Mitchell enabled feminists to analyze the constructedness of sexuality within culture (not the physical body). Her analyses of the psychoanalytic theories of Freud and Lacan reveal the construction of femininity at the heart of their separation of the biological and the psychological in the question of sexual difference. In all of her writings on the connections among feminism, literature, and psychoanalysis, Mitchell consistently distinguishes between the ideal and the historical in the constructedness of the subject.

Mary Anne Stewart Boelcskevy

References

Mitchell, Juliet. *Psychoanalysis and Feminism*. New York, Pantheon, 1974.
———. *Woman's Estate*. New York: Pantheon, 1971, 1986.
———. *Women, the Longest Revolution*. New York: Pantheon, 1984.

Modleski, Tania

Since the publication of *Loving with a Vengeance* in 1982, Tania Modleski has championed the female reader/viewer's stake in narrative texts. *Loving with a Vengeance* argues that the formulaic nature of Harlequin novels, gothic romances, and television soap operas ensures that the reader knows more than the female protagonist; thus, while the heroine struggles in the throes of passion the reader is able to maintain a healthy distance. Indeed, Modleski notes, the open-ended format of the soap opera serves many of the goals of feminism: nonlinear narrative, shifting identifications and distanciation from the text, and extended "familial" relationships with an indefinite number of others. Perhaps the most important point Modleski makes in *Loving with a Vengeance* is that the enactment of female victimization in Harlequins, gothic novels, and soaps "testif[ies] to women's extreme discontent with the social and psychological processes which transform them into victims."

The idea that a popular narrative might usefully dramatize women's victimization is expanded into the central tenet of Modleski's next book, *The Women who Knew Too Much*. In the course of reading seven Hitchcock films—*Blackmail, Murder, Rebecca, Notorious, Rear Window, Vertigo,* and *Frenzy*—Modleski argues that the female viewer of these apparently misogynistic films "can find pleasure in acknowledging and working through [her] anger [at oppression by the patriarchy], especially when that anger has long been denied or repressed." However, in *The Women who Knew*

Too Much Modleski begins to complicate the theoretical basis of her feminist criticism. She challenges the Marxist/feminist endorsement of "distance" as the proper mode of engagement with a text, objecting that if feminists enshrine distance as the politically correct stance for a viewer they risk "participat[ing] in the repression of the feminine typical of the patriarchal 'semiotic system' known as classical . . . cinema." Modleski's interest in Hitchcock's films centers around the way the films demonstrate that "the desire for distance itself [is] . . . bound up with the male's insistence on his difference from woman." Modleski proposes that narrative empathy, spectatorial passivity, and the unconscious imaginary are feminine, and she speculates that Hitchcock's male protagonists and Hitchcock himself are only partially successful in repressing these feminine forces. The violence that pervades Hitchcock's films, Modleski argues, is the result of Hitchcock's extreme reaction to outbreaks of the "feminine" in his work.

A feminist essentialism is implicit in *The Women who Knew Too Much,* and it becomes explicit in Modleski's most recent book, *Feminism without Women,* where Modleski warns that "male power frequently works to efface female subjectivity by occupying the site of femininity." To save feminism, and femininity, for women, Modleski emphasizes the responsibility of the writer in speaking for the shared experience of women.

Taking J.L. Austin's "performative" speech acts as her model, Modleski seeks to cut through the dizzying theoretical disputes that obscure much feminist film criticism. The essays in *Feminism without Women* critique contemporary images of women on film and television, but they also argue for the personal stake of the writer in any feminist project. Modleski's book risks irritating feminists wary of her charge that a feminist critique must speak in the name of an essential feminism; and also humanists who recognize Modleski's position of address but do not agree with her relentless attack upon the patriarchy. Nonetheless, Modleski's willingness to interrogate her personal stake in the subjects of her writing remains an exemplary—and hard-won—point of departure for feminist criticism.

Ellen Draper

References

Modleski, Tania. *Feminism Without Women: Culture and Criticism in a "Postfeminist" Age.* New York: Routledge, 1991.

————. *Loving with a Vengeance: Mass-Produced Fantasies for Women.* Hamden, Conn.: Archon, 1982. London: Methuen, 1985.

————. *The Women who Knew Too Much: Hitchcock and Feminist Theory.* New York: Methuen, 1988.

Moers, Ellen

Moers is known as a veritable pioneer in feminist literary scholarship for her 1976 publication of *Literary Women.* This text, largely the product of work begun in the early 1960s, was significantly informed by the rising feminist awareness of the early 1970s. While seeking to establish an alternative canon based on the works of women authors, Moers's book considers how these authors function in a woman's tradition.

Literary Women, in its discussion of English, American, and French women authors, focuses on a primarily Western tradition and within that tradition Moers chooses to discuss writers whom she deems "major literary figures of the latter eighteenth and the whole of the nineteenth century." Viewing the increase in female authorship as a phenomenon that begins in the eighteenth century, Moers acknowledges her own project as one driven primarily by a concern for the literary canon. What does it "matter to literature" that "so many of the great writers of modern times have been women?" What does it mean "to be at once a woman and a writer?" What impact does the gender of an author have on a text?

Moers's preface positions her project as the tracking of the "deep creative strategies of the literary mind at work upon the fact of female." According to Moers, female bodies influence the work of women writers both biologically—by affecting women's "senses" and "imagery"—and socially—women are "assigned roles in the family and in courtship" creating experiences that are reflected in their texts. To ignore the existence of these female bodies would be to ignore "whatever was special about being a woman in their time and class and place." Consequently these women writers would then be only "narrowly human" and not much "good as writers."

The reader positioned at the end of the twentieth century, informed by current feminist and postcolonial thought, may be struck by

Moers's essentialism, Western bias, and her seemingly uncritical acceptance of the category of "great" works and writers. One might accuse her of adhering to a Western male paradigm of humanist thought. Recent critiques of Moers's book, such as that by Sydney Kaplan, comment on its "[h]ighly idiosyncratic" preferences for certain authors and "oddly unsystematic" organizational structure. Other critics, like Bonnie Zimmerman, on its homophobic, heterosexist strain. Kaplan also asks why Moers does not question the scarcity of women writers and the silencing of many talented women. For the most part, however, these critics still acknowledge Moers's groundbreaking work and emphasize the importance of historicizing Moers's text so that *Literary Women*'s valuable contribution to feminist literary scholarship is, and can continue to be, acknowledged.

Maria Jerinic

References

Kaplan, Sydney Janet. "Varieties of Feminist Criticism." In *Making a Difference: Feminist Literary Criticism*, edited by Gayle Greene and Coppélia Kahn, 37–58. London: Methuen, 1985.

Moers, Ellen. *Literary Women: The Great Writers*. New York: Oxford University Press, 1985.

Zimmerman, Bonnie. "What Has Never Been: An Overview of Lesbian Feminist Criticism." In *Making a Difference: Feminist Literary Criticism*, edited by Gayle Greene and Coppélia Kahn, 177–210. London: Methuen, 1985.

Moi, Toril

As a Norwegian feminist scholar and literary critic, Moi's primary emphasis in her work is, as she herself explains, on deconstructing the "death-dealing binary oppositions of masculine and feminine." Her most well-known and influential work is *Sexual/Textual Politics*. Moi begins *Sexual/Textual Politics* with a call to recover and rediscover early feminist writers, particularly Virginia Woolf. Moi emphasizes that the debt that contemporary feminist scholars, including herself, owe to Woolf and other pioneering feminist writers needs to be both acknowledged and explored. In *Sexual/Textual Politics,* Moi combines powerfully and persuasively deconstruction, Marxism, and psychoanalysis, to create a particularly confrontational

kind of feminism. She illuminates with crystal clarity, the negative and the positive in some of the most influential Anglo American and French feminist thought. For example, Moi takes issue with Elaine Showalter's disturbingly patriarchal espousal of liberal humanism, questions Sandra Gilbert's and Susan Gubar's insistence on the dictatorial control of the "angry feminist" authorial voice in all women's texts, and she objects to French feminists, Hélène Cixoux's and Luce Irigaray's romanticized essentialism. Throughout the text, Moi maintains a continuous dialogue in which she explores and questions both "schools" of feminist thought, while at the same time blurring the lines between "masculine and feminine."

In her later works, Moi concentrates more specifically on French feminist thought, editing two collections of French feminist essays, *The Kristeva Reader* and *French Feminist Thought: A Reader*. In the first collection, Moi traces the development of one of the most influential of the French feminist critics, paying particular attention to Kristeva's radical start as a feminist scholar and ending with her gradual retreat from the political realm. In *French Feminist Thought,* Moi concentrates on some of the earlier, lesser known, but equally influential feminist thinkers who developed their theories in the aftermath of the 1968 intellectual revolution that took place in Paris. She includes essays by critics such as Annie Leclerc, Christine Delphy, Michele Montrelay, Anne Tristran, and Annie dePisane.

Most recently, Moi has turned her attention to the controversial figure of Simone de Beauvoir. Her 1990 book, *Feminist Theory and Simone de Beauvoir,* was written, according to Moi, to "document and explore a particularly striking aspect in Beauvoir criticism: the unusual number of condescending, sarcastic, sardonic, or dismissive accounts." As she did with Woolf, Moi advocates a reclaiming of de Beauvoir, despite the latter's own assertion that she was not a feminist. Moi also emphasizes the link between de Beauvoir's feminism and Marxism as a truly radical concept that needs further exploration, implying perhaps that it is in this link that the future of feminism lies.

Susan M. Frankson

References

Kristeva, Julia. *The Kristeva Reader.* Edited by Toril Moi. New York: Columbia University Press, 1986.

Moi, Toril. *Feminist Theory and Simone de Beauvoir*. Oxford: Basil Blackwell, 1990.
———. *Sexual/Textual Politics: Feminist Literary Theory*. London and New York: Methuen, 1985.
———, ed. *French Feminist Thought: A Reader*. Oxford: Basil Blackwell, 1987.

Montagu, Lady Mary Wortley (Pierrepoint)

Letter-writer, poet, essayist, Lady Mary Wortley Montagu (1689–1762) has long been acknowledged as one of the most important and notorious *femmes philosophes* of eighteenth-century England by scholars of history and religion. Her place in literary studies has been far less certain, however, beginning to improve only with the modern publications of her biography, her complete letters (1965–1967), and a collected edition of her work. Recent feminist scholarship focusing on the importance of the familiar letter (a genre in which the female voice has been granted privilege and authority throughout its history as a literary form) in eighteenth-century British literature has drawn attention to the work of Lady Mary, and she has become a significant figure in the countercanon of eighteenth-century studies.

Lady Mary's "Turkish Embassy Letters," first published in an unauthorized edition in 1763, were universally praised by contemporaries ranging from early feminist Mary Astell (who wrote a preface to the circulating manuscript of the letters in 1724), to Voltaire to Dr. Samuel Johnson. She wrote the letters in 1716–1718, when she traveled across Europe to Constantinople accompanying her husband, Edward Wortley Montagu, who had been named ambassador to Turkey. The letters demonstrate the unique perspective available to an eighteenth-century female traveler in their descriptions of the seraglio and the Turkish women's baths. The clear-sighted observation displayed therein, combined with a forthright tolerance and sympathy for the Islamic Turkish culture, contributed greatly to an exchange of ideas with Christian Europe, and firmly established Lady Mary as a major figure in the European Enlightenment.

Feminist scholars have recognized Lady Mary as one of a vocal contingent of eighteenth-century Englishwomen who insisted in their lives and writings on women's intellectual potential. Self-taught through extended forays into her father's library, Lady Mary was an avid reader who did not hesitate to breach the walls of male knowledge, mastering the Latin language and writing juvenilia under both male and female pseudonyms. Following her Turkish travels, she campaigned vigorously in England to establish inoculation against smallpox (a practice she had learned in Turkey), despite resistance from the male-dominated medical profession. In response to a Tory periodical, she anonymously produced her own political journal, *The Nonsense of Common-Sense* (1737–1738), devoting number six to a feminist essay censuring popular attitudes that denied women's ability to reason and instead encouraged them to value themselves only by their looks and their virtue. Several points of her argument mirror the present-day feminist debate over whether women are morally superior to men. Lady Mary's writings also include biting social commentary letters to her sister, and a long series of intimate, reflective letters to her daughter, the Countess of Bute, written from her self-exile in France and Italy at the end of her life. Lady Mary died in London of breast cancer in 1762.

Kathleen B. Grathwol

References

Grundy, Isobel. "The Politics of Female Authorship: Lady Mary Wortley Montagu's Reaction to the Printing of Her Poems." *Book Collector* 31 (1982): 19–37.

Halsband, Robert. *The Life of Lady Mary Wortley Montagu*. Oxford: Clarendon, 1956.

Lowenthal, Cynthia. "The Veil of Romance: Lady Mary's Embassy Letters." *Eighteenth-Century Life* 14 (1990): 66–82.

Montagu, Lady Mary Wortley. *The Complete Letters of Lady Mary Wortley Montagu*. Edited by Robert Halsband. Oxford: Clarendon, 1965–1967.

———. *Lady Mary Wortley Montagu: Essays and Poems and Simplicity, A Comedy*. Edited by Robert Halsband and Isobel Grundy. Oxford: Clarendon, 1977.

Perry, Ruth. "Two Forgotten Wits." *Antioch Review* 39 (1981): 431–438.

Rubenstein, Jill. "Women's Biography as a Family Affair: Lady Louisa Stuart's 'Biographical Anecdotes' of Lady Mary Wortley Montagu." *Prose Studies* 9 (1986): 3–21.

Spacks, Patricia Meyer. "Borderlands: Letters and Gossip." *Georgia Review* 37 (1983): 791–813.

Moon

Like the witch, the moon is an icon that encapsulates a dichotomy of feminine traits that society considers both dangerous and alluring, and witchcraft has complex and myriad connections to the moon in many cultures. The moon is representative of the feminine principal in the indigenous cultures of North and South America, Africa, Australia, Polynesia, India, China, Mongolia, the Arabic world, and even Greenland; and of course the Greco-Roman and Celtic traditions combine to produce the many allusions to the moon as feminine force in English literature.

Originally representing the oldest religious beliefs of the power of women, especially reproduction, the moon came to be known as the "Lesser Light" of the sky as monotheism, centered around a male god, came to replace older religions. Its symbolism reflects the danger of essentializing the nature of woman: her fierceness and her sexuality, for instance, may be celebrated, or may be reviled, depending on the text's relationship to the power represented by the moon. The heavenly body representing women, the moon reappears constantly throughout the millennia and today as an emblem of their spirituality, as in the phrase "drawing down the moon."

Related both to the power of the body (childbirth) and of the mind, the moon (the Latin *mens* meaning both moon and mind) and the symbols most closely related to it, especially the bird and the tree, are considered by followers of C.G. Jung to be part of the wellspring of archetypes that all human minds may tap; these symbols are associated in literature as well as in dreams.

Judith Tabron

References

Adler, Margot. *Drawing down the Moon: Witches, Druids, Goddess-Worshippers, and Other Pagans in America Today.* Boston: Beacon, 1986.

Harding, Mary Esther. *Woman's Mysteries, Ancient and Modern: A Psychological Interpretation of the Feminine Principle as Portrayed in Myth, Story and Dreams.* New York: Putnam, for the C.G. Jung Foundation for Analytical Psychology, 1971.

Perez, Janet. "The Triple Lunar Goddess in Aura and 'In a Flemish Garden.'" *Review of Contemporary Fiction* 8 (1988): 189–198.

Sasaki, Michiru. "The Metamorphoses of the Moon: Folk Belief in Lunar Influence on Life and the Symbolic Scheme of a Midsummer Night's Dream." *Shakespeare Studies* (Tokyo) 23 (1984–1985): 59–93.

Walker, Barbara G. *The Woman's Dictionary of Symbols and Sacred Objects.* San Francisco: Harper and Row, 1988.

Moraga, Cherríe

As a contributing co-editor of *This Bridge Called My Back: Writings by Radical Women of Color,* Cherríe Moraga, together with Gloria Anzaldúa, stands at the forefront of the development of a U.S. Third-World feminism. The first anthology of its kind, the book contains prose, poetry, personal narrative, and analysis by African American, Asian American, Latina and Native American feminists. As a challenge to the cultural imperialism of Anglo American feminism, the project represents an early effort to theorize a feminist politics that takes into account the multiple oppressions of race, class, and sexuality. In her essay "La Güera," Moraga discusses the psychic dislocation of fair-skinned Chicanas who "pass for white," and confronts the internalized racism and classism that underlie the phenomenon. In response to movements such as Anglo American feminism (which privileges gender oppression over that of race and class), and Chicano nationalism (which privileges race and class oppression over that of gender), Moraga argues against the ranking of different kinds of oppression. She argues that the hierarchical ranking of oppressions denies the full complexity of the lived reality of the multiply oppressed woman, and leaves her no ground from which to begin to change her life.

In her more recent work, Moraga has gone on to elaborate some of the issues and concerns she first addressed in *Bridge. Loving in the War Years,* an autobiographically inflected collection of short fiction, poetry, and testimonial essay, gives voice to Moraga's effort to develop a specifically Chicana feminist theory—one that derives from her experience as both Chicana and lesbian. Moraga's lesbianism, which brought her both to writing and to political consciousness, has been crucial to her development as a Chicana theorist. It has provided her with a location from which to investigate the sexuality of Chicanas, both hetero- and homosexual, and to begin to name the culturally specific ways in which the Chicano family participates in the acculturation and oppression of its female members.

As poet, playwright, editor, teacher, and co-founder of Kitchen Table: Women of Color Press, Moraga has been crucial to the production, the dissemination, and the theoretical understanding of literature by Chicanas and other women of color in the United States.

Paula Moya

References

Moraga, Cherríe. *Giving up the Ghost: Teatro in Two Acts.* Los Angeles: West End, 1986.

———. *Loving in the War Years: lo que nunca paso por sus labios.* Boston: South End, 1983.

———, and Gloria Anzaldúa, eds. *This Bridge Called My Back: Writings by Radical Women of Color.* Watertown, Mass.: Persephone, 1981.

———, et al., eds. *Cuentos: Stories by Latinas.* New York: Kitchen Table: Women of Color Press, 1983.

Morris, Meaghan

As a translator instrumental in disseminating Continental theory within Australia, and as the author of essays on postmodernist theory and British cultural studies, Meaghan Morris has experienced what it means to enter debates in which the terms have been set elsewhere—not in Australia, but in America, England, or France. This experience has helped her to devise new ways of theorizing the spatial categories with which feminists organize their relationship to academic theories and institutions. In *The Pirate's Fiancée,* she advocates a critical practice that does not situate itself either "inside" or "outside" masculine-dominated debates, but refuses that binary opposition. Drawing on discourse analysis, she proposes that feminists' aim should be neither to abandon nor to salvage such debates, but to find "possible places for women's speech"; feminists might equip those debates with new terms of reference and make women's work the context in which the debates might proceed.

Noting that even theories attentive to differences of race, class, and gender make universalist claims that they ought to shed as they travel from site to site in the global economy, Morris stresses the difference her Australian situation makes. Postmodernists like Jean-François Lyotard likewise give priority to "the local" while advocating a retreat from humanist absolutes. However, as Morris indicates, in constituting postmodernity as a field, postmodern thought has left women no place from which to speak. The same, Morris argues, is true of cultural studies, which aims to respect everyday pleasures, rather than viewing popular culture as a site of debased taste or oppression. For Morris, cultural studies often defines itself and its object, "ordinary people," through an act of exclusion discrediting feminist viewpoints or the voice of any "unambivalently discontented . . . subject."

Morris's own essays in cultural studies and on postmodern culture—on women's experiences of shopping centers, motels, and tourist attractions—thus aim to associate "everyday life" with a range of moods extending beyond pleasure. These accounts of women's work interrogate the home/voyage opposition that separates movement from location as it links the former with men's travel and history-making and the latter with women's confined, static place. Morris argues that "home" should be conceptualized not as the blank a priori of the voyage, but as an "eventful" space where, historically, women have produced modernity.

Deidre Lynch

References

Morris, Meaghan. "At Henry Parkes Motel." *Cultural Studies* 2 (1988): 1–16, 29–47.

———. "Banality in Cultural Studies." In *Logics of Television: Essays in Cultural Criticism,* edited by Patricia Mellencamp, 14–43. Bloomington: Indiana University Press, 1990.

———. "Identity Anecdotes." *Camera Obscura* 12 (1984): 41–65.

———. *The Pirate's Fiancée: Feminism, Reading, Postmodernism.* London: Verso, 1988.

———. "Things to Do with Shopping Centres." In *Grafts: Feminist Cultural Criticism,* edited by Susan Sheridan, 193–225. London: Verso, 1988.

Morrison, Toni

The first African American to be awarded the Nobel Prize in literature, in 1993, Toni Morrison is widely praised both for her lyrical, innovative prose style and for her nuanced portrayals of African American history and traditions. While her six novels are taught under rubrics ranging from "women writers" and "black writers" to "magical realism" and "postmodernism," her work has been of particular importance for black feminist literary theory because the main subjects of Morrison's complex artistry are usually African American women.

Born Chloe Anthony Wofford in Depression-era Ohio, Morrison earned critical praise for her first novel, *The Bluest Eye,* which combined magical realism with an uncompromising indictment of the harsh toll exacted on young black girls by dominant caucasian standards of beauty. The fabulistic *Sula* expanded these thematic concerns by exploring a lifelong friendship between Sula Peace and Nel Wright, the former of whom defies all the traditional expectations of black womanhood that the latter has uncritically upheld. Together with her role as editor of *The Black Book* and her prominent *New York Times Magazine* article "What the Black Woman Thinks of Women's Lib," these novels demonstrate Morrison's early efforts to distance herself not only from the valorization of violence and black manhood that were common among her contemporaries in the black arts movement, but also from the privilege accorded middle-class white identity among second-wave feminists.

With the publication of *Song of Solomon,* a mythopoeic rendering of the Great Migration that won the National Book Critics Circle Award for fiction, Morrison solidified her place in the black literary canon and increased her already-substantial cross-racial readership. She followed the commercially successful but critically unacclaimed *Tar Baby* with a powerful exploration of the effects of slavery on black families in *Beloved,* which was awarded the Pulitzer Prize for fiction. The novel's haunting refrain that "this is not a story to pass on" is indicative of Morrison's refusal to evade even the most painful historical and psychological realities of black life in America. Her most recent novel, *Jazz,* confronts the black urban scene by portraying a tragic love affair in (and, perhaps, with) jazz-age Harlem.

As a senior editor at Random House, Morrison has helped bring into print the work of other African Americans, including women such as Angela Davis, Toni Cade Bambara, and Gayl Jones. She has, moreover, recently taken an active role in political and academic debates by editing a volume of essays on the Anita Hill—Clarence Thomas hearings, *Race-ing Justice, En-gendering Power,* and by publishing a book of literary criticism, *Playing in the Dark,* which explores the construction of racial identities by numerous white American writers. While Morrison is generally viewed as less of a polemicist than peers such as Alice Walker, her extraliterary activities and her stated belief that "all good art has always been political" would suggest that she adheres to an understanding of the writer's role that transcends any straightforward belief in the aesthetic purity of art, as Danille Taylor-Guthrie explains.

Morrison's most salient legacy is her success in situating African American women at the forefront of contemporary American literature. By focusing extensively on her writings, black feminist critics such as Barbara Christian, Deborah McDowell, Valerie Smith, and Mae Gwendolyn Henderson have likewise created a space in the academy where African American women are recognized both as innovative scholars and as vital subjects of scholarship.

Doris Witt

References

Middleton, David L. *Toni Morrison: An Annotated Bibliography.* New York: Garland, 1987.

Morrison, Toni. *Beloved.* New York: Knopf, 1987.

———. *The Bluest Eye.* New York: Simon and Schuster, 1970.

———. *Jazz.* New York: Knopf, 1992.

———. *Playing in the Dark: Whiteness and the Literary Imagination.* Cambridge: Harvard University Press, 1992.

———. *Song of Solomon.* New York: Knopf, 1977.

———. *Sula.* New York: Knopf, 1973.

———. *Tar Baby.* New York: Knopf, 1981.

———. "What the Black Woman Thinks about Women's Lib." *New York Times Magazine* 6 (August 22, 1971): 14ff.

———, ed. *The Black Book.* Compiled by Middleton Harris. New York: Random House, 1974.

———, ed. *Race-ing Justice, En-gendering Power: Essays on Anita Hill, Clarence Thomas, and the Construction of Social Reality.* New York: Pantheon, 1992.

Taylor-Guthrie, Danille, ed. *Conversations with Toni Morrison.* Jackson: University Press of Mississippi, 1994.

M

Motherhood

Though it is so obviously a central fact of female experience, until recently motherhood was seldom theorized for its own sake. When it has been part of theoretical debate, motherhood traditionally has been used to elucidate or contextualize some other problem. The most important example of this phenomenon for feminist considerations of motherhood is the position of the mother in the Oedipal narrative developed by Freud and revised variously by subsequent psychoanalytic critics. According to Freud's basic paradigm, the mother functions as a site of desire for both father and son, and a competition between the males is waged over the maternal body. Further, the development of a healthy (male) personality is largely dependent, in Freud's narrative, on the behavior of the mother. So "classical" psychoanalysis defines the mother in two somewhat contradictory ways: as a passive object to be contested, and as an enormously responsible (and always guilty) subject.

Freud's explanatory narrative—and the double bind in which it places mothers—gave rise to a multitude of questions and elaborations. But it was not until the 1970s that the experiences of actual mothers and the social formation of maternal behavior emerged as important feminist concerns in their own right. Most significant for feminist thinking about motherhood at that time were Adrienne Rich's *Of Woman Born* and Nancy Chodorow's *The Reproduction of Mothering*. These works inaugurated new ways of thinking about motherhood and exemplified the two distinct (though related) directions that feminist theory about motherhood would take.

Rich argued that motherhood is at once both an intensely female experience and an institution defined and controlled by patriarchy. The tensions between these two aspects of motherhood are Rich's subject. She grounds her work historically, in her own experience as both mother and daughter. Perhaps Rich's greatest contribution to feminist thought about motherhood was her insistence that motherhood must be understood as a political institution, historically changing, capable of being redefined.

Chodorow's different effort to understand and redefine motherhood begins not from particular experience, but from the totalizing theory of psychoanalysis. According to the Freudian narrative, the "pre-Oedipal" stage—a time of entire and (potentially) satisfying identification between mother and infant—is followed by a new phase of "Oedipal" separation. Chodorow relied on this narrative, but argued that the shift from pre-Oedipal to Oedipal relation occurs quite differently for girls than for boys: boys separate more completely from the pre-Oedipal stage of nurturant symbiosis with their mothers, while girls never do fully separate. For this reason, according to Chodorow, women are more capable of empathy and demonstrative love than are men. Family structures where mothers have primary child care responsibility reproduce these gendered capacities for nurturance: girls learn to identify with others, boys learn to deny relationality. Neither female nurturance nor male distance are biologically determined; more equally shared parenting that would give richer emotional options to men and end the exclusion of women-as-mothers from public life.

After Rich and Chodorow, feminists thinking about motherhood were able to work from new assumptions. Women's capabilities for nurturance were seen as a great strength; furthermore, that strength was available to men, since such capacities for nurturance were culturally, not biologically, determined. Indeed, motherhood itself (or what Sara Ruddick famously called "maternal thinking") was seen to be a constructed category, determined by cultural pressures and political relationships, not "natural" or eternally the same.

Armed with these insights, Anglo American feminists turned attention during the 1980s to new maternal theory coming out of France and popularly associated with a group of women variously influenced by poststructuralist theory and by Jacques Lacan's revisions of psychoanalysis. These theories were leading many feminists to the belief that radical change might not be possible within existing cultural frameworks; not only the organization of domestic routines needed to change, but also much more fundamental and less easily revised frameworks, including language itself and the hierarchical, exclusionary habits of mind it engenders.

The French theorist and analyst Julia Kristeva looked to the kind of language and symbiotic relationship shared between mothers and newborn infants during the pre-Oedipal stage for alternatives to phallocentric patterns of thought and behavior. Kristeva's essay "Stabat Mater" comprises both an argument for and an exemplification of the potential she found in motherhood to destabilize traditional language and social relations. The main body of the text is a meditation on the figure of the mother in Western culture, epitomized by the Virgin Mary in Roman Catholic tradition. But the calm reasoning and development of this argument is ruptured at irregular intervals by a textual representation of maternal language: nonsemiotic, emotive, contingent, personal. Kristeva's essay attempts to enact the insufficiencies of notions like linear argument, unified identity, and stable meaning; it pits maternal experience, in its multiplicity and materiality, against abstract binaries like nature/culture, self/other, and body/mind. Motherhood becomes the paradigm of *jouissance*, a joyous, pluralizing disruption, an alternative to reductive certainty.

Under these varied influences, Anglo American feminist writing on motherhood has expanded dramatically since the 1980s. Much important work, especially in feminist film theory, continues to use psychoanalytic rubrics in attempting to revise patterns of maternal silencing and to valorize maternal language and desire. Nevertheless, the limitations of psychoanalysis for feminists theorizing motherhood have remained troubling, even to its practitioners. Several important feminist critiques of the use of psychoanalytic explanation to discuss motherhood have emerged, most notably essays by Marianne Hirsch and Jane Gallop. Despite this rigorous questioning, however, many theorists and critics continue to use psychoanalytic tools, believing that the problem of imbeddedness in oppressive assumptions is inescapable and that the psychoanalytic rubric, while seriously flawed, remains useful.

Others have come to feel that although women-as-mothers (and other "others") must necessarily speak in languages that simultaneously silence them, all such languages are not created equal, and psychoanalysis may not make available as much alterity as certain other rubrics when it comes to thinking about motherhood. For these feminists, Gallop's call for a "divorce" between feminist theorizing of motherhood and psychoanalytic assumptions signaled a change of direction. Recent work on motherhood like that of Ruth Perry and Felicity Nussbaum deploys new rubrics, reimagining the subversive functions of motherhood in history, and attempting to remain alert to differences among mothers—especially differences of race, economic and social class, and cultural context. These critics resist theorizing motherhood as a single entity or a stable position, choosing instead to consider how varieties of motherhood function historically both to abet and to subvert patriarchy (itself a multiple and unstable phenomenon).

To draw too firm a distinction between psychoanalytic feminist theorists of motherhood and those who work within a more historically sensitive frame, however, would be to obscure what may be the central insight that has emerged in feminist maternal theory since the 1970s: that a particular methodology may be less important than the cunning and alertness with which it is deployed. Theorists of motherhood, whatever their theoretical commitments, tend now to look for forms of resistance and alterity that exist alongside, even as part of, instances of cooptation. The effort to find "the difference within"—places where oppressive discourses and practices are undercut by dissonance, rupture, or contradiction—rather than a (doomed) effort to move outside phallocentric discourse altogether, now occupies feminists interested in reenvisioning motherhood.

Toni Bowers

References

Chodorow, Nancy. *The Reproduction of Mothering: Psychoanalysis and the Sociology of Gender*. Berkeley: University of California Press, 1978.

Flax, Jane. "The Conflict between Nurturance and Autonomy in Mother-Daughter Relationships and within Feminism." *Feminist Studies* 4 (1978): 171–189.

Gallop, Jane. "Reading the Mother Tongue: Psychoanalytic Feminist Criticism." *Critical Inquiry* 13 (1987): 314–329.

Garner, Shirley Nelson, Claire Kahane, and Madelon Sprengnether, eds. *The (M)other Tongue: Essays in Feminist Psychoanalytic Interpretation*. Ithaca, N.Y.: Cornell University Press, 1985.

Gelpi, Barbara Charlesworth. *Shelley's Goddess: Maternity, Language, Subjectivity*. Oxford University Press, 1992.

Hirsch, Marianne. *The Mother-Daughter Plot: Narrative, Psychoanalysis, Feminism*. Bloomington: Indiana University Press, 1989.

———. "Review Essay: Mothers and Daughters." *Signs* 7 (1981): 200–222.

Homans, Margaret. *Bearing the Word*. Chicago: University of Chicago Press, 1986.

Johnson, Barbara. "Apostrophe, Animation, and Abortion." *Diacritics* 16 (1986): 29–39.

Kristeva, Julia. "Stabat Mater" [1983]. Reprinted in *The Kristeva Reader,* edited by Toril Moi, 160–186. New York: Columbia University Press, 1986.

Nussbaum, Felicity. *Torrid Zones: Maternity, Sexuality, and Empire in 18th Century English Narrative.* Baltimore, Md.: Johns Hopkins University Press, 1995.

O'Barr, Jean F., Deborah Pope, and Mary Wyer, eds. *Ties that Bind: Essays on Mothering and Patriarchy.* Chicago: University of Chicago Press, 1990.

Perry, Ruth. "Colonizing the Breast: Sexuality and Maternity in Eighteenth-Century England." *Journal of the History of Sexuality* 2 (1991): 204–234.

Rich, Adrienne. *Of Woman Born: Motherhood as Experience and Institution.* New York: W.W. Norton, 1976, 1986.

Sprengnether, Madelon. *The Spectral Mother: Freud, Feminism, and Psychoanalysis.* Ithaca, N.Y.: Cornell University Press, 1990.

Stanton, Domna C. "Difference on Trial: A Critique of the Maternal Metaphor in Cixous, Irigaray, and Kristeva." In *The Poetics of Gender*, edited by Nancy K. Miller, 157–182. New York: Columbia University Press, 1986.

Treblicot, Joyce, ed. *Mothering: Essays in Feminist Theory.* Totowa, N.J.: Rowman and Allanheld, 1984.

Mouth

See ORALITY

Mulatto

Though the term is commonly thought to stem etymologically from "mule"—thus connoting the product of an "unnatural" union—agreement upon the word's origin is not universal among historians. In its strictest conception, the term denotes a person who is half black and half white, though it has been employed historically to apply to persons of mixed race more generally. Feminist scholarship continues to contest the role of the mulatto as a literary figure, seeing it variously as an assimilationist device designed to quell the anxieties of a white middle-class readership, or, more recently, as a figure of mediation allowing for the imaginative reworking of existing race relations in the nineteenth and twentieth centuries.

The term is often discussed in connection with the figure of the "tragic mulatto," first popularized in the 1840s in the stories of white abolitionist activist and writer Lydia Maria Child. Beautiful and refined, these mulatta characters (for they they are usually female) are typically betrayed by their white master/lovers and sold into slavery, where they eventually either go mad or meet a violent death trying to escape. Alternatively, especially toward the end of the century, the fictional mulatto tends to appear in an exemplary role, inspiring the black community toward racial uplift, as in Frances E.W. Harper's *Iola Leroy; or, Shadows Uplifted.*

Barbara Christian has articulated a widely held criticism of black writers for appeasing a white middle-class readership in their idealized representations of light-skinned characters who approximate whites. However, Hazel Carby, in her groundbreaking work, *Reconstructing Womanhood: The Emergence of the Afro-American Woman Novelist,* challenges that view, instead positing the mulatto figure as "a narrative device of mediation." Carby is among other contemporary critics who are reexamining the African American literary tradition to probe the multiple and contradictory political valences associated with representations of the mulatto.

Eva Allegra Raimon

References

Berzon, Judith R. *Neither White nor Black.* New York: New York University Press, 1978.

Carby, Hazel V. *Reconstructing Womanhood: The Emergence of the Afro-American Woman Novelist.* New York: Oxford University Press, 1987.

Christian, Barbara. *Black Feminist Criticism: Perspectives on Black Women Writers.* New York: Pergamon, 1985.

Frederickson, George M. *The Black Image in the White Mind: The Debate on Afro-American Character and Destiny, 1817–1914.* New York: Harper and Row, 1971.

Gillman, Susan. "The Mulatto, Tragic or Triumphant? The Nineteenth-Century American Race Melodrama." In *The Culture of Sentiment,* edited by Shirley Samuels, 221–243. New York: Oxford University Press, 1992.

Harper, Frances E.W. *Iola Leroy; or, Shadows Uplifted* [1892]. Boston: Beacon, 1987.

Hopkins, Pauline. *Contending Forces: A Romance Illustrative of Negro Life North and South* [1900]. New York: Oxford University Press, 1988.

Jordan, Winthrop D. *White over Black: American Attitudes toward the Negro, 1550–1812.* Chapel Hill: University of North Carolina Press, 1968. New York: W.W. Norton, 1977.

Larsen, Nella. *Passing.* New York: Knopf, 1929.

Nelson, Dana, D. *The Word in Black and White: Reading "Race" in American Literature, 1638–1867.* New York: Oxford University Press, 1992.

Twain, Mark. "The Tragedy of Pudd'nhead Wilson." In *The Unabridged Mark Twain,* Vol. 2. Philadelphia: Running, 1979.

Williamson, Joel. *New People: Miscegenation and Mulattoes in the United States.* New York: New York University Press, 1984.

Yellin, Jean Fagan. *The Intricate Knot: Black Figures in American Literature, 1776–1863.* New York: New York University Press, 1972.

———. *Women and Sisters: The Antislavery Feminists in American Culture.* New Haven: Yale University Press, 1989.

Mulvey, Laura

In 1975 Laura Mulvey published "Visual Pleasure and Narrative Cinema," the essay that proposed that the camera's gaze is male. In this influential essay Mulvey argued that classical (that is, Hollywood) cinema is a patriarchal institution partaking of a universal symbolic order that "speaks castration and nothing else." Lacking a penis, a woman symbolizes the threat of castration that motivates the formation of the symbolic order. When the male gaze of the camera is directed at the image of a woman, the gaze rekindles the trauma of castration and the film must devalue or punish the woman to remove her as a threat. When the masculine gaze of the camera looks at a male body, on the other hand, it finds an ego ideal. Whereas in classical Hollywood films men move freely in deep space, Mulvey argued, women are depicted in shallow focus and in close-up, literally pinned against a backdrop, confined and dismembered by the frame of the camera.

"Visual Pleasure and Narrative Cinema" was the first feminist film theory to propose that the process of cinematic signification, rather than the signified narrative, might be gendered and oppressive to women. Mulvey's call for a feminist cinema that rejects the pleasure of narrative continuity and spectacle in order to liberate women from "to-be-looked-atness," and her cinematic production, with Peter Wollen, of the feminist film *Riddles of the Sphinx,* influenced countless avant-garde feminist film-makers, and laid the groundwork for almost all of the feminist film theory written since 1975.

Ellen Draper

References
Mulvey, Laura. *Visual and Other Pleasures.* Bloomington: Indiana University Press, 1989.

———. "Visual Pleasure and Narrative Cinema." *Screen* 16 (1975): 7–19. Reprinted in *Feminism and Film Theory,* edited by Constance Penley, 67–79. New York: Routledge, 1988.

———, and Colin McCabe. *Godard: Images, Sounds, Politics.* London: Macmillan, 1982.

Mysticism

Mysticism for women, especially in the Middle Ages but also today, means a search for spiritual fulfillment above and beyond everyday spiritual life, a search for a definition of their souls that exalts them rather than denigrates them as they are denigrated in many aspects of the dogma of the Christian church. Medieval women mystics were characterized by their burning passion for Christ, their complete and utter devotion to Him and to His teachings even when they overstepped the boundaries imposed on them by their society's gender roles. Christina Mirabilis, Marie d'Oignies, Hildegard of Bingen, Catherine of Siena, Julian of Norwich and her contemporary Margery Kempe, and Teresa of Avila were women who sought union with God, defied the teachings of their local clergy, and spoke to priest and layman alike, giving them the word of God as they had received it.

Medieval mystics ranged from the illiterate (whose works were recorded by male amanuenses) to the spectacular intellectual Hildegard of Bingen, one of the most important theologians of the twelfth century. They had in common the courage to escape their arranged marriages, declaring their bodies sacred to Christ and gaining some measure of mental and physical as well as spiritual freedom. These women forged their own languages with which to speak their minds, bodies, and souls, with which to convey the ecstasy of their love of God. In the twentieth century that passion arose again in the person of Simone Weil, noted French intellectual and revolutionary, in whom the "burning love" for God recalls the ecstasies of the medieval mystics without ever relinquishing her commitment to her own intellect and reason.

Judith Tabron

References

Bynum, Caroline. "'. . . And Woman His Humanity': Female Imagery in the Religious Writing of the Later Middle Ages." In *Gender and Religion: On the Complexity of Symbols,* edited by Caroline Walker Bynum, 1–20. Boston: Beacon, 1986.

Hohlwein, Kathryn. "Armed with a Burning Patience: Reflections on Simone Weil." In *The Feminist Mystic and Other Essays on Women and Spirituality,* edited by Mary E. Giles, 142–157. New York: Crossroads, 1982.

Lagorio, Valerie M., ed. *Mysticism: Medieval & Modern.* Salzburg: University of Salzburg, 1986.

Petroff, Elizabeth Alvilda, ed. *Medieval Women's Visionary Literature.* New York and Oxford: Oxford University Press, 1986.

Wiethaus, Ulrike, ed. *Maps of Flesh and Light: The Religious Experience of Medieval Women Mystics.* Syracuse, N.Y.: Syracuse University Press, 1993.

Myth

As described by Estelle Lauter in *Women as Mythmakers,* a myth is an "unusually potent story" that is repeated, in oral or written form, until it becomes accepted as truth, often achieving sacred status. The most influential mythological traditions in Western literature are those from the classical Greek and Roman cultures and those from the early Judeo-Christian culture as represented in the Old and New Testaments. Folk and fairy tales, forms of popular mythology, are also influential in our literature. All of these types of myth pose a problem for feminist literary theorists. Because these mythologies are deeply grounded in patriarchal, misogynistic traditions, they often perpetuate gender inequities in a particularly powerful and covert way by portraying a world in which female figures, according to Carolyne Larrington in *The Feminist Companion to Mythology,* are viewed "reductively, purely in terms of their sexual function."

Yet myths are also enormously important, forming the basis of much of our literary tradition, providing characters, plots, psychological depth, and cultural coherence to literary works. Traditional myths, however drenched in patriarchal attitudes and hostile to female power they may be, cannot simply be dismissed. Feminist literary theorists and writers have therefore devised a number of strategies for dealing with myth, beginning with active feminist critique of traditional Western mythology in general and certain myths in particular. Using the insights garnered from this critique, feminist literary critics can then employ a revised version of what Maggie Humm, in *Feminist Criticism: Women as Contemporary Critics,* calls "myth criticism" as their primary critical methodology, and female writers can create literary works based on revisions of existing myths or creation of new, gynocentric myths.

Recognizing that, as Larrington points out, "myths about women are not necessarily women's myths" and that historically "women have been disbarred from the means to fix their myths in literary form," feminist critique opens myths to the same kinds of feminist literary analysis as might be applied to any other male-authored, male-centered texts. Feminist critique often focuses on the role of myths in perpetuating patriarchy and reveals the misogyny embedded in traditional mythological stories. Such critique might note the valorization of rape in Greek myths, for example, or point out the victimization of young females in fairy tales. Yet feminist critique also reveals a hidden core of female power in myths. This duality creates what Jane Caputi, in "On Psychic Activism: Feminist Mythmaking," calls the twofold task of contemporary feminists, a task involving "both patriarchal myth-smashing and woman-identified myth-making."

The literary practice of creating such gynocentric myth takes a number of forms. In revisionary mythmaking, female writers and poets often employ characters and plots from classical and biblical myths, as well as fairy and folk tales, but they revise the myths by telling them from the "other" side, centering the story around the formerly muted female characters. This is not a new strategy: Christine de Pizan's fifteenth-century revisions of such mythic women as Medea, Isis, Minerva, and Ceres in her *Book of the City of Ladies* are meant to both expose the "massive ingratitude of men" who tell misogynistic tales and to reclaim these women as benefactors to the human race. Anne Sexton's revisions of such fairy tales as "Cinderella" and "Rapunzel"; H.D.'s long poetic explorations of women from Greek tales, such as Helen of Troy and Eurydice; Toni Morrison's rewriting of folk tales in her novels: all are examples of twentieth-century revisionary myth-making. At the heart of this revision is what Alicia Ostriker, in "The Thieves of Language: Women Poets and Revisionist Mythmaking," calls "the challenge to and correction of gender stereotypes embodied in myth." Female writers working with revisionary myth-making recognize the richness and usefulness of traditional myth, as well as the need to claim it as one's own, or, in Rachel DuPlessis's terms, to offer "the possibility of speech to the female in the case, giving voice to the muted."

Other feminist writers use mythological figures somewhat differently, adopting, for example, mythic goddess figures as symbolic representations of their own life experiences, as does Christine Downing in *The Goddess: Mythological Images of the Feminine*, claiming that by exploring a kind of psychic sisterhood with mythological figures like Artemis, Hera, and Aphrodite, women may "come to recognize the *mythos,* the connecting thread, the *story* of our life." Some feminist writers, however, reject patriarchal Western mythologies entirely, seeking instead female representations in alternative mythologies, including those of Native American, Celtic, and African cultures. Others choose to invent completely new mythologies, feminist in nature; many of Suniti Namjoshi's tales in *Feminist Fables* are attempts at newly minted gynocentric myths.

Practitioners of feminist myth criticism, as described by Humm, try to "analyse structures of meaning in myths" and to discover the uses of myths in literary works. Such critics recognize classical and biblical myths as male constructs and they critique them as such, while also working "to discover the force and outline of early, more specifically female, mythologies." Feminist myth critics named by Humm include Virginia Woolf, Annis Pratt, Audre Lorde, and Leslie Silko.

Whether working as literary theorists, crit-ics, or creative writers, feminists engaged in the critique, analysis, and re-creation of myths are involved in what Caputi calls "one of the most significant developments to emerge out the contemporary feminist movement . . . the quest . . . to discover, revitalize, and create a female oral and visual tradition and use it, ultimately, to change the world."

Hollis Seamon

References

Caputi, Jane. "On Psychic Activism: Feminist Mythmaking." In *The Feminist Companion to Mythology,* edited by Carolyne Larrington, 425–440. London: Pandora, 1992.

Daly, Mary. *Gyn/Ecology: The Metaethics of Radical Feminism.* Boston: Beacon, 1978.

Downing, Christine. *The Goddess: Mythological Images of the Feminine.* New York: Crossroads, 1989.

DuPlessis, Rachel. "The Critique of Consciousness and Myth in Levertov, Rich and Rukeyser." In *Shakespeare's Sisters: Feminist Essays on Women Poets,* edited by Sandra Gilbert and Susan Gubar, 280–300. Bloomington: Indiana University Press, 1979.

———. "'Perceiving the Other-side of Everything': Tactics of Revisionary Mythopoesis." In *Writing beyond the Ending,* 105–122. Bloomington: Indiana University Press, 1985.

Humm, Maggie. *Feminist Criticism: Women as Contemporary Critics.* New York: St. Martin's, 1991.

Larrington, Carolyne, ed. *The Feminist Companion to Mythology.* London: Pandora, 1992.

Lauter, Estelle. *Women as Mythmakers: Poetry and Visual Art by Twentieth-Century Women.* Bloomington: Indiana University Press, 1984.

Lefkowitz, Mary. *Women in Greek Myth.* Baltimore: Johns Hopkins University Press, 1986.

Namjoshi, Suniti. *Feminist Fables.* London: Sheba Feminist Press, 1981.

Ostriker, Alicia. "The Thieves of Language: Women Poets and Revisionist Mythmaking." In *The New Feminist Criticism,* edited by Elaine Showalter, 314–338. New York: Pantheon, 1985.

M

N

Name of the Father

A term coined by French psychoanalytic theorist Jacques Lacan to indicate the symbolic dimension of paternal authority in the founding of the subject. The Name of the Father designates that place outside the subject that functions as the source and locus of authority in a primordial sense. Lacan develops this term from the notion of the "dead father" in Freud's *Totem and Taboo*. In this essay, Freud traces the founding of civilization to the establishment of fundamental laws against murder and incest that result from the remorse and debt incurred through the killing of the ancient, mythic father by his sons. The father, as well as his prohibitions, becomes Law, comes to stand for authority. Thus the law is invoked in the name of the father.

Lacan adopts this explanation to support his theory of the development of individual subjectivity. For Lacan, the subject is constituted through a split or lack precipitated by the subject's entrance into the symbolic world of language. This division gets figured by the introduction of the father into the imaginary, seamless connection between mother and child. The introduction of the father acts as a bar or interdiction in general, as an authority that founds the subject as both symbolic and historical. The father thus comes to stand for symbolic law, for the idea of authority. Name of the Father stands for the authority of law as an ancient, transcendent authority to which the individual is subjected, through which the individual is constituted as subject.

Anna Geronimo

References

Freud, Sigmund. *Totem and Taboo*. Edited and translated by James Strachey. New York: W.W. Norton, 1950.

Lacan, Jacques. *Feminine Sexuality: Jacques Lacan and the école freudienne*. Edited by Juliet Mitchell and Jacqueline Rose. Translated by Jacqueline Rose. New York: W.W. Norton, 1982.

———. "Of the Subject of Certainty." In *The Four Fundamental Concepts of Psycho-Analysis,* edited by Jacques-Alain Miller, 29–41. Translated by Alan Sheridan. New York: W.W. Norton, 1978.

———. "On a Question Preliminary to Any Possible Treatment of Psychosis." In *Ecrits,* translated by Alan Sheridan, 179–225. New York: W.W. Norton, 1977.

Narratology

As defined by Gerald Prince, narratology is "the (structuralist-inspired) theory of narrative," focusing on "the nature, form, and functioning" of texts that tell stories. Narratologists seek to identify what "all and only narratives have in common" as well as "what enables them to be different from one another." Feminist narratologists look for the commonalities and differences that can be attributed to gender. This can mean attending to the gender of a character, an author, a narrator, a reader, or some combination of these figures.

For the purposes of analysis, narratology generally separates a narrative text—whether it be a novel, novella, short story, film, oral narrative, or any other form that recounts events in a time sequence—into two levels: story and discourse. "Story" is what happens in a narrative; "discourse" is how the story gets rendered in language. Characters' traits, events, and context (historical, geographical, and cultural) constitute the level of "story"; narration, management of perspective (called "focalization" by Gérard Genette), and temporal ordering constitute the level of "discourse." The narratologist compares and contrasts the ways these functions operate in individual texts with the goal of drawing generalizations about how all narrative operates.

Grounded in structuralism (and named in 1969 by Tzvetan Todorov in *Grammaire du Décaméron*), narratology is a set of highly organized theories. Structuralist narratologists tend to make charts and diagrams of narrative patterns, and narrative theory has often depended upon categories arranged in binary opposition to each other (such as "story" and "discourse"). Although narratologists have continually coined new and unfamiliar-looking terms to describe the phenomena they are observing (Genette is especially notorious in this respect), they generally try to be very clear about the definitions of those terms and very specific about the distinctions they are making among types and functions of narratives.

Poststructuralist feminist theorists have raised questions about the validity of a system of thought that depends so strongly on binary oppositions. Feminist narratologists have attempted, since the 1980s, to move away from an "either/or" model of describing narrative, to include more possibilities among narrative forms. Also, feminist narratologists have noted that many structuralists based their theories on examples that were written almost exclusively by men. Feminist revisions of narratology have proposed categories for analysis that include, rather than exclude, women's ways of writing.

Like other branches of structuralism, narratology originally made claims to universal applicability: the structures it purported to uncover were supposed to be properties of all narratives, regardless of their historical, social, or cultural origins. However, since the mid 1980s, feminist narratologists have insisted upon considering the context in which a narrative was produced. Susan Suleiman's *Authoritarian Fictions*, though not a specifically feminist study, provided a model for analyzing narrative formations within political and cultural contexts. Like Suleiman, feminist narratologists tend to describe narrative patterns in a particular genre or period, working from the assumption that such factors as the race, class, gender, sexual orientation, and nationality of a writer may have significant impact upon the narrative forms he or she employs.

Feminist narratologists, such as Sally Robinson, are also interested in the ways narrative may construct these categories within culture.

The feminist narratology that arose in the late 1970s (and continued through the 1980s) concentrated first on the roles of female characters in narrative. In *The Heroine's Text*, Nancy K. Miller analyzes the plots of eighteenth-century novels written in France and England, to show that there are only two possible fates for a central female character in that genre: in the end, she can get married or she can die. Mieke Bal's *Lethal Love* focuses on biblical narratives, seeking to dismantle "a monolithically misogynist view of those biblical stories wherein female characters play a role, and a denial of the importance of women in the Bible as a whole." Such works look for patterns in the actions assigned to female characters within a given genre.

Feminist narratology has also investigated narrative discourse, asking whether the gender of an author or narrator has an impact upon the ways in which a narrative gets told. Rachel Blau DuPlessis's *Writings beyond the Ending* analyzes feminine revisions of plot formations; Robyn R. Warhol's *Gendered Interventions* identifies gendered patterns in Victorian narrators' uses of direct address to the reader. Susan Lanser's groundbreaking essay "Toward a Feminist Narratology" proposed a gender-conscious revision of narratology's formulation of "voice," and became the cornerstone of her important book *Fictions of Authority*, the most comprehensive narratological analysis of women's writing to date. A collection of feminist-narratological essays, edited by Kathy Mezei (who introduces the collection with an excellent survey of the field) is forthcoming.

Robyn R. Warhol

References

Bal, Mieke. *Lethal Love: Feminist Literary Readings of Biblical Love Stories.* Bloomington: Indiana University Press, 1987.

DuPlessis, Rachel Blau. *Writings beyond the Ending: Narrative Strategies of Twentieth-Century Women Writers,* Bloomington: Indiana University Press, 1985.

Genette, Gérard. *Narrative Discourse: An Essay in Method.* Translated by Jane E. Lewin. Ithaca, N.Y.: Cornell University Press, 1980.

Lanser, Susan S. *Fictions of Authority: Women Writers and Narrative Voice.*

Ithaca, N.Y.: Cornell University Press, 1992.

Mezei, Kathy, ed. *Ambiguous Discourse: Feminist Narratology and British Women Writers.* Chapel Hill: University of North Carolina Press, forthcoming.

Miller, Nancy K. *The Heroine's Text: Readings in the French and English Novel, 1722–1782.* New York: Columbia University Press, 1980.

Prince, Gerald. *A Dictionary of Narratology.* Lincoln and London: University of Nebraska Press, 1987.

Robinson, Sally. *Engendering the Subject: Gender and Self-Representation in Contemporary Women's Fiction.* New York: State University of New York Press, 1991.

Suleiman, Susan Rubin. *Authoritarian Fictions: The Ideological Novel as a Literary Genre.* New York: Columbia University Press, 1983.

Warhol, Robyn R. *Gendered Interventions: Narrative Discourse in the Victorian Novel.* New Brunswick, N.J.: Rutgers University Press, 1989.

Native American Feminist Literary Theory

As an intended approach to literary criticism or practice, feminism has been cautiously defined as such by Native writers. Many writers "of color" have challenged feminism for "cultural imperialism," "shortsightedness" in defining gender in terms of "middle-class, white experiences," and for its "internalization of racism, classism, and homophobia" (Mohanty 1991). Likewise, Native writers have distanced themselves from "feminism" for a shared suspicion of its neglect of Native histories. (See Jaimes and Halsey. They go so far as to suggest that Native women and feminism are unequivocally incompatible.) Native writers who have formulated a feminist critique or practice do so through careful definitions of their suspicions, departures from, and invitations of particular feminisms. Their formulations can be said to cluster around three main issues: tribal sovereignty as the recognition of rights to self-governance and land-base jurisdiction; cultural survival defined as the means to maintain traditional practices often by juridical access to specific lands and resources (though survival is not "dependent" on sovereign status); and the diverse tribal understandings of gender roles and sexuality.

In 1982, Rayna Green chronicled some of the concerns addressed by Native women at various political meetings in which she participated from 1977 to 1981 in her essay "Diary of a Native American Feminist." Her observations are important to understanding the diverse contexts under which tribal women have formed alliances for social change. Green remarks that in this context Indian feminism is as various as are tribal perspectives, and that the conflicting sites of tradition and federal policy demand constant renegotiation within and between Native peoples for their respective communities. The "facts and resources" that close the essay draw attention to Native women's health, employment, and education and the organizations seeking to make interventions within these areas (including Ohoyo Resource Center and Women of All Red Nations). Green's comments represent Native women's negotiation of their involvement within and apart from the "white women's movement."

Kathryn Shanley's 1984 essay "Thoughts on Indian Feminism" argues that while alliances between Indian women and the "white feminism movement" are important, Indian women have too often been made into "tokens" for a movement that has ignored their particular struggles and beliefs. Shanley maintains that tribal sovereignty and tradition are not merely supplementary to Indian feminism but absolutely fundamental in defining participation in and self-definition with anything feminist. She posits that because Indian women have traditionally occupied a central place within their tribe's cultural, spiritual, economic, and political lives, concerns characteristic of the "white women's movement" over oppressions of the "nuclear family" and its hierarchically defined sociopolitical confinement of the women to the private/domestic sphere has little translation into Indian communities and worldviews. For Shanley, Indian feminism values and is constituted by home(land) and tradition.

The plethora of Native anthologies that have proliferated since the 1970s can be understood as significant interventions not only in the voids of U.S. literary canons but as attempts to raise political awareness of Native struggles for self-determination and cultural survival. Among the first were Jane B. Katz's edition *"I Am the Fire of Time": The Voices of Native American Women* and Carolyn Niethammer's *Daughters of the Earth: The Lives and Legends of American Indian Women.* Recent collections include the Telling It Book Collective's *Telling It: Women and Language across Cultures: The Transformation of a Conference* and Connie Fife's *The Colour of Resistance: A Contemporary Collection of Writing by Aboriginal Women*; see also a forthcoming edition by Inés Hernández-Ávila entitled *On Our Own Terms: Critical/Creative Representations by Native American Women*. Together, the anthologies do the important work of breaking down national and patriarchal territories that want to police Native "Indianness" and sexuality by providing the places through which Native writers reclaim their histories and identities.

Concurrent with these editions are innumerable critiques written by Native scholars about gender roles and sexuality. In *The Hidden Half: Studies of Plains Indian Women*, Patricia Albers and Beatrice Medicine offer a collection of critical studies written by Natives about the representation of Plains Indian women within the disciplines of anthropology and history. In *American Indian Women: Telling Their Lives*, Gretchen M. Bataille and Kathleen Mullen Sands analyze the complexities of Native women's autobiographies. Both of these texts directly oppose the historically racist and patriarchal theorizing of Native gender roles that have perpetuated stereotypes about Native men and women that have served to foreclose cross-cultural understandings of Native women's central place within traditional societies and the complexities of Native experiences with and against colonization as well as tribal traditions around sexuality. In like purpose, Walter L. Williams's *The Spirit and the Flesh: Sexual Diversity in American Indian Culture* and Will Roscoe's compilation *Living the Spirit: A Gay American Indian Anthology* counter racist and "compulsory heterosexual" patriarchal (mis)understandings of Native sexualities. Both of these texts analyze the roles and significance of gay, lesbian, bisexual, and "third gender/sex" peoples within tribal communities.

Though not specifically "literary," tribal sovereignty and tradition inform how Native writers have formulated a feminist (literary) criticism and practice. In 1986, Paula Gunn Allen's *The Sacred Hoop: Recovering the Feminine in American Indian Traditions* located Native women and the feminine within Native literature and art while critiquing (U.S.) patriarchal and colonial attempts to not merely suppress but destroy tribal gynocratic societies and their women-centered communities. Allen's text offers important interpretive tools for reading

and understanding Native women/feminine traditions such as within the works of Leslie Marmon Silko and the powerful feminine "deities" within tribal beliefs. Criticisms of Allen's work point out her overgeneralizations and so essentialisms of Native women and what constitutes the "tribal" as she tends to define all Natives from her own Keres (Laguna Pueblo) history.

In 1990, Laura Coltelli edited a collection of interviews entitled *Winged Words: American Indian Writers Speak*. Allen, Joy Harjo, Linda Hogan, and Wendy Rose discuss the effects of feminism within their respective works. Though Coltelli did not ask the men she interviewed what their positions were in respect to feminism, the collection is important for understanding the negotiations of Native women with and against feminism at the level of methodology.

Inés Hernández-Avila's 1995 essay "Relocations upon Relocations: Home, Language and Native American Women's Writings" addresses the works of Native women in relation to "homes, positions, and (re)locations" and language (forthcoming in *American Indian Quarterly*). As an interrogation of the terms "feminism" and "feminist politics," Hernández-Avila's essay locates Native women's writing practices as cultural activism from tribal histories of relocation. Native women's various emphases on homelands and traditions within their writings remap and renegotiate the "territories" of feminism by subverting its definition of the home as private and giving voice to Native peoples and their beliefs. For Hernández-Avila, the implications of these configurations are for understandings of the historical issues facing Native peoples (home always belonging to the very public process of relocation), as well as the formation of alliances between Native women—across national and tribal borders—toward tribal sovereignty and continuance. Forthcoming projects by Native writers promise to likewise disrupt feminist (literary) practices with tribal histories of survival as opposition and voice (re)claiming.

Please note that herein I use "Native American," "Native," "Indian," and "tribal" interchangeably to refer to the indigenous peoples of the North Americas. These terms are equally contested as (il)legitimate signifiers for indigenous Americans. For instances of the concerns with the ideological etymologies of the terms, see Robert F. Berkhofer, Jr.'s *The White Man's*

Indian (1978), Glenn T. Morris's essay "International Law and Politics: Toward a Right to Self-Determination for Indigenous People" in M. Annette Jaimes's edition *The State of Native America* (1992), and Haunani-Kay Trask's *From a Native Daughter* (1994).

Joanne Marie Barker

References

Albers, Patricia, and Beatrice Medicine, eds. *The Hidden Half: Studies of Plains Indian Women.* Lanham, Md.: University Press of America, 1983.

Allen, Paula Gunn. *The Sacred Hoop: Recovering the Feminine in American Indian Traditions.* Boston: Beacon, 1986.

Bataille, Gretchen M., and Kathleen Mullen Sands. *American Indian Women: Telling Their Lives.* Lincoln: University of Nebraska Press, 1984.

Berkhofer, Robert F. *The White Man's Indian: Images of American Indian from Columbus to the Present.* New York: Knopf, 1978.

Coltelli, Laura, ed. *Winged Words: American Indian Writers Speak.* Lincoln: University of Nebraska Press, 1990.

Emberley, Julia. *Thresholds of Difference: Feminist Critique, Native Women's Writings, Postcolonial Theory.* Toronto: University of Toronto Press, 1993.

Fife, Connie, ed. *The Colour of Resistance: A Contemporary Collection of Writing by Aboriginal Women.* Toronto: Sister Vision, 1993.

Green, Rayna. "Diary of a Native American Feminist." *Ms.* (August 1982): 170–172, 211–213.

Jaimes, M. Annette, and Theresa Halsey. "American Indian Women: At the Center of Indigenous Resistance in North America." In *The State of Native America: Genocide, Colonization, and Resistance,* edited by M. Annette Jaimes, 311–344. Boston: South End, 1992.

Katz, Jane B., ed. *"I Am the Fire of Time": The Voices of Native American Women.* New York: Dutton, 1977.

Mohanty, Chandra Talpade. "Introduction." In *Third World Women and the Politics of Feminism,* edited by Ann Russo Mohanty and Lourdes Torres, 150. Bloomington: Indiana University Press, 1991.

Morris, Glenn T. "International Law and Politics: Toward a Right to Self-Determination for Indigenous People" in *The State of Native America: Genocide, Colonization, and Resistance,* edited by M. Annette Jaimes, 55–86. Boston: South End, 1992.

Niethammer, Carolyn, ed. *Daughters of the Earth: The Lives and Legends of American Indian Women.* New York: Collier, 1977.

Roscoe, Will, comp. *Living the Spirit: A Gay American Indian Anthology.* New York: St. Martin's, 1989.

Shanley, Kathryn. "Thoughts on Indian Feminism." In *A Gathering of Spirit: A Collection by North American Indian Women,* edited by Beth Brant, 213–215. Ithaca, N.Y.: Firebrand, 1984.

Telling It Book Collective, eds. *Telling It: Women and Language across Cultures: The Transformation of a Conference.* Vancouver: Press Gang, 1990.

Trask, Haunani-Kay. *From a Native Daughter: Colonialism and Sovereignty in Hawai'i.* Monroe, Me.: Common Courage, 1993.

Williams, Walter L. *The Spirit and the Flesh: Sexual Diversity in American Indian Culture.* Boston: Beacon, 1986.

Nature

There are at least two fundamental philosophical issues involved in the feminist critique of the dominant Western conception of nature. The first issue is whether, and to what extent, humanity is part of nature. The second issue is whether, and to what extent, women are part of humanity. These two questions are connected in significant ways that many feminist authors have explored. Briefly, the critique centers upon the conception of nature as feminine, the domination of that feminine force by science and the way in which that contributes to the subjugation of women.

The first question is whether nature is conceived of as including the human. Some cultures place humans within nature; Western civilization, though, is noted for separating the human world from that of nature—and for considering humans superior to the elements and beasts of the natural world. With the rise of science in the West, many believe that the perceived difference between humanity and nature was maximized, and the relationship became one of domination and exclusion. The second question is whether women are fully human. Western civilization, like so many patriarchal cultures, excludes women from full human status. Women have been considered different and essentially lesser than men, as incomplete humans or irrational, emotional humans. Science has been utilized in attempts to justify these beliefs about women, and to further their subjugation. Woman, like nature, is essentially different from man—and man's role is to dominate and control both.

As Carolyn Merchant, in *The Death of Nature*, documents, early-sixteenth-century Europeans saw the whole of nature as an organism, and as female—a nourishing mother, the source of life. Humans were considered a part of this greater whole, with harmony and cooperation being the primary relation. With the Scientific Revolution, nature lost its life, independence, and sentience to become pure material, passively governed by laws that science was to discover. Philosophical mechanism, championed by Descartes, held sway over vitalism; nature as matter-in-motion took precedence over nature as a life force. Nature, though still feminine, was no longer a generally benevolent yet powerful force with which one cooperated, but a machine to be conquered and placed in the service of humanity by science and technology. The primary metaphor used for this process of domination has been of active male (scientist) who, by "rape" or by "seduction" gains knowledge of the passive female (nature).

Susan Griffin's *Women and Nature* approaches the same questions, but with a much different style. Rather than offering a scholarly work that attempts to convince the reader of the reality of the patriarchal exploitation of women and of nature, she draws the reader to experience nature and women through what she believes are their own voices. The book is a dialogue between the voice of the patriarchy that purports to be objective, emotionless, and supremely rational and the voices of nature and women, which are portrayed as subjective, descriptive, emotive. In this way Griffin offers her criticism of the dominant paradigm of Western civilization in which, she argues, the real experiences of women and of nature are minimized and marginalized.

A major component of Western civilization is science, and its understanding and control of nature is often considered our highest achievement. However, science did more than subjugate nature; many would argue that it was, and

is, an effective tool in the subjugation of humans one deems "other," or different from oneself. In *Science and Sexual Oppression,* Brian Easlea presents science as masculine, and chronicles its far-reaching negative consequences for the feminine, and the women, in the world. In this work, and others, he argues for the democratization of science and its philosophical underpinnings to bring about liberation rather than domination.

Merchant's and Griffin's works, among others, are often cited as foundational to the ecofeminist movement. Ecofeminism connects the subjugation of feminine nature with that of women at the hands of the masculine culture, and, especially, its science. Although ecofeminists differ on the particulars, generally they argue for a shift to a worldview that is more holistic and inclusive, and that reveres nature, and woman, as the life-source and nurturer of the world, and of humanity, respectively. *Reclaim the Earth* is a classic collection of essays on ecofeminism. Two more recent, and readily available, collections of essays that provide a good sense of the movement and the views of its members are *Healing the Wounds* and *Ecofeminism*. For one woman's conception of this new worldview that ecofeminism offers, see Elizabeth Dodson Gray's *Green Paradise Lost*. Paula Gunn Allen, in *The Sacred Hoop*, offers another such view, based on the traditions and current reformulation of the culture of Native Americans. Janet Biehl, in *Rethinking Ecofeminist Politics,* offers a critical view of ecofeminism, considering it an incoherent movement that would, if successful, return us to an irrational and mystical world in which everyone (women as well as men) would suffer.

Susan M. Mooney

References

Allen, Paula Gunn. *The Sacred Hoop: Recovering the Feminine in American Indian Traditions*. Boston: Beacon, 1986.

Biehl, Janet. *Rethinking Ecofeminist Politics.* Boston: South End, 1991.

Caldecott, Leonie, and Stephanie Leland, eds. *Reclaim the Earth: Women Speak out for Life on Earth.* London: Women's, 1983.

Easlea, Brian. *Science and Sexual Oppression: Patriarchy's Confrontation with Women and Nature*. London: Weidenfeld and Nicholson, 1981.

Gaard, Greta, ed. *Ecofeminism: Women, Animals, Nature.* Philadelphia: Temple University Press, 1993.

Gray, Elizabeth Dodson. *Green Paradise Lost*. Wellesley, Mass.: Roundtable, 1979.

Griffin, Susan. *Women and Nature: The Roaring inside Her*. New York: Harper and Row, 1978.

Merchant, Carolyn. *The Death of Nature: Women, Ecology and the Scientific Revolution*. New York: Harper and Row, 1980.

Ortner, Sherry. "Is Female to Male as Nature Is to Culture?" In *Woman, Culture, and Society*, edited by Michelle Rosaldo and Louise Lamphere, 67–87. Stanford: Stanford University Press, 1974.

Plant, Judith. *Healing the Wounds: The Promise of Ecofeminism*. Philadelphia: New Society Publishers, 1989.

Neurosis

Although often associated with Sigmund Freud, the term "neurosis" has a long history in the medical literature preceding his discovery of the unconscious. For scholars of feminist theory, "neurosis" is a significant term because neurotics—especially so-called hysterical neurotics—were usually women whose ambitions, behavior, and sexuality differed from expected, heterosexual norms.

According to Sacks and Rousseau, the term "neurosis" was first coined in 1769 by William Cullen, an Edinburgh physician. In the late eighteenth century, neurosis referred to a set of diseases that were considered "affections of the nervous system"—that is, they had some (supposedly) palpable somatic cause. However, neurosis during the Enlightenment was broadly defined: such diseases as chorea, apoplexy, paralysis, hypochondria, tetanus, epilepsy, whooping cough, diarrhea, diabetes, hysteria, melancholia, and mania were all considered by Cullen to be "neuroses." In the case of hysteria, Cullen had, in fact, taken a step backward from such physicians as Thomas Sydenham (1621–1698), who had perceived for the first time that the causes of hysterical neurosis could be both psychological and societal—that is, that "hysteria imitates culture"—and that it could afflict men as well as women. Cullen, however, reverted back to the ancient theory that hysteria was caused by the "wandering womb," which would, if not satisfied by sufficient heterosexual intercourse, detach from its moorings and wander the body's internal cavities, causing a wide variety of somatic symptoms. Clearly, this hysteria was a "women's disease."

During the 150 years following Cullen's coining of the term "neurosis," actual physical causes were found for many of the illnesses that had fallen under the neurotic rubric. What remained classified as "neurotic," according to Sacks, were illnesses like hypochondria, hysteria, and cataplexy—"nervous" disorders for which no physical cause could be found (although physicians remained confident that the neuroses had organic, rather than psychological, causes). At this time, the neuroses were also differentiated from the psychoses, which were major mental illnesses ("lunacy") often leading to commitment to the lunatic asylums of the nineteenth century.

In the middle of the nineteenth century, the French physician Jean-Martin Charcot took up the study of neurosis, especially hysteria. Charcot treated many neurotics, both male and female, in his clinic at the Salpêtrière asylum. He believed that hysterical symptoms—especially the famous attacks of *grande hystérie*, prolonged and sometimes ecstatic seizures "performed" by female hysterics at his clinic—could be relieved by placing pressure on certain hysterogenic zones on the hysteric's body (found especially, according to Elaine Showalter, in the ovarian region). Charcot believed that hysterical attacks in men were precipitated by violent accidents, and that such attacks in males could be stopped by compressing the testicles (as Showalter comments, at least one of Charcot's staff physicians at the Salpêtrière found that "squeezing the patient's testicles made the convulsions stronger").

Charcot was famous for lecture-demonstrations, at which he "exhibited" his female hysterical patients, hypnotizing them in front of large audiences. Indeed, according to Showalter, Charcot emphasized the visual manifestations of hysteria and presented the "hysterical body as an art object," publishing volumes of photographic iconographies that were idealized by some artists, especially members of the Surrealist movement.

Sigmund Freud studied with Charcot and took up his study of hysteria and the neuroses. In his *Introductory Lectures on Psychoanalysis*, Freud proposed a detailed classification of the neuroses. First, he identified two broad types of neuroses: the "actual neuroses," in which physiological symptoms were caused by sexual frustration (including anxiety neurosis and hypochondria); and the "psychoneuroses," which were psychological in origin, usually the result of some sort of childhood trauma. The "psychoneuroses" were further classified into two categories: transference neuroses (which included phobias, hysteria, and "obsessional neurosis"); and narcissistic neuroses (paranoia, "hallucinatory confusions," and melancholia). Freud considered only the so-called transference neuroses to be amenable to psychoanalytic treatment (what he classified as "narcissistic neuroses" would today be considered major psychoses).

According to Freud, the symptoms of neurosis were symbolic; often, the symptoms mimicked traumatic events of the past that had been forgotten by the patient precisely because of their threatening nature. Symptoms could also be caused by unfulfilled forbidden wishes, repressed by the patient because they, too, were unacceptable and threatening (such wishes might include sexual or violent impulses toward the parents, for example). The neurotic patient, Freud said, is always ignorant of the meaning of the symptoms, because the symptoms are created by "unconscious processes"; when the forbidden thoughts become conscious, the threatening wishes or memories can be acknowledged and dealt with by the patient—and then the symptoms disappear. Thus, the work of psychoanalysis is largely that of "making the unconscious conscious."

Freud and his colleague Joseph Breuer were among the first investigators of neurosis to actually listen to their women patients and take their problems seriously. However, according to Showalter, Freud's initial "sympathy with women's intellectual and creative frustrations" began to falter as he became more invested in his psychoanalytic system and as his methods became more rigid and codified. His paper *Dora: Fragment of an Analysis of a Case of Hysteria,* has become a famous example of how Freud's rigid thinking sometimes silenced his women patients. Numerous critics have noted that in this famous case (Freud's only full-length paper on a female analysand), Freud imposed his own interpretations upon Dora's experience, going so far as to label as "hysterical" her behavior in rejecting the sexual overtures of a much older man, the husband of her father's mistress; as a result, Dora broke off the analysis.

Feminist thinkers have viewed hysteria in widely differing manners. For some, like Hélène Cixous, the hysterical woman (in particular, Dora) is a rebel, one who revolts against society's expectations. Others, like Catherine Clément, do not see hysteria as a powerful form of feminine subversion; rather, they see the hysteric as a woman who must express herself through symptoms because she cannot participate in the dominant societal discourse. Lisa Kasmer, in an explication of Charlotte Perkins Gilman's story "The Yellow Wallpaper" (about a woman's hysteria and the punishing "rest cure" forced upon her, which drives her mad), notes that the narrator's madness is not a successful attempt to create a new discourse, but rather a process of being overcome by an ultimately alienating masculine discourse. In tearing down the yellow wallpaper, the narrator "destroys her only access to symbol, through which she can consciously understand her own thoughts."

Lori A. Baker

See also HYSTERIA

References

Bernheimer, Charles, and Claire Kahane, eds. *In Dora's Case: Freud—Hysteria—Feminism.* New York: Columbia University Press, 1990.

Breuer, Joseph, and Sigmund Freud. *Studies on Hysteria.* Edited and translated by James Strachey. London: Hogarth, 1955.

Cixous, Hélène. "The Laugh of the Medusa." Translated by Keith Cohen and Paula Cohen. In *The Signs Reader,* edited by Elizabeth Abel and Emily Abel, 279–297. Chicago: University of Chicago Press, 1983.

———, and Catherine Clément. *The Newly Born Woman.* Translated by Betsy Wing. Minneapolis: University of Minnesota Press, 1986.

Drinka, George Frederick. *The Birth of Neurosis: Myth, Malady, and the Victorians.* New York: Simon and Schuster, 1984.

Freud, Sigmund. *The Complete Introductory Lectures on Psychoanalysis.* Edited and translated by James Strachey, 243–466. New York: W.W. Norton, 1966.

———. *Dora: Fragment of an Analysis of a Case of Hysteria.* New York: Macmillan, 1963.

Kasmer, Lisa. "Charlotte Perkins Gilman's 'The Yellow Wallpaper': A Symptomatic Reading." *Literature and Psychology* 36 (1990): 1–15.

Rousseau, G.S. "'A Strange Pathology': Hysteria in the Early Modern World, 1500–1800." In *Hysteria beyond Freud,* edited by Sander Gilman, Helen King, Roy Porter, G.S. Rousseau, and Elaine Showalter, 91–224. Berkeley: University of California Press, 1993.

Sacks, Michael. "Introduction to the Neuroses." In *Psychiatry: The Personality Disorders and Neuroses,* edited by Arnold M. Cooper, Allen J. Frances, and Michael H. Sacks, 315–323. New York: Basic, 1986.

Showalter, Elaine. "Hysteria, Feminism, and Gender." In *Hysteria beyond Freud,* edited by Sander Gilman, Helen King, Roy Porter, G.S. Rousseau, and Elaine Showalter, 286–344. Berkeley: University of California Press, 1993.

Strong, Beret E. "Foucault, Freud, and French Feminism: Theorizing Hysteria as Theorizing the Feminine." *Literature and Psychology* 35 (1989): 10–26.

New Criticism

For poetry studies in America, New Criticism was the leading theory from the 1940s through the early 1960s. New Critics such as I.A. Richards, John Crowe Ransom, and Cleanth Brooks maintained that poems should be read in ways that focus attention on the use of language and the unity of composition. By attending to the words themselves, their order and meaning, New Critics avoided references to external influences such as culture, life circumstances, historical situation, or social status on the work and its writer. While New Critics did not view the evolution of a literary form or a writer's previous use of a form as relevant to the poem's interpretation, they held that the form organized the meaning of the work.

Generally, feminist criticism is opposed to the tenets of New Criticism. In particular, gynocriticism is antithetical to New Criticism, as the former conscientiously draws attention to the women writers as women and to the challenges women writers face culturally, socially, emotionally, historically, and personally. The role of women as producers of literature and the types of subjects upon which they commonly wrote, identifiable as "women's issues," are the targets of study for gyno/feminist critics. While New Criticism and feminist critics share surface interests in language and meaning, gynocritics stress the women's voices heard in the diction

and form of the works. This interest in writing as women's writing, combined with a desire to uncover the distinctively female worldview within women's writing, is incompatible with the independent approach to literature New Critics employed.

Beverly Schneller

References
Gilbert, Sandra, and Susan Gubar. *The Madwoman in the Attic.* New York: W.W. Norton, 1979.

Ransom, John Crowe. *Practical Criticism.* Norfolk, Conn.: New Directions, 1941.

Welleck, Rene, and Austin Warren. *Theory of Literature.* New York: Harcourt, Brace, 1956.

New Historicism

New Historicism is a type of historical criticism, developed in the 1980s under the influence of various poststructuralist theories—feminism, Marxism, psychoanalytic criticism, reader-response criticism, and deconstruction—that reconceptualizes history and literature, as well as their relationship to one another. New Historicists see the boundaries between the literary and the social to be shifting and highly permeable, a view that has encouraged a reevaluation of the traditional literary canon. As a result, many works previously considered outside the scope of scholarly study have been revalued as works of literary merit or cultural importance. This is of particular significance to feminist critics, for many newly "discovered" works are those written by, for, and about women. Moreover, New Historicists have argued, as have feminists, that works of literature and criticism are not apolitical or ahistorical activities, as both sorts of texts are produced within historically specific contexts that cannot be ignored. Just as any text is implicated by its place within history, the critic must recognize herself or himself as both a product and producer of a certain kind of literary history.

Like feminists who have reacted against the objectifying formalist strategies of New Criticism, a school of criticism that privileges a restricted canon of literary masterpieces and dissects these works as isolated aesthetic objects of individual (and typically male) genius, New Historicists have sought to "historicize" texts, examining them within their specific historical contexts. For the New Historicist, literature is not separate from, nor necessarily superior to, other discursive practices; instead it acts as a participant within a larger system of cultural production. A second dimension of New Historicism is the "textualizing" of history. As cultural anthropologist Clifford Geertz argues, in *The Interpretation of Culture*, there is no "human nature independent of culture," that human beings themselves are "cultural artifacts." He further maintains that as "the culture of a people is an ensemble of texts" the study of culture is necessarily textual. The past is transmitted through texts and our only access to the past is through those texts. From a New Historicist perspective, then, history is no longer simply a backdrop to literature, nor is literature simply a passive reflector of social realities. In other words, any literary text exists in a complicated dialectic with its context, both produced by and capable of influencing material conditions.

Such redefinitions of history, literature, and the relationship between the two have a significant impact on the examination of the texture and textuality of women's lives, as well as women's texts and the images of women *within* texts. In order to achieve a fuller exploration of literary texts, New Historicists break down the barrier between literature and other fields of research, drawing upon the discourses of medicine, the law, sociology, anthropology, religion, education, and so forth. Poststructuralist Mikhail M. Bakhtin, in *The Dialogic Imagination: Four Essays* (1981), describes this intertextuality through the terms "heterglossia" and "dialogism," which define a text as composed of "a multiplicity of social voices." By destabilizing the "binary oppositions"—male/female, culture/nature, literary/nonliterary—that have informed much critical thinking and undermining hierarchical and exclusionary interpretative practices, New Historicists and feminists are able to hear and to explore many previously unheard voices. Of particular importance for feminists is the recognition of the fluidity and mutual dependence of what have long been considered public (male) and private (female) discourses. Texts long considered to be strictly female (and thus unimportant), such as romance novels, diaries, mothers' journals, conduct books, and ladies' magazines, have been reevaluated and these reevaluations have led to more informed reading of texts produced both by female and male authors.

The work of historian/philosopher Michel Foucault, which has informed many New His-

torical studies, also is significant to feminist studies. In such works as *Discipline and Punish* (1978), Foucault describes how the individual subject is produced by and exists within a structural grid of power and knowledge that saturates and circumscribes the individual life. Foucault argues, however, that power is not merely repressive force. "In fact," he asserts in *Discipline and Punish*, "power produces; it produces reality; it produces domains of objects and rituals of truth." Gender is one of the objects and vehicles of power, as Foucault demonstrates in *The History of Sexuality* (1978), where he describes "the way in which sex is 'put into discourse,'" demonstrating that "sexuality is a very real historical formation." Part of this process was the "hysterization of women's bodies," as they were saturated with sexuality through the combined efforts of various discursive practices and constituted as "texts" to be read within the context of power relations.

A number of feminist New Historians have exhibited the ways in which femininity and female identity are historically constructed, as well as the ways in which gender has played an essential role in the formation and deployment of literary texts. Two examples include Nancy Armstrong's *Desire and Domestic Fiction* (1987) and Felicity Nussbaum's *The Autobiographical Subject* (1989). Armstrong, through her exploration of the ideology of conduct books and novels of the eighteenth and nineteenth centuries, demonstrates how the discourse of sexuality shaped the novel and how domestic fiction helped to produce the modern subject, who is, according to Armstrong, female. Nussbaum examines various genres of self-definition—scandalous memoirs, spiritual autobiographies, mothers' journals—to show how women across the eighteenth century inhabited these forms and employed them as a means to define and to empower themselves as women and as writers.

Beyond the charge made by some feminists, such as Judith Newton, that feminist historians have been doing for years what New Historicism suggests are critical innovation, feminists have offered at least two significant complaints against New Historicism. The first is that Foucauldian versions of history offer a totalizing vision of power structures within which there is no individual agency and from which there is no escape through change. Moreover, feminists have argued that New Historicists ignore gender as a significant component of any historical moment or erase the centrality of gender differences within any historical context. As Wai-Chee Dimock argues in "Feminism, New Historicism, and the Reader," what is necessary is the "engendering of history," a recognition that gender is a necessary component of historical change.

Despite these valid arguments, the conjunction of New Historicism and feminism has proven fruitful. For instance, New Historicism has encouraged feminists to recognize that gender is not an ahistorical and immutable category of difference. As Dimock asserts, "Gender is most useful as an analytic category . . . when it is understood to be constituted in time and constrained by time, propelled by temporal necessity and subject to temporal reconfiguration." In short, just as history must be engendered, gender must be historicized. Merging these two theories combines New Historicist synchronic view of history with the feminist diachronic view, allowing for both a careful description of specific historical moments in women's history and a recognition of the potential for change. Moreover, New Historicism's critical self-consciousness has enriched feminist appraisals of canon formation because, as Ellen Pollak argues, it encourages us "not simply to repudiate traditional standards of literary value but to rethink the entire process of exclusion by which canons are defined and then sustained."

Judith Burdan

References

Armstrong, Nancy. *Desire and Domestic Fiction: A Political History of the Novel.* New York: Oxford University Press, 1987.

Bakhtin, M.M. *The Dialogic Imagination: Four Essays.* Edited by Michael Holquist. Translated by Caryl Emerson. Austin: University of Texas Press, 1981.

Dimock, Wai-Chee. "Feminism, New Historicism, and the Reader." *American Literature* 63 (1991): 601–622.

Foucault, Michel. *Discipline and Punish: The Birth of the Prison.* Translated by Alan Sheridan. New York: Random House, 1978.

———. *The History of Sexuality.* Vol. 1. Translated by Robert Hurley. New York: Random House, 1978.

Geertz, Clifford. *The Interpretation of Culture.* New York: Basic, 1973.

Greene, Gayle, and Coppelia Kahn, eds.

Making a Difference: Feminist Literary Criticism. New York: Methuen, 1985.

Newton, Judith, and Deborah Rosenfelt, eds. *Feminist Criticism and Social Change: Sex, Class and Race in Literature and Culture.* New York: Methuen, 1985.

Nussbaum, Felicity. *The Autobiographical Subject: Gender and Ideology in Eighteenth-Century England.* Baltimore, Md.: Johns Hopkins University Press, 1989.

Pollak, Ellen. "Feminism and the New Historicism." *The Eighteenth Century: Theory and Interpretation* 29 (1988): 281–286.

Thomas, Brook. *The New Historicism and Other Old-Fashioned Topics.* Princeton: Princeton University Press, 1991.

Veeser, H. Aram, ed. *The New Historicism.* New York: Routledge, 1989.

N

Newton, Judith Lowder

Since the publication of her book *Women, Power, and Subversion* in 1981, Judith Lowder Newton has been well recognized as a leading theorist of Marxist-feminist literary criticism. Committed both to rendering visible the difference gender makes within bourgeois society and to considering how class and gender together shape cultural values and ideas, Newton was among the first literary critics to insist that feminist scholarship be historically grounded.

In *Women, Power, and Subversion,* Newton argued that the nineteenth-century relegation of women to a "sphere of influence" separate from the sphere of activity accorded to men served primarily to deprive women of what small share of economic power they previously enjoyed. Examining a variety of novels by women, she demonstrated how their authors subtly resist "influence" as appropriate female behavior by such narrative strategies as undercutting traditional power relations within the text and creating strong, active heroines.

Newton's more recent work includes such influential essays as her introduction (with Deborah Rosenfelt) to *Feminist Criticism and Social Change,* in which she theorizes a "materialist-feminist critical practice" that is broad enough to embrace feminist approaches that are not specifically socialist while still emphasizing the social construction of gender and the material conditions determining culture.

Newton has continually insisted upon the importance of material conditions and class considerations to an understanding of women's writing and of feminist theory more broadly. For Newton, feminism is not only an interpretive strategy, but a meaningful political act.

Eileen Gillooly

References

Newton, Judith Lowder. "History as Usual? Feminism and the 'New Historicism.'" In *The New Historicism,* edited by Aram Veeser, 152–167. New York and London: Routledge, 1989.

———. *Women, Power, and Subversion: Social Strategies in British Fiction 1778–1860.* Athens: University of Georgia Press, 1981.

———, and Deborah Rosenfelt, eds. *Feminist Criticism and Social Change: Sex, Class, and Race in Literature and Culture.* New York and London: Methuen, 1985.

———, Mary P. Ryan, and Judith R. Walkowitz, eds. *Sex and Class in Women's History.* History Workshop Series. London and Boston: Routledge and Kegan Paul, 1983.

Nin, Anais

The author of short stories, novels, journals, and erotic literature, Anais Nin encouraged early feminists to claim a distinctly female experience of the world, especially of sexuality. She believed that including the erotic in literature was "like life itself" and validated early feminist interest in female literary characters who claimed their own power and desires.

While living in Paris in the 1920s, Nin began to write erotica at a dollar per page for an unknown patron. Later published under the titles *Delta of Venus* and *Little Birds,* Nin's erotica form the center of her literary canon and explicitly depict women in the active pursuit and achievement of sexual satisfaction. Her journals, too, which she kept from the time she was thirteen until the day she died, are considered among her most significant writing because they document, in great detail, the course of a woman's life. Two of these journals, published posthumously at Nin's request, reinforce her assertion that sexuality can never be "abnormal." *Henry and June* (1986) describes her adulterous affair with the writer Henry Miller, and her bisexual relationship with his wife, June. *Incest* (1992), Nin's last journal, records her sexual relationship with her own father, a man she had been separated from since she began her journals decades earlier. Nin's fiction, which she valued more than either the erotica or the journals as her most serious writing, also depicts female sexual experience but probes the psychological relationships between men and women as well. Nin has been criticized for her stilted literary style, her idealization of an essential feminine nature, and her self-conscious construction of the persona Anais Nin. The erotica are also problematic because they frequently rely on the exploitative use of the racial or classed Other to create sexual arousal. Nonetheless, Nin was a pioneer in the feminist project of claiming and writing about women's experience and desire.

Sara E. Quay

References

Nin, Anais. *The Delta of Venus.* New York: Bantam, 1977.

———. *D.H. Lawrence: An Unprofessional Study.* Chicago: Swallow, 1964.

———. *The Diary of Anais Nin: Volumes I–VII.* New York: Harcourt Brace Jovanovich, 1966–1980.

———. *Henry and June.* New York: Harcourt Brace Jovanovich, 1986.

———. *Incest.* New York: Harcourt Brace Jovanovich, 1992.

———. *Ladders to Fire.* Chicago: Swallow, 1959.

———. *Little Birds.* New York: Bantam, 1979.

———. *A Spy in the House of Love.* Chicago: Swallow, 1954.

O

Object Relations Theory

Although the term "object relations" has been used by different theorists to refer to slightly different therapeutic methods, its essential tenet is that it views interpersonal relationships as the foundation of personality development. Feminist theorists have adopted the principles of object relations theory as tools with which to understand aspects of mothering, gender differences, and the connection between the human psyche and the external, social world.

Developed by theorists like Melanie Klein, D.W. Winnicott, and Margaret Mahler, object relations theory differs from its Freudian roots in several important ways. It locates the origins of development in the child's primary relationship rather than in biological drives; sees developmental stages in terms of interpersonal relationships rather than biosexual stages such as the oral, anal, and phallic; and considers adult psychopathology to be a result of unsatisfying primary relationships rather than conflicts between competing aspects of the mind such as the id, ego, and superego. The focus of object relations theory is the mother-child relationship, upon which the healthy development of the child rests. That development depends upon the child's ability to project inner images of the self and others first onto external people—"objects"—especially the mother, and then to reintegrate them into his or her own psychic structure. According to object relations theory, the infant's relationship to the mother must go through two phases, attachment and separation. Attachment consists of the child's sense of oneness or union with the mother, a sense that is gradually replaced by a tolerance of her absence, and finally a recognition of her separateness. If this process is completed, the child will be able to exist in relation to, but not be dependent upon, other people and will be able to negotiate competing aspects of the psyche such as love and hate. If the child is unable to either attach to, or separate from, the mother, the self fails to develop in a way that will allow him or her to engage in adult interpersonal relationships. Moreover, those relationships will be characterized by defense mechanisms such as splitting, projection, and projective identification culminating in a fragmented sense of both the self and the world.

Feminist theorists have contested the basic tenets of object relations theory on several points. They have, for instance, argued that it reproduces gender and parenting roles by assuming that the infant's primary caretaker is always the biological mother. In doing so, the theory normalizes the idea that women are "natural" mothers and that men, as fathers, should exist only as figures peripheral to the caretaking of children. As a result of this gender-role dichotomy, object relations theory also legitimates the cultural tendency to devalue motherhood and to blame mothers (and therefore women) for all adult problems, failures, and pathology. It also demonizes the woman who chooses not to have children, who chooses instead to have a career, or who makes a bid for an autonomous life. Object relations theory additionally fails feminism by leaving unaddressed the misogyny implicit in the very term "object relations," which not only reinforces the cultural perception of women as objects, but defines them as objects from which separation must be attained in order to reach healthy adulthood. For in valorizing separation and individuation, the mother, and by association women in general, become objects that must be rejected. In addition, by claiming that separation and individuation are the necessary elements to healthy adulthood, object relations also overlooks what some feminists see as the primary aspect of female development: connection to other people. Finally, object relations theory defines the individual in very limited terms: a white, Western male who is cared for by a full-time mother. As a result of this bias, object relations fails to take into consideration alternative approaches to parenting; historical changes in approaches to parenting; and the reality of racial and class difference in family structure.

Although these weaknesses have made object relations theory problematic for some feminists, others, such as Nancy Chodorow and Dorothy Dinnerstein, have used such failings to pursue feminist agendas. First, they have emphasized the fact that the theory sees the individual as more than a sum of his or her biological drives, taking into account the social aspect of the human condition. As a result, object relations theory enables feminists to claim that women tend to be the primary caretakers of children not because of a biologically based maternal instinct but because of the fact that they are mothered by women, a fact that emphasizes the social, rather than the natural, reproduction of women as mothers. In addition, because object relations theory foregrounds motherhood and the role it plays in development, it enables feminist theorists to analyze the relationship between mothering and gender. For instance, feminist research has examined the effect a child's sex has on the mother-child dyad. Such research has led to the conclusion that men and women experience the world differently because the process of separation that object relations dictates is different for both. Whereas boys must separate from mother, girls must remain to some extent attached in order to form their identity as female. Feminists like Carol Gilligan have used this insight to validate women's unique developmental path as one that takes place through a network of relationships, beginning with the mother. Despite some of its problematic roots, object relations theory has provided feminist theorists with a useful tool with which to counter psychoanalytic and biological interpretations of human nature, allowing them to reclaim important social aspects of women's psychological development.

Sara E. Quay

References

Chodorow, Nancy. *The Reproduction of Mothering: Psychoanalysis and the Sociology of Gender.* Berkeley: University of California Press, 1978.

Dinnerstein, Dorothy. *The Mermaid and the Minotaur: Sexual Arrangements and Human Malaise.* New York: Harper and Row, 1976.

Gilligan, Carol. *In a Different Voice: Psychological Theory and Women's Development.* Cambridge: Harvard University Press, 1982.

Klein, Melanie. *Love, Guilt and Reparation and Other Works: 1921–1945.* London: Hogarth, 1975.

Mahler, Margaret. *On Symbiosis and the Vicissitude of Individuation.* New York: International Universities Press, 1968.

Winnicott, D.W. *The Family and Individual Development.* New York: Basic, 1965.

———. *Playing and Reality.* New York: Basic, 1971.

Orality

The concept of orality is important in literary theory, first, in opposition to literacy and, secondly, in the context of the pregenital "oral stage" of psychoanalysis. Both meanings of orality lead to a consideration of women's relationship to language, as well as to oral and literary tradition. The mythological Philomela has provided feminist theorists with a crucial figure for women's construction of a literary tradition in the face of the violent silencing of women's voices. The turn to body criticism should prompt reflection not merely on mythology and corporeal metaphors but on actual women's lips, tongues, and teeth.

The literary theorist most noted for studies of the opposition between orality and literacy is Walter Ong, who has attempted to recover a sense of human consciousness in a state of primary orality—that is, in a world with no knowledge of writing. Since Ong deliberately deemphasizes the social consequences of the shifts from oral to scribal and then print culture, he has at best a minor interest in gender questions. However, his description of the opposition between the oral and literate mind resembles that between women's and men's conversational styles, and emotional and intellectual dispositions, as these have been described, for example, in Carol Gilligan's *In a Different Voice*. According to Ong, in *Orality and Literacy*, oral thought tends, among other things, to be "aggregative rather than analytic," traditional rather than concerned with experimentation and discovery, "empathetic and participatory rather than objectively distanced," "situational rather than abstract," communal rather than private and self-conscious, and characterized by dialogue rather than totalization and by proverbs instead of facts. The process of oral composition, moreover, has traditionally been described by means of a weaving metaphor that would include, if not focus on, women's work: "*rhapsoidein*, to 'rhapodize,' basically means in Greek 'to stitch songs together.'" Despite his description of an orality that sounds stereotypically "feminine," Ong believes that women were excluded from the primary orality of the classical world as it survived vestigially in the Latin rhetorical education of European men from the medieval period through the nineteenth century.

Ong's focus on the orality of ancient Greece leads him to ignore the lower literacy rates for women in early modern Europe, which were connected with their relative lack of involvement in a commercial marketplace. Their distance from new capitalist economic relations led women to assume the role of preservers of a traditional culture that was to a large extent oral. In the past, women's connection with oral tradition has been dismissed as "old wives' tales" or gossip. However, participating in a general rehabilitation of folk culture, feminists have examined the roles of "wise women" and women healers. Contemporary women writers are well aware of women's historical responsibility for preserving traditional values. Maxine Hong Kingston, in *The Woman Warrior*, observes that the Chinese men who came to the United States for work expected the women they left behind "to keep the traditional ways" and "to maintain the past against the flood." While Kingston distances herself from a Chinese culture that imposes such expectations on women while largely denying them individuality and value, she nonetheless draws upon traditional oral sources of song and "talk-story." Like other women writers, Kingston thematizes the silencing of women, the power of women's speech, and the alternately enabling and inhibiting matrilineal verbal inheritance. She treats these themes powerfully in her depiction of an imaginary or real oral mutilation: her mother's cutting the frenum of her tongue either to restrain rebellious speech or to liberate linguistic abilities.

The oral stage of psychoanalysis is the first stage in the pregenital organization of infantile sexuality. While Sigmund Freud has more to say about the anal or sadistic stage, he offers an important description of the oral stage in *Three Essays on the Theory of Sexuality*. The mouth or labial region is an erotogenic or "pleasure-producing" zone that is first awakened in an infant, through the instinct for self-preservation, by taking nourishment, in the Freudian model, at the maternal breast. Freud terms the oral stage cannibalistic because "the sexual *aim* consists in the incorporation of the object." Later, this autoerotic oral pleasure becomes separated from the function of nourishment, when, in many cases, an infant indulges in rhythmic sucking—thumb-sucking, for example.

The oral stage offers psychoanalytic feminists a symbiotic fusion of mother and child, prior to sexual differentiation, as well as semiotic ("signifying") practices that escape the paternal prohibitions of the Oedipal stage. Drawing upon the French Freudian Jacques Lacan, Julia Kristeva posits a distinction between pregenital, corporeal semiotic practices and the Oedipal symbolic realm dominated by grammar, logic, and abstraction. Kristeva situates semiosis in what she terms a *chora* (from a Greek word meaning "enclosure" or "womb"), which embodies instinctual drives and heterogeneous vocal impulses that, even after the advent of the symbolic, remain as the destabilizing rhythmic elements of language. In *Powers of Horror* Kristeva focuses on the modern novelist Louis-Ferdinand Celine as one who seeks "to make writing oral" and who attempts to resurrect from the "maternal abyss" a musical language for emotion and the unnamable. Despite her focus on the maternal, the material, and the corporeal, Kristeva insists that the writers who provide access to the semiotic may be men as well as women. She wishes to incarnate speech without "biologizing language," thus avoiding the potential for biological essentialism in the works of other psychoanalytic feminists, such as Hélène Cixous.

In related reflections on writing and the body, feminist theorists have discussed the tale of Philomela, narrated most famously in Book 6 of Ovid's *Metamorphoses*, and echoed by Shakespeare in his early tragedy *Titus Andronicus*. Philomela is raped by Tereus, the husband of her sister, Procne. To prevent her from revealing his crime, Tereus cuts out Philomela's tongue, but she communicates her story in the form of an artfully woven tapestry that Procne interprets. Philomela is subsequently transformed into a nightingale, a bird that serves as a figure for the lyric poet for such writers as Milton, Anne Finch, Coleridge, and Keats—just as her weaving serves Ovid as a metaphor for the making of the narrative text. Ann Rosalind Jones and Patricia Joplin have argued that male poets and critics have effaced male violence from this Ovidian narrative in favor of pastoralism or archetypal universalizing, whereas women writers have found in Philomela and Procne a "voice of the shuttle" that survives rape and oral mutilation, as well as an empathetic mode of feminist interpretation of that resistant voice.

Recent feminist theory has supplemented explorations of myth and literary tradition with discussion of the body, though little has yet been written on the history of oral mutilation and modification. Modifications of lips and teeth, in accordance with the demands either of ritual or beauty, are common in many cultures including the United States in the late twentieth century. Among the Sara of central Africa and the Botocudo of Brazil, wooden disks, called labrets, were inserted into the lips, which were sometimes stretched to a circumference as great as twenty-nine inches. Such extreme modifications may have been intended as a sign of honor or, as April Fallon (citing Desmond Morris) states in "Culture in the Mirror," to make "the females of the tribes look unattractive to the Arab slave traders." The labial region has recently been the site of changing ideals of beauty. In *Face Value*, Robin Lakoff and Raquel Scherr note that some African American women have elected cosmetic surgery for lip reduction. On the other hand, an article in the April 1991 *Ebony* magazine, entitled "They Took Our Music . . . Now They're 'Taking' Our Lips," states that the once caricatured lips of many people of African heritage—given the celebrated beauty of "pouty-mouthed White stars such as Michelle Pfeiffer, Julia Roberts, Kim Basinger"—are now being sought by many white women through lip augmentation surgery involving collagen injections. While standards of beauty still require the alteration of women's bodies, perhaps at the end of the twentieth century ethnocentrism is beginning to yield to a racially and ethnically syncretic ideal. The rise of body criticism ought to encourage exploration of the representations of mouths in art and literature, perhaps especially in the rhetorical

device of the blazon: the head-to-toe descriptions that so frequently dissected women into beautiful parts.

James Carson

References

Fallon, April. "Culture in the Mirror: Socio-cultural Determinants of Body Image." In *Body Images,* edited by Thomas F. Cash and Thomas Pruzinsky, 80–109. New York: Guilford, 1990.

Freud, Sigmund. *Three Essays on the Theory of Sexuality.* In vol. 7 of *The Standard Edition of the Complete Psychological Works of Sigmund Freud,* translated by James Strachey, 125–245. London: Hogarth, 1953.

Gilligan, Carol. *In a Different Voice.* Cambridge: Harvard University Press, 1982.

Jones, Ann Rosalind. "New Songs for the Swallow: Ovid's Philomela in Tullia d'Aragona and Gaspara Stampa." In *Refiguring Woman,* edited by Marilyn Migiel and Juliana Schiesari, 263–277. Ithaca, N.Y.: Cornell University Press, 1991.

Joplin, Patricia Klindienst. "The Voice of the Shuttle Is Ours." *Stanford Literary Review* 1 (1984), 25–53.

Kingston, Maxine Hong. *The Woman Warrior* [1975]. New York: Vintage, 1989.

Kristeva, Julia. *Powers of Horror.* Translated by Leon S. Roudiez. New York: Columbia University Press, 1982.

Lakoff, Robin Tolmach, and Raquel L. Scherr. *Face Value.* Boston: Routledge and Kegan Paul, 1984.

Norment, Lynn. "They Took Our Music . . . Now They're 'Taking' Our Lips." *Ebony* 46 (April 1991): 118–122.

Ong, Walter J. *Orality and Literacy.* London: Routledge, 1982.

Orientalism

Formerly a term designating the scholarly study of the Middle East and Asia, Orientalism has, since Edward W. Said's landmark book *Orientalism,* come to be understood as a discourse that enabled Western Europe not only to understand the Orient, but to have power over it. The primary features of this discourse, which first emerged in the late eighteenth century, are its tendency to dichotomize the human world into "us and them," Europe and East, to essentialize the other (to make categorical statements about the Oriental mind, personality, and so on), and to deny the other a voice. Said shows that, far from constituting a body of disinterested academic knowledge, Orientalism prepared the way, justified, and was deeply implicated in Western European colonialism and imperialism. (For a different account of Orientalism, see Raymond Schwab's *The Oriental Renaissance*.)

For feminist literary theory, Said's radical redefinition of Orientalism raises questions about how women were involved in and affected by Orientalism. First, one can make a connection between the ways in which the Orient and woman are represented as other. Such a connection is authorized by Orientalism's feminization of the East: the Orient is figured both as an erotic feminine territory, which the Westerner penetrates, possesses, and controls, and as an unruly, inferior body, which (like woman) must be contained and civilized within patriarchal structures. Seeing the parallel between women and the Oriental subject permits one to examine the links between colonialism and patriarchalism and to analyze the discursive strategies employed to subordinate woman as the "other within."

Another area of interest concerns whether and how women participated in the production of Orientalist discourse. Here Said's reorganization of the field becomes problematic. Said's book has been faulted for doing what it accuses Orientalism of doing: determined to represent Orientalism as a monolithic, "sheer knitted-together" discourse, Said acknowledges no dissenting voices or internal debates and ends up totalizing and essentializing Orientalism, just as Orientalists supposedly did to the East. Absent from *Orientalism*, for example, are the writings of women who traveled to the East in large numbers and wrote significant works about their experiences.

How do these writings fit into Orientalist discourse? Were they subsumed within it, or did they articulate experiences that conflicted with it and colonialist structures? Billie Melman's *Women's Orients* argues that women's writing on the East contributed to the emergence of "an alternative view of the Orient which developed . . . along side the dominant one." She claims that encounters with new institutions, systems of manners, and social arrangements (concubinage, polygamy, sequestration of females) led many Western women "to self-criti-

cism" and to "an identification with the other that cut across barriers of religion, culture and ethnicity." Melman's study fruitfully complicates Said's account of Orientalism. It suggests that Western women's contact with Eastern cultures altered and expanded their ideological horizons, enabling them to reevaluate their own marginalized status and to generate writings that challenged the authority and assumptions of the dominant discourse.

For feminist literary theory, Melman's work has rich implications: it valorizes the study of women's writing—especially writing traditionally classified as subliterary—and shows how women's travel and travel writing could serve as a form of cultural critique.

Terence Bowers

References

Bevis, Richard. *Bibliotheca Cisorientalia: An Annotated Checklist of Early English Travel Books on the Near and Middle East*. Boston: G.K. Hall, 1973.

Melman, Billie. *Women's Orients: English Women and the Middle East, 1718–1719*. Ann Arbor: University of Michigan Press, 1992.

Said, Edward W. *Orientalism*. New York: Pantheon, 1978.

———. "Orientalism Reconsidered." In *Essex Conference on the Sociology of Literature: Europe and the Other,* edited by Francis Barker, 14–27. Colchester: University of Essex Press, 1985.

Schwab, Raymond. *The Oriental Renaissance: Europe's Rediscovery of India and the East, 1680–1880*. Translated by Gene Patterson-Black and Victor Reinking. New York: Columbia University Press, 1984.

Ostriker, Alicia Suskin

Though her approach has been considered essentialist, Ostriker has contributed to feminist literary history by defining an American female poetic tradition, in which as a poet she also participates. Like many contemporary American feminists, Ostriker began her critical work with formal studies of male writers. Her *Vision and Verse in William Blake* concentrated on metrical techniques and structures in the verse. She has also edited Blake's *Complete Poems*.

Next, Ostriker turned to contemporary American women poets, writing extensively on

H.D., Sylvia Plath, and Anne Sexton. *Writing like a Woman,* which includes work on these and other women poets, as well as two personal essays on writing poetry, anticipated Ostriker's controversial *Stealing the Language.* Ostriker distrusts theory, and addresses poetry as a poet. In this study she employed an "inductive" method of reading and a gynocritical approach grounded in the poets' lives, their focus on female experiences, and their development of gender-specified forms and styles.

Ostriker's third phase of scholarly production focused on Judaism and culture, and has contributed to recent biblical analyses in women's studies. *Feminist Revision and the Bible* addressed the relation of the female writer to the male literary tradition, and combined modern biblical criticism and mainstream feminist approaches to show that women writers resist biblical misogyny yet relate to transgressive biblical discourses. A work in progress, entitled *The Nakedness of the Fathers,* contains critical rewritings of biblical narratives that are both mythical revision and cultural analysis.

Ronna C. Johnson

References

Ostriker, Alicia Suskin. *A Dream of Springtime: Poems 1970–78.* New York: Smith/ Horizon, 1979.

———. *Feminist Revision and the Bible.* Oxford: Basil Blackwell, 1993.

———. *Green Age.* Pittsburgh: University of Pittsburgh Press, 1989.

———. *The Imaginary Lover.* Pittsburgh: University of Pittsburgh Press, 1986.

———. *Songs.* New York: Holt, Rinehart, and Winston, 1969.

———. *Stealing the Language: The Emergence of Women's Poetry in America.* Boston: Beacon, 1986.

———. *A Woman under the Surface: Poems and Prose Poems.* Princeton: Princeton University Press, 1982.

———. *Writing like a Woman.* Ann Arbor: University of Michigan Press, 1983.

Other

The genealogy of this word can be traced in disciplines as varied as philosophy, anthropology, and psychoanalysis, and in critical approaches like feminism and postcolonial theory. It is most often used as a figure for sexual and racial difference within a binary structure of thought. Jacques Derrida has persuasively argued that Western metaphysics is based on binary oppositions, a structure that easily subsumes the idea of the self as the stable, normative point of reference, and the other, as constituted by the exclusions of this self.

Enlightenment thought in Europe posited the masculine subject as normative and women as the unstable, undefinable other. This has been pointed out by a number of feminist thinkers; most prominent among them are Hélène Cixous and Luce Irigaray. Cixous works against the binary oppositions of male and female to posit the heterogeneous, ever-changing, ungraspable quality of "female" writing. As Toril Moi explains in *Sexual/Textual Politics,* in Cixous's definition, "the feminine, libidinal economy is open to difference, willing to be 'traversed by the other,' characterized by spontaneous generosity." Luce Irigaray, working more directly against Western philosophy and Freudian psychoanalysis, writes that in these two traditions, women are always defined by a lack. If Western philosophy is constituted by self-reflexivity, the only way in which it can represent women is as a negative of its own reflection. This, she argues, is the inescapable logic of castration anxiety, which, in order to bolster up the male psyche, defines women in terms of a deficiency.

Race, which has been one of the most important cognitive and theoretical categories in recent critical work, is also a figure for Otherness. In the introduction to *"Race," Writing, and Difference,* Henry Louis Gates defines race as "a trope of ultimate, irreducible difference between cultures, linguistic groups, or adherents of specific belief systems which—more often than not—also have fundamentally opposed economic interests." This irreducible difference fed into the binary logic of much Western thought to constitute the Other, which Gates describes as "that odd metaphorical negation of the European defined as African, Arabic, Chinese, Latin American, Yiddish, or female." There is an interesting homology here between racial and sexual difference that raises the possibility of transposing one for the other in equally oppressive ways. This idea is the central theme of Sander Gilman's "Black Bodies, White Bodies," an essay that ranges over nineteenth-century art, medicine, and literature to draw a relation between the representation of the racial Other and female sexuality. Gilman relates the intense interest in the Hottentot Venus's anomalous genitalia in nineteenth-century anatomy and art to the tradition of representing black women as excessively sexualized and therefore closest to prostitutes. In this double move, anatomy becomes a way to pathologize the raced and classed Other, and a way to establish "normative" female sexuality.

Gayatri Spivak complicates the category of the Other, which she defines as the underprivileged and dispossessed Third-World woman who is found beyond the margins of representation. In her "Can the Subaltern Speak?" she points out that a theory of the subject that effectively obliterates questions of mediation through sign-systems leads to the conclusion that the oppressed can speak for themselves. This implies that the subject so represented is transparent and immediately accessible to meaning. Spivak thinks this involves an "interested" refusal by Western intellectuals to recognize their institutional power, to recognize that "everything they read, critical or uncritical, is caught within the debate of the production of that Other, supporting or critiquing the constitution of the Subject as Europe."

Chandra Mohanty in "Under Western Eyes: Feminist Scholarship and Colonial Discourses" reads the "composite, singular, 'Third World woman'" as a product of much of Western feminism's unreflective adoption of humanist positions that involve "the necessary recuperation of the 'East' and 'Woman' as Others." She writes that "the relationship between 'Woman'—a cultural and ideological composite Other constructed through diverse representational discourses (scientific, literary, judicial, linguistic, cinematic, etc.)—and 'women'—real, material subjects of their collective histories—is one of the central questions the practice of feminist scholarship seeks to address." She does not see this relationship as one of "direct identity, or a relation of correspondence or a relation of simple implication." Working against broad generalizations that are a legacy of Orientalizing habits of thought, anthropological discourses and a paternalistic rhetoric of humanism, Mohanty lays great emphasis on a strategy of reading the Other within its own social, economic, and political materialities.

Shuchi Kapila

References

Cixous, Hélène. "The Laugh of the Medusa." Translated by Keith Cohen and Paula Cohen. *Signs* 1 (1976): 875–899.

———, and Catherine Clément. *The Newly Born Woman*. Translated by Betsy Wing. Minneapolis: University of Minnesota Press, 1986.

Gates, Henry Louis, Jr. "Introduction." In *"Race," Writing, and Difference*, 1–20. Chicago: University of Chicago Press, 1985.

Gilman, Sander. "Black Bodies, White Bodies: Toward an Iconography of Female Sexuality in Late Nineteenth-Century Art, Medicine, and Literature." In *"Race," Writing, and Difference*, edited by Henry Louis Gates, 223–261. Chicago: University of Chicago Press, 1985.

Irigaray, Luce. *The Speculum of the Other Woman*. Translated by Gillian C. Gill. Ithaca, N.Y.: Cornell University Press, 1985.

Mohanty, Chandra. "Under Western Eyes: Feminist Scholarship and Colonial Discourses." In *Third World Women and the Politics of Feminism*, edited by Chandra Mohanty, Ann Russo, and Lourdes Torres, 51–80. Bloomington: Indiana University Press, 1991.

Moi, Toril. *Sexual/Textual Politics*. London: Methuen, 1985.

Said, Edward. *Orientalism*. New York: Vintage Books, 1979.

Spivak, Gayatri. "Can the Subaltern Speak?" In *Marxism and the Interpretation of Culture*, edited by Cary Nelson, 272–312. Urbana: University of Illinois Press, 1988.

———. "French Feminism in an International Frame." In *In Other Worlds: Essays in Cultural Politics*, 134–153. New York: Routledge, 1988.

———. "Three Women's Texts and a Critique of Imperialism." In *"Race," Writing, and Difference*, edited by Henry Louis Gates, 262–280. Chicago: University of Chicago Press, 1985.

O

P

Passing

Passing is an individual's assumption of the appearance and lifestyle of another group so well, or to such a degree, that one passes for a member of that group. Examples include a woman who passes as a man and an African American who passes as white. Passing is most often discussed in one direction, as when a member of a minority group passes as a member of the majority, although it occurs in the other direction as well.

A common theme in Renaissance drama (for example, several of Shakespeare's heroines pass as boys), passing also received attention in the eighteenth century, when women who had lived as men were tried for fraud. The choice of a passing lifestyle was coded at the time as desire for rights and privileges, rather than indicating sexual deviance. Harriet Beecher Stowe, in *Uncle Tom's Cabin*, presents passing as a white young man an effective way for a young slave woman to escape to the north. In the twentieth century, Nella Larsen's novella *Passing* foregrounds some of the issues of racial passing.

The mechanism of passing is the effective performance of an identity, a performance so perfect that it cannot be distinguished from or by the "real" members of that group. As such, it foregrounds the performative nature of identity more generally. Recent work, such as that of Marjorie Garber, in *Vested Interests,* has focused on the way in which the choice of a passing lifestyle is not the rejec-tion of one identity in favor of another as much as it is an embracing of both simultaneously.

Dara Tomlin Rossman

References

Friedli, Lynne. "'Passing Women'—A Study of Gender Boundaries in the Eighteenth Century." In *Sexual Underworlds of the Enlightenment,* edited by G.S. Rousseau and Roy Porter, 234–241. Chapel Hill: University of North Carolina Press, 1988.

Garber, Marjorie. *Vested Interests: Cross-dressing and Cultural Anxiety.* New York: Routledge, 1992.

Ramsey, Priscilla. "A Study of Black Identity in 'Passing' Novels of the Nineteenth and Early Twentieth Century." *Studies in Black Literature* 7 (1976): 1–7.

Paternal Metaphor

A term coined by French psychoanalytic theorist Jacques Lacan to denote the particular symbolic nature of the role of the father in the development of subjectivity. Lacan developed this term in response to what he felt was a misunderstanding of Freud's theories of castration and the Oedipus complex by other psychoanalytic theorists, mainly by object relations theorists. Object relations holds that the child develops its subjective identity purely in response to the mother as object and in response to frustration and anger directed at the mother. Lacan felt that such theories fail to account for the role played by the paternal function, which serves to introduce a more symbolic notion of desire. While object relations explains that the child desires to possess or even devour the mother, Lacan asserts that what the child desires is to be the object of the mother's desire. Yet the child's desire refers not to the mother but beyond her; in fact, it refers to what Lacan calls "the symbolic."

Lacan asserts this by reinserting the paternal function into the picture. According to Lacan, the father "triangulates" the seamless mother-child dyad. That is, he takes up a role in relation to the mother that supplants the child as the primary object for the mother's desire. The paternal function in the family drama figures or represents the division that marks the individual's entrance into the Lacanian "symbolic" and is a fundamental condition of subjectivity. Thus, although an actual father is not necessary for this function to operate (indeed, Lacan asserts that the absence of an actual father tends to intensify the paternal function), Lacan emphasizes the metaphorical nature of the paternal role.

"Paternal metaphor" refers not only to the specific function of the paternal in inscribing the subject, but also to a larger, more comprehensive privileging of the notion of representation within Lacan's theories. Because his primary contention is that we are subjects because we exist within language, we are inscribed as "symbolic" subjects. The "symbolic" function, the function of representation or substitution, is critical to the complex of Lacan's theories. Ultimately, for Lacan, the key to the significance of the phallus and the role of sexuality in relation to subjectivity is to understand them all as metaphorical.

Anna Geronimo

References

Lacan, Jacques. *Feminine Sexuality: Jacques Lacan and the ecole freudienne.* Edited by Juliet Mitchell and Jacqueline Rose. Translated by Jacqueline Rose. New York: W.W. Norton, 1982.
———. "On a Question Preliminary to any Possible Treatment of Psychosis." In *Écrits*: A Selection, translated by Alan Sheridan, 179–225. New York: W.W. Norton, 1977.

Penis

In biological terms, the penis is the male organ of urination, reproduction, and sexual pleasure. As a marker of sexual difference, the penis has been invested with symbolic and cultural meanings that make it a sign of masculine authority in patriarchal societies. Femininity is defined as the absence of a penis, or lack. In Freudian terms, the male is always threatened with loss of the penis (castration); the female is always deprived and wants what the male has (penis envy). Feminist critics challenge this phallocentric model in their revisions of the literary tradition.

For example, in *Sexual Politics,* Kate Millett uncovers the mythical status of the penis in canonical male texts. Sandra Gilbert and Susan Gubar analyze the metaphoric connection between pen and penis, emphasizing the relationships between authorship and masculine power that have made it possible to exclude women writers from literary canons. In order to displace the singular authority of the penis, French feminists, such as Hélène Cixous, Luce Irigaray, and Monique Wittig, posit theories of feminine writing (*écriture féminine*) centered on the multiple pleasure sites of the female body.

Jacques Lacan and his followers distinguish the penis from the term "phallus," a signifier for the social and linguistic order of patriarchal society. The penis, then, is a biological organ, while the phallus is a symbolic function. Though, in Western culture, the phallus as signifier is inseparable from the privileged status of the penis, Lacanian critics argue that the phallus in fact signifies the elusive nature of power.

Ashley J. Cross

See also PENIS ENVY

References

Cixous, Hélène. "The Laugh of the Medusa." Translated by Keith Cohen and Paula Cohen. *Signs* 1 (1976): 778–894.
Gallop, Jane. *Reading Lacan.* Ithaca, N.Y.: Cornell University Press, 1985.
Gilbert, Sandra, and Susan Gubar. *The Madwoman in the Attic: The Woman Writer and the Nineteenth-Century Literary Imagination.* New Haven and London: Yale University Press, 1979.
Greene, Gayle, and Coppélia Kahn, eds. *Making a Difference: Feminist Literary Criticism.* London: Routledge, 1985.
Irigaray, Luce. *Speculum of the Other Woman.* Translated by Gillian C. Gill. Ithaca, N.Y.: Cornell University Press, 1985.
Millett, Kate. *Sexual Politics.* Garden City, N.Y.: Doubleday, 1970.
Moi, Toril. *Sexual/Textual Politics.* New York: Methuen, 1985.
Wittig, Monique. "The Mark of Gender." In *The Poetics of Gender,* edited by Nancy Miller, 63–73. New York: Columbia University Press, 1986.
———. "The Straight Mind." *Feminist Issues* 1 (1980): 103–111.

Penis Envy

According to classical Freudian theory, the notion that women suffer from a repressed desire to possess the phallus. In "The Infantile Genital Organization of the Libido" Freud presented his view that the female, discovering her lack of the identifying male organ, becomes convinced that she has been castrated and blames her insufficiency on the mother. Soon afterwards, German American psychoanalyst Karen Horney put forward the first of her well-known challenges to Freudian female sexuality in a paper on penis envy, claiming, as did Alfred Adler, that it signified women's wish to enjoy status equal to that of men. In more recent times the theory and its male counterpart, the castration complex, have been berated, perhaps nowhere more vigorously than in feminist criticism.

Kate Millet's influential *Sexual Politics* polemicized against the male bias in Freud's psychoanalytic theory. By analyzing selected passages from the works of Henry James, D.H. Lawrence, and Norman Mailer, Millet claims to uncover evidence in the texts echoing that in Freud of a cultural dynamic that functions covertly so as to promote the idea of male supremacy, or to degrade and objectify women as a passive sexual commodity. Drawing in part on Horney's groundbreaking neo-Freudian studies, Millet and other feminist critics have reacted against what Jacques Derrida terms the "phallogocentric" rhetoric that informs Western literature, as it does Freudian discourse. More recently, Mary Jacobus and Sarah Kofman have examined the arbitrary but univocal masculinist readings that Freud assigned to literary texts. In citing fiction to uphold assumptions that support his psychoanalytic theory, Jacobus argues, Freud committed acts of "violence against literature." Both critics repudiate what is seen as Freud's strategic attempts to interpret behavior and text in ways that reiterate cultural male prejudices already in play. By privileging the phallus, Jacobus claims, Freud's theory works to the advantage of the male and against the female, who is defined by her lack as an incomplete male.

Susan P. Reilly

See also PENIS

References

Freud, Sigmund. "The Infantile Genital Organization of the Libido." In *The Complete Psychological Works of Sigmund Freud,* edited by James Strachey, Vol. 19. London: Hogarth, 1974.

Horney, Karen, M.D. *Feminine Psychology.* Edited by Harold Kelman, M.D. New York: W.W. Norton, 1967.

Jacobus, Mary. *Reading Woman: Essays in Feminist Criticism.* New York: Columbia University Press, 1986.

Kamuf, Peggy. *Fictions of Feminine Desire: Disclosures of Heloise.* Lincoln and London: University of Nebraska Press, 1982.

Kofman, Sarah. *The Enigma of Woman: Woman in Freud's Writings.* Translated by Catherine Porter. Ithaca, N.Y.: Cornell University Press, 1985.

———. *Freud and Fiction.* Translated by Sarah Wykes. Boston: Northeastern University Press, 1991.

Krupnick, Mark, ed. *Displacement: Derrida and After.* Bloomington: Indiana University Press, 1983.

Lacan, Jacques. *Feminine Sexuality: Jacques Lacan and the école freudienne.* Edited by Juliet Mitchell and Jacqueline Rose. Translated by Jacqueline Rose. New York: W.W. Norton, 1982.

Millet, Kate. *Sexual Politics.* Garden City, N.Y.: Doubleday, 1970.

Performance

While in common parlance "performance" suggests acting, display, and exhibition, for feminist literary criticism the term bears many additional meanings. A specific narrow reference is to performance art, which has recently and increasingly been referred to simply as performance. Wide-ranging and contradictory in mode, intention, and effect, performance art is not a movement or a collective. It is not quite theater, not quite consciousness-raising, not quite live sculpture, stand-up comedy, or musical concert. Much of performance art has grown in the 1960s and 1970s out of a turn from the commodification and commercialization of the visual arts, toward works of immediacy and presence that could not be bought or sold but only experienced. In the 1980s and 1990s much of performance art seems to be turning toward increasing theatricality. As a medium of expression and representation, performance art is especially important to feminist critics because it has embraced gender studies almost from its start. Suzanne Lacy's *Three*

Weeks in May, for example, raised consciousness about rape, while Carolee Schneeman's *Interior Scroll,* in which she pulled a text of a male critic's negative words about her from her vagina, externalizes women's internalizations of patriarchy. Other important female or feminist performance artists include Laurie Anderson, Sandra Bernhard, Valie Export, Karen Finley, Vanalyne Green, the Guerilla Girls, Holly Hughes, Robbie McCauley, Linda Montano, Adrian Piper, Rachel Rosenthal, Anna Deveare Smith, Split Britches (Peggy Shaw and Lois Weaver), and Urban Bush Women.

"Performance" in a broader sense, as a manner of representation on stage, is also an important area of feminist activity. Explorations of theatrical gestures and how they are gendered, particularly in modern dance, have been undertaken within performance itself by, for example, Pina Bausch, Trisha Brown, Meredith Monk, and Twyla Tharpe, as well as in critical scholarship.

Recently, in work extremely important for feminism, the term "performance" has taken on an even broader meaning yet, to include all bodily movements, acts, and gestures, whether onstage or off. The work of Judith Butler and others suggests that performance is the basis of gender constitution. For Butler, "Gender is in no way a stable identity or locus of agency from which various acts proceed; rather, it is an identity tenuously constituted in time—an identity instituted through a *stylized repetition of acts* . . . [and] through the stylization of the body." If performance is the means of gender constitution, it can also be a means of gender deconstruction: "The possibilities of gender transformation are to be found in the arbitrary relation between [repeated] acts, in the possibility of a different sort of repeating, in the breaking or subversive repetition of that style."

Deborah Thompson

References

Butler, Judith. *Gender Trouble: Feminism and the Subversion of Identity.* New York: Routledge, 1990.
———. "Gender Trouble, Feminist Theory, and Psychoanalytic Discourse." In *Feminism/Postmodernism,* edited by Linda J. Nicholson, 324–339. New York: Routledge, 1990.
———. "Performative Acts and Gender Constitution: An Essay in Phenomenology and Feminist Theory." In *Performing Feminism: Feminist Critical Theory and Theatre,* edited by Sue-Ellen Case, 270–228. Baltimore, Md.: Johns Hopkins University Press, 1990.
Case, Sue-Ellen. *Feminism and Theatre.* New York: MacMillan, 1988.
Juno, Andrea, and V. Vale, eds. *Re/Search: Angry Women.* San Francisco: Re/Search, 1991.

Perry, Ruth

Working within the traditionally male-identified genres of literary history and biography, Ruth Perry was among the first feminist critics to point out the difference gender makes in interpreting public history and private lives. In *Women, Letters, and the Novel,* Perry explored the relationship between the ascendancy of the novel in the eighteenth century and the decline in middle-class women's economic status during the same period. As industrialization increasingly deprived women of paid labor, leaving them little more than marriage and mothering as an outlet for their energies or as a means of support, heroine-centered epistolary novels emerged that romanticized marriage and patriarchal authority, thereby serving, Perry noted, to naturalize both women's relegation to the domestic sphere and their economic disadvantage. In her introduction to *Mothering the Mind,* Perry illustrated that while mentoring and literary influence—both "masculine" activities—have been well explored, the artist's relationship to a "mothering" figure who provides the facilitating environment necessary for the artist to create has been largely ignored. And in *The Celebrated Mary Astell*—an account of one of the most important, if historically forgotten, eighteenth-century women of letters—Perry theorized feminist biography as not only the presentation of an individual life (a method associated with masculine biography), but a portrait of the common feminine experience of a historical era as well.

Formulating questions previously unasked in literary inquiry—such as, how did the rise of the novel affect women specifically? or, how might feminist life-writing be methodologically distinct from traditional modes?—Perry's work has been crucial in defining what it is to be a feminist literary historian and biographer.

Eileen Gillooly

References
Perry, Ruth. *The Celebrated Mary Astell: An Early English Feminist.* Chicago and London: University of Chicago Press, 1986.
———. *Women, Letters, and the Novel.* New York: AMS, 1980.
———, and Martine Watson Brownley, eds. *Mothering the Mind: Twelve Studies of Writers and Their Silent Partners.* New York and London: Holmes and Meier, 1984.

Persephone

The myth inscribed in the Homeric hymn "To Demeter" in the seventh century B.C. tells of Persephone, daughter of Zeus and Demeter, goddess of grain and fertility who was abducted by Hades, god of the underworld. Distraught, Demeter withholds her fertility from the land until her daughter is restored to her. Because Persephone ate some pomegranate seeds while in the underworld, she must spend part of each year in that realm. Thus, on one of its many levels, the story explains the cycles of birth, death and rebirth, and the seasons. Other versions, such as the Babylonian Innana or Egyptian myths, feature a goddess powerful on earth and in the underworld. Charlene Spretnak conjectures that the rape was added to the story when a patriarchal social order supplanted a matrifocal one.

The rape version that prevails in our literature is both politically and psychologically compelling. On the political level, Persephone's separation from and reunion with her mother speaks to the loss of wholeness, the marginalization and powerlessness, and the quest for community of women in patriarchal societies. In psychological terms, Julia Kristeva describes loss of the mother as the beginning of individuation and entrance into the world of the symbolic, the world of language, and of "the law of the father." Writers such as Meridel Le Sueur, Margaret Atwood, and Alice Walker write varieties of the myth. Alicia Ostriker argues that contemporary American women poets tell the story of daughters searching for their mothers. The myth is a female *bildungsroman* of innocence lost, of suffering transformed into joy, of death and rebirth, of fragmentation made whole, of maturation, of the young woman reaching adulthood to reunite with her mother literally and figuratively. Most of all it is a story of women's quest.

Karen F. Stein

References
Kristeva, Julia. *Black Sun: Depression and Melancholia* [1987]. Translated by Leon S. Roudiez. New York: Columbia University Press, 1989.
Ostriker, Alicia. *Stealing the Language: The Emergence of Women's Poetry in America.* Boston: Beacon, 1986.
Spretnak, Charlene. "The Myth of Demeter and Persephone." In *Weaving the Visions: New Patterns in Feminist Spirituality,* edited by Judith Plaskow and Carol P. Christ, 72–76. San Francisco: Harper and Row, 1989.

Phallic Mother

The phallic mother—a woman with breasts and penis—is an image occurring in dreams and fantasies and taking two main forms: that of a woman who carries the male organ or a phallic attribute externally and that of one who has kept the phallus inside her own body. According to psychoanalysis, these two representations take different though interrelated symbolic meanings. Whereas the first is interpreted as an archetypal object of desire, uniting female fecundity and nurturance with the male capacity for insemination, the second figures male fears of self-sufficient female sexuality and reproductive powers. In both cases, the phallic mother relates to the primal fantasy of an originary bisexuality, an ambivalent sexual identification that is dissolved by an image of autonomy and immanence. At the same time, the image both defies and attests to woman's castration and thus creates a coexistence of opposites. According to Julia Kristeva the image represents the fact that woman cannot be thought of outside of the phallic symbolic order. At the same time, Kristeva underscores the significance of the phallus not as a biological organ, but as a symbol of power which, as the fantasy of the phallic mother implies, can be taken on by both men and women. Her notion that the image at the same time disrupts the alliance between father, phallus, and power, however, has itself been criticized as a misleading fantasy. The popular pejorative usage of the term "phallic woman" labels a female with supposedly masculine or authoritative features.

Sabine Sielke

References

Gallop, Jane. "The Phallic Mother: Fraudian Analysis." *The Daughter's Seduction, Feminism and Psychoanalysis*, 113–131. London: Macmillan, 1982.

Gauthier, Lorraine. "The Phallic Mother: Platonic Meta-physics of Lacan's Imaginary." In *The Hysterical Male: New Feminist Theory*, edited by Arthur Kroker and Marilouise Kroker, 212–234. New York: St. Martin's, 1991.

Ian, Marcia. *Remembering the Phallic Mother: Psychoanalysis, Modernism, and the Fetish*. Ithaca, N.Y.: Cornell University Press, 1993.

Phallocentrism

Literally meaning centering on the phallus. Despite Lacan's repeated assertions to the contrary, for example in "The Signification of the Phallus," feminist critics regard as insufficient, and therefore male-privileging, the division between biological penis and symbolic phallus. Lacan's reliance, indeed, that of much psychoanalytic theory, on a male metaphor in discussions of desire, and the castration complex, may therefore be termed phallocentric. This problem was recognized as early as 1927 by a writer in the *International Journal of Psycho-Analysis,* who wrote that "there is a healthy suspicion growing that men analysts have been led to adopt an unduly phallo-centric view of the problems in question." Also in the first part of the twentieth century, Ernest Jones warned that psychology as a whole underestimated the importance of female sexuality, this being illustrated by male practitioners' phallocentric bias.

Feminist works that offer alternatives to phallocentrism include Luce Irigaray's questioning of the Freudian concept of penis envy. In "The Blind Spot of an Old Dream of Symmetry," she argues that since the little girl has several sexual organs, why should she desire one penis at all? Psychoanalytic discourse errs in its phallocentric definition of women's desire in terms of that of men. In *This Sex Which Is Not One* Irigaray further challenges psychoanalysis where the masculine is the norm, again encouraging women to rejoice in their multiplicity. This multifaceted female desire, in its confrontation with phallocentrism, "upsets the linearity of a project, undermines the goal-object of desire, diffuses the polarization toward a single pleasure, disconcerts fidelity to a single discourse." In 1975, Laura Mulvey in "Visual Pleasure and Narrative Cinema" observed the ambiguous position into which phallocentrism places women, excluding them and yet being reliant on their emblematic castrated presence.

Phallocentrism, when applied to structures of language, society, or philosophy, gives primacy to ideas that have a logical, rational, linear, unified argument and aim. Feminist critics argue that such characteristics are masculine and depend on a phallogocentric conception of language where words and ideas are ordered into a set of binary oppositions in such a way that one of the pair appears to dominate its partner. Hélène Cixous, both in the form and content of her writing, offers a direct challenge and alternative to the logical linearity of phallocentric writing and thought. In "The Laugh of the Medusa," a good example of *l'écriture féminine*, Cixous writes in a nonlinear, antilogical, feminine way. Some of her metaphors, however, such as a woman's "white ink" often displease those feminists who are uneasy with being too strictly tied to the biological. Her discussion of "parental-conjugal phallocentrism" clearly delineates this phenomenon as a cultural construct maintained at least in part by patriarchal notions of the family. Further, the histories of writing and of rationality exist in an interdependent relationship with phallocentrism.

In her 1991 work *Mothering Psychoanalysis*, Janet Sayers contends that because of the work of Helene Deutsch, Karen Horney, Anna Freud, and Melanie Klein, psychoanalysis has witnessed a shift away from a predominantly patriarchal and phallocentric tendentiousness to a "gynocentric" preeminence being granted to the feminine.

Emma L.E. Rees

See also PHALLOGOCENTRISM

References

Cixous, Hélène. "The Laugh of the Medusa." *Signs* 1 (1975): 875–893.

Culler, Jonathan. *On Deconstruction: Theory and Criticism after Structuralism*. Ithaca, N.Y.: Cornell University Press, 1982.

International Journal of Psychoanalysis 8 (1927).

Irigaray, Luce. *Speculum of the Other Woman*. Translated by Gillian C. Gill. Ithaca, N.Y.: Cornell University Press, 1985.

———. *This Sex Which Is Not One.* Translated by Catherine Porter with Carolyn Burke. Ithaca, N.Y.: Cornell University Press, 1985.

Jones, Ann Rosalind. "Writing the Body: Toward an Understanding of *L'Ecriture Féminine.*" *Feminist Studies* 7 (1981): 247–263.

Lacan, Jacques. "The Signification of the Phallus." In *Écrits: A Selection,* translated by Alan Sheridan, 281–291. New York: W.W. Norton, 1977.

Mulvey, Laura. "Visual Pleasure and Narrative Cinema." *Screen* 16 (1975): 7–19.

Sayers, Janet. *Mothering Psychoanalysis.* London: Hamish Hamilton, 1991.

Phallogocentrism

A word formed by combining phallocentrism (literally, "centering on the phallus"), and logocentrism (that which is "word-centered"). "Logos" implies a rational, singular linguistic meaning or aim, logocentrism thus indicating the masculinist system of thought predicated on such unitary meanings. In phallogocentrism, it is the phallus that is the logos at the center of Western metaphysical thought. Logos, signifying in Christian theology the word of God incarnate, reflects patriarchal justification of its own power through reference to a hidden external authority. The father's power in psychoanalytic discourses is likewise only implicit, no explanation for it being forthcoming.

Ann Rosalind Jones in "Writing the Body" cites Julia Kristeva, Luce Irigaray, Hélène Cixous, and Monique Wittig as opponents to the patriarchal systems of thought that perpetuate the phallogocentric nature of Western culture. Western culture traditionally views the rest of the world only in terms of its relation to the phallus. The feminist project aims in part to establish a new perspective that might allow for some illumination of the structures of phallogocentric society.

In his *On Deconstruction*, Jonathan Culler points out Jacques Derrida's relationship with the concept of the phallus as Western symbol of truth and subjectivity, and he makes clear how the tendency of Freudian psychoanalysis to define the female psyche in terms of a lack is a good example of phallogocentrism. That is, the phallus can be regarded as the signifier or norm, the central point of reference, all other objects and ideas being defined in relation to it. In her

"Sorties," Hélène Cixous, in speaking of a fundamental opposition of man and woman, implies that logocentrism has always sought to justify phallogocentrism, thereby giving primacy to the masculine order.

In some ways, *jouissance* (being a secular bliss, a direct and reflexive enjoyment of female sexuality) may be understood to be the feminist opponent of phallogocentrism. Women's bodily experiences thus oppose the phallic/symbolic order. The immediacy of libidinal *jouissance* challenges the phallogocentric binary system of meaning whereby linguistic structures are oppositional, so that one partner in each pair, the masculine, repeatedly assumes dominance over the other.

Emma L.E. Rees

See also PHALLOCENTRISM

References
Cixous, Hélène. "Sorties." In *New French Feminisms,* edited by Elaine Marks and Isabelle de Courtivron, 90–98. New York: Schocken Books, 1981.

Culler, Jonathan. *On Deconstruction: Theory and Criticism after Structuralism.* Ithaca, N.Y.: Cornell University Press, 1982.

Felman, Shoshana. "Women and Madness: The Critical Phallacy." *Diacritics* 5 (1975): 2–10.

Irigaray, Luce. *This Sex Which Is Not One.* Translated by Catherine Porter with Carolyn Burke. Ithaca, N.Y.: Cornell University Press, 1985.

Jones, Ann Rosalind. "Writing the Body: Toward an Understanding of *L'Ecriture Féminine.*" *Feminist Studies* 7 (1981): 247–263.

Lacan, Jacques. "The Signification of the Phallus." In *Écrits: A Selection,* translated by Alan Sheridan, 281–291. New York: W.W. Norton, 1977.

Phallus

The "phallus" acquired its present significance as a term in feminist psychoanalytic theory through the work of the French psychoanalyst Jacques Lacan. In "The Meaning of the Phallus," first presented in German in 1958 and later published in Lacan's *Écrits* and in English translations in 1977 and 1982, Lacan states that the phallus is not a fantasy, an imaginary effect or an object, nor is it "the organ, penis or clitoris, which it symbolises." The phallus is a signifier, "the privileged signifier of that mark where the share of the logos is wedded to the advent of desire." Here Lacan postulates that the phallus signifies the child's recognition that the mother desires something other than the child, and that the child's (and the mother's) desire is therefore located in some order beyond the mother-child dyad. The phallus thus signifies the moment when the law of the "father" (understood as figurative) precipitates the child into the symbolic order of difference and signification. Lacan calls this moment "castration," a term that refers equally to both sexes and that designates a necessary loss of the imaginary relation with the mother, for if the individual is not differentiated in this way he or she will be psychotic. The phallus thus signifies both loss and the initiation of desire. Feminist critics have taken up a wide range of positions concerning Lacan's theory of the phallus. In "Cosi Fan Tutti," Luce Irigaray objects to Lacan's claim that women don't know what they're saying [about their sexuality], and comments that in taking discourse itself as the object of its investigations, psychoanalysis "remains caught up in phallocentrism."

In "Phallus/Penis: Same Difference," Jane Gallop questions the Lacanian separation of the phallus from the penis, pointing out that, though "the signifier phallus functions in distinction from the signifier penis . . . it also always refers to penis." She also notes that "[s]uch attempts to remake language to one's own theoretical needs, as if language were merely a tool one could use, bespeaks [sic] a very un-Lacanian view of language." In *The Daughter's Seduction*, Gallop links Lacan's essay on the phallus to his 1958 reading of Ernest Jones's 1916 essay on the supposed centrality of phallocentric symbolism in language and literature. And in *Reading Lacan*, Gallop points out that in saying that "the unconscious castration complex has the function of a knot," Lacan is using a word, noeud or knot, which "is a well-known crude term for 'penis.'"

In her 1982 introduction to Lacan's theory, Jacqueline Rose defends Lacan against the charge of phallocentrism, for the phallus is a "fraud" in that neither sex actually possesses it. Since the phallus stands for the "precariousness of any identity assumed by the subject," it cannot represent "an unproblematic assertion of male privilege." Rose distinguishes between Lacan's earlier work, in which he assigns unity

to the imaginary, and his work from the 1970s on, where he locates the fantasy of sameness in language and the symbolic. The phallus thus circulates only in its own imaginary circuits and woman becomes a "symptom," an object of total fantasy such that she can be said not to exist. Although Rose acknowledges that Lacan's statements about the status of the woman are problematic, she emphasizes that, "for Lacan, men and women are only ever in language" and that since "all speaking beings must line themselves up on one side or the other of this [phallic] division . . . anyone can cross over and inscribe themselves on the opposite side from that to which they are anatomically destined."

In *Lacan in Contexts*, David Macey notes that Lacan's references to the phallus and to the question of femininity begin in the 1950s, when Simone de Beauvoir's *The Second Sex* was having a major cultural impact, although Lacan chooses to ignore this. Macey likens psychoanalytic debates about femininity to "travellers' tales" about the "dark continent" and comments that claims "to the effect that Lacanian psychoanalysis has something to offer feminism must first refute its implicit genital determinism." In *Jacques Lacan: A Feminist Introduction*, Elizabeth Grosz posits that in Lacan's theory the phallus is "the valorized signifier around which both men and women define themselves as complementary or even supplementary subjects," and that therefore no one has a privileged relation to the phallus. But she comments that "the phallus envelops the penis as the tangible sign of a privileged masculinity, thus in effect naturalizing male dominance," and that, "although Lacan's account is directed to the phallus as signifier, not to the penis as an organ, it is committed to an a priori privilege of the masculine that is difficult, if not impossible, to dislodge."

In *Lacan*, Malcolm Bowie states that although both the subject and desire are genuinely genderless in Lacan's "The Meaning of the Phallus," "the agent that is called upon to tie the two views together, to give the subject 'his' desire by signifying it for him, is the male genital, transcendentalized," and that Lacan's dialectic involves him in "a monomaniacal refusal to grant signifying power to the female body." Bowie proposes that Lacan's "model" could be reinvented from the female point of view, meaning that "the drama of possession and privation, of absence and presence, of promise and threat, could be retained and perhaps even enhanced if the principals were breast, clitoris, vagina and uterus."

In the spring 1992 issue of *differences: A Journal of Feminist Cultural Studies*, subtitled "The Phallus Issue," Kaja Silverman interrogates instances of slippage between phallus and penis in Lacan's texts, demonstrating that the Lacanian phallus can be defined not only as imaginary and symbolic but as the Law or "Name-of-the-Father." In each of these three definitions, however, the phallus requires the anatomical support of the penis. She points out that, "astonishingly," some of Lacan's commentators have enthusiastically elaborated on Lacan's suggestions that the mother's "veneration" for the father should extend to his authority as representative of the law. Finally, she demonstrates that in his 1964 seminar, Lacan postulates no necessary link between primary repression and the paternal metaphor, and she concludes by challenging "the notion that there is any such necessary or privileged signifier [as the phallus]." Judith Butler elaborates a theory of the plasticity and transferability of the phallus. If the body is not a purely discursive construction but consists of "sites which vacillate between the psychic and the material," then the morphological imaginary may be rewritten as a "lesbian phallus." Butler argues that the phallus appears to be the privileged signifier of the symbolic order only as an imaginary effect of the transformation of an imaginary body part (the penis) into a "centering and totalizing function." She posits that the phallus might symbolize body parts other than the penis, but that "what is needed is not a new body part . . . but a displacement of the hegemonic Symbolic of (heterosexist) sexual difference."

Paula Bennett, in "Critical Clitoridectomy: Female Sexual Imagery and Feminist Psychoanalytic Theory," takes feminist psychoanalytic critics to task for their neglect of clitoral symbolism in women's writing. Working with nineteenth-century American women's poetry, she argues that a language of flowers was employed to represent women's genitals, and that feminist critics have reinstated phallic primacy in their attention to Lacan's theory of the phallus.

Mary Wilson Carpenter

References

Bennett, Paula. "Critical Clitoridectomy: Female Sexual Imagery and Feminist Psychoanalytic Theory." *Signs* 18 (1993): 235–259. Reprinted in *Revising the Word and the World: Essays in Feminist Literary Criticism,* edited by Vévé A. Clark, Ruth-Ellen Joeres, and Madelon Sprengnether, 115–142. Chicago and London: University of Chicago Press, 1993.

Bowie, Malcolm. *Lacan.* Cambridge: Harvard University Press, 1991.

Butler, Judith. "The Lesbian Phallus and the Morphological Imaginary." *differences* 4 (1992): 133–171. Reprinted in *Bodies that Matter: On the Discursive Limits of "Sex"* by Judith Butler, 57–92. New York and London: Routledge, 1993. *differences* 4 (1992). "The Phallus Issue."

Gallop, Jane. *The Daughter's Seduction: Feminism and Psychoanalysis.* Ithaca, N.Y.: Cornell University Press, 1982.

———. "Phallus/Penis: Same Difference." In *Men by Women: Women and Literature,* edited by Janet Todd, 243–251. New York: Holmes and Meier, 1981. Reprinted in *Thinking through the Body* by Jane Gallop, 124–133. New York: Columbia University Press, 1988.

———. *Reading Lacan.* Ithaca, N.Y., and London: Cornell University Press, 1985.

Grosz, Elizabeth. *Jacques Lacan: A Feminist Introduction.* London and New York: Routledge, 1990.

Irigaray, Luce. "Cosi Fan Tutti" [1975]. Translated by Catherine Porter with Carolyn Burke. *This Sex Which Is Not One,* 86–105. Ithaca, N.Y.: Cornell University Press, 1985.

Lacan, Jacques. "The Meaning of the Phallus" [1958]. Translated by Jacqueline Rose. In *Feminine Sexuality: Jacques Lacan and the école freudienne,* edited by Juliet Mitchell and Jacqueline Rose, 74–85. New York: W.W. Norton, 1982.

Macey, David. *Lacan in Contexts.* London and New York: Verso, 1988.

Silverman, Kaja. "The Lacanian Phallus." *differences* 4 (1992): 84–115.

Physical Disability

Even in the 1980s and 1990s, literary criticism tends to follow the tradition of New Criticism (1940s–1950s) by treating representations of physical disability under the rubric of "the grotesque," a literary convention that focuses on the aesthetic and metaphoric possibilities for interpreting anomaly or "abnormality." Thus, criticism usually considers the many physically disabled characters who are scattered about the edges of literature by authors as diverse as Dickens, Flannery O'Connor, or Samuel Beckett to be "grotesques" whose rhetorical purpose is to establish a mood, symbolize degeneracy or despair, or signify some psychic imperfection. Such an aesthetic convention discourages viewing disabled characters from a politically conscious perspective that might analyze the relations between literary representations and actual people who have physical disabilities. However, feminism's insistent focus in the 1970s and 1980s upon the social, political, and personal consequences of the way that culture interprets bodies—as well as the social identities that refer to bodily variation—has begun in the 1990s to shift academic perspectives on disability away from symbolic readings and toward a more politicized view of disability both in literary interpretation and the social relations of the academic community. Interpreting disability as a cultural rather than an individual or a medical issue dovetails with the insistence by both feminism and ethnic studies upon examining power relations rather than assigning deviance when analyzing cultural representations of oppressed groups.

Both inside and outside the academy in the 1990s, feminism is still struggling to articulate theory and practice that adequately address cultural and corporeal differences within women as a group. In its effort to highlight gender, feminism has sometimes obscured other identities and categories of cultural analysis such as race, ethnicity, sexuality, class, and physical ability. As feminism recognizes this omission, however, the voices of and for women with disabilities are beginning to be heard in literary criticism and women's studies, as exemplified by Rosemarie Thomson and Barbara Hillyer. The most crucial literary critical application of the politics and sociology of seeing the body as a culturally determined artifact is analyzing and questioning the rhetorical uses of disability in literary representation. Critics need to probe the cultural narratives of disability that recur in literature, especially those that coincide with stereotypical gender scripts. For example, the narrative of courageous overcoming; the pathetic, dependent disabled figure; and the bitter, villainous figure with a disability are all stock representations that limit the range of possibilities disabled people can imagine for themselves and nondisabled people envision for those with disabilities. Feminist crit-

ics should also become aware of the parallels between how gender as a social, legal, and political category shapes women and how disability as a cultural institution similar to gender and race shapes the lives of "the disabled" and invests their bodies with meaning. Moreover, in the spirit of making the personal political, critics should follow the lead of Roberta Galler, Marsha Saxton and Florence Howe, and Anne Finger by focusing both teaching and scholarship on narratives that either invest disabled characters with subjectivity or center the perspective of the disabled figure.

Finally, feminist politics and theory in general need to investigate further the way some of its political positions affect the situations and struggles of disabled women. The biologist Ruth Hubbard, for instance, points out as oppressive the argument embedded in the rhetoric of abortion rights for eliminating "defective" fetuses that are destined to be disabled individuals. The philosopher Susan Wendell questions as well the feminist ideology of independence that often makes it difficult for disabled women to ask for the assistance they require. The feminist emphasis on the sexual objectification of women tends to ignore the cultural tendency to deny disabled women's sexuality and reproductive capabilities, leaving them in a marginalized position that Fine and Asch call "rolelessness." The politicized perspective of feminism that so permeates contemporary literary criticism has only begun to consider the many textual and cultural representations of disability as well as their intersections with gender; much work remains to be done in the 1990s and beyond.

Rosemarie Garland Thomson

References
Browne, Susan E., Debra Connors, and Nancy Stern, eds. *With the Power of Each Breath: A Disabled Women's Anthology.* Pittsburg, Pa.: Cleis, 1985.
Fine, Michelle, and Adrienne Asch, eds. *Women with Disabilities: Essays in Psychology, Culture, and Politics.* Philadelphia: Temple University Press, 1988.
Finger, Anne. *Past Due: A Story of Disability, Pregnancy and Birth.* Seattle, Wash.: Seal, 1990.
Galler, Roberta. "The Myth of the Perfect Body." In *Pleasure and Danger,* edited by Carol Vance, 165–172. Boston: Routledge and Kegan Paul, 1984.
Hillyer, Barbara. *Feminism and Disability.*

Norman: University of Oklahoma Press, 1993.

Hubbard, Ruth. "Who Should and Who Should Not Inhabit the World." In *The Politics of Women's Biology*, 179–198. New Brunswick, N.J.: Rutgers University Press, 1990.

Saxton, Marsha, and Florence Howe, eds. *With Wings: An Anthology by and about Women with Disabilities*. New York: Feminist, 1987.

Thomson, Rosemarie Garland. "Speaking about the Unspeakable: The Representation of Disability as Stigma in Toni Morrison's Novels." In *Courage and Tools: The Florence Howe Award for Feminist Scholarship 1974–1989*, edited by Joanne Glasgow and Angela Ingram, 239–251. New York: MLA, 1990.

Wendell, Susan. "Toward a Feminist Theory of Disability." *Hypatia* 4 (1989): 104–126.

Plath, Sylvia

Due perhaps to her highly publicized suicide, which led in turn to speculation about her personal struggles, and because her best-known poems are often filled with images of illness, suffering, violence, and death, Plath's life has inspired a number of biographies, and her work has become the focus of recent feminist criticism. Her writing remains at the center of a number of disputes in the drama concerning femininity and writing and has been the subject of legal battles over literary control. What happens when the law is asked to judge the effect or intention of a work of fiction is a concern that continues to generate interest for journalists like Janet Malcolm in the formation and development of the Plath canon.

Feminist criticism has been divided on the subject of Plath. Some feminists have stressed the representative nature of her work, and how it is concerned with injustice in a patriarchal world. Carole Ferrier has analyzed Plath's bee poems as expressions of what is seen as the dilemma faced by women raised in such a culture: "self-destruction or motivation toward revolutionary social change." More recently, Sandra Gilbert and Susan Gubar have considered how Plath describes through her work a "sexual battle that was not just intensely physical but notably linguistic, with combat carried on through words, whispers, promises, vows."

The themes of victimization and response were taken up as early as 1978 by Jane Marcus and by Barbara Charlesworth Gelpi the following year. More radical feminists have attempted to portray Plath as an artist who was abused and betrayed by men. Manju Jaidka identifies a "ritual of exorcism" in "Daddy," a ritual performed to deliver female personae from the male "masters" who oppress them. Other critics see Plath as aggressor and view her writing as alternately self-indulgent and masochistic, a product of self-loathing that produces hostilities toward the female condition. From this perspective, Plath is thought to have stereotyped the feminist as a failed woman or a destroyer of men. Jane Marcus sees *The Bell Jar* as a work that "harnessed" Plath's hatred of men, while others sees her art as an expression of self-directed torture and rage that culminated in her suicide. Albert Wilhelm finds in the mixed messages of the poems signals of Plath's own ambivalence toward womanhood. The fervid and spiteful poetic portraits, the images of entrapment, guilt, and despair in her work are seen as arising from her own frustration at failing to attain a conventional ideal of womanhood.

Jacqueline Rose takes issue with conventional feminist readings of the poems and combines deconstructive and psychoanalytic criticism with feminist ideology in *The Haunting of Sylvia Plath*. Another more tempered and objective view of her work is offered by David Young, who sees those who portray Plath as "feminist martyr, romantic prodigy, and helpless psychotic" as misguided. His assessment of her poetry is free of the biographical associations that dog much of Plath criticism. Young and others examine Plath as a gifted poet who grew out of, and in some cases surpassed, the works of her predecessors Thomas, Lowell, and Roethke.

Susan P. Reilly

References

Alexander, Paul. *Rough Magic: A Biography of Sylvia Plath*. New York: Viking, 1991.

Butscher, Edward. *Sylvia Plath: Method and Madness*. New York: Seabury, 1976.

Ferrier, Carole. "The Beekeeper's Apprentice." In *Sylvia Plath: New Views on the Poetry*, edited by Gary Lane, 203–217. Baltimore, Md.: Johns Hopkins University Press, 1979.

Gelpi, Barbara Charlesworth. "A Common Language: The American Woman Poet."

In *Shakespeare's Sisters: Feminist Essays on Women Poets*, edited by Sandra M. Gilbert and Susan Gubar, 245–260. Bloomington: Indiana University Press, 1979.

Gilbert, Sandra M., and Susan Gubar. *No Man's Land*. New Haven: Yale University Press, 1988.

Gustafson, Richard. "'Time is a Waiting Woman': New Poetic Icons." *Midwest Quarterly* 16 (1975): 318–327.

Hayman, Ronald. *The Death and Life of Sylvia Plath*. Secaucus, N.J.: Birch Lane, 1991.

Jaidka, Manju. "Sentimental Violence: A Note on Diane Wakoski and Sylvia Plath." *Notes on Contemporary Literature* 14 (1984): 2.

Malcolm, Janet. *The Silent Woman: Sylvia Plath and Ted Hughes*. New York: Knopf, 1994.

Marcus, Jane. "Nostalgia Is Not Enough: Why Elizabeth Hardwick Misreads Ibsen, Plath, and Woolf." *Bucknell Review* 24 (1978): 157–177.

Rose, Jacqueline. *The Haunting of Sylvia Plath*. Cambridge: Harvard University Press, 1992.

Stevenson, Anne. *Bitter Fame: A Life of Sylvia Plath*. New York: Houghton Mifflin, 1989.

Wagner-Martin, Linda. *Sylvia Plath: A Biography*. New York: Simon and Schuster, 1987.

Wilhelm, Albert E. "Sylvia Plath's Metaphors." *Notes on Contemporary Literature* 1980 (10): 8–9.

Young, David. "Poetry 1981: Review Essay." *Field: Contemporary Poetry and Poetics* 26 (1982): 77–86.

Pleasure

See DESIRE; *JOUISSANCE*

Poetics

See FEMINIST POETICS

Poovey, Mary

As a literary theorist of ideology, social constructions of gender, and poststructuralism, Mary Poovey has written articles as well as two books about nineteenth-century British culture, *The*
Proper Lady and the Woman Writer: Ideology as Style in the Works of Mary Wollstonecraft, Mary Shelley, and Jane Austen and *Uneven Developments: The Ideological Work of Gender in Mid-Victorian England.*

Poovey's first book considers how women balanced late-eighteenth-century standards for femininity with the desire to write. Courtesy books, religious pamphlets, and popular magazines taught women "proper" femininity: chastity, self-effacement, modesty, and reticence. Authorship connoted ambition, worldliness, notoriety, hence, impropriety. The writing styles of Wollstonecraft, Shelley, and Austen illustrate "strategies of indirection, obliqueness, and doubling," verbal analogues to the paradoxical lives of those seeking acceptance as writers and women.

The second book examines mid-Victorian debates that highlighted contradictions between accepted femininity and women's actual lives. These debates addressed the use of chloroform during childbirth, the feminization of literature, and Florence Nightingale and her nurses. "Oppositional voices" challenged the belief that masculinity and femininity were fixed characteristics determined by biology. Just as important, Poovey shows that while these debates provided nontraditional middle-class men and women with opportunities to protest constraining gender roles, the debates also supported the illusion that "everyone" shared the beliefs, values, and behaviors of white, middle-class heterosexuals. Thus the focus on one set of conflicts—based on gender difference—helped silence the oppositional voices of working-class activists, people of color, and citizens of countries colonized by Britain.

Teresa Mangum

References

Poovey, Mary. *The Proper Lady and the Woman Writer: Ideology as Style in the Works of Mary Wollstonecraft, Mary Shelley, and Jane Austen*. Chicago: University of Chicago Press, 1984.

———. *Uneven Developments: The Ideological Work of Gender in Mid-Victorian England*. Chicago: University of Chicago Press, 1988.

Popular Culture

Whereas "culture" in a traditional sense refers to the highest achievements in music, theater, art, and literature, "popular culture" encompasses the flood of products and images produced by the mass media: television, movies, advertising, pop music, and best-selling novels. Since the consumption of such products may constitute the only truly common culture of the late twentieth century, it is important that feminists pay close attention to the images of women the mass media provide. Feminist theorists have begun to use tools of analysis honed by the study of literature to understand how images of women are constructed, circulated, and consumed within popular culture.

An examination of the work such critique has produced in America should proceed from an understanding of two fields from which popular culture study borrows: British cultural studies and feminist film theory.

British cultural studies began in the early 1960s at the University of Birmingham's Centre for Contemporary Culture Studies (CCCS). Grounded in Marxist politics and prompted by a desire to distance their work from that of traditional literary critics, CCCS scholars focused less upon the contents of mass media forms than upon their consumption. The work of Stuart Hall and Dick Hebdige, among others, documented the many ways in which male working-class "subcultures" used popular forms to create personal style. The Women's Studies Group, formed in the CCCS to address this imbalance, brought a feminist viewpoint to culture studies when they published *Women Take Issue: Aspects of Women's Subordination* in 1978. At the same time, feminists on both sides of the Atlantic were creating an impressive body of film criticism. Theorists such as Laura Mulvey, Pam Cook, and Claire Johnston produced compelling readings of classic Hollywood cinema based upon psychoanalytic theory rather than audience research.

The study of popular culture borrows from both of these disciplines. Like culture studies, it may seek out the meanings that consumers draw from popular forms; like film theory, it may elaborate complex readings of individual texts. Its primary difference lies in its object of study. Unlike film criticism or culture studies, which have found a home within academia, popular culture studies examines mass media images, material that seemingly lies beyond the bounds of serious analysis. Its constitution as a unified discipline has therefore been problematic; popular culture theorists can be found sprinkled throughout any number of different university departments.

These difficulties notwithstanding, popular culture scholars have produced a rich expanse of writing. When such writing proceeds from a feminist perspective, the study of popular culture can yield fascinating results, as proven by several recent books and articles. Janice Radway's *Reading the Romance: Women, Patriarchy, and Popular Literature,* for example, combines culture studies' hands-on ethnographic approach with astute textual analysis. Extensive interviews with women in the middle-class community of "Smithton" led Radway to the conclusion that romance readers interpret romance heroines as being strong, intelligent, and independent—as being, though the readers themselves might not use the term, feminist. For Radway's readers, romance novels function as instruction books for negotiating the contradictory demands patriarchy makes of women. Far from being simply escapist fluff, romance novels provide a system of interpretation as varied, complex, and personally meaningful for the women who consume them as feminism itself.

Other feminist scholars have directed their attention to visual media not included under the banner of film studies. Their efforts contribute to an ongoing reworking within feminist film theory of some of that discipline's most basic concepts. E. Ann Kaplan's examination of MTV, for instance, questions the assumption that filmed representations necessarily assume a male viewer. In *Rocking around the Clock: Music Television, Postmodernism and Consumer Culture,* Kaplan defines MTV's look as fundamentally different from that of Hollywood cinema. Music videos seem to offer "a wide range of gazes with different gender implications," including a "genderless address," allowing men and women equal visual pleasure.

Carol Clover and Linda Williams approach film theory through genres of popular film commonly thought to be hopelessly misogynist, horror and pornography. Though neither woman denies that these genres offer many deeply disturbing images, both are interested in moving beyond the question of whether any individual image is positive or negative. Instead, each proposes to describe the systems of representation through which the images of horror and of pornography gain meaning. Their close study of dozens of films leads Clover and Williams to the conclusion that, unlike mainstream cinema, which tends to marginalize women, modern horror and pornography make women the center of their narrative universes. Though

P

not all these depictions may be what every feminist would call "positive," both Clover and Williams argue that such images, because they are the main focus of attention in almost all of the genres' films, encourage male viewers to identify with the women they see on screen, rather than with the male characters who persecute or pursue them.

Kaplan, Clover, and Williams have all been influenced by the mass of critical theory grouped together under the term "postmodernism." In their writing, the blurring of gender boundaries that characterizes much postmodern thought, and which enables male viewers to imaginatively occupy the position of "female" on-screen, is part of an identifiably feminist agenda. Not all feminists have been equally optimistic that postmodern theory can serve feminist ends. Tania Modleski warns that a theoretical position that allows men to assume the role of "woman" is of questionable value for feminism. Her most recent work combines a clear summary of postmodern theory with illustrations of how this theory is embodied in many popular films. Feminists must be suspicious, she insists, of theories that allow men to occupy the position of "woman," or they may find themselves squeezed out of the frame altogether.

African American and lesbian feminists have voiced similar misgivings about current critical theory. In *Black Looks: Race and Representation,* bell hooks reminds readers that theoretical sophistication should not come at the expense of a coherent African American identity. If postmodern theory opens up the possibility that ethnic as well as gender boundaries may be crossed with ease, it also poses the threat that such crossings will deny the ongoing reality of racism and sexism. Hooks notes the prevalence of mass-media images of black women that perpetuate racist/sexist notions, and insists that race must continue to be a category for the interpretation of popular culture.

Lesbian intervention in this debate has taken place mainly within the realm of film theory. Writing in the collection *How Do I Look?: Queer Film and Video,* Teresa de Lauretis and Judith Mayne address the virtual exclusion of lesbian concerns from feminist consideration of film. Mayne notes the way in which the possibility of desire between women has been ignored in feminist readings of the films of Dorothy Arzner, one of the few women directors to emerge from the Hollywood studio system. Teresa de Lauretis examines the way that Sheila McLaughlin's 1987 film *She Must Be Seeing Things,* through its focus on a lesbian couple, not only enlarges the realm of what can be seen on screen, but helps create a new position from which to view: that of the lesbian spectator.

Though neither de Lauretis nor Mayne addresses mass media images directly, their work is similar to that of the critics discussed earlier in this entry: sexual orientation, like race, like the designation "woman" itself, can and should be important issues for popular culture critics. *The Madonna Connection: Representational Politics, Subcultural Identity, and Cultural Theory,* edited by Cathy Schwichtenberg, exemplifies the ways that these considerations can interact in popular culture studies. The critics in this anthology use the figure of Madonna to explore the tangled intersections of race, sex, and gender in popular culture. The collection encompasses the most promising aspects of feminist popular culture studies: attention to audiences, theoretical sophistication, and a feminism that has become ever more inclusive in composition and outlook.

Kim Hicks

References

Bad Object-Choices, eds. *How Do I Look?: Queer Film and Video.* Seattle: Bay, 1991.

Camera Obscura 16 (January 1988). Special issue: "Television and the Female Consumer."

Clover, Carol. *Men, Women and Chain Saws: Gender in the Modern Horror Film.* Princeton: Princeton University Press, 1992.

Dent, Gina. *Black Popular Culture: A Project by Michele Wallace.* Seattle: Bay, 1992.

hooks, bell. *Black Looks: Race and Representation.* Boston: South End, 1992.

Kaplan, E. Ann. *Rocking around the Clock: Music Television, Postmodernism and Consumer Culture.* New York: Routledge, 1987.

Modleski, Tania. *Feminism without Women: Culture and Criticism in a "Postfeminist" Age.* New York: Routledge, 1991.

———, ed. *Studies in Entertainment: Critical Approaches to Mass Culture.* Bloomington: University of Indiana Press, 1986.

Radway, Janice. *Reading the Romance:*

Women, Patriarchy, and Popular Literature. Chapel Hill: University of North Carolina Press, 1984.

Schwichtenberg, Cathy, ed. *The Madonna Connection: Representational Politics, Subcultural Identities, and Cultural Theory*. Boulder, Colo.: Westview, 1993.

Williams, Linda. *Hard Core: Power, Pleasure, and the "Frenzy of the Visible."* Berkeley: University of California Press, 1989.

Women's Studies Group, Centre for Contemporary Cultures Studies, University of Birmingham, eds. *Women Take Issue: Aspects of Women's Subordination*. London: Hutchinson, 1978.

Pornography

Pornography has historically been an ambiguous term obscured by protracted legal wranglings over questions of free speech and morality. The Greek *pornoeraphia* (*porne*, prostitute + *graphein*, to write), originally "writing about prostitutes," is generally accepted as any text or image depicting sexually explicit behavior intended to arouse sexual excitement. Since the 1970s, feminist criticism has been polarized into two camps: libertarian feminism, which challenges the censorship of pornography; and "antipornography" feminism (Linda Williams's term) which defines pornography in terms of power, rather than sexuality. Recently, however, attempts have been made to establish a middle position that would engage the term in a more flexible, fluid manner.

Libertarian feminists treat pornography as positive force that redefines sexuality and gender relations. The Feminist Anti-censorship Taskforce (FACT), for example, argues that pornography is fundamentally anarchic and revolutionary, undermining both the traditional (that is, male) notions of morality and the insistence upon female purity that have historically been used to subordinate women. Libertarian feminists consider ultraconservative right-wing antipornography movements to be not only a threat to civil rights, but the embodiment of antisexual attitudes that are the source of attacks on abortion, homosexuality, and free access to birth control materials. The libertarian view, however, has been criticized as somewhat naive, because during the 1960s and 1970s women often found themselves expected to prove their sexual liberation by granting virtu-ally any male unlimited access to their bodies; to refuse was tantamount to a confession that one was "hung-up" and sexually repressed. Additionally, it is argued that pornography's violence and brutality toward women exposes its supposedly egalitarian nature as illusory. An "erotic classic" such as *Fanny Hill* may appear to present a comparatively enlightened alternative culture in which women are as free to enjoy sexual experience as men, and use it to acquire wealth and power of their own. Yet Fanny's experiences have little to do with the actual life of an eighteenth-century prostitute, and her history reinforces the myth that women are purely physical creatures constantly seeking sexual gratification.

Antipornography feminists such as Andrea Dworkin argue that pornography is not a matter of morality or free speech, but of power: specifically, male authority and control manifested as the reification and debasement of women. Pornography is viewed as propaganda that presents women as either helpless but willing victims, or sexual insatiables yearning to be overpowered by any available virile male. Antipornography feminists argue that every man who uses pornographic photographs for sexual gratification reduces a very real human being to a sexual object. In doing so, he may easily come to see all women (or homosexuals, or children) in equivalent terms, as objects to be used for his own purposes. He will not only believe that the women in the pornographic images choose to be there because they gain power over men through their sexual attractiveness and submissiveness, but that all women feel—or would like to feel—the same way. It does not matter that such an assertion has little basis in reality: most women have little wish to expose their bodies publicly, nor is there much power inherent in becoming the visual property of any male with the financial wherewithal to purchase a pornographic magazine. But women can have little control in how they are perceived, because, as Dworkin points out, pornography reduces all females to *pornes*, the lowest class of prostitute, available to virtually any male. The pornographic consciousness groups them into pejorative categories devoid of individuality: they may be perceived as sluts, bitches, cunts, fucks, or pieces of ass, but never as human beings—they exist outside human experience. They are dehumanized commodities in an androcentric industry dedicated not only to sex discrimination, violence against women, misogyny, and sexual

P

abuses, but also to the perpetuation of such horrors. Dworkin's definition of pornography as any text or image that reduces a human being to an object makes the supposedly ambiguous term abundantly clear.

It is pervasive as well, permeating not only advertising, film, and literature, but real life—if one accepts Robin Morgan's celebrated assertion that "pornography is the theory, and rape the practice." Antipornography feminists also draw analogies between pornography, historical imperialism, and the institution of slavery, since the fundamental premise underlying all of these is identical—women do not own their bodies in the same sense that native nonwhite peoples do not own their lands, culture, or persons. For antipornography feminists, the erotic heroines of supposed "classics" such as Pauline Reage's *The Story of O* and the Marquis de Sade's *Justine*—along with their literary sisters Eve, Lucrece, Clarissa, Lolita, and so on—emerge as victims of genital imperialism, and part of the cycle by which males maintain power over women.

Feminists such as Linda Williams, however, challenge the antipornography feminist model, arguing that it not only oversimplifies a complex and frequently contradictory issue, but places women in a no-win situation. Although Williams recognizes pornography's potential harm to women, she suggests that instead of damning such materials, feminists should demystify them. Such a process results in the deconstruction of binary hierarchies such as male/female, sadist/masochist, active/passive, and subject/object that are the foundation of the pornographic consciousness. One might argue, for example, that pornography is as much about male inadequacy as male power, since its focus is the power of female sexuality—a source of significant male anxiety.

Williams's paradigm does provide some room—even hope—for ameliorative change. Such change is imperative, for, if pornography is indeed everywhere, and if all men ("even the best of them," Dworkin asserts) are indeed conditioned by it, then women have few options. Critics who ignore such materials marginalize themselves, not the pornography. Critics who engage them from the perspective of the excluded subject establish a model that privileges women as good and damns men as evil; in short, they merely invert the androcentric gender hierarchy. Attempts to redefine the sexual landscape by promoting egalitarian, nonhierarchical erotica seem similarly futile: reading and

viewing are not passive acts, and thus the reader/viewer is invariably placed in a position of power when s/he uses the erotic subjects for sexual gratification. Clearly, pornography needs not only new rules, but an entirely different playing field. Designing such a site will involve new methodologies, new paradigms, and new approaches to sexuality and gender.

Darby Lewes

References

Barry, Kathleen. *Female Sexual Slavery.* Englewood Cliffs, N.J.: Prentice-Hall, 1984.

Caputi, Mary. *Voluptuous Yearnings: A Feminist Theory of the Obscene.* Lanham, Md.: Rowman and Littlefield, 1994.

Dworkin, Andrea. *Pornography: Men Possessing Women.* New York: Perigee, 1981.

Ellis, Kate, with Nan Hunter, Beth Jaker, Barbara O'Dair, and Abby Tallmer. *Caught Looking: Feminism, Pornography, and Censorship.* New York: Feminist Anticensorship Taskforce (FACT) Book Committee, 1986.

Faust, Beatrice. *Women, Sex, and Pornography.* New York: Macmillan, 1980.

Garry, Ann. "Pornography and Censorship." In *Philosophy and Sex,* edited by Robert Baker and Frederick Elliston, 312–326. Buffalo, N.Y.: Prometheus, 1984.

Gibson, Pamela Church, and Roma Gibson, eds. *Dirty Looks: Women, Pornography, Power.* London: British Film Institute, 1993.

Griffin, Susan. *Pornography and Silence.* New York: Harper Colophon, 1981.

Gubar, Susan, and Joan Hoff. *For Adult Users Only: The Dilemma of Violent Pornography.* Bloomington: Indiana University Press, 1989.

Kappeler, Susanne. *The Pornography of Representation.* Minneapolis: University of Minnesota Press, 1986.

Lederer, Laura, ed. *Take Back the Night: Women on Pornography.* New York: William Morrow, 1980.

Lewes, Darby. "Nudes from Nowhere: Pornography, Empire, and Utopia." *Utopian Studies* 4 (1993): 66–73.

MacKinnon, Catherine A. "Not a Moral Issue." *Yale Law and Policy Review* 11 (1984): 321–345.

Morgan, Robin. "Theory and Practice: Pornography and Rape." In *The Word of a*

Woman: *Feminist Dispatches, 1968–1992.* New York: W.W. North, 1992, pp. 78–89.

Myers, Kathy. "Towards a Feminist Erotica." In *Visibly Female: Feminism and Art: An Anthology,* edited by Hillary Robinson, 283–296. London: Camden Press, 1987.

Russell, Diana. *Against Pornography: The Evidence of Harm.* Berkeley, Calif.: Russell, 1993.

Russo, Ann. "Conflicts and Contradictions among Feminists over Issues of Pornography and Sexual Freedom." *Women's Studies International Forum* 10 (1987): 103–112.

Sontag, Susan. "The Pornographic Imagination." In *Styles of Radical Will.* New York: Delta, 1978.

Stimpson, Catherine, and Ethel Spector Person. *Women: Sex and Sexuality.* Chicago: University of Chicago Press, 1980.

Williams, Linda. *Hard Core: Power, Pleasure, and the "Frenzy of the Visible."* Berkeley: University of California Press, 1989.

Postcolonialism

The prefix "post" indicates this term's defining relationship with the period after colonization. While *Webster's New Collegiate Dictionary* limits "postcolonialism" to the era following a "colony's achieving independence," literary and cultural critics often use the term more broadly to include responses to colonization as it occurs, as well as after the colonizers leave. Feminist literary critics concerned with postcolonialism focus on a variety of issues, such as the history and structures of colonialism evident in literature, and the roles female characters and women writers play in relation to colonization.

In the late 1970s and early 1980s, postcolonialism introduced several important revisions to feminist criticism. One postcolonial model of criticism argues that the dynamics of colonization—the domination of one culture by another—can also be found in other relationships, such as those between cultures and groups within the United States, or between a masculine and a feminine. Thus as Chandra Talpade Mohanty explains, some "feminist women of color in the U.S." speak of the "appropriation of their experiences and struggles by hegemonic white women's movements" as colonization. As Mohanty suggests, postcolonialism supplies a way to recognize differences and "heterogeneities" in women's movements previously dominated by mainstream white culture.

Postcolonialism also suggests ways feminist literary critics can reexamine works of literature previously studied without reference to the contexts of colonialism and imperialism. Gayatri Chakravorty Spivak gives such a reading of *Jane Eyre,* demonstrating that earlier feminist readings of the novel, which focused on the development of Jane, missed its connections to imperialism. Spivak argues that Bertha Mason, Rochester's "mad" first wife from the West Indies, links *Jane Eyre* to the British colonization of the West Indies and incorporates the complicated role played by "imperialism, understood as England's social mission." With postcolonialism, the "madwoman in the attic" of *Jane Eyre* must be interpreted in the context of nineteenth-century England's imperialism and its attitudes toward the people of its colonies.

In addition to critiquing literary and cultural colonialism, feminist literary critics use postcolonialism to study the works of "colonized" writers, the writing produced within a particular region during and after its colonization. These studies serve several purposes: they introduce writers whose works have not been included in the literary canon and place canonical works in the context of colonial and postcolonial writings. They provide another side to literary history and offer a way of seeing canonical writing as part of a larger conversation, instead of a literary monologue.

Susan B. Taylor

References

Ashcroft, Bill, Gareth Griffiths, and Helen Tiffin. *The Empire Writes Back: Theory and Practice in Post-Colonial Literatures.* London and New York: Routledge, 1989.

Mohanty, Chandra Talpade. "Under Western Eyes: Feminist Scholarship and Colonial Discourses." *Boundary* 2, nos. 12/13 (1984): 333–358.

Parry, Benita. "Problems in Current Theories of Colonial Discourse." *Oxford Literary Review* 9 (1987): 27–58.

Spivak, Gayatri Chakravorty. *The Post-Colonial Critic.* New York: Routledge, 1990.

———. "Three Women's Texts and a Critique of Imperialism." *Critical Inquiry* 12 (1985): 243–261.

Viswanathan, Gauri. *Masks of Conquest:*

Literary Study and British Rule in India. New York: Columbia University Press, 1989.

Postfeminism

A term popularized by the media during the early 1980s to refer to what was alleged to be a new phase of gender politics. Like other "post" words of the late twentieth century, most notably "postmodernism," postfeminism means different things to different people. One version of postfeminism claims that society has advanced beyond sexism and that feminism is no longer necessary. Another version promotes the view that feminism is obsolete, not because feminist goals have been met, but because women have finally come to their senses and realize that they do not want to "have it all." No version of postfeminism accurately reflects the situation of most women in the late twentieth century.

One of the most striking features of the so-called postfeminist movement is its conservative character. Postfeminism disavows the need for social change. Within the academy, some critics have embraced the concept of postfeminism in an effort to dissociate themselves from feminism's political empiricism; in so doing, they inevitably renounce the social agenda that is essential to feminism. As Tania Modleski points out, texts that herald the advent of postfeminism are "actually engaged in negating the critiques and undermining the goals of feminism—in effect, delivering us back into a prefeminist world."

The concept of postfeminism is intimately connected with antifeminist backlash and thus predates the twentieth century, appearing whenever feminism has been perceived as a threat to the status quo. Such a backlash occurred after the period of feminist controversy in 1790s England, which witnessed the appearance of Mary Wollstonecraft's *A Vindication of the Rights of Woman* and numerous other feminist tracts: journalists of the early nineteenth century boasted that women of their day no longer clamored for rights or sought to rival men in their pursuit of liberty. Likewise, as Susan Faludi explains, shortly after women won the vote in the United States, antifeminists launched a campaign portraying the perils of equality for women, invoking the postfeminist claim that women no longer wanted to be bothered with "all that feminist pother." A key facet of much postfeminist propaganda is the argument that women should accept subordination for their own good. Many postfeminists claim that too much freedom would make women unhappy and potentially unmarriageable.

The ambiguity of the term "postfeminism" helps to mask its antifeminist usage. Its proponents can simultaneously deplore the historically unequal status of women and discourage women from acting in their own interests. Similarly, in postfeminist discourse, the rhetoric of feminism is often used as a tool to obfuscate feminist issues. For example, women are urged to "choose" family over career as though there were no alternative options, to exercise their right to be feminine as though femininity conflicted with political rights, to celebrate yet again the "year of the woman" as though feminism had reached its peak and one year would compensate for several millennia's worth of the year of the man. From the postfeminist perspective, women are equal enough in theory that they can let down their guard and enjoy their actual subordination.

By referring to a period as postfeminist, opponents of feminist goals capitalize on the optimism of the women's movement. Women's rights activists have always hoped that there would be a time when patriarchy became obsolete and feminist politics would thus be unnecessary. Postfeminism in this sense would be a feminist utopia. Unfortunately, feminism still has a long way to go before it can arrive at that utopian "post."

Audrey Bilger

References

Faludi, Susan. *Backlash: The Undeclared War against American Women.* New York: Crown, 1991.

Modleski, Tania. *Feminism without Women: Culture and Criticism in a "Postfeminist" Age.* New York: Routledge, 1991.

Rosenfelt, Deborah Silverton. "Feminism, 'Postfeminism,' and Contemporary Women's Fiction." In *Tradition and the Talents of Women,* edited by Florence Howe, 268–291. Urbana: University of Illinois Press, 1991.

Russo, Mary. "Notes on 'Post-feminism.'" In *The Politics of Theory,* Proceedings of the Essex Conference on the Sociology of Literature, July 1982, edited by Francis Barker et al., 27–37. Colchester: University of Essex, 1983.

Poststructuralism

Poststructuralism works as an umbrellalike term used to describe some elements of the theoretical practices of deconstruction, feminisms, new historicism, neo Marxism, cultural studies, and psychoanalysis, to name a few. A common denominator in poststructuralist criticism is a relentless questioning of ideologies and concepts that appear to be "natural," "stable," and "known." Much of feminist criticism may be said to be "poststructuralist" because of its interest in examining the assumptions upon which fixed notions of gender (for instance, that women and men are naturally different) are based, and in its desire to work toward transforming these assumptions. In addition, feminist poststructuralists seek to change the sociohistorical practices that participate in reproducing stable or "traditional" ways of defining men and women and their places in literature, history, or society.

The attempt both to define and to historically locate poststructuralism can become problematic for the poststructuralist for whom definitions and histories are not transparent or transcendent explanations of "truths." Rather, poststructuralists tend to call into question how "truths" are produced. For example, one might write, "Poststructuralism is usually thought of as beginning in the late 1960s when Jacques Derrida's lecture "Structure, Sign and Play in the Discourse of the Human Sciences" displaced the idea that structure is a stable system.'" However, the preceding sentence attempts to establish a point of origin (the late 1960s, or 1966, the year the essay was written); to suggest a closed system of meaning (namely, that the ideas in Derrida's essay are responsible for the shift from structuralism to poststructuralism); and lastly seems to place the genesis of this origin and system in the unified "self" of Derrida. Thus the poststructuralist critic, while recognizing the need for definition, is also aware of the implications of such an act of definition.

When examining the creation of points of origin, closed systems of meaning, and unified selves, poststructuralists notice that these creations imply a structure of meaning in which there is always an unquestioned "center." For example, an introductory paragraph in an anthology that reads "Emily Dickinson is one of America's best women poets" contains one unwritten center of meaning that assumes that male poets and female poets are judged by different criteria; Emily Dickinson is not labeled as "one of America's best poets," but categorized by her gender. Similarly, the sentence on Emily Dickinson creates centers of nationality (American) and of the aesthetic (best). A poststructuralist might ask, among other things, "What does this text mean by 'America'?," and "How does this text produce an idea of what is 'best'? What are the implications of using these words to define Emily Dickinson? How and why is the relationship between Emily Dickinson and the poetry solidified and unquestioned? Who is served by these constructions?"

Poststructuralists realize that one of the results of this kind of inquiry is the inevitable creation of another system, or structure, with another center. Thus, any attempts to question the nature of "definitions" and "history" is simultaneously producing a definition and a history. Although the production of more "centers" may seem like a futile endeavor, some poststructuralists argue that the very process of examining how these centers are made and the subsequent creation of new centers destabilizes and disrupts more traditional structures. Thus it creates different possibilities for ways of defining, interpreting, and historicizing.

Two seminal texts that engage in this process are Jacques Derrida's "Structure, Sign and Play" and Julia Kristeva's essay "Semiotics: A Critical Science and/or a Critique of Science." Both essays challenge the structuralist precept that texts are part of systems that can be scientifically analyzed. Derrida critiques Lévi-Strauss's structural anthropology for its assumption that one can stand outside a structure and analyze it. According to Derrida, Lévi-Strauss's opposition between culture and nature is fallacious because one can never be external to culture. Kristeva, using the works of Marx and Freud, critiques the structuralism and semiotic system set forth by Saussure, arguing for the use of semiotics and structuralism, not only as "sciences," but also as systems that simultaneously critique science by calling into question the assumptions about "truth" and "method" upon which scientific inquiry is based. By incorporating history and psychology into a structuralist system, Kristeva transforms structuralism from a closed system of signs that can be "mastered" to a dynamic of production that reflects social constructs and signifying systems.

The work of these critics and the vast field of poststructuralist criticism that has followed has created a mixed reaction among feminists. Many feminists feel that poststructuralism is a counter to feminist goals because it represents theory as elitist, white, and male; thus, to participate in poststructuralism is to, in some sense, take on the tools and the language of the oppressor. Nina Baym articulates this concern in "The Madwoman and Her Languages: Why I Don't Do Feminist Literary Theory," stating that "theory is an agenda for the way women might or should write in future; to me it seems a guarantee of continued oppression. The most militant theorists do not use the language they call for." Many feminists are also troubled by poststructuralism because they see it as divorced from the kind of tangible political action that impelled the feminist movement in the first place. Hortense J. Spillers describes this as "a fairly complete breach between matters of feminist social theory and feminist metatheory [that] appears beyond repair." Yet, even as Spillers and others locate this breach, their work often attempts to bridge this gap.

Joan Scott argues for poststructuralism, stating, "Until we understand how the concepts work to constrain and construct specific meanings, we cannot make them work for us." The possibility for exploring and reshaping these "concepts" and "meanings" is one of poststructuralism's greatest appeals for feminists. In *Gender Trouble*, Judith Butler uses poststructuralism to argue that both gender and sex are cultural products and thus, neither is more "natural" than the other; both are productions of power. In her essay, "Postmodern Blackness," bell hooks implements poststructuralism "to critique essentialism while emphasizing the significance of 'the authority of experience.'" The implications of these and other poststructuralist texts for feminism are multiple in that they create visionary and re-visionary ways of looking at issues of gender, sex, race, and class.

If poststructuralism is an umbrella term for one of the ways in which theory is practiced today, it is an umbrella that is permeated by other influences. To call any text or critic simply "poststructuralist" would ignore the nuances and the call for multiple and shifting categorizations that poststructuralism tries to enact. Whether or not individual feminists consider the many deployments of poststructuralism to be useful methods of interpretation, feminism, in general, seems to have benefited from the lively political debate that poststructuralism has engendered.

Kathleen Gormly

References

Baym, Nina. "The Madwoman and Her Languages: Why I Don't Do Feminist Literary Theory." In *Feminist Issues in Literary Scholarship*, edited by Shari K. Benstock, 45–61. Bloomington: Indiana University Press, 1987.

Butler, Judith. *Gender Trouble: Feminism and the Subversion of Identity*. New York: Routledge, 1990.

Carby, Hazel V. "'Woman's Era': Rethinking Black Feminist Theory." In *Reconstructing Womanhood: The Emergence of the Afro-American Woman Novelist*, 3–21. New York: Oxford University Press, 1987.

Derrida, Michel. "Structure, Sign and Play in the Discourse of the Human Sciences." In *The Languages of Criticism and the Sciences of Man*, edited by Richard Macksey and Eugenio Donato, 247–265. Baltimore, Md.: Johns Hopkins University Press, 1970.

Ferguson, Margaret, and Jennifer Wicke, eds. *Feminism and Postmodernism*. Durham, N.C.: Duke University Press, 1994.

Fuss, Diana. *Essentially Speaking: Feminism, Nature and Difference*. New York: Routledge, 1989.

Hirsch, Marianne, and Evelyn Fox Keller, eds. *Conflicts in Feminism*. New York: Routledge, 1990.

hooks, bell. *Yearning: Race, Gender, and Cultural Politics*. Boston: South End, 1990.

Kristeva, Julia. *The Kristeva Reader*. Translated by Toril Moi. New York: Columbia University Press, 1986.

Scott, Joan. *Gender and the Politics of History*. New York: Columbia University Press, 1988.

Spillers, Hortense J. "'An Order of Constancy': Notes on Brooks and the Feminine." *Centennial Review* 29 (1989): 223–248.

Weedon, Chris. *Feminist Practices and Poststructuralist Theory*. Oxford: Basil Blackwell, 1987.

Praxis

In its most basic meaning, this term denotes action or practice, as opposed to abstract theory. Accordingly, it could be applied to much of the pioneering feminism and feminist criticism that valued political activism over theoretical concerns. Many Anglo American feminists of the 1970s and early 1980s approached female-authored texts through a generally empirical mode of criticism that focused primarily on women's experiences. Toril Moi observes that such critics often perceived literary theory as an antifeminist and "hopelessly abstract 'male' activity." Nina Baym, for example, rejected theory as "irretrievably misogynist."

Defining praxis simply by what it is not, however, fails to acknowledge that praxis is inevitably based on a theoretical or ideological premise. A creative use of praxis can be found in the works of many contemporary feminist novelists, including Fay Weldon, Margaret Atwood, and Emma Tennant, among others, who practice literary criticism not through the traditional mode of analytical and theoretical critical essays, but rather through fictions that appropriate and subvert traditional canonical metanarratives in order to reinscribe them from a female perspective. Patricia Waugh and Carol McGuirk, among others, cite this form of praxis as a frequently employed feminist mode of postmodernism. Of particular interest as an example of praxis as criticism is Weldon's *Letters to Alice on First Reading Jane Austen,* an epistolary metafiction in which the narrator qua author "Aunt Fay," explains Austen's fictions through the practical advice she imparts to a fictional niece. Praxis, thus, can and should be seen as a counterpart to rather than the binary opposite of theory in the methodologies of feminist criticism.

Patricia Juliana Smith

References

Atwood, Margaret. *Lady Oracle.* New York: Simon and Schuster, 1976.

Baym, Nina. "The Madwoman and Her Languages: Why I Don't Do Feminist Literary Theory." In *Feminisms: An Anthology of Literary Theory and Criticism,* edited by Robyn R. Warhol and Diane Price Herndl, 154–167. New Brunswick, N.J.: Rutgers University Press, 1991.

McGuirk, Carol. "Drabble to Carter: Fiction by Women, 1962–1992." In *Columbia History of the British Novel,* edited by John Richetti et al., 939–965. New York: Columbia University Press, 1994.

Moi, Toril. *Sexual/Textual Politics: Feminist Literary Theory.* New York: Methuen, 1985.

Tennant, Emma. *Sisters and Strangers: A Moral Tale.* London: Paladin, 1991.

Waugh, Patricia. *Feminine Fictions: Revisiting the Postmodern.* London: Routledge, 1989.

Weldon, Fay. *Letters to Alice on First Reading Jane Austen.* London: Michael Joseph, 1984.

P

Procreation

See REPRODUCTION

Prostitution

Legal statutes define prostitution as the performing of sex acts in exchange for money. Feminist responses to prostitution have attempted to confront the cultural assumptions behind the trade in women, rather than the prostitute herself. Feminist support for movements to abolish the sexual exploitation of women derives from a recognition that the sale of the female body reflects a pervasive ideology of sexual violence and objectification of women. Yet, many feminists resist such movements, based on the conflicting recognition that government efforts to control prostitution have attacked the problem by attacking the woman, ignoring the masculine ideology and economic inequities that drive women onto the streets. Feminist historians, such as Judith Walkowitz, note that such government solutions have responded more to the ideological needs of male power than the plight of the prostitute, culminating in the further restriction of women's sexual, economic, and political freedoms.

As an issue for feminist literary theory, prostitution is inextricably linked to pornography. As Andrea Dworkin notes, "The word *pornography,* derived from the ancient Greek *porne* and *graphos,* means 'writing about whores.'" Pornography and prostitution share the central image of the woman objectified, debased, reduced to the *porneia,* the cheapest of sexual slaves. Within the text of pornography, the prostitute's body becomes metaphoric, an object to be used by men to represent all women in passive acquiescence to male power. Since Mary Wollstonecraft, feminist writers have challenged this ideology by seizing control of the prostitute's metaphoric status and wielding it against the structures of patriarchy; early feminists' recognition of an analogy between prostitution and the economics of marriage reverses the metaphor by noting the commodification of female sexuality at the heart of mainstream culture. Recent feminist criticism goes further by rejecting the metaphor's implicit division of female experience strictly on the basis of sexuality—madonna or whore—and exploring the central role this metaphor has played in the production of a privileged male subjectivity and the literary canon that affirms it.

Shannon Bell challenges the metaphor at its origins, in the suppression by male philosophers of the figure of the *hetairae*—the courtesan philosophers of ancient Greece, acknowledged by Socrates as his teachers—in Plato's *Symposium.* By reinscribing the prostitute at the origins of Western philosophy, the feminist critic destabilizes the male authority that traditional readings have assigned to canonical texts. Plato's text constructs philosophy as female, laying the groundwork for a central metaphor of Western literary tradition: the equation of text with prostituted female body, a source of pleasure accessible to any man privileged with literacy and leisure. While early modern culture viewed the prostitute as barren, a vessel unresponsive to male seed, the image of the prostitute proved fertile ground for the male imagination as a commodity to be sold within the literary marketplace. According to Peter Brooks, the prostitute is the embodiment of all that can be narrated, a model of the sexual transgression and criminality that inspires fascination and desire in a male reader. In popular fictions like Defoe's *Moll Flanders,* Cleland's *Fanny Hill,* and Zola's *Nana,* the prostitute's narrative transforms literary commerce into an image of her own erotic transaction: her sexual adventures inspire both the male writer's pen and an outpouring of coins from the reader's purse. The prostitute has also served as a metaphor for theatricality according to Joseph Lenz, a vehicle for moral satire writes Vern Bullough, and as a figure who provokes pity, affirming the male reader's subjectivity by her wretched state explains Daniel Harris.

More important for feminist criticism, the image of the prostitute became during the eighteenth and nineteenth centuries a weapon in the hands of male critics seeking to deny the moral and stylistic legitimacy of women writers, as Catherine Gallagher and Jacqueline Pearson have demonstrated: "Whore is scarce a more reproachful Name/Than Poetess." As Charles Bernheimer notes, prostitution, by its Latin etymology, means to set or place *(statuere)* in public *(pro);* used as a metaphor for literary publication, the image of the prostitute deprives the woman writer of her voice by inscribing her text with the culture's contempt for the prostitute's soiled and sold body.

Since the 1980s, the literary representation of prostitution has been challenged by women writing and speaking their own experience in the life. This act of speaking out—in prostitutes' rights groups and in recent performance art by prostitutes who challenge the image of women in the sex industry—rejects the idea of the prostitute as an object displayed in the marketplace, or a metaphor to be contested by literary critics. By claiming the role of author, the prostitute poses a challenge both from and to feminist theory, demanding both a voice and an identity as women who work, desire, laugh, and talk back.

Sergei Lobanov-Rostovsky

References

Alexander, Priscilla. "Prostitution: A Difficult Issue for Feminists." In *Sex Work: Writings by Women in the Sex Industry,* edited by Frederique Delacoste and Priscilla Alexander, 184–214. Pittsburgh, Pa.: Cleis, 1987.

Bell, Laurie, ed. *Good Girls/Bad Girls: Feminists and Sex Trade Workers Face to Face.* Seattle, Wash.: Seal, 1987.

Bell, Shannon. *Reading, Writing and Rewriting the Prostitute Body.* Bloomington: Indiana University Press, 1994.

Bernheimer, Charles. *Figures of Ill Repute: Representing Prostitution in Nineteenth-Century France.* Cambridge: Harvard University Press, 1989.

Brooks, Peter. "The Mark of the Beast: Prostitution, Melodrama, and Narrative." In *Melodrama,* edited by Daniel Gerould and Jeanine Parisier, 125–140. New York: New York Literary Forum, 1980.

Bullough, Vern L., et al. *A Bibliography of Prostitution.* New York: Garland, 1977.

Dworkin, Andrea. *Pornography: Men Possessing Women.* New York: Putnam, 1981.

Gallagher, Catherine. "George Eliot and *Daniel Deronda*: The Prostitute and the Jewish Question." In *Sex, Politics and Science in the Nineteenth Century Novel,* edited by Ruth Bernard Yeazell, 39–62. Baltimore, Md.: Johns Hopkins University Press, 1986.

Harris, Daniel A. "D.G. Rossetti's 'Jenny': Sex, Money and the Interior Monologue." *Victorian Poetry* 22 (1984): 197–215.

Lenz, Joseph. "Base Trade: Theater as Prostitution." *ELH* 60 (1993): 833–855.

Millett, Kate. *The Prostitution Papers.* New York: Ballantine, 1973.

Pearson, Jacqueline. *The Prostituted Muse: Images of Women and Women Dramatists 1642–1737.* New York: St. Martin's, 1988.

Walkowitz, Judith R. *Prostitution and Victorian Society: Women, Class and the State.* Cambridge: Cambridge University Press, 1980.

Wollstonecraft, Mary. *A Vindication of the Rights of Woman* [1792]. Baltimore, Md.: Penguin, 1975.

Psychoanalysis

When he published *The Interpretation of Dreams* in 1900, Sigmund Freud laid the foundation for a new field of humanistic knowledge, psychoanalysis, that would alter the shape of feminist literary theory and, in fact, virtually all other fields, for years to come. With a thorough understanding of biology, Freud, a doctor of medicine, studied psychic phenomena like dreams and fantasy that take root in infancy and childhood. He found that dreams and fantasy give shape to an individual's physic, emotional, and intellectual life as it develops out of the early attachment to the parents. Freud showed how dreams, for instance, are versions of childhood scenarios in which the parents play a major role. Once a part of the mother's body, the child begins to use the language of dreams to represent the mother as a forbidden sexuality and the father as an authority figure at the center of social life.

Freud's focus on the language used to represent the parents, coupled with the new readings of his work in the 1960s and 1970s in France, helps to explain his impact on feminist literary theory. Paul Ricoeur's and Jacques Lacan's analyses, for instance, legitimize psychoanalysis as a model for a critical interpretation of Western cultures.

Freud studied dreams and fantasy in the words his patients used to discuss their mental life. He showed how free association in the language of these patients, many of whom were diagnosed as hysterics, revealed conflicts and tensions in a culture that created a taboo out of sexuality.

In an analysis of his own dream in a train heading for summer vacation, for example, he showed how he was better able to cope with excessive ambition and the sexual drives to which it is connected once he understood how it grew out of the megalomania of his childhood. Here and throughout his work, Freud created a precise vocabulary in which concepts become dynamic and dramatize psychic conflicts. These concepts include the unconscious, the ego, the id, the superego, the manifest, the latent, inhibition, and repression.

Psychoanalysis recognizes and examines the role of the unconscious using manifest phenomena, that is, material freely exhibited, as the point of departure. Under Freudian analysis, the words patients use to describe their dreams are manifest phenomena that reveal latent desires: physical and emotional longings growing out of their unconscious or early attachments to the parents. In this context, Freud distinguishes among the ego, the id, and the super-ego as the three principal voices or "agencies" in a conflicted psyche.

The ego is the most complicated of Freudian agencies. Freud developed the idea of the ego in his second theory of the psyche as an agency that is both conscious and unconscious and that adapts to reality. The id performs unconscious functions and is perhaps best understood as the set of biological drives, the material base upon which the individual lives. The super-ego is the simplest psychic voice. Either conscious or unconscious, it is a kind of censor or guard enforcing social regulation and is identified with the phallus in the work of Jacques Lacan. His imaginative reading of Freud and especially his concept of the role of a phallus, deriving from, but not limited to, the actual sexual organ, creates new interest in psychoanalysis as a critique of phallocentric societies.

Paul Ricoeur's reading of Freud offers a philosophical ground for feminist literary theory and its critique of essentialism, logical positivism, and metaphysics, though he does not discuss feminism directly. Ricoeur shows that psychoanalysis is not an experimental science or an essentialist biology but rather a human science with radical implications for European philosophy.

That is, because dreams are one form of the conflicted structures of desire giving shape to philosophical and artistic creation, the psychoanalysis of dreams is a model for the analysis of art and for the work of interpretation in general. For Ricoeur, Freud connects psychoanalysis and a philosophy of creation in ways that suggest that artists mobilize energy deriving from earlier sexual experience and move forward through their creative works to forge new meanings.

Drawing on philosophical thought and literary traditions at the turn of the century, Freud's analysis of the conflicts created by a forbidden sexuality and an authoritarian censor implicitly underline "difference" and "the other." In approaching psychic dilemmas that are also social, psychoanalysis draws connections among radically different components of subjectivity, the private (attachment to the mother, for instance) and the public (the social contract that creates language and taboos). In this way, psychoanalysis plays a major role in shaping concepts and convictions central to feminist theory: difference, "the other," the connections between the personal and the political.

Until the 1970s, many feminist theorists were hostile to Freud, especially in the United States and England, where an essentialist reading of psychoanalysis prevailed. Despite Lacan's and Ricoeur's work, some feminists, philosophers, and, especially, social and physical scientists, measure the legitimacy of Freud's assumptions, methodology, and conclusions by using quantitative empirical criteria and a pragmatic, positivist approach.

In *Feminism and Psychoanalytic Theory,* Nancy Chodorow, an American sociologist who acknowledges a debt to Freud in elaborating her own psychoanalytic theory of mothering and male dominance in Western cultures, documents feminist theorists' initial hostility and subsequent interest in Freud beginning in the 1970s and growing ever since. Juliet Mitchell, in *Psychoanalysis and Feminism,* and Adrienne Rich in *Of Woman Born,* are two of her other examples of this growing interest.

For feminist literary theory, a more serious critique of psychoanalysis warns of its tendency to describe the psyche in ways that universalize human nature and fail to consider cultural and historical difference. Paul Bové discusses psychoanalysis's two weaknesses—its disregard for cultural and historical change and its implicit rejection of Marx and of the Marxist critique of imperialist practices. Here Bové echoes some of the concerns of earlier commentators

of Freud, for example Eric Fromm in his "Method and Function of an Analytic Social Psychology" in *The Essential Frankfurt School Reader.*

Psychoanalysis in its most useful versions leads to work that is neither essentialist nor ahistorical. Freud's writing serves as a catalyst to reexamine sexuality and personal life in their connections to politics and public life. His anthropological work in *Moses and Monotheism* is a good example. The psychoanalyst illuminates the mystery, creativity, strength, and conflicts of a psychic life that helps to shape sexuality. In this way, psychoanalysis reveals sexism and other forms of oppression and works toward the well-being of the individual and the group.

Carol Mastrangelo Bové

References

Bové, Paul. "Afterward." In *Writing and Fantasy in Proust: "La Place de la madeleine,"* by Serge Doubrovsky, translated by Carol Mastrangelo Bové, 148–158. Lincoln and London: University of Nebraska Press, 1986.

Chodorow, Nancy J. *Feminism and Psychoanalytic Theory.* New Haven and London: Yale University Press, 1989.

Freud, Sigmund. *Beyond the Pleasure Principle.* Vol. 18 of *The Standard Edition of the Complete Psychological Works of Sigmund Freud,* translated by James Strachey, 7. London: Hogarth and Institute of Psychoanalysis, 1950.

———. *The Interpretation of Dreams.* Vols. 4 and 5 of *The Standard Edition of the Complete Psychological Works of Sigmund Freud,* translated by James Strachey. London: Hogarth and Institute of Psychoanalysis, 1955.

Fromm, Erich. "The Method and Function of an Analytic Social Psychology: Notes on Psychoanalysis and Historical Materialism." In *The Essential Frankfurt School Reader,* edited by Andrew Arato and Eike Gebhardt, 477–496. New York: Continuum, 1982.

Graybeal, Jean. *Language and "the Feminine."* Bloomington: Indiana University Press, 1990.

Lacan, Jacques. *Écrits: A Selection.* Translated by Alan Sheridan. New York and London: W.W. Norton, 1977.

Laplanche, J., and J.B. Pontalis. *The Lan-*

guage of Psychoanalysis. Translated by Donald Nicholson-Smith. New York and London: W.W. Norton, 1973.

Mitchell, Juliet. Psychoanalysis and Feminism. New York: Random House, 1974.

Rich, Adrienne. Of Woman Born. New York: Bantam, 1976.

Ricoeur, Paul. Freud and Philosophy: An Essay on Interpretation. Translated by Denis Savage. New Haven and London: Yale University Press, 1970.

Psychoanalytic Criticism

Broadly defined as the study of artistic production in the context of Freud's discovery of the unconscious, psychoanalytic criticism considers literature as a representation of consciousness where the unconscious is latent. With Freud's *Interpretation of Dreams* as their model, psychoanalytic critics read the multiple meanings of the text as Freud would analyze a dream. These multiple meanings include the manifest content (often simply "content" in Freud) or ideas present and freely expressed, and the latent content or thoughts absent and desired by the dreamer or writer. Because of its representation of the mother, on the one hand, as a forbidden sexuality, and of the father, on the other, as the social order controlling that sexuality, psychoanalytic criticism stimulates lively debate among feminist literary theorists.

Psychoanalytic critics maintain a dialogue with earlier approaches to literature and take these approaches, and Freud, in a new direction. They have developed psychic concepts like condensation, displacement, and identification and have related them, respectively, to formalist notions like metaphor, metonymy, and point of view. In this way they combine the study of subjectivity, or the subject, with objectivity, or the textual object, and often raise questions about the status of each. With clear implications for feminism, Julia Kristeva's criticism, for instance, demonstrates the extent to which Western cultures shape a tradition of the subject that is rational and male. Her work constitutes a critique of phallocentric and imperialist practices.

Like Kristeva, many psychoanalytic critics, especially those who are European, have been influenced by Karl Marx and Jacques Lacan. For these critics, art channels sexual and aggressive drives not to provide therapy for the individual nor to maintain the cultural order but, on the contrary, to enable the writer to live more fully by subverting middle-class values and the social contract. Given that the cultural order is patriarchal, psychoanalytic criticism focusing on subversion, like that of Serge Doubrovsky, Jacqueline Rose, Jane Gallop, and Julia Kristeva, is of special use to feminist literary theory.

Doubrovsky, for example, probes the unconscious voices subverting aristocratic authority in Proust's novel and removes the Symbolist veneer from *The Remembrance*. Rose, a British critic, shows how useful psychoanalytic concepts can be in exploring persistent stereotypes of the feminine in film. Claude Richard uses psychoanalysis to reread American classics like "The Purloined Letter" and to contribute to contemporary debates on the role of fantasy in literature and culture. Jane Gallop demonstrates how Lacan can help to write a feminist theory aware of the complex workings of the psyche as a subject both "male" and "female," conflicted by violence and desire. She uses feminism to politicize a theory that, on American soil, often focuses on sublimation and accommodation to an unjust social contract.

Julia Kristeva's work grows out of Russian and American Formalism, French Structuralism, and Lacanian psychoanalytic theory. She derives her notion of the speaking subject from Lacan's version of the Freudian unconscious as a linguistic process. According to Lacan, the psyche precariously constructs itself in language as an alternation of conscious and unconscious voices under the watchful eye of the father figure or phallus. Building on Lacanian theory but shifting the focus away from the phallus, Kristeva studies literature's role in reconnecting the individual or speaking subject to emotional, sensual, and sexual experience that more purely formalist criticism and the sociopolitical forces supporting such criticism were responsible for severing.

For Kristeva, psychoanalytic criticism dramatizes the problems of twentieth-century cultures that define the human being and the ethical mainly in terms of the rational and the spiritual. According to Kristeva, Freud forces us to recognize the ways we have cut off the emotional and sexual components of our being and to reattach these components. She develops a psychoanalytic criticism and theory that shows the relationship between the individual's conflicts and those of the society of which he or she is a part. In *Strangers to Ourselves,* for instance, she traces the history of Western treatment of foreigners. She uses Freud to show how this history emerges from Western psychic structures and from the capitalist and patriarchal societies they support.

Rejecting feminism when it is understood as a set of orthodox values, Kristeva's work is feminist to the degree that she bases her critique of Western societies on an analysis of the psyche that acknowledges the voice of "the other," often a woman or foreigner. She shows how texts reach deep into the unconscious to maternal sources of pleasure and subversion. For Kristeva, writers reactivate these sources in an effort to reconfigure patriarchal society.

Kristeva first lays out her theory linking "the foreign" within, that is, unconscious drives, to "the foreign" without, the immigrant or minority. She then analyzes the rhetoric used in political texts of different historical periods. She studies the language of the French Revolution, to take one example, in terms of both its openness to, and its persecution of foreigners.

Critics of Kristeva and of psychoanalysis in general charge that it speaks of the psyche in a universal way, minimizing the impact of cultural and historical difference and of Western imperialist practices. Nancy Fraser also makes such an argument in a recent article on French discourse theories, in which she concludes that psychoanalytic criticism is of little use to feminism. Psychoanalytic critics in the United States, often shaped by pragmatism and political conservatism, do frequently speak of the psyche in a universal way when they stress the notion of sublimation in Freud. According to these versions of psychoanalytic criticism, creative writers channel or "sublimate" forbidden sexual and aggressive drives in their work. For critics as otherwise different as Lionel Trilling, *The Liberal Imagination,* and Jeffrey Mehlman, *A Structural Study of Autobiography,* artists produce texts that are therapeutic and socially valued. With Jane Gallop's work a notable exception, much psychoanalytic criticism in the United States helps to build and maintain the cultural order.

Critical of that order, Kristeva is keenly aware of cultural difference, of historical change, and of the horrors of colonialism in *Strangers to Ourselves.* In her chapter on the French Revolution in this volume, she shows how the rhetoric of political texts of the period shapes France's changing relationships to the foreigner. Like Malek Alloula's analysis of France's treatment of Algerian women in postcards in *The Colonial Harem, Strangers to Ourselves* reveals the conflicted psychology underpinning France's relationship to the foreigner.

Kristeva and Alloula describe and offer a theory of the psyche that connects the individual to the particular society of which he or she is a member. *Strangers to Ourselves* and *The Colonial Harem* show that psychoanalytic criticism bridges cultural and historical boundaries while acknowledging and analyzing these boundaries and the patriarchal and imperialist practices they may conceal.

Carol Mastrangelo Bové

See also KRISTEVA, JULIA

References

Alloula, Malek. *The Colonial Harem.* Translated by Myrna Godzich and Wlad Godzich. Minneapolis: University of Minnesota Press, 1986.

Doubrovsky, Serge. *Writing and Fantasy in Proust: "La Place de la madeleine."* Translated by Carol Mastrangelo Bové. Lincoln and London: University of Nebraska Press, 1986.

Fraser, Nancy. "The Uses and Abuses of French Discourse Theory for Feminist Politics." *Boundary 2,* no. 17 (1990): 82–101.

Freud, Sigmund. *The Interpretation of Dreams.* Vols. 4 and 5 of *The Standard Edition of the Complete Psychological Works of Sigmund Freud,* translated by James Strachey. London: Hogarth and The Institute of Psychoanalysis, 1955.

Gallop, Jane. *The Daughter's Seduction: Feminism and Psychoanalysis.* Ithaca, N.Y.: Cornell University Press, 1982.

Garner, Shirley N., et al., eds. *The M(Other) Tongue.* Ithaca, N.Y.: Cornell University Press, 1985.

Kristeva, Julia. *Strangers to Ourselves.* Translated by Leon S. Roudiez. New York: Columbia University Press, 1991.

Lacan, Jacques. "The Mirror Stage as Formative of the Function of the I." In *Écrits: A Selection,* translated by Alan Sheridan, 1–7. New York and London: W.W. Norton, 1977.

Richard, Claude. "Destin, Design, Dasein: Lacan, Derrida and 'The Purloined Letter.'" *Iowa Review* 1981 (12): 1–11.

Rose, Jacqueline. *Sexuality in the Field of Vision.* London: Verso, 1986.

Wright, Elizabeth. *Psychoanalytic Criticism:*

Theory in Practice. London and New York: Methuen, 1984.

Public Sphere

The masculine half of an ideological division of the social world into public and private realms that developed with the industrialization of the Western world in the nineteenth century. Feminist theorists have demonstrated that this division and the masculinization of the public worlds of economic and cultural production and political action have served to support the exploitation and marginalization of women in patriarchal societies.

Feminist literary theory has engaged the concept of the public sphere by questioning the pronouncements of the patriarchy, by exploring the role women authors have played in the public realm of literature, and by working to undermine the binary division that makes the concept of a masculine public sphere possible. While the simple assumption that there are easily separable public and private spheres has become more problematic since the advent of poststructuralism, the public sphere remains an important area of inquiry for feminist literary theory in that it is, by definition, the realm where both literature and literary criticism operate.

Christopher Wells

References

Belsey, Catherine, and Jane Moore. "Introduction: The Story So Far." In *The Feminist Reader: Essays in Gender and the Politics of Literary Criticism,* edited by Catherine Belsey and Jane Moore, 1–20. New York: Basil Blackwell, 1989.

Elshtain, Jean Bethke. *Public Man, Private Woman: Women in Social and Political Thought*. Brighton, U.K.: Harvester, 1982.

Janeway, Elizabeth. *Man's World, Women's Place: A Study in Social Mythology*. New York: Dell, 1971.

P

Q

Queer Theory

This term has come to signify a body of scholarly work, generated primarily by lesbians and gay men, that crosses disciplinary, methodological, and thematic lines. It focuses on sex, gender, and sexuality, with particular attention to the social construction of sexualities, and to the discourses and social control practices that surround them. At the intellectual center of the nascent field of lesbian and gay studies, queer theory also parallels the emergence of queer politics in the 1980s. While queer theory is strongly interdisciplinary, no field has been more powerfully impacted by it than literature, where many important queer theorists do their work. And although the moniker "queer" may be read as shorthand for lesbian and gay, or for the more unwieldy "lesbian, gay, bisexual, transgendered (transvestite, transsexual), and questioning," the body of work under the queer theory umbrella surpasses even these categories.

While scholarship about homosexuals and homosexuality dates back to the invention of those terms in the late nineteenth century, antihomophobic scholarship by out-of-the-closet lesbians and gay men did not find its way into the academy until over a century later. *The History of Sexuality, Volume 1*, by Michel Foucault, which was translated into English in 1978, is widely seen as heralding the mainstreaming of queer theory into Anglophone academia. Foucault's stature helped to legitimate the emergence of queer theory and opened the floodgates for what was to become an unprecedented groundswell of lesbian and gay scholarship.

The emergence of queer theory also depended on increasing use of the term "queer" among a vocal segment of the lesbian, gay male, bisexual, and transgendered (transsexual, transvestite) communities in the 1980s. The popularity of the term points to an unprecedented level of coalition politics among these divergent communities, particularly in organizations such as ACT-UP (The AIDS Coalition to Unleash Power) and its short-lived spin-off Queer Nation. Although traditionally a derogatory term, "queer" was appropriated by these groups to signify pride, antiassimilationism, and an "in-your-face" radicalism typical of queer political activism and, to some extent, queer theory.

As the term implies, queer theory involves the study of "queer" people. It also encompasses research in the academic disciplines from queer standpoints. Queer theory strives to add excluded perspectives to the disciplines, filling in gaps and redressing ignorance and bigotry spawned by heterocentricity. These are formidable tasks in and of themselves. But like feminist theory, queer theoretical works also tend to share a more radical deconstructivist aim: to unsettle the foundational categories around which academic disciplines, social norms, and even the production of knowledge are arranged by introducing queer perspectives, readings, and epistemological practices. Foucault's contention that desire is socially constructed, rather than inherent or natural, became a foundational truism of much of the queer theory that followed. His social constructivism also in many ways paralleled feminist theory's crucial disaggregation of biological "sex" and culturally imposed "gender." As Eve Kosofsky Sedgwick writes in *Epistemology of the Closet,* "[A]n understanding of virtually any aspect of modern Western culture must be, not merely incomplete, but damaged in its central substance to the degree that it does not incorporate a critical analysis of modern homo/heterosexual definition."

Queer theory has a complex relationship with feminist theory. Much queer scholarship—particularly that written by lesbians—is outspokenly feminist, and would be equally relevant in the contexts of women's studies and lesbian/gay studies. Conversely, reading other works of queer theory, one barely discerns the existence of women, much less feminism, with predictably sexist outcomes. The majority of queer theoretical scholarship falls somewhere in the middle, often in contradictory ways: work that at least nods in the direction of feminism, using its insights or methods, but without an overtly feminist perspective or agenda.

Where feminist theory focuses primarily on the issues of women, gender, and sexuality, queer theory generally posits sex and sexuality as its fundamental categories of analysis. Queer theory has borrowed much from the early feminist articulation of the difference between sex and gender, which allowed women to name their oppression as resulting from sexism, rather than as determined by biology. Queer theory's interpretation of sexual schema (such as the homo/hetero binary) as historically specific and oppressive inventions, rather than as immutable "natural" facts, has opened up exciting new avenues for research. Queer theorists are likely to raise questions about sexual power relations. Such deconstructive theoretical moves have begun to challenge scholars across the disciplines to question assumptions about the "naturalness" of heterosexuality as currently organized, and to acknowledge the homophobia inherent in the presumption of normative heterosexuality.

A strong, self-described "sex-positive" current underlies much queer theoretical work, particularly as it relates to issues around HIV disease, with an emphasis on the validity of all forms of sexuality. While women's right to control their own bodies is axiomatic within feminist theory, feminist theorists are also attentive to the extensive sexual violations of women and children in our society, and to the painful reality that sex, for women and children at least, is not always "positive." This difference is one of the sharpest between queer and feminist theories, and mirrors divisions among certain feminists as well. In addition, some theorists argue that queer theory's emphasis on sexuality perpetuates the demeaning stereotypical equation of gays with sex. Others, however, contend that the need for such sex-centered scholarship, from

queer perspectives, is essential to the fight against homophobia.

While queer theory, like feminist theory, sees itself as oppositional to and deconstructive of existing gender regimes, its relationship to the academy places it in a contradictory political position. On the one hand, it is almost always dangerous professionally, and sometimes personally, to do queer scholarship, as it once was to do feminist scholarship. Homophobia is still the order of the day on and off campus (in journals and on dissertation, hiring, and tenure committees). Those who risk their professional futures by producing such scholarship may be rightly lauded for their antihomophobic intellectual work, for they are often jeopardizing their professional futures, and they know it.

On the other hand, the conventional scholastic standards that inhere in queer theory, such as years of specialized training and research in professionally elite environments, place it firmly within the academic disciplines, with all their ingrained privileges and access to legitimacy. In addition, much queer theoretical writing shares with other texts in the "postmodern" camp a dense, jargon-filled, and often impenetrable rhetorical style. Both of the above points open queer theorists to charges (brought by feminist theorists, among others) of elitism and political irrelevance.

Tensions and conflicts between queer theory and feminist theory in the academy reflect political conflicts in the wider world. As Lisa Duggan discusses in "Making it Perfectly Queer," lesbian activists and scholars, who in the 1970s were primarily identified with feminism, found themselves torn in the 1980s between "women's" and "queer" communities, concerns, and even identities. Lesbian/gay coalition politics precipitated by the AIDS crisis are reflected in queer theoretical production, where we find (mostly lesbian) women writing about gay men, their books, films, dress, history, bodies, culture, and sexuality. We do not, however, find a similar level of interest on the part of male queer theorists (even those who use feminist insights and methodologies) in lesbians and their works and lives.

It is precisely these points of contention between queer theory and feminist theory that point to the sorts of questions that will demand investigation in the coming years. What is the place of lesbians and lesbian studies in queer theory? Will conflicts between the ethos of sexual libertarianism and that of feminism widen into an impassable chasm between queer and feminist theories? Or will common ground in their academic and political interests help engender a more mutually enhancing relationship? As the queer theory canon solidifies, what types of concerns and perspectives will be considered appropriate to it? Hundreds of lesbian and gay studies courses are now taught in the halls of higher education in the United States, most of which have queer theoretical texts at their center. How will such a radical and oppositional field change and adjust as its increasing institutionalization unleashes struggles over authority and control in the academic power structure?

If anything seems certain in this rapidly evolving field, it is that queer theorists, like feminist theorists, will continue to navigate/negotiate the line between loyalty to the political interests of their communities and the demands of academia. What will be lost and what will be found in this process remains to be seen.

Amy Agigian

References

Abelove, Henry, Michèle Aina Barale, and David Halperin, eds. *The Lesbian and Gay Studies Reader*. New York and London: Routledge, 1993.

Butler, Judith. *Gender Trouble: Feminism and the Subversion of Identity*. New York and London: Routledge, 1990.

Duggan, Lisa. "Making It Perfectly Queer." *Socialist Review* 1 (1992): 11–31.

Foucault, Michel. *The History of Sexuality, Vol. 1: An Introduction*. Translated by Robert Hurley. New York: Pantheon, 1978.

Fuss, Diana, ed. *Inside/Out: Lesbian Theories, Gay Theories*. New York: Routledge, 1991.

Garber, Marjorie. *Vested Interests: Cross Dressing and Cultural Anxiety*. New York and London: Routledge, 1992.

Sedgwick, Eve Kosofsky. *Epistemology of the Closet*. Berkeley: University of California Press, 1990.

Querelle des Femmes

The *querelle des femmes* refers to a series of written documents on the equality of the sexes, particularly on the condition and supposed character of women, dating from the late fourteenth century through the seventeenth century. Although mainly French, this written debate engages writers throughout Europe and originates in ancient times. Many Classical and late antique writers are cited during the *querelle* as justification for what we would consider to be misogyny. Aristotle, for instance, argues that women are naturally inferior to men, and that, as wives must be subject to the will of their husbands, so women must be subject to men in the political arena. The misogyny at times apparent in Roman writers such as Horace, Juvenal, or Ovid, as well as in Church fathers such as Paul or Jerome, resurfaces and fuels the debate. Prior to the *querelle,* some individuals—such as Sappho—do write favorably about women; however they may not expressly address this misogynistic tradition.

It is not until Christine de Pizan writes *The Book of the City of Ladies* in 1399 that a direct purposeful written dialogue begins, criticizing previous attacks on women made by male writers and defending womankind from such attacks. Christine reacts to the long tradition of written attacks against women as embodied in *The Romance of the Rose,* the second part of which, detailing the rape of the rose, was written by Jean de Meun. In this first phase of the *querelle des femmes,* known as the *Querelle du Roman de la Rose,* Christine attacks Jean de Meun's immorality and lack of *courtoisie,* or courtesy. She takes issue with the latter's stance that all women are evil and that young men need lessons in how to conquer women against their will. Siding with Christine is Jean Gerson, who writes the "Traité contre *le Roman de la Rose.*" Opposing Christine's position and supporting Jean de Meun are Jean de Montreuil, Gontier Col, and Pierre Col. In *The Book of the City of Ladies,* Christine furthers her argument in a discussion by *Justice, Droiture,* and *Raison,* enumerating illustrious literary and historical women. Although Christine's views cannot be considered "feminist" by today's standards, her courage and outspoken conviction make her a leader of women's rights in her time and the primary force behind the *querelle des femmes.* Soon after this exchange, Martin Le Franc in his *Champion des Dames* also offers examples of successful or famous women and criticizes attacks on women made by Jean de Meun. In order to refute the restrictions and limitations of traditional stereotypes, feminist writers in the sixteenth century also adopt this format of presenting literary and historical examples in support of women's attributes and accomplishments.

As the *querelle des femmes* unfolds in the

sixteenth century, the debate repeatedly considers questions such as whether women are the cause of all suffering in the world and whether they are inferior to men, or whether they are superior to men in virtue and ability and are indeed the inventors of civilization. Similarly, are women fickle and unfaithful, or are they just following men's example? Writers of the *querelle* also consider more overtly political issues such as women's legal status, marital contracts, and "suitable" occupations. Still other questions of a theological nature arise from opposing interpretations of Genesis: being made after man, is woman as inherently flawed? Or, being the final act of creation, does woman embody the most perfect form of humankind? At the end of the century, one anonymous writer uses polemical theological arguments, taken to the extreme, to try to prove that women are not human beings at all. On the antifeminist side of the *querelle* in the sixteenth century are Rabelais in *Gargantua*, Montaigne in his *Essays,* and many others who in certain works present conventional patriarchal and limited views of women. Some writers, such as Erasmus, seem to further both sides of the debate in various works, while others may state that they support the feminist cause but may not appear very "feminist" to us. The more or less feminist side then includes among others Ariosto, Heinrich Cornelius Agrippa von Nettesheim, Hélisenne de Crenne, and Marguerite de Navarre and her circle, which advocated a spiritual, Platonic love. A discussion of these theories and works is found in Lula McDowell Richardson.

While many of the writers engaged in the *querelle des femmes* both praise and criticize womankind, the praise even from the profeminist side is sometimes patronizing or seriously inadequate by our standards. For example, some writers argue that women should be taught to read but be "allowed" only limited subjects, or that, even if educated, women must be prohibited from assuming leadership roles in government. Yet each work represents a reaffirmation or progression in the debate, inspiring thinkers on both sides to publish their views. Feminists of today would find some fault with almost all the works on both sides of the *querelle,* which typically accept some subordination of women to men and rarely if ever advocate true equality. In the face of institutionalized discrimination, however, the feminists of the *querelle* undertake considerable risk in

making their position known, showing great courage and foresight for their time.

A.M. Dropick

References

Alexis, Guillaume, Sir Thomas Elyot, and Henricus Cornelius Agrippa. *The Feminist Controversy of the Renaissance*. Edited by Diane Bornstein. Delmar, N.Y.: Scholars' Facsimiles and Reprints, 1980.

Baird, Joseph L., and John R. Kane, eds. *La Querelle de la Rose: Letters and Documents*. Chapel Hill: University of North Carolina Press, 1978.

Christine de Pizan. *The Book of the City of Ladies*. Translated by Earl Jeffrey Richards. New York: Persea, 1987.

Ferguson, Margaret F., Maureen Quilligan, and Nancy J. Vickers, eds. *Rewriting the Renaissance*. Women in Culture and Society Series. Chicago: University of Chicago Press, 1986.

Kelly, Joan. "Early Feminist Theory and the *Querelle des Femmes,* 1400–1789." *Signs: Journal of Women in Culture and Society* 8 (1982): 4–28.

Richardson, Lula McDowell. *The Forerunners of Feminism in French Literature of the Renaissance from Christine of Pisa to Marie de Gournay*. Dissertation, Johns Hopkins Studies in Romance Literatures and Languages 12. Baltimore, Md.: Johns Hopkins University Press, 1929.

Wellington, James E. "Renaissance Anti-Feminism and the Classical Tradition." In *Sweet Smoke of Rhetoric. A Collection of Renaissance Essays,* edited by Natalie Grimes Lawrence and J.A. Reynolds, Vol. 7, 1–17. University of Miami Publications in English and American Literature. Coral Gables, Fla.: University of Miami Press, 1964.

Willard, Charity Cannon. *Christine de Pizan: Her Life and Works*. New York: Persea, 1984.

Wilson, Katherina M., ed. *Women Writers of the Renaissance and Reformation*. Athens: University of Georgia Press, 1987.

Quilting

Typically associated with the folk craft of the patchwork quilt, quilting has provided motifs and symbols in women's writings, that have engaged feminist literary critics. Additionally, critics use quilting metaphorically to describe the structure and process of women's writing, the female aesthetic, and even feminist critical approaches.

Practiced in Europe, Africa, and Asia, the complex of quilting techniques, aesthetics, and language developed with the patchwork quilt in the United States, through contributions of British colonists and African slaves. The typical three-layered patchwork quilt has a pieced or appliqued top, a filling or batting, and a bottom lining. These layers are quilted with a running stitch or knotted (tacked or tied) with strong thread or yarn at intervals. This multicultural history and technology offer rich metaphorical possibilities for writers and critics.

In "Common Threads," the final chapter of *Sister's Choice*, Elaine Showalter compares quilting and women's writing: both were ignored and devalued by the patriarchal worlds of art and literature; both were created in the interstices of time in the women's sphere, and both have been rediscovered. Paralleling the rediscovery of women's writing in the 1960s and 1970s, the revival of interest in quilting, which raised quilting to an art, was spurred by Patricia Mainardi's "Quilts: The Great American Art," published in *Feminist Art Journal* and *Ms.* in 1973.

Even though rural women continued quilting throughout the twentieth century, women's writing about quilts is most prolific from the 1800s through the early 1900s and after 1970. Both Showalter and Elaine Hedges examine these writers' uses of quilting motifs. Among the literary pieces discussed are Harriet Beecher Stowe's *The Minister's Wooing*, Susan Glaspell's "A Jury of Her Peers," Alice Walker's "Everyday Use" and *The Color Purple*, Joyce Carol Oates's "The Celestial Timepiece," and Adrienne Rich's "Natural Resources." Writers after the 1970s quilt revival often use quilt imagery as a symbol of heritage or women's "common language," binding them in the women's sphere.

Showalter surveys feminists' use of piecing and quilt patterns to describe the female aesthetic and the structure of women's texts; the nonhierarchic pieced quilt serves as a metaphor for the "decentered structure" of the "verbal quilt" of the feminist text. For example, Showalter suggests that Stowe's *Uncle Tom's Cabin* is structured like the "Log Cabin" quilt pattern, operating "through a cumulative effect of blocks of event[s] structured on a par-allel design." Similarly, Torsney terms feminists' variety of critical approaches a "critical quilt."

Contemporary feminists usually view the relationship between piecing and writing positively, but Hedges cautions not "to ignore this adversarial relationship" between the needle and the pen, noting that many women rebelled against domestic sewing chores. While quilt-making could be burdensome, critics find the quilt an expressive means for voicing the concerns of muted cultures. Elsley illustrates this with the Names Project AIDS Quilt, analyzing it as symbolic communication that "invites a reading." Thus, after reading stories about quilting and discovering the multivocal nature of the quilt, feminist critics are joining folklorists in anthropological approaches to read quilts' narratives.

Susan Roach

References

Elsley, Judy. "The Rhetoric of the Names Project Aids Quilt: Reading the Text(ile)." In *Aids: The Literary Response*, edited by Emmanuel Nelson, 187–196. New York: Twayne, 1992.

Ferrero, Pat, Elaine Hedges, and Julie Silbur. *Hearts and Hands: The Influence of Women and Quilts in American Society*. San Francisco: Quilt Digest, 1987.

Hedges, Elaine. "The Needle or the Pen: The Literary Rediscovery of Women's Textile Work." In *Tradition and the Talents of Women*, edited by Florence Howe, 338–364. Urbana: University of Illinois Press, 1991.

Mainardi, Patricia. "Quilts: The Great American Art." *Feminist Art Journal* 2 (1973): 18–23.

Roach, Susan. "The Kinship Quilt: An Ethnographic Semiotic Analysis of a Quilting Bee." In *Women's Folklore, Women's Culture*, edited by R.A. Jordan and S.J. Kalcik, 54–64. Philadelphia: University of Pennsylvania Press, 1985.

Showalter, Elaine. *Sister's Choice: Tradition and Change in American Women's Writing*. Oxford: Clarendon, 1991.

Torsney, Cheryl B. "The Critical Quilt: Alternative Authority in Feminist Criticism." In *Contemporary Literary Theory*, edited by G. Douglas Atkins and Laura Morrow, 180–199. Amherst: University of Massachusetts Press, 1989.

Q

Wahlman, Maude Southwell, and John Scully. "Aesthetic Principles in Afro-American Quilts." In *Afro-American Folk Art and Crafts,* edited by William Ferris, 79–98. Jackson: University of Mississippi Press, 1983.

R

Racism

Commonly understood, racism is the ranking of human beings on the grounds of perceived biological differences—such as skin color, hair texture, and features—that are then stigmatized as marks of social, intellectual, and cultural inferiority. Within feminist theory, racism has recently emerged as its most salient problematic as it raises in simultaneity issues often regarded in isolation, such as antiessentialism and the assertion of identity (dealt with by psychoanalytical and cultural studies feminists); social difference and equality (dealt with by legal studies scholars, Marxist feminists); and language and representation (dealt with by feminist semioticians, literary and film theorists, philosophers). Within dominant feminism, the issue of race compels women to shift their attention away from differences between the sexes to differences among and between women. As Ramazanoglu suggests in . . . *Contradictions* . . . , for Third-World and minority women the divisions between women are much more obvious than any sense of shared identity on the basis of gender.

Hazel Carby in *Reconstructing Womanhood* argues that the critique of dominant feminism by nonwhite women can be traced back to the works of black women such as the ex-slave Harriet Jacobs and the educationist Anna Julia Cooper, which bear testimony to the racism of the suffrage and temperance movements, and effectively indict white women for perpetuating the "racist patriarchal order against all black people," instead of allying themselves with black women. Today that debate between women has expanded to include postcolonial and immigrant women, who now produce what can be termed as the internal critique of feminism.

De Lauretis has pointed out that the issue of race has polarized feminist theory insofar as women of color have directed their criticism not at male power but at white women. Dominant feminism is charged with perpetuating racism on several counts: Barbara Smith in "Toward A Black Feminist Criticism" accused several prominent feminist literary theorists of racism for having excluded and ignored the contributions of black women of letters. Alice Walker has coined the term "Womanist" to refer to the specificity of black women's struggles. The Combahee River Collective, a socialist lesbian group, was formed in 1974 to examine the multilayered texture of black women's lives and to enable black women to represent themselves. Hull et al.'s anthology *All the Women Are White, All the Men Are Black, but Some of Us Are Brave* sought to redress the gap in representations of black women in discourses of feminism and race. Moraga and Anzaldúa's classic anthology *This Bridge Called My Back* attempted to theorize the intersections of ethnicity and race under the rubric of "women of color," or U.S. Third World Feminism. In Britain, minority women such as Amos and Parmar in their essay "Challenging Imperial Feminism" have sought to decenter the priorities of white women—such as the critique of the nuclear family, reproductive rights and sexual liberty, and the antinuclear campaign—as signs of inattention to black women's needs.

Aside from these consciousness-raising critiques, other more disciplinary studies pointing to differences between women have emerged. In literary theory, Gayatri Spivak in her essay "Three Women's Texts and a Critique of Imperialism" has analyzed the historical specificity of feminist individualism through a reading of *Jane Eyre* and *Wide Sargasso Sea* to demonstrate that the white woman's individuation is made possible through the exclusion of the other woman. Chandra Mohanty in "Under Western Eyes" has pointed to the homogenizing and objectifying strategies of much feminist ethnographic and sociological work on so-called Third-World women, which renders them as passive victims of patriarchy; she has also problematized the notion of sisterhood as a universal symbol of sexual oppression. These issues have pedagogical consequences for literary studies in that multicultural pluralism, with its attempt to include other women, is shown to be ideologically counterproductive. More recently, Vron Ware in *Beyond the Pale* has called upon white women to think of themselves as racially embodied in order to better come to terms with the painful history of racism within the women's movement.

The issue of sexuality and race is addressed by several critics: Hortense Spillers, most notably in "Mama's Baby, Papa's Maybe," interrogates fundamental categories of feminist analysis such as the sex-gender system in psychoanalytic terms. A controversial issue that discloses the imbrication of race and sex is interracial rape: the representation of the rape of white women as a political weapon, often used to justify lynching and colonialism, is analyzed by Valerie Smith through a reading of Alice Walker's short story "Advancing Luna" in "Split Affinities," and by Jenny Sharpe in *Allegories of Empire*. In a related vein, cultural critic Michele Wallace in *Black Macho* traces the sexism in African American novels such as *Native Son*, popular culture, and political movements to racist representations of black male sexuality.

Today, the question of race has become indispensable for feminist analysis, which has increasingly attempted to become a discourse for the analysis of power as such. Some of the problems confronting women today are the universalizing impulse of dominant feminism especially witnessed in feminist literary histories such as Gilbert's and Gubar's *Norton Anthology of Literature by Women;* the inability of dominant feminists to identify with the experiences of other women and to learn from their traditions; the unquestioning identity of so-called white women who have not fully examined the historical and metaphoric implications of calling themselves "white," and the reinforcement (by so-called women of color) of the untenable binary between the singular category of "white" and the homogeneity of "colored"; and finally the intellectual hubris of dominant

feminism that often seeks to tutor other women in the rules of feminism. These are among the most pressing issues for feminism today as it negotiates its contradictory internal tensions as proof of its vitality.

Kalpana Seshadri-Crooks

References

Amos, Valerie, and Pratibha Parmar. "Challenging Imperial Feminism." *Feminist Review* 17 (1984): 3–19.

Carby, Hazel. *Reconstructing Womanhood: The Emergence of the Afro-American Woman Novelist.* New York: Oxford University Press, 1987.

de Lauretis, Teresa. "Upping the Anti (sic) in Feminist Theory." In *Conflicts in Feminism,* edited by Marianne Hirsch and Evelyn Fox-Keller, 255–270. New York: Routledge, 1990.

Hull, Gloria T., et al., eds. *All the Women Are White, All the Men Are Black, but Some of Us Are Brave.* New York: Feminist, 1982.

Mohanty, Chandra. "Under Western Eyes: Feminist Scholarship and Colonial Discourses." In *Third World Women and the Politics of Feminism,* edited by Chandra Mohanty et al., 51–80. Bloomington: Indiana University Press, 1991.

Moraga, Cherríe, and Gloria Anzaldúa. *This Bridge Called My Back: Writings by Radical Women of Color.* Watertown, Mass.: Persephone, 1981. New York: Kitchen Table: Women of Color Press, 1983.

Ramazanoglu, Caroline. *Feminism and the Contradictions of Oppression.* London: Routledge, 1989.

Sharpe, Jenny. *Allegories of Empire: The Figure of Woman in the Colonial Text.* Minneapolis: University of Minnesota Press, 1993.

Smith, Barbara. "Toward a Black Feminist Criticism." In *The New Feminist Criticism,* edited by Elaine Showalter, 168–185. New York: Pantheon, 1985.

Smith, Valerie. "Split Affinities: The Case of Interracial Rape." In *Conflicts in Feminism,* edited by Marianne Hirsch and Evelyn Fox-Keller, 271–287. New York: Routledge, 1990.

Spillers, Hortense. "Mama's Baby, Papa's Maybe: An American Grammar Book." *Diacritics* 17 (1987): 65–81.

Spivak, Gayatri. "Three Women's Texts and a Critique of Imperialism." In *Critical Inquiry in Race, Writing, and Difference,* edited by H.L. Gates, 262–280. Chicago: University of Chicago Press, 1986.

Wallace, Michele. *Black Macho and the Myth of the Superwoman.* New York: Dial, 1979. New York: Verso, 1990.

Ware, Vron. *Beyond the Pale: White Women, Racism and History.* London: Verso, 1992.

Radway, Janice

Radway is the author of *Reading the Romance: Women, Patriarchy and Popular Literature,* a complex study of the social process of producing and consuming romance novels. In her more recent work, Radway investigates how the Book of the Month Club challenged literary authority by uniting cultural production with mass consumption and distribution.

Reading the Romance is an ethnographic study of a bookstore employee named Dot Evans and her regular clientele of romance readers, whom Radway calls the Smithton women. Radway makes use of reader theorist Stanley Fish's notion of "interpretive communities" to investigate how this group makes meaning of romance texts. Radway seeks to contrast literary critical interpretations of the novels with those of the "fans of the genre." Contrary to the belief that readers are passive consumers of mass culture, Radway shows the Smithton women are actively engaged in distinguishing between "failed" and "ideal" romances. Using the psychoanalytic theory of Nancy Chodorow, Radway argues a successful romance helps readers negotiate their "partial dissatisfaction" with patriarchal marriage, by representing a heroine who ends up in a nurturing heterosexual relationship that resembles the mother-daughter dynamic. For feminists, this work is important because it reveals a community of women for whom the event of reading is a subversive means of claiming time and privacy for themselves.

Mary Thompson

References

Radway, Janice. "Mail-Order Culture and Its Critics: The Book-of-the-Month Club, Commodification and Consumption, and the Problem of Cultural Authority." In *Cultural Studies,* edited by Lawrence Grossberg, Cary Nelson, and Paula Treicheler, 512–527. New York: Routledge, 1992.

———. *Reading the Romance: Women, Patriarchy and Popular Literature* [1984]. Chapel Hill: University of North Carolina Press, 1991.

———. "The Scandal of the Middlebrow: The Book-of-the-Month Club, Class Fracture, and Cultural Authority." *South Atlantic Quarterly* 89 (1990): 703–736.

Rape

Although *Webster's II New Riverside University Dictionary* defines rape as the "crime of forcing another person to submit to sexual intercourse," the legal definition varies depending on which legal system, or which individual, does the defining. Inherent in the understanding of rape, the problem of definition spills over into the field of literary scholarship and studies of such violence in literature. From New Criticism, which ignored instances of rape or viewed them only in relation to the text itself, to the rise of feminist theory, which examines in great detail representations of rape in literature, rape has been a theme of interest to literary theorists. Feminist theorists are especially invested in the study of rape because of the relationship between examples of rape in literature and the violence of rape that is perpetrated on real women.

Although not specifically literary, social attitudes toward the act of rape play an important role in how rape has been read in literature. Historically, rape was viewed as a sexual act done by a man to a woman as a way of claiming property or as part of a legal right to the woman's body. Women in this context were considered passive participants in rape, which was somehow a natural aspect of their social existence. With the rise of psychoanalytic theory, social attitudes began to change as rape was interpreted as a sexual act deeply implicated in the unconscious mind. More than simply a sexual act done to women, psychoanalysis asserted that rape is something women desire, a sort of masochism that they seek and enjoy at an unconscious level. Helene Deutsch elaborated on this notion, asserting that masochism is an inherent aspect of femininity and that rape fantasies are instinctive in women. Such ideas have perpetuated the myth that women want to be raped, thereby undermining the traumatic experience that being raped involves.

It was not until 1975, when the publication of Susan Brownmiller's *Against Our Will* raised the general public's consciousness about the history of rape and the injury it inflicts on the victim, that rape became identified as a crime of violence. Departing from the pejorative psychoanalytic understandings of rape, Brownmiller claimed that rape "is nothing more or less than a conscious process of intimidation by which *all* men keep *all* women in a state of fear." This assertion, made in the midst of the highly active women's movement, offered feminists a way of understanding rape that considered its effectiveness as a powerful weapon designed to oppress women. In response to work like Brownmiller's, women began to view rape as a serious and unacceptable crime whose future was to be denied.

Building on the feminist concept of rape as violence done to women, the 1970s gave way in the 1980s to a feminist concern with the social structures that perpetuate that sexual violence. In 1983, Catharine MacKinnon's influential article "Feminism, Marxism, Method and State" posited an ideological analysis of the existence of rape. MacKinnon suggested that rape is not only an act used to intimidate women, but also a violence so inherent in Western culture that one must ask how woman has come to occupy so vulnerable a position. Charging the judicial system itself as a participant in the social reproduction of rape, MacKinnon argued for a reconceptualization of the crime, its victims, and the social system in which they exist. Since then, feminist activists have been concerned not only with the consequences of rape for the victim, but with the position of the victim in the larger social structure. The judicial system, too, has taken the experience of the rape victim more seriously and begun to define rape in a more aggressive fashion. Despite improvements in the legal treatment and understanding of rape, however, social attitudes toward rape and the rape victim continue to be based to a large extent on conventional stereotypes. Women are implicitly questioned, if not blamed, for the violence done to them, and courts of law frequently fail to render justice in rape cases.

In many ways, the importance of rape to literary theory parallels the changing social attitudes toward such violence. Early literary criticism paid little, if any, attention to examples of rape in literature. As a topic of scholarly interest, in fact, rape did not become a subject heading in the *Humanities Index* until 1974, just a year before the publication of Brownmiller's work. It was not a regular category of literary analysis until four years later in 1978. Formalism, the predominant mode of literary criticism until the 1950s, reflected the prefeminist attitude toward rape. Interested in the text as a work of art, formalism considered instances of sexual violence in literature as significant only in terms of the narrative itself. When interpreting Yeats's "Leda and the Swan," for example, New Criticism would have been unconcerned with the fact that the poem's metaphor for the birth of Greek civilization is a woman being raped. Like the social system, which historically misclassified and misunderstood rape, ignoring the victim while attending to the perpetrator, formalist criticism ignored the significance that examples of rape in literature might have for women.

Since the advent of feminism and the publication of feminist texts such as Brownmiller's, instances of rape in literature have become the focus of serious academic scholarship. Once feminist criticism began to question the representation of women in literary texts, in fact, the field exploded into an array of new interpretations of rape. Concerned with the ways that literary representations of women present a false picture of women's real experience, such criticism was first concerned with examining specific instances of rape from a mimetic standpoint. Of central concern was the relationship between literary representations of rape and the lived experience of real women. Although feminist critics have since come to recognize that a "real" woman is not being raped in the texts they study, it was important during this first wave of feminist thought to explore such moments as if it were. The rape of Samuel Richardson's Clarissa, for instance, could be studied mimetically as a literary example of a "real" woman who is raped by a "real" suitor, someone she had come to trust. In this early phase of feminism, the importance of literary victims of rape like Clarissa was their response to the rape and how that response corresponds to reactions of real rape victims. What, for example, are the myths and stereotypes inherent in the literary representations of women who are raped? What are the implications of such representations for real rape victims? How is the rape a result of patriarchal society? What, in the end, does the text teach its readers about rape?

Examining narratives in which rape occurs has been important to feminist theory for it has allowed scholars to draw attention to moments of violence in literature where they have been previously overlooked. Since the 1980s, however, feminist theory has extended its commentary on representations of rape to include the theorization of the representations themselves. With the rise of deconstruction, feminists began to explore how language itself is a violence done to women, a metaphorical rape perpetrated by the text and author. More recent feminist theorists might ask about the reader/critic as "rapist," either because of some voyeuristic pleasure gained by reading about the rape, or as a result of an incessant analytic "rape" of the text itself. The significance of textual gaps or ellipses in the structure of the text where the rape takes place (as in Thomas Hardy's *Tess of the D'Urbervilles*) is another area of interest to feminist theory. What is the meaning of such deletions? How does the rape victim's silence act as a metaphor for women's silence regarding their own authority? What does it mean for a female author to write about a rape, as Charlotte Perkins Gilman does in *Herland*? Theorists interested in political analysis draw parallels between rape and colonialism in texts like E.M. Forster's *A Passage to India,* exploring the ideologies at play in the representation of rape. Contemporary American texts have also begun to deal with rape more explicitly. Gloria Naylor's *The Women of Brewster Place*, for example, graphically depicts the brutality of gang rape. Such texts move feminist theory into another position from which to read rape, one, perhaps, in which the impact of rape must be theorized as an all too common trauma to the psyche of Western culture.

In the future it is certainly important to continue to study examples of rape in literature and to continue to move beyond familiar readings in an attempt to change assumptions about rape that perpetuate a passivity toward such violence. How woman is constructed as an object to be raped, for example, is a possible direction in which to move. In this light, rape victims like Tess become more than literary characters and more than representations of real life. They are viewed, instead, as vehicles through which literary theory can understand the political, social, and cultural factors that perpetuate the act of rape. In examining characters like Tess as complex figures whose material and psychological circumstances interact with the society in which they are a part, feminist theory continues to gain insight into how women are placed in a position vulnerable enough to be raped.

Sara E. Quay

References

Brownmiller, Susan. *Against Our Will*. New York: Simon and Schuster, 1975.

Estrich, Susan. *Real Rape*. Cambridge: Harvard University Press, 1987.

Ferguson, Frances. "Rape and the Rise of the Novel." *Representations* 20 (1987): 88–112.

Hermann, Dianne. "The Rape Culture." In *Women: A Feminist Perspective,* edited by Jo Freeman, 41–63. Palo Alto, Calif.: Mayfield, 1984.

Higgins, Lynn V., and Brenda Silver, eds. *Rape and Representation*. New York: Columbia University Press, 1991.

Horney, Karen. *Feminine Psychology*. New York: W.W. Norton, 1967.

Lant, Kathleen Margaret. "The Rape of the Text: Charlotte Gilman's Violation of *Herland*." *Tulsa Studies in Women's Literature* 9 (1990): 291–308.

MacKinnon, Catharine. "Feminism, Marxism, Method and State: Toward Feminist Jurisprudence." *Signs: Journal of Women in Culture and Society* 8 (1983): 635–658.

Naylor, Gloria. *The Women of Brewster Place*. New York: Penguin, 1982.

Plaza, Monique. "Our Damages and Their Compensation, Rape: The Will Not to Know of Michel Foucault." *Feminist Issues* 7 (1981): 25–35.

Quay, Sara. "'Lucrece the Chaste': The Construction of Rape in Shakespeare's 'The Rape of Lucrece.'" *Modern Language Studies* 15 (1995): 3–17.

Sanday, Peggy Reeves. "Rape and the Silencing of the Feminine." In *Rape,* edited by Sylvana Tomaselli and Roy Porter, 84–101. Oxford: Basil Blackwell, 1986.

Sharpe, Jenny. "The Unspeakable Limits of Rape: Colonial Violence and Counter-Insurgency." *Genders* 10 (1991): 25–46.

Tanner, Laura E. "Reading Rape: Sanctuary and the Women of Brewster Place." *American Literature* 62 (1990): 559–582.

Warner, William Beatty. "Reading Rape:

Marxist-Feminist Figurations of the Literal." *Diacritics* (1983): 13–32.

Reader-Response Criticism

Although it has become a widely inclusive term, applied to many disparate approaches, all reader-response criticism shares one central belief: that the meaning of a work of literature, rather than inhering statically in the text itself or being recoverable from the author's intentions, is produced dynamically through the interaction between text and reader. Although its various incarnations prove useful to a wide range of feminist approaches to literature, all reader-oriented criticisms have in common with feminism an interactive approach to meaning-making, a validation of personal experience, and a belief in pluralism.

Proponents of reader-response criticism vary in the amount of power they attribute to each party to the collaboration that creates meaning. From this variation arises the diversity of reader-response theories and methodologies. Those who believe that the reader brings a disproportionate share of meaning to a relatively inert text make real readers the focus of their attention; they may examine these readers in several ways. This psychological mode of reader-response criticism is exemplified by Norman Holland, who studies the actual responses of real readers and discern the effects of their psychological makeup and defining concerns or obsessions on the meanings they construct. Others, such as Stanley Fish, while also stressing the centrality of real readers, take a more sociological approach, in the belief that one's construction of meaning is always constrained and guided by the conventions adopted by an "interpretive community." Still others, in what has become known as "reception theory" following Hans Robert Jauss, look at the changes in these communities, their conventions, their expectations, and their readings, over the course of history.

Those, on the other hand, who believe that the text (its language, its structure, its literary devices) exerts equal or greater control over meaning-making than do readers, focus on the text's construction of any or several of a range of fictional "readers" and its guidance of those readers in the generation of meaning. These constructed readers can include narratology's "narratee" (the counterpart of the narrator), as well as the "implied reader" in its various incar-

nations, which have been called "mock," "model," "virtual," "authorial," and "ideal" readers. The implied reader is a construct of the text which, depending on the particular theory, has more or less in common with the external reader and which acts as a mediator between that reader and the text. The text defines the implied reader through a range of direct and indirect methods, and manipulates it into certain kinds of responses by leaving it gaps to fill in and by giving it cues to follow in doing so. This process results in the interactive construction of a continually evolving meaning.

The fact that reader-response theories are predicated on an interaction in which the reader is active rather than passive means opportunities for readers to collaborate with texts in the generation of meanings, rather than aiming merely to absorb the author's intentions. The model's emphasis on relationships between participants, rather than the authoritarian imposition of one individual's understanding on another, echoes feminism's own preferred modes of interaction. Moreover, since the orientation toward the reader means some degree of freedom of interpretation, it results in a pluralism that subverts the patriarchal notion of a single transcendent meaning to which one must have privileged access.

If the focus is on individual real readers, a reader-response approach leads to the kind of validation of individuals' experiences that feminism often aims to achieve; and the exploration of the psychology of readers can lead to studies of gender differences in reading. When the focus is expanded to the interpretive community, the feminist reader-response critic can examine both the constraints and exclusions of a male-centered interpretive community and the possibilities of different conventions offered by a feminist interpretive community. The historicizing nature of reception theory enables feminists to place a work and its changing readership in appropriate cultural contexts, including gender-based ones; Jaussian reception theory, which uses the relationship between the text and its readers' "horizon of expectations" as a criterion for evaluating "artistic value," might also open one route to the expansion of the canon. And studies of the implied reader enable the feminist critic to understand the role gender differences play both in the reader's actualization of meaning and in the author's or narrator's methods or ideological underpinnings.

Jonathan Culler, in his essay "Reading as a

Woman," outlines three "moments" in the history of feminist criticism: a focus on the relationship between women's (individual real readers') experiences of the world and their experiences of literature; a questioning of the conventions by which patriarchal interpretive communities (groups of real readers) limit and define possible readings; and a contextualizing of these conventions and an exploration of alternatives to them. This linear scheme obscures the fact that all three of these strands of feminist reader-response criticism continue to hold sway and to influence one another. In Jane Tompkins's *Sensational Designs*, it became clear that the second form of feminist reader-response criticism implicitly requires the third: in laying bare the historically specific assumptions that have underwritten critical judgments, Tompkins both undermines the notion of timeless literary value and proposes an alternative yardstick, consciously bound to culture and history, which leads to the formation of a countercanon of works that had profound effects on their contemporaneous readers.

Such discussions of canon formation concentrate heavily on the real reader, but feminist reader-response criticism concerns itself with implied readers as well. A number of theorists have attempted to specify feminist theories of reader response that take into account both real and implied readers (and often the disjunction between them). For instance, Judith Fetterley has developed and applied the concept of the "immasculation" of the female reader and one available response to it—resistance; Patrocinio Schweickart has examined the split subject position which many men's texts force upon the feminist reader, and has proposed divergent approaches to the reading of "male" and "female" texts; and such critics as Annette Kolodny, Jean Kennard, and Dale Bauer have explored gender-specific reading strategies and the conventions of feminist interpretive communities.

In response to the growing recognition among feminists of the diversity of both women and feminists, theorists have begun to specify reader-response criticisms for smaller subsets of feminists. All such theories must keep in mind the divergent needs that underlie both reader-response criticism and feminism: a healthy pluralism that allows for diversity, and a set of acceptable conventions that are the prerequisite for any mutually comprehensible dialogue, whether between reader and text, or between reader and reader.

Debra Malina

References

Bauer, Dale M. *Feminist Dialogics: A Theory of Failed Community*. Albany: State University of New York Press, 1988.

Culler, Jonathan. "Reading as a Woman." In *On Deconstruction: Theory and Criticism after Structuralism*, 43–64. Ithaca, N.Y.: Cornell University Press, 1982.

Fetterley, Judith. *The Resisting Reader: A Feminist Approach to American Fiction*. Bloomington: Indiana University Press, 1978.

Flynn, Elizabeth A., and Patrocinio P. Schweickart, eds. *Gender and Reading: Essays on Readers, Texts, and Contexts*. Baltimore, Md.: Johns Hopkins University Press, 1986.

Kennard, Jean M. "Convention Coverage or How to Read Your Own Life." *New Literary History* 13 (1981): 69–88.

Kolodny, Annette. "A Map for Rereading: Or, Gender and the Interpretation of Literary Texts." *New Literary History* 11 (1980): 451–467.

Schweickart, Patrocinio P. "Reading Ourselves: Toward a Feminist Theory of Reading." In *Gender and Reading: Essays on Readers, Texts, and Contexts*, edited by Elizabeth A. Flynn and Patrocinio P. Schweickart, 31–62. Baltimore, Md.: Johns Hopkins University Press, 1986.

Suleiman, Susan R., and Inge Crosman, eds. *The Reader in the Text: Essays on Audience and Interpretation*. Princeton: Princeton University Press, 1980.

Tompkins, Jane. *Sensational Designs: The Cultural Work of American Fiction 1790–1860*. New York: Oxford University Press, 1985.

———, ed. *Reader-Response Criticism: From Formalism to Post-Structuralism*. Baltimore, Md.: Johns Hopkins University Press, 1980.

Reading

Based on reader-oriented criticism, feminist approaches to reading literature stress a consideration of the reader and the text and the relationship between them. Early feminist reading focused on the depiction of women in literature and on the importance for feminists of becoming "resisting readers." The field has gradually expanded to incorporate vexed questions of socially constructed gendered reading positions, under the auspices of gynocriticism.

One goal of early feminist readings of literature was to study images of women in the text. Ellen Moers, Elaine Showalter, Josephine Donovan, and Sandra Gilbert and Susan Gubar, for instance, focused their interpretations of literature on the characterization of women in their (restricting) historical, economic, social, and cultural contexts. Such criticism recovered the significance of female characters in literature and mimetically revealed issues that concern real women. In response to the newly developing field of reader-response theory, which was dominated by male critics like Roland Barthes and Stanley Fish, other first-wave feminist critics insisted that male-centered reader theory acknowledge a female response to misogynistic literature written by men.

As a result of recognizing the oppressive impact of having been taught to see things "as men," feminist reading has frequently been subversive. The goal of critics like Judith Fetterley, for instance, is to "raise consciousness" of readers in order to reveal androcentric viewpoints, creating "the resisting reader" who is aware of and resists being subject to male authorial and critical models. "Reading against the grain," based on the reader-response notion that texts are capable of bearing different interpretations depending on the orientation of readers, aims at discovering covert texts. Feminist reading has also emphasized marginal positions, while "bracketing off" dominant patriarchal ideology to reveal female anger at male dominance submerged beneath orthodox plots. Instead of promoting dominant belief systems, such reading positions encourage recognition of latent discourses in order to construct negotiated or oppositional readings that allow for an interrogation of patriarchy. Such reading relies on the idea that all reader response is learned, culturally determined, and mediated by gender.

The emphasis on subversive feminist readings, while not entirely superseded, has gradually given way to gynocriticism. This second-wave approach stresses women as writers, invoking the difference between adversarial or resistant feminist readings of male texts and sympathetic feminist readings of female texts that emphasize connection. Such criticism also reads gaps in texts—which are frequently coded as feminine—as problematic, and theorizes the use of the feminine as a literary trope.

One of the current challenges in feminist reader criticism is what it means to define gendered readers. What does it mean to read and write as a "man" or as a "woman"? Is there an essential "male" or "female" writer or reader? Can a man read as "a woman"? Are there significant variations in the reader response of women of different classes, races, religions, nationalities, sexual preferences? Feminist reader criticism will no doubt continue to address these questions, even as it continues to analyze the depiction of women in the text, to construct subversive readings, and to rescue women's texts from oblivion, ensuring the recognition of a female tradition in literature.

Deborah D. Rogers

References

Fetterley, Judith. *The Resisting Reader.* Bloomington: Indiana University Press, 1978.

Flynn, Elizabeth A., and Patrocinio P. Schweickart, eds. *Gender and Reading: Essays on Readers, Texts, and Contexts.* Baltimore, Md.: Johns Hopkins University Press, 1986.

Fuss, Diana. "Reading like a Feminist." *differences* 1 (1989): 77–92.

McConnell-Ginet, Sally, Ruth Borker, and Nelly Furman, eds. *Women and Language in Literature and Society.* New York: Praeger, 1980.

Realism

Literary realism has been defined in three ways: as the mimetic tendency in literature visible from Antiquity through the present (according to Auerbach); as the generic domain of the novel, which emerged in the eighteenth century (according to Watt); and as the socially conscious, densely detailed novel that flourished from the mid nineteenth century in Europe (and from the late nineteenth century in America) through the first two decades of the twentieth century. The latter, most specialized definition—which overlaps considerably with "naturalism"—is the concern of this entry. Historically, then, realism emerges beside the "New Woman," and participates in the production of multiple images of women in fields such as art, psychology, sociology, and advertising. Rachel Bowlby's comment about the title character of George Gissing's *Eve's Ransom*, written in 1895, could apply to many realist protagonists: "She is the center of a problem which is not of her own making." Recent scholarship that emphasizes, in Amy Kaplan's words, the "social construction" of realism can complement feminist interpretations. Realist novels spotlight many issues central to feminist theory: women's work, sexuality, the marriage market, and women's restricted sphere.

Literary realism carries considerable baggage because of the layperson's sense of "realistic" (that is, accurate) representation. However, most scholars now agree that realism represents, rather than transcribes, reality. Because of differing assumptions about the real, and the imprecision of literary-historical terminology, one reader may term Thomas Hardy's *Tess of the D'Urbervilles* realistic, another call it early modernist. George Eliot's *Middlemarch* is simultaneously realistic and Victorian. Feminist theory permits one to cut a number of Gordian knots by asking: whose reality is depicted in a given text?, and does "reality" differ for men and women? Furthermore, the feminist challenge to Western oppositional logic (for example, male versus female, culture versus nature, essence versus detail) also permits one to imagine "realism" as a continuum of possibilities rather than a fixed category. Feminists may insist, finally, on "realism*s*."

Numerous men have written realist novels featuring female protagonists. Inaugural realist novels such as Gustav Flaubert's *Madame Bovary* and Leo Tolstoy's *Anna Karenina* center on women's lives—and their deaths. Gissing's *The Odd Women* and Arnold Bennett's *The Old Wives' Tale* are two exemplary British treatments of the "woman question." American men have been especially prolific: Henry James's *The Portrait of a Lady* and *The Bostonians*, William Dean Howells's *A Modern Instance*, Stephen Crane's *Maggie*, Theodore Dreiser's *Sister Carrie* and *Jennie Gerhardt*, and Sinclair Lewis's *Main Street* and *The Job* all center on women. Feminist readers may ask: why are male realists so interested in women who work outside the home, discuss political change, demonstrate independent thought, divorce their husbands, dream of lives outside those scripted for women, or behave as if their sexuality were their own business? Are they fellow-travelers with feminism; does women's independence exist only in the fantasies of male authors; or are male realists more subtly objectifying women through literary representations?

Such questions are complicated because in *Sister Carrie* a male author, Dreiser, breaks the tradition that the "fallen woman" must die, even while contemporary women realists continued to depict death as the outcome for women who have sex outside of marriage (as in Kate Chopin's *The Awakening*), or who are simply so accused (as in Edith Wharton's *The House of Mirth*). Another complication is that many realist novels—from *The Bostonians* to Dreiser's *An American Tragedy,* from Wharton's *The Age of Innocence* to Sherwood Anderson's *Winesburg, Ohio*—manifest anxiety about the power that women (allegedly) have over men.

Realist novels by women reveal their own stress points. One is the problematic ending, particularly notable in Wharton's novels. In *The House of Mirth*, Lily Bart's death is shrouded by questions: is it suicide? what is "the word" that passes between the frustrated lovers? Wharton's *The Custom of the Country*, a brilliant investigation of women's "work" on the marriage market, also ends ambiguously, with the protagonist remarried to the man who was her husband before the action of the novel begins. And what is woman's work in the realist novel? Realism usually manifests class consciousness. Rebecca Harding Davis's pioneering "Life in the Iron Mills" and Anzia Yezierska's *Bread Givers* empathetically describe the back-breaking labors of poor women. But upon closer observation, their female protagonists seem no more constricted than the affluent heroines of, say, Wharton and James. An early work in feminist theory, Charlotte Perkins Gilman's *Women and Economics,* demonstrates how turn-of-the-century middle- and upper-class women were forced into constraining "work" as slaves to their homes and the sexual demands of husbands.

The productions of "local colorists," which constitute, as Josephine Donovan says, a "women's tradition" that overlaps with realism, may initially seem less ambiguous. Sarah Orne Jewett's *The Country of the Pointed Firs* and Willa Cather's novels celebrate women's work and their relationship to nature. But why, then, must the narrator in *Pointed Firs* leave the happy woman-centered community in Maine? Why does Cather depict *My Antonia* through a male narrator? Biographical considerations further complicate feminist interpretations, for Jewett and Cather efface their woman-centered sexuality in their writings.

Recent scholarship points out ways that

realism may be of fundamental interest to feminists. Alfred Habegger and Michael Bell describe male-authored realism as a defensive, compensatory reaction to fears about the "feminization" of culture and the authors' "sissified" social role. Naomi Schor notes that the pronounced attention to details characteristic of realism has always been coded as feminine and, consequently, devalued. Schor calls for feminists to shift their focus from the "representation of woman" to seek out the "relationship between woman and representation." The success of feminist inroads into realism is, ironically, confirmed by the backlash, as is well illustrated by James Tuttleton's complaint about the "takeover" of Wharton criticism. The resistance to feminist readings of realism indicates that there is far more work to be done

Clare Virginia Eby

References

Ammons, Elizabeth. *Conflicting Stories: American Women Writers at the Turn into the Twentieth Century.* New York: Oxford University Press, 1992.

Auerbach, Erich. *Mimesis: The Representation of Reality in Western Literature.* Translated by Willard R. Trask. Princeton: Princeton University Press, 1953.

Bell, Michael Davitt. *The Problem of American Realism: Studies in the Cultural History of a Literary Idea.* Chicago: Chicago University Press, 1993.

Bowlby, Rachel. *Just Looking: Consumer Culture in Dreiser, Gissing and Zola.* New York: Methuen, 1985.

Donovan, Josephine. *New England Local Color Literature: A Women's Tradition.* New York: Frederick Ungar, 1983.

Gilbert, Sandra M., and Susan Gubar. *No Man's Land: The Place of the Woman Writer in the Twentieth Century.* Vol. 2. *Sexchanges.* New Haven: Yale University Press, 1989.

Gilman, Charlotte Perkins. *Women and Economics: A Study of the Economic Relation between Men and Women as a Factor in Social Evolution.* Boston: Small, Maynard, 1898.

Habegger, Alfred. *Gender, Fantasy, and Realism in American Literature.* New York: Columbia University Press, 1982.

Kaplan, Amy. *The Social Construction of American Realism.* Chicago: University of Chicago Press, 1988.

Schor, Naomi. *Breaking the Chain: Women, Theory, and French Realist Fiction.* New York: Columbia University Press, 1985.

Tuttleton, James W. "The Feminist Takeover of Edith Wharton." *New Criterion* 7 (1989): 6–14.

Watt, Ian. *The Rise of the Novel.* Berkeley: University of California Press, 1957.

Renaissance Studies

Feminist literary criticism has flourished in Renaissance studies since its powerful emergence in the mid 1970s. Although various studies had already been published on the representation of women in the literature of Shakespeare and his contemporaries, such as Anna Jameson's *Characteristics of Women, Moral, Poetic, and Historical* (1887), Helena Faucit Martin's *On Some of Shakespeare's Female Characters* (1885), and Agnes Mure MacKenzie's *Women in Shakespeare's Plays* (1924), all of which, generally speaking, find Shakespeare's women courageous but unwomanly when they behave unconventionally or insubordinately, it was not until the publication of Juliet Dusinberre's controversial book *Shakespeare and the Nature of Women* in 1975 that feminism advanced significantly in Renaissance studies.

Like several of her predecessors, such as Violet Wilson in *Society of Women in Shakespeare's Time,* published in 1924, Dusinberre endeavors to link modern English and American feminism to the humanist and Puritan philosophies of the English Renaissance, which she says allowed women substantially more authority and freedom than they had been hitherto permitted. To demonstrate this positive change in attitudes toward women, Dusinberre examines an assortment of Elizabethan and Jacobean drama, which she claims is "feminist in sympathy." Dusinberre's argument is representative of the then-fashionable approach in feminist criticism to celebrate female protagonists in canonical texts without considering the possible ways in which their characterizations, when contextualized both historically and culturally, reinforce rather than challenge patriarchy.

This feminist approach to Renaissance literature was notably responded to by Joan Kelly-Godal in her seminal essay "Did Women Have a Renaissance?" Kelly-Godal locates in Jacob Burckhardt's classic *The Civilization of the Renaissance in Italy* the origins of the view that Renaissance women and men shared a new-fangled social equality, and attempts to refute this view by showing how the male-dominated literature of the period reveals and rationalizes a remarkably different, more restricted social and historical experience for Renaissance women than Renaissance men. Criticism like that of Kelly-Godal spurred scholars to be more inclusive in their analyses, to venture outside the traditional canon, and give the myriad texts written by Renaissance women greater treatment.

The Modern Language Association Special Session on Feminist Criticism of Shakespeare in 1976 was the first of its kind and the next major event for feminism in Renaissance studies after the publication of *Shakespeare and the Nature of Women*. This event encouraged communication and solidarity among feminist critics of the English Renaissance; it led immediately to the collaborative editorial effort made by Carolyn Ruth Swift Lenz, Gayle Greene, and Carol Thomas Neely to publish for the first time a collection of feminist essays on Shakespeare, entitled *The Woman's Part: Feminist Criticism of Shakespeare*. According to Lenz, Greene, and Neely, "The critics in this volume liberate Shakespeare's women from the stereotypes to which they have too often been confined; they examine women's relations to each other; they analyze the nature and effects of patriarchal structures; and they explore the influence of genre on the portrayal of women." In addition to its feminist commitment, *The Woman's Part* is exemplary of a pivotal moment in the history of Renaissance studies. Notwithstanding the analytical methods associated with the New Criticism, which are prominent in its essays, such as in their rigorous close readings of passages, many of the essays in *The Woman's Part* show a strong interest in the connections between literary texts and social and historical phenomena that were becoming a principal concern for Renaissance scholars in the late 1970s and early 1980s, and are now characteristic of Renaissance studies in the 1990s. This analytical shift in Renaissance studies is chiefly due to the recent advent of New Historicism and cultural materialism, both poststructuralist and Marxist literary-cultural critical approaches that are largely responsible for the intense politicization of current Renaissance studies. Although feminist criticism has thrived under the auspices of both New Historicism and cultural materialism, some feminist critics have found these new political discourses to be too male-dominated and elitist.

The debates between feminists, New His-toricists and cultural materialists that surfaced at the 1986 World Congress of the International Shakespeare Association culminated in the Seminar on Materialist Feminist Criticism of Shakespeare that met at the Shakespeare Association of America conference in 1989. This seminar led to the publication of *The Matter of Difference: Materialist Feminist Criticism of Shakespeare*. Valerie Wayne, its editor, asserts that feminism must not defend itself against New Historicism by returning to or calling for an extension of "the methods of *The Woman's Part* and a feminist criticism that is predominantly psychoanalytic." Instead, we must acknowledge the "productive complexity of this particular moment" and realize that "some practices of new historicism and cultural materialism" could serve "a more historically grounded feminism" that attempts to "speak from the differences among and within women and from a further recognition of the importance of racial, economic, social and erotic categories to assert the value of individually and collectively situated knowledges." Materialist feminism is clearly the present direction of feminist literary-cultural studies of the English Renaissance.

Bryan Reynolds

References

Dollimore, Jonathan, and Alan Sinfield, eds. *Political Shakespeare: New Essays in Cultural Materialism*. Ithaca, N.Y.: Cornell University Press, 1985.

Dusinberre, Juliet. *Shakespeare and the Nature of Women*. London: Macmillan, 1975.

Ferguson, Margaret W., Maureen Quilligan, and Nancy J. Vickers, eds. *Rewriting the Renaissance: Discourses of Sexual Difference in Early Modern Europe*. Chicago: University of Chicago Press, 1986.

Jardine, Lisa. *Still Harping on Daughters: Women and Drama in the Age of Shakespeare*. Brighton: Harvester, 1983.

Kelly-Godal, Joan. "Did Women Have a Renaissance?" In *Becoming Visible: Women in European History*, edited by Renate Bridenthal and Claudia Koonz, 175–199. Boston: Houghton Mifflin, 1977.

Lenz, Carolyn Ruth Swift, Gayle Greene, and Carol Thomas Neely, eds. *The Woman's Part: Feminist Criticism of Shakespeare*. Urbana: University of Illinois Press, 1980.

Neely, Carol Thomas. "Constructing the Sub-

R

ject: Feminist Practice and the New Renaissance Discourses." *English Literary Renaissance* 18 (1988): 3–18.

Waller, Gary F. "Struggling into Discourse: The Emergence of Renaissance Women's Writing." In *Silent but for a Word: Tudor Women as Patrons, Translators, and Writers of Religious Works,* edited by Margaret Patterson Hannay, 238–256. Kent, Ohio: Kent State University Press, 1985.

Wayne, Valerie, ed. *The Matter of Difference: Materialist Feminist Criticism of Shakespeare.* Ithaca, N.Y.: Cornell University Press, 1991.

Woodbridge, Linda. *Women and the English Renaissance.* Urbana: University of Illinois Press, 1984.

Zimmerman, Susan, ed. *Erotic Politics: Desire on the Renaissance Stage.* New York: Routledge, 1992.

Reproduction

Given that biologically, women literally and figuratively bear the burden of human reproduction, our reproductive capacity has been variously viewed by feminists as either a means of empowerment or a source of enslavement. In each view, women's power depends on our ability to control birth and what results from conception. Central, then, to feminist discourse on reproduction is women's right to bodily self-determination.

While the relationship between a woman's reproductive capabilities and her cultural status has been a subject of Western feminist inquiry at least since the Renaissance *querelles des femmes,* women's primary role as mothers was left largely unaddressed by feminists until the 1960s, when the publication of Betty Friedan's *Feminine Mystique,* depicting the virtual enslavement of the suburban housewife, coincided with the development and wide-scale dissemination of the pill.

Hailing the new disassociation of reproduction and women's sexuality, American feminists of the 1960s and 1970s asserted the rights of women to control their own bodies: through birth control, through abortion (legalized in 1973), and through knowledge of their own bodies and bodily functions. Groups such as the Boston Women's Health Collective, authors of the best-selling *Our Bodies/Ourselves* encouraged women to reclaim their bodies from patri-

archal medicine, to look at their own cervixes and to be able to understand the choices finally available to them.

For the radical feminists of the period, the male desire to control women's bodies epitomizes the systematic oppression of women at the foundation of patriarchal society. In *The Dialectic of Sex,* Shulamith Firestone argued this oppression to be rooted in women's reproductive biology. Replacing the Marxist concept of "production" with "reproduction," Firestone sees society as split into two conflicting biological classes based on male and female reproductive functions. The key to women's release from the "barbaric" prison of pregnancy is through the development of artificial means of reproduction and the dissolution of the family as we know it, enabling men and women to achieve true equality in a world in which "genital distinctions between the sexes" will have no cultural meaning.

This antibiological view of reproduction, coinciding with the advent of *in vitro* fertilization (IVF) in 1978, was extremely influential for both feminist theorists and science fiction writers such as Marge Piercy, whose *Woman on the Edge of Time* depicts a feminist utopia in which women have relinquished their unique biological power in order to create a nonhierarchical society. But while some feminists, like Firestone, denigrated biological reproduction as the means by which men enslaved and controlled women, others followed the lead of Adrienne Rich, whose *Of Woman Born* (1976) distinguished between the experience of mothering as a potential source of power for women and the institution of motherhood as controlled by the patriarchy. According to Rich, Firestone confused the victimizing experience of childbirth under patriarchy with the potential experience of childbirth "in a wholly different emotional and political context." Presenting a history of Western midwifery and obstetrics that emphasized the way that patriarchal medicine has gradually sought hegemony over women's health, Rich argues that the solution to women's oppression lies not in technology, which invites further male incursions into the previously all-female sphere of childbirth praxis, but in a return to woman-centered birth.

Rich's concept of empowering birth is informed by the work of birth activists such as Sheila Kitzinger and Suzanne Arms, who view the process of childbirth not as disease or medical emergency but as a natural life cycle event most appropriately controlled by women themselves. In *Immaculate Deception II*, Arms vehemently denounces "routine" practices such as episiotomies, anesthesia, and pubic shaves, which deny women their active role as birth-givers. The birth activists of the 1970s are still important voices in the 1990s, for the growth of procedures such as artificial insemination, embryo transfer, and IVF has both been facilitated by and increased the use of "everyday" technologies such as ultrasound, amniocentesis, and electronic fetal monitoring, while the quest for "the perfect baby" (along with medical fears of malpractice suits) has led to skyrocketing c-section rates.

Virtually all feminist discussions of reproduction in the 1980s and 1990s have addressed in some way the question of technology. The rapid development of techniques such as IVF, and new reproductive categories such as surrogacy, artificial insemination by donor (AID), and open adoption have been harshly critiqued by many theorists. Like Adrienne Rich, Margaret O'Brien believed patriarchy to be man's response to his detachment from reproduction. While for women, conception, gestation and parturition are part of a continuum, male insemination—whether artificial or through coitus—is temporally and spatially removed from birth. Paternity is, perforce, far from certain. If we accept the reality of this male alienation as a cause of patriarchal oppression, technological "advances" such as IVF must be viewed as a means for men to increase their hegemony in the reproductive process. Ultimately, then, argued Janice Raymond in 1993, to promote "technological and contractual reproduction" is to undermine women's reproductive rights, especially the right to abortion.

Although some feminists in the 1980s continued to insist on the possibilities for arrangements such as surrogacy and open adoption to create community among women, technology, according to 1980s writers such as Andrea Dworkin and Margaret Atwood, not only reaffirms existing patriarchal structures but creates divisions between women, whether by class (economically disadvantaged women bearing the children of the privileged) or by function (mothers versus breeders). Similar, the fragmentation of conception into independently movable—and purchasable—reproductive parts (such as egg, sperm, embryo, uterus) has caused some feminists to consider the exploitation of young, lower-class women through surrogacy, adoption, and egg harvesting as a form of prostitution.

Yet some feminists such as Patricia Spallone find that the focus on the problematic status of high-tech conception or parturition obscures an insidious class bias or even racism on the part of those formulating the critique. In this reading, the gravest threat to the bodily autonomy of many disabled, poor, or minority women is not technologically advanced infertility cures or even fetal monitors, but far more overtly oppressive practices such as coercive contraception, eugenic abortion, or the lack of access to prenatal care. The question should not be whether IVF reinforces patriarchal hegemony, but why some women have access to this technology and others do not.

While the above theorists have considered the ethical issues at stake in the use of reproductive technologies, literary and cultural critics of the 1980s and 1990s have examined the language and images by which reproduction is culturally constructed. Just as patriarchal medicine pathologizes the natural events of the female life cycle, so the seemingly "objective" language of medicine alienates and indeed objectifies the subjects of its enquiry. In a new twist on the analysis of reproduction as production, Emily Martin explores how medical texts employ metaphors of production to transform the body into a machine whose contractions function "efficiently" or "inefficiently." Martin then appropriates those metaphors for her own discourse, describing the acts of resistance by which women achieve the births they desire. The spread of linguistic analyses such as Martin's is accompanied by a growing critical interest in the literature that expresses women's own experiences of life in the body. For example, Delese Wear and Lois Nixon contrast medical descriptions with women's writings on reproductive experiences from menarche to menopause, while Alice Adams offers a psychoanalytic reading of images of childbirth in texts ranging from Hemingway to Atwood to feminists poets such as Toi Derricotte.

As reproductive technologies became more entrenched, and the political climate continued its move to the right, the question of the mother-fetus relationship came to the fore in the late 1980s and 1990s. Changes in technology and public discourse have, in Barbara Duden's terms, "reframed" the mother as "ecosystem" and fetus as "endangered species." The language of medicine makes the doctor the ally of the fetus, opposed to the mother, while the humanization and construction of the fetal image grants it an iconic status. Studies by a range of feminist cultural critics demonstrate how the now-pervasive visual representations of the fetus—ranging from ultrasound "snapshots" to the antiabortion *Silent Scream* to the amazing fiber-optical photos of Lennart Nillson—have not taught us to recognize the reality of the fetus; rather, we have been taught to read a fetus—indeed, a baby—into a series of often unrecognizable images. Such images, these critics argue, threaten women's reproductive freedom by promoting and perpetuating the myth of the "autonomous," innocent fetus, with rights supplanting those of the woman who houses her. This most recent criticism of a society that privileges women's reproductive capacities over their subjectivity is a unifying theme among theorists as disparate in time and ideology as Firestone and Adams, who, while arguing against "abstract dichotomies" such as "mother/fetus," nevertheless privilege the autonomy of the mother.

Naomi Yavneh

References

Adams, Alice. *Reproducing the Womb: Images of Childbirth in Science, Feminist Theory, and Literature*. Ithaca, N.Y.: Cornell University Press, 1994.

Arms, Suzanne. *Immaculate Deception II*. Berkeley, Calif.: Celestial Arts, 1994.

Atwood, Margaret. *The Handmaid's Tale*. New York: Fawcett Crest, 1985.

Corea, Genea. *The Mother Machine: Reproductive Technologies from Artificial Insemination to Artificial Wombs*. New York: Harper and Row, 1985.

Davis-Floyd, Robbie E. *Birth as an American Rite of Passage*. Berkeley and Los Angeles: University of California Press, 1992.

Duden, Barbara. *Disembodying Women: Perspectives on Pregnancy and the Unborn*. Translated by Lee Hoinacki. Cambridge, Mass., and London: Harvard University Press, 1993.

Dworkin, Andrea. *Right-wing Women*. New York: Coward-McCann, 1983.

Firestone, Shulamith. *The Dialectic of Sex*. New York: Bantam, 1970.

Martin, Emily. *The Woman in the Body: A Cultural Analysis of Reproduction*. Boston: Beacon, 1987, 1992.

O'Brien, Margaret. *The Politics of Reproduction*. Boston: Routledge and Kegan Paul, 1981.

Petchesky, Rosalind Pollack. "Fetal Images: The Power of Visual Culture in the Politics of Reproduction." In *Feminist Studies* 13 (Summer 1987): 263–292.

Raymond, Janice G. *Women as Wombs: Reproductive Technologies and the Battle over Women's Freedom*. San Francisco: Harper, 1993.

Rich, Adrienne. *Of Woman Born*. New York: W.W. Norton, 1976, 1986.

Rothman, Barbara Katz, ed. *Encyclopedia of Childbearing: Critical Perspectives*. Phoenix, Ariz.: Oryx, 1993.

Spallone, Patricia. *Beyond Conception: The New Politics of Reproduction*. Amherst, Mass.: Bergin and Garvey, 1989.

Wear, Delese, and Lois LaCivita Nixon. *Literary Anatomies: Women's Bodies and Health in Literature*. Albany, N.Y.: SUNY Press, 1994.

Revision

Often spelled as "re-vision" by feminist writers, the word derives from "revise" which means, according to *Webster's New Collegiate Dictionary*, "to look over again in order to correct and improve." When applied to literary history and literary works, such revisionary reexamination enables feminist theorists to recognize and to reveal the previously hidden and often unconscious assumptions about gender that pervade all areas of traditional literary study, a study based almost entirely on male literary experiences. This recognition and revelation, in turn, help to create new and improved versions of literary study that restore the works of female writers, critics, and theorists while actively critiquing traditional male-oriented literary paradigms.

Revisionary reading and writing have been central tenets of contemporary feminist theory since the early 1970s. "When We Dead Awaken: Writing as Re-vision," an essay by Adrienne Rich published in 1972, provided feminist theorists with a germinal concept of revision; Rich's definition of revisionary reading and writing underlies many subsequent feminist works. Calling for a "radical critique of literature, feminist in its impulse," Rich sees revision as the central action necessary for producing such a critique: "Re-vision—the act of looking back, of seeing with fresh eyes, of entering an old text from a new critical direction—is for us more than a chapter in our cultural history: it is an act of survival." The purpose of such revision is to liberate the female writer from the paralyzing effects of a male literary tradition that "negates everything she is about." Revision, for Rich as for many subsequent feminists, requires reading the work of female writers and the rejection of male-imposed standards of literature.

Many feminist critics of the late 1970s and early 1980s adopted Rich's concept of revision as a primary tenet of their own work, whether that work involved feminist critique of male-authored literature, resurrection and study of female writers, or both. In a pioneering work of feminist critique, *The Resisting Reader: A Feminist Approach to American Fiction*, Judith Fetterley uses Rich's terminology of survival, calling her book "a self-defense survival manual for the woman reader." Fetterley calls for revisionary reading, a practice that allows female readers to resist the process of "immasculation," whereby they have been taught to accept as normal and legitimate the misogynistic system of values that pervades American literature.

In 1979, in *The Madwoman in the Attic*, Sandra Gilbert and Susan Gubar use the term "revision" to describe their critical methodology in analyzing the works of nineteenth-century female writers and they apply the concept of revision to the literary practice of the women they study, as well, claiming that the female writer's "battle for self-creation involves her in a revisionary process" in which she actively seeks female precursors as literary examples and models to counteract the prevailing patriarchal notions of literary authority as a solely male prerogative.

In 1980, in her article "What Do Feminist Critics Want? A Postcard from the Volcano," Gilbert sets a revisionary agenda for all kinds of feminist criticism, calling for a "revisionary imperative" involving a process whereby feminist critics must revise one thousand years of Western culture: "We must review, reimagine, rethink, revise, and reinterpret the events and documents" that constitute that culture. As part of this overall cultural revision, Gilbert calls for rediscovery of female writers and advocates a broad revision of literary study, including a reexamination of all the "secret intersections of sexuality and textuality" that inform traditional literary studies.

In addition to describing critical methodologies, the term "revision" is frequently used by feminist critics to describe a particular kind of female literary practice. Under this usage, revision is most often seen as a literary strategy by which female writers alter traditional male literary conventions and expectations, whether overtly or covertly, consciously or unconsciously. Among contemporary female poets, for example, as described by Marge Piercy in *Early Ripening: American Women's Poetry Now,* this is a revision in which "*vis-a-vis* almost any institution or holiday or habit or idea, there is a confrontational aspect, a remaking, a renewing, a renaming, a reexperiencing and then recasting." Another kind of revisionary literary practice, called "revisionist mythmaking," in which classical and biblical myths, folktales, and fairy tales are revised by female writers in order to reveal the previously hidden female presence within male-dominated mythologies, has been carefully analyzed by a number of feminist critics, including Rachel DuPlessis and Alicia Ostriker.

Throughout its recent history, feminist literary theory has also been aware of the need for constant self-revision. In 1978, Fetterley described feminist criticism as a "growing, changing, constantly self-transforming phenomenon," and it has continued in that ever-changing mode, mainly because of a willingness to revise its own tenets. During the turbulent decade of the 1980s, mainstream academic feminist critics received challenges from many feminists who felt disenfranchised by the predominantly white, middle-class, heterosexual assumptions of feminist criticism. Black, Third-World, lesbian, working class, and other feminists challenged mainstream feminist literary theorists to examine their own assumptions about race, class, and sexuality and to revise their practice accordingly. New kinds of feminist literary theory developed, as feminists learned to embrace the diversity of their many constituencies.

This ability to undertake continual revisionary readings of itself is perhaps the most dynamic and promising aspect of feminist literary theory today. Isobel Armstrong, in *New Feminist Discourses,* characterizes current feminist literary theory by its revisionary core, saying, "It is in the very nature of feminist thought to disinvest customary orderings of their unity and authority by transforming them." Revision—of every aspect of literary study, including itself—is the very heart of feminist literary practice.

Hollis Seamon

References

Armstrong, Isobel, ed. *New Feminist Dis-*

courses: *Critical Essays on Theories and Texts.* New York: Routledge, 1992.

DuPlessis, Rachel. *Writing beyond the Ending.* Bloomington: Indiana University Press, 1984.

Ezell, Margaret. *Writing Women's Literary History.* Baltimore, Md.: Johns Hopkins University Press, 1993.

Fetterley, Judith. *The Resisting Reader: A Feminist Approach to American Fiction.* Bloomington: Indiana University Press, 1978.

Gilbert, Sandra. "What Do Feminist Critics Want? A Postcard from the Volcano." In *The New Feminist Criticism,* edited by Elaine Showalter, 29–45. New York: Pantheon, 1985.

———, and Susan Gubar. *The Madwoman in the Attic.* New Haven, Conn.: Yale University Press, 1979.

Ostriker, Alicia. "The Thieves of Language: Woman Poets and Revisionist Mythmaking." In *The New Feminist Criticism,* edited by Elaine Showalter, 314–338. New York: Pantheon, 1985.

Piercy, Marge, ed. *Early Ripening: American Women's Poetry Now.* London: Pandora, 1987.

Rich, Adrienne. "When We Dead Awaken: Writing as Re-vision." In *On Lies, Secrets, and Silence: Selected Prose, 1966–1978.* New York: W.W. Norton, 1979.

Rhetoric

Although "rhetoric" is frequently used in literary criticism to refer to narrative strategies or to an ideologically significant vocabulary, its historical reference is to a discipline seeking to regulate all aspects of communication, from bodily movement or "delivery" to figurative language or "elocution." Literary critics have been interested in rhetoric mainly from a historical perspective, tracing the influence of prescriptions made in rhetorical treatises on literary style. However, as these prescriptions are imbued with ideological assumptions often (though not exclusively) concerning women, analyzing the discourse of rhetoric is of importance to feminist literary theory. Feminist theorists have begun to be interested in rhetorical treatises as cultural sites for the imbrication of misogynist ideology and language, and have been showing how these treatises weave derogatory notions of female sexuality and conduct into components of communication, from gestures and intonations to the smallest units of linguistic form.

Although not specifically feminist, the work of Michel Foucault on "The Discourse on Language" is crucial for understanding rhetoric as a cultural institution complicit in the marginalization of the feminine. Debunking the conventional notion of rhetoric as motivated by a veneration of language, Foucault pointed out that rhetoric involved "taboos . . . and limits" whose purpose is to relieve language "of its most uncontrollable elements"—those linked with "desire and power." This definition of rhetoric implies that it is designed to "disarmed heterosexuality and pacify politics" at large, and it opens up for feminist theorists an important question: how it was deployed to disarm specifically female sexuality and to pacify potential political insurrections of women?

In 1981, this question was addressed at the margins of Naomi Schor's article on "Female Paranoia," where Schor suggested that the figure of synecdoche, which the rhetorical tradition had constructed as a detail representing a whole, was thus culturally coextensive with the clitoris as understood by psychoanalytic theory. It is the rhetorical tradition's association of synecdoche with an aspect of female sexuality depreciated by psychoanalysis, Schor suggested, that underlies its marginalization in or omission from influential metalinguistic theories of the twentieth century, such those of Jakobson and Lacan (which focus on metonymy).

It was not until 1987, however, that full-scale studies devoted to the interface between rhetorical theory and gender politics began to be published. Barbara Johnson's *A World of Difference,* aiming throughout to demonstrate that "political issues can be structured like, and by the contours of figurative language," includes an essay on "Apostrophe, Animation and Abortion," which argues that the figure of apostrophe, associated by rhetorical treatises with "language's ability to give life and human form to something dead or inanimate," is thus linked with medical and legal questions concerning gestation and abortion. In literature, this link is manifest not only in the poems cited by Johnson, where thematic concerns with pregnancy are structured "by something akin to apostrophe," but also in a book such as Oriana Fallaci's "Letter to a Child Never Born," where apostrophe itself is the organizing form of a narrative documenting the generation and loss of a fetus.

Also published in 1987, Patricia Parker's *Literary Fat Ladies: Rhetoric, Gender, Property,* which combines a feminist focus with New Historicist methodologies, provides groundbreaking insights concerning the misogynist assumptions underwriting the discourse of rhetorical treatises, especially in the Renaissance. Parker shows that Renaissance rhetoric was gynophobic not only in excluding women from its study, but also in attaching stereotypes of the feminine to its berated categories. Thus, discursive "copia" or "dilation" is associated with misogynistically construed aspects of female sexuality: both with the pregnant female body, necessary for the perpetuation of patriarchy, and with unbridled licentiousness, which patriarchy seeks to control. "Disposition," the second of the five parts of classical rhetoric, concerned with the organization of an argument, has affinities with the gynecological conception of the male's role in generation as "disposing" or shaping the otherwise uncontrollable female body. "Katachresis," the "far-fetched" or extreme metaphor, perjoratively distinguished by rhetorical treatises as "abuse" "from the 'shamefast' and 'maydenly' way that metaphor should by contrast behave," is thus gendered as a transgressive female, analogous to Shakespeare's "unruly and undomesticated 'Kate.'"

Analyzing the definitions of these and other rhetorical categories, such as "paralepsis," constructed as an "incivill dame," or "metalepsis," described as a woman "carried away" with emotion, Parker has mapped the course for a feminist inquiry into the hidden misogynist agenda at work in the ostensibly neutral discourse on the art of speech. It is important to continue this course, and especially to scrutinize definitions of figures of speech devalued on account of their imaginary association with female sexuality, such as temporal inversion, dubbed "hysterologia" (womb-speech) and described as a threat to linguistic decorum, or simile, whose construction as a "less attractive" metaphor in Aristotle's *Rhetoric* is parallel to Aristotle's influential definition of the female as a botched male.

Such figures of speech become not only potential vehicles for, but also manifestations of, misogynist ideology, which they carry into the texts where they are deployed. Consequently, another question of interest to feminist theory is the significance of the use of rhetorical forms gendered as feminine in literary texts, whether or not thematically focused on gender. For example, what are the implications of the use of hysterologia to structure the plot of detective fiction for the gender ideology of this genre? What does it mean for a woman writer like Virginia Woolf to appropriate figures of speech that had been devalued by the rhetorical tradition? In addressing these issues through the examination of definitions of figures of speech and other components of communication not as descriptive statements but as expressions of cultural anxieties concerning femininity, feminist theory continues to gain insight into how rhetoric has been implicated in the dissemination of misogyny and the marginalization of women in Western culture.

Shirley Sharon-Zisser

References

Foucault, Michel. "The Discourse on Language." In *The Archaeology of Knowledge and the Discourse on Language,* translated by A.M Sheridan Smith, 215–237. New York: Pantheon, 1972.

Jarrat, Susan C., ed. *Feminist Rereadings in the History of Rhetoric. Rhetoric Society Quarterly* 22 (1992).

Johnson, Barbara. *A World of Difference.* Baltimore, Md.: Johns Hopkins University Press, 1987.

Ong, Walter J. *Rhetoric, Romance and Technology: Studies in the Interaction of Expression and Culture.* Ithaca, N.Y.: Cornell University Press, 1971.

Parker, Patricia. *Literary Fat Ladies: Rhetoric, Gender, Property.* London: Methuen, 1987.

Schor, Naomi. "Female Paranoia: The Case for Psychoanalytic Feminist Criticism." *Yale French Studies* 62 (1981): 204–219.

Sharon-Zisser, Shirley. "Undoing the Tyranous Advantage: Renaissance Rhetoric and the Subduing of Female Power." *Women's Studies* 24 (1994): 247–271.

Sutton, Jane. "Unconscious Assumptions in the Method of Rhetoric." Paper presented at the ninth biennial conference of the International Society for the History of Rhetoric, Turin, July 20–24, 1993.

Vickers, Nancy. "Diana Described: Scattered Woman and Scattered Rhyme." *Critical Inquiry* 8 (1981): 265–279.

Rich, Adrienne

As the American women's movement of the late

1960s progressed, feminist literary criticism focused on the surge of contemporary literature by women. Women writers struggled to articulate their own unique experience. Rich is primarily known for her poetry, in which she seeks to discover language capable of representing women's experience. Her poetry concentrates on themes and issues rising directly from her own experience, to examine sexual politics, power, and the power of language to transform that experience through re-vision. Rich's poetry moved from her negative analysis of women's power in a patriarchal culture with, for example, her early poem "Aunt Jennifer's Tigers," to the female-identified, gynocentric vision of *Dream of a Common Language* in 1978. The scope of Rich's poetic vision chronicles her individual experience as a source and resource to employ the scars received from male-dominated institutions to understand the origins and results of female oppression. In 1993, with the publication of *Adrienne Rich's Poetry and Prose*, Barbara Gelpi and Albert Gelpi note that Rich's ability to use this intense method of scrutiny and self-healing in her writings "has also been her central, but by no means her single, contribution to the methodology at the core of all feminist theorizing."

In both her prose and poetry, Rich explored the connections to other women writers, tracing a female literary tradition. Rich's classic essay "When We Dead Awaken: Writing as Re-Vision" proposes a revision, a new way of viewing text contrary to traditional literary analysis. This feminist reading theory reorders the text from the perspective that readers can view "how the very act of naming has been till now a male prerogative, and how we can begin to see and name—and therefore live—afresh." Rich's revision sought literary mothers and sisters in past women's writings. This feminist approach to reading resulted in the collection *On Lies, Secrets, and Silence*. These critical essays provide new insights to women writers such as Emily Dickinson, Anne Bradstreet, and Charlotte Brontë, as well as crystallizing the issues developed in Rich's own poetry.

The landmark work *Of Women Born: Motherhood as Experience and Institution* combines Rich's experience as a mother and daughter with a historical, cross-cultural analysis of motherhood. She identifies the ways in which the institution of motherhood has dominated women and limited their potential. Her vision of a new motherhood emerges, a motherhood filled with potential for all women and free of patriarchal control. Rich posits the possibility to reclaim female power based on the biological power of the mother. She employs this female critique in the further development of her gynocentric theory. *Of Women Born* also applies these insights in an analysis of female relationships in several literary works by women.

Rich identifies the concept of a "lesbian continuum to include a range—through each woman's life and throughout history—of woman-identified experience" in "Compulsory Heterosexuality and Lesbian Existence." The concept of lesbianism expands to "embrace many more forms of primary intensity between and among women." Rich's term "lesbian existence" signifies the historical existence of lesbians and the evolving nature of that term. Rich asserts a primal connection between women that seeks to include all types of female bonding. This essay sparked debate among feminist theorists. The appropriation of black women's writing to the lesbian continuum is problematic because it may not allow sufficient room for cultural differences. Further questions arise concerning whether this theory allowed for clear lesbian identification or even differences within lesbianism itself.

Rich continues to explore themes of power, ethics, and personal identity as they relate to her revision of women and their sociohistorical reality. She created a feminist poetics to embody women's experience and redefine reality according to a female aesthetic. The significance of Rich's work makes her an important reference point for feminist literary theory.

Mary A. Danahey

References

Cooper, Jane Roberta, ed. *Reading Adrienne Rich: Reviews and Re-visions, 1951–81*. Ann Arbor: University of Michigan Press, 1984.

Diaz-Diocaretz, Myriam. *Translating Poetic Discourse: Questions on Poetic Strategies in Adrienne Rich*. Philadelphia: John Benjamins, 1985.

Keyes, Claire. *The Aesthetics of Power: The Poetry of Adrienne Rich*. Athens: University of Georgia Press, 1986.

Martin, Wendy. *An American Triptych: Anne Bradstreet, Emily Dickinson, Adrienne Rich*. Chapel Hill: University of North Carolina Press, 1984.

Rich, Adrienne. *Adrienne Rich's Poetry and*

Prose. Edited by Barbara Gelpi and Albert Gelpi. New York: W.W. Norton, 1993.

———. *Adrienne Rich's Poetry and Prose: Selected Bibliography*. Edited by Barbara Gelpi and Albert Gelpi. New York: W.W. Norton, 1993.

———. *Blood, Bread, and Poetry*. New York: W.W. Norton, 1986.

———. *A Change of World*. New Haven, Conn.: Yale University Press, 1951.

———. "Compulsory Heterosexuality and Lesbian Existence." *Signs: Journal of Women in Culture and Society* 5 (1980): 631–660.

———. *The Diamond Cutters and Other Poems*. New York: Harper, 1955.

———. *Diving into the Wreck*. New York: W.W. Norton, 1973.

———. *The Dream of a Common Language*. New York: W.W. Norton, 1978.

———. *Leaflets*. New York: W.W. Norton, 1966.

———. *Necessities of Life*. New York: W.W. Norton, 1966.

———. *Of Woman Born: Motherhood as Experience and Institution*. New York: W.W. Norton, 1976.

———. *On Lies, Secrets, and Silence: Selected Prose, 1966–1978*. New York: W.W. Norton, 1979.

———. *Snapshots of a Daughter-in-Law*. New York: Harper and Row, 1963.

———. *Time's Power*. New York: W.W. Norton, 1989.

———. *Twenty-one Love Poems*. Emeryville, Calif.: Effie's, 1976.

———. *A Wild Patience Has Taken Me This Far*. New York: W.W. Norton, 1981.

———. *Your Native Land, Your Life*. New York: W.W. Norton, 1986.

Riviere, Joan

A translator of Freud's works, and herself a psychoanalyst, Riviere's main contribution to feminist theory is her 1929 essay on womanliness as masquerade. In this documentation of her analysis of a strong, successful, therefore "masculine" female subject, Riviere recounts how her subject adopted what Riviere identified as "feminine" behavior. Immediately after Riviere's female subject had given public lectures, an activity associated at that time with men, she underwent a period of flirtation and coquettishness. This seemed to Riviere to be behavior designed to counteract her violation of established behavioral norms for the sexes. In effect, her subject donned a "mask" of femininity to divert attention from her usual "masculinity."

Feminist theorists have more recently used Riviere's work as evidence that femininity and masculinity must be considered socially constructed and mutable, as opposed to essential and fixed categories. The concept of the masquerade has also been employed in feminist film theory to articulate the complex identificatory or distancing processes the female spectator undergoes as she confronts her own image on the cinema screen.

Jenifer K. Ward

References

Doane, Mary Ann. "Film and the Masquerade: Theorizing the Female Spectator." *Screen* 23 (1982): 74–87.

Heath, Stephen. "Joan Riviere and the Masquerade." In *Formations of Fantasy*, edited by Victor Burgin, James Donald, and Cora Kaplan, 45–61. London and New York: Methuen, 1986.

Riviere, Joan. "Womanliness as a Masquerade." In *Formations of Fantasy*, edited by Victor Burgin, James Donald, and Cora Kaplan, 35–44. London and New York: Methuen, 1986.

Romance

Though now often synonymous with Harlequins, bodice rippers, and the novels of Danielle Steel, romance has a record of diverse use as a literary term referring to distinguishable genres, as well as to an ideological position and style opposed to realism. Its origins lie some eight centuries ago, during the medieval period, when it was a genre of literature written in the vernacular (that is, a language derived from the Romans' Latin) and was characterized by its representation of a chivalric age in which knights undertook fantastic adventures in order to win a lady's favor. Nonetheless, romance as a genre is paradoxically associated with women writers and readers as a phenomenon largely of this century. Derogated for this association with women, it has been criticized for its formulaic sameness by those unfamiliar with the differences to be expected from a large body of literature written by women and men from at least three continents and published by various companies with diverse writing guidelines. The romance novel today is divided into such subgenres as the Gothic, the Regency, the family saga, and the short contemporary romance, to name but a few.

The least common denominator of the romance genre has come to be its focus on the romantic relation between a woman and a man (although lesbian romances are available), usually—but not always and not always exclusively—written from the woman's point of view. This woman may be young and virginal or not, a point connected with when the work was published, by which publisher, and in what subgenre it belongs, as well as what audience it addresses. The romance also generally has a happy ending. Distinctions among subgenres often depend on setting and time period. Some authors are associated with only one subgenre—Georgette Heyer, for example, is credited with creating the Regency romance—while others write various types, sometimes employing different pseudonyms.

Some scholars argue that romances appear in ancient Greek literature. The title of Clara Reeve's *The Progress of Romance through Times, Countries, and Manners with Remarks on the Good and Bad Effects of It, on Them Respectively,* written in 1785, suggests the work's intent to present the history and nature of romance in order to evaluate it. To some extent, Reeve, herself a romance writer, was reacting to the novel's growing dominance. The conflict between the two forms rests on the degree of realism present in characters, setting, and action, a distinction Hawthorne notably expresses in his 1851 preface to *The House of the Seven Gables*. While Hawthorne himself wrote romances, he also condemned those "damned scribbling women," domestic sentimentalists such as Susan Warner, Charlotte M. Yonge, and E.D.E.N. Southworth, with whom he competed unsuccessfully for popular and financial success.

The criticism of both romances and novels harks back to Plato's condemnation of the arts generally for placing false, illusory, but enchanting worlds before us. Feminists from Wollstonecraft on have objected to romance as purveying escapist fantasies that distract women from acting to change their real circumstances. Contemporary feminist critics like Ann Snitow and Joanna Russ have objected to or ridiculed the romance's emphasis on clothing and food, and its almost excessive concern with the minutest

details of the heroine's subjective experience. Reading these works as sympathetic to the patriarchal status quo, they criticize romances as pornographic, escapist, and badly written. More positively, Tania Modleski, Janice Radway, Mariam Darce Frenier, and others see romances as reflecting and expressing contemporary women's experience, especially their fears of the violence and uncertainties that surround them. Most positively, Carol Thurston argues that the erotic romances that followed the publication of Kathleen Woodiwiss's *The Flame and the Flower* in 1972 express, in response to reader demand, a feminist sensibility by presenting stronger female and more sensitive male protagonists. Feminist students of popular culture have celebrated romances as manifestations of a thriving female subculture, a point the professional organization Romance Writers of America (founded in 1981) makes in the many references to sisterhood that appear in its own literature and that of its regional affiliates.

Romance is not the first genre to address a female audience. Eighteenth-century conduct books containing practically useful information and morally uplifting sentiments were also directed at women; it is not surprising that characteristics of these two genres should appear in works by the same author: a late example is Emily Post who, before her etiquette guide established her as an authority on that subject, wrote novels such as *The Title Market,* dealing with heroines whose fate could be determined by their ability to behave properly according to the code governing their social circle. The many novels of Grace Livingston Hill, usually falling into the "inspirational romance" subgenre, often deal more with religious or social duty than with romantic conflict and its resolution.

While individual authors like Daphne du Maurier and Heyer were successful in the first half of this century, the overwhelming response to Victoria Holt's hardback *Gothic Mistress of Mellyn* in 1961 signaled the beginning of a general romance boom. In the 1970s trade publications proclaimed that publishing romances was equivalent to printing money, and for twenty years romances have represented about 40 percent of the paperback market. Harlequin Enterprises, a Canadian business that entered the romance market in 1949 with paperback reprints of Mills's and Boon's English originals, saw sudden sales growth in the 1970s after employing mass marketing techniques adapted from those used to sell soap products. In 1976

Harlequin published its first novel by a U.S. author, Janet Dailey's *No Quarter Asked*. Since then Dailey's success includes the regular appearance of her works on the *New York Times* best-seller list.

Acknowledgment as a best-seller, however, does not guarantee respect as an author. Even as scholarly work on women's romance novels increases, aesthetic prejudices against the romance novels and negative stereotypes of romance readers continue to exist. Although these books are accepted now as of interest to sociology, cultural studies, and women's studies, the literary status of these romance novels remains contested.

Harriet E. Margolis

References

Fallon, Eileen. *Words of Love: A Complete Guide to Romance Fiction*. New York: Garland, 1984.

Frenier, Mariam Darce. *Good-bye Heathcliff: Changing Heroes, Heroines, Roles and Values in Women's Category Romances*. New York: Greenwood, 1988.

Henderson, Lesley, ed. *Twentieth-century Romance and Historical Writers*. Chicago: St. James, 1990.

Jensen, Margaret. *Love's Sweet Return: The Harlequin Story*. Bowling Green, Ohio: Bowling Green State University Press, 1984.

Modleski, Tania. *Loving with a Vengeance: Mass-produced Fantasies for Women*. New York: Methuen, 1984.

Mussell, Kay. *Fantasy and Reconciliation: Contemporary Formulas of Women's Romance Fiction*. Westport, Conn.: Greenwood, 1984.

Radway, Janice A. *Reading the Romance: Women, Patriarchy, and Popular Literature*. 2nd ed. Chapel Hill: University of North Carolina Press, 1991.

Ramsdell, Kristin. *Happily Ever After: A Guide to Reading Interests in Romance Fiction*. Littleton, Colo.: Libraries Unlimited, 1987.

Russ, Joanna. "Somebody's Trying to Kill Me and I Think It's My Husband: The Modern Gothic." *Journal of Popular Culture* 6 (1973): 666–691.

Snitow, Ann. "Mass Market Romance: Pornography for Women Is Different." In *Powers of Desire: The Politics of Sexuality*, edited by Ann Snitow, Christine Stansell, and Sharon Thompson, 245–263. New York: Monthly Review, 1983.

Thurston, Carol. *The Romance Revolution: Erotic Novels for Women and the Quest for a New Sexual Identity*. Urbana: University of Illinois Press, 1987.

Romanticism

The status of Romanticism within feminist studies is markedly ambivalent. In part because the British Romantic canon was long dominated by a handful of male poets, Romanticism has been seen as a fundamentally masculine tradition in which women are objectified, silenced, and equated with a mute Nature. Other critics, noting longstanding associations between Romanticism and attributes conventionally coded as feminine—feeling, intuition, sympathy, empathy—argue that the canonical Romantic writers appropriate allegedly feminine qualities and characteristics, viewing Romanticism as a feminized tradition although dominated by men. Still others have posited partial analogies between Romanticism and feminism as revolutionary movements that value community, validate feeling, and underscore the destabilizing operations of desire and the unconscious in their understandings of subjectivity.

The notion of Romanticism as a "masculine tradition" inhospitable to women writers is developed by Margaret Homans in her influential study *Women Writers and Poetic Identity*. Homans argues that the figure of the poet and the speaking voice are coded as male throughout Romantic poetry, and such key Romantic values as vision, transcendence, and the "strong self" are in effect male prerogatives. Women within Romanticism are doubly objectified, as objects of the masculine poet's desire closely associated with Nature. The strong (male) Romantic subject asserts itself through dominating or internalizing otherness, typically identified as feminine. The woman writer remains alien to this tradition, writing out of her very difficulties with its governing terms. In subsequent work, Homans, drawing critically upon Lacan, finds Wordsworth's Romantic myth of language acquisition to be normative for Western culture. The (male) subject's acquisition of language demands the death or rejection of the mother, thereafter identified with the "literal" (or absent referent). For women, who maintain (as Nancy Chodorow argues) an identification with the mother, symbolic or figurative language remains problematic. Women are relegated to, and can most readily adapt, what Homans calls "literal language," a vague concept variously identified with the referent "outside language," with the child's "presymbolic language," and with a writing style that is "as literal as possible."

Susan Levin and Meena Alexander also view Romanticism as a masculine movement alien to the concerns and practices of women writers. For Levin, drawing on such "difference" or "self-in-relation" feminists as Chodorow and Gilligan, the woman writer chooses community, relational bonds, domesticity, and an "equipoise of self and the phenomenal world" over the assertive subjectivity of the (male) Romantic. Similarly for Alexander, Romantic-era women writers write from quotidian experience, an ethic of nurturing, and a knowledge rooted in the body, eschewing the symbolic, visionary mode and heightened self-consciousness of their male contemporaries. Yet Alexander also acknowledges that the canonical male Romantics valorized feeling and empathy, implicitly validating "femininity and the functions previously reserved for women," despite the objectification of women and feminine figures in their works. This point is made more centrally by Alan Richardson, who argues that male Romantic writers "colonize" perceived feminine characteristics and modes, wishfully absorbing the feminine through such means as infantile fantasies of introjecting the mother and myths of androgynous fusion, in an essay included by Anne Mellor in *Romanticism and Feminism*. Similar arguments have since been worked out more fully in relation to Lacanian and other psychoanalytic models by Diane Long Hoeveler and by Barbara Charlesworth Gelpi, who provides crucial historical context in an extended discussion of the "maternal ideology" developed prior to and during the Romantic era.

Sonia Hofkosh, Karen Swann, and Marlon Ross also contributed key essays to *Romanticism and Feminism*. Hofkosh outlines an exemplary historicist account of the male Romantic writer's anxious implication in a literary field increasingly dominated by female writers and readers, showing in particular how Byron's self-image, literary relations, and ambivalence toward the economics of publishing were all manifestly inflected by gender concerns. Influenced by feminist appropriations of Lacan, Swann finds comparable anxieties at work in Keats, yet asks whether such anxieties may not be productive, facilitating the male protagonist's (and poet's) entrance into a masculine symbolic regime. Ross's essay makes part of his major study *The Contours of Masculine Desire*, which places canonical Romanticism in the context of a feminized literary marketplace and the rise of a women's poetic tradition. Like Homans, Ross sees Romanticism as primarily masculine, characterized by literary rivalry, a doomed will to autonomy ("self-possessing individuation"), and a compulsion to mastery over nature; woman figures chiefly as the Romantic poet's internalized object or "anchor of desire." And yet the very aggressivity of Romanticism arises as a defensive reaction to the feminization of the literary profession and the considerable market successes of Felicia Hemans, Letitia E. Landon, and others. Against Romanticism, Ross sets the development of a distinct feminine poetic tradition leading from eighteenth-century bluestockings to "affectional" poets like Hemans and Landon, who write from within a domestic ideology that they at once endorse and refashion.

In addition to these psychoanalytically and sociohistorically inflected accounts, feminist readings of Romanticism have been produced that attend more closely to linguistic and philosophical issues, notably by Mary Jacobus and Julie Ellison. In an early essay on *Villette*, Jacobus poses analogies between Romanticism and feminism as revolutionary impulses "buried" within Victorian culture, noting, however, the Romantic tendency to equate the feminine with the irrational. Her more recent essays on sexual difference in Wordsworth's *Prelude*, drawing on deconstructive theory, demonstrate how conflicts or impasses in Romantic representations of femininity signal impasses in the very workings of representation. Ellison, studying interrelations of gender, hermeneutics, and ethics in Romantic texts, sees Romanticism as marked by ambivalence toward the feminine yet as sharing certain affinities with feminism, including a respect for the cognitive validity of feeling, an anxiety regarding violence, and critiques of authority and of the stable subject.

Much important work remains to be done in relation to the recovery of Romantic-era poetry by women: how might this considerable body of texts be theorized, and to what extent will its recuperation further problematize theories of Romanticism? Building on the work of Ross and others, Anne Mellor raises these issues in *Romanticism and Gender,* which in addition touches on a broad range of texts by women too often disregarded in studies of Romanticism: the conduct book and domestic novel, journals and other autobiographical forms, the Gothic, the feminist writings of Wollstonecraft and Hays, children's books and "popular" fiction. Although flawed by its tacit shifting among conflicting theoretical positions and by its admittedly "crude" dichotomies, this study, in its scope and in the questions it poses, suggests a productive new basis for feminist studies of Romanticism. Whether Romanticism will come to be regarded as merely one historical tendency (masculine or not) among several or be dismissed altogether as a misleading and anachronistic term remains to be seen.

Alan Richardson

References

Alexander, Meena. *Women in Romanticism: Mary Wollstonecraft, Dorothy Wordsworth and Mary Shelley*. London: Macmillan, 1989.

Ellison, Julie. *Delicate Subjects: Romanticism, Gender, and the Ethics of Understanding*. Ithaca, N.Y.: Cornell University Press, 1990.

Gelpi, Barbara Charlesworth. *Shelley's Goddess: Maternity, Language, Subjectivity*. Oxford: Oxford University Press, 1992.

Hoeveler, Diane Long. *Romantic Androgyny: The Women Within*. University Park: Pennsylvania State University Press, 1990.

Homans, Margaret. *Bearing the Word: Language and Female Experience in Nineteenth-Century Women's Writing*. Chicago: University of Chicago Press, 1986.

———. *Women Writers and Poetic Identity: Dorothy Wordsworth, Emily Brontë, and Emily Dickinson*. Princeton: Princeton University Press, 1980.

Jacobus, Mary. *Reading Woman: Essays in Feminist Criticism*. New York: Columbia University Press, 1986.

———. *Romanticism, Writing, and Sexual Difference: Essays on the Prelude*. Oxford: Clarendon, 1989.

Levin, Susan. *Dorothy Wordsworth and Romanticism*. New Brunswick, N.J.: Rutgers University Press, 1987.

Mellor, Anne K. *Romanticism and Gender*. New York: Routledge, 1993.

———, ed. *Romanticism and Feminism*. Bloomington: Indiana University Press, 1988.

Ross, Marlon B. *The Contours of Masculine Desire: Romanticism and the Rise of Women's Poetry*. New York: Oxford University Press, 1989.

R

Rose, Jacqueline

In works addressing the complex relation of psychoanalysis, politics, and feminism, Jacqueline Rose argues for a feminist discourse that accommodates the language of fantasy, desire, and sexuality. Rose takes issue with feminist accounts of psychoanalysis that understand psychic life as the unmediated effect of social reality. Such accounts, Rose asserts, ignore the concept of the unconscious—that is, the notion of a "divided and disordered subjectivity." While acknowledging the phallocentrism of Freudian and Lacanian psychoanalysis, Rose nonetheless applauds psychoanalysis for bringing difficult questions of female (and male) subjectivity into the political arena. Rose refutes the notion that a discussion of women's unconscious fantasies necessarily denies the reality of female victimization and oppression.

Rose's first book offers readers a lucid introduction to the complexities of Lacanian thought. Co-edited with Juliet Mitchell, *Feminine Sexuality: Jacques Lacan and the école freudienne* includes Rose's translations of papers by Lacan and members of his school of psychoanalysis on the question of female sexuality. Two essays, one by Mitchell on the history of the debate in the 1920s and 1930s surrounding Freud's theories of femininity, and one by Rose on Lacan's place within that debate, compose the two-part introduction to the works that follow. In particular, Rose's exposition of several fundamental aspects of Lacanian psychoanalysis provides readers with an exceptionally helpful supplement to his work.

Sexuality in the Field of Vision collects ten of Rose's most important papers on feminism and psychoanalysis. Part one, entitled "Femininity and Representation," includes, among other essays, studies of George Eliot, *Hamlet*, and Julia Kristeva. Part two, entitled "The Field of Vision," includes works that consider the intersection of feminism, Lacanian psychoanalysis, and film theory.

It is Rose's commitment to a feminist discourse in which politics and fantasy might coexist that inspired her recent literary critical study of the writings of Sylvia Plath. Informed by the poststructuralist theories of Lacan, Jacques Derrida, and Julia Kristeva, Rose's book *The Haunting of Sylvia Plath* considers negative or violent aspects of Plath's writing while resisting "turning them against her." Celebrating the play of voices within Plath's texts, Rose emphasizes the need for a similar heterogeneity within feminism.

Davida Pines

References

Payne, Michael, and Maire Jaanus. "An Interview with Jacqueline Rose." In *Why War? Psychoanalysis, Politics, and the Return to Melanie Klein.* In *The Bucknell Lectures in Literary Theory,* edited by Michael Payne and Harold Schweizer, 231–255. Oxford: Blackwell, 1993.

Rose, Jacqueline. *The Case of Peter Pan or the Impossibility of Children's Fiction.* London: Macmillan, 1984; Rev. ed. Philadelphia: University of Pennsylvania Press, 1992.

———. *The Haunting of Sylvia Plath.* London: Virago, 1991. Cambridge: Harvard University Press, 1992.

———. *Sexuality in the Field of Vision.* London: Verso, 1986.

———, and Juliet Mitchell, eds. *Feminine Sexuality: Jacques Lacan and the école freudienne.* London: Macmillan, 1982.

Weyant, Nancy. "Jacqueline Rose: A Bibliography, 1974–1992." In *Why War? Psychoanalysis, Politics, and the Return to Melanie Klein.* In *The Bucknell Lectures in Literary Theory,* edited by Michael Payne and Harold Schweizer, 256–261. Oxford: Blackwell, 1993.

Rowbotham, Sheila

Rowbotham made her mark as an English Marxist and feminist. Rowbotham brought to feminist theory the crucial concept that gender issues are inextricably linked to class issues. Beginning in the early 1970s, she published several works with the goal of bringing women into history and analyzing women's history from a Marxist perspective. For example, she explained how female reformers lobbied for equality within their respective economic situations; whether it be middle-class women fighting against male dominance or working-class women fighting against appalling factory conditions, both groups struggled for economic autonomy within distinct economic contexts.

In her 1972 work *Women, Resistance and Revolution,* Rowbotham argued that women will become liberated only when the masses are liberated, a revolution brought about by a militant feminist movement. Rowbotham's *Hidden from History,* published in 1973, presented a history of women in England from the beginnings of the modern era through the 1930s, showing both how historical changes affected women and how women affected historical change. She presented women as historical agents, and included the lives of both working-class and middle-class women in her discussion. Her most recent work, published in 1989, traces the history of the modern feminist movement in Britain from the 1960s to the 1980s. Rather than looking at books, she looks at leaflets, magazines, letters and internal papers in order to try to gain unique insights into the movement.

Rowbotham's most important contribution to feminist theory to date is her insistence on contextual gender analysis, specifically regarding class, which ushered in an era of more sophisticated examinations of gender where feminist historians began to analyze gender with sensitivity not only to class but ethnicity, sexuality, and other significant differences as well.

Gina Hames

References

Rowbotham, Sheila. *Dreams and Dilemmas: Collected Writings.* London: Virago, 1983.

———. *Hidden from History: 300 Years of Women's Oppression and the Fight against It.* London: Pluto, 1973.

———. *The Past Is before Us: Feminism in Action since the 1960s.* London: Pandora, 1989.

———. *Women, Resistance and Revolution: A History of Women and Revolution in the Modern World.* New York: Pantheon, 1972.

Rubin, Gayle

An anthropologist by training, Gayle Rubin is a central voice in feminist theorizing on gender, sexuality, and their interconnections. Perhaps her best-known work is "The Traffic in Women," in which she takes on Karl Marx, Friedrich Engels, Claude Lévi-Strauss, Sigmund Freud, and Jacques Lacan in order to analyze the origins and processes of the oppression of women. In this article, Rubin proposes the concept of the "sex/

gender system," which she defines as "the set of arrangements by which a society transforms biological sexuality into products of human activity, and in which these transformed sexual needs are satisfied"—that is, the social and cultural practices through which human infants, female and male, become gendered beings, women and men. Rubin analyzes and deconstructs such concepts and practices as the incest taboo, the exchange of women, the Oedipal complex, and the sexual division of labor. Lévi-Strauss and Freud posit these constructs as essentially constitutive of culture; Rubin asserts that they are constitutive only of a particular kind of culture in which men dominate, a dichotomous, complementary gender system is enforced, and heterosexuality is compulsory.

Her next major article, "Thinking Sex," in contrast to "Traffic in Women," argues for a conceptual separation of sexuality and gender as distinct, though often interactive, aspects of identity and social organization. Rubin's newer work focuses on more nuanced understandings of genders as complex sets of social and cultural signs that individuals employ to signal their personal styles, erotic desires, senses of identity, political stances. "Of Catamites and Kings," for example, discusses lesbian genders and transsexualism.

Rubin has also been an important voice in the feminist "sex debates," arguing against the antipornography movement and for tolerance of and legal freedoms for sexual minorities such as sado-masochists, prostitutes, transsexuals, and child-lovers. She makes a distinction in "Thinking Sex" between these kinds of sexual practices in and of themselves and sexual practices that involve harm and coercion, which she points out can occur in any form of sexual practice.

Diana L. Swanson

References

Rubin, Gayle. "Of Catamites and Kings: Reflections on Butch, Gender, and Boundaries." In *The Persistent Desire: A Femme-Butch Reader,* edited by Joan Nestle, 466–482. Boston: Alyson, 1992.
———. "The Leather Menace: Comments on Politics and S/M." In *Coming to Power: Writings and Graphics on Lesbian S/M,* edited by Samois, 192–227. Boston: Alyson, 1982.
———. "Misguided, Dangerous, and Wrong: An Analysis of Antipornography Politics." In *Bad Girls and Dirty Pictures:*

The Challenge to Reclaim Feminism, edited by Allison Assiter and Avedon Carol, 18–40. London: Pluto, 1993.
———. "Thinking Sex: Notes for a Radical Theory of the Politics of Sexuality." In *Pleasure and Danger: Exploring Female Sexuality,* edited by Carole S. Vance, 267–319. New York: Routledge and Kegan Paul, 1984.
———. "The Traffic in Women: Notes on the Political Economy of Sex." In *Toward an Anthropology of Women,* edited by Rayna Reiter, 157–210. New York: Monthly Review, 1975.

Russ, Joanna

Russ is best known for her critical work *How to Suppress Women's Writing* and her science-fiction antinarrative *The Female Man.* Her critical work celebrates the visionary nature and flexibility of science fiction, which, she argues in "What Can a Heroine Do?" give women writing in the genre the freedom to experiment with forms and literary myths that legitimize female culture. The lyric structure of *The Female Man,* for example, disrupts traditional notions of linear plot development by blurring the perspectives of the four time-traveling female protagonists. As the title suggests, this frequently satiric work resists defining women's experience in terms of male experience. In *How to Suppress Women's Writing,* Russ exposes the "premature burial" of women's writing by patriarchal culture. She argues that a female literary tradition has been concealed and denigrated by "suppressing context," the separation of writing from experience, the personal from the political, private from public, and women from their own tradition. Recovering this tradition, Russ predicts, will require a paradigmatic shift in the way texts are evaluated.

In addition to her success in science fiction, a genre written primarily by and for men, Russ's work is important for feminist theorists for two reasons: first, she reveals how women's writing is excluded from the literary canon; and second, she offers empowering strategies for reevaluating literature.

Mary Thompson

References

Russ, Joanna. *The Female Man.* New York: Bantam, 1975.
———. *How to Suppress Women's Writing.*

S

Sappho

Celebrated by Plato as the "Tenth Muse" and by both her contemporaries and succeeding commentators as "the Poetess," Sappho is considered to be the first woman poet of Western civilization. Little of her work and less of the known facts of her life have survived to our day; of the thousands of poems she is known to have written, only two apparently intact poems and many fragmentary stanzas and lines are extant. Sappho's poems are personal, concerned largely with matters of everyday life and the affairs of those around her. She presided, in an unknown role, over a large circle of girls and young women, and her poems are filled with details of dress and behavior. Many of her poems are epithalamia, or wedding songs, celebrating the marriage ceremony. Others, reflecting her passionate love for other women, have given rise to our contemporary definition of "lesbian," the word deriving from Sappho's island home of Lesbos in the Aegean Sea. These were also cause for the destruction and repression of much of her work over the centuries. Despite this, her reputation prevailed and her work was periodically "rescued" by poets, usually male (for example, Swinburne), who refashioned it to suit the style and themes popular in their own time. Thus, modern translations of her poetry, beginning in the seventeenth century, were frequently more representative of their translator and the age than reflective of the originals. Her advocates often repressed her love for other women (at times re-creating her as a prostitute) and defended her righteously against those who expressed moral outrage. Through the eighteenth century, the term "Sappho" was commonly bestowed upon women poets (including such authors as Aphra Behn,

Lady Mary Wortley Montagu, and Madeleine de Scudery) as a flattering courtesy. In other cases it was appropriated by young women poets. Possibly the most significant of these was Renee Vivien (1877–1909), for whom Sappho was not only a crucial subject for her poems but also a historical figure with whom she identified (indeed of whom she felt herself to be the reincarnation). As more recent translations of the poems have made explicit Sappho's lesbianism, her name is more frequently and popularly associated with her sexuality than with her poetry. The commonly used "sapphic," synonomous with "lesbian," demonstrates an evolving disjunction between the name and the historical figure. Thus the history of her reception reflects a continuing privileging of particular aspects of her life and legend over others, depending on the agenda of her admirers or detractors.

Kathleen Mackin

References

Blankley, Elyse. "Return to Mytilene: Renee Vivien and the City of Women." In *Women Writers and the City,* edited by Susan Merrill Squier, 45–67. Knoxville: University of Tennessee Press, 1984.

De Jean, Joan. *Fictions of Sappho: 1546–1937*. Chicago: University of Chicago Press, 1989.

Lipking, Lawrence. "Sappho Descending: Eighteenth-Century Styles in Abandoned Women." *Studies in the Eighteenth Century* 12 (1988): 40–57.

Sappho. *Lyrics in the Original Greek*. Translated by Willis Barnstone. New York: Anchor, 1945.

Satire

Defining satire is one of literary theorists' greatest challenges, since satire is associated with parody, burlesque, irony, wit, comic writing, and pornography. Elements of satirical tone can be found across the genres and in a spectrum of the arts as well. The misogynistic nature of satire is of special interest to feminist critics, since women were often the target of satirical writing from ancient to modern times. Both male and female writers have used satire to critique society; however, male authors' satirical works generally attract more comment from feminist literary theorists.

In the ancient world, satire was often written in the formal verse style in which an *adversarius* was used to provoke the poem's speaker into conversation in which he speaks out against social vices, follies in general, and corruption. Horace and Juvenal, among other Roman satirists, exercised the most influence on English literary satire flourishing in the eighteenth century. Horatian satire, as popularized by Alexander Pope, employs an intelligent, broad-minded but serious speaker, who is happy to satirize his own shortcomings as well as those of the people around him. Juvenalian satire, exemplified in Samuel Johnson's "London" and "The Vanity of Human Wishes" is moralistic in tone, grave in spirit, and designed to sadden or anger its readers, who should be humbled by the recognition of their shortcomings. Menippean satire, used by Petronius in *The Satyricon,* is written in alternating prose and verse featuring a sequence of debates or conversations wherein learned speakers consider various viewpoints on established topics.

Feminist readers of satirical texts are interested in the portrayal of women and the effect these portrayals have on social attitudes toward women and sexuality. The debate among feminist scholars centers on whether such works are harmful to women's perceptions of themselves and to how others perceive them. Semonides's pornographic *Satyr on Women* is one example where women are assigned characteristics of beasts as expressions of their sexuality and natural characters. In commenting upon this work, Joseph Addison in *The Spectator* 209 wrote, "A Satyr should expose nothing but what is corrigible, and make due discrimination between those who are and those who are not the proper object of it." Alexander Pope and Jonathan Swift are the foci of some feminist eighteenth-century scholars such as Felicity

Nussbaum, who in *The Brink of All We Hate* shows her readers the various treatments women receive at the pens of these authors.

Antifemale satire typically calls attention to women's "vices" of vanity and pseudo-intellectualism; some modern readers, such as Gail Kern Paster, see such satire as a screen behind which men hide their fears of the female body. In addition, theories of commodification of women, expressed by Laura Brown among others, stress how women were made the excuses for male rapacity in the acquisition of goods. In another instance of antifemale satire, Lord Byron's *The Blues: A Literary Eclogue,* which takes its name from the Bluestocking Circle of eighteenth-century women intellectuals, displays the fear of female wit.

Thus feminist critics involved in rereading older satirical literature seek to expose its underlying misogynistic treatment of women. Where applicable, they also question the overall value of such literature. Feminist critics seem divided over the way to respond to the issue of satire and pornography's influence on social attitudes toward their women subjects.

Beverly Schneller

References

Berger, Ronald J., et al. *Feminism and Pornography.* Westport, Conn.: Praeger, 1991.

Brown, Laura. *The Ends of Empire.* Ithaca, N.Y.: Cornell University Press, 1992.

Guilhamet, Leon. *Satire and the Transformation of Genre.* Philadelphia: University of Pennsylvania Press, 1987.

Hutchins, Linda. *A Theory of Parody.* London: Methuen, 1989.

Lloyd-Jones, Hugh, ed. *The Female of the Species: Semonides on Women.* London: Duckworth, 1975.

Nussbaum, Felicity. *The Brink of All We Hate.* Lexington: University Press of Kentucky, 1984.

Paster, Gail Kern. *The Body Embarrassed.* Ithaca, N.Y.: Cornell University Press, 1992.

Pollard, Arthur. *Satire.* London: Methuen, 1987.

Schor, Naomi

Naomi Schor brings to her work an understanding of feminism seen through the transition from structuralism to deconstruction. Sandra Gilbert's and Susan Gubar's attic, Peggy Kamuf's crypt, and Nina Auerbach's woman-demon are her predecessors in the feminist project of mapping representational strategies that Schor continues in *Breaking the Chain: Women, Theory, and French Realist Fiction*. Focusing on the detail of the foot, the classic fetish for the clitoris, she proposes "a poetics of reading which not only takes over details referring to woman's body but also breaks with the linearity of the signifying chain." In the first part of her book, she groups five essays under "Reading (for) the Feminine" explicitly to mime her own "working through" process as a female critic entering into patriarchal theoretical discourse. Rather than Irigaray's "mimeticism" or Kolodny's "playful pluralism," Schor names this process "patriody" in order to emphasize that "the inherently linguistic nature of woman's playful relationship to paternal theoretical discourse" contains elements both of parody and parricide. Her interrogation of the reading models proposed by Jacques Derrida, Roland Barthes, Jacques Lacan, and René Girard reveals the lingering man/woman hierarchies in poststructuralism. Returning to Lacan and his developmental model in which the paternal signifier mediates the mother-child dyad in order to form the speaking subject, Schor claims that in order for the feminist critic to break her earlier illusory mirror relationship with her symbolic father(s), a recognition of the maternal must intervene.

Reading in Detail: Aesthetics and the Feminine continues Schor's project; instead of her earlier examination of reading practice as female paranoia, she examines male paranoia in reading the detail. Citing her study as "both a defense of the detail and an illustration of its lures," Schor offers a feminist archaeology of the detail in which she traces its progress from the neoclassicist denigration of the particular through its rise at the birth of realism to its current prominence. Schor argues that by viewing the negative aspects of the detail as ornamental (and thus effeminate and decadent) or everyday (and thus domestic in its "prosiness"), the gendered nature of the concept is revealed. From this insight, Schor is able to demonstrate not only "the gendering that underpins neoclassical aesthetics" but the "persistent association of idealist aesthetics with the discourse of misogyny" through her readings of Reynold, Hegel, Wey, Loos, and Lukács. Schor draws on Freud's theory of displacement to "make intelligible and legitimate the multiple modes of investment in the trivial" and cautions that fascination with the trivial may be problematic: "Does the triumph of the detail signify a triumph of the feminine with which it has so long been linked? or has the detail achieved its new prestige by being taken over by the masculine, triumphing at the very moment when it ceases to be associated with the feminine, or ceasing to be connoted as feminine at the very moment when it is taken up by the male-dominated cultural establishment?"

Mary Anne Stewart Boelcskevy

References

Schor, Naomi. *Breaking the Chain: Women, Theory, and French Realist Fiction*. New York: Columbia University Press, 1985.
———. "Feminist and Gender Studies." In *Introduction to Scholarship in Modern Languages and Literatures,* edited by Joseph Gibaldi, 262–287. New York: Modern Language Association of America, 1992.
———. *Reading in Detail: Aesthetics and the Feminine*. New York: Routledge, 1987.

Sedgwick, Eve Kosofsky

Sedgwick, queer theorist and literary critic, has crucially contributed to feminism by articulating the relationship between gender and (homo)sexuality. In *Between Men: English Literature and Male Homosocial Desire*, Sedgwick argues that the paradigmatic rivalry between men over a mediating woman, which undergirds patriarchal culture, lies on a continuum with male same-sex desire. However, in Anglo American society, this continuum was disrupted with the advent of the homo/heterosexual binary, so contemporary male homosocial culture repudiates any connection with homosexuality. She opposes this fractured masculine continuum to a relatively seamless one between female homosociality and homosexuality, an opposition that has been criticized by theorists like Teresa de Lauretis.

In *Epistemology of the Closet,* Sedgwick suggests that while gender and sexuality are implicated, they constitute conceptually distinct realms; thus, analyzing sexuality purely in gendered terms is heterosexist. Further, in exploring the incoherence of the homo/heterosexual binarism, a binarism that she contends centrally informs a wide range of other cultural dualities, Sedgwick demonstrates the contradictory roles historically attributed to gender in gender separatist and integrative models of homosexuality. Rather than selecting between these inconsistent paradigms, she explores the multiple political effects of these conceptual contradictions.

Sedgwick uses deconstructive, feminist, and Foucauldian theories in unexpected, constantly skeptical ways. While she mainly analyzes canonical Euro-American texts, her readings are often provocatively interdisciplinary. Her syntactically difficult, frequently confessional, even exhibitionistic, witty, and highly performative prose constantly challenges the conventions of literary academic criticism.

Stephen da Silva

References

de Lauretis, Teresa. *The Practice of Love: Lesbian Sexuality and Perverse Desire.* Bloomington: Indiana University Press, 1994.

Sedgwick, Eve Kosofsky. *Between Men: English Literature and Male Homosocial Desire.* New York: Columbia University Press, 1985.

———. *Epistemology of the Closet.* Berkeley: University of California Press, 1990.

———. *Tendencies.* Durham: Duke University Press, 1993.

Self

A term used to signify the individual's conscious experience of separate identity within a collective whole. A feminist concept of self is defined by a fundamental tension and interaction between individual and collective identity. Thus, for many feminists, the self is multifarious, dynamic, relational, as well as unique.

A feminist concept of self challenges a number of preexisting notions about the experience of separate identity. Most persistent is the Enlightenment concept of a unitary, essentially rational self that is differentiated between mind and body and that discounts the efficacy of various types of social relations in its creation. This essentialist self is often stereotypically assumed to be white, Western, and masculine, feminists argue. This version of the self is based upon the stories of the experiences and problems of a privileged group. However, positing this self as the norm has implications for women, who are conflated with the irrational and the corporeal, their stories left untold.

Postmodernist attacks on classical thought, and particularly its notion of the rational, self-reflective subject have also been a target of feminist criticism. Arguing that the Enlightenment concept of self displaces or derogates its "other," postmodernist deconstructors have been accused of rendering subjectivity meaningless to the extent that they see the self as no more than an effect of discourse or a construct of language, as an anachronistic and irrelevant fiction. In response, some feminist theorists locate the self not only in fictive or textual conventions, but also in concrete social relations. They ascribe to it both agency and autonomy within a complex web of real human relationships that are essential to its assertion.

This feminist concept of self is directly connected to object-relations psychoanalysis in its stress on the central importance of sustained, intimate personal relationships, especially with the mother or her substitutes, in the development and experience of a separate identity. It develops as well from the recognition that gender is only one of several determining influences on the individual's life. Social factors such as race, class, and ethnicity as well as the physical experience of bodily integrity thus lead the individual to a sense of self that is simultaneously embodied, gendered, social, and discrete. Such a view challenges not only the Enlightenment concept of an essential self, but also the postmodern attempt to render subjectivity meaningless, a project that threatens the feminist effort to retrieve women from the margins of patriarchal culture at just the point when they are articulating and analyzing their subjectivity, when they are asserting their selfhood.

Linda C. Pelzer

See also AUTONOMY

References

Chodorow, Nancy. *The Reproduction of Mothering. Psychoanalysis and the Sociology of Gender.* Berkeley: University of California Press, 1978.

Felski, Rita. *Beyond Feminist Aesthetics: Feminist Literature and Social Change.* London: Hutchinson Radius, 1989.

Flax, Jane. *Thinking Fragments. Psychoanalysis, Feminism, and Postmodernism in the Contemporary West.* Berkeley: University of California Press, 1990.

Gallop, Jane. *The Daughter's Seduction.*

Feminism and Psychoanalysis. Ithaca, N.Y.: Cornell University Press, 1982.

Gilligan, Carol. *In a Different Voice: Psychological Theory and Women's Development.* Cambridge: Harvard University Press, 1982.

McNay, Lois. *Foucault and Feminism: Power, Gender, and the Self.* Boston: Northeastern University Press, 1992.

Miller, Jean Baker, ed. *Psychoanalysis and Women.* Boston: Beacon, 1976.

Semiotic

In feminist literary theory, Julia Kristeva uses the word "semiotic" in opposition to "symbolic" to refer to the two components of the signifying process that constitutes language. The semiotic is characterized by the pre-Oedipal drive and energies, by rhythmic pulsions, by disruptions, by contradictions, and by heterogeneity. It is associated with "oral and anal drives" that are oriented and structured around the mother's body. In contrast, the symbolic is connected with the Law of the Father. The "dialectic" between the semiotic and the symbolic determines the type of discourse (narrative, metalanguage, theory, poetry, and so on) that is produced. Kristeva believes that the subject is always both semiotic and symbolic; hence, no signifying system one produces can be either exclusively semiotic or symbolic, and is instead necessarily marked by an indebtedness to both.

Influenced by insights of psychoanalysis, Kristeva first explained her theories of the semiotic in *La révolution du langage poétique* in 1974, translated as *Revolution in Poetic Language* in 1984. According to Kristeva, the semiotic is articulated by "flow and marks": facilitation, energy transfers, the cutting up of the corporeal and social continuum as well as that of signifying material. It is bound up with the body as *jouissance.* Semiotic energies or drives articulate the *chora,* a mobile and provisional space constituted by movements and their ephemeral stases. Our discourse moves with and against the *chora* in the sense that it simultaneously depends upon and refuses it. This *chora* is the locus of the drive activity underlying the semiotic.

For Kristeva, the language of the semiotic is potentially subversive because it serves as a means of undermining the symbolic order. Semiotic force is revolutionary as it can disturb, question, and destabilize the symbolic order.

The semiotic is closely linked to femininity, but is by no means a language exclusive to women. Because of its fluid and plural nature, it can be used in opposition to all fixed, transcendental significations associated with patriarchy and authority. In literature, certain kinds of writing, such as avant-garde modernist texts, exhibit characteristics of the semiotic. The semiotic creates a different textual pleasure or *jouissance* that has to do with excess of language and the play of the unconscious and the preverbal. Semiotic writing is therefore transgressive and disrupts the unity of symbolic language.

Some feminist critics such as Judith Butler point out that Kristeva's strategy of subversion is doubtful because her theory depends on the privileging of paternal law. The dimension of language that Kristeva highlights is repressed and seems to be a kind of language that cannot be consistently maintained. Displacement and disruption of the Law of the Father are temporary. Thus, her theories suggest that patriarchal hegemony will always reassert itself.

Eleanor Ty

References

Butler, Judith. *Gender Trouble: Feminism and the Subversion of Identity.* New York: Routledge, 1990.

Kristeva, Julia. *Desire in Language: A Semiotic Approach to Literature and Art.* Edited by Leon S. Roudiez. New York: Columbia University Press, 1980.

———. *The Kristeva Reader.* Edited by Toril Moi. New York: Columbia University Press, 1986.

———. *Revolution in Poetic Language.* Translated by Margaret Waller. New York: Columbia University Press, 1984.

Semiotics

Semiotics, a term coined by Charles Sanders Peirce, is the study of signs. A recent and growing field, semiotics developed out of Peirce's pragmaticism and the structuralism of Ferdinand de Saussure. Semiotics speaks always to the relation between a sign and what it stands for and understands that relation to be both arbitrary and diacritical. Pierce claimed that any sign can be taken as something in itself, or in relation to its object, or as a mediating factor between the two. In his own investigation of "the life of signs in society," de Saussure, the founder of modern linguistics, saw language as a binary system consisting of an arbitrarily related signifier (the sound) and signified (the concept). Jacques Lacan developed this concept of the nature of the sign as both arbitrary and diacritical, a fundamental concept of sexuality in Freudian psychology, into a psychoanalytic theory that has had great impact on feminist theory. Jacques Derrida argued from the basis of this arbitrary and diacritical nature of the sign that language is essentially indeterminate—that there is no origin of meaning—and that there is no prelinguistic self. Because the issue of gender is fundamentally an issue of representation, for feminists the study of signs has become the study of gendered signs, and the arbitrary and diacritical nature of the sign is the site where semiotics and feminism intersect.

Arbitrariness means that the relation between the sign and its referent is neither a necessary nor natural one. From here, we could argue against claims of an essential nature of woman, because woman as a sign is a constructed category. A complication that arises from this constructedness is that, because the recognition of women as a distinct social group was a founding moment for feminism, the arbitrariness of the sign at first seems to threaten a fundamental aspect of feminism, that is, its claim that there is a category called woman. But by denaturalizing the category, the arbitrariness of the sign opens up for analysis the many ways in which woman is constructed as subject within an oppressive system.

In its diacritical nature, the sign takes on its meaning only out of its difference from other signs. This meaning-making through difference has led to the insight that the categories of man and woman stand in diacritical relation to one another and, moreover, that this binary opposition is at the heart of language. Hélène Cixous argued that Western philosophy and literary thought is a series of male/female oppositions which, no matter the terms, always translate in a patriarchal value system into positive/negative. To this binary system, Cixous opposes a multiple, heterogeneous difference as the feminine.

Feminist semiotics has fostered a wide range of inquiries, in particular questions about the representation and the reading of the female body in a variety of texts: literature, theory, and cinema. Film theory became feminist film theory with feminist film-maker Laura Mulvey's "Visual Pleasure and Narrative Cinema." In her article, Mulvey traced the "system of looks" constructed by the triangulated structure of camera/projector, profilmic/cinematic image, and spectator. Positing that such a system creates the gaze of a masculine voyeur as the only possibility, Mulvey opened the Hollywood narrative to further feminist readings. Kaja Silverman and Teresa de Lauretis are just two of the theorists who have extended Mulvey's insights. In *Acoustic Mirror: The Female Voice in Psychoanalysis and Cinema*, Silverman reads the complex interaction of visual and aural experience in cinema where she finds a dissociation between the male body and voice coupled with an overinvestment in the female body. Cinematic practice, she argues, privileges the disembodied voice, just as our reading practices give us the omniscient third-person narrator as the site of narrative authority. In *Technologies of Gender: Essays on Theory, Film, and Fiction,* by gendering Michel Foucault's theory that sexuality is deployed through discourses of power, Teresa de Lauretis explores both how gender is constructed and repressed. The gender-neutrality of discourses—whether social scientific, philosophical, historical, critical, modernist, or postmodernist—can be seen, de Lauretis argues, as acts of violence because they draw our attention away from women toward a representation of woman.

Although signs are always virtual, we tend to conceive of them as actual. Hollywood and literary codes are part of larger cultural codes through which we read signs. Thus, the texts semiotics opens for investigation are not only theory, film, and literature but the female body in the world. Feminist semiotics explores, on a broad basis, how gender is reproduced. One area of inquiry asks how a female body can be read as authoritative when authority itself is often seen as a male domain. In "Presence of Mind, Presence of Body: Embodying Positionality in the Classroom," for example, Ann Ardis explores how a student audience's reading of a female teacher's body can support or undermine her discursive authority. The visible signs inscribed on a speaker's body are not limited to gender, however. Another recent focus of concern for feminist semiotics, in response to criticism that feminism itself has often thought too reductively of the category "woman," has been an investigation of how the conjunction of gender, race, class, and sexuality affects readings of the female body. While the Saussurean dichotomous approach to signs has had a stronger influence on early feminist semiotics, the Peircean triadic system offers feminist theorists a promising alternative to Saussure's binary oppositions.

Mary Anne Stewart Boelcskevy

References

Ardis, Ann. "Presence of Mind, Presence of Body: Embodying Positionality in the Classroom." *Hypatia* 7 (1992): 167–176.

Butler, Judith. *Bodies that Matter: On the Discursive Limits of "Sex."* New York: Routledge, 1993.

———. *Gender Trouble: Feminism and the Subversion of Identity*. New York: Routledge, 1990.

Cixous, Hélène. "The Laugh of the Medusa." Translated by Keith Cohen and Paula Cohen. *Signs* 1 (1976): 875–899.

Colapietro, Vincent M. *Glossary of Semiotics*. New York: Paragon, 1993.

de Lauretis, Teresa. *Technologies of Gender: Essays on Theory, Film, and Fiction*. Bloomington: Indiana University Press, 1987.

Derrida, Jacques. *Of Grammatology*. Chicago: University of Chicago Press, 1976.

Foucault, Michel. *The History of Sexuality*. 3 vols. Translated by Robert Hurley. London: Allen Lane, 1979–1988.

Hull, Gloria T., Patricia Bell Scott, and Barbara Smith, eds. *All the Women Are White, All the Blacks Are Men, But Some of Us Are Brave*. Old Westbury, N.Y: Feminist, 1982.

Lacan, Jacques. *Écrits: A Selection*. Translated by Alan Sheridan. New York: W.W. Norton, 1977.

Mulvey, Laura. *Visual and Other Pleasures*. Bloomington: Indiana University Press, 1989.

———. "Visual Pleasure and Narrative Cinema." *Screen* 16 (1975): 6–18.

Peirce, Charles Sanders. *Semiotic and Significs: The Correspondence between Charles S. Peirce and Victoria Lady Welby*. Edited by Charles S. Hardwick. Bloomington: Indiana University Press, 1977.

Saussure, Ferdinand de. *Course in General Linguistics*. Translated by Wade Baskin. New York: McGraw-Hill, 1969.

Silverman, Kaja. *Acoustic Mirror: The Female Voice in Psychoanalysis and Cinema*. Bloomington: Indiana University Press, 1988.

———. *The Subject of Semiotics*. New York: Oxford University Press, 1983.

Spelman, Elizabeth V. *Inessential Women: Problems of Exclusion in Feminist Thought*. Boston: Beacon, 1988.

Sentimentality

The *Oxford English Dictionary* shows that the term was originally defined in a favorable sense to mean "characterized by or exhibiting refined and elevated feeling" but later shows its meaning to have shifted to have more negative connotations: "addicted to indulgence in superficial emotion; apt to be swayed by sentiment" and "arising from or determined by feeling rather than by reason." This shift in meaning is attributable to the gendering of "sentimentality" as it developed as a "set of cultural practices" from the eighteenth through the twentieth century. The central question for feminists is whether sentimentality is fundamentally conservative or radical in nature.

The idea of sentimentality developed in the late seventeenth and early eighteenth centuries. Originally, the word grew out of the term "sensibility," which Fred Kaplan describes as "a response to external stimuli" rather than the "innate moral sentiment" usually associated with the term "sentimentality." It is significant that the term had its first usage in the eighteenth century, a time when women were being pushed toward the domestic rather than the public sphere by a strong social impulse toward reformation and morality. From its beginnings, sentimentality was aligned with women in an essentialist way. Samuel Richardson's Clarissa Harlowe is frequently cited as the quintessential eighteenth-century sentimental character. John Mullan points out that in many of the sentimental novels of this era, sentimentality is "an investment in a particular version of the feminine—tearful, palpitating, embodying virtue whilst susceptible to all the vicissitudes of 'feeling.'" Thus, ironically, while sentimentality may indicate a kind of moral superiority, it also coincides with physical weakness or inferiority that is coded as female.

The nineteenth century is considered the apex of sentimentality in literature and culture. Howard Fulweiler asserts that the most important subjects in sentimental literature during this period were "the status of women, romantic love, marriage, and the family"—all traditionally "female" subjects. Charles Dickens and

Alfred Tennyson frequently employed sentimentality when dealing with these subjects. In America, sentimentality was closely aligned with the abolitionist movement after the successful publication of *Uncle Tom's Cabin*. Shirley Samuels in *The Culture of Sentiment* argues that sentimentality, which evokes an emotional response from the reader or viewer, "produces or reproduces spectacles that cross race, class, and gender boundaries."

At the beginning of the twentieth century, writers rejected sentimentality. Suzanne Clark describes how the rejection of sentimentality had a gendered undercurrent: "Women writers were entangled in sensibility, were romantic and sentimental by nature, and so even the best might not altogether escape this romantic indulgence." Modernist writers furthered this gendering of sentimentality through a series of binaries, male/female, serious/sentimental, critical/popular, which associated the female, sentimental literature with a now disdained popular culture.

Feminism's conflicting approaches to sentimentality are most clearly displayed in the 1977 *Feminization of American Culture* by Ann Douglas and the 1985 response by Jane Tompkins, *Sensational Designs*. Douglas felt that the "sentimental undermines the serious," and that while it provided a means for female expression, it did not serve as an impetus for political action. Tompkins, on the other hand, argued that the nineteenth-century sentimental tradition was important for feminism because it had an impact on society as "a political enterprise . . . that both codifies and attempts to mold the values of its time." While feminist critics like Douglas feared that sentimentality sought to reinforce social control, most critics now agree that it actually sought to produce radical reform.

Sigrid King

References

Clark, Suzanne. *Sentimental Modernism: Women Writers and the Revolution of the Word*. Bloomington and Indianapolis: Indiana University Press, 1991.

Douglas, Ann. *The Feminization of American Culture*. New York: Avon, 1977.

Fulweiler, Howard. "'Here a Captive Heart Busted': From Victorian Sentimentality to Modern Sexuality." In *Sexuality and Victorian Literature*, edited by Don Richard Cox, 234–250. Knoxville: University of Tennessee Press, 1984.

Kaplan, Fred. *Sacred Tears: Sentimentality in Victorian Literature*. Princeton: Princeton University Press, 1987.

Mullan, John. *Sentiment and Sociability: The Language of Feeling in the Eighteenth Century*. Oxford: Clarendon, 1988.

Samuels, Shirley, ed. *The Culture of Sentiment: Race Gender and Sentimentality in Nineteenth-Century America*. New York and Oxford: Oxford University Press, 1992.

Tompkins, Jane. *Sensational Designs: The Cultural Work of American Fiction 1790–1860*. New York: Oxford University Press, 1985.

Separate Spheres

A cultural ideology that developed with the industrialization of the Western world in the nineteenth century, positioning women in a domestic sphere centered on the home, and men in the larger world of commerce outside the home. This division and its marginalization of women is a cornerstone of patriarchal culture.

Janet Wolff has charted the developing separation of public and private life in the nineteenth century through changes in ideology, economics, geography, and architecture. Elizabeth Janeway and other critics have explored the ideological element of this division as a social myth that has supported the corollary myth that women are powerless. Feminist anthropology has argued that the extent to which women are subordinated in a given society is directly related to the degree to which the domestic and public realms are separated. Juliet Mitchell's *Women: The Longest Revolution* further explores the complex relationship between the public and domestic worlds, arguing that understanding this relationship is necessary if feminism is to have an effect on both realms.

This area of inquiry remains vital in feminist literary theory. The declaration that "the personal is political" is based on the assumption that social existence cannot be neatly divided into more and less important spheres.

Christopher Wells

References

Janeway, Elizabeth. *Man's World, Women's Place: A Study in Social Mythology*. New York: Dell, 1971.

Kelly, Joan. *Women, History & Theory: The*

Essays of Joan Kelly. Chicago: University of Chicago Press, 1984.

Mitchell, Juliet. *Women: The Longest Revolution.* Somerville, Mass.: New England Free Press, 1966.

Rosaldo, Michelle, and Louise Lamphere, eds. *Woman, Culture & Society.* Stanford: Stanford University Press, 1974.

Wolff, Janet. "The Culture of Separate Spheres: The Role of Culture in Nineteenth-Century Public and Private Life." In *The Culture of Capital: Art, Power, and the Nineteenth-Century Middle Class,* edited by Janet Wolff, 117–134. Manchester: Manchester University Press, 1988.

Shakespeare

Feminist criticism of Shakespeare addresses the role of gender in Shakespearean drama. Oppositional feminist readers see in the plays and poetry archetypal blueprints for patriarchal control, yielding the shrewlike tamings of the comedies, the all-male imperatives—the Salic law, *"in terram Salicam mulieres ne succedant" (Henry V)*—of the histories, and the violent snuffing out of all female sexuality in the tragedies. More sympathetic feminists find in these various male-dominated agendas a saving irony, or see in the plays elaborate strategies for undoing and resisting the very historical imperatives they necessarily bring to the stage. Sometimes less polemical considerations of Shakespearean mothers, daughters, sisters, wives, and lovers enrich and enlarge the inherently revisionist project of feminism.

The feminist reevaluation of Shakespeare may be conveniently divided into two phases, the first formative (1832–1975), the second institutional (1975–present). Though feminist-minded challenges to Renaissance representations of women go back at least as far as Jane Angar's 1589 *Protection of Women,* which assailed many of the stereotypes of women condemned by later feminist readers of Renaissance literature, the first phase of feminist Shakespearean criticism may be said to begin with the publication in 1832 of Anna Jameson's pioneering *Shakespeare's Heroines: Characteristics of Women.* In the centuries between Angar's assault on euphuistic romance and Jameson's study, important responses to Shakespearean women by women include Aphra Behn's preface to *The*

Dutch Lover (1673), Elizabeth Montagu's *Essay on the Writings and Genius of Shakespeare* (1769), Elizabeth Griffith's *The Morality of Shakespeare's Drama Illustrated* (1775), and Mary Lamb's *Tales from Shakespeare* (1807). Jameson's book, however, offers the first full-scale critique of women in Shakespeare.

Influenced in part by Jameson's work, a circle of activist women writers in the later nineteenth century furthered the feminist reevaluation of Shakespeare in studies like Mary Clarke's *The Girlhood of Shakespeare's Heroines* (1850) and Elizabeth Wormeley Latimer's *Familiar Talks on Some of Shakespeare's Comedies* (1886). In 1897, George Bernard Shaw condemns in decidedly feminist terms Shakespeare's lord-of-creation moral in *The Taming of the Shrew* (see below). In the 1920s and 1930s, Virginia Woolf further fuses feminism and Shakespeare while working through her own complicated identification as "Shakespeare's sister." In the first decades of the postwar period, numerous essays but only a handful of books and dissertations like Betty Bandel's *Shakespeare's Treatment of the Social Position of Women* (1951) further examine the changing critical perceptions of women in Shakespeare.

The second, institutional phase of feminist criticism of Shakespeare begins with the publication of Juliet Dusinberre's *Shakespeare and the Nature of Women* in 1975, the first explicitly feminist engagement with the poetry and plays. Dusinberre's study was soon followed by several books, anthologies, and essays arguing for either a more sympathetic, or a more polemical, response to the role played by women. In conjunction with developments in the criticism and theory associated with feminism, subsequent readers have examined in closer detail issues of gender and genre, patriarchy and power, phallocentrism and misogyny, and subversion and containment. As a greater consensus has been gradually achieved, so, paradoxically but perhaps predictably, has the institutional and extrainstitutional debate over Shakespeare and the nature of women intensified and deepened.

This ongoing debate within feminist criticism of Shakespeare may be conveniently illustrated by the archetypal instance of *The Taming of the Shrew,* for among feminist readers the play has provoked decidedly conflicted and opposed responses. Revisionist critics see in Kate's final speech a send-up, rather than a celebration, of the domesticating moral that so troubled Shaw. The earliest such readers of the play include Margaret Webster in 1942, who finds in Kate's speech a "delicious irony," and Nevill Coghill in 1950, who sees in the same speech's commitment to serve, honor, and obey a liberating, self-reliant credo "generously and charmingly asserted by Katerina at the end." Still earlier, in 1886, Constance O'Brien proposed a similar reading; indeed, Coghill's "but it is a total misconception to suppose that she has been bludgeoned into it" strikingly recalls O'Brien's "it is all nonsense to talk as if this bit of merry comedy expresses Shakespeare's serious ideas of the proper relations between husband and wife." In studies since 1975, a number of feminist critics have appealed to a similar irony while seeking to make the play not more, but less, patriarchal than it might at first appear.

Antirevisionist readers, on the other hand, take *The Taming of the Shrew* at its word, and its lord-of-creation moral literally. First among those to take issue with the revisionist attention to irony is Robert Heilman in "The *Taming Untamed, or The Return of the Shrew*" (1966), and while the argument here cannot be described as feminist, many feminist readers have followed Heilman and Shaw in balking at the play's patriarchal master-plot, and at revisionist attempts to redeem it. Still other feminist readers have sought a compromise between the foot-in-mouth literalism of antirevisionist readings and the tongue-in-cheek irony of revisionist accounts.

These various readings of *The Taming of the Shrew* thus mirror and roughly chronicle the progress of the larger critical debate in feminism over Shakespeare's relative patriarchy, a debate whose lack of resolution only heightens the transformative force and influence of feminism's engagement with Shakespeare.

Stephen Bretzius

References

Dusinberre, Juliet. *Shakespeare and the Nature of Women*. New York: Barnes and Noble, 1975.

Kolin, Philip C. *Shakespeare and Feminist Criticism: An Annotated Bibliography and Commentary*. New York: Garland, 1991.

Lenz, Carolyn Ruth Swift, Gayle Greene, and Carol Thomas Neely, eds. *The Woman's Part: Feminist Criticism of Shakespeare*. Urbana: University of Illinois Press, 1980.

Novy, Marianne, ed. *Women's Re-Visions of Shakespeare: On the Responses of Dickinson, Woolf, Rich, H.D., George Eliot, and Others*. Urbana: University of Illinois Press, 1990.

Woolf, Virginia. *A Room of One's Own*. New York: Harcourt, Brace and World, 1928.

Showalter, Elaine

With the appearance of *A Literature of Their Own*, Elaine Showalter firmly established herself as one of the founders of feminist literary criticism in the United States. Her examination of the apparent lack of a common female literary heritage or "unifying voice" for women in literature from the 1840s to the 1960s exposed several crucial flaws in the canonical assessment of female writers. Against a patriarchal literary history that derived its theories from the works of a few "great" female authors and either expounded accepted stereotypes of femininity or tended to desex women writers entirely, Showalter argued that writing women formed a vital, powerful "subculture" within a larger male-dominated social framework. Similarly, her most recent book, *Sexual Anarchy*, develops the concept of "subculture" in demonstrating how social constructions of both femininity and masculinity are called into question in the chaotic, apocalyptic, centennial environments of the 1890s and 1990s. Throughout her theory, women are "figures of disorder," inhabiting a "mysterious and frightening wild zone" on the fringes of (but not outside of) mainstream patriarchal culture. However, this description also contains Showalter's important point that women, and women writers, should be considered within their larger social, economic, and cultural contexts, and not simply or merely as members of the female sex.

Showalter distinguishes between two types of feminist literary criticism: "feminist critique" deals with women as readers of works by male authors, while the much broader "gynocritics" looks at women as writers, the nature of female creativity, and "the history, themes, genres and structures of literature by women." In *A Literature of Their Own*, she uses her gynocritical approach as a valuable means of examining the female subculture of authorship. She divides female literary history into three stages: the "feminine" period (1840–1880), when women internalized patriarchal ideologies and strove to imitate works from the dominant literary tradition; the "feminist" era (1880–1920), characterized by protest of and rebellion against those previously unquestioned values; and the "female" age (1920–1960), when women turned to self-exploration, self-discovery, and a search for a specifically female identity. The modern purpose of women's writing, she later adds, is to articulate female experience, "to discover the new world."

Although the certainties implied by this historical model have been questioned by subsequent critics, Showalter's gynocritical approach has had many valuable effects. Her insistence on breaking free of traditional perceptions of female writers, on transcending the stereotypical themes and images assigned to women's works, and on rediscovering previously ignored or neglected women writers and examining them in the company of other female authors and in a broad cultural context has opened many doors for modern feminists in their approaches to female texts. Feminist critics, she writes in *The New Feminist Criticism,* must concentrate on "what women actually write, not in relation to a theoretical, political, metaphoric, or visionary ideal of what women ought to write."

Alexandra Bennett

References

Hirsch, Marianne, and Evelyn Fox Keller, eds. *Conflicts in Feminism.* New York: Routledge, 1990.

Moi, Toril. *Sexual/Textual Politics: Feminist Literary Theory.* New York: Routledge, 1985.

Showalter, Elaine. *The Female Malady: Women, Madness, and Culture in England, 1830–1980.* New York: Pantheon, 1986.

———. *A Literature of Their Own: British Women Novelists from Brontë to Lessing.* Princeton: Princeton University Press, 1977.

———. *Sexual Anarchy: Gender and Culture at the Fin de Siecle.* New York: Viking, 1990.

———. *Sister's Choice: Tradition and Change in American Women's Writing.* Oxford: Clarendon, 1991.

———, ed. *The New Feminist Criticism.* New York: Pantheon, 1985.

———, ed. *Speaking of Gender.* New York: Routledge, 1988.

Signs: Journal of Women in Culture and Society

S

Since Catharine R. Stimpson founded *Signs* in 1975, it has maintained its status as *the* journal of new feminist scholarship, including rigorous research about women, sexuality, sex roles, pertinent social institutions, and culture. As its title implies, *Signs* represents a variety of academic disciplines and so functions as a quarterly digest of feminist perspectives upon all topics that concern women around the world.

Signs's first edition in 1975 announced that it would, first, publish new scholarship about women that would lead to "an accurate understanding of men and women, of sex and gender, and of large patterns of human behavior, institutions, ideologies, and art"; second, publish interdisciplinary work; and third, present a number of points of view, which would provide several theoretical perspectives within feminism.

Indeed, *Signs*'s advisory board, representing various academic disciplines from many countries, is a testament to the large scope of its mission, which still holds true today. A further testament to its democratic ideals, the journal changes editors every five years to ensure that no single group dominates.

Perhaps the best indication of *Signs*'s success and influence can be seen outside of the academic community. The discoveries and conclusions of its scholarly research have been cited in local publications across the country, which suggests the magnitude of its value to a wide range of readers. This in turn suggests that *Signs* facilitates at all levels—from academia to the grassroots—the improvement of the material conditions of women's lives.

Michelle L. Deal

References

Fox-Genovese, Elizabeth. "Signs: Journal of Women in Culture and Society." *Times Literary Supplement* (March 17, 1995): 25–26.

McMillen, Liz. "Ground-Breaking Feminist Journal Grapples with Its Own Success." *Chronicle of Higher Education* 39, no. 27 (1993): A7–A9.

Stimpson, Catharine R. "Editing Signs." In *The Horizon of Literature,* edited by Paul Hernadi, 241–248. Lincoln: University of Nebraska Press, 1982.

———, et al. "Editorial." *Signs: Journal of Women in Culture and Society* 1 (1975): v–viii.

Silence

As a noun meaning an absence of voice, silence has become a metaphor for woman's historical powerlessness within Western culture; as a verb meaning to suppress, silence betrays the political mechanisms behind that powerlessness. Both meanings are important for the feminist literary critique of silence. While textual silences are not unique to women's writing, and have often been analyzed in gender-neutral terms, feminist theorists argue that silence holds special significance for women, as writers and as literary characters, because of their political marginalization.

The study of silence as it relates to women and writing, has, however, changed dramatically in the past twenty-five years; while feminist critics continue to probe the ways that silence has been used against women, they are also investigating the ways in which women have used silence to subvert and critique the narrative and political structures of a male-dominated society, and more recently, to critique other forms of domination, including imperialism and racism.

For feminists of the 1960s and 1970s, "silence," with its inescapable connotations of invisibility and censorship, was a negative term. Tillie Olsen's *Silences,* for example, listed the personal and social reasons that kept women from writing. Other critics invoked the notion of a conspiracy of silence to describe women's reticence in writing honestly about subjects like motherhood and lesbianism. The "images of women" school of feminist criticism (1970s) explored connections between the idealized depiction of silent women in texts, from folktales to conduct books, and the repressive socialization of women as readers, writers, and critics.

Moving beyond an examination of the social constraints upon women, feminist sociolinguists of the 1970s targeted the male bias historically present within specific languages, particularly English. The French feminists (1970s and 1980s), drawing upon the psychoanalytic theories of Freud and Lacan, also emphasized the male-centeredness of language, but in a more fundamental way; in Lacan's distinction between the masculine or symbolic, which includes discursive language, and the feminine or semiotic, which is prelinguistic, woman is alienated from rational language, relegated to hysteria or silence. Rejecting literal silence as a trap for women, Hélène Cixous advocated a kind of writing that would privilege those dissonant, disruptive, and hysterical elements previously devalued as feminine and irrational. Julia Kristeva, on the other hand, reinterpreted the position of silent observer and listener as potentially empowering.

Both viewpoints influenced the feminist study of literary silence in the 1980s and 1990s. Instead of reading the blanks, gaps, and ellipses surrounding the representation of women, in texts by men as well as women, as mimetic representations of absence, feminist critics reinterpreted them as sites of ideological and narratological strain or resistance. Thus, in an analysis of George Eliot's *Daniel Deronda,* Ellen Rosenman argued that the gaps and silences of the novel's female confessions not only dramatize the impossibility of a woman's self being expressed in the available social and literary structures (including institutions like marriage), but also disrupt the coherence of the male-centered narrative and thereby expose the arbitrary nature of narrative coherence. For other feminist critics, silence, in a variety of senses, became the sign of women's writing, the means by which women offered their critique of Western culture. Patricia Laurence, for instance, claimed Virginia Woolf as inheritor of a specifically female relation to silence, one that implicitly assigns power to woman as silently observing subject, in contrast to a masculine perspective that defines woman as observed object.

Reflecting feminist theory's growing emphasis upon the analysis of differences other than gender, feminist critics of the 1990s are paying close attention to the way that women within texts, by both men and women, have been silenced by virtue of race and class. How, for instance, have colonial women been deprived of voice? The example of Bertha, Rochester's mad Creole wife in Charlotte Brontë's *Jane Eyre,* comes to mind, but there are many others. Feminist critics are also examining the complicity of white middle-class women writers in silencing other persons with regard to race and class. What does it mean that an educator like Hannah More did not believe in teaching lower-class women to write? Did white middle-class women writers in the nineteenth century appropriate the imagery and voices of slavery in order to further their own self-determination? Of special interest is the recovery of the voices of women who write from outside white middle-class Anglo American culture. How are postcolonial women writers subverting the silences imposed upon them by political repression and censorship?

Increasingly, feminist critics have argued that privileging silence(s) in woman's writing presumes falsely that all women, regardless of class, race, ethnic or historical status, share the same experience of language. There is a nagging suspicion that modern feminists may, in their own way, simply be perpetuating the cultural stereotypes about women and silence that they have claimed to revise. In light of the escalating violence and abuse that is directed toward real women, one wonders whether it is self-deluding to equate silence, in any form, with empowerment.

Marla Harris

References

Busia, Abena P.A. "Silencing Sycorax: On African Colonial Discourse and the Unvoiced Female." *Cultural Critique* (1989–1990): 81–104.

Cameron, Deborah, ed. *The Feminist Critique of Language: A Reader*. London: Routledge, 1990.

Cheung, King-Kok. *Articulate Silences: Hisage Yomamoto, Maxime Hong Kingston, Joy Kowaga*. Ithaca, N.Y.: Cornell University Press, 1993.

Cixous, Hélène. "The Laugh of the Medusa." Translated by Keith Cohen and Paula Cohen. *Signs* 1 (1976): 778–894.

Kristeva, Julia. *About Chinese Women*. Translated by Anita Barrows. New York: Urizen, 1977.

Landy, Marcia. "The Silent Woman." In *The Authority of Experience: Essays in Feminist Criticism*, edited by Arlyn Diamond and Lee R. Edwards, 16–27. Amherst: University of Massachusetts Press, 1977.

Laurence, Patricia Ondek. *The Reading of Silence: Virginia Woolf in the English Tradition*. Stanford: Stanford University Press, 1991.

Olsen, Tillie. *Silences*. New York: Delacorte, 1978.

Rosenman, Ellen B. "Women's Speech and the Roles of the Sexes in Daniel Deronda." *Texas Studies in Literature and Language* 31 (1989): 237–256.

Stout, Janis P. *Strategies of Reticence: Silence and Meaning in the Works of Jane Austen, Willa Cather, Katherine Anne Porter, and Joan Didion*. Charlottesville: University Press of Virginia, 1990.

Sister

Although this term is generally used in its biological sense to denote a woman in relation to other people born of her parents, it has a much broader meaning and a varied history within feminism. The *Oxford English Dictionary* includes definitions of "sister" as "one who is reckoned as, or fills the place of, a sister. In modern specific uses . . . a (fellow) feminist," and "a female holding a similar position to another." For many years, the ideals of fellowship and solidarity implied in the concept of sisterhood were taken for granted by feminists. More recently, however, critics have denounced this term as a dangerous and misleading omission of the concerns and obstacles that tend to divide women, such as race, class, and sexual preference. The controversies that have arisen out of the concept of sisterhood pose crucial questions about the nature of female relations, both in life and in literature.

Intriguingly, the *Oxford English Dictionary* also defines "sisterhood" as a term "used loosely to denote a number of women having some common aim, characteristic, or calling. Often in a bad sense. Recently also *spec.* of feminists." Bad sense or no, the concept of a universal sisterhood of women grew out of the fight for female suffrage in the late nineteenth and early twentieth centuries, and was fundamental to the women's movement during the late 1960s and through the early 1970s. The literary works of writers such as Adrienne Rich and Alice Walker, and the theory of Kate Millett all illustrate this importance. The biological link emphasized in sisterhood was also a neat encapsulation of the common struggle women faced against patriarchy—sisters bonded together to rebel against the tyranny of the omnipresent father figure. Sisterhood was a "woman-to-woman dyad" that had the power to constitute "a threat within patriarchy." Experience was held to be the key link between all women: the repression brought on by repressive ideological definitions was "shared by every woman," and this "common oppression" provided the basis of female unity. For many, sisterhood was one of the most rewarding aspects of the painful struggle for women's liberation: as Gloria Steinem wrote with relief in 1972, "women understand."

But the essentialist universality of these "deep and personal connections" among women has not gone unchallenged. Although these common interests and goals were hailed by feminists of the 1960s and 1970s as having the power to transcend "barriers of age, economics, worldly experience, race, [and] culture" in the worldwide battle for sexual equality, they did not prove to be either as ubiquitous or as constant as those theorists had hoped. Instead, the concerns of smaller groups of women gradually grew to overshadow the sororal bonds that the earlier movement had forged. Even as early as 1970, one lesbian writer described herself as "social anathema, even to you brave ones" involved in feminist endeavors. The language of sisterhood and female solidarity began to fray most noticeably at the edges during the late 1970s and the 1980s, when women of different classes, races, sexual preferences, ages, and educations began to articulate their fundamental difference from one another. Feminists, instead of proclaiming the common identity of women that sisterhood seemed to imply, began to formulate theories "on the basis of disagreement and opposition." As Audre Lorde commented in a 1985 address, feminists found it difficult to "deal constructively" with the "genuine differences" between them—the close familial bond appeared to be replaced by multiple family squabbles.

However, the concept of sisterhood has not been abandoned entirely. More recently, feminist critics such as Amy Levin, Helena Michie, and the contributors to *Conflicts in Feminism* have stressed that "unity does not require that we be identical to each other." The automatic and erroneous equation of "sister" with "friend," Levin argues, allows theorists to ignore "the frequent friction . . . that is so much at odds with ideals of sisterhood."

Instead of insisting that all women experience exactly the same oppression simply by virtue of being women, these critics point out that relationships between blood sisters frequently involve anger, conflict, jealousy, and competition, yet lose none of their strength or value. A sister is "a special kind of double," who may be one's mirror image and one's polar opposite at the same time. Thus, one possible solution to the conflicts that have arisen within this facet of feminism is to acknowledge and attempt to work within the "negotiation of sameness and difference, identity and separation" that the complex sororal bond involves.

The varied history of the concept of sisterhood has interesting implications for the feminist study of literature. The more recent questioning of the ideal of universal sisterhood has widened the spectrum through which female characters can be read, enabling us to look beyond a "self-imposed censorship on certain feelings that women consider unacceptable." For example, competition, jealousy, envy, and obsession are fundamental aspects of Julia Corbett's relationship with her sister Cassandra in A.S. Byatt's *The Game*. Similarly, Aurora's relationship to Marian Erle in Elizabeth Barret Browning's *Aurora Leigh* takes on multiple levels of new meaning when distinctions of class, elements of sexual rivalry, and their competitiveness with each other and with virtually all of the other women in the poem are taken into account. Women's attachments to each other in literary texts have been simultaneously rendered richer and infinitely more problematic with the redefinition of sisterhood as reality instead of as ideal.

The shifting implications of what it means to be a sister raise important questions for feminism and feminist literary study. Faced with the complexities that the trope of sisterhood is now seen to embody, how can feminism exist as a unified movement? Under what circumstances could common aspects of female existence reach beyond individual special interests? In what ways does individuality contrast with communality in stories involving pairs or groups of sisters? Can these oppositions ever be reconciled? In examining the roles and relations of characters like Aurora Leigh, critics are able to gain insight into both the legacy of liberal feminism and the possible paths that can be mapped out within the expanded discourse of sisterhood.

Alexandra Bennett

References

Hirsch, Marianne, and Evelyn Fox Keller, eds. *Conflicts in Feminism*. New York: Routledge, 1990.

Levin, Amy K. *The Suppressed Sister: A Relationship in Novels by Nineteenth- and Twentieth-Century British Women*. London: Associated University Presses, 1992.

Lorde, Audre. *I Am Your Sister: Black Women Organizing across Sexualities*. Latham, N.Y.: Kitchen Press: Women of Color Press, 1985.

McNaron, Toni A.H., ed. *The Sister Bond: A Feminist View of a Timeless Connection*. New York: Pergamon, 1985.

Martin, Wendy, ed. *The American Sisterhood: Writings of the Feminist Movement from Colonial Times to the Present*. New

York: Harper and Row, 1972.

Michie, Helena. *Sororophobia: Differences among Women in Literature and Culture.* Oxford: Oxford University Press, 1992.

Morgan, Robin, ed. *Sisterhood is Powerful: An Anthology of Writings from the Women's Liberation Movement.* New York: Vintage Books, 1970.

Rich, Adrienne. *Adrienne Rich's Poetry.* Edited by Barbara Charlesworth Gelpi and Albert Gelpi. New York: W.W. Norton, 1975.

Steinem, Gloria. "Sisterhood." In *Current Issues and Enduring Questions,* edited by Sylvan Barnet and Hugo Bedeau, 566–571. Boston: Bedford, 1993.

Slave Narratives

It is estimated that between 1703 and 1944 six thousand former slaves had related their stories of captivity as a testimonial to the horrors of chattel slavery. Henry Louis Gates has asserted that black slaves in the United States were unique "in the long history of human bondage" in their creation of a genre of literature that simultaneously attested to the violence of slavery and "bore witness to the urge of every black slave to be free and literate." Intended primarily to inspire political support in the struggle for abolition, slave narratives by both men and women appealed to the humanity and sympathy of a predominantly white Northern audience. Women's narratives, however, differed in their detail and frankness about the sexual abuse endemic in slavery, and thus defied nineteenth-century conventions of "true womanhood" that dictated decorum and silence about sexual matters. In voicing their stories, these women called for justice, not merely sympathy. They became models for feminist suffragists who were agitating for women's rights in Seneca Falls. Both Frederick Douglass, easily the most famous slave narrator, and Sojourner Truth attended their conventions, and Douglass signed the "Declaration of Sentiments" in 1848. These women's rights advocates went on to adopt the abolitionist slogan and symbol that depicted a kneeling female slave with the caption "Am I Not A Woman And A Sister?" In so doing they linked women's oppression with racial subjugation, but they also blurred the real distinctions between the oppression of chattel slavery and marriage.

Slave narratives have been important documents for feminist historians and theorists. In the mid 1980s, the Schomburg Library of Nineteenth Century Black Women Writers began publishing many previously unpublished women's slave narratives, thus providing scholars with easy access to these historically significant texts. Perhaps the most famous narrative for feminists has been Harriet Jacobs's *Incidents in the Life of a Slave Girl.* Long considered to have been authored by the white abolitionist Lydia Maria Child, Jean Fagan Yellin in 1981 proved Jacobs the author of her own narrative. A considerable amount of scholarly work has been done on this narrative since then, and it is now required reading in most American literature classes. Sojourner Truth's narrative has similarly been important to feminist scholars. Her famous phrase "Ar'n't I a Woman?," delivered in a renowned address to the 1851 Women's Rights Convention in Akron, Ohio, is widely referred to by feminist historians and literary critics.

Slave narratives have been important to feminist theorists from the nineteenth century abolitionists and suffragists to current historians and critics as well as fiction writers. Toni Morrison in *Beloved,* Sherley Anne Williams in *Dessa Rose,* and Octavia Butler in *Kindred* have demonstrated in their fiction a strong literary relation with slave narratives. That all of these texts function as revisionary slave narratives is a testimony to how influential the slave narratives have been as a literary genre. That feminist theorists have been influenced by this genre can be seen in the vast number of critical texts and histories that have burgeoned since the republishing effort by the Schomburg library and others since the early 1980s.

Lisa Marcus

References

Andrews, William L. *To Tell a Free Story: The First Century of Afro-American Autobiography, 1760–1865.* Urbana: University of Illinois Press, 1986.

———, ed. *Six Women's Slave Narratives.* New York: Oxford University Press, 1988.

Davis, Charles H., and Henry Louis Gates, Jr., eds. *The Slave's Narrative.* New York: Oxford University Press, 1985.

Douglass, Frederick. *Narrative of the Life of Frederick Douglass, an American Slave* [1845]. New York: Penguin, 1982.

Foster, Frances Smith. *Witnessing Slavery: The Development of Antebellum Slave Narratives*. Westport, Conn.: Greenwood, 1979.

Gates, Henry Louis, Jr., ed. *The Classic Slave Narratives*. New York: New American Library, 1987.

Jacobs, Harriet. *Incidents in the Life of a Slave Girl*. Edited by Jean Fagan Yellin. New York: Oxford University Press, 1987.

McDowell, Deborah E., and Arnold Rampersad. *Slavery and the Literary Imagination*. Baltimore, Md.: Johns Hopkins University Press, 1989.

Sekora, John, and Darwin T. Turner, eds. *The Art of the Slave Narrative*. Macomb: Western Illinois Press, 1982.

Washington, Margaret, ed. *Narrative of Sojourner Truth*. New York: Vintage, 1993.

Wilson Starling, Marion. *The Slave Narrative: Its Place in American History*. Boston: G.K. Hall, 1982.

Yellin, Jean Fagan. *Women and Sisters: The Antislavery Feminists in American Culture*. New Haven: Yale University Press, 1989.

Slavery

In the United States of America, slavery is and has always been synonymous with race slavery, which is the economic and social system in which people of Africa and their descendants became chattel, movable property, and had their labor stolen from them by their white "owners." Sometimes used figuratively to suggest other oppressions, the history and discursive elaboration of slavery remain central to feminist literary theory not only because of slavery's persisting social fallout in American culture, but also because the history and literary imaginings of slavery raise central feminist questions. Deborah E. McDowell and Arnold Rampersad call slavery "the American heart of darkness, the historic national sin that no holy water will ever wash away."

Among literary critics and theorists, the study of slavery centers on the slave narratives and on other literary representations of slavery; these representations of slavery serve different functions in different historical moments. Harriet Jacobs's now famous *Incidents in the Life of a Slave Girl* (1861) is a vitally important representation of slavery because not only does she—as all slave narrators do—tell her own tale of bondage, forced labor, familial separation, and sadistic cruelty as a plea for those still in bondage, but she also addresses for the first time the way in which enslaved women endured sexual terrorism at the hands of their white male masters. For many enslaved African American women, the system of slavery stole both labor power and sexual "purity." Jacobs's text raises fundamental feminist questions about the intersections of race, gender, and sexual ideologies; she shows how slavery renders the notion of "true womanhood" unrealizable for enslaved women.

One of the most widely reproduced and disseminated texts about slavery, however, forwards a white woman's view of the "peculiar institution," as slavery is sometimes called. Harriet Beecher Stowe's *Uncle Tom's Cabin, or, Life among the Lowly* swept the country in 1852 and was followed by untallied spin-off tales, plays, and souvenirs. Stowe is credited with having written "the little book that started the big war," and her hugely popular novel certainly furthered the abolition of slavery. Twentieth-century readers, however, find that Stowe's arguments for abolition do not derive from claims for racial equality. To many, her "Uncle Tom" is a docile, exoticized caricature of subservient, emasculated Christian obedience; his character derives from racist discourses and therefore represents some white people's impressions of "black" character.

While Stowe exerted tremendous influence over antebellum representations of slavery, the elaboration and diversification of slavery's meanings persist well into the twentieth century. The WPA collected first-hand accounts of slavery until 1940. In 1983, Harriet Wilson's 1859 text *Our Nig, or Sketches from the Life of a Free Black* was rediscovered. Wilson's novel shows how "slavery's shadows fell" in the North, and thereby questions the "freedom" of the free states. Margaret Walker's 1966 novel *Jubilee* marked a resurgence in narratives about slavery and has recently been followed by Shirley Ann Williams's *Dessa Rose* and Toni Morrison's *Beloved*.

The meaning of slavery in feminist literary criticism and theory is also currently a matter of discussion and elaboration. Those interested in British feminism note that, as early as the publication of *Oroonoko* by Aphra Behn in 1688, British women writers have referred to slavery; at the end of the eighteenth century, they sometimes used slavery as a metaphor for their own condition. In the United States, Hortense Spillers writes that there is no single origin of or representation of slavery; she argues that "the cultural synthesis we call 'slavery' was never homogeneous in its practices and conceptions." Slavery's many meanings still signify differently to various feminist theorists. Gillian Brown—in her discussion of *Uncle Tom's Cabin*—emphasizes slavery's dismantling of the central tenets of nineteenth-century womanhood. She writes, "The distinction between work and family is eradicated in the slave, for whom there is no separation between economic and private status." Karen Sanchez-Eppler has argued that white women abolitionists appropriated slavery as a metaphor for their own oppression, frequently eliding the plight of the enslaved. Hazel Carby observes the paradoxical flickering of slavery in African American writing; she maintains that slavery is central, socially and economically, but that it is "rarely the focus" of Afro-American novels. Deborah McDowell concludes that the rewritings of slavery in the late twentieth century—she focuses on *Dessa Rose*—serve to set the record straight, to tell the story of slavery one more time from the imagined vantage point of those who endured it. The necessity of retelling slavery is, for McDowell, both to get the story right and to see the current world and its discriminations in relation to the legacy of slavery. She suggests that a central project of literary criticism, fiction—and of feminist literary theory as well—is to stave off the "cultural amnesia that has begun to reenslave us all."

Mary V. Dougherty

References

Brown, Gillian. "Getting in the Kitchen with Dinah: Domestic Politics in Uncle Tom's Cabin." *American Quarterly* 36 (1984): 503–523.

Carby, Hazel. "Ideologies of Black Folk: The Historical Novel of Slavery." In *Slavery and the Literary Imagination,* edited by Deborah E. McDowell, 125–143. Baltimore, Md.: Johns Hopkins University Press, 1989.

Ferguson, Moira. *Subject to Others: British Women Writers and Colonial Slavery, 1678–1834.* New York: Routledge, 1992.

Foner, Philip. *History of Black Americans: From the Emergence of the Cotton King-dom to the Eve of the Compromise of 1850.* Westport, Conn.: Greenwood, 1983.

Franklin, John Hope, and Alfred Moss, Jr. *From Slavery to Freedom: A History of Negro Americans.* New York: McGraw-Hill, 1988.

Genovese, Eugene. *Roll, Jordan, Roll: The World the Slaves Made.* New York: Pantheon, 1974.

Gutman, Herbert. *Power and Culture: Essays on the American Working Class.* Edited by Ira Berlin. New York, 1987.

McDowell, Deborah E., and Arnold Rampersad. *Slavery and the Literary Imagination.* Baltimore, Md.: Johns Hopkins University Press, 1989.

Pryse, Marjorie, and Hortense Spillers, eds. *Conjuring: Black Women, Fiction, and Literary Tradition.* Bloomington: Indiana University Press, 1985.

Sanchez-Eppler, Karen. "Bodily Bonds: The Intersecting Rhetorics of Feminism and Abolition." *Representations* 24 (1988): 28–59.

Spillers, Hortense. "Changing the Letter: The Yokes, the Jokes of Discourse, or, Mrs. Stowe, Mr. Reed." In *Slavery and the Literary Imagination,* edited by Deborah E. McDowell, 25–61. Baltimore, Md.: Johns Hopkins University Press, 1989.

White, Deborah Gray. *Ar'n't I a Woman?: Female Slaves in the Plantation South.* New York: W.W. Norton, 1985.

Smith, Barbara

Activist Barbara Smith is a forerunner in the field of African American feminist studies, both for publishing the earliest theoretical statement of black feminist criticism, and for co-founding Kitchen Table: Women of Color Press in 1981, the first press specifically devoted to the work of women of color. In her landmark essay "Toward a Black Feminist Criticism," published in 1977, Smith pointed out that male and feminist critics alike had undervalued or ignored the literature of black women. She then called for a new black feminist critical approach based on the shared language and cultural experience of black women, one that would identify a distinct black female literary tradition as well as its often lesbian subtexts. Significantly, her analysis of Toni Morrison's *Sula* marked the first lesbian reading of a female relationship in an African

American literary work. While subsequently labeled essentialist by some feminist literary critics, her essay is nevertheless seen as the groundbreaking statement that facilitated the emergence of black feminist criticism as a field of inquiry, and more specifically, as a tool for literary analysis.

Smith also helped develop the first interdisciplinary reference text and pedagogical tool published for black feminist studies as co-editor (with Gloria Hull and Patricia Bell Scott) of *All the Women Are White, All the Blacks Are Men, but Some of Us Are Brave: Black Women's Studies,* a collection of essays, bibliographies, and sample course syllabi. Smith next edited Kitchen Table's first major publication, *Home Girls: A Black Feminist Anthology,* an unconventional collection of fiction, poetry, dialogue, speech, essays, and intergeneric forms by African American women addressing a range of feminist and lesbian issues.

In addition to her work at Kitchen Table: Women of Color Press, Smith continues to teach and write on a number of issues affecting feminists of color, particularly lesbians. Her work remains important for feminist literary criticism in that she was one of the first to point out the blind spots of white feminists, to foster the study of black women's writing, and therefore to diversify the field of academic feminism.

Kimberley Roberts

References

Smith, Barbara. "Toward a Black Feminist Criticism" [1977]. In *All the Women Are White, All the Blacks Are Men, but Some of Us Are Brave: Black Women's Studies,* edited by Gloria T. Hull, Patricia Bell Scott, and Barbara Smith, 157–175. Old Westbury, N.Y.: Feminist, 1982.

————, ed. *Home Girls: A Black Feminist Anthology.* Latham, N.Y.: Kitchen Table: Women of Color Press, 1983.

————, et al., eds. *All the Women Are White, All the Blacks Are Men, but Some of Us Are Brave: Black Women's Studies.* Old Westbury, N.Y.: Feminist, 1982.

————, et al., eds. *Yours in Struggle: Three Feminist Perspectives on Anti-Semitism and Racism.* Ithaca, N.Y.: Firebrand, 1984.

Smith-Rosenberg, Carroll

Smith-Rosenberg radically changed the conceptualization of nineteenth-century gender relations with her pioneering 1975 article "The Female World of Love and Ritual." She argued that women act as agents of their own history and are not merely acted upon. Specifically, she analyzed the nature of women's long-lasting, intimate friendships within a particular social and cultural setting, sparking the "separate spheres" debate for nineteenth-century gender history. Women's friendships resulted from a gendered division of labor, the so-called "separate spheres." Smith-Rosenberg's study broke away from a strictly psychosexual, or Freudian, perspective, which had been the common path of analysis. Instead, she called this world of women homosocial, bringing to light a new set of questions for further research. "Disorderly Conduct," Smith-Rosenberg's book of essays published in 1985, included "Love and Ritual" and explored many other issues surrounding nineteenth-century women, their relationships, and their sexuality. Some of her articles in this volume have been criticized for being reductionist because she treats sexuality only as a metaphor for social structures, when, particularly in the case of homosexuality, sexual issues represent much more than metaphors and sexuality in itself influences society.

Gina Hames

References

Smith-Rosenberg, Carroll. "The Body Politic." In *Coming to Terms: Feminism, Theory Politics,* edited by Elisabeth Weed, 101–121. New York: Routledge, 1989.

————. *Disorderly Conduct: Visions of Gender in Victorian America.* New York: Knopf, 1985.

————. "The Female World of Love and Ritual: Relations between Women in Nineteenth-Century America." *Signs: Journal of Women in Culture and Society* 1 (1975): 1–29.

Social Contract

Originating with liberal philosophers Thomas Hobbes and John Locke, this term from political theory describes the binding agreement made among individuals to form an organized society. In the mid eighteenth century, Jean-Jacques Rousseau stressed the importance of language and education rather than force as the source of the contract's authority. The social contract naturalizes power relations through language. Following the work of Jean Bethke Elshtain, feminist critics have emphasized the ideological nature of the social contract, showing how it is also a sexual contract that defines women's identities, social roles, and writing styles.

The sexual contract divides social reality into two spheres, public/political and private/domestic, defining women's realm as the domestic sphere of the household and family. The sexual/social contract has excluded women's voices from the public sphere, and thus from literary canons, and has limited women's writing to domestic ("nonpolitical") concerns. As Adrienne Rich and Monique Wittig have shown, the contract demands heterosexuality and denies lesbian existence. At the same time, it depends on what Eve Sedgwick calls homosocial desire, the social bonds between men, to support its exclusions of women.

Feminist literary critics, such as Christine Froula and Judith Lowder Newton, show how literature both reinforces and challenges the social contract. Nancy Armstrong argues that the domestic novel participates in the sexual/social contract by translating the political into the psychology of sexual relations. Feminist criticism continues to study the ideological relationship between the social contract and literary representation.

Ashley J. Cross

References

Armstrong, Nancy. *Desire and Domestic Fiction: A Political History of the Novel.* New York: Oxford University Press, 1987.

Elshtain, Jean Bethke. *Public Man and Private Woman: Women in Social and Political Thought.* Princeton: Princeton University Press, 1981.

Froula, Christine. "When Eve Reads Milton: Undoing the Canonical Economy." *Critical Inquiry* 10 (1983): 321–347.

Newton, Judith Lowder. *Women, Power, and Subversion: Social Strategies in British Fiction 1778–1860.* Athens: University of Georgia Press, 1981.

Pateman, Carole. *The Sexual Contract.* Stanford: Stanford University Press, 1988.

Rich, Adrienne. "Compulsory Heterosexuality and Lesbian Existence." *Signs* 5 (1980): 631–660.

Rousseau, Jean-Jacques. *The Social Contract.* Translated by Maurice Cranston. New York: Penguin, 1968.

Sedgwick, Eve Kosofsky. *Between Men: English Literature and Male Homosocial Desire.* New York: Columbia University Press, 1985.

Wittig, Monique. "On the Social Contract." *Feminist Issues* 9 (1989): 3–12.

Socialist Feminism

Socialist feminism may be distinguished from both radical or liberal feminism by its insistence that capitalism and patriarchy are equal, but different, systems of oppression. Less concerned with determining which has historical priority, socialist feminism argues that only a dialectical method of exploring their interrelation can provide a viable means of undoing social injustice. This entails a two-pronged attack—on Marxist exclusions of women from theories of production and on feminist argument where it fails to take account of the fissuring effects of social class in its discussion.

The late 1960s saw the emergence of a vocal, and specifically feminist, group of Marxist women thinkers on both sides of the Atlantic who were instrumental in developing a critique of both Leninist "vanguardist" methods of organization and New Left theories. An article by Juliet Mitchell, "Women: The Longest Revolution," adapted Louis Althusser's theory of ideology to lead the departure of socialist feminists toward psychoanalysis as a means of explaining the "complex unity" of women's oppression under patriarchy. Mitchell argued that a socialist analysis of women's oppression should not be confined to the economic determinism of understanding the family (women and children) as a form of private property (for men), and stressed the importance of assessing the role of ideology in containing and constructing "women" as sexual subjects in capitalist patriarchy. In America, a similar debate developed over the "unhappy marriage" of Marxism and feminism. Zillah Eisenstein argued for an analysis that attended to "the mutually reinforcing dialectical relationship" between hierarchies of class and sex that she termed "capitalist patriarchy," while Heidi Hartmann pointed out that patriarchal interest on the part of men in the labor movement has significantly undermined their struggle with capitalist exploitation.

In literary and cultural criticism, these theoretical insights have resulted in a socialist feminist critical praxis with a distinctive set of preoccupations and methodologies. The most striking are an insistence on exploring the historical specificity of particular literary and cultural forms and their negotiation with the intersection of gender, class, and race in textual production; the development of collaborative methods of reading, writing, and interpreting literary and cultural texts; and an exploration of the relation between text and social reality, which has resulted in an interrogation of categories of "aesthetic value" as historically and socially determined rather than absolute and given. Much socialist feminist criticism has been concentrated in nineteenth-century studies. Essays by Cora Kaplan ("Pandora's Box") and Gayatri Chakravorty Spivak ("Three Women's Texts and a Critique of Imperialism") interrogated conventional feminist readings of Charlotte Brontë's *Jane Eyre* that see Jane as a prototype of the autonomous feminist subject, pointing out that her (middle-class) autonomy and individualism is purchased at the cost of the suppression and demonization of more radical (working class and antiimperialist) forms of feminist resistance symbolized in the overdetermined figure of Bertha Rochester. This critique of feminist humanism extends into socialist-feminist discussions of popular and mass culture. Ros Coward's influential essay "Are Women's Novels Feminist Novels?" stressed the distinction between women-centered literature and a feminist politics in writing; representations of gender difference are not coterminous with a critique of sexual inequality. Critics like Coward and Michèle Barrett in Britain, Tanya Modleski and Teresa de Lauretis in the United States, and Meaghan Morris and Susan Sheridan in Australia, focus on the importance of establishing a feminist culture, resistant to capitalist and patriarchal modes of production and consumption, and hence providing the necessary conditions for a radical artistic practice to develop.

Ros Ballaster

References

Barrett, Michèle. "Feminism and the Definition of Cultural Politics." In *Feminism, Culture and Politics*, edited by Rosalind Brunt and Caroline Rowan, 37–58. London: Lawrence and Wishart, 1982.

Coward, Rosalind. "Are Women's Novels Feminist Novels?" In *The New Feminist Criticism*, edited by Elaine Showalter, 225–239. London: Virago, 1986.

Eisenstein, Zillah R., ed. *Capitalist Patriarchy and the Case for Socialist Feminism*. New York: Monthly Review, 1970.

Hartmann, Heidi. "The Unhappy Marriage of Marxism and Feminism." In *Women and Revolution*, edited by Lydia Sargent, 1–42. Boston: South End, 1981.

Kaplan, Cora. "Pandora's Box: Subjectivity, Class and Sexuality in Socialist Feminist Criticism." In *Sea Changes: Culture and Feminism*, 147–176. London: Verso, 1986.

Mitchell, Juliet. "Women: The Longest Revolution" [1966]. In *Women: The Longest Revolution*, 12–54. London: Virago, 1984.

Sargent, Lydia, ed. *The Unhappy Marriage of Marxism and Feminism: A Debate on Class and Patriarchy*. London and Sydney: Pluto, 1981.

Spivak, Gayatri Chakravorty. "Three Women's Texts and a Critique of Imperialism." *Critical Inquiry* 12 (1985): 62–80.

Sororophobia

A term coined by Helena Michie to explore both the possibilities and the limitations of the metaphor of sisterhood within the lexicon of feminism. Michie argues that the familial term "sister" both reveals and obscures the complex quality of women's relationships to one another. For, while the ideal of sisterhood suggests a close-knit bond between women united against patriarchy and provides a safe space in which to articulate the friction between them, it also covers over numerous differences irreducible to the paradigm of the nuclear family. The negative impact of such differences, when they are ignored, is apparent in conflicts between academic feminisms and "street" feminisms, frictions between straight and lesbian feminists and within the lesbian community itself, racial tensions, and in other areas in which the agendas of different feminist groups come into conflict. Sororophobia provides a paradigm for reading these conflicts by recalling "competition, racism, betrayal, argument, homophobia, classism, jealousy, envy, [and] hostility" into the vocabulary of feminism, not simply to suggest a "phobic" relationship between women, but also to suggest that which must be negotiated in order to form more effective and cohesive feminist coalitions.

"Sororophobia," Michie writes, "is about

negotiation; it attempts to describe the negotiation of sameness and difference, identity and separation, between women of the same generation, and is meant to encompass both the desire for and the recoil from identification with other women. . . . [It] is not so much a single term as it is a matrix against and through which women work out—or fail to work out —their differences." Turning a feminist analysis on feminism itself, Michie points toward work that might be done between women in order to strengthen their alliances without covering over their differences.

Rebecca F. Stern

References

Hirsch, Marianne, and Evelyn Fox Keller, eds. *Conflicts in Feminism*. New York: Routledge, 1990.

Michie, Helena. *Sororophobia*. New York: Oxford, 1992.

Space

Whether explicitly or implicitly, on many different levels the problem of space is always already at the heart of the various projects of feminist literary theory. In the most basic terms, "space" denotes a limited area, a site, zone, or place. In feminist theoretical terms, "space" can be understood as a culturally saturated category of invented order; "space" thus produces and reflects social division. Both literally and figuratively, this means that "spaces" are defined and identified by sociocultural forces that finally enforce limitations, laws, and practices pertaining to "inclusion" and "exclusion." Historically, women have been distinctly excluded from and assigned to particular spaces; the idea of woman's "proper place" is then a construction that informs the "space" of gender itself. As much as racial segregation (written into the law) is about keeping spaces separate and unequal, a similar "separate and unequal" sociospatial atmosphere structures relations between women and men. Feminist literary theory has noted that by designating particular spaces "feminine," a society invested in gender segregation has ultimately deprived women of the opportunities that the "public" masculine sphere offers to (privileged white) men. If a feminist theoretical point of view is, after all, a view from a different location (different, that is, from the dominant masculine point of view that has historically constructed, produced, defined

and validated the "reality" of social experience), the question of "space" is clearly endemic to feminist theory.

On one level, this question has been taken up in the form of a critique of geographic and architectural spatial arrangements. Daphne Spain points out in her book *Gendered Spaces* that "women and men are spatially segregated in ways that reduce women's access to knowledge and thereby reinforce women's lower status relative to men's." Gendered spaces "separate women from knowledge used by men to produce and reproduce power and privilege." In the United States, such a critique dates back to the nineteenth century. As Dolores Hayden shows in her book *The Grand Domestic Revolution: A History of Feminist Designs for American Homes, Neighborhoods, and Cities*, "Between the end of the Civil War and the beginning of the Great Depression, three generations of material feminists raised fundamental questions about what was called 'woman's sphere' and 'woman's work.' They challenged two characteristics of industrial capitalism: the physical separation of household space from public space, and the economic separation of the domestic economy from the political economy." Among the nineteenth-century American feminist theorists who pioneered this new consciousness were Catherine Beecher, Harriet Beecher Stowe, and Charlotte Perkins Gilman. Issues pertaining to women's domestic confinement were also raised in fictional works. For example, in "The Yellow Wallpaper" Gilman portrays women's affliction within dominant constructions of "space" by telling the story of a nameless woman who, under the authority of her physician-husband, is confined to an upstairs bedroom, denied pen and paper, and finally, driven to a state of utter despair.

In the first half of the twentieth century feminist critiques of spatial circumstances continued. Virginia Woolf's nonfictional polemic *A Room of One's Own* argues that "a woman must have money and a room of her own if she is to write." Highlighting the relationship between economics, space, and "freedom," Woolf and others extended Gilman's work, characterizing "woman's sphere" as an economic-spatial arrangement designed to produce and maintain a system that deprives and exploits women.

In asserting such critiques, feminist theorists are always already in the business of transgressing boundaries, for they venture beyond the

S

zones to which they are definitively confined as women. On one hand, because the space of writing itself has always been a "masculine" territory, women writers are staking ground. In this sense, feminist theorists are, and must be, trespassers. On another hand, however, feminist theory invents a space that has not yet been traversed; as feminist philosopher Mary Daly articulates in *Beyond God the Father: Towards a Philosophy of Women's Liberation,* feminist thought moves into a "new space" on the boundaries of patriarchy or patriarchal space. Space is then a concept that is always already challenged by, and challenges, feminist criticism.

In the second half of the twentieth century, the popular claim by feminist theorists that the "personal is political" continued to challenge the durability of the public/private split. By centralizing the "personal," by claiming or situating the "personal" as the "political," feminist theory relocated sexual politics as a public issue. In this way, feminist theory enacted a powerful spatial strategy rooted in inversion and invasion. More abstractly, recent years show feminist theory to be highly conscious of, and increasingly reliant on, sociospatial references and terminologies. Feminist discourses often refer to the margins or marginality, boundaries, borders, barriers, and limitations, and frequently call for the construction of "new" and renovated spaces that would demolish traditional conceptions of gender and allow for the architecture of new identities. Much of the work of feminist literary theory is about carving out a space in which "women," "women's" issues, and women writers can be central to literary analysis and history. In the process of challenging the literary canon, feminist literary theory also establishes a space for women critics in the field of literary criticism.

As critics of the history of feminist theory have astutely pointed out, these spatial concerns have unfortunately proven to be quite ironic, for feminist theory maintains its own boundaries and exclusive practices. It has been a space in which white, heterosexual, middle-class women discourse about "women" at large without acknowledging the diversity of women's experiences in this world. Even as feminist theory initially grew out of a need to protest and amend a situation that exploited and excluded women in different aspects of culture and cultural production, feminist theory itself reproduced patterns of domination and hierarchy characteristic of the patriarchy by excluding (and exploiting) women of color, poor women, and lesbians. To the extent that white, heterosexual, middle-class feminists have remained silent on issues concerning lesbians, women of color, and poor women, feminist theory has remained another space in which women's voices are silenced. The construction of space is thus intimately and intricately bound up with the history of feminist theory; it both implicates and explains it. Perhaps the revolutionary potential of feminist theory is then dependent on its ability to constantly refigure space.

Kim Savelson

References

Cott, Nancy F. *The Bonds of Womanhood: "Woman's Sphere" in New England 1780–1835.* New Haven: Yale University Press, 1977.

Daly, Mary. *Beyond God the Father: Towards a Philosophy of Women's Liberation.* Boston: Beacon, 1971.

Fuss, Diana, ed. *Inside/Out: Lesbian Theories, Gay Theories.* New York: Routledge, 1991.

Gilman, Charlotte Perkins. *Women and Economics.* Boston: Small, Maynard, 1898.

———. *The Yellow Wallpaper.* Old Westbury, N.Y.: Feminist, 1973.

Hayden, Dolores. *The Grand Domestic Revolution: A History of Feminist Design for American Homes, Neighborhoods, and Cities.* Cambridge: MIT Press, 1981.

hooks, bell. *Feminist Theory: From Margin to Center.* Boston: South End, 1984.

Lakoff, Robin. *Language and Woman's Place.* New York: Harper and Row, 1975.

Rich, Adrienne. *On Lies, Secrets, and Silence.* New York: W.W. Norton, 1979.

Rosenberg, Rosalind. *Beyond Separate Spheres: Intellectual Roots of Modern Feminism.* New Haven: Yale University Press, 1982.

Spain, Daphne. *Gendered Spaces.* University of North Carolina Press, 1992.

Stowe, Catherine Beecher, and Harriet Beecher. *The American Woman's Home.* Hartford, Conn.: Stowe-Day Foundation, 1869.

Woolf, Virginia. *A Room of One's Own.* Orlando, Fla.: Harcourt Brace Jovanovich, 1929.

Spacks, Patricia Meyer

Already an accomplished critic, Patricia Meyer Spacks became with the publication of *The Female Imagination* a pioneer in Anglo American feminist literary theory as well. Considering a wide range of theoretical, fictional, and autobiographical texts by English-speaking, middle-class women dating from the seventeenth through late twentieth centuries, Spacks noted the thematic persistence of a number of conflicts that, though not exclusive to women, occupied special concern in their writing, conflicts such as the desire both for dependency and independence, for community and for autonomy, for passivity and for agency. In so doing, she argued for a "female imagination" that was in its viewpoints and psychic preoccupations fundamentally different from its male counterpart.

Spacks's subsequent books have concentrated on ideas and issues recurrent in women's writing. *Gossip* explores the ways in which the eponymous subject is marked as feminine: devalued, trivialized, denied authority, gossip yet wields extraordinary subversive and constitutive power both in fiction and in life. *Desire and Truth* focuses on the struggles in eighteenth-century novels between "truths" of plot and those of desire, between "masculine" and "feminine" values (like reason and feeling), and between the "authorial intention" of the plot and its historically conditioned receptions.

With remarkable breadth of reference, Spacks has written more extensively than any other feminist critic on eighteenth- and nineteenth-century English narrative. Her work has brought to critical attention a number of women writers forgotten by literary history and has been particularly useful in clearing space within putatively universal ideas (imagination, desire, truth) for a recognition of feminine difference.

Eileen Gillooly

References

Spacks, Patricia Meyer. *The Adolescent Idea: Myths of Youth and the Adult Imagination.* New York: Basic, 1981.
———. *Desire and Truth: Functions of Plot in Eighteenth-Century English Novels.* Chicago: University of Chicago Press, 1990.
———. *The Female Imagination.* New York: Knopf, 1975.
———. *Gossip.* New York: Knopf, 1985. Chicago: University of Chicago Press, 1986.
———. *Imagining a Self: Autobiography and Novel in Eighteenth-Century England.* Cambridge: Harvard University Press, 1976.

Spectacle

Spectacle involves a visual display, designed to provide intense sensory stimulation. By appealing primarily to the senses, it thereby discourages critical engagement and lends itself to consumption or commodification. It is most often associated with the public sphere and is marked by its staged or designed qualities. The excess and artifice of the spectacle serve to thwart recognition of both its status as a substitution for the real, as well as the fact of one's actual physical separation from the spectacular vision or event. Further, the consideration of spectacle assumes a noninteractive relationship between the seer and the seen. The spectacle is the object of sight, rather than the subject.

Feminist theory has used the split between subject and object inherent in spectacle, as well as the connotations of the display and the primacy of the visible, to consider the function of sexual difference in visual representation. Laura Mulvey, in her landmark essay on visual pleasure in the classical Hollywood narrative cinema, identified what she referred to as the male gaze: the effect of a complex relationship between the looks of the spectators in the audience, the characters at each other, and the camera itself. Mulvey argued that because of the structuring of these looks, the spectator identified with the male protagonist, and that the female in the cinematic narrative was thus objectified in a voyeuristic and fetishistic way, by all three looks. Mulvey concluded that the construction of the woman as spectacle was thus unavoidable in narrative cinema.

More recent work has complicated and expanded Mulvey's original theory, especially by positing the presence of an active female spectator or subject, as well as a male object of visual pleasure in cultural productions and in televised sports, and by pointing out the limits of the invocation of spectacle for feminist film theory. Certainly, theories that point to an unstable or oscillating sexuality must also be taken into account, before any attempt to fix spectacle in what is by now conventional gendered terms.

In addition, the notion of the woman as spectacle in cinema has been useful in the articulation of theories of difference, production, and spectatorship or reception in the other arts, performance, and theater.

Dyer, Richard. "Don't Look Now: The Male Pin-Up." *Screen* 23 (1982): 61–73.

Flitterman, Sandy. "Thighs and Whiskers: The Fascination of Magnum, P.I." *Screen* 26 (1985): 42–58.

Mayne, Judith. "The Limits of Spectacle." *Wide Angle* 6 (1984): 6.

Mulvey, Laura. "Visual Pleasure and Narrative Cinema." *Screen* 16 (1975): 6–18.

Pollock, Griselda. "What's Wrong with Images of Women?" *Screen Education* 24 (1977): 25–33.

Roof, Judith. "Marguerite Duras and the Question of a Feminist Theater." In *Feminism and Psychoanalysis,* edited by Richard Feldstein and Judith Roof, 323–340. Ithaca, N.Y., and London: Cornell University Press, 1989.

Stacey, Jackie. "Desperately Seeking Difference." *Screen* 28 (1987): 48–61.

Straub, Kristina. *Sexual Suspects: Eighteenth-Century Players and Sexual Ideology.* Princeton: Princeton University Press, 1992.

Spender, Dale

Australian feminist and author/editor of over twenty books, Dale Spender researches and writes about many subjects, always with an aim toward reconstructing the role of women in Western, patriarchal society. Her foremost concerns address women's language, education, and literary pursuits. With the publication of her first book, *Man Made Language,* Spender began a veritable crusade that continues into the present, a crusade based on the premise that men have used their power over women to control women's speech, women's writing, and women's access to knowledge. Spender is adamant in her view that the responsibility for women's oppression lies with men. Throughout her works, Spender urges women not to succumb to reactionary stances that would compromise women's struggle for a redistribution of patriarchal power.

Spender's investigation into the history of women's writing has demonstrated how men have devalued and suppressed the texts of women who voiced opposition to the patriarchal power structure—a paradigm that denied women access to education, marginalized their artistic achievements, and ridiculed their polemical statements. Through her research, Spender found that women protested their devaluation within their society, but that subsequently, these protests were "edited out" of the literature. In addition, any record of the few, temporary instances when women did gain a comparable footing with men was suppressed; hence, a subsequent generation of women, Spender found, began the protest again, believing they were without precedent. Many of Spender's books, such as *Mothers of the Novel,* and *Living by the Pen: Early British Women Writers,* provide us with that "missing" history of women's voices: they engage in the project of claiming a place for and a value in women's experience.

Spender's theoretical premise is that knowledge is socially constructed. Spender explores the politics of knowledge, and gathers together essays written by women scholars that address feminism's influence in their respective academic disciplines as well as the powerful influence of women's studies outside the traditional disciplinary framework. Spender wants to break the cycle of women's protest and their subsequent silencing. The key to breaking the cycle, Spender believes, is control of how knowledge is generated and distributed. Women need to control the publication of their writing, and gain significant purchase on the extensive possibilities offered by electronic information systems.

Spender is her own best example of the policy she recommends. With the legacy of women's heritage and traditions Spender's work provides, present and future feminist theorists have access to centuries of women's voices on which to base their own speech, their own writing, and their own quest for equal participation in the generation of and distribution of knowledge.

Kramarae, Cheris, and Dale Spender, eds. *The Knowledge Explosion: Generations of Feminist Scholarship.* New York: Viking Penguin, 1991.

Spender, Dale. *Feminist Theorists: Three Centuries of Key Women Thinkers.* New York: Pantheon, 1983.

———. *For the Record: The Making and*

Meaning of Feminist Knowledge. London: Women's, 1985.

———. *Living by the Pen: Early British Women Writers*. New York: Teachers College Press, 1992.

———. *Man Made Language*. London: Routledge and Kegan Paul, 1980.

———. *Mothers of the Novel: 100 Good Women Writers before Jane Austen*. London: Pandora, 1986.

———. *There's Always Been a Women's Movement This Century*. London: Pandora, 1983.

———. *Women of Ideas and What Men Have Done to Them: from Aphra Behn to Adrienne Rich*. London: Routledge and Kegan Paul, 1982.

———. *The Writing or the Sex? or, Why You Don't Have to Read Women's Writing to Know It's No Good*. New York: Pergamon, 1989.

Spillers, Hortense J.

A premier scholar of African American literature and women's studies, Hortense Spillers draws on feminist theory, anthropology, semiotics, and cultural studies to theorize gender and African American women's subjectivity. The clearest articulation of her argument can be found in "Mama's Baby, Papa's Maybe: An American Grammar Book," where she posits that the violence and domination experienced by African Americans under slavery has left them ungendered and outside the law, and therefore removed from participation in patriarchal power structures. According to Spillers, gender in the United States is merely an instrument of racial solidarity in the Anglo American rise to power; thus because some people have it, and some do not, Spillers sees gender as a socially constructed category, much like race or class. She further maintains that this marginal position vis-à-vis gender leaves both female and male African Americans uniquely poised to enact a radical revision to white male dominance.

As feminist theory has typically been the domain of white feminists, Spillers considers it crucial for African American women scholars to theorize gender and sexuality in ways that are specific to African American experience. While Spillers draws on thinkers like Freud and Foucault, her work does not merely appropriate existing theories, but rather accounts for the deficiencies in white Western critical models.

For example, in contrast to a poststructuralist stance that typically negates any appeal to experience, Spillers considers the historic experiences of African American women crucial to any articulation of black feminist thought. Further, she envisions a "dialectics of process" that can acknowledge the multiple and shifting identities of black women. Put simply, her theory conflates the insights of contemporary critical discourse with the diverse lived experience of black women.

Spillers's theories of gender also inflect her position on the black women's literary tradition; in contrast to other black feminist critics who assume a unified and linear tradition, and thereby imply a kind of monolithic black female experience, Spillers considers the tradition radically discontinuous. The most fruitful critical paradigm for black feminist inquiry, then, is not to establish a line of literary mothers and daughters, but rather to embrace the widely divergent vocabularies and possibilities for black female experience.

Thus her contribution to feminist literary theory lies in her radical approach to gender as a racial category of analysis. In addition, her work is a model of interdisciplinary sophistication and aptly illustrates how feminist theory is enriched by intersection with other critical modes.

Kimberley Roberts

References

Spillers, Hortense J. "Mama's Baby, Papa's Maybe: An American Grammar Book." *Diacritics: A Review of Contemporary Criticism* 17 (1987): 65–81.

———. "'The Permanent Obliquity of an In[pha]llibly Straight': In the Time of the Daughters and the Fathers." In *Changing Our Own Words: Essays on Criticism, Theory, and Writing by Black Women*, edited by Cheryl Wall, 127–149. New Brunswick, N.J.: Rutgers University Press, 1989.

———, ed. *Comparative American Identities: Race, Sex, and Nationality in the Modern Text*. New York: Routledge, 1991.

———, ed. *Conjuring: Black Women, Fiction, and Literary Tradition*. Bloomington: Indiana University Press, 1985.

Spinster

Although most contemporary readers would

immediately understand a spinster to be: "A woman still unmarried; *esp.* one beyond the usual age for marriage, an old maid" (*Oxford English Dictionary*, def. 2b.), the word originally meant a woman who spun (spin + feminine ending -ster). *Brewer's Dictionary of Phrase and Fable* (Harper and Row, 1981) explains that a young woman was not considered ready for marriage until she had spun a complete set of linens. Hence, a maiden was referred to as a spinner or spinster and, from the seventeenth century on, unmarried women were legally known as spinsters.

Like many originally neutral terms associated with women, however, "spinster" underwent what Muriel Schulz refers to as "semantic derogation." The productive elements of the term were dismantled over the years (indeed, spinster briefly meant "mistress" or "prostitute,"), until it took on the negative connotation it bears today. While few, if any, unmarried women would currently be referred to as spinsters, the adjective "spinsterish" is still used to imply a certain fussy, prissy demeanor.

The derogation of the term "spinster" appears to have begun with the decline in status of unmarried women, prompted by a decline in their economic status. In the eighteenth century the economic bases were shifting from home-centered industry to a market economy, and this new economy was one that increasingly excluded women's labor. As textiles began to be produced in factories, there was less need of traditionally feminine skills such as weaving or spinning. In addition, men were appropriating such traditionally feminine fields as midwifery. With few respectable economic options available to them, unmarried women became increasingly dependent on their families, but yet outside the patriarchal control of husbands. The combination of dependency and potential liberty (unmarried women had in fact more legal rights than their married counterparts) made them seem a frightening presence to society and increasingly ugly stereotypes grew up around them, often reflected and promulgated in literature. The problem of "redundant women" seemed especially acute in the nineteenth century, prompting social scientists to suggest numerous causes and remedies, most of which centered on emigration, and few of which centered on legitimate employment. Through the twentieth century the spinster image underwent several metamorphoses, from the prim "old maid" to the independent and self-confident "new woman," changes that were noted accordingly.

Although earlier literary critics may have focused on specific literary spinsters (such as Miss Havisham in *Great Expectations*, for example), the subject of the spinster figure in literature has been most fully explored with the advent of feminist theory. Rather than accepting these literary portrayals as actual or even wishful representations of spinsterhood, feminist theorists evaluate the various elements that produce such portrayals, revealing everything from the forces that suppressed women to the subversive messages with which fictional spinsters were entrusted.

This work, of course, is the work feminist theorists do on all literature. The application of such a lens to the spinster figure has proved quite illuminating, however, as it reveals a writer's, and hence often a society's, concern with elements such as woman's sexuality or cultural role. From the eighteenth into the twentieth century Western woman's role has been marriage, childbirth, the generation and maintenance of society. The stories that surround women who do not fulfill that role are fertile ground for feminist theorists. Some critics simply track the portrayals of old maids against what is known about a historical age, testing those portrayals against other cultural artifacts. Other theorists, such as Jean Kern, examine what happens when women writers take on such a characterization. Are they sympathetic or hostile? Do they promulgate, deny, or rework the stereotypes? Still other critics, Nina Auerbach among them, suggest a more subversive view, challenging our notions of what it meant to be an unmarried woman "of a certain age" in a given culture. Recent studies illuminate the transformation of the characterization, redefining the terminology in the light of historical progress and our own new perspective. Issues of class, sexuality, and economics rise to the forefront. Do only white, middle-class women qualify as spinsters? Is celibacy a necessity for spinsterhood? What about lesbians? With such questions, feminist critics are expanding the base of what had initially been a fairly circumscribed topic.

Although the term "spinster" feels anachronistic, there are contemporary feminist theorists such as Mary Daly who are attempting to reclaim it in their work. Harkening back to the literal, productive origins of the word "to spin," Daly resists limiting "the meaning of this rich and cosmic verb," insisting that spinsters, women who do not define their selves by relation to men or children, take part "in the whirling movement of creation"(3). While Daly's spinsters are outside of patriarchal norm there is nothing desiccated or powerless about them. Such arguments resonate with Native American mythology, which contains powerful female spider/spinner figures. Critics' increasing awareness of alternative worldviews further enlarges the scope of previously limited characterizations.

All of these theorists, however, regardless of their focus, approach the subject with an understanding that there is something new to be gleaned about culture or literature from applying feminist viewpoints to such a topic. As our critical view expands so does the quaint figure of the spinster; she is no longer only a stereotypic character who at best acts as a historical signpost. Spinsters are being reclaimed and reevaluated across the literary spectrum, showing us both where we have been, and offering clues as to where we might travel.

Sarah Amyes Hanselman

References

Auerbach, Nina. *Woman and the Demon: The Life of a Victorian Myth.* Cambridge: Harvard University Press, 1982.

Daly, Mary. *Gyn/Ecology: The Metaethics of Radical Feminism.* Boston: Beacon, 1978.

Doan, Laura L., ed. *Old Maids to Radical Spinsters: Unmarried Women in the Twentieth Century Novel.* Urbana: University of Chicago Press, 1991.

Hickok, Kathleen. *Representations of Women: Nineteenth Century British Women's Poetry.* Westport, Conn.: Greenwood, 1984.

Jeffreys, Sheila. *The Spinster and Her Enemies: Feminism and Sexuality, 1880–1930.* London: Pandora, 1985.

Kern, Jean. "The Old Maid, or 'To Grow Old, and Be Poor, and Laughed at.'" In *Fettr'd or Free? British Women Novelists, 1670–1815,* edited by Mary Anne Schofield and Cecilia Macheski, 201–214. Athens: Ohio University Press, 1986.

Kramarae, Cheris, and Paula A. Treichler, eds. *Amazons, Bluestockings, and Crones: A Feminist Dictionary.* London: Pandora, 1985.

Schulz, Muriel. "The Semantic Derogation of Women." In *Language and Sex: Difference and Dominance,* edited by Barrie Thorne and Nancy Henley, 64–75. Rowley: Newbury House, 1975.

Vicinus, Martha. *Independent Women: Work and Community for Single Women, 1850–1920.* Chicago: University of Chicago Press, 1985.

Spirituality

While the types and aims of feminist spirituality vary widely, the major unifying principle is a desire to challenge patriarchal religious traditions and to affirm women as spiritual beings and authorities concerning their own spiritual experience. Spiritual feminists recognize that male-dominated religion is a major factor in the legitimation and perpetuation of patriarchy. In relation to literary enterprise, feminist spirituality necessitates that women challenge canonical texts and readings of those texts, and create new stories and modes of interpretation. American feminists have led in this task, possibly due to the traditions of religious invention and pluralism in this country, and the women's suffrage movement in America.

One of the first phases of feminist literary criticism involved examining male-authored texts for accurate or biased and faulty depictions of female experience. In the nineteenth century, spiritual feminists began a similar twofold approach in their critique of patriarchal religions and texts. First, they focused on the lack of positive female representation in dominant literary texts, especially the Bible. Women began to reinterpret biblical texts with an eye to revealing "hidden" positive comments or stories about women, aspects that had been overlooked by a misogynistic priesthood. Others focused their reading by looking for traditionally "feminine" traits in the Christian God/ Jesus, with the hope that this reexamination would in turn lead to a view of the female as other than a temptress or inducer to sin. Some, such as Elizabeth Cady Stanton, in *The Woman's Bible,* vociferously challenged the sexism found in these texts.

Another task of feminist literary criticism has been the recovery of "lost" or neglected works by female authors. In the twentieth century, especially during the 1960s revivification of the women's movement, spiritual feminists continued efforts that are often labeled "reformist" (that is, working within a dominant religious tradition), but expanded their efforts in two ways. First, like their literary counterparts, spiritual feminists began to recover and promote neglected works by women involved in spiritual enterprises, such as Hildegard of Bingen. The second approach was to reexamine female Old and New Testament figures and emphasize their stories as demonstrating specifically feminist traits and values. Scholars such as Rosemary Ruether, working in the Christian tradition, and Judith Plaskow, working in the Jewish tradition, exemplify this approach. Many feminists continue these efforts, some also working to incorporate nonsexist language into liturgies and hymns.

Again reflecting the tendencies of feminist criticism as a whole, a number of spiritual feminists developed a consciously gynocentric approach. Increasing numbers of feminists felt it was not possible to reform the Judeo-Christian tradition, and that women's spirituality needed its own words, texts, and interpretations. Many turned to the revival of Old-European pre-Christian religion, or Wicca (otherwise known as witchcraft), with its emphasis on a Goddess or goddesses rather than a God. Rather than merely signifying a gender change for deity, women felt that the use of this one term, "Goddess," implied a revolutionary paradigm shift. They reasoned that if divine order not only included femaleness but actually focused on it, then women would also be placed at the center. Though later some chose to go outside of Wicca, the rediscovery of the Goddess was tremendously influential, and remains so at the time of this writing. For literary scholars, this rediscovery resulted in revisions of archetypal theory, especially regarding the quest motif, and in a view of storytelling as a sacred female endeavor.

Feminist archetypal criticism shifted from traditional views of female mythological figures or symbols as helpers and guides on a male's quest or spiritual journey, to a reexamination of these figures and symbols in light of women's experiences. Jean Bolen, for example, discusses the Greek goddesses as they exemplify stages or experiences in women's lives, as opposed to the usual discussions of these goddesses as they relate to or serve male gods. Charlene Spretnak, suspicious of the agenda that reduced many of the Greek goddesses to helpers of males, undertook a literary excavation of earlier, less androcentric tales involving these goddesses.

Given the weight of Greco-Roman influence on Western literary tradition and interpretation, such projects amount to a challenging of traditionally accepted cornerstones of culture. In a similar fashion, Barbara Walker examined a variety of symbols from a fresh feminist perspective, while Maureen Murdock criticized the quest motif as an enterprise of male triumph and transcendence. She found that this pattern was not applicable to women's lives; instead, woman's quest is viewed as a descent that leads to unity.

The telling of women's stories became a central focus as well, for, as Carol Christ bluntly put it, "Women's stories have not been told." While this comment reflects a larger feminist focus, the distinguishing slant that feminist spirituality offers is a view of the storytelling process as the means for women to create a new mythology that is not only personally healing, but has the potential to heal society as well by transforming the symbol systems of our culture. This goal places the spiritual focus in line with a common feminist political agenda. Gloria Orenstein observes that this is not accomplished by erecting a female monomyth to replace a male one, but rather by weaving a tapestry of voices that reflects the diverse stories that women have to tell. She also notes that noncanonical genres such as fantasy fiction are well suited for this myth-making, and serve to spread it at the level of popular culture.

In spite of this goal, diversity remains a challenge for spiritual feminists. While texts such as Jacqueline deWeever's *Mythmaking and Metaphor in Black Women's Fiction* challenge the Eurocentric, middle-class dominance in many of the writings on women's spirituality, there remains much work to be done before all women's voices are represented. As with other areas of feminism and literary theory, culture, race, class, and other variables must be understood if any broad pronouncements are to be valid.

Janice Crosby

References

Bolen, Jean S. *Goddesses in Everywoman: A New Psychology of Women.* New York: Harper and Row, 1984.

Carson, Anne. *Feminist Spirituality and the Feminine Divine: An Annotated Bibliography.* Trumansburg, N.Y.: Crossing, 1986.

———. *Goddesses & Wise Women: The Literature of Feminist Spirituality 1980–*

1992: *An Annotated Bibliography*. Freedom, Calif.: Crossing, 1992.

Christ, Carol. *Diving Deep and Surfacing: Women Writers on Spiritual Quest*. 2nd ed. Boston: Beacon, 1986.

———, and Judith Plaskow, eds. *Womanspirit Rising: A Feminist Reader in Religion*. San Francisco: Harper and Row, 1979.

deWeever, Jacqueline. *Mythmaking and Metaphor in Black Women's Fiction*. New York: St. Martin's, 1991.

Murdock, Maureen. *The Heroine's Journey: Woman's Quest for Wholeness*. Boston: Shambhala, 1990.

Orenstein, Gloria. *The Reflowering of the Goddess*. New York: Pergamon, 1990.

Ruether, Rosemary. *Sexism and God-Talk: Toward a Feminist Theology*. Boston: Beacon, 1983.

Spretnak, Charlene. *Lost Goddesses of Early Greece: A Collection of Pre-Hellenic Myths*. Boston: Beacon, 1981.

Stanton, Elizabeth C., ed. *The Woman's Bible*. New York: European, 1895.

Walker, Barbara. *The Woman's Dictionary of Myth and Symbol*. San Francisco: Harper and Row, 1988.

Spivak, Gayatri Chakravorty

A specialist in deconstruction (she translated Derrida's *Of Grammatology*), Marxism, and psychoanalytic criticism, and a critic linked with subaltern studies, Gayatri Spivak has contributed to feminist literary theory in at least two major ways. First, aided partly by the deconstructive strategies of reversal and displacement, she has revealed how Marxism and Freudianism exclude or marginalize women's experience (how Marxism ignores female reproductive labor in its theory of the production; how psychoanalysis effaces the womb and the clitoris in its theorizing of consciousness and sexuality) and has suggested how these theoretical narratives might be rewritten from a feminist perspective and reapplied to literary texts. But second and more important, while this approach can radically "redo the terms of our understanding," Spivak insists on the provisionality and strategic employment of these reconstituted terms: deconstruction, after all, allows for no fixed, "rigorous definition of anything."

This insistence on provisionality counteracts a major trend in feminism that seeks to define woman and the feminine in essentialist terms. Essentialist feminism, Spivak claims, suppresses the heterogeneity of women's identity and situations, especially those of Third-World women. "The First World Feminist must stop," Spivak warns, "from feeling privileged *as a woman*"; otherwise one reproduces a colonialist relationship.

Terence Bowers

See also SUBALTERN STUDIES

References

Spivak, Gayatri Chakravorty. "Can the Subaltern Speak?" In *Marxism and the Interpretation of Culture*, edited by Cary Nelson and Lawrence Grossberg, 271–313. Urbana: University of Illinois Press, 1988.

———. "Displacement and the Discourse of Women." In *Displacement: Derrida and After*, edited by Mark Krupnick, 169–191. Bloomington: Indiana University Press, 1983.

———. "French Feminism Revisited: Ethics and Politics." In *Feminists Theorize the Political*, edited by Judith Butler and Joan Scott, 54–85. New York: Routledge, 1992.

———. *In Other Worlds: Essays in Cultural Politics*. London: Methuen, 1987.

———. *The Post Colonial Critic: Interviews, Strategies, Dialogues*. Edited by Sarah Harasym. New York: Routledge, 1990.

Stein, Gertrude

Gertrude Stein has the dubious distinction of being one of modernism's most challenging writers. Her writing, with its extreme use of disruptive techniques (repetition, punning, extensive line breaks) and its unusual punctuation (periods between each word or phrase; her famous refusal of commas), radically questions most reading practices. While feminist criticism has, since the 1970s, done much to bring Stein's work into the critical theorization of modernist literature, there has been little agreement within feminist literary criticism as to the most basic question about her work: namely, can it be called "feminist"? While her early *Three Lives* tells the story of three economically and socially disenfranchised women in Baltimore in fairly conventional narrative form, her work after 1909 turns to nonnormative linguistic practices as its primary compositional mode.

These works, with the exception of her two autobiographies, are more concerned with subverting linguistic structures than with putting forward an easily recognizable feminist platform.

As Stein subverts linguistic structures, her work continually muddies the gender categories of male and female. Throughout Stein's writing, the subject is neither singularly nor exclusively gendered. There is in her engagements with gender a continual confusion of categories. Her first full-length piece, *Q.E.D.*, is a narrative exploration of a lesbian love triangle, in which the character Adele mimics Shakespeare's Rosalind, when she is dressed as Ganymede, by saying "Thank God I was not born a woman." Similarly, the 1917 "Lifting Belly," a poem that resituates the heterosexual love poem into a lesbian space, encourages a crossing of gender boundaries when it urges "please be the man."

"Patriarchal Poetry" is perhaps the most challenging to feminist interpretative frames. This poem was written in 1927, Stein's period of her most extreme use of nonstandardized linguist practices. Despite the suggestive title, in "Patriarchal Poetry" gender relations, and even what Stein might mean by the term "patriarchal poetry," are not clear. Instead the heavily repetitive style of the poem raises more questions than it answers: is this work an ironic mimicry of the patriarchal poetic tradition, which is full of repetition, of recycled forms, metaphors, similes? Or is it an escape from the poetry of patriarchy, a space where through repetition words are freed from the stereotypical meaning? Or is it both, a parody in which Stein wants to treat the words of patriarchy as she does nouns, to "refuse them by using them"?

Stein's feminism becomes less ambiguous, without being any less complicated, in her final opera, *The Mother of Us All*. In this piece, Susan B. Anthony engages Daniel Webster and other patriarchal figures in "discussions" about suffrage, marriage, and the word "man." This opera, which was never produced on stage in Stein's lifetime, usefully highlights the fact that Stein's work is intimately connected with democratic and feminist ideals regarding the right to choose (in the opera—the right to vote) theoretical and gender positions.

Juliana Spahr

References

Stein, Gertrude. *Fernhurst, Q.E.D., and Other Early Writings*. New York: Liveright, 1973.
———. *Last Operas and Plays*. New York: Rinehart, 1949.
———. *The Selected Writings of Gertrude Stein*. Edited by Carl Van Vecten. New York: Vintage, 1962.
———. *A Stein Reader*. Edited by Ulla Dydo. Evanston, Ill.: Northwestern University Press, 1993.
———. *Three Lives*. New York: New American Library, 1985.
———. *The Yale Gertrude Stein*. New Haven: Yale University Press, 1980.

Stimpson, Catharine R.

Catharine Stimpson directly positions culture (an area of relative power for women) as a political battleground in which feminist critics should further women's causes. Combining politics and scholarship herself, Stimpson was founding editor in 1975 of the influential *Signs: A Journal of Women in Culture and Society*.

Stimpson's critical work on lesbian texts leads to an emphasis on the differences female texts present behind a structure of apparent conformity. In "Zero Degree Deviancy," her study of lesbian novels, Stimpson finds two patterns, the "dying fall" and the "enabling escape," by which lesbian authors expressed their sexuality within a society stigmatizing homosexuality. Similarly, in "The Mind, the Body, and Gertrude Stein," she argues that Stein "coded" her homosexuality behind a persona both male and of genius in order to escape "normal" strictures put on the female body and the average mind.

In "On Differences," Stimpson celebrates literature as a force for acceptance of cultural and sexual difference. Readers encounter and become used to "otherness." In "Are the Differences Spreading?" and "Reading for Love," Stimpson suggests the feminist reader should reveal, amplify, and celebrate difference, also unveiling female rebellion and challenge hidden in texts of conformity. Rather than accept textual moral unity imposed by a repressive culture, feminist critics should separate rebellion and explain the (re)subordination of women characters or women authors required by their own cultural context. Such a reconstruction of feminist foremothers turns culture from social tool of repression to political tool of female freedom in difference.

Lynn L. Sharp

References

Stimpson, Catharine R. "Are the Differences Spreading? Feminist Criticism and Postmodernism." *English Studies in Canada* 15 (1989): 364–382.

———. "The Mind, the Body, and Gertrude Stein." *Critical Inquiry* 3 (1977): 489–506.

———. "On Differences." *PMLA* 106 (1991): 402–411.

———. "Reading for Love: Canons, Paracanons, and Whistling Jo March." *New Literary History* 21 (1990): 957–976.

———. *Where the Meanings Are, Feminism and Cultural Spaces.* New York: Methuen, 1988.

———. "Zero Degree Deviancy: The Lesbian Novel in English." *Critical Inquiry* 8 (1981): 363–379.

Subaltern Studies

The term "subaltern" according to *Webster's Dictionary* signifies "subordinate," as in a "subaltern officer," who (specifically in regard to the British army) holds "an army commission below that of captain." In general, then, "subaltern" refers to someone of "lower rank."

Within feminist theory, the term "subaltern" has resonances with the project(s) of Third-World and postcolonial feminism/s—generally considered as "subordinate" fields within the universalizing gestures of Western feminism. Clearly, part of the task of postcolonial feminist theorists is to challenge the tendentious claims of such scholarship either to universal representation through appropriation (speaking on behalf of women everywhere) or, in its poststructural variants, to maintaining the sense of the West as Self (and therefore universal) by constituting the colonial female subject as its Other. Gayatri Chakravorty Spivak's essay "Can the Subaltern Speak?" published in 1988, is a seminal text in this arena. She refers to the work of a group of Indian historiographers called the Subaltern Studies group, as a precursor to her own project. That work, led by Ranajit Guha, purports to rewrite the history of Indian nationalism from the perspective of "the people," an essential undertaking because, as Guha notes, "The historiography of Indian Nationalism has for a long time been dominated by elitism—colonialist elitism and bourgeois-nationalist elitism . . . shar[ing] the prejudice that the making of the Indian nation and the development of the consciousness . . . were exclusively or predominantly elite achievements." Spivak, herself a Marxist critic, is sympathetic to such a project, because she realizes that "certain varieties of the Indian elite are at best native informants for First-World intellectuals interested in the voice of the Other"—thus contributing to the continuing imperialism of First-World theory and knowledge, of which feminist theoretical production is a part. Nevertheless, Spivak also realizes that the "colonized subaltern subject," including the subaltern female subject, is "irretrievably heterogeneous." What this means is that although it is indeed important to challenge the hegemony of white Western (bourgeois) feminism by letting Third-World women speak for themselves, it is equally important to recognize the diversity in these subject-positions, in which gender is but one constitutive factor. Even within a particular class and ethnic group, there are a variety of subject-positions and "voices" to be heard and represented. Finally, it is the problem of "representation" that forecloses the possibility of letting the subaltern speak. "The subaltern cannot speak" because there is no subaltern "essence," male or female, from whence to generate an "authentic" or unmediated, class-neutral perspective. The best that we, as postcolonial feminists, can do, according to Spivak, is to "unlearn" our female privilege—which I take to mean our privilege as members of an intellectual class within the North American or European academy.

Several Indian scholars, primarily in the fields of history, political science, and women's studies have contributed in recent years to the growing body of material referred to as subaltern studies—which, in a feminist light, signifies what Kum Kum Sangari and Sudesh Vaid have called a "feminist historiography." By this they mean a historiography that "acknowledges that each aspect of reality is gendered," and thus, such historiography can be feminist without being exclusively women's history. Above all, such investigations and rewritings of history eschew theoretical generalizations in favor of more nuanced "materially specific studies of patriarchal practice, social regulation and cultural production" that pay attention to the "regional, class and caste variation of patriarchal practices and their diverse histories." Clearly, such work, occurring at the interface of several disciplines, and investigating the effects of colonial rule on gender and patriarchy in different class and caste formations, is very much in keeping with Spivak's notions for a viable postcolonial feminist interventionary practice.

Fawzia Afzal-Khan

References

Chatterjee, Partha. *Nationalist Thought and the Colonial World: A Derivative Discourse?* Minneapolis: University of Minnesota Press, 1993.

Guha, Ranajit, and Gayatri Spivak, eds. *Selected Subaltern Studies.* New York: Oxford University Press, 1988.

Mani, Lata. "Contentious Traditions: The Debate on Sati in Colonial India." In *Recasting Women,* edited by Kum Kum Sangari and Sudesh Vaid, 88–127. New Brunswick, N.J.: Rutgers University Press, 1990.

Sangari, Kum Kum, and Sudesh Vaid. *Recasting Women.* New Brunswick, N.J.: Rutgers University Press, 1990.

Spivak, Gayatri C. "Can the Subaltern Speak?" In *Marxism and the Interpretation of Culture,* edited by C. Nelson and L. Grossberg, 271–313. Basingstoke: Macmillan Education, 1988.

———. "Imperialism and Sexual Difference." In *Contemporary Literary Criticism: Literary and Cultural Studies,* edited by Robert Con Davis and Ronald Scheifer, 517–529. New York: Longmans, 1989.

———. *In Other Worlds: Essays in Cultural Politics.* New York: Routledge, 1988.

———. *The Post-Colonial Critic: Interviews, Strategies, Dialogues,* edited by Sarah Harasym. New York: Routledge, 1990.

———. "Three Women's Texts and a Critique of Imperialism." In *"Race," Writing and Difference,* edited by Henry Louis Gates, Jr., 262–280. Chicago: University of Chicago Press, 1985.

Sublime

Most often used by literary critics to characterize specific moments in Romantic poetry, the term "sublime" designates a sensation of terrifying but transportive empowerment resulting from the individual's confrontation and ultimate identification with one of the following entities, depending upon the philosophical tradition invoked: supremely powerful discourse (Longinian), an object or conception of tremen-dous or even infinite magnitude (Kantian), or the revelation of paternal power (psychoanalytic). Wary of the sublime's emphasis on the appropriation and suppression of the Other and alienated by its masculinist bias, feminists have until recently ignored the sublime as a potentially valuable aesthetic for women. Within the past decade, however, a number of female theorists have suggested that the term can be and in specific cases has already been regendered, albeit problematically, to empower, authorize, and inspire the woman writer.

In her landmark article on the sublime and the beautiful in the writing of Edmund Burke, Frances Ferguson argued that the two categories were both gendered and hierarchical. Setting an individualist, antisocial, and masculine sublime against a domestic, social, and feminine beautiful, Burke—according to Ferguson—privileges the former as the realm of authentic, authoritative existence while revealing the latter to be a seductively dangerous realm of emasculation and death. The first feminist critic to address the gender anxieties within sublime aesthetics, Ferguson initiated an ongoing debate about their significance for both male and female writers.

Five years after Ferguson's article appeared, Mary Arensburg published a collection on the sublime that expanded the debate about the sublime and gender in important new ways. Using male modernist poet Wallace Stevens as her subject, Arensburg illustrated and expanded psychoanalytic critic Neil Hertz's theory that the sublime experience actually originates in a pre-Oedipal wish to be incorporated by the mother. Meanwhile, in the same volume, and later in her 1990 book, Joanne Feit Diehl further challenged the idea that the sublime is a privileged masculine experience by pointing to women poets like Emily Dickinson, H.D., and Marianne Moore who employ various strategies to achieve it. Conceding that sublime identification will be difficult for the woman writer as long as authority is centered in the patriarch, Diehl nevertheless argues that it is not altogether impossible.

In 1989, Patricia Yaeger—perhaps the most well known feminist theorist on the sublime—went even further than Diehl to argue that a "female sublime" is both a possible and necessary experience for literary women. Sketching out basic strategies that writers like Cixous, Irigaray, Bishop, Welty, and Giovanni have used to mitigate the violent and appropriative nature of the traditional (masculine) version, Yaeger identifies a "failed" sublime, gesturing toward but never achieving transcendence; a "sovereign" sublime, emphasizing horizontal rather than vertical movement as well as the immediate expenditure of transportive energy; and a pre-Oedipal sublime, celebrating the woman's connection with the mother and the female body. Later, Yaeger added a fourth category, a "maternal" sublime, which draws its authorizing energy from the female experience of parturition.

Feminist critics are racing to add to Yaeger's list. Most recently, in her comparative discussion of the male and female Romantics, Anne Mellor identified sublime strategies among female Gothic writers. While male Romantic poets center their sublime experiences around individual transcendence and the destruction of the Other, their female contemporaries strive to envision a mode of transport that is not predicated on the erasure of either the (female) body or other minds; indeed, Mellor argues that for women writers like Ann Radcliffe, the sublime ideally generates a "renewed appreciation of the equal value and dignity of other people." Thus, if the male version emphasizes isolation and discontinuity, this female form of the sublime builds off experiences of "co-participation" and communality.

With its emphasis on transgression, empowerment, and authorization, the sublime continues to be an appealing mode for feminists. However, the same characteristics that make it attractive have also raised concerns among those, like Lee Edelman, who wonder if the sublime's original association with violence and domination can really be avoided and whether any "female" sublime could preserve differences within gender experience, such as race and sexual orientation. Yet despite these controversies—or perhaps even because of them—reimagining the sublime is a project that seems unlikely to be abandoned anytime soon.

Lisa Rado

References

Arensburg, Mary. *The American Sublime*. Albany: State University of New York Press, 1986.

Diehl, Joanne Fiet. *Women Poets and the American Sublime*. Bloomington: Indiana University Press, 1990.

Edelman, Lee. "At Risk in the Sublime: The Politics of Gender and Theory." In *Gender and Theory*, edited by Linda Kauffman, 213–224. New York: Basil Blackwell, 1989.

Ferguson, Frances. *Solitude and the Sublime*. New York: Routledge, 1992.

———. "The Sublime of Edmund Burke, or the Bathos of Experience." In *Glyph 8*, edited by Walter Benn Michaels, 62–78. Baltimore, Md.: Johns Hopkins University Press, 1981.

Freeman, Barbara. *The Feminine Sublime*. Berkeley: University of California Press, 1995.

Hertz, Neil. *The End of the Line*. New York: Columbia University Press, 1985.

Mellor, Anne. *Romanticism and Gender*. New York: Routledge, 1993.

Yaeger, Patricia. "The Language of Blood: Towards a Maternal Sublime." *Genre 25* (1992): 5–24.

———. "Toward a Female Sublime." In *Gender and Theory*, edited by Linda Kauffman, 191–212. New York: Basil Blackwell, 1989.

Suleiman, Susan Rubin

"Writing and Motherhood," first published in 1984, was one of the first studies to investigate the relationship between motherhood, writing, and the subjectivity of the creating mother. In this article, Suleiman challenges psychoanalytic assumptions about the incompatibility of writing and motherhood, showing that they can coexist, although not without conflict. Analyzing works of fiction, autobiography, and theory, Suleiman examines the triangle of the writing mother, her work, and her child. "Maternal Splitting," first published in 1988, expands upon these issues by examining the mother's guilty rivalry with the maternal surrogate. Suleiman challenges the debilitating myth of maternal omnipotence that assigns the mother exclusive responsibility for the child's wellbeing. Maintaining that parenting models should emphasize collaboration and compromise, Suleiman calls for new representations of maternity and the creation of a nurturing environment for contemporary American families.

In *Subversive Intent*, Suleiman examines the relationship of avant-garde women artists to their male precursors and collaborators. She suggests that women artists feel a double allegiance, sharing formal experiments and some cultural goals with male avant-gardes while constructing a feminist critique of dominant sexual ideologies. Suleiman introduces her theory of the "laughing mother" as a figure that embodies the power of feminist humor and parody. This emphasis has led to her promotion of "feminist postmodernists" such as Angela Carter and Christine Brooke-Rose.

Most recently, in *Risking Who One Is,* Suleiman examines the concept of "the contemporary" and the role of autobiography as a genre that puts the writer's self at risk and into play.

Through her description of a feminist poetics and her focus on women's avant-garde artistic practices, Suleiman's research has consistently examined the relationship between gender, culture, aesthetics, and politics.

Clare Olivia Parsons

References

Suleiman, Susan Rubin. "Maternal Splitting: 'Good' and 'Bad' Mothers and Reality." In *Risking Who One Is: Encounters with Contemporary Art and Literature,* 38–54. Cambridge: Harvard University Press, 1994.

———. *Subversive Intent: Gender, Politics, and the Avant-Garde.* Cambridge: Harvard University Press, 1990.

———. "Writing and Motherhood." In *Risking Who One Is: Encounters with Contemporary Art and Literature,* 13–37. Cambridge: Harvard University Press, 1994.

———, ed. *The Female Body in Western Culture: Contemporary Perspectives.* Cambridge: Harvard University Press, 1986.

Surrealism

Surrealism, a movement in literature and the visual arts, was founded in 1924 by the French poet André Breton. In his first *Manifesto of Surrealism,* which set forth the philosophy of the movement, Breton called for the restoration of the irrational in art and in life: in order to be effective, Breton and his followers felt, art must include elements of dream, of fantasy, and of chance. The surrealists had a social agenda, as well: they called for the downfall of bourgeois society, which had, they felt, allowed the depredations of the First World War. The surrealists were, for a brief time, supporters of communism and decried the institution of marriage and the necessity for work. Perhaps more than any other modernist movement in art, surrealism both deified and vilified images of the feminine: for the surrealists, "Woman" was the embodiment of a mysterious "Other," associated with madness and with access to the irrational contents of the unconscious mind. The result of this cult of the "Woman as Other" was an ambivalence about women's rights and about the role of women artists in the surrealist movement itself. Some well-known members of the surrealist group included, among poets, Paul Éluard, René Crevel, Philipe Soupault, Benjamin Péret, and Robert Desnos; among the visual artists, Salvador Dali, René Magritte, Max Ernst, Man Ray, Joan Miró, Yves Tanguy, and André Masson.

Ambivalence about the feminine was, from the beginning, inherent in the tenets of surrealism, since its focus on the irrational was heavily based on Sigmund Freud's discovery of the unconscious and of the meaning of dreams—and on the work of French psychiatrist Pierre Janet, who discovered the existence of psychic automatism in women hysterics at the Salpetriére Asylum. The Surrealists, drawing on Freud, believed that artists could tap into the repressed contents of the unconscious mind through such compositional methods as automatic writing (which was, according to Breton, the written equivalent of Freud's verbal "free association"); collaborative "surrealist games" that were dependent on chance associations; and, in the visual arts, the use of collage, found objects, and found images. The other important route of direct access to the unconscious was Woman: as Rudolf Kuenzli notes, Freud's theories imply that women are "closer to the unconscious than men." Thus, the Surrealists saw Woman—especially the young, sexually free waif, or *femme-enfant*—as the "child muse," as man's mediator with nature and with the irrational.

The Surrealists idealized the image of the hysteric; as art historian Whitney Chadwick puts it in her seminal book *Women Artists and the Surrealist Movement,* they "raised the status of Hysteria from a mental disorder to a poetic precept." In 1928, the Surrealists celebrated the "fiftieth anniversary" of the discovery of hysteria by publishing a series of photos, obtained from the Salpetriére hospital archives, showing women patients in the ecstatic states that Janet had called *l'amour fou,* or mad love. Hysteria was not an illness, the Surrealists maintained in their journal, *La Révolution Surréaliste,* but a transformative state, a "supreme means of expression." In his novel *Nadja*, Breton recounts the story of his encounter and brief relationship with a disturbed young woman, Nadja, who embodies the qualities of the intuitive madwoman and dependent *femme-enfant*.

However, Chadwick and other critics of the surrealist movement have noted that the surrealist idealization of madness had a quality of clinical detachment: madness was sublime, as long as it was the madness of the Other. Woman, Chadwick writes, "completes the male vision by absorbing into herself those qualities that man recognizes as important but does not wish to possess himself." Although Breton and fellow poet Paul Éluard composed poems in states of simulated madness, published in the 1930 volume entitled *The Immaculate Conception,* they were careful to maintain distance from and control over their own "altered states." And in the novel *Nadja,* Breton quickly abandons the young woman when it becomes evident that she is disturbed enough to be committed to an asylum.

According to Suleiman, the Surrealists' ideal of the "feminine" may have created their paradoxical attitudes toward real women. France of the 1920s was repressive toward women: birth control was not permitted, and French women did not receive the right to vote until 1946. Yet although the Surrealists promoted free love and disdained the idea that women should be expected to marry, they did not support women's rights; rather, they rejected the image of the working woman as a product of the despised bourgeoisie. Perhaps as a consequence, the women writers and artists associated with the surrealist movement struggled for acceptance and recognition as mature artists in their own right. Although women were present in the surrealist circle, none were official members of the movement in the years between 1924 and 1933. Only later, when the movement had begun to disperse because of the Second World War, were women allowed to become "official" members; indeed, their work has begun to be noticed by scholars, critics, and the public only in the last twenty years. Important female artists and writers associated with the movement include Eileen Agar, Leonora Carrington, Ithell Colquhoun, Leonor Fini, Valentine Hugo, Frida Kahlo, Joyce Mansour, Lee Miller, Meret Oppenheim, Valentine Penrose, Gisèle Prassinos, Kay Sage, Dorothea Tanning; Toyen, Remedios Varo, and Unica Zurn.

Each of these women struggled, in various ways, to find a unique and empowering means of self-expression within a movement that variously denied women artists' need for self-definition. Many later disclaimed their association with the surrealist movement. According to Chadwick, they often turned to the self-portrait, or self-portrayal in literature and poetry, as a means of creating an image of the feminine that matched their own experience. Their response to the male artists' renderings of the objectified female body (often distorted or dismembered) are reflected, according to Cottenet-Hage, in an underlying concern with bodily integrity, fear of and desire for penetration, the risk of fusion, and in the frequent representation of female sickness and aging. Some of the women artists, like Meret Oppenheim and Leonora Carrington, sought affirmation in the less phallocentric psychology of Carl Jung, and drew on images from hermeticism and Celtic goddess-worship, especially in works created in the decades following the Second World War.

Lori A. Baker

References

Breton, André. *Manifestoes of Surrealism.* Translated by Richard Seaver and Helen R. Lane. Ann Arbor: University of Michigan Press, 1969.

———. *Nadia.* Translated by Richard Howard. New York: Grove, 1960.

Chadwick, Whitney. *Women Artists and the Surrealist Movement.* New York: Little, Brown, 1985.

Cottenet-Hage, Madeleine. "The Body Subversive: Corporeal Imagery in Carrington, Prassinos, and Mansour." *Dada-Surrealism* 1990 (18): 76–95.

Ellenberger, Henri F. *The Discovery of the Unconscious.* New York: Basic, 1970.

Éluard, Paul, and André Breton. *The Immaculate Conception.* Translated by Jon Graham. London: Atlas, 1990.

Gauthier, Xavière. *Surréalisme et sexualité.* Paris: Gallimard, 1971.

Kuenzli, Rudolf. "Surrealism and Misogyny." *Dada/Surrealism* 18 (1990): 17–26.

Orenstein, Gloria Feman. "Reclaiming the Great Mother: A Feminist Journey to Madness and Back in Search of a Goddess Heritage." *Symposium* 36 (1982): 45–70.

———. "Women of Surrealism." *Feminist Art Journal* 2 (1973): 1.

Raaberg, Gwen. "The Problematics of

Women and Surrealism." *Dada/Surrealism* 18 (1990): 1–10.

Suleiman, Susan Rubin. "A Double Margin: Reflections on Women Writers and the Avant-garde in France." *Yale French Studies* 75 (1988): 148–172.

———. *Subversive Intent: Gender, Politics, and the Avant-Garde*. Cambridge: Harvard University Press, 1990.

Symbolic

Using psychoanalytic and linguistic theories, Jacques Lacan developed a new concept of subjectivity that became the basis for much of the work done by French feminists such as Julia Kristeva and Luce Irigaray. One key term Lacan introduced is the "symbolic," which he opposed to the "imaginary." Lacan wished to reformulate the work of Sigmund Freud and rewrote the castration and Oedipus complex in the light of poststructuralist theories of discourse. According to Lacan, at the "imaginary" stage, the infant has no clear distinction between self and others. It is only through language that the child recognizes that she or he is separate from the mother. The acquisition of language coincides with the moment when the father, associated with authority and the phallus, interrupts and forbids the mother-and-child relation. The child then experiences a sense of loss of the maternal body. Symbolization begins when the child substitutes words for the objects that she or he desires. Entry into the symbolic order necessarily entails acceptance of the sexualized world of the father and mother, as well as the world of prohibitions and repressions.

Kristeva's theories of signifying practice are derived from this Lacanian model. She distinguishes between what she calls the "semiotic" and the "symbolic," the latter term very similar to Lacan's notion. While Kristeva agrees that the symbolic is the stable, unifying force that allows a subject to speak coherently, she constructs a dialectical view of subjectivity. The chaotic, heterogeneous impulses of the semiotic or the preverbal are incompletely repressed when the paternal order intervenes in the mother and child dyad. Both the semiotic and the symbolic, which is the "logical" and "syntactic functioning" of language associated with the father, have a part in the construction and constitution of the subject. They continually cross each other in the social, subjective, and textual worlds. Though the symbolic is dominant in everyday life and conscious activity, both are present in signifying practice. The symbolic mode owes a debt of existence to the unrepresentable and maternal semiotic.

Luce Irigaray does not simply adopt the notion of the symbolic from Lacan. She uses it critically to raise the issue of sexual difference. Irigaray envisions two different accounts of subjectivity for the two sexes, two kinds of ways of knowing. She argues that the Freudian notion of pre-Oedipal and Oedipal and Lacan's imaginary and the symbolic explain only the development of the male subject. Irigaray refuses to accept Lacan's system of the symbolic where he has stated that "woman does not exist." She asserts the need for a female symbolic that takes into account mother-daughter relations and does not reject elements usually associated with the feminine. A different social and symbolic order would not represent women with the usual psychoanalytic tendencies, such as hatred of mothers or female rivalry, which are destructive to women.

Eleanor Ty

References

Grosz, Elizabeth. *Jacques Lacan: A Feminist Introduction*. New York: Routledge, 1990.

Irigaray, Luce. *Speculum of the Other Woman*. Translated by Gillian C. Gill. Ithaca, N.Y.: Cornell University Press, 1985.

———. *This Sex Which Is Not One*. Translated by Catherine Porter. Ithaca, N.Y.: Cornell University Press, 1985.

Kristeva, Julia. *Desire in Language: A Semiotic Approach to Literature and Art*. Edited by Leon S. Roudiez. New York: Columbia University Press, 1980.

———. *The Kristeva Reader*. Edited by Toril Moi. New York: Columbia University Press, 1986.

Lacan, Jacques. *Écrits: A Selection*. Translated by Alan Sheridan. New York: W.W. Norton, 1977.

T

Tate, Claudia

Claudia Tate has been instrumental in fostering the contemporary emergence of African American women's literature. Tate's *Black Women Writers at Work,* in which she interviews fourteen black women authors, pointed—in her introduction and through the words of the writers—to the need for critical attention that would examine the craft, technique, and artistry of these authors and their historical, cultural, and intellectual contexts. Tate contends that these writers possess a perspective that allows them to "cut through layers of institutionalized racism and sexism and uncover a core of social contradictions and intimate dilemmas which plague all of us, regardless of our race or gender." For the Schomburg Library of Nineteenth Century Black Women Writers, Tate edited *The Works of Katherine Davis Chapman Tillman.* With *Domestic Allegories of Political Desire: The Black Heroine's Text at the Turn of the Century,* Tate produced a work that many predict will be one of the defining studies in the field. In these books and in articles on Gwendolyn Brooks, Ralph Ellison, Nella Larsen, Alice Walker, Richard Wright, African American literary culture, and the development of black feminist criticism, Tate consistently emphasizes the necessity of attention to both race and gender.

Domestic Allegories of Political Desire focuses on the eleven extant post-Reconstruction novels written by African American women between 1890 and 1910. These novels, about courtship, marriage, and family dynamics, were authored by Frances E.W. Harper, Pauline E. Hopkins, Amelia Johnson, Emma Dunham Kelley-Hawkins, and Katherine Tillman and were aimed at middle- and working-class black people struggling through an era of intense racial hatred and violence. Tate follows the work of Cathy N. Davidson and Jane Tompkins in demanding we be responsive to the ideological and economic situations of sentimental and domestic fiction authors; Tate shows the error inherent in the assumption that these authors were apolitical when compared to the racial protest fiction of their black male contemporaries by illustrating that it was the widely held view of turn-of-the-century African Americans that full citizenship and integration into mainstream society "would result as much or more from demonstrating their adoption of the 'genteel standard of Victorian sexual conduct' as from protesting racial injustice." These domestic allegories countered retrogressionism, the theory that blacks were reverting to barbarism. In place of such racist discourse, they offered images of successful, civic-minded black families while their plots fulfilled the desire for "acquisition of authority for the self both in the home and in the world." Tate situates this era in African American literature into the larger tradition by considering connections to and discontinuities with the earlier slave narratives of Harriet Jacobs and Harriet Wilson and the later "domestic tragedies" of Angelina Weld Grimké. Noted for offering a model of meticulous scholarship that delves deeply into the historical and cultural contexts of its subjects, *Domestic Allegories* has also been praised for its rigorous, insightful, and engagingly interesting close readings.

Kathryn West

References

Tate, Claudia. "Anger So Flat: Gwendolyn Brooks's Annie Allen." In *A Life Dis-*

tilled: *Gwendolyn Brooks, Her Poetry and Fiction,* edited by Maria K. Mootry and Gary Smith, 140–150. Urbana: University of Illinois Press, 1987.

———. *Domestic Allegories of Political Desire: The Black Heroine's Text at the Turn of the Century.* New York: Oxford University Press, 1992.

———. "Laying the Floor; Or, the History of the Formation of the Afro-American Canon." *Book Research Quarterly* 3 (1987): 60–78.

———. "Notes on the Invisible Woman in Ralph Ellison's Invisible Man." In *Speaking for You: The Vision of Ralph Ellison,* edited by Kimberly W. Benston, 163–172. Washington: Howard University Press, 1987.

———. "On Black Literary Women and the Evolution of Critical Discourse." *Tulsa Studies in Women's Literature* 5 (1986): 111–123.

———. "Pauline Hopkins: Our Literary Foremother." In *Conjuring: Black Women, Fiction, and Literary Tradition,* edited by Marjorie Pryse and Hortense Spillers, 53–66. Bloomington: Indiana University Press, 1985.

———. "Reshuffling the Deck; Or, (Re)Reading Race and Gender in Black Women's Writing." *Tulsa Studies in Women's Literature* 7 (1988): 60–78.

———, ed. *Black Women Writers at Work.* New York: Continuum, 1983.

———, ed. *The Works of Katherine Davis Chapman Tillman.* New York: Oxford University Press, 1991.

Theater

"Theater" and "literary criticism" have had a troubled relationship of mutual distrust. Within English departments, for example, the position of theater in relation to literature has paralleled the position of women in relation to patriarchy: it is considered wanton, more frivolous, more trivial, less universal, and, in Derridean terms, "supplementary." Because drama is an embodied as well as a textual medium, it is often thought of in English departments as an impure literature, and dramatic texts except for those of Shakespeare (often read as extended poems or novels) are deemphasized. Nevertheless, the exclusion of drama's performative aspects within literature departments is beginning to be discussed.

The debate over the "textuality" of dramatic performance is also central to contemporary drama and drama criticism. Indeed, one major impulse in the creation of the medium of performance art was to escape from what was perceived as the hegemony of the script. Many women in particular have seen the hegemony of (generally male-authored) scripts as part and parcel of a more general patriarchal hegemony. Some women, who have found male scripts (or the maleness of writing, male prescriptions) especially constraining, have posed the body and body-focused performances as alternate sites for dramatic exploration. (This movement, most active in the 1970s and early 1980s, resonates with the "French feminism" simultaneously developing in the critical genre, as well as "consciousness-raising" activities occurring in the United States.) The dialectic between male scripts and female bodies is particularly exemplified in Carolee Schneemann's *Interior Scroll,* in which, appearing naked on stage, Schneemann slowly unraveled a scroll from her vagina. On this scroll were the words of a male critic's deprecations of her body art. She read these words out loud as she removed them from her body, thereby dramatically exteriorizing and bringing to consciousness the interiorized proscriptions and prescriptions inhabiting women's bodies and expressions.

Women's bodies, of course, aren't necessarily binarized in an essentialist way from male texts (though dramatizing such an essentialist binarism has at times been an expedient political strategy); rather, feminist theater itself can productively become an arena for staging and rewriting the terms of the debate, and for deconstructing the binarism even as the theater dramatizes the powerful hegemony of this binarism on the construction of our identities and the running of our daily lives.

This binarism between (male) texts and (women's) bodies is often played out through tropes; there is a widespread tendency to use theatricality (particularly the melodramatic sort) as a trope for the feminine, and vice versa. (Jonas Barish, for example, in his *The Antitheatrical Prejudice,* presents persuasive and ample evidence of such troping in literary and critical works from Plato to Yvor Wintors.) This textual complicity of antitheatricality with antifeminism would be of great interest to feminist critics. Some of the most interesting feminist work in current theater studies, for example, involves the revaluation and retheorization of melodrama. Conversely, theoretical debates over masquer-ade, cross-dressing, exhibitionism, Irigaray's *"mimétisme,"* Foucault's "surveillance" and Panoptic gazes, and Judith Butler's speculations on the "performativity" of gender, all bear dramatic overtones and reverberations. Stemming from the common Greek root *thea*, theater and theory have become vehicles for each other, as well as vehicles with which to check against each other. Hélène Cixous's *Portrait of Dora*, for example, simultaneously theatricalizes feminist theory and theorizes feminist theater. Indeed, this simultaneity leads Jane Gallop to ask, in her reading of this play, "Cannot a theoretical text also be theatrical? In fact, is theory not always theatrical, a rhetorical performance as well as a quest for truth?" (As Gallop's discourse suggests, there is a trend in the realm of theory toward an ever-expanding inclusiveness in the term "theater," which may now include happenings, demonstrations, protest, sit-ins, hunger-strikes, Senate hearings, WAC (Women's Action Coalition) attacks, therapy sessions, and classroom dynamics.)

Theoretically impossible, and practically difficult as it is to separate the categories "theorist" and "theater worker," it is often equally artificial to separate the categories "playwright" and "poet" or "novelist." Alice Childress, Marguerite Duras, and ntozake shange, for example, move among "literary" and "dramatic" modes with striking fluidity. Should shange's "choreopoems" (such as *for colored girls who have considered suicide/ when the rainbow is enuf*) be thought of as poetry, dance, or theater? shange's plays, and the guerrilla theater of groups such as the Guerrilla Girls (performance artists/activists) and WAC, among many examples, dramatize the difficulties involved in separating even "feminist activism" from "feminist theater." Activism and theater have been extensively interactive in feminism.

Indeed, much of feminist theater is precisely about putting traditional binaries, such as literary/ nonliterary, theory/theater, and acting/ activism, under investigation. Feminist theater, if it is locatable at all, can be found most readily at the borderlines (or at the undoing of the borderlines) between literary and nonliterary, theory and theater, text and body.

Deborah Thompson

References

Barish, Jonas. *The Antitheatrical Prejudice.* Berkeley: University of California Press, 1981.

Butler, Judith. *Gender Trouble: Feminism and the Subversion of Identity*. New York: Routledge, 1990.

———. "Gender Trouble, Feminist Theory, and Psychoanalytic Discourse." In *Feminism/Postmodernism,* edited by Linda J. Nicholson, 324–339. New York: Routledge, 1990.

———. "Performative Acts and Gender Constitution: An Essay in Phenomenology and Feminist Theory." In *Performing Feminism: Feminist Critical Theory and Theatre,* edited by Sue-Ellen Case, 270–282. Baltimore, Md.: Johns Hopkins University Press, 1990.

Case, Sue-Ellen. *Feminism and Theatre.* New York: Macmillan, 1988.

Gallop, Jane. *The Daughter's Seduction: Feminism and Psychoanalysis.* Ithaca, N.Y.: Cornell University Press, 1982.

Juno, Andrea, and V. Vale, eds. *Re/Search: Angry Women.* San Francisco: Re/ Search, 1991.

Schneemann, Carolee. *More Than Meat Joy: Complete Performance Works and Selected Writings.* Edited by Bruce McPherson. New Paltz, N.Y.: Documentext, 1979.

Third-World Women

In recent years, feminist cultural and literary theory in the U.S. academy has come under increasing attack by women writers, sociologists, and cultural critics from the so-called Third World for paying scant attention to the issues and problems confronting nonwhite, middle-class women—in other words, for being Eurocentric. As Patricia Hill Collins (a professor of Afro-American studies) notes, "Even though Black women intellectuals have long expressed a unique feminist consciousness about the intersection of race and class in structuring gender, historically we have not been full participants in white feminist organizations. . . . Even today African American, Hispanic, Native American, and Asian American women criticize the feminist movement and its scholarship for being racist and overly concerned with white, middle-class women's issues." Thus, one of the primary aims of Third-World feminist theory has been to bring to the foreground the voices and perspectives of

Third-World women of color long marginalized or excluded from the dominant discourses of the West, both male and female.

Yet, it is best to use the term "Third-World women" advisedly, for, as many who are thus designated point out, such a term perpetuates a (false) "three worlds theory" as though these worlds were somehow unrelated, whereas it is more accurate to note, in the words of a well-known postcolonial theorist, "There is only one world and it is profoundly unequal." Thus, the task of "Third-World" feminists has been two-fold and seemingly paradoxical: (a) to counter the unequal treatment they have received at the hands of white Western feminists by asserting the need for voices of "Third-World" women to challenge the dominant discourse of Western feminism that has excluded them, and (b) at the same time to critique the very notion of a unified Third-World "essence" that not only does not differentiate between diverse groups of "Third-World" women, but implicitly valorizes a concept of "authenticity" that lends itself to using certain "Third-World" women as "tokens" speaking for all Third-World women. Such an approach, dangerous in itself, also absolves white women of the need to articulate their solidarity with and acquire knowledge of the lives and words of Third-World women and women of color. It allows white women academics like Patricia Meyer Spacks to write books of literary theory and criticism, such as *The Female Imagination*, that deliberately ignore the contributions of nonwhite women by offering the following lame (and ultimately racist) excuse: "As a white woman, I'm reluctant and unable to construct theories about experiences I haven't had."

A further problematic within "Third-World" feminist theory is the question of who is designated by the term. So far, the term "Third-World women" seems to exist interchangeably with "postcolonial" as well as "women of color." It might, in this sense, be worthwhile to differentiate between "U.S. Third-World feminism" and feminists from those parts of the globe that were once colonies of Europe or are currently under the control of U.S. imperialism, who could be more properly designated as "postcolonial"—such as, for example, the noted Indian literary and cultural critic Gayatri Spivak. In fact, the term "postcolonial"—itself a hotly contested one—seems to have been coined by, and most applicable to, theorists and writers of the South Asian diaspora, including the influential group of South Asian historiographers who call themselves the Subaltern Studies collective. Most postcolonial feminists are either Marxists (like Spivak) or are strongly left-leaning in their political orientation—such as the noted sociohistorian Chandra Talpede Mohanty, who writes of the need for Third-World women to challenge the universalizing tendency of much Euro-American feminist theory and scholarship shaped "Under Western Eyes"—that is, under interlocking systems of oppression such as capitalism and colonialism.

Yet, even the term "U.S. Third-World feminist" denotes women who are separated by differential physiognomies, languages, classes, and sexual preference. The point to note here is that the term has allowed for women from diverse groups of "people of color" to forge a unified oppositional consciousness in the face of common forms of oppression. As Chela Sandoval observes, "The theory and method of oppositional consciousness . . . is visible in the activities of the recent political unity variously named 'U.S. Third World feminist,' 'feminist women of color,' and 'womanist.' This unity has coalesced across differences in race, class, language, ideology, culture, and color." To this list could also be added the term "postcolonial women of color"—to indicate the political solidarity implied by the very notion of a "Third-World feminism."

Fawzia Afzal-Khan

References

Collins, Patricia Hill. *Black Feminist Thought: Knowledge, Consciousness, and the Politics of Empowerment.* New York: Routledge, 1991.

hooks, bell. *Talking Back: Thinking Feminist, Thinking Black.* Boston: South End, 1989.

Hull, Gloria T., Patricia Bell Scott, and Barbara Smith, eds. *But Some of Us Are Brave.* New York: Feminist, 1982.

Minh-ha, Trinh T. *Woman, Native, Other: Writing Postcoloniality and Feminism.* Bloomington: Indiana University Press, 1989.

Mohanty, Chandra Talpede, Ann Russo, and Lourdes Torres, eds. *Third World Women and the Politics of Feminism.* Bloomington: Indiana University Press, 1991.

Moraga, Cherríe, and Gloria Anzaldúa, eds. *Writings By Radical Women of Color.*

New York: Kitchen Table: Women of Color Press, 1981.

Sandoval, Chela. "U.S. Third World Feminism: The Theory and Method of Oppositional Consciousness in the Postmodern World." *Genders* 10 (1991): 1–24.

Sangari, Kum Kum, and Sudesh Vaid, eds. *Recasting Women: Essays in Indian Colonial History*. New Brunswick, N.J.: Rutgers University Press, 1990.

Spivak, Gayatri. *In Other Worlds*. New York: Routledge, 1988.

———. *The Post-Colonial Critic*. Edited by Sarah Harasym. New York: Routledge, 1991.

Todd, Janet

Feminist scholar and teacher, Todd is perhaps best known for her books *Sensibility: An Introduction* and *Feminist Literary History*. In *Sensibility* Todd explores the sentimental impulse in literature of the eighteenth century; she connects the devaluation of sentimental writing with its label as "feminine," and with the increase in the number of eighteenth-century women reading and writing. *Feminist Literary History* is both a chronicle and defense of feminist criticism in America starting in the 1960s. Specifically, Todd highlights the debate between French psychoanalytic and American sociohistorical feminisms; against the French feminists' charge that American feminism lacks intellectual and theoretical sophistication, Todd offers a contextualized perspective, citing the importance of American feminism as a precursor to contemporary critical modes. Additionally, Todd has edited numerous anthologies including *Be Good Sweet Maid: An Anthology of Women and Literature*, *British Women Writers: An Anthology from the 14th Century to the Present* (co-edited with Dale Spender), and *British Women Writers: A Critical Reference Guide*, and has written on various women writers from Mary Wollstonecraft to Aphra Behn.

Melissa Tedrowe

References

Todd, Janet. *Feminist Literary History*. New York: Routledge, 1988.

———. *Sensibility: An Introduction*. New York: Methuen, 1986.

———, ed. *Be Good Sweet Maid: An Anthology of Women and Literature*. New York: Holmes and Meier, 1981.

———, ed. *British Women Writers: A Critical Reference Guide*. New York: Continuum, 1989.

———, and Dale Spender, eds. *British Women Writers: An Anthology from the 14th Century to the Present*. London: Pandora, 1989.

Tompkins, Jane

Best known for her book *Sensational Designs*, Jane Tompkins has influenced feminist readings of literature through her revisionary definition of what makes a literary text "classic"; her validation of the nineteenth-century woman-authored sentimental novel; and her insistence on the connection between personal experience and professional writing.

In *Sensational Designs*, a study of American literature, Tompkins challenges the idea that literary works are inherently valuable and therefore naturally canonical. Developing her work in reader-response theory, Tompkins suggests that a text's significance depends not on its aesthetic nature or transcendent themes, but on the circumstances in which it is produced and the community of readers in which it is read. By tapping into deeply rooted societal concerns, beliefs, and anxieties, literature does "cultural work," constructing and interpreting the world for its readers. A text's ability to successfully do such work will determine the extent to which it is read. What makes a text "classic," Tompkins claims, is its ability to sustain "the scrutiny of successive generations of readers, speaking with equal power to people of various persuasions."

Tompkins's argument opens up the canon to marginalized writers such as women, discredited genres such as popular novels, and nonfictional writing such as advice books. In particular, she recuperates the significance of nineteenth-century domestic novels like Harriet Beecher Stowe's *Uncle Tom's Cabin* and Susan Warner's *The Wide, Wide World*. These novels, she writes, were immensely popular in their time yet have been discredited by literary critics because of their emphasis on female values, especially female sentiment. Tompkins suggests that the characteristics that have marginalized the domestic novel in literary history are those that are most significant to the feminist critic. For such texts envision a matriarchal society and do so not through formalist methods of symbolism and style but by depicting familiar situations, colloquial language, and powerful emotions to which readers easily relate and respond. In *West of Everything,* Tompkins suggests that the cult of domesticity—in which sentimental novels participated—was responded to by "the Western"— novels and, later, movies—which reject the very values the sentimental novel embraces, including female authority, temperance, Christianity, and the private sphere.

Tompkins's interest in the power of sentiment is apparent in the style of her critical writing—which is often autobiographical—and in her insistence on the relationship between public writing and private feeling. In "Me and My Shadow" she revises her earlier assertion that appropriating the terms of literary criticism offers feminist scholars access to power. Instead, she strongly encourages male and female critics alike to move away from theory, recuperating the personal aspects of writing which, like the sentimental novel, are associated with the feminine and therefore rejected from academic prose. In the epilogue to *West of Everything* she extends this assertion, warning feminist critics against academic "showdowns" in which women target one another's scholarship in the pursuit of their own careers.

By validating the power of the reader and the significance of interpretation, Jane Tompkins has provided feminist literary theorists with critical tools used to open the canon to authors, texts, and subjects previously thought to be insignificant. Her recuperation of the marginalized of literary studies has helped to validate the academic study of ethnic and minority literature. Finally, her belief in the relationship between feminist studies and academic scholarship continues to remind feminist scholars of the crucial relationship between the personal and the professional, challenging feminist academics to retain their link to feminism's activist and social roots.

Sara E. Quay

References

Tompkins, Jane. "'All Alone, Little Lady?'" in *The Uses of Adversity: Failure and Accommodation in Reader Response,* edited by Ellen Spolsky, 190–196. Lewisburg, Pa.: Bucknell University Press, 1990.

———. "'Indians': Textualism, Morality and the Problem of History." *Critical Inquiry* 13 (1986): 101–119.

———. "Me and My Shadow." In *Femi-nisms,* edited by Robyn Warhol and Diane Price Herndl, 20–39. New Brunswick, N.J.: Rutgers University Press, 1991.

———. *Reader-Response Criticism: From Formalism to Post-Structuralism.* Baltimore, Md.: Johns Hopkins University Press, 1980.

———. *Sensational Designs: The Cultural Work of American Fiction, 1790–1860.* New York: Oxford University Press, 1985.

———. "A Short Course in Post-Structuralism." In *Conversations: Contemporary Critical Theory and the Teaching of Literature,* edited by Charles Moran and Elizabeth Penfield, 19–37. Urbana, Ill.: National Council of Teachers of English, 1990.

———. *West of Everything: The Inner Life of Westerns.* New York: Oxford University Press, 1992.

Traffic in Women

The anthropologist Gayle Rubin first introduced this term in a now-classic 1975 essay of the same name. It describes the phenomenon whereby men consolidate power and form alliances among and between themselves through the ritualized exchange of women in marriage. Since the political and economic power that passes through a woman and to her male kin is never actually available to her, these transactions fix woman's status in patriarchal heterosexual culture as an object rather than a subject: even the woman who "chooses" her marital partner still has no choice but to be transacted within a system of power that uses her body as its basic medium of exchange.

Rubin maintains that subjects are enculturated, not born, to participate in the traffic in women. In keeping with her self-defined aim of "taking up [Friedrich] Engels' project of extracting a theory of sex oppression from the study of kinship," she accounts for the process whereby a biological woman becomes a domesticated wife by drawing upon Marxist theories of class oppression rather than essentialist formulations of gender and sexuality. Rubin describes "the set of arrangements by which a society transforms biological sexuality into products of human activity, and in which these transformed needs are satisfied" as a "sex/ gender system," and she provides examples of its form and function through her "exegetical" readings of canonical works by the fathers of modern anthropology and of psychoanalysis.

Rubin regards Claude Lévi-Strauss's major kinship study, *The Elementary Structures of Kinship*, and Sigmund Freud's central theories of human psychosexual development, the Oedipal and Electra complexes, as technologies for the production of human personalities well suited to heterosexual patriarchal culture rather than treating them as merely descriptive narratives. Through her careful analysis of the sex/gender system that structures and is structured by each of their works, Rubin demonstrates how the theories of both Lévi-Strauss and Freud make possible the ideological and practical conditions necessary for the free circulation of women as property between men.

In light of the current essentialist/constructivist controversies and the recent popularity of Michel Foucault, Rubin's claim that "sex as we know it—gender identity, sexual desire and fantasy, concepts of childhood—is itself a social product" seems particularly prescient. Two decades later, her work still informs contemporary trends in gender and sexuality studies.

Nancy Goldstein

References

Engels, Friedrich. *The Origin of the Family, Private Property, and the State, in the Light of the Researches of Lewis H. Morgan.* New York: International Publishers, 1972.

Foucault, Michel. *The History of Sexuality, Volume I: An Introduction.* Translated by Robert Hurley. New York: Pantheon, 1975.

Freud, Sigmund. *The Standard Edition of the Complete Works of Sigmund Freud.* Translated by James Strachey. London: Hogarth and the Institute for Psychoanalysis, 1953–1974.

Irigaray, Luce. "When the Goods Get Together." In *New French Feminisms,* edited by Elaine Marks and Isabelle de Courtivron, 107–111. New York: Schocken Books, 1981.

Lévi-Strauss, Claude. *The Elementary Structures of Kinship.* Boston: Beacon, 1969.

Rubin, Gayle. "Thinking Sex." In *Pleasure and Danger: Exploring Female Sexuality,* edited by Carole S. Vance, 267–319. New York: Routledge and Kegan Paul, 1984.

———. "The Traffic in Women: Notes on the 'Political Economy' of Sex." In *Toward an Anthropology of Women,* edited by Rayna R. Reiter, 157–210. New York: Monthly Review, 1975.

Sedgwick, Eve Kosofsky. *Between Men: English Literature and Male Homosocial Desire.* New York: Columbia University Press, 1985.

Translation

The work of the translator in Western literature has long been deemed worthy of praise only when it proved to be transparent and faithful to the letter of the original text. Recent studies, however, in literary theory, anthropology, cultural studies, linguistics, psychoanalysis, and women's studies have considered translation as a dynamic, interactive practice that engages some of the most widely debated issues in contemporary theory. Many of those issues intersect with feminist concerns, and translation figures increasingly in feminist theoretical discussions not only of texts translated into English but also of cross-cultural texts originally composed in English.

Unquestionably, the principal contribution of women-identified translation theory and practice has been the heightened valorization of the translator's work. Although such valorization is consistent with the demythologization of the "author" and the "original" in much current literary criticism, feminist translators position themselves specifically within that wider effort. Their feminism, as Sherry Simon has explained, provides a "framework" that both foregrounds the fact of mediation and identifies the translator's "ideological cards."

In their writing, feminist translators define their principal task as the development of specific strategies for expressing in appropriate English the innovations of a given writer. They also address, however, the need to deconstruct the gendered metaphorics that has characterized the representation of translation for centuries; they study the work of women translators from the past; and they probe the extent to which feminism—or any ideological commitment—can serve as an enabling identification. In addition, some feminist translators stress the need to integrate their concerns about gender with the concerns of race, class, and nationality while others point out the fallacy of assuming that gender definitions are consistent across cultures. Still other feminists suggest that translation offers a singular opportunity for questioning all fixed identifications.

Within this feminist framework, then, translations are affirmed as original works in their own right, works for which translators demand adequate compensation and recognition and for which they are willing to assume concomitant responsibilities. Of those responsibilities, none is more pressing than the paradoxical bond felt by the feminist translator with the work she translates. Because her feminist praxis will lead her to translate—in some cases exclusively—work by women writers and women writers who are little known in English, she will often accompany her own rendition of a work with introductory material that situates it within a given cultural or historical context. Even when she identifies her translation as subversive or transgressive, she also feels a strong sense of commitment to authors she is unwilling to declare "dead" before their writing has been read with the attention it merits.

That sense of commitment has been expressed eloquently by "First-World" translators who work with "Third-World" texts. As Gayatri Chakravorty Spivak has observed, the most appropriate strategy for translating those texts may leave key words, phrases, or even concepts untranslated. Rather than offer the highly "readable" versions demanded by the North American marketplace, such a strategy endeavors to engage readers in the activity of translation and make clear the need for intensive preparation if they are to understand an unfamiliar culture.

Carol Maier

References

Benstock, Shari. "Unveiling the Textual Subject: *Helen in Egypt* and *Ulysses*." In *Textualizing the Feminine: On the Limits of Genre,* 163–189. Norman: University of Oklahoma Press, 1991.

Chamberlain, Lori. "Gender and the Metaphorics of Translation." *Signs* 13 (1988): 454–472.

de Lotbinière-Harwood, Susanne. *Re-Bellet et Infidèle. La traduction comme practique de réécriture au féminin/The Body Bilingual. Translation as a Rewriting in the Feminine.* Quebec: Les éditions du remue-ménage/Women's, 1991.

Diaz-Diocaretz, Myriam. *Translating Poetic Discourse: Questions on Feminist Strate-*
gies in Adrienne Rich. Amsterdam/Philadelphia: John Benjamins, 1985.

Godard, Barbara. "Theorizing Feminist Discourse/Translation." In *Translation, History and Culture,* edited by Susan Bassnett and André Lefevere, 87–96. London: Pinter, 1990.

Kaminsky, Amy. "Translating Gender." In *Reading the Body Politic: Feminist Criticism and Latin American Women Writers,* 1–13. Minneapolis: University of Minnesota Press, 1993.

Levine, Suzanne Jill. "Epilog: Traduttora, Traditora." In *The Subversive Scribe: Translating Latin American Fiction,* 181–184. St. Paul, Minn.: Greywolf, 1991.

Patai, Daphne. *Brazilian Women Speak: Contemporary Life Stories.* New Brunswick, N.J.: Rutgers University Press, 1988.

Simon, Sherry. "Out from Undercover." In *Mapping Literature: The Art and Politics of Translation,* edited by David Homel and Sherry Simon, 49–54. Montreal: Véhicule, 1988.

Spivak, Gayatri Chakravorty. "The Politics of Translation." In *Destabilizing Theory: Contemporary Feminist Debate,* edited by Michèle Barrett and Anne Phillips, 177–202. Stanford: Stanford University Press, 1992.

Transvestism

In ordinary usage, the term "transvestism," which comes from *trans* ("across") and *vestis* ("dress"), refers to the practice of adopting the dress, the manner, and frequently the sexual role of the opposite sex. From a psychoanalytic viewpoint, the practice of cross-dressing indicates an abnormal or repressed desire whereby pleasure requires an imaginary condition of identity that simulates a bodily ego in order to transcend a preconstructed gender-specific body. Cross-dressing takes on a special significance with the rise of feminist theory, where transvestism in literature and film is examined as a subversion and reappropriation of gender roles.

Transvestism has been part of a deeply rooted tradition that dates back to biblical times; in Deuteronomy 22:6 we are told that "the woman shall not wear that which pertainth to man, neither shall a man put on a woman's garments: for all that do so are abomination unto the Lord thy God." Nevertheless, both Classical and Christian writings point to a long history of cross-dressing practices. Herodotus refers to the Skyths living on the shores of the Black Sea, who would wear female clothes and do the work of women. Although historically the male transvestite has surfaced more frequently than the female, St. Augustine referred to women who changed into men. In Renaissance England, the theater provided parts for women played by men, while featuring in a number of comedies women characters cross-dressed as men. Furthermore, writings have been collected from the seventeenth and eighteenth centuries that reveal over one hundred cases of women living as men in the Netherlands, and at least fifty cases have been discovered in Great Britain.

Although for men, transvestism has been depicted by some twentieth-century psychoanalysts as perverted, cross-dressing by women has not always been so linked to strictly erotic or libidinal motives. Most female transvestites experience no sexual excitement through cross-dressing, but rather seek to appropriate the masculine role in order to break out from the conventional confines of male oppression. While the tradition of female transvestism dates back to medieval times, the practice became more visible in the 1890s. Women, for instance, began to associate male clothing with freedom. Cross-dressing for women became a way of socially and politically defining the inequalities existing between masculinity and femininity. Inverting the female role came to be seen by some as an attempt to invert the traditional "privileged system that lends primacy to men."

Contemporary feminist philosophers are also concerned with the motives of male feminism, which could be seen as another kind of cross-dressing. In film, for instance, Elaine Showalter questions the "sudden appeal of serious female impersonation," observing that the "white fathers" of male criticism are involved in what she terms as critical cross-dressing— appropriating feminists' language. Showalter demonstrates how film critics see the female impersonator (such as Dorothy Michaels in *Tootsie*) as the "first genuinely mainstream feminist heroine of our era."

In her book *Vested Interests: Cross-dressing and Cultural Anxiety*, Marjorie Garber observes that literary and cultural critics have recently looked at cross-dressing as a sign of constructed gender categories. According to Garber, many critics want to "subsume [the figure of the transvestite] within one of the two traditional genders, . . . to *appropriate* the transvestite for particular political and critical aims." But Garber insists on recognizing what has in the past been called the "third sex" as a "mode of articulation, a way of describing a space of possibility." In her own discussions of literature, Garber demonstrates how characters with gender-specific bodies learn to transcend their preconstructed condition by cross-dressing, which allows them to imagine a crossover to another condition of identity. Garber uses examples of Peter Pan and Captain Hook in *Peter and Wendy* to show how these characters can occupy a "safe" space in literature where they can be both a "boy" and a "woman" at once. Garber also includes a chapter on detective fiction to show how writers "deliberately make use of the appropriation of the cross-dresser" by incorporating "grammatical clues" to clothe gender. In one of Dorothy Sayer's short stories, for instance, the character Jacques Larouge is also known as Sans Culotte (meaning "without dress") and functions to veil the who-done-it. Thus, cross-dressing in literature creates a "safe" space for anxieties over gender.

Much of the capacity for gender bending exists within the text, where feminine characters can be suspended between male and female. Reading forms of transvestism may come to play an important part in the deconstruction of identity. As Judith Butler notes, "If identities were no longer fixed as the premises of a political syllogism, and politics no longer understood as a set of practices derived from the alleged interests that belong to a set of ready-made subjects, a new configuration of politics would surely emerge from the ruins of the old. Cultural configurations of sex and gender might then proliferate . . . confounding the very binarism of sex, and exposing its fundamental unnaturalness."

Ron May

References

Butler, Judith. *Gender Trouble: Feminism and the Subversion of Identity*. New York: Routledge, 1990.

Garber, Marjorie. *Vested Interests: Cross-dressing and Cultural Anxiety*. New York: Routledge, 1992.

Modleski, Tania. *Feminism without Women: Culture and Criticism in a "Postfeminist" Age*. New York: Routledge, 1991.

Showalter, Elaine. "Critical Cross-Dressing: Male Feminists and the Woman of the Year." *Raritan* 3 (1983): 130–149.

Tulsa Studies in Women's Literature

Founded in 1982 by Germaine Greer as the organ of the now defunct Tulsa Center for the Study of Women's Literature, TSWL is the longest-running academic journal devoted to the study of women's literature. In its earliest stages, the journal concentrated on archival research and the excavation of neglected women's work. In her germinal essay "The Tulsa Center for the Study of Women's Literature: What We Are Doing and Why We Are Doing It," Greer explained that "investigating the vast mass of female product that is our inheritance . . . can help to illumine the other side of the coin struck by official historians . . . [in order to] revolutionize the concept of history itself." After struggling with a lack of financial and political support from the University of Tulsa, Greer severed connections with the university in 1983 and the editorship was taken up by Shari Benstock. Under Benstock's leadership, the journal began to include theoretically oriented essays and won the MLA Conference of Editors of Learned Journals Award for best special issue in 1985. When Benstock resigned in 1986 to protest the same conditions that caused Greer's departure, the journal was headed by guest editors until its third editor, Holly Laird, took the helm. In her first editorial essay, Laird pronounced the journal an "institution" with a "strong identity and a life of its own," pledging that it would "remain . . . primarily dedicated to women's literature . . . includ[ing] the feminist criticism and theory being written by and for women."

Jeslyn Medoff

References

Benstock, Shari, ed. *Feminist Issues in Literary Scholarship*. Bloomington: Indiana University Press, 1987.

U

Unconscious

The theory of the unconscious, considered to be the founding idea of modern psychoanalysis, is attributed to Sigmund Freud as one of his most significant discoveries. J. Laplanche and J.B. Pontalis, in *The Language of Psychoanalysis*, characterize the Freudian unconscious as a psychic system composed of contents, mostly unconscious ideas representing childhood wishes and instincts, that have been denied access to the consciousness through the operation of repression. These contents are thus sealed off from direct communication with the consciousness, structured according to the laws of displacement and condensation, and accessible only through the distorted lenses of dreams, jokes, and slips of the tongue. French Freudian psychoanalyst Jacques Lacan expanded Freud's view by arguing that the unconscious is structured like a language, thus making explicit the links to a poetics of signs and literature. Other psychoanalysts developed views of the unconscious with varying relationships to Freud's founding theory, among them Carl Jung, Melanie Klein, and R.D. Laing. Jung's theory of the collective unconscious, for example, spurred the development of literary analyses of archetypal patterns in literature. In recognizing the connections between a textual unconscious in literature and "woman" as the unconscious of masculine culture, the more current work of feminist theorists like Hélène Cixous, Julia Kristeva, Luce Irigaray, Jane Gallop, and Alice Jardine, among others, has become central to the movement to invert phallocentric psychoanalytic insights, suggesting the potential for innovative feminist readings and interpretations.

An early work, *The Interpretation of Dreams* (1900), was Freud's major breakthrough to establishing the dream as a "rebus" and the "royal road" to the unconscious. In the same text, Freud introduced his theory of the Oedipal complex, where the male child's repression of his forbidden desire for the mother opens the space of the unconscious and initiates him into a culturally acceptable masculine role. Much later, in "Female Sexuality" (1931) and "Femininity" (1933), Freud finally recognized the complicated nature of a woman's entrance into society, claiming that women spend a longer pre-Oedipal period of attachment to their mothers than boys. He was unable, however, to clarify the consequences for women of such a substantially different formative period. Freud's interpretations of culture and society further essentializes woman by equating her with the unconscious, effectively demonstrated by his reading of Shakespeare, Greek myth, and folklore in "The Theme of the Three Caskets" (1913). Here Freud assigns meaning to conclude that woman symbolizes death, a reading that situates woman as the underground, the tomb (casket) of Mother Earth and a space synonymous with the unconscious.

Jacques Lacan called for a return to Freud's theory of the unconscious and a rejection of ego psychology, extending Freud's description of the unconscious to argue in *Écrits* that "what the psychoanalytic experience discovers in the unconscious is the whole structure of language." For Lacan, the unconscious is that part of the subject's discourse that is outside of his/her control and that part of his/her history that is marked by a blank, where a censored truth has been inscribed and can only be revealed through its symptoms. Building upon the linguistic theories of Ferdinand de Saussure, Lacan shows that the splitting of the linguistic sign (S/s) into signifier and signified creates a barrier to signification where language may "signify something quite other than what it says." Lacan adapts Freud's model of the dream as a puzzle to theorize the unconscious as a lost language, perhaps even preexisting consciousness, where what is found is the discourse of the Other. In his efforts to continue the debate on female sexuality and hold onto Freud's insight of sexual difference as symbolically constructed, Lacan acknowledged in *Seminar XX, Encore* the cultural exclusion of woman by the very nature of society and language and reinforced the notion of woman as radically Other from man and positioned as his unconscious. Lacan also extended his theories beyond his own discipline to offer seminars that interpreted a textual unconscious through the interplay of structures and signifiers in works like Poe's "The Purloined Letter" and Joyce's *Finnegan's Wake.*

The work of Lacan on Freud, essentially continuing the blind spots of a phallocentric psychoanalytic tradition, inspired several French feminists and theorists to react. In "The Laugh of the Medusa," for example, Hélène Cixous connects woman to the poetry she might write and to the unconscious as the place where both have been repressed. Cixous proposes in "Castration or Decapitation?" a feminine unconscious and textuality concerned with giving, with beginning everywhere at once, with operating in excess, and with reactivating that which phallocentric language tries to cut out—the voice of the mother. Julia Kristeva, in "La Femme Ce N'est Jamais Ça," theorizes quite similarly to Cixous, writing: "In 'woman' I see something that cannot be represented, something that is not said, something above and beyond nomenclatures and ideologies." In poetic language, Kristeva argues, a semiotic process transgresses the laws of the symbolic, allowing for the emergence of drives emanating from the unconscious. This "revolution" reactivates the relationship to the mother, an incestuous invasion of forbidden territory, that the symbolic process has repressed. Woman is a specialist in the unconscious, Kristeva concludes in "About Chinese Women," equating women with poetic language, the semiotic process, repression, and the movement toward revolution and transgression of the law. Luce Irigaray insists in *This Sex Which Is Not One,* along with Kristeva and Cixous, that the importance of the mother in the theory of the unconscious has been ignored. Arguing as well that woman is the unconscious in *Speculum of the Other Woman,* Irigaray challenges women to look for those blanks in discourse that track women's exclusion and to reinscribe those blanks in order to disrupt the logical process of the reader-writer. Alice Jardine, in *Gynesis: Configurations of Woman and Modernity,* connects woman as man's unconscious to the text as cultural unconscious in a merger of American and French feminisms, revising Lacanian and Freudian insights to uncover the repressed "woman-in-effect" in the text.

Several recent collections of feminist psychoanalytic theory and criticism indicate that feminist critics have not only returned to Freud's treatment of his young female patient Dora in his *Fragment of an Analysis of a Case of Hysteria* (1905) to reinterpret the unspoken and repressed of that text, they have also explored Lacanian texts, especially his "Seminar on the Purloined Letter" for his repression of the feminine. Feminist scholars have applied their insights about the unconscious to a wide array of literary texts, including *Jane Eyre,* "The Yellow Wallpaper," and the novels of Virginia Woolf, among others. Furthermore, building upon French feminism and object-relations theory from Melanie Klein and expanded in Nancy Chodorow's *The Reproduction of Mothering: Psychoanalysis and the Sociology of Gender,* feminists continue to examine female acculturation, the institutionalization of motherhood, and the repression of a lengthy pre-Oedipal mother-daughter relationship as these become embedded in texts. The future of this area of critical exploration of texts will indeed advance the demand for an ongoing feminist exploration of the nature of the unconscious, of its relationship to language, and of the differences of its formation in females for whom fear of castration can never present a threat.

Merry M. Pawlowski

References

Barr, Marleen S., and Richard Feldstein, eds. *Discontented Discourses: Feminism/Textual Intervention/Psychoanalysis.* Urbana: University of Chicago Press, 1989.

Chodorow, Nancy. *The Reproduction of Mothering: Psychoanalysis and the Sociology of Gender.* Berkeley: University of California Press, 1978.

Cixous, Hélène. "Castration or Decapitation?" *Signs* 7 (1981): 41–55.

———. "The Laugh of the Medusa." In *New French Feminisms,* edited by Elaine Marks and Isabelle de Courtivron, 245–264. New York: Schocken Books, 1981.

Ellenberger, Henri. *The Discovery of the Unconscious: The History and Evolution of Dynamic Psychiatry.* New York: Basic, 1970.

Freud, Sigmund. *The Standard Edition of the Complete Psychological Works of Sigmund Freud.* 24 vols. Translated by James Strachey et al. London: Hogarth, 1953–1974.

Gallop, Jane. *The Daughter's Seduction: Feminism and Psychoanalysis.* Ithaca, N.Y.: Cornell University Press, 1982.

Irigaray, Luce. *Speculum of the Other Woman.* Translated by Gillian C. Gill. Ithaca, N.Y.: Cornell University Press, 1985.

Jardine, Alice. *Gynesis: Configurations of Woman and Modernity.* Ithaca, N.Y.: Cornell University Press, 1985.

Kiell, Norman. *Psychoanalysis, Psychology, and Literature: A Bibliography.* Metuchen, N.J.: Scarecrow, 1982.

Kristeva, Julia. *The Kristeva Reader.* Edited by Toril Moi. New York: Columbia University Press, 1986.

Lacan, Jacques. *Écrits: A Selection.* Translated by Alan Sheridan. New York: W.W. Norton, 1977.

Laplanche, Jean, and J.B. Pontalis. *The Language of Psychoanalysis.* Translated by Donald Nicholson Smith. New York: W.W. Norton, 1973.

Mitchell, Juliet. *Psychoanalysis and Feminism.* London: Allen Lane, 1974.

———, and Jacqueline Rose, eds. *Feminine Sexuality: Jacques Lacan and the école freudienne.* New York: W.W. Norton, 1982.

Uterus

Also known as the womb, the uterus is one of the primary reproductive organs in a woman's body. Due to its capacity for supporting the development of new life during pregnancy, the uterus has come to be associated with powers of femininity in both physical reproduction and artistic creation. At the same time, the uterus has been represented as a source of female fluidity and instability, both through its link with the physical flows of blood in menstruation and childbirth and through historical associations connecting disorders such as hysteria with a "wandering womb." For feminist theorists, the uterus has served as a locus for debates regarding the relation between women's reproductive capabilities and social and cultural definitions of female subjectivity.

The earliest source of recorded medicine, the Egyptian *Kahun Papyrus* (c. 1900 B.C.), associated certain behavioral disorders with aberrations in the position of the womb. In the Hippocratic writings, these disturbances were given the name "hysteria," from *hystera,* the Greek word for womb, and treatments were prescribed in order to induce the uterus to move downward to its proper position. Plato and Aristotle described the womb as an animal within an animal, with its own consciousness, capable of moving around within the lower part of the body and upsetting the bodily economy with its disturbed state. Such conceptions supported stereotypes of feminine error and changeability.

In midwifery manuals of sixteenth-century England, the womb was represented as so greedy for male seed that it could descend to snatch and suck semen, indicating the unsettling power of female sexual desire. Other metaphoric associations across history include the womb as house and prison for the infant, as harbor with its own port and gates, as well-watered field that attracts seed, as voracious stomach that finally helps expel the child into the world, and as cocoon that spins or weaves the child through a series of layered membranes. In her collection of feminist essays on motherhood as experience and institution, Adrienne Rich emphasizes connections between the uterus and the "earth-womb," from which life originates and to which it returns, and juxtaposes the liquidity of the uterus with the ocean, "whose tides respond, like woman's menses, to the pull of the moon," and whose water "corresponds to the amniotic fluid in which human life begins."

The uterus has played an important part in revisionary developments in psychoanalytic theory in the twentieth century. While Freud represented the mother first as phallic and then as castrated, privileging the phallus in the constitution of the body image from the child's point of view, Melanie Klein argued that both sexes identify first with the mother, leading to the development of a femininity complex for boys (by contrast to the Freudian castration

U

complex for girls) that results in womb envy. In challenging the emphasis upon the phallus in traditional psychoanalytic theories, feminist theorists have critiqued the concomitant representation of women's bodies as lacking, which attempts to ignore or erase the potentially powerful significance of the uterus.

Revising Lacan's phallic account of the origins of language, Julia Kristeva and Luce Irigaray have developed models for the preverbal underpinnings of culture that reclaim the value of the maternal figure for feminine discourse. Kristeva argues that the semiotic is composed of pre-Oedipal, prelinguistic forces associated with the nonsymbolic contact between mother and child, and uses the term *chora,* also derived from the Greek word for womb, to denote a receptacle or maternal space that underlies the symbolic. In finding that the speaking subject is both "generated and negated" in the *chora,* Kristeva constructs the maternal body as a locus of origin as well as of loss.

In *Speculum of the Other Woman* Irigaray analyzes the erasure of the mother in the Platonic allegory of the cave, arguing that even as the cave can be read as a metaphor "of the den, the womb or Hystera," the material womb itself is superseded by a uterine metaphor, so that the womb is "transmuted by/for analogy into a circus and a projection screen, a theater of/for fantasies." More recently, Irigaray has focused on the placental relation between mother and child *in utero.* Through an interview with a biology teacher named Helene Rouch, Irigaray establishes the significance of the placenta as a mediating space between mother and fetus, with its own autonomy, which allows the difference between "self" and "other" to be continuously negotiated. In *je, tu, nous,* Irigaray describes the organization of the "placental economy" as "one not in a state of fusion, which respects the one and the other," and calls attention to the consequences of the ignorance of the placental economy on the male cultural imaginary, "in particular regarding the relationship to the so-called mother tongue," where the materiality of relationship to the maternal body is erased.

Scrutinizing psychoanalytic preoccupation with the phallus, Marcia Ian suggests that "the phallus might be a screen image, a phobic substitute for something else," that something else being the umbilical cord, "for it is the umbilical cord after all, and not the penis, which constitutes the historic 'locution and link of ex-change' from which the subject must be 'missing' if he is to be a subject and not a permanent appendage of the mother." Given that the umbilical cord links the bodies of mother and fetus even as the placenta preserves their distinction, Ian observes that the umbilical cord defines difference at once through connection and separation. Feminist attention to the functions not only of the uterus but also of the placenta and umbilical cord opens new possibilities for constructions of the subject in material as well as metaphoric terms.

Recent advances in reproductive technologies have altered both treatment and representations of the uterus, with significant implications for conceptions of maternity and subjectivity. Michelle Stanworth examines the coexistence of feminist hostility and support for the development of artificial wombs with the capacity to make biological motherhood redundant, and finds that the debates regarding conceptive technologies provide a way of talking about different cultural conceptions of motherhood as potentially debilitating or empowering. Alice Adams suggests that the artificial womb can be viewed as a "sanitized mother," cleansed of the threat of maternal agency posed by the biological alternative, and endlessly accessible to view.

Moving from reproductive technologies focused on the uterus to the development of medical-photographic discourse focused on the fetus, E. Ann Kaplan analyzes the implications of the treatment of the maternal body in Lennart Nilsson's striking series of photographs of the fetus during gestation, produced in *A Child is Born* (1965). In magnifying the inside of the woman's uterus until it looks like outer space, Nilsson's book manages to render inception and gestation in cosmic terms, observes Kaplan, while reducing the material mother to a holding vessel, "the non-subject that makes possible the child's subjectivity." Along similar lines, Adams notes that images of the fetus *in utero* construct the woman's womb as "the inner frame which contextualizes the surface image of the fetus" so that "the history of the intelligible fetus begins with the mother's retrospective erasure."

Even as Irigaray finds the womb treated as a "projection screen" in Plato's allegory of the cave, so contemporary medical photographs of the fetus *in utero* can be found to produce the same effect, with the dark female space of the uterus now apparently penetrated by the light of (implicitly masculine) scientific observation.

In maintaining that the most recent conceptive technologies reproduce old myths of self-generation that displace the presence of the mother, contemporary feminist theorists begin to engage in reconstituting the material significance of the uterus for constructions of women as not only mythical but also historical agents of their own reproduction.

Naomi J. Miller

References

Adams, Alice. *Reproducing the Womb: Images of Childbirth in Science, Feminist Theory, and Literature*. Ithaca, N.Y.: Cornell University Press, 1994.

Erickson, Robert A. *Mother Midnight: Birth, Sex, and Fate in Eighteenth-Century Fiction*. New York: AMS, 1986.

Ian, Marcia. *Remembering the Phallic Mother: Psychoanalysis, Modernism, and the Fetish*. Ithaca N.Y.: Cornell University Press, 1993.

Irigaray, Luce. *Je, tu, nous: Toward a Culture of Difference*. Translated by Alison Martin. New York: Routledge, 1993.

———. *Speculum of the Other Woman*. Translated by Gillian C. Gill. Ithaca, N.Y.: Cornell University Press, 1985.

Kaplan, E. Ann. *Motherhood and Representation: The Mother in Popular Culture and Drama*. London: Routledge, 1992.

Klein, Melanie. "Early Stages of the Oedipus Conflict," In *The Selected Melanie Klein*, edited by Juliet Mitchell, 69–83. Harmondsworth: Penguin, 1986.

Kristeva, Julia. *Revolution in Poetic Language*. Translated by Margaret Waller. New York: Columbia University Press, 1984.

Paster, Gail Kern. *The Body Embarrassed: Drama and the Disciplines of Shame in Early Modern England*. Ithaca, N.Y.: Cornell University Press, 1993.

Rich, Adrienne. *Of Woman Born: Motherhood as Experience and Institution*. New York: W.W. Norton, 1986.

Stanworth, Michelle. "Birth Pangs: Conceptive Technologies and the Threat to Motherhood." In *Conflicts in Feminism*, edited by Marianne Hirsch and Evelyn Fox Keller, 288–304. New York: Routledge, 1990.

Veith, Ilza. *Hysteria: The History of a Disease*. Chicago: University of Chicago Press, 1965.

Utopianism

The study of utopia consists of two strands: the first is the study of literary works that imagine a perfect society; the second is the study of intentional communities that attempt to actualize a harmonious social order. This essay considers the first strand, and, in particular, utopian novels by women writers.

By definition, utopianism hinges on a paradox: it is a vision of a better world, but one that does not exist. This paradox is embodied in the coinage of the word, from the Latin eu-topia, the "good place," or *ou-topia*, "no place." The first utopian novel, Thomas More's *Utopia* (1516), depicts the travels of a visitor from our world to an imagined world of harmony and order. While purportedly about the future, utopias are really about the past and present, formulating critiques of what is. The utopian vision is one of promise and hope, while its opposite, the dystopian vision, is satirical, cynical.

A further paradox inheres in utopian literature. The author's vision of a perfect society may not match the reader's. It is noteworthy that virtually all the utopian societies imagined by male writers (starting with More's *Utopia*) fail to transform the social arrangements that keep men in positions of power relative to women. Feminist utopias address the question of power, favoring a democratic or communal power structure rather than a hierarchal one. These works create new roles for women in the home and society, and pay particular attention to childbirth and child care.

Most utopias (by both men and women) are pastoral, often antitechnological. Some feminist utopias relegate technology to the background or dedicate it to the service of ecology. For example, in Charlotte Perkins Gilman's *Herland,* the women drive cars, but we never see the factories that produce them. In *Woman on the Edge of Time,* Marge Piercy depicts both a pastoral utopian world where technology preserves nature, and a nightmare technological world, thick with pollution. Similarly, in Ursula K. Le Guin's *Always Coming Home,* the warlike male society of the Condors invests heavily in armaments, but denies education to women. In contrast, the peaceful Kesh are agrarian, and live simply, but provide all their people access to a highly sophisticated network of computerized information. Cyborgs and androids are now entering utopian fiction: in Marge Piercy's *He, She and It* a sensitive android becomes the heroine's lover.

Utopian fiction written by women usually considers such questions as women's work (both in and out of the house), family structure, political and personal power, government, and childbirth. Often the government in a feminist utopia is set up along family lines. Values such as caretaking and motherhood are paramount, as in Gilman's *Herland* or Marion Zimmer Bradley's *The Ruins of Isis.*

Critics have argued the merits of single-sex utopias. The all-woman society may be seen as a metaphor for an ideal world: writers eliminate men in order to show the utopian possibilities when women have political and social power. On the other hand, some critics argue that a world of women may be a pessimistic vision suggesting that women believe that they cannot achieve equality when there are men around.

As might be expected, the problems of reproduction are important in an all-woman society. Some writers imagine parthenogenesis or cloning, others develop unusual possibilities. Suzy McKee Charnas writes of women mating with horses in *Motherlines,* published in 1978.

The technology of reproduction is an issue in utopian fiction as well. Does mechanized childbirth represent an advance or a retreat? The dystopian satire *Brave New World* by Aldous Huxley depicts a world where children are "decanted" off an assembly line, already programmed to become members of a particular social class. In contrast, in Piercy's *Woman on the Edge of Time* mechanical childbirth allows men to participate equally with women in nurturing and caring for infants.

Utopian fiction seems to flower in times of social change. The 1890s and 1970s were both times that produced feminist utopian fictions. Utopias tend to reflect contemporary political and social thinking, and thus may not seem utopian when seen in the light of other times. For example, Mary E. Bradley Lane wrote *Mizora* about a world of blonde, white-skinned women, a vision that we would now perceive as racist. In the 1970s, many feminist utopias portrayed worlds of powerful women.

Political skepticism has led many to question the idea of utopia, emphasizing the impracticality of utopia or the dangers of a static society. In response to these problems, the concept of process has come to describe the utopian project. Similarly, Le Guin coined the term "ambiguous utopia" as the subtitle of her novel *The Dispossessed,* in which she explores the problem of political stagnation in an isolated utopia. Her short story "The Ones Who Walk Away from Omelas" questions the moral basis of a utopia that coexists with injustice.

Utopian literature is a mirror in which authors reflect their concerns, the hopes and fears of their times, and their yearnings for a more golden future.

Karen F. Stein

References

Albinski, Nan Bowman. *Women's Utopias in British and American Fiction.* London, New York: Routledge, 1988.

Barr, Marleen, and Nicholas D. Smith, eds. *Women and Utopia.* Lanham, Md.: University Press of America, 1983.

Bartkowski, Frances. *Feminist Utopias.* Lincoln and London: University of Nebraska Press, 1989.

Bradley, Marion Zimmer. *The Ruins of Isis.* New York: Pocket, 1978.

Gilman, Charlotte Perkins. *Herland* [1915]. New York: Pantheon, 1979.

Huxley, Aldous. *Brave New World* [1946]. New York: Harper Collins, 1989.

Jones, Libby Falk, and Sarah Webster Goodwin, eds. *Feminism, Utopia, and Narrative.* Knoxville: University of Tennessee Press, 1990.

Kessler, Carol Farley, ed. *Daring to Dream: Utopian Stories by United States Women, 1836–1919.* Boston: Pandora, 1984.

Lane, Mary E. Bradley. *Mizora* [1880–1881]. New York: Gregg, 1975.

Le Guin, Ursula K. *Always Coming Home.* New York: Harper and Row, 1985.

———. *The Dispossessed: An Ambiguous Utopia.* New York: Avon, 1974.

Piercy, Marge. *He, She and It.* New York: Knopf, 1991.

———. *Woman on the Edge of Time.* New York: Knopf, 1976.

Sargent, Lyman Tower. *British and American Utopian Literature, 1516–1985: An Annotated Chronological Bibliography.* New York: Garland, 1988.

V

Veil

The Islamic veil, *chador*, a large black square of fabric falling from the head to the ankles, is part of the *hijab*, the traditional Islamic dress for women. The chador covers all of a woman's skin except for the eyes and hands and is, according to Islamic law, to be worn by women when in public. Fundamentalist Islamic women may appear unveiled only before other women, their husbands, and close male relatives within the privacy of the home. In countries such as Iran, the legal penalties for women appearing in public unveiled are severe. While in 1935 the shah banned the chador as part of a plan to Westernize the country, the fundamentalist revolution in 1967 signaled a return to traditional Islamic ways, and the chador was again made a requirement for women. The readoption of the chador, or veil, in Islamic countries corresponds to a return to fundamentalist values.

European women have also worn the veil, though its use is rare in modern times. Critic Elaine Showalter asks, "Why was the veil linked with femininity? First of all, veiling was associated with female sexuality and the veil of the hymen. The veil thus represented female chastity and modesty; in rituals of the nunnery, marriage, or mourning, it concealed sexuality." The veil that covers a woman's face during the marriage ritual functions as a symbolic boundary between chastity and sexual initiation. This identification of the veil with both privacy and femininity causes it, according to Gilbert and Gubar, to function as "an image of confinement different from yet related to the imagery of enclosure that constantly threatens to stifle the heroines of women's fiction." They claim that "the recording of what exists behind the veil is distinctively female because it is the woman who exists behind the veil in patriarchal society, inhabiting a private sphere invisible to public view."

Veiled women in the Salome myth, Gothic novels, and novels such as Hawthorne's *Blithedale Romance* are often depicted in a sinister or threatening way, perhaps, as Showalter notes, because "the veiled woman who is dangerous to look upon also signifies the quest for the mystery of origins, the truth of birth and death." Gilbert and Gubar observe that "the veiled lady of male literature is frequently identified with spiritual powers," and veiled or blindfolded women in the visual arts often stand for Truth. "Clearly," asserts Doane, "one can trace a poetics or theoretics of the veil in the texts of literature, psychoanalysis, and philosophy as well as the cinema." Traditionally, only women wear the veil, and the veil's appearance in narrative, film, and visual arts signifies femininity. While the veil's cultural meanings are multiple, and have shifted according to the historical moment, it remains a powerful symbol of both female confinement and feminine sexuality.

Lisa Nakamura

References

Ahmed, Leila. *Women and Gender in Islam: Historical Roots of a Modern Debate.* New Haven and London: Yale University Press, 1992.

Brooks, Geraldine. *Nine Parts of Desire: The Hidden World of Islamic Women.* New York: Anchor Doubleday, 1995.

Doane, Mary Ann. *Femmes Fatales: Feminism, Film Theory, Psychoanalysis.* New York and London: Routledge, 1991.

Gilbert, Sandra, and Susan Gubar. *The Mad-*

woman in the Attic. New Haven: Yale University Press, 1979.

Sedgwick, Eve Kosofky. "The Character in the Veil: Imagery of the Surface in the Gothic Novel." *PMLA* 96 (1981): 255–270.

Showalter, Elaine. *Sexual Anarchy: Gender and Culture at the Fin de Siecle.* New York: Penguin, 1990.

Vickers, Nancy J.

Nancy Vickers's work on representations of the female body in Petrarch, Dante, Cellini, and Shakespeare has had an enormous impact on the study of gender in early-modern literature and culture. Her most influential article, "Diana Described: Scattered Woman and Scattered Rhyme," examines the violence and anxiety implicit in conventional descriptions of female beauty. She focuses on Petrarch's *Rime Sparse,* where the beloved Laura "is always presented as a part or parts of a woman," and reads this "descriptive dismemberment" as a defensive strategy of the male spectator in the presence of an overpowering female. In contrast to Ovid's Actaeon, who is metamorphosed and dismembered after seeing the naked Diana, it is Petrarch's Laura who is dismembered in images as Petrarch "scatters her [body] through his scattered rhymes." Similarly, in "'The blazon of sweet beauty's best,'" Vickers examines the dynamics of male competition and conquest that inform the anatomical blazon in Shakespeare's *Lucrece.* Vickers has edited many books, the most influential of which is *Rewriting the Renaissance: The Discourses of Sexual Difference in Early Modern Europe.* This volume contains a series of well-known essays that expand questions of gender difference to include questions of social, racial, and national difference in the early modern period. The text, which is divided into three parts ("The Politics of Patriarchy: Theory and Practice," "The Rhetorics of Marginalization: Consequences of Patriarchy," and "The Works of Women: Some Exceptions to the Rule of Patriarchy"), brings together feminist, new historicist, psychoanalytic, Marxist, and deconstructive methodologies in an effort to rethink representations of identity and difference in the drama, prose, and poetry of Early Modern Europe. Vickers is currently working on gender, technology, and the lyric in contemporary culture.

Carla J. Mazzio

References

Ferguson, Margaret W., Maureen Quilligan, and Nancy Vickers, eds. *Rewriting the Renaissance: The Discourses of Sexual Difference in Early Modern Europe.* Chicago: University of Chicago Press, 1986.

Vickers, Nancy J. "'The Blazon of Sweet Beauty's Best': Shakespeare's *Lucrece.*" In *Shakespeare and the Question of Theory,* edited by Geoffrey Hartman and Patricia Parker, 95–115. London: Methuen, 1985.

———. "Diana Described: Scattered Woman and Scattered Rhyme." *Critical Inquiry* 8 (1981): 265–279.

———. "The Heraldry in Lucrece's Face." *Poetics Today* 6 (1985): 171–184.

———. "Maternalism and the Material Girl." In *Embodied Voices: Female Vocality in Western Culture,* edited by Leslie C. Dunn and Nancy A. Jones, 230–246. Cambridge: Cambridge University Press, 1994.

———. "The Mistress in the Masterpiece." In *The Poetics of Gender,* edited by Nancy R. Miller, 19–41. New York: Columbia University Press, 1986.

———. "'Vital Signs': Petrarch and Popular Culture." *Romanic Review* 79 (1988): 184–195.

———. "Widowed Words: Dante, Petrarch, and the Metaphors of Mourning." In *Discourses of Authority in Medieval and Renaissance Literature,* edited by Kevin Brownlee and Walter Stephens, 97–108. Hanover, N.H., and London: University Press of New England, 1989.

———, and Ann R. Jones. "Canon, Rule and the Restoration Renaissance." *Yale French Studies* 75 (1988): 9–25.

Victorian Studies

Today many literary scholars claim they study culture rather than literature. Victorianists often irascibly insist this is what they have done for decades. Thus, feminist literary studies of Victorian women writers, female characters, women's novels, women readers, or constructions of gender are likely to be contextualized in debates over women's property rights or custody laws or medical treatments or advertisements. Feminist critics view literary texts as part of a complexly gendered system of representations.

Twentieth-century feminist Victorian studies gained a stronghold in American universities during the 1970s. Martha Vicinus edited two collections of multidisciplinary essays, *Suffer and Be Still: Women in the Victorian Age* and *A Widening Sphere: The Changing Roles of Victorian Women,* which cover marriage, sexuality, motherhood, and employment (from writing to governessing to industrial labor to prostitution). Explicitly, literary feminist studies focused on women characters in literature by men or on the few women who were taught regularly: George Eliot, Charlotte Brontë, and Emily Brontë. Then Elaine Showalter published *A Literature of Their Own: British Women Novelists from Brontë to Lessing.* By recovering a long-forgotten tradition of women writers, this sweeping overview changed the curriculum of Victorian studies. Feminist scholars also changed Victorianists' conceptions of well-known novels and poems. Sandra Gilbert's and Susan Gubar's study *The Madwoman in the Attic: The Woman Writer and the Nineteenth-Century Literary Imagination* finds currents of anger and madness beneath the surfaces of passive, pure, self-effacing femininity. They explore the burning, threatening creative genius seething in the art of women writers who fought their way into the public world of publishing.

Middle-class Victorians often wrote of the separate spheres, arguing that the private, domestic sphere was the proper place for women while men belonged in the public world of commerce and government. Many 1980s studies asked whose interests were served by this fantasy and why so many women promoted it.

Nina Auerbach found one answer in Victorian images of women such as the victim, queen, angel, and demon in *Woman and the Demon: The Life of a Victorian Myth.* Margaret Homans used psychoanalytic studies of language acquisition to understand how the private bonds between mothers and daughters affected women's writing in *Bearing the Word: Language and Female Experience in Nineteenth-Century Women's Writing.*

Other feminists turned to Marxist analyses of class struggle and Foucault's argument that individuals are disciplined into proper beliefs and behaviors through social institutions like prisons and clinics. For example, Nancy Armstrong's *Desire and Domestic Fiction: A Political History of the Novel* proposes that novels like *Emma, Jane Eyre,* and *Shirley* taught readers to value home as the center of moral, spiritual authority. Consequently, "female" qualities—sentimentality, emotion, love, maternal feeling—emerged as an alternative form of power in response to the aggressive, competitive "public" world.

Mary Poovey also discusses Victorian gender as Victorian ideology in her book *Uneven Developments: The Ideological Work of Gender in Mid-Victorian England.* She shows how public debates over issues like childbirth practices reveal that gender behaviors are learned rather than innate. Ironically, the same debates that inspired women to speak silenced people oppressed due to class or color by fixing attention on white, middle-class gender conflicts.

Most recently, feminist criticism has asked how literature participated in British imperialism. The late Victorian period marked the high point of Victorian colonialism. White women played an often-ignored role in the imaginative as well as geographical subjugation of India, Africa, and the Caribbean while women of color suffered the consequences.

Late Victorian fears of social degeneration dominated 1890s literature. Elaine Showalter's *Sexual Anarchy: Gender and Culture at the Fin De Siecle* suggests that fears of homosexuality and changing masculinities at home promoted imperialism abroad. Anita Levy's *Other Women: The Writing of Class, Race, and Gender, 1832–1898* asks how Victorian anthropological and scientific theories about color, race, and national differences that the Victorians used to justify imperialism entered the purportedly domestic space of the novel. Critics like Suvendrini Perera, the author of *The Reaches of Empire: The English Novel from Edgeworth to Dickens,* teach us to see how the politics of empire saturate the novels. Other studies examine the travel writing and diaries of British women who lived in the colonies, as in the case of Sara Mills's *Discourses of Difference: An Analysis of Women's Travel Writing and Colonialism.*

Feminist Victorianists continue their multifaceted labor of recovering neglected texts and lost voices, exploring the complex relations among artifacts of Victorian culture, and deciphering the beliefs, values, contradictions, and differences in the language of the last century. Perhaps our greatest challenge is to understand how this near literary past still powerfully influences our present.

Teresa Mangum

References

Armstrong, Nancy. *Desire and Domestic Fiction: A Political History of the Novel.* New York: Oxford University Press, 1987.

Auerbach, Nina. *Woman and the Demon: The Life of a Victorian Myth.* Cambridge: Harvard University Press, 1972.

Gilbert, Sandra M., and Susan Gubar. *The Madwoman in the Attic: The Woman Writer and the Nineteenth-Century Literary Imagination.* New Haven: Yale University Press, 1979.

Homans, Margaret. *Bearing the Word: Language and Female Experience in Nineteenth-Century Women's Writing.* Chicago: University of Chicago Press, 1986.

Levy, Anita. *Other Women: The Writing of Class, Race, and Gender, 1832–1989.* Princeton: Princeton University Press, 1991.

Mills, Sara. *Discourses of Difference: An Analysis of Women's Travel Writing and Colonialism.* New York: Routledge, 1991.

Perera, Suvendrini. *The Reaches of Empire: The English Novel from Edgeworth to Dickens.* New York: Columbia University Press, 1991.

Poovey, Mary. *Uneven Developments: The Ideological Work of Gender in Mid-Victorian England.* Chicago: University of Chicago Press, 1988.

Showalter, Elaine. *A Literature of Their Own: British Women Novelists from Brontë to Lessing.* Princeton: Princeton University Press, 1977.

―――. *Sexual Anarchy: Gender and Culture at the Fin De Siecle.* New York: Penguin, 1990.

Vicinus, Martha, ed. *Suffer and Be Still: Women in the Victorian Age.* Bloomington: Indiana University Press, 1972.

―――, ed. *A Widening Sphere: The Changing Roles of Victorian Women.* Bloomington: Indiana University Press, 1977.

Violence

Feminist analyses of violence have circulated around a number of central issues, namely, the history of power and domination and the structure of political and social hierarchies. Feminist theories of violence are especially concerned with the relationships between patriarchal power and authority, representation, and the nature and origin of violence.

Feminist analyses of power and violence have focused on the family, and on types of violence inherent to the domestic sphere. Such examinations identify the patriarchal structure of the nuclear family as being a microcosm of the patriarchal power of the state, which recognized the rights of women and children only toward the end of the nineteenth century. Sociological studies of domestic violence, like Lenore Walker's *The Battered Woman Syndrome,* have influenced literary analyses of what Nancy Armstrong termed domestic fiction. In these literary analyses, the novel exists both as the disseminator of domestic ideology and the narrative and imaginative space in which the boundaries of domestic power can be challenged and subverted (see, for example, Kate Ferguson Ellis's *The Contested Castle*). Critical readings of literature, when attenuated by extensive consideration and analysis of domestic situations' structures of power—intersections of state, religious, and family ideology, for example—may deconstruct what appear to be naturalized, sanctioned or commonsensical representations of gender, race, sexuality, economic relations, and power.

Many postcolonial literary and cultural theorists (Frantz Fanon, Abdul Jan Mohamed, Gayatri Spivak) have, like feminist theorists, identified the violence and oppressiveness of colonial culture as being directly related to the extreme patriarchal structure of colonial cultures, which authorized and stabilized their authority based on "reason" of the alleged essential differences between European and non-Western "native" cultures and peoples. Colonial power rationalized its dominance using the same kinds of metaphysical binaries utilized to define the supposed biological or natural differences between men and women in traditional European philosophical frameworks. In the colonial setting however, disparaging or submissive constructions of race and gender were mingled and manipulated, disseminated and recirculated to socially and discursively determine or fix "native" populations as subject-races, racial Others subjected to the will and domination of the ruling imperial power. In this sense, "native" men and women occupied the dark underside of these Manichean binary constructions; native passivity and irrationality, for example, are defined as opposite Western-European activity (intelligence, creativity) and rationality. These constructions of racial and cultural difference attempted to legitimize the colonial project and led to the (total or partial) destruction of indigenous peoples and the disruption of their cultures and traditions. Nullifying the legacy of imperialism's linguistic, epistemological, and actual violence is identified by numerous postcolonial critics as one of the primary challenges of contemporary postcolonial and Western European cultures.

The work of political philosopher Hannah Arendt has conducted less gender specific analyses of power to focus instead on the nature of modern state and the possibilities of rebellion, resistance, and the redefinition of society within those states. Arendt's *On Violence,* "written against the backdrop of the twentieth century," examines the role violence has always played in politics, while attempting to come to terms with the shrinking power and authority of Western states alongside those states' accumulation of massively destructive weaponry. In Arendt's view, the reality of total destruction in modern culture alters the age-old traditional use of violence, which Arendt identifies as the means by which a particular political goal (action) could be realized. In the essay she additionally argues that the increasing bureaucratization of life and politics and people's growing lack of confidence in representative governments practically guarantees that citizens will respond to their lessening power and authority defensively, aggressively, and frequently, with violence. While Arendt's is not a feminist position—for example, her arguments are rhetorically and theoretically built around the philosophical/universal subject "man"—her understanding of short-term, rational, and revolutionary violence as a means by which reform has been and can be stimulated makes *On Violence* worthy of inclusion. If one considers the examples of what Arendt considers "justifiable" uses of violence as a political catalyst, such as the student rebellions in the United States, Germany, and France, one can appreciate the logic of her argumentation. The limitations, dangers, and excesses of violence are acknowledged in the work; however, selective use of violence as an agent of change in repressive states and situations is recognized as "man's faculty of action" and represents, Arendt suggests, "the ability to begin something new."

Elaine Scarry's *The Body in Pain: The Making and Unmaking of the World* also concentrates on less gender-specific examples of violence with its examination of acts of terror and torture, the suffering of the body, and the inexpressibility of pain. Scarry analyzes the ways in which the undeniable "certainty" of a victim's pain "shatters" language by reverting speech to a state of prelanguage, which makes the experience of pain and violence especially difficult to represent to another. *The Body in Pain* examines the degree to which pain's lack of referentiality inspires a sense of doubt in the person hearing about the victim's pain after the fact of torture or abuse. The nonsufferer's sense of doubt, Scarry argues, has serious political consequence since what is not verbally represented or representable is often doomed to remain politically and publicly invisible, unrepresented. Refusing and recovering from pain's silencing effect on the body and mind, making the experience of pain representable provides the victim of trauma, male or female, victim of political torture, rape, or ordinary pain associated with illness, what Scarry refers to as the "language of agency."

Violence remains a crucial concern for feminists, primarily because social advancements have not lessened the degree of violence experienced by women in their homes and on the streets. Legal and textual representation are cited as the cause of violence against women. For example, rape victims frequently experience a kind of judicial violence in the court room when constructions of "the feminine" work against them: their testimony isn't believed because they've been sexually active women; or their clothing or behavior—ranging from public drinking to being out late at night alone—are deemed inappropriately feminine. Legislative and artistic forms of representation are also considered possible avenues for social change; many feminist theorists believe that once definitions and interpretations of gender, language, and behavior are broadened and expanded, progressive change will follow. It seems apparent that feminist discussions of violence will continue to highlight forms and practices of representation. By examining fictive and real acts of violence, feminists aim to understand the plight of women in literature and society in an attempt to define a feminism that acknowledges a history of victimization without losing sight of feminism's original goals, which include the rights of equal protection and personal safety.

Mia E. Carter

References

Ackley, Katherine Anne, ed. *Women and Violence in Literature: An Essay Collection.* New York: Garland, 1990.

Arendt, Hannah. *On Violence, The Crises of the Republic.* New York: Harcourt Brace Jovanovich, 1969.

Armstrong, Nancy, and Leonard Tennenhouse, eds. *The Violence of Representation: Literature and the History of Violence.* London: Routledge, 1989.

Ellis, Kate Ferguson. *The Contested Castle: Gothic Novels and the Subversion of Domestic Ideology.* Urbana: University of Illinois Press, 1989.

Girard, René. *Violence and the Sacred.* Baltimore, Md., and London: Johns Hopkins University Press, 1977.

Harlow, Barbara. *Resistance Literature.* New York: Methuen, 1987.

Munson, Deats, and Sara and Lagretta Tallent Lenker, eds. *The Aching Hearth: Family Violence in Life and Literature.* New York and London: Plenum, 1991.

Scarry, Elaine. *The Body in Pain: The Making and Unmaking of the World.* New York: Oxford University Press, 1985.

Sharpe, Jenny. "The Unspeakable Limits of Rape: Colonial Violence and Counter Insurgency." *Genders* 10 (1991): 25–46.

Walker, Lenore. *The Battered Woman Syndrome.* New York: Springer, 1984.

Voyeurism

Derived from the French verb *voir* meaning "to see," voyeurism has been mainly understood to denote an exaggerated interest in viewing sexual objects or activities to obtain sexual gratification. Often referred to as scopophilia, voyeurism includes subjecting the object to a controlling and curious gaze. Children, too, perform voyeuristically when peeping at forbidden body parts and functions. The voyeur, who is concerned with remaining invisible, seeks a spectacle as a violation of personal perimeters. Voyeurism offered a means by which many nineteenth-century writers could cross social boundaries to obtain first-hand experience with what was considered the dark and mysterious Other. From a feminist perspective, voyeurism broadly denotes the masculine gaze that fixes the female figure as an erotic object.

In the 1800s, male voyeurism was accomplished through the activity of slumming. Although "nightwalking" was a playful male sport noted in urban accounts as early as Elizabethan times, during the nineteenth century such urban spectatorship was considered investigative social reporting, which would result in reform of the lower classes. The privileged bourgeois male, disguised in a spirit of reform, crossed boundaries of social classes in order to obtain a fascinated gaze at the other, and his primary object was none other than the woman in public. Between 1840 and 1880, the prostitute, described by Judith Walkowitz as "repudiated and desired, degraded and threatening," and symbolized as the lower-class, sexually disordered figure of nineteenth-century urban life, served as the central spectacle of bourgeois male voyeurism. Newspapers and journals featured voyeuristic descriptions of street women and "muscular women at work."

Especially notable in much of nineteenth-century literature, voyeurism acts as a power of spectatorship. Walkowitz notes that, as a representation of a privileged gaze, voyeurism structured a variety of texts on social investigation, social policy, tourism, exploration, and discovery. According to Walkowitz, fictional forms "ratified sexual difference and contained scenarios of considerable sexual ambiguity" where "through fantasy, elite men were able to project their sexual fears and anxieties on to a 'male killing force,' but in the person of the detective hero they quickly invoked a super-rational superego to hunt down those same repressed desires and to restore order." Along with the Sherlock Holmes detective stories, sensational novels such as *Dracula, The Strange Case of Dr. Jekyll and Mr. Hyde, The Picture of Dorian Gray,* and *The Island of Dr. Moreau* "stimulated a widespread male fascination" with crime and the male hero. These novels exhibit a voyeuristic preoccupation with the "secret pleasures" and "nocturnal adventures" of closeted sexual desires.

In the 1900s, as Laura Mulvey demonstrates, silent and narrative film constructed the female on display as not only the sexual object for characters in the film, but for the eye of the camera itself and for the audience of viewers as well. Mulvey sees the male viewer as identifying with the ego of his likeness on the screen, the male voyeur character, and she argues that the image of woman is constructed as "passive raw material for the active gaze of man." According to Mulvey, the mainstream cinema has become a main source of pleasure for the voyeur who views the female other as object. The contrast between the dark auditorium and the play of lighting on the screen creates the illusion of private spectatorship from a discreet position. A perfect example is the 1926 version of Fritz Lang's silent film *Metropolis*, where the inventor Rotwang stalks the innocent Maria through the dark catacombs. For the most part, Rotwang remains off screen as the beam of his flashlight continually searches for Maria, pinning her to every wall until she reaches the end of a cul-de-sac. The beam's voyeuristic probing of Maria from bottom to top creates an illusion of rape in which the viewer participates. Similar constructions of the female character as erotic object continue into narrative film.

American horror films of the 1970s and 1980s, which dedicate much time to looking at women, have been seen as voyeuristic modes for male viewers who identify with screen female victim-heroes in fear and pain, and Carol Clover points out that the target audience for such films is adolescent males. The camera-as-viewer invites the young male viewer to participate as voyeur in a drama where the primary victim is almost always female and the monster is always male. Clover suggests that male viewers may take voyeuristic pleasure in the torment of woman, or at least, "horror cinema offers such pleasures." Against such practices, feminists expose male constructs of women as erotic object for voyeuristic audiences. Perhaps this exposure will discourage authors and directors from modeling cinema and narratives on the male gaze.

Ron May

V

References

Clover, Carol J. *Men, Women, and Chainsaws: Gender in the Modern Horror Film.* Princeton: Princeton University Press, 1992.

Freedman, Barbara. *Staging the Gaze.* Ithaca, N.Y.: Cornell University Press, 1991.

Mulvey, Laura. *Visual and Other Pleasures.* Bloomington: Indiana University Press, 1981.

Walkowitz, Judith R. *City of Dreadful Delight: Narratives of Sexual Danger in Late-Victorian London.* Chicago: University of Chicago Press, 1992.

Williams, Linda. *Hard Core: Power, Pleasure, and the "Frenzy of the Visible."* Los Angeles: University of California Press, 1989.

W

Walker, Alice

Novelist, essayist, poet, short story writer, and author of children's books, Alice Walker is best known for her Pulitzer Prize–winning novel *The Color Purple*. In it, Walker used an epistolary form and rural black vernacular to chronicle the abuse and subsequent healing of Celie, a poor Southern woman. Through her work in different genres, Walker's writing contributes to a dialogue about cultural practices as potentially damaging to women, and raises the question of how Western feminists interpret and critique rituals within and outside their own locales. For example, her novel *Possessing the Secret of Joy* exposes and explores the details of female circumcision as an initiation into adulthood among certain cultures in Africa, the Middle East, and Asia.

Walker's multigenre work contributes to feminist theory and to black feminist theory in several significant ways. She identifies herself as a "womanist," a term she defines as "a black feminist or feminist of color . . . who loves other women, sexually and/or nonsexually . . . committed to survival and wholeness of entire people, male *and* female." Walker's womanism is part of her attempt to integrate and enrich women's lives through political engagement, psychic liberation, and relatedness that is woman-centered, but not necessarily separatist; she is at once concerned with black women's specific subjectivities and a more inclusive vision that is connected to nature, spirituality, and challenging oppression.

Walker also engages in the feminist project of recuperating lost or marginalized female writers. She acknowledges Zora Neale Hurston as an important precursor and role model, and has been instrumental in restoring Hurston to her place as a great American writer and key figure in the African American literary canon. She edited a collection of Hurston's work, wrote a forward to a Hurston biography, as well as several essays about her in *In Search of Our Mothers' Gardens: Womanist Prose*.

Finally, Walker has built upon and revised the works of other key feminist writers and theorists, notably Virginia Woolf. Walker applies Woolf's dictum "For we think back through our mothers if we are women" in terms of literary and literal mothers. In the essay "In Search of Our Mothers' Gardens," Walker expands key points from Woolf's *A Room of One's Own* to address the issue of black woman's creativity, which can take forms other than those that have been valorized for men or white women. Enslaved, raped, often bearing the burden of caretaker, black women's creativity bears the mark of "contrary instincts" (Woolf's term) or contradictory identities. Walker examines the poetry of the slave Phillis Wheatley, stating that her loyalties were completely divided, as was, without question, her mind. "How could this be otherwise?" Walker asks. By revising Woolf, and looking at cases such as Wheatley's with historic specificity, Walker illuminates the limits of certain feminist theory to fully account for the experience of black women. This is a critique that black feminists and other feminist scholars have used to dispel the notion of "universal sisterhood."

By drawing on the case of her mother and anonymous black women, Walker reminds us that the stories, gardens, quilts, and other creations of mothers and grandmothers who could not be artists, because of historical circumstances, are often contained (if not always acknowledged) in their daughters' signatures.

Cheryl Fish

References

Banks, Erma Davis, and Keith Byerman. *Alice Walker, An Annotated Bibliography, 1968–1986.* New York: Garland, 1989.

Butler-Evans, Elliot. *Race, Gender and Desire: Narrative Strategies in the Fiction of Toni Cade Bambara, Toni Morrison and Alice Walker.* Philadelphia: Temple University Press, 1989.

Callaloo 12 (1989). Special issue devoted to Alice Walker. Baltimore, Md.: Johns Hopkins University Press.

Gates, Henry Louis, Jr., and K.A. Appiah, eds. *Alice Walker: Critical Perspectives Past and Present.* New York: Amistad/Penguin USA, 1993.

Pratt, Louis H. *Alice Malsenior Walker: An Annotated Bibliography, 1968–1986.* Westport, Conn.: Meckler, 1988.

Walker, Alice. *The Color Purple.* New York: Harcourt Brace Jovanovich, 1982.

———. *Her Blue Body Everything We Know: Earthling Poems, 1965–1990.* San Diego: Harcourt Brace Jovanovich, 1991.

———. *In Search of Our Mothers' Gardens: Womanist Prose.* New York: Harcourt Brace Jovanovich, 1984.

———. *Living by the Word: Selected Writings, 1973–1988.* San Diego: Harcourt Brace Jovanovich, 1988.

———. *Possessing the Secret of Joy.* San Diego: Harcourt Brace Jovanovich, 1992.

———. *The Temple of My Familiar.* San Diego: Harcourt Brace Jovanovich, 1989.

———. "Zora Neale Hurston—A Cautionary Take and a Partisan View." Foreword to *Zora Neale Hurston: A Literary Biography* by Robert Hemenway. Urbana: University of Illinois Press, 1977.

———, ed. *I Love Myself When I Am Laughing . . . A Zora Neale Hurston Reader.* New York: Feminist, 1979.

Wilenz, Gay. *Binding Cultures: Black Women Writers in Africa and the Diaspora.* Bloomington: Indiana University Press, 1992.

Winchell, Donna Haisty. *Alice Walker.* New York: Twayne, 1992.

Walkerdine, Valerie

Initially trained as a primary teacher, Valerie Walkerdine went on to get a Ph.D. in developmental psychology and to concentrate on studying the teaching of mathematics to girls. In examining this, Walkerdine developed an analysis and critique of assessments of girls' mathematical abilities. She pointed out that there were substantial discrepancies between the girls' actual (early) achievements in their work and tests, and the teachers' evaluations of their ability: while girls' good results were attributed to conscientious hard work and rote learning, boys were often labeled as having "potential," even if they did not achieve much. Walkerdine and her colleague Rosie Walden called this "the just or only phenomenon," indicating that the girls' good performances were dismissed as "just" or "only" the result of some negligible factor, while successful boys, in contrast, were seen as having real understanding or insight. Walkerdine elaborated a nonessentialist theoretical approach from and for this work, based on the discourse-theory of the French theorist Michel Foucault, in which culture is seen to allocate rationality to the very definition of the "male," and irrationality to the "female." Therefore "women" are constructed as embodying the irrational, and ultimately incapable of grasping mathematics. Importantly, Walkerdine analyzed classroom practices and educational and psychological theories further in detail using this perspective and psychoanalysis, and argues that the "child" is a constructed category overall, and not an essential "natural" reality. Walkerdine's work illustrates how this "child" and its gender are produced as a "reality" in society, and specifically in education, for its own purposes. Thus Walkerdine reads gender and childhood as text, deriving her methodology from postmodern literary theory.

Karín Lesnik-Oberstein

References

Steedman, Carolyn, Cathy Urwin, and Valerie Walkerdine, eds. *Language, Gender, and Childhood.* London and Boston: Routledge and Kegan Paul, 1984.

Walden, Rosie, and Valerie Walkerdine. *Girls and Mathematics: From Primary to Secondary Schooling.* London: Heinemann, 1983.

———. *Girls and Mathematics: The Early Years: A Review of Literature and an Account of Original Research.* London: Heinemann, 1982.

Walkerdine, Valerie. *The Mastery of Reason: Cognitive Development and the Produc-*

tion of Rationality*. London: Routledge, 1989.
———. *Schoolgirl Fictions*. London: Verso, 1990.
———, and the Girls and Mathematics Unit. *Counting Girls Out*. London: Virago, 1989.
———, and Helen Lucey. *Democracy in the Kitchen: Regulating Mothers and Socializing Daughters*. London: Virago, 1989.

Wallace, Michele

Michele Wallace's frequently anthologized 1975 essay "Anger in Isolation: A Black Feminist's Search for Sisterhood" was groundbreaking in its expression of anger and anguish over black women's exclusion from both the white-dominated feminist movement and the male-dominated black civil rights movement. Wallace continued her analysis of the double bind of being black and female in her controversial 1979 book *Black Macho and the Myth of the Superwoman*. Her central argument was that the Black Power movement had embraced white patriarchal values by blaming black women in part for the subjugation of black men. Denouncing men's attempts to silence black women, Wallace called for women to take their liberation into their own hands.

Blending autobiography with incisive analyses of American popular and academic cultures, the essays in Wallace's *Invisibility Blues: From Pop to Theory* form a tour de force of feminist theory in both content and methodology. In her examinations of how African American music, movies, literature, and theory are resistant to and implicated in the intersecting oppressions of class, race, and gender, Wallace combines close-to-the-bone self-examination with systematic theorizing. She focuses on the ways American culture transforms black women into highly visible but mute objects. Her powerful interweaving of autobiography with Marxist-feminist-African-Americanist critical theory exposes the "endlessly specific and contextual" ways that patriarchy, white supremacy, and capitalism maintain cultural dominance.

Kari J. Winter

References

Wallace, Michele. "Anger in Isolation: A Black Feminist's Search for Sisterhood." *Village Voice* 28 (1975): 6–7.
———. *Black Macho and the Myth of the Superwoman*. New York: Dial, 1979. New York: Verso, 1990.
———. *Invisibility Blues: From Pop to Theory*. New York: Verso, 1990.

War

Traditionally and historically, war has been considered an exclusively male experience: "War is men's business not ladies," Rhett Butler declares in the film *Gone with the Wind*. This myth—that the domain of war belongs properly to men—persists despite the ever-increasing civilian involvement in war. It has promoted a concept of war that is undoubtedly polarized and gendered, equating men with war and women often with peace and always with something other than real war. In 1983, in *Does Khaki Become You? The Militarization of Women's Lives*, Cynthia Enloe claimed that the military was "society's bastion of male identity" and that in order to preserve this status quo "it must categorize women as peripheral, as serving safely at the 'rear' on the 'home front.'" "The military," she continues, "has to constantly redefine 'the front' and 'combat' as wherever 'women' are not."

By extension, this gendered conception of war has shaped literary texts and formed the literary canon. Until very recently, the narration of war was a male-dominated field with the tale of the battlefield as the privileged (and usually the only) war story in the canon. As women's war activities have been viewed as subordinate and peripheral to those of men, female war texts have also been proportionally discounted. They have often disappeared or been thought of as telling the story of something other than the true face of war.

Despite these (assigned) subordinate roles, however, women were often held to be responsible for war. Writers as disparate as Homer, John Ruskin, and Pearl Buck have in different ways held them accountable. Homer's Helen was both the pretext and the cause of the Trojan wars. In "Of Queen's Garden's," Ruskin argues that women are responsible for war because they fail to prevent men from fighting. In 1940, the then-popular American writer Pearl Buck revived this theme; men were fighting because women had failed to create "moral character" in their sons while they were still at home. The anger of the English World War I war poets was often specifically directed toward women and accused them of ignorance, idealism, and, indirectly, of complicity with the state in sending the men to war.

In the 1970s and 1980s, the task in front of feminist literary critics and war theorists was to set the record straight: to examine the gendered conception of war with its polarities and contradictions. A beginning was made by looking at what the women themselves had to say. Women's war texts were sought out and, where possible, reprinted—Rebecca West's novel *The Return of the Soldier* and the collections of women's poetry from the two World Wars edited by Catherine Reilly, for example. The result of this work was the realization that there was a polyphony of women's wartime voices ranging from the pacifist, through those filled with sadness, remorse, and guilt, to the purely militaristic.

In 1983, Sandra Gilbert's groundbreaking article "Soldier's Heart: Literary Men, Literary Women, and the Great War" appeared in *Signs*. The article addresses the "sexual implications" of World War I, arguing that "as young men became increasingly alienated from their prewar selves, increasingly immured in the muck and blood of No Man's Land, women seemed to become, as if by some uncanny swing of history's pendulum, ever more powerful." Gilbert was among the first to examine in literature the apparent reversal of the gender roles in wartime. Susan Gubar picked up the theme of the war between the sexes in "This Is My Rifle, This Is My Gun," which claims that much of the literature about World War II documents women's sense that "the war was a blitz on them."

The 1980s also saw the appearance of other important articles and books on the relationship of women and war. Feminist literary and social critics examined the images of women in wartime and found that, despite their real and mythic exclusion from the battlefront, women had been assigned passive or reactive parts, what feminist war theorist Nancy Huston identified as "supporting roles." Women, Huston claims, in an essay entitled "Tales of War and Tears of Women," can be "the pretext" for war (Helen of Troy), or "the booty or recompense," for example. In their "reactive" roles, they can be "trained as sympathetic nurses . . . as seductive spies . . . as cheerleaders . . . waving goodbye to departing men." They can also be "castrating bitches . . . miracle mothers . . . wistful wives . . . and cooperative citizens." Nancy Hartsock and Judith Stiehm demonstrated that the masculine role of the "warrior-hero" has played a central role in the conceptualization of politics.

"Tales of War and Tears of Women" also argues for the cyclical interdependence of warmaking and war-writing: "War imitates war narratives imitating war." For Huston, there is a cyclical interdependence of war-making and war-writing and a profound contradiction between a pacifist critique of the illogic embedded in warmongering and the narrative impulse to "make sense" of suffering.

In 1987, the essays in *Behind the Lines: Gender and the Two World Wars* took up the task of examining the gender balance of power during wartime and the postwar period. The two World Wars permanently changed Western civilization. However, they did little or nothing to change the relationship between the sexes. Despite their wartime assumption of greater economic and social power, once the wars were over, women found themselves relegated to their prewar status and still subordinate to men.

Jean Bethke Elshtain's *Women and War* in turn exploits and then explodes the preconception of traditional and accepted polarities of gendered thinking: men are militaristic and go to (and with) war; women, pacifist by nature, are aligned with peace. The dichotomy that identifies man as the warrior-hero and woman as peace-maker (and often as mother) distorts the role that women have always played in telling and participating in the war story. Elshtain questions and challenges our (America's) discourses about war—newspapers, films, television, and political theory are all grist to her analytical mill. She focuses on the links between women and war, and insists that women move from their place in the wings and see themselves as they are—active and complicitous actors on the political scene as it constructs the discourses that perpetuate war.

A recent and useful addition to the growing literature on the relationship of women and war is Claire Tylee's *The Great War and Women's Consciousness*. Tylee focuses on World War I, drawing on Paul Fussell's *The Great War and Modern Memory* as a model, and offers useful analyses of the problematic of language. She also reflects on methodologies appropriate to dealing with ideology in fiction, and confronts problems of aesthetic evaluation as they are filtered by a gendered ideology.

The issue of women's complicity in the institution of war is one with which theorists and critics continue to grapple. It is clear now that women's role in relation to war is far more complex and complicitous than the conventional conceptions of war and its narrative would have us believe. The image of women as somehow removed from the arena and the story of war is a false one.

It is true, however, that female war experience is not the monolithic one of the battlefield, even though in modern warfare the "battlefield" encompasses towns, cities, and their civilian inhabitants. "Experience" therefore becomes "experiences" differing from woman to woman, from social class to social class, and from country to country.

Despite the enormous recent interest in the subject of women and war, much work remains to be done. There is still a reliance on a male-centered historiography and literature, still a need to distinguish among types of war narrative and to interrogate the gaps in official documents and logics, for example. "It is," as Charlotte Perkins Gilman noted in 1911, in *The Man-Made World,* "still hard for us to see what warfare really is in human life," and that remains the principal challenge facing us today.

Jennifer Clarke

See also VIOLENCE

References

Elshtain, Jean Bethke. *Women and War.* New York: Basic, 1987.

———. "Women as Mirror and Other: Toward a Theory of Women, War, and Feminism." *Humanities in Society* 5 (1982): 32.

———, and Sheila Tobias. *Women, Militarism, and War.* Totowa, N.J.: Rowman and Littlefield, 1990.

Enloe, Cynthia. *Does Khaki Become You? The Militarization of Women's Lives.* Boston: South End, 1983.

Fussell, Paul. *The Great War and Modern Memory.* London, Oxford, and New York: Oxford University Press, 1975.

Gilbert, Sandra M. "Soldier's Heart: Literary Men, Literary Women, and the Great War." *Signs* 8 (1983): 422–450.

Gubar, Susan. "This Is My Rifle, This Is My Gun." In *Behind the Lines: Gender and the Two World Wars,* edited by Margaret Randolph Higonnet, Jane Jenson, Sonya Michel, and Margaret Collins Weitz, 227–259. New Haven and London: Yale University Press, 1987.

Hartsock, Nancy C. "Prologue to a Feminist Critique of War and Politics." In *Women's View of the Political World of Men,* edited by Judith H. Stiehm, 121–150. Dobbs Ferry, N.Y.: TransNational, 1984.

Higgonet, Margaret Randolph, Jane Jenson, Sonya Michel, and Margaret Collins Weitz, eds. *Behind the Lines: Gender and the Two World Wars.* New Haven: Yale University Press, 1987.

Huston, Nancy. "The Matrix of War: Mothers and Heroes." In *The Female Body in Western Culture: Contemporary Perspectives,* edited by Susan Rubin Suleiman, 120–136. Cambridge: Harvard University Press, 1986.

———. "Tales of War and Tears of Women." *Women's Studies International Forum* 5 (1982): 271–282.

Reilly, Catherine, ed. *Chaos of the Night: Women's Poetry and Verse of the Second World War.* London: Virago, 1984.

———, ed. *Scars upon My Heart: Women's Poetry and Verse of the First World War.* London: Virago, 1981.

Ruddick, Sara. "Preservative Love and Military Destruction: Some Reflections on Mothers and Peace." In *Mothering: Essays in Feminist Theory,* edited by Joyce Trebilcot, 231–262. Totowa, N.J.: Rowman and Allanheld, 1984.

Scarry, Elaine. *The Body in Pain: The Making and Unmaking of the World.* New York and Oxford: Oxford University Press, 1985.

Tylee, Claire M. *The Great War and Women's Consciousness: Images of Militarism and Womanhood in Women's Writings, 1914–64.* Iowa City: University of Iowa Press, 1990.

Washington, Mary Helen

Mary Helen Washington has helped introduce American readers to a wide variety of African American women writers from the nineteenth century to the present, some of whose works had been previously little known or out of print. She was one of the first critics, for example, to bring focused attention to the long-neglected works of Zora Neale Hurston. Throughout her career, Washington has worked to develop a rhetoric of black women's literary tradition that would help reveal and explain the intricacies of that tradition.

Washington's essay "'Taming All That Anger Down': Rage and Silence in Gwendolyn Brooks's *Maud Martha*" is representative of her literary criticism, providing a feminist analysis of a little-discussed novel. Washington argued that Maud Martha's repressed silence is reflected in the novel's terse, condensed form. Washington then examined the ways in which Maud Martha's "double consciousness"—her ability to imagine alternative selves—reflects her fragmentation as a result of racism and sexism. Washington's analysis of the rhetorical complexities of Brooks's novel demonstrated the richness of African American women's writing and investigated ways in which racism and sexism inflect literary form.

Washington's works are designed to appeal to both general and scholarly readers. Her academic writings, book reviews, and articles in the popular press have established her as a public intellectual and activist who seeks to educate a large audience.

Lisa Jadwin

References

Washington, Mary Helen. "Introduction: Zora Neale Hurston: A Woman Half in Shadow." In *I Love Myself When I Am Laughing . . . And Then Again When I Am Looking Mean and Impressive: A Zora Neale Hurston Reader,* edited by Alice Walker. New York: Feminist, 1979.

———. "I Sign My Mother's Name: Alice Walker, Dorothy West, Paule Marshall." In *Mothering the Mind: Twelve Studies of Writers and Their Silent Partners,* edited by Ruth Perry and Martine Watson Brownley, 142–163. New York: Holmes and Meier, 1984.

———. "'Taming All That Anger Down': Rage and Silence in Gwendolyn Brooks's *Maud Martha.*" *Massachusetts Review* 24 (1983): 453–466.

———. "These Self-Invented Women: A Theoretical Framework for a Literary History of Black Women." In *Politics of Education: Essays from Radical Teacher,* edited by Robert C. Rosen, Leonard Vogt, and Michael Apple, 89–98. Albany: State University of New York Press, 1990.

———, ed. *Black-Eyed Susans: Classic Stories by and about Black Women* Garden City, N.J.: Anchor, 1975.

———, ed. *Invented Lives: Narratives of Black Women, 1860–1960.* New York: Doubleday, 1990.

———, ed. *Memory of Kin: Stories about Family by Black Writers.* New York: Doubleday, 1991.

———, ed. *Midnight Birds: Stories by Contemporary Black Women Writers.* Garden City, N.J.: Anchor, 1980.

Wharton, Edith

In nineteen novels and nearly one hundred novellas and short stories, Edith Wharton explored her society's construction of femininity, depicting women as both victims of, and accomplices in, their own diminishment. From total self-abnegation to ruthless self-assertion, Wharton's heroines express the range of late-Victorian and post-Victorian norms of female behavior.

In novels like *The House of Mirth, The Custom of the Country,* and *The Age of Innocence,* Wharton explored women's complicity in their own infantilization, repression, and objectification in old New York society, satirizing a culture whose minutely articulated system of matrimonial exchange precisely mirrored the system of financial exchange that formed its material support. All three novels suggest the tragedy and horror of a society in which woman has become the ultimate commodity.

Feminist critics have been interested in the ways Wharton's novels allude to and revise traditional themes of women's fiction, such as the "seduced and abandoned" plot, to expose the relentless operation of social convention in the lives of both men and women. *The Reef* and *Summer* dramatize the problematics of female sexuality, its expression and repression, in a society dominated by a rigid sexual double standard. Recent critics have also been interested in Wharton's depiction of relationships among women, which range from bitter rivalry and subtle manipulation to intense mutual solidarity and empathy, in a postmatriarchal world where heterosexual commerce prevails. Wharton's complex and often ambivalent treatment of such relationships has led to a rich critical conversation in recent years.

While some feminist critics have seen in Wharton's work a condemnation of patriarchal oppression of women, recent critics identify the object of Wharton's critique as the constricting social norms that stifled and deformed the lives of both men and women in her old New York society. Wharton's portrayals of alienated individuals, paralyzed by convention, form an important aspect of the protomodernist tradition.

Nancy Disenhaus

References

Ammons, Elizabeth. *Edith Wharton's Argument with America*. Athens: University of Georgia Press, 1980.

Bauer, Dale M. *Feminist Dialogics: A Theory of Failed Community*. Albany: State University of New York Press, 1988.

Fryer, Judith. *Felicitous Space: The Imaginative Structures of Edith Wharton and Willa Cather*. Chapel Hill: University of North Carolina Press, 1986.

Gilbert, Sandra M., and Susan Gubar. *No Man's Land: The Place of the Woman Writer in the Twentieth Century*. New Haven: Yale University Press, 1989.

Goodman, Susan. *Edith Wharton's Women: Friends and Rivals*. Hanover, N.H.: University Press of New England, 1990.

Olin-Ammentorp, Julie. "Edith Wharton's Challenge to Feminist Criticism." *Studies in American Fiction* 16 (1988): 237–244.

Papke, Mary Suzanne. *Verging on the Abyss: The Social Fiction of Kate Chopin and Edith Wharton*. Westport, Conn.: Greenwood, 1990.

Showalter, Elaine. *Sister's Choice: Tradition and Change in American Women's Writing*. Oxford: Clarendon, 1991.

Waid, Candace. *Edith Wharton's Letters from the Underworld: Fictions of Women and Writing*. Chapel Hill: University of North Carolina Press, 1991.

Wershoven, Carol. *The Female Intruder in the Novels of Edith Wharton*. Rutherford, N.J.: Fairleigh Dickinson University Press, 1982.

Wicca

See WITCH

Williams, Patricia

Primarily known as a critical race theorist, law professor Patricia Williams has legitimated and popularized the discursive methods typical of both critical race theory and feminist jurisprudence. Her publications in law journals and theory collections have influenced more than a decade of law professors, law students, and feminists. In her most widely available work, *The Alchemy of Race and Rights: Diary of a Law Professor*, Williams combines autobiography, legal analysis, family history, and literary allusion to challenge definitions of both legal scholarship and public discourse. Rejecting the limitations imposed by law's faith in categorization, judicial objectivity, and universal truths, Williams asserts the importance of subject position or identity to legal decision-making, in part through emphasizing the contribution her own identity makes to her work as lawyer, law professor, and cultural critic.

Williams "breaks form" with legal scholarship by introducing her personal history (she is the great-great-granddaughter of a slave named Sophie and a white lawyer named Austin Miller) and by confronting the reader with a multiplicity of images, ideas, and feelings that call into question the simplistic legal thinking that continues to protect the public/private dichotomy, the Anglo American connection between private property and rights, and, in the largest sense, American racism itself. As she says, "Little bits of law and pieces of everyday life fly out of my mouth in weird combinations." But by containing such "weird combinations" in a literary tour de force that demonstrates a deep understanding of legal, social, and philosophical discourse, Williams simultaneously protests legal scholarship's tendency to naturalize objectivity and celebrates the transformative, even alchemical, power of the personal.

Kathryn Temple

References

Greene, Linda S. "Breaking Form." *Stanford Law Review* 44 (1992): 909–925.

West, Robin. "Murdering the Spirit: Racism, Rights, and Commerce." *Michigan Law Review* 90 (1992): 1771–1796.

Williams, Patricia. *The Alchemy of Race and Rights: Diary of a Law Professor*. Cambridge: Harvard University Press, 1991.

———. "And We Are Not Married: A Journal of Musings upon Legal Language and the Ideology of Style." In *Consequences of Theory,* edited by Jonathan Arac and Barbara Johnson, 191–208. Baltimore, Md.: Johns Hopkins University Press, 1991.

Williamson, Judith

In her 1979 book on advertising *(Decoding Advertisements)* and in subsequent essays on popular media, Judith Williamson gives a Marxist-feminist inflection to semiotics. Semiotics postulates that meaning is a function, not of a correspondence between signs and things, but of structures of difference, that a word derives its meaning from being what all other words are not. Early semiotic studies insisted that a system of meaning should be understood as referring primarily to its own formal structure; Williamson, by contrast, analyzes how the differential structure of signification structures social reality.

In *Decoding Advertisements*, Williamson demonstrates how the language of advertising actively manufactures differences, the better to distinguish and market particular brand names. When a product is portrayed as securing an identity for its consumer, the viewer of the ad is re-created as a subject who differs from others according to what she buys. The "totemisms" packaging us as Pepsi people or Breck girls distract consumers from real social divisions. According to Williamson, a similar effect transpires as "femininity" is circulated as a sign in mass culture. Images of women are often images of Nature or family life and so evoke aspects of experience that seem to transcend history and cut across class. By this means, "femininity" functions to conceal politics. Omnipresent reminders of sexual difference cover up the class antagonisms consumer culture cannot afford to acknowledge. Williamson shows what this form of ideological coverup shares with exoticism, as she notes that, although capitalism, rooted in imperial conquests, operates by destroying different value systems, in order to signify it also needs constructs of difference. For this reason, consumers are bombarded with images of timeless, exotic locales and feminized "primitives"; entire societies must be repackaged to help reflect capitalism's view of itself, while being "robbed of their own meanings and speech." Journalists' and advertisers' iconography of the family functions similarly: it provides an alibi for a capitalist economy that privileges competition and profit and that actively opposes the values it confines within the private sphere.

The fact that "woman" is mass culture's primary vehicle for representing otherness sets feminism a challenge: to develop an oppositional practice that acknowledges those social differences that a preoccupation with sexual difference helps to contain. Williamson argues that when feminists concentrate on sexual rather than class or race interpellation, or study the construction of "the" unconscious, they reinforce the system of meaning they mean to contest.

Deidre Lynch

References

Williamson, Judith. *Consuming Passions: The Dynamics of Popular Culture.* London: Marion Boyars, 1986.

——. *Decoding Advertisements: Ideology and Meaning in Advertising.* London: Marion Boyars, 1978.

——. "How Does Girl Number Twenty Understand Ideology?" *Screen Education* 40 (1981–1982): 80–87.

——. "Woman Is an Island: Femininity and Colonization." In *Studies in Entertainment: Critical Approaches to Mass Culture,* edited by Tania Modleski, 99–118. Bloomington: Indiana University Press, 1986.

Willis, Susan

In the Marxist theory of revolution, the men of Europe's proletarian underclass figure as the source of historical definition and agent of social change. In her literary history *Specifying,* Susan Willis brings American feminism to Marxism: she assigns this revolutionary role to the heroines created by African American women novelists. Similarly, in her essays in cultural studies, *A Primer for Daily Life,* Willis identifies domesticity as a source for a vision of nonalienated social relations: she redefines a traditional site of female disempowerment as a zone where one can imagine change.

For Willis, the importance of novels like Toni Morrison's *The Bluest Eye* for historical thinking is not just that they demonstrate how the stories of individuals are inextricable from the story of the African American community's experience of twentieth-century capitalism—a story about migration from the agrarian South to the industrial North and about the transition to a wage-labor economy. By recovering the community's past, these novels also envision social modes not contained by capitalism, forms of economic independence not prompted by the profit motive: they thereby represent alternative futures. Their depictions of remembered communal pleasures—fish fries in *The Bluest Eye* or

African dancing in Paule Marshall's *Praisesong for the Widow*—gain a utopic force from being juxtaposed with the atomizing of community and the false gratifications that characterize consumer society.

Commodity capitalism's reproduction of oppressive social structures is the chief concern of Willis's essays on suburbia, everyday practices (housework, grocery shopping), and mass-cultural commodities (toys, exercise machines, Michael Jackson videos). However, Willis also emphasizes the contradictions defining the commodity, an amalgam of exchange value and use value, which at once negates the social relations of production and requires the social for its production. The commodity necessarily bears traces of an alternative social formation. Recognizing such contradictions is a prerequisite to developing a revolutionary perspective on everyday life. Willis contends that, if women think about the ambiguous status their unpaid domestic labor has in the capitalist economy, and if they listen to their children (who have not yet learned to substitute commodities for human relationships), that perspective can be theirs.

Deidre Lynch

References

Willis, Susan. "Disney World: Public Use/ Private State." *South Atlantic Quarterly* 92 (1993): 119–137.

———. *A Primer for Daily Life*. London: Routledge, 1991.

———. *Specifying: Black Women Writing the American Experience*. Madison: University of Wisconsin Press, 1987.

Witch

The word "witch" has always identified men as well as women; its first known use, in a text of 890 C.E., refers to a man, and modern witchcraft may be practiced by men as well as women. However, the witch trials of Europe and America, extending over most of the early modern period (sixteenth and seventeenth centuries), indelibly identified the term "witch" with the primarily female objects of their proceedings.

The witch trials created an image of witches that is reflected in literature up to the present time. A witch brought to trial was usually accused after she had cursed someone, often a person who had attempted to take her property or abuse her person. The trial involved connecting her offensive words to some subsequent destruc-tive act, followed by reports (often from other women) of the accused's relationship to the Devil or pagan activities, and the revelation of physical signs of her witchcraft on her own body. The proving upon the body of the accusation of witchcraft was a process intimately tied to the misogynistic fear of female sexuality and reproductive capability; for instance, the woman's body was searched for moles, supposed to be extra nipples at which the Devil suckled her milk. Often trial testimony consisted of descriptions of the accused woman's sexual liaisons with the Devil, which almost always included charges of sodomy or bestiality.

A witch, then, was a woman who spoke out of turn or defensively, and whose sexuality exceeded society's prescription. Ostensibly an offense against Christianity, witchcraft more often consisted of offenses against neighboring men, consolidating their wealth in an age of burgeoning capitalism, by women tainted with "abnormal" sexuality or physical defects (including signs of age). This duality is expressed to the present day, especially in children's and fantasy literature, in the dichotomy between the young, beautiful, and often sexually alluring witch, and the old, haggard, ugly witch. Characters often reveal their nature as witches—as dangerous females—by switching quickly between one stereotype and the other (the evil queen of Disney's "Snow White" is a good example).

The witch thus encapsulates a set of uncontrollable female stereotypes whose necessary suppression and simultaneous attractiveness reflects the concurrent goals of patriarchy and capitalism. The struggle between misogyny and titillation within the reification of this symbol was so overt in James VI's *Demonologie* that even contemporary witch-hunters decried it as absurd, saying that if everything in it were true, every woman would be a witch—a revealing analysis. Today campaigns against woman politicians like Maggie Thatcher reflect similar ideas, with slogans like "She's a witch," considered by sloganeers to be interchangeable with "She's a bitch." The connection of danger to her body makes the witch image a negative expression of a certain sort of inescapable essential femininity that must be controlled for the good of the populace.

On the other hand, witchcraft (or Wicca, from the Old English word for witch) has been reclaimed by modern American and European women. These religious groups are essentially revivalist in nature, and thus neopagan rather than pagan. Modern witches, or Wiccans, like Z. Budapest and Starhawk, are searching for a means of spiritual expression not afforded them by patriarchal religions and organize holidays and ceremonies around a symbolism inclusive of, or exclusively composed of, women's lives and women's bodies. They have therefore made of an otherwise misogynistic label a self-celebratory liberation.

Judith Tabron

See also SPIRITUALITY

References

Adler, Margot. *Drawing down the Moon: Witches, Druids, Goddess Worshippers, and Other Pagans in America Today.* Boston: Beacon, 1986.

Budapest, Zsuzsanna. *The Holy Book of Women's Mysteries.* Berkeley: Wingbow, 1980, 1989.

Christ, Carol P., and Judith Plaskow, eds. *Womanspirit Rising: A Feminist Reader in Religion.* San Francisco: Harper and Row, 1979.

Dekker, Thomas, William Rowley, and John Ford. "The Witch of Edmonton" [1623]. In *The Best Plays of Thomas Dekker,* edited by Ernest Rhys. The Mermaid Series. London and New York: T. Fisher Unwin, Charles Scribner's Sons, n.d.

Larner, Christina. *Witchcraft and Religion: The Politics of Popular Belief.* Edited by Alan Macfarlane. Oxford and New York: Basil Blackwell, 1984.

Levack, Brian P. *The Witch-hunt in Early Modern Europe.* London and New York: Longmans, 1987.

Starhawk. *Dreaming the Dark: Magic, Sex and Politics* [1982]. Boston: Beacon, 1988.

Thomas, Keith Vivian. *Religion and the Decline of Magic.* New York: Charles Scribner's Sons, 1971.

Wittig, Monique

The work of Monique Wittig, French novelist and feminist theorist living and teaching in the United States, grew out of the author's political activism in the student and workers' revolt of the late 1960s and the radical feminist and lesbian movement in France. Her writings are usually—and rightfully so—discussed in the context of French feminist theory, but need to be clearly contrasted to the work of Cixous, Irigaray, and Kristeva.

Wittig's experimental feminist and frequently utopian fictional texts put into practice central theoretical concerns of feminist poststructuralism. They foreground the materiality of language, deemphasize binary oppositions *(Les guérillères),* underscore the violence inherent in the division of the subject in language *(The Lesbian Body),* and perform Irigaray's notion of women's discourse as mimicry. Wittig's political goals, however, are generally opposed to that of French feminist thought, oftentimes leaning toward Anglo American feminist criticism instead. While she insists on the necessity to represent female experience and attempts to undo the postmodernist "death of the author," Wittig rejects the concept of an *écriture féminine,* the privilege placed on the female body as a site of *différance* as well as the metaphorization of the body. Any such celebration of female "otherness," she argues, perpetuates women's oppression, which itself is responsible for the culturally constructed sexual binarism of male and female. Based on the assumption that language is a means of both women's oppression and the fight against that oppression, Wittig's writing instead reappropriates for her own feminist purposes established literary genres or canonical texts such as the *Bildungsroman* in *L'opoponax* (1964); the epic in *Les guérillères;* and Dante's *Divine Comedy* in *Virgile, non* (1985), in this way reworking and revising cultural conventions and myths.

In opposition to Irigaray, who came to argue the significance of a gender-specific legislation, Wittig opts for a complete abolishment of sex and gender. Instead, she aims at the universalization of a third, a lesbian perspective, at a lesbian body politic devoid of sexual difference and beyond the categories of gender. According to Wittig's utopian political agenda, only a lesbian subject and society based on total reciprocity and equality subverts and escapes the familiar economic, political, ideological, and physical subordination of women by men. Thematized in her early novel *Les guérillères,* this agenda also informs Wittig's lesbian dictionary *Brouillon pour un dictionnaire des amantes* (1976), which tries to eliminate male culture, as well as her numerous essays. While Wittig is generally praised for her focus on concrete political reality, it remains a paradox of her work that she pairs her "anti-essentialist materialism" (Fuss) with an ahistorical romantic vision of an undifferentiated and exclusive lesbian world.

Sabine Sielke

References

Crowder, Diane Griffin. "Amazons and Mothers? Monique Wittig, Hélène Cixous and the Theories of Women's Writing." *Contemporary Literature* 24 (1983): 117–144.

Fuss, Diana. "Monique Wittig's Anti-Essentialist Materialism." In *Essentially Speaking: Feminism, Nature and Difference*, 39–53. New York: Routledge, 1989.

Ostrosky, Erika. *A Constant Journey: The Fiction of Monique Wittig*. Carbondale: Southern Illinois University Press, 1991.

Rosenfeld, Marthe. "A Linguistic Aspect of Sexual Conflict: Monique Wittig's *Le corps lesbien*." *Mosaic* 17 (1984): 235–241.

Shaktini, Namascar. "Displacing the Phallic Subject: Wittig's Lesbian Writing." *Signs* 8 (1982): 29–44

Wenzel, Helene Vivienne. "The Text as Body/Politics: An Appreciation of Monique Wittig's Writing in Context." *Feminist Studies* 7 (1981): 264–287.

Wittig, Monique. *Les guérillères* [1969]. Translated by David Le Vay. Boston: Beacon, 1985.

———. *The Lesbian Body* [1973]. Translated by David Le Vay. Boston: Beacon, 1986.

———. *The Straight Mind and Other Essays*. Boston: Beacon, 1992.

Woodhull, Winnie, and Patricia S. Yaeger. "By Myriad Constellations: Monique Wittig and the Writing of Women's Experience." In *Power, Gender, Values*, edited by Judith Genova, 13–30. Edmonton: Academic, 1987.

Wollstonecraft, Mary

Educator, essayist, political reformer, novelist, book reviewer, writer of a travelogue, letters, and stories for children, Mary Wollstonecraft is an important figure in women's studies and in literary history because she established herself as one of England's first middle-class female writers and feminist polemicists. In her *Vindication of the Rights of Woman* (1792), which was written partly in response to the fervor and liberal ideas following the French Revolution of 1789, she argued for the moral and rational worth of women. Wollstonecraft attacked the system of education prevalent in the eighteenth century, which she felt kept women in "ignorance" under the name of "innocence." She argued that society failed to cultivate women's understanding. Instead it decked women with "artificial graces" that did not give them the means to support themselves with dignity, should they not have a chance to marry. Wollstonecraft disagreed with writers such as the French philosopher Jean Jacques Rousseau and the Scottish physician Dr. John Gregory, who believed that women were naturally inferior and should therefore be submissive and subservient to men. She points out that women who are taught to be artful, vain, silly, and frivolous, make undesirable companions. For her, education becomes the key to improvement, and she looks forward to a "revolution in female manners."

What is most significant about the *Rights of Woman* is its observations about the constructions of gender difference. Women are not inherently weak or foolish, but are encouraged by society to be "creatures of sensation," dependent upon men for their existence. By placing the blame on the ideologies of femininity rather than on women themselves, Wollstonecraft makes it possible for later sociologists, educators, and literary scholars to go beyond essential qualities of women and to seek social change. In her unfinished novel *The Wrongs of Woman, or Maria* (1798), Wollstonecraft continues to explore the theoretical and material conditions that make women "slaves" in society. The work renders in fiction her arguments made earlier in her prose tracts. Though she was aware that there were differences in women because of class, Wollstonecraft contends that women were united through the various ills and oppressions they suffered. The metaphor of the world as a "vast prison" is used to suggest the condition in which most women lived.

In addition, through its focus on the relationship between the mother, Maria, and her infant daughter, and through its depiction of female bonding and friendship in the characters of Maria and her jailer, Jemima, *The Wrongs of Woman* envisions alternative subject positions and relational possibilities for women. Through her rebellious heroine, Wollstonecraft questions the proper role of wives, mothers, and daughters in late-eighteenth-century English society. The adulterous but articulate and passionate

Maria also challenges stereotypical notions of the mistress, the fallen woman, and the prostitute as found in the literature of the period. Wollstonecraft reveals her own attraction, and at the same time, resistance to, sentimentalism and romantic gratification. The novel's fragmentary conclusion hints at further disappointments and loss, reinforcing Wollstonecraft's notion of female powerlessness and oppression.

Eleanor Ty

References

Todd, Janet M. *Mary Wollstonecraft: An Annotated Bibliography*. New York: Garland, 1976.

Wollstonecraft, Mary. *Collected Letters of Mary Wollstonecraft*. Edited by Ralph M. Wardle. Ithaca, N.Y.: Cornell University Press, 1979.

———. *Letters Written during a Short Residence in Sweden, Norway, and Denmark*. Edited by Carol Poston. Lincoln: University of Nebraska Press, 1976.

———. *Mary and the Wrongs of Woman*. Oxford: World's Classics, 1976.

Wollstonecraft, Mary. *A Vindication of the Rights of Woman*. Edited by Carol Poston. New York: Norton Critical Edition, 1975.

Womanist

Simply put, a womanist is what Alice Walker has called a "feminist of color." But she also defines womanist as "a woman who loves other women, sexually and/or nonsexually." Likewise, a womanist "loves herself." Walker's definitions of the word have expanded to include a branch of feminist criticism that is different from black feminist criticism. In addition to studying black women's writing, womanist criticism includes the study of images of black women in men's literature. Womanist is also frequently cited as a descriptive term for contemporary types of African and African American literary genres, pedagogy, and religious rites.

Walker coined "womanist" in her first collection of essays, *In Search of Our Mothers' Gardens*. Here she explored the theories and practices of feminists and feminism. Within that tradition, she incorporated the "womanist" tradition and prose of black women. A year after its publication, Walker's book inspired feminist literary critics such as Sherley Anne Williams to further develop the term as a theory. Womanist

inquiry rereads "negative, stereotyped images of black women" as "only a part of the problem of phallocentric writings by black males." To better understand this problem, Williams believes it is necessary for womanist critics to "turn to what black men have written about themselves."

Etymologically, womanist derives from "womanish," what Walker calls a black mother's expression used to describe a daughter who is acting "like a woman," *"willful,"* "responsible. In charge. *Serious.*"

Since Walker first defined "womanist" in 1983, people in and out of the academy have welcomed the term and have expanded its original meaning to include diverse attitudes and cultural practices.

Michelle L. Deal

References

Walker, Alice. *In Search of Our Mothers' Gardens*. New York: Harcourt, 1983.

Williams, Sherley Anne. "Some Implications of Womanist Theory." In *Reading Black, Reading Feminist*, edited by Henry Louis Gates, Jr., 68–75. New York: Meridian, 1990.

Womb

See UTERUS

Woolf, Virginia

A pioneer in feminist literary theory, Virginia Woolf (1882–1941) was the first writer to articulate some of the most important ideas in feminist literary thought in two major essays, *A Room of One's Own* and *Three Guineas,* and in numerous shorter works. Woolf's essays have proven a fertile source of ideas for feminist thinkers since they were published, and especially since the 1960s. Her arguments continue to influence feminist literary theory as well as feminist scholarship in history and psychology.

Her central idea is that there is a persistent inequality between men and women evident in every aspect of social life. Her argument is rooted in the world she knew personally—England of the late nineteenth and early twentieth centuries—but she implies that this inequality exists across cultures and time. The unequal power of men and women she sees everywhere: from the domestic tyranny of fathers and privilege of sons in families, to men's control of governments, universities, business, law, finance, religion, and the press; from the masculine drive for power that lies behind colonialism, imperialism, and dictatorships, to the paternal analogies used to justify foreign conquest. The corollary of men's power is women's marginality, Woolf argues. She sees women pushed out of the centers of power and onto the margins, and she uses the word "patriarchy"—the rule of the fathers—to summarize this inequality. "The most transient visitor to this planet," she remarks, "could not fail to be aware . . . that England is under the rule of a patriarchy."

Woolf argues that patriarchal values pervade literature and literary criticism as completely as they pervade the political and social spheres. The starting point of literary theory for Woolf is the material world. She examines the connection between material circumstances and women's writing at many levels, beginning with the most basic: the body. In a memorable passage in *A Room of One's Own,* Woolf attempts to account for the absence of women among writers of the English Renaissance. She invents the story of "Judith Shakespeare," an imaginary sister of William who was as "wonderfully gifted" as he. The story demonstrates that Judith's female body—her appealing face and capacity to be made pregnant—and the reaction of men to her body were in themselves reasons it would have been impossible for Judith to be a poet-playwright like her brother. The very fact of having a female face and body, Woolf's story shows, militates against having the life of a writer.

Woolf argues that social history must precede feminist literary theory. To understand a woman's writing, a literary critic must understand her practical daily life: "Fiction is like a spider's web, attached ever so lightly perhaps, but still attached to life at all four corners." However, when Woolf looks for information to help her understand women's lives in the past, she is frustrated by the absence of women in history books. She declares, "A new kind of history is wanted," and proposes that women college students and women scholars do research on the real lives of real women in every period: "At what age did she marry; how many children had she as rule; what was her house like; had she a room to herself; did she do the cooking; would she be likely to have a servant?" For Woolf, literary theory requires answers to such questions. Woolf's influence lies behind the tremendous surge in feminist historical scholarship since the 1960s.

Woolf argues that psychological forces also affect women's literary achievement. For example, Woolf considers the ways girls of middle and upper classes were socialized in England in the late nineteenth century, and the assumptions about proper feminine behavior that such young women would internalize. One force that prevents women from writing Woolf calls the ideology of "femininity": the expectation that women should be nice and sympathetic rather than forceful, outspoken, or intellectually vigorous. This expectation she named "the angel in the house" after the Patmore poem, and she claims she had to "kill" that phantom before she herself could write. Further, she says women inevitably remember other people's spoken scorn, discouragement, and opposition. These memories lower a woman writer's vitality and sap her strength, Woolf argues. Women are therefore less likely than men to complete their work or complete it as they had planned. Feminist psychologists since the 1960s have followed Woolf's hint that internalized assumptions about gender limit women's aspirations and thwart their achievement. Such research has also led psychologists to analyze how low expectations and active discouragement limit the achievement of people marginalized by race or social class as well as gender.

The critical reception of books by women demonstrates patriarchal attitudes, Woolf finds. When women write fiction, their books are judged by critics who hold patriarchal values. A critic will therefore value men's writing more than women's and will say, "This book is important because it deals with war; this book is trivial because it deals with the feelings of women in a drawing room." Woolf's insight about the differential reception of books by men and women writers has inspired recent literary scholars to examine the gender politics of publication, book reviewing, and the politics of creating a "canon." Woolf's influence also may be felt in movements to bring African American, Latino, gay and lesbian, and other literatures into university and school curricula.

Yet paradoxically, Woolf argues, women's marginality has kept them free. In *A Room of One's Own,* after the writer has been ordered to stop walking on the grass and denied access to a library because she is a woman, she reflects on "how unpleasant it is to be locked out," yet immediately comments, "I thought how it is worse perhaps to be locked in." It is an advantage to be a woman, Woolf argues, because women can be free from destructive emotions like patriotism or desire for fame. Relishing women's position on the margins, she proposes in *Three Guineas* that women—especially the "daughters of educated men"—should form a "Society of Outsiders" in order to maintain independence of "unreal loyalties." Women's marginal position creates an alternative consciousness which, Woolf argues, can redeem society.

Placing value on being female gives Woolf a distinctive stance as a feminist literary theorist. She remarks, "The truth is, I often like women. I like their unconventionality. I like their subtlety. I like their anonymity." Friendliness toward women and women writers appears repeatedly in Woolf's writing. It informs her relation to her putative audience in *A Room of One's Own*—a room full of women university students at her lecture, and the women who are indirectly addressed in *Three Guineas*. It comes through in her description of reading a contemporary novel (probably an imaginary one) portraying the friendship between two women: "Chloe liked Olivia. They shared a laboratory together." It pervades her three greatest novels, *Mrs. Dalloway, To the Lighthouse,* and *Orlando.*

The concept of androgyny offers Woolf a resolution to the separation between the sexes. In the last chapter of *A Room of One's Own* Woolf speculates that healthy personality includes male and female elements in both men and women. The word "androgyny" (andro = man/gyny = woman) suggests a uniting of male and female, and Woolf suggests that a "marriage" of female and male qualities in each personality signals psychological wholeness. Woolf's very interest in the separation between male and female domains led her to question the idea that maleness or femaleness is biological or innate. This thought led her to speculate about what recent theorists call the "social construction of gender"—the idea that femininity and masculinity are created by social expectations. Woolf therefore experimented with erasing gender boundaries. In her novel *Orlando,* the central character changes sex—from man to woman—in the middle of the book.

Woolf's literary theory comes with a distinctly activist slant. She encourages her readers to translate anger into action, to transform ignorance into knowledge, and by writing to illuminate, dramatize, and thus improve the lives of women. Her activism is implicit in her understanding of the writer's role as political and in her belief that if women write, they can stop war, they can change culture. Her activism is explicit in her call for women to do feminist scholarship and research. Woolf's activist intent also comes through in her demand for a new fiction by and about women: "There is the girl behind the counter too—I would as soon have her true history as the hundred and fiftieth life of Napoleon."

Woolf's approach to literary history is to look for poetry, fiction, and drama by women, and if she finds none, to look for letters and diaries. In *A Room of One's Own,* she boldly goes to the shelves and looks century by century for writing by women. Her curiosity about women's lives in the past leads her to value fragmentary or fugitive texts that let us glimpse "lost" female experience and inner lives. Her desire to recover the texts of forgotten women writers has opened up fruitful avenues of feminist literary history.

Woolf has led feminist literary critics to ask questions about the "canon" of books accepted as great, about who determines what books are part of that canon, about the assumptions behind the idea of "literary greatness," and about the power relations in publication, reviewing, and teaching some books and not others. Even her casual questions have opened up feminist theoretical debate: is there a "natural" literary form for women? Is there a female style? What should be the relation between a woman writer and a woman reader? between a woman writer and any reader? Who are the literary models for women writers?

Woolf's style is a part of her point. The form of *A Room of One's Own* enacts the connection between daily life and fiction because the essay begins as a story in the life of its writer. Chapters one and two, in particular, show the writer in the process of developing thoughts out of experience. Its narrative method gives *A Room of One's Own* a warmth, immediacy, and modesty that have been seen by some recent feminist critics as the source of its power and suggestiveness. Yet some other feminist literary scholars deplore the essay's witty indirectness, and see its tone as evidence that Woolf unconsciously acquiesced to an ideology of feminine politeness and decorum, denied her own anger, and deprived her writing of authority. Woolf's tone in *A Room of One's Own*—witty, tentative, ironic, modest, speculative—partly accounts for its effectiveness in suggesting new directions for feminist scholarship. The tone of *Three Guineas*—objective, measured, full of statistics, occasionally scornful and despairing—make it a thornier work that is less widely read and taught, but it is perhaps a more typical model for writers of feminist literary theory.

Woolf's importance as a feminist literary theorist lies in her application of the concept of patriarchy to literary study, the daringly subjective tone of her critical writing, her insistence on the relevance of her own experience to large theoretical questions, and her trust that examining her own responses would enable her to come up with ideas about literature. The advice she gives to women writers she followed herself and found it accurate: "Be truthful, one would say, and the result is bound to be amazingly interesting. Comedy is bound to be enriched. New facts are bound to be discovered." Both innovative and suggestive, Woolf has been a major, generative force in feminist literary theory.

Marcia McClintock Folsom

References

Bell, Quentin. *Virginia Woolf: A Biography.* New York: Harcourt Brace Jovanovich, 1972.

Marcus, Jane. *New Feminist Essays on Virginia Woolf.* London: Macmillan, 1981.

———. *Virginia Woolf: A Feminist Slant.* Lincoln: University of Nebraska Press, 1987.

Marder, Herbert. *Feminism and Art: A Study of Virginia Woolf.* Chicago: University of Chicago Press, 1968.

Woolf, Virginia. *The Diary of Virginia Woolf.* Vols. 1–6. Edited by Anne Olivier Bell. London: Hogarth, 1977.

———. *The Letters of Virginia Woolf.* Vols. 1–6. Edited by Nigel Nicholson and Joanne Trautmann. New York: Harcourt Brace Jovanovich, 1975–1980.

———. *Moments of Being: Unpublished Autobiographical Writings.* Edited by Jeanne Schulkind. New York: Harcourt Brace Jovanovich, 1976.

———. "Professions for Women." In *Virginia Woolf: Women and Writing,* edited by Michele Barrett, 57–63. New York: Harcourt Brace Jovanovich, 1979.

———. *A Room of One's Own.* New York: Harcourt Brace Jovanovich, 1929.

———. *Three Guineas.* New York: Harcourt Brace Jovanovich, 1938.

———. *A Writer's Diary.* Edited by Leonard Woolf. New York: Harcourt Brace Jovanovich, 1953.

Work

Before feminists began to analyze work as a gendered concept and practice, work had been defined as that which was paid, took place within the "public" sphere, and was performed and produced primarily by men. Whereas women were bound culturally by their roles as wives, mothers, and daughters, men were permitted to occupy public spaces as workers, and the experiences of male workers and male-defined notions of culturally valuable work were dominant. Feminist opposition to male-centered theories of labor has influenced feminist literary theories concerning the canon, literary value, and cultural production. Indeed, feminist literary critics have documented through literature that women did participate in the work force as wage laborers and as producers of culturally valuable work. Challenging the male-defined notions of work, feminist literary critics show how labor within the family and among the community is work, although women's labor and voices both outside the home and within it often have been muted, erased, or forgotten.

Given the historical absence of women within existing studies of the work force, feminist literary scholars looked to novelists and writers as evidence of women's participation in paid production. Mary Kelly's *Private Woman, Public Stage* studies nineteenth-century woman writers in the United States and the domestic roles that shaped their professional identities, describing their labor as "literary domesticity." It is in part because many of the "literary domestics," who earned livings for themselves and their families through their writing, wrote about the "private" sphere that their work was not considered artistic or literary, despite the fact that their writings enjoyed enormous popularity at the time of publication. Feminist literary theorists turned theories of the marketplace into questions about literary value, asking why literature produced by women often became neglected and unread. Literary critics such as Nina Baym, Elaine Showalter, and Jane Tompkins have recovered the neglected texts of women writers, reconstructing what Tompkins calls in *Sensational Designs* the "cultural work" their literary productions performed in their time.

Tompkins's study opens the literary canon and questions the aesthetic values that previously have encouraged the erasure or ridicule of women's texts. Feminist literary scholars continue to recover cultural productions by women, challenging the devaluation of women's work that has pervaded the political, economic, and academic system.

For feminist literary theorists, the rediscovery of women's work inspired new studies of writers who themselves had produced critiques of domestic labor, writers such as Charlotte Perkins Gilman in *Women and Economics* and Olive Schreiner in *Woman and Labor*. Building upon the early insights of women writers, more recent feminist theories have expanded the category of labor to include work inside the home, from the reproduction of the work force (children) to the labor of writing itself. Literary critics such as Nancy Armstrong, in *Desire and Domestic Fiction,* for instance, have examined the primary role of domestic fiction in the production of economic and social life.

Feminist literary critics influenced by Marxist theory have recognized the failure of Marxist theories of labor to adequately analyze the sexual division of labor, a division that assigns work according to gender, allowing men to occupy public spaces as workers and women to continue domestic production untheorized and unpaid. Mary Poovey in her book *Uneven Developments* successfully unhinges some of the binary oppositions posed by the domestic and the public, the nonworking woman and the working man, arguing that the literary man and his literary labor stood at the "crossroads of a capitalist economy . . . dependent upon representations of non alienated natural domestic women to accomplish its tasks." Through her readings of both *Jane Eyre* and the writings attributed to Florence Nightingale, Poovey demonstrates that women's paid work was dependent upon the twofold representation of woman both as the sexless and classless breeder of the domestic sphere and the unmarried or working woman who is oversexed and dangerous. Literature, for Poovey, is a cultural text that can exemplify not only the uneven development of economic relations between the sexes, but also offers insights into how "an entire system of institutional practices and conventions at mid-century in Britain" functioned.

If gender and class have become distinct categories of inquiry, with the help of feminist literary theorists, by the 1980s critics also began to rethink the ways in which work can differentiate women according to race, class, ethnicity, and sexuality. Domestic ideology and the literary conventions of the "literary domestics" in the nineteenth-century United States, for instance, often excluded black women and working women from the very definitions of "woman." Hazel Carby argues in *Reconstructing Womanhood* that in order for black women to be heard as orators or writers they had to "confront the dominant domestic ideologies and literary conventions of womanhood which often excluded them from the definition of 'woman.'" Indeed, Margaret Fuller suggested that the difference in the kinds of work black and white women performed exposed a contradiction in men's assumptions about women's capabilities in antebellum America. She argued in *Woman in the Nineteenth Century*: "Those who think the physical circumstances of Woman would make a part in the affairs of national government unsuitable, are by no means those who think it impossible for negresses to endure field work, even during pregnancy." From the earliest days of slavery, compulsory labor had controlled black women's lives. Thus unlike many middle and upper-class white women who wrote about and within the private sphere, work outside the home was mandatory for black women, and consequently, domesticity, work, and writing may have different cultural meanings for all women.

Literary critics from Mary Poovey to Wai Chee Dimock and Amy Schrager Lang have recently offered new methods for considering the concept of class as a generative axis for analyses by rethinking the relation between gender and modes of production. A recent collection of essays, *Rethinking Class: Literary Studies and Social Formations,* seeks to reintroduce class, not as a self-evident subject, but as an evolving category of analysis, a category in which the issues of gender, literature, and history are foregrounded. In her essay "Class, Gender, Metonymy," for instance, Dimock reads the memoirs and letters of women workers next to the stories of Herman Melville and Rebecca Harding Davis in order to analyze the dependency of Marxian notions of class on the bodily (gendered) subject. The collection offers feminist literary critics and all scholars paths by which to return to questions about class, labor, and work as inquiries central to the understanding of literature and culture.

What defines work, who performs it, and

who controls the kinds of meanings produced by it, continue to be central questions for feminist literary theory. Conceptualizing gender as an analytic category in the construction of work has helped all feminists theorize the gendering of skill, value, class, as well as the literary itself.

Jennifer Travis

References

Armstrong, Nancy. *Desire and Domestic Fiction: A Political History of the Novel.* Oxford: Oxford University Press, 1987.

Baym, Nina. *Novels, Readers, and Reviewers: Responses to Fiction in Antebellum America.* Ithaca, N.Y.: Cornell University Press, 1984.

Carby, Hazel. *Reconstructing Womanhood: The Emergence of the Afro-American Woman Novelist.* Oxford: Oxford University Press, 1987.

Dimock, Wai Chee, and Michael T. Gilmore, eds. *Rethinking Class: Literary Studies and Social Formations.* New York: Columbia University Press, 1994.

Fuller, Margaret. *Woman in the Nineteenth Century and Other Writings.* Edited by Donna Dickenson. New York: Oxford, 1994.

Gilman, Charlotte Perkins. *Women and Economics: The Relation between Men and Women as a Factor in Social Evolution.* Boston: Small, Maynard, 1899.

Kelly, Mary. *Private Woman, Public Stage: Literary Domesticity in Nineteenth-Century America.* Oxford: Oxford University Press, 1984.

Poovey, Mary. *Uneven Developments: The Ideological Work of Gender in Mid-Victorian England.* Chicago: University of Chicago Press, 1988.

Schreiner, Olive. *Woman and Labor.* New York: Frederick A. Stokes, 1911.

Showalter, Elaine. *A Literature of Their Own: British Women Novelists from Brontë to Lessing.* Princeton: Princeton University Press, 1977.

Tompkins, Jane. *Sensational Designs: The Cultural Work of American Fiction 1790–1860.* Oxford: Oxford University Press, 1985.

W

Y

Yaeger, Patricia

Behind all of Patricia Yaeger's scholarship is a fierce determination to transform the image of the woman writer from silent sufferer to empowered author. While most French and Anglo American feminists, from Julia Kristeva to Sandra Gilbert and Susan Gubar, have tended to emphasize women's alienation from and struggle with language, Yaeger continues to present evidence of female authors' reveling in the pleasure of words. Perhaps best known for her groundbreaking work on the sublime, she has also reread the categories of the patriarchy and the grotesque to illustrate their potential for the woman writer.

Challenging the reigning feminist doctrine that speech is both agonizing and dangerous for women excluded from the patriarchal discursive realm, Yaeger argued in her influential book *Honey-Mad Women* that women writers of the past and present have consistently experienced empowerment and enjoyment through language. Constructing an alternate "mythology" of female discourse, she combines the *jouissance* of contemporary French feminists with the historical awareness of their Anglo American counterparts to illustrate women writers' insatiable hunger for words. Disputing the argument that language is inherently a masculine sign system, Yaeger identifies various emancipatory strategies of nineteenth- and twentieth-century female authors, particularly what she describes, in Bakhtinian terms, as a "poetics of play."

As part of her continuing effort to emphasize this less painful vision of female creativity, Yaeger has revealed the sublime and the Southern grotesque to be narrative strategies women have reconceptualized and employed to authorize their writing and address the deforming effects of the patriarchal political tradition. Moreover, by refiguring the Father as a human with breasts, a vulnerable body whose flesh is inscribed with both Oedipal and pre-Oedipal significations, she has helped to mitigate the terror traditionally associated with his image.

Patricia Yaeger has been a major force behind the movement to shift feminist emphasis from female victimage to female valor. As a result of her efforts, future generations will most likely regard their literary precursors less as silenced and suffering Niobes than honey-mad women, intoxicated and empowered by the irresistible sweetness of speech.

Lisa Rado

References

Yaeger, Patricia. *Honey-Mad Women.* New York: Columbia University Press, 1988.

———. "The Language of Blood: Towards a Maternal Sublime." *Genre* 25 (1992): 5–24.

———. "The Poetics of Birth." In *Sexuality: From Aristotle to Aids,* edited by Domna Stanton, 262–295. Ann Arbor: University of Michigan Press, 1992.

———. "Toward a Female Sublime." In *Gender and Theory,* edited by Linda Kauffman, 191–212. New York: Basil Blackwell, 1989.

———, and Beth Kowaleski-Wallace, eds. *Refiguring the Father.* Carbondale: Southern Illinois University Press, 1989.

Z

Zimmerman, Bonnie

Bonnie Zimmerman's lesbian feminist criticism has consisted of two aspects—first, an examination of the role experiential-based personal narratives play in constructing a politics of identity, and second, the publication of a book on lesbian fiction that critiques the representation of lesbianism. Among other questions, Zimmerman asks: "What role does lesbianism play in thinking, reading, and writing?" "Is there a 'lesbian?'" "Who is a 'lesbian?'" "Can one read as a 'lesbian?'" "Is lesbian feminism different from feminist criticism?" "What would a lesbian feminist criticism and aesthetics consist of?" "Does it belong in the academy?" "Is it necessary to establish a lesbian canon?"

Zimmerman grapples with representation by focusing on heterosexism, arguing that it is necessary and possible to read as a "lesbian" and interrogate and disrupt heterosexist representations that distort language and sexuality with absences, encodings, and stereotypes, and that marginalize lesbianism by making it invisible, or excluding it altogether.

Two excellent examples of Zimmerman's work are her readings of lesbian vampire films and the letters and novels of George Eliot, and the assertions that: first, even though lesbian vampire films are encoded with nineteenth century stereotypical representations of lesbianism, they also contain representations of sexual attraction between women that can be read as a threat to a male-dominated society; and, second, Eliot's expressions of a lesbian consciousness disappeared in 1860 when the scientific community began to theorize homosexuality as congenital, thus indicating her awareness of the stigmatization of lesbianism.

Kay Hawkins

References

Zimmerman, Bonnie. "The Dark Eye Beaming: Female Friendship in George Eliot's Fictions." In *Lesbian Texts and Contexts—Radical Revisions*, edited by Karla Jay and Joanne Glasgow, 126–144. New York: New York University Press, 1990.

———. "Daughters of Darkness: Lesbian Vampires." *Jump Cut* 24–25 (1981): 23–24.

———. "What Has Never Been: An Overview of Lesbian Feminist Criticism." *Feminist Studies* 7 (1981): 451–476.

Index

The main entry for each topic is listed in **boldface**.

Bell, Shannon 320
Belsey, Catherine **42**, 96
Benjamin, Jessica **42**, 102
Bennett, Paula 307
Benstock, Shari **43**, 404
Berger, John 209
Bible 36, 280, 296 *(see also Myth, Spirituality)*
Biehl, Janet 284
Bildungsroman 7, 59, 195, 303
Bilingualism **43** *(see also Translation)*
Binary Opposition **44**, 116, 172, 173, 218, 280, 364, 396 *(see also Helene Cixous, Jacques Derrida)*
Biography 193
Biological Determinism **45** *(see also Essentialism)*
Birth **47** *(see also Ecriture Feminine, Maternal, Reproduction)*
Bisexuality 78
Black Feminist Criticism (African American) **48**, 65, 165, 199, 200, 239, 240, 395
Black Feminist Criticism (other than African American) **51**, 84
Black Power Movement 421
Blazon 412
Bleier, Ruth 46
Bloom, Harold 30
Blues **52**, 66
Body **53**, 186 *(see also Anorexia, Hysteria, Orality)*
Books. See Reading, Reader-Response Theory
Boose, Lynda 149, 211
Bordo, Susan 54, 129
Boston Women's Health Collective 344
Breast **56** *(see also Body, Motherhood, Object Relations Theory, Reproduction)*
Breastfeeding 56
British Feminism **58** *(see also Socialist Feminism)*
Brontë, Charlotte **59**, 180, 315
Browning, Elizabeth Barrett 251
Brownmiller, Susan 39, **60**, 336
Brownstein, Rachel 194
Brumberg, Joan Jacobs 19
Bunch, Charlotte 61
Butch-Femme 232
Butler, Judith **61**, 147, 152, 197, 205, 211, 235, 302, 306, 318
Bynum, Caroline Walker 129

C

Cameron, Deborah 230
Campbell, Beatrix **63**
Canada 28
Canon 13, 38, **63**, 242, 266, 287 *(see also New Criticism)*
Capitalism 109
Caputi, Jane 189, 276
Carby, Hazel **65**, 274, 323, 434
Care, Ethic of Care. See Carol Gilligan
Carnival 35, **66**
Carribean Identity 80
Carter, Angela 66, **67**, 137

Castellanos, Rosario **68**
Castle, Terry 133, 246
Censorship **69**, 209 *(see also Pornography, Silence)*
Centre for Contemporary Cultural Studies 95, 311
Chadwick, Whitney 392
Charcot, Jean-Martin 285
Chaucer, Geoffrey 257
Chernin, Kim 18, **70**
Chesler, Phyllis 213, 214
Chicana Feminism 71
Chicana Theory **71**, 141 *(see also Alarcon, Norma, Anzaldua, Gloria, Moraga, Cherrie)*
Chicanas 269
Child, Lydia Maria 274
Childhood 420
Children **72**
Children's Literature **73**
Chinese-Americans 223
Chodorow, Nancy 7, **74**, 102, 124, 139, 250, 254, 272, 292, 322
Chopin, Kate **76**
Chow, Rey 52, 98
Christ, Carol **76**, 386
Christian, Barbara 274
Christianity 101, 250
Christine de Pizan 12, 237, 329
Cinema. See Film
Cisneros, Sandra 44
Cixous, Hélène 47, 53, 54, **77**, 102, 125, 164, 213, 231, 250, 255, 259, 286, 296, 304, 364, 406
Class **78**, 207 *(see also Marxism, Materialist Feminism)*
Clément, Catherine 67, **80**, 202, 230, 286
Cliff, Michelle **81**
Clitoridectomy 307, 419
Clothes. See Fashion
Clover, Carol 70, 311, 417
Cohen, Paula Marantz 146, 211
Collins, Patricia Hill 397
Colonialism **82**, 412 *(see also Postcolonialism)*
Colonization **84**
Combahee River Collective 243, 248, 333
Comedy **84** *(see also Laughter, Satire)*
Coming Out **86** *(see also Compulsory Heterosexuality, Lesbianism)*
Commodities 427
Community **86** *(see also Identity)*
Compulsory Heterosexuality **87** *(see also Adrienne Rich)*
Consciousness Raising 137, 158, 162
Consumption **88**, 146, 426
Cornell, Drucilla 156, 157
Cornillon, Susan Koppelman 17, 164
Cosmetic Surgery 294
Costume **90** *(see also Crossdressing, Masquerade, Performance, Transvestism)*
Cott, Nancy F. **91**
Courtship **9**
Coward, Ros 378
Cowie, Elizabeth 248
Creativity **93**, 419 *(see also Feminist Aesthetics)*

Materialist Feminism 94, 245, **247**, 289 *(see also Marxism, New Historicism, Postcolonialism)*
Maternal **250** *(see also Maternity, Maternal Thinking, Mother, Motherhood)*
Maternal Thinking **252**, 272
Maternity 4, **253**, 391
Matrocentric **256**
Matrophobia **257**
Mayne, Judith 312
Mc Cullers, Carson 8
McDowell, Deborah 48, **239**
McKay, Nellie **240**, 242
Mead, Margaret 7
Meat 130
Medicine 345, 407
Medieval Studies **257** *(see also Mysticism)*
Medusa 78, **259**
Meese, Elizabeth A. 138
Mellor, Anne 354, 391
Melman, Billie 295
Melodrama 264
Men in Feminism **260**
Menstruation 56
Merchant, Carolyn 284
Mercier, Cathryn 74
Metafiction 185
Metaphor. See Rhetoric
Metaphysics, Western 109
Mexican Feminism 68
Mexico 68
Michie, Helena 54, 129 *(see also Sorophobia)*
Middle Ages 257 *(see also Medieval Studies)*
Military, and Women. See War
Mill, John Stuart **261**
Miller, Nancy 31, **261**, 280
Millett, Kate 17, 136, 137, 164, **262**, 300, 301
Mimesis **262**
Minh-ha, Trinh 51, 141, 205, **263**
Mirror Stage **263**
Miscegenation **264**
Misogyny 36 *(see also Antifeminism, Dinnerstein, Dorothy)*
Mitchell, Juliet 148, 203, 247, **264**, 377
MLF. See Mouvement de Liberation des Femmes
Modern Language Association 200, 343
Modernism 43, 191 *(see also H.D., Stein, Gertrude)*
Modleski, Tanya 177, **265**, 312, 316
Moers, Ellen **266**
Mohanty, Chandra 51, 233, 297, 315, 334
Moi, Toril 58, **267**
Montagu, Lady Mary Wortley **268**
Moon **269**
Moraga, Cherríe 87, **269**
Morgan, Robin 314
Morris, Meaghan **270**
Morrison, Toni **270**, 426
Mother-Child Dyad 112, 292, 300
Motherhood **270**, 391 *(see also Object Relations Theory)*
Mothers and Daughters 102, 195

Mouth. See Orality
Mouvement de Liberation des Femmes 132
MTV 311
Mulatto **274** *(see also Miscegenation)*
Multiculturalism 65, 142, 144 *(see also Asian American Feminist Literary Theory, Chicana Literary Theory, Black Feminist Literary Theory, Native American Feminist Literary Theory)*
Mulvey, Laura 162, 163, 176, 177, 209, **275**, 304, 364, 381, 416
Munich, Adrienne 259
Mysticism **275** *(see also Medieval Studies)*
Myth 70, 223, **276**, 303 *(see also Fairy Tales, Revision, Spirituality)*
Mythology 259

N
Name-of-the-Father **279** *(see also Lacan, Jacques)*
Narrative Theory. See Narratology
Narrative. See Narratology
Narratology 36, **279**, 338 *(see also Feminist Poetics, Gynocritics, Semiotics)*
Native American Feminist Literary Theory **281**
Nature 186, **283**
Naylor, Gloria 337
Nestle, Joan 232
Neurosis **285** *(see also Hysteria, Psychoanalysis, Unconscious*
New Criticism **287**, 336
New Historicism **287** *(see also Cultural Studies, Foucault, Michel, Poststructuralism)*
Newton, Judith Lowder 288, **289**
Nightingale, Florence 310
Nin, Anais **290**
Nochlin, Linda 209
Novels 24, 135
Nursing. See Breast
Nussbaum, Felicity 133, 273, 288, 360

O
O'Brien, Margaret 345
Object Relations Theory **291** *(see also Chodorow, Nancy, Gilligan, Carol)*
Oedipus Complex 75, 202
Okin, Susan Moller 253
Old Maid. See Spinster
Olsen, Tillie 136, 370
Ong, Walter, J. 292
Opera 80
Orality **292** *(see also Beauty, Ecriture Feminine, Silence)*
Orientalism **294** *(see also Colonialism)*
Ortner, Sherry 39
Ostricker, Alicia 231, 277, **295**
Other **296** *(see also Orientalism, Postcolonialism)*
Other, Woman as 392

P
Parenting 75, 116
Parker, Patricia 349